D0205919

RESEARCH GUIDE TO BIOGRAPHY AND CRITICISM

Volume I
A-LAND

Edited By
Walton Beacham

Library of Congress
Cataloging in Publication Data

Research guide to biography and criticism: literature/ edited by Walton Beacham— Washington, D.C.: Research Publishing, 1985.
2 v.; 24 cm.

Bibliography.
Includes index in v. 2.

Description and evaluation of the most important biographical, autobiographical, and critical sources for 335 British, American, and Canadian writers.

1. English literature—History and criticism—Bibliography. 2. English literature—Bio-bibliography. 3. Authors, English—Biography—Bibliography. 4. American literature—History and criticism—Bibliography. 5. American literature—Bio-bibliography. 6. Authors, American—Biography—Bibliography.
I. Beacham, Walton, 1943-

Z2011.R47 1985 016.82'09 85-2188
(PR85)

Library of Congress Catalog Card Number: 85-2188

Complete Set ISBN: 0-933833-00-8
Volume 1 ISBN: 0-933833-01-6
Volume 2 ISBN: 0-933833-02-4

Printed in the United States of America
First Printing, July 1985
Second Printing, November 1985
Third Printing, January 1986

PREFACE

With so many biographical and critical works available in most libraries, it is often difficult for students to know which sources relate to their specific needs, or for general readers to know which biographies interest them the most.

The *Research Guide to Biography and Criticism* has been designed to assist students in narrowing and researching topics for term papers and essay exams, and to provide librarians with a tool which will help them lead students to valuable, accessible resources. The guide is especially useful for libraries which might have limited holdings on a particular author. With clear content description and exact bibliographical information for every book reviewed, it is much easier to locate the needed resources in other libraries.

With these expressed goals, the Research Guide has limited its scope to those authors who are most often studied. The contents in no way reflect any editorial opinion as to a writer's historical importance, or to the quality of his work. The contents were compiled with the assistance and advice of some three hundred university professors and librarians.

The second criterion for including an author is the amount and availability of biographies, autobiographies, and critical materials about him. Most contemporary writers have not been included because there is yet no full biographical or critical treatments of their lives. Most dramatists and world authors are not included because Research Publishing has scheduled their inclusion in a separate, parallel set in 1985. These two volumes contain British and American poets, novelists, and prose writers.

The third criterion is that the sources discussed are generally available in United States libraries. Books which are out-of-print or difficult to locate are clearly distinguished from the resources which a librarian could reasonably expect to find.

Finally, an auxilliary Contents has been prepared which groups authors generally by their literary periods. This is intended only as an aid for researching specific periods, not to organize writers into schools. The index contains the writers included, as well as all the principal books and articles which have been *explained.* There are many more resources contained in the articles. Book and article titles which are not self-explanatory contain in parentheses the author whom the book discusses. Where there are two or more biographies with the same title, the biographers' names are placed in parentheses.

Research Publishing is continually interested in producing books which are devoted to improving the research capabilities of students. We welcome any suggestions for revising this title or ideas for other types of books. Write to: Research Publishing, 2113 "S" Street, NW, Washington, D.C. 20008.

Walton Beacham

CONTRIBUTORS

David L. Ackiss

Timothy Dow Adams

Consuelo M. Aherne, S.S.J.

Barbara Taylor Allen

David G. Allen

Andrew J. Angyal

Stanley Archer

Robert A. Armour

Edwin T. Arnold

Marilyn Arnold

Stephen C. B. Atkinson

Dennis Baeyen

Margaret Ann Baker

Jane L. Ball

Melissa E. Barth

Richard H. Beckham

Sue Bridwell Beckham

Thomas Becknell

James P. Bednarz

Kirk H. Beetz

Anthony Bernardo

Winifred Farrant Bevilacqua

Robert G. Blake

Leslie Rebecca Bloom

Harold Branam

Jeanie R. Brink

Carl W. Brucker

Larry Brunner

Mitzi M. Brunsdale

Hallman B. Bryant

Elizabeth Buckmaster

Paul Budra

Marilyn S. Butler

Marilyn D. Button

Richard J. Calhoun

Susan L. Carlson

Thomas Carmichael

John Carpenter

Michael Case

S. Catharine Christi, S.S.J.

John R. Clark

Pamela J. Clements

Samuel Coale

William Condon

John J. Conlon

Fred D. Crawford

Gloria L. Cronin

Richard H. Dammers

Frank Day

Dennis R. Dean

Phyllis T. Dircks

Richard J. Dircks

Robert DiYanni

Henry J. Donaghy

David C. Dougherty
William R. Drennan
Gweneth A. Dunleavy
John J. Dunn
Margaret M. Dunn
Phyllis Fahrie Edelson
Bruce L. Edwards, Jr.
Richard A. Eichwald
Robert P. Ellis
Ann W. Engar
Bernard F. Engel
Robert C. Evans
Patricia A. Farrant
Richard Fine
Benjamin Franklin Fisher, IV
James Flynn
Anne-Marie Foley
John Miles Foley
Howard L. Ford
Robert J. Forman
Thomas C. Foster
Warren French
Robert A. Gates
Edward V. Geist
Scott Giantvalley
Richard B. Gidez
James R. Giles
C. Herbert Gilliland
Joe Glaser
Alan Golding
Liela H. Goldman
Dennis M. Goldsberry
Sidney Gottlieb
Kenneth B. Grant
Glenn A. Grever
Edward Guereschi
Lyman B. Hagen
Jay L. Halio
David Mike Hamilton
Gertrude K. Hamilton
Katherine Hanley, C.S.J.
Maryhelen C. Harmon
John P. Harrington
Henry Hart
Joseph M. Hassett
William J. Heim
Terry Heller
Michael Hennessy
John T. Hiers
Maria Hinkle
Barbara Horwitz
Kenneth A. Howe
Dolan Hubbard
Mary Anne Hutchinson
James M. Hutchisson
John L. Idol, Jr.
S. E. Jackson
Philip K. Jason

Ed Jewinski
Irma M. Kashuba, S.S.J.
Steven G. Kellman
Rebecca Kelly
James M. Kempf
Barbara A. King
Lawrence F. Laban
Mary Lago
Thomas M. Leitch
Joan M. Lescinski, C.S.J.
Michael M. Levy
Leon Lewis
Henry J. Lindborg
James C. MacDonald
R. D. Madison
James Maloney
Stella Maloney
Joseph Marotta
Kathleen Massey
Charles E. May
Laurence W. Mazzeno
George E. McCelvey
Kathleen McCormick-Leighty
Linda E. McDaniel
Carmela Pinto McIntire
Thomas F. Merrill
Richard E. Meyer
Jim Wayne Miller
Ray Miller, Jr.
Joseph R. Millichap
Sally Mitchell
Gene M. Moore
Robert A. Morace
Ann R. Morris
Robert E. Morsberger
Claire Clements Morton
Gerald William Morton
Michael Mott
Kevin Mulcahy
John Mulryan
Lisa A. Murray
Marilyn K. Nellis
Robert D. Nixon
George O'Brien
James M. O'Neil
Robert Otten
Cóilín Owens
Richard J. Panofsky
Sandra Manoogian Pearce
Nancy W. Prothro
Steven Reece
James A. W. Rembert
Jack Wright Rhodes
Thomas Jackson Rice
Marinelle Ringer
Samuel J. Rogal
Mary Rohrberger
Lucy E. W. Rollin

Robert L. Ross
David Sadkin
Dale Salwak
Joachim Scholz
Margaret K. Schramm
Lisa M. Schwerdt
Wanda LaFaye Seay
Barbara Kitt Seidman
Steven Serafin
Lynne P. Shackelford
Eric Paul Shaffer
Allen Shepherd
William David Sherman
John C. Shields
Jack Shreve
R. Baird Shuman
Charles L. P. Silet
Dale W. Simpson
Thomas J. Slater
Marjorie Smelstor
Charlotte Spivack
Marlene Springer
L. Robert Stevens
William B. Stone
H. R. Stoneback
Michael L. Storey
Edmund M. Taft, IV
Daniel Taylor
Joseph R. Taylor
Welford Dunaway Taylor
Michael S. Tkach
Thomas J. Travisano
E. F. J. Tucker
A. Gordon Van Ness
Nancy Walker
Robbie Jean Walker
Ronald G. Walker
Gary F. Waller
Tomasz Warchol
John Chapman Ward
Mark A. Weinstein
Judith A. Weise
Charmaine Wellington
Craig Werner
Faye Pauli Whitaker
Edward P. Willey
Donald E. Winters
Stephen F. Wolfe
Chester L. Wolford
John A. Wood
Dorena Allen Wright
Eugene P. Wright
Linda Yoder
Bruce W. Young
Eugene Zasadinski

CONTENTS BY LITERARY PERIODS
BRITISH

CONTENTS BY LITERARY PERIODS AMERICAN, CONTEMPORARY BRITISH/AMERICAN, CANADIAN

Colonial American

American Romanticism

American Realism/Naturalism

Modern American

HAROLD ACTON
1904

Author's Chronology

Born July 5, 1904, Villa La Pietra, Florence, Italy, of Anglo-Neapolitan and American parents; *1918* enters Eton; *1922 The Eton Candle,* edited by Brian Howard, publishes eleven poems, a chapter from a novel, "A Note on Jean Artur Rimbaud, and three of his poems done into English" by Acton, receives excellent reviews, goes into a second printing, and leads to an offer to publish Acton's first book; the same year Acton enters Oxford; *1923 Aquarium* published; *1924* with Peter Quennell jointly edits *Oxford Poetry; 1926–1932* receives the B.A., leaves Oxford, continues to publish books of poetry, novels, and his first important historical work, *The Last Medici; 1932–1939* moves to Peking and begins his study of Chinese art and literature, lectures at the National University, publishes his translations of Chinese poetry and drama, and contributes an essay to Nancy Cunard's *Negro* anthology; *1941* joins the R.A.F.; *1945* returns to Florence and La Pietra; *1948* publishes his *Memoirs of an Aesthete; 1965* awarded the C.B.E. (Commander, Order of the British Empire); *1974* knighted; *1984* publishes his twenty-ninth book.

Author's Bibliography (selected)

Aquarium, 1923 (poems); *An Indian Ass,* 1925 (poems); *Five Saints and an Appendix,* 1927 (poems); *Cornelian,* 1928 (prose fable); *Humdrum,* 1928 (novel); *This Chaos,* 1930 (poems); *The Last Medici,* 1932 (history); *Modern Chinese Poetry,* 1936 (translation); *Famous Chinese Plays,* 1937 (translation); *Peonies and Ponies,* 1941 (novel); *Memoirs of an Aesthete,* 1948 (autobiography); *Prince Isidore,* 1950 (novel); *The Bourbons of Naples,* 1956 (history); *The Last Bourbons of Naples,* 1961 (history); *Old Lamps for New,* 1965 (novel); *More Memoirs of an Aesthete,* 1970 (autobiography); *Tit for Tat and Other Tales,* 1972 (short stories); *Nancy Mitford: A Memoir,* 1975 (biography); *The Pazzi Conspiracy,* 1979 (history); *The Soul's Gymnasium and Other Stories,* 1982 (short stories); *Three Extraordinary Ambassadors,* 1984 (history).

Overview of Biographical Sources

Though Acton as poet, novelist, short story writer, essayist, translator from the Chinese, historian, and memoirist has published twenty-nine books, contributed to forty-seven others, published several hundred articles, had twelve of his works translated into Italian, and though he is a leading figure in all accounts of Europe's dazzling social and literary scenes between the wars, no true full-length biography has yet been written. Martin Green's *Children of the Sun: A Narrative of "Decadence" in England After 1918* (1976) is an attempt "to describe the imaginative life of English culture after 1918 and to trace the prominence within it, the partial dominance over it, established by men of one intellectual temperament, . . . England's Children of the Sun." The life of Acton and of fellow poet Brian Howard is used to "provide the narrative nexus" of the study. *Oxford, China and Italy: Writings in Honour of Sir Harold Acton,* edited by Edward Chaney and Neil Ritchie (London and New York: Thames and Hudson, 1984) contains several excellent short biographical pieces by Anthony Powell, Joan Haslip, John Lehmann, and Laurence Sickman. Acton's Oxford days are discussed in essays entitled "The Undergraduate" by Peter Quennell, "An Oxonion Aesthete" by Christopher Sykes, and "The Good-Natured Man" by A. L. Rowse. Many of the details of Acton's life are, of course, found in the biographies of such friends and fellow writers as Evelyn Waugh, who dedicated *Decline and Fall* to him, the Sitwells, Norman Douglas, Bernard Berenson, Nancy Cunard, and Brian Howard.

Evaluation of Selected Biographies

Green, Martin, *Children of the Sun: A Narrative of "Decadence" in England After 1918.* New York: Basic Books, Inc., 1976. Green opens his study with a "Prologue: A Visit to La Pietra" in which he describes Acton as having "planted the banner of Pierrot on the ramparts of Oxford and London" and having "captured all England for his flamboyant Sunchildren. Pierrot—that was the identity I was trying to detect . . ." Green tries too hard to force Acton's life into that mold, but it is not an uninteresting book, and Green does organize a great many facts of both literary and social history, though not all of them are accurate, into a single, readable volume.

Autobiographical Sources

Acton's two volumes of memoirs, *Memoirs of an Aesthete* (London: Methuen, 1948) and *More Memoirs of an Aesthete* (London: Methuen, 1970) are among his most highly praised and critically esteemed works. The first volume, which covers the years 1904–1938, deals with the artistic and social world of Florence in the early days of this century, the English literary scene in the 1920's and early 1930's, and life in China from 1932 until the Japanese invasion. Acton writes about his own life and his association with the other literary, social, and artistic giants of that era with frankness, great wit, and a good bit of modesty and self-criticism. The second volume picks up where the first leaves off and continues to 1966. Together they represent one of the most sparkling autobiographies of this century and might aptly be compared to Logan Pearsall Smith's *Unforgotten Years* and Kenneth Clark's *Another Part of the Wood* and *The Other Half.*

Overview of Critical Sources

The most important critical work that has been undertaken on Acton is Neil Ritchie's *Harold Acton: A Bibliography* (Florence, 1984). Essays on Acton as translator, historian, and poet appear in *Oxford, China and Italy: Writings in Honour of Sir Harold Acton.* Green's *Children of the Sun: A Narrative of "Decadence" in England After 1918* attempts to evaluate some of Acton's work in the context of his overriding and unwieldy "Sonnerkind" thesis.

Evaluation of Selected Criticism

Birch, Cyril, "Harold Acton as a Translator from the Chinese," in *Oxford, China and Italy: Writings in Honour of Sir Harold Acton.* edited by Edward Chaney and Neil Ritchie, pp. 37–44. New York: Thames and Hudson, 1984. Birch discusses Acton's translations of *Modern Chinese Poetry, Famous Chinese Plays,* and the *Peach Blossom Fan.* He concludes that "Acton puts all lovers of Chinese literature in his debt."

Ritchie, Neil, *Harold Acton: A Bibliography.* Florence, 1984. Ritchie's bibliography is a model of the bibliographer's art. It describes in detail and provides a commentary on the English, American, and Italian first and subsequent editions of all twenty-nine of Acton's books, the forty-seven books Acton has made contributions to, and provides an annotated list of 196 contributions to periodicals. The bibliography also provides a complete and very thorough index. The volume is a necessity for all Acton scholars.

Wood, John A. "Harold Acton as a Poet," in *Oxford, China and Italy: Writings in Honour of Sir Harold Acton.* edited by Edward Chaney and Neil Ritchie, pp. 25–33. Wood attempts to explain why Acton's poetry has not received the critical attention he feels it deserves. He discusses each of Acton's four volumes of poetry and concludes that Acton's work is a poetry of celebration and joy. He quotes six complete poems and selections from several others, thereby bringing back into print some of Acton's work that has been neglected since the publication of his last book of poems in 1930.

Selected Dictionaries and Encyclopedias

The Author's and Writer's Who's Who, Hafner Publishing, 1971. Brief biography.

Contemporary Authors, Gale Research, 1962. Brief biography.

Who's Who, St. Martin's Press, 1984. Brief biography.

World Authors 1950–1970, H. W. Wilson, 1975. Excellent biographical entry with short essay by Acton, appraisal of his work, and short bibliography.

John A. Wood
McNeese State University

JOSEPH ADDISON
1672–1719

Author's Chronology

Born May 1, 1672, Milston, England, the son of an Anglican clergyman; *1686* attends Charterhouse School where he meets Richard Steele; *1687* enters Queen's College, Oxford, to prepare for ordination; *1689* elected fellow at Magdalen College; *1694* publishes several English poems and translations from Latin; *1699* edits a volume containing seven of his Latin poems and receives a pension to tour the Continent in preparation for government service; *1700–1702* tours France, Italy, and Germany; *1704* appointed Commissioner of Appeals as reward for poem in praise of Duke of Marlborough; *1705* publishes an account of his travels; *1706* appointed Undersecretary of State; *1707* sees his opera produced; *1708* elected to Parliament and appointed secretary to the Lord Lieutenant of Ireland; *1710* contributes regularly to Steele's *Tatler; 1711* begins publishing the *Spectator* with Steele; *1713* his *Cato* plays for twenty-five nights; *1714* appointed secretary to Regency government; *1715* appointed a Commissioner of Trade and marries Countess of Warwick; *1717* appointed Secretary of State; *1718* resigns because of ill-health; *1719* dies on June 17.

Author's Bibliography (selected)

"A Letter from Italy," 1701 (poem); "The Campaign," 1704 (poem); *Remarks Upon Several Parts of Italy,* 1705; *Rosamond,* 1707 (opera); essays contributed to the *Tatler,* 1709–1710, the *Spectator,* 1711–1712, 1714, and the *Guardian, 1713; Cato,* 1713 (tragedy); *The Freeholder,* 1715–1716 (periodical); *The Drummer,* 1716 (comedy); *Dialogues Upon the Usefulness of Ancient Medals,* 1721.

Overview of Biographical Sources

There are seven major biographies about Addison, ranging in length from a long article to monograph-length to several hundred pages. There is little to choose among them for accuracy since the facts of Addison's life are documented and the landmarks of his political and literary careers are agreed upon. There are two gaps in the biographical record that no work has been able to fill because of a lack of materials: Addison's life prior to his entrance to the university, and his private life during adulthood. Addison's letters, collected by Walter Graham (Oxford: Oxford University Press, 1941) are no window to his heart; they treat routine business and political matters. Unable to chart any dramatic points in a life progressively but mildly successful, most biographers have retold Addison's life against the background of England's hectic "Augustan Age" (1688 to 1715) when the nation underwent critical shifts in political structure, social patterns, and cultural attitudes. Thus biographers have judged

Addison's life against their assumptions about the historical period. The student should therefore be aware of the biographer's perspective about the period before accepting his interpretation of his subject. Addison's biographers fall into three groups each of which sees a different meaning to the age. The groups are, chronologically, the late eighteenth-century biographers who emphasize culture sophistication; the Victorian biographers who emphasize moral reform; and the early twentieth century biographers who attack philistinism and conformism. The most recent biography is the first to emphasize Addison's life as an individual experience rather than as representative of larger issues.

Evaluation of Selected Biographies

Aikin, Lucy, *The Life of Joseph Addison.* 2 vols. London: Longmans and Green, 1843. Aikin's book is the most adoring, the one most given to reproducing passages from Addison that the author thinks are beautiful, and the one most tedious for the student to read.

Courthope, W. J. *Addison.* London: English Men of Letters Series, 1884. This survey is readable and compact. It provides some literary criticism, but mainly contrasts Addison's praise of virtue to the Restoration's glorification of vice.

Dobree, Bonamy, "The First Victorian," in *Essays in Biography.* Oxford: Oxford University Press, 1925. The title is indicative: Dobree finds the origin of Victorianism in Addison's personal smugness and middle-brow horizons which translate into writings filled with self-satisfaction and complacent ideas.

Johnson, Samuel, "The Life of Addison," in *The Lives of the Poets.* London: J. Nichols, 1779. Every student of Addison should start with Johnson's account. The work is half-biography and half-literary criticism. The biographical portion traces the rise of a new kind of author, the public writer. The critical half focuses on Addison's achievement as a comic writer and a stylist.

Smithers, Peter, *The Life of Joseph Addison.* Oxford: Clarendon Press, rev. ed. 1968. Smithers' book is the most objective and meticulous biography. Smithers is unusually attentive to Addison's political career and to educated guesses about his private life. This is the work to read after Johnson's.

Sutherland, James, "The Last Years of Joseph Addison," in *Background for Queen Anne.* London: Metheun, 1939, pp. 127–144. Sutherland dislikes Addison personally and depicts him as a posturer in, rather than proponent of, Christian virtue.

Tyers, Thomas, *An Historical Essay on Mr. Addison.* London, 1773. This short work does not provide much specific information, but Tyers argues that Addison's popular success changed the nature of authorship: writers became authorities to the public and could expect to earn a respectable living at their trade.

Overview of Critical Sources

Most of the important criticism about Addison has been written in the last twenty-five years. As long as Addison was enthroned as a moralist, literary critics tended to ignore him as a writer. Once the revisionist biographies by Dobree and Sutherland toppled Addison from the pedestal, criticism was free to appreciate him as both a product and a producer of an intense and active literary age. Most of the criticism falls into three categories. The first treats Addison's literary theory as a transition stage between a Neo-classic and a Romantic aesthetic. The second shows that the label "essay" poorly describes the original, rich and varied pieces that Addison contributed to several periodical papers. The third defines the qualities of Addison's middle style which helped to establish prose as a literary language equal to poetry.

Evaluation of Selected Criticism

Bloom, Edward A. and Lillian D. Bloom, *Joseph Addison's Sociable Animal. In the Market Place, on the Hustings, in the Pulpit.* Providence, RI: Brown University Press, 1971. The Blooms synthesize Addison's views on politics, economics, and religion into a coherent philosophy about human nature.

Bloom, Edward A. and Lillian D. Bloom, eds. *Addison and Steele: The Critical Heritage.* London: Routledge and Kegan Paul, 1980. A useful collection of reviews and essays tracing the reputation of the *Tatler* and *Spectator.* The volume reprints commentaries by Addison's contemporaries as well as the famous Victorian evaluations that became the interpretive cliches which modern critics set out to destroy.

Elioseff, Lee Andrew, *The Cultural Milieu of Addison's Literary Criticism.* Austin: University of Texas Press, 1963. Elioseff's book identifies what was new and what was inherited wisdom in Addison's thinking about tragedy and epic.

Evans, James E. and John N. Wall, Jr. *A Guide to Prose Fiction in the "Tatler" and the "Spectator."* New York: Garland, 1977. This book has two uses: it provides an issue-by-issue summary of several hundred contributions, and it points out how much imaginative writing—and how little straightforward essay composing—Addison and Steele really did.

Kay, Donald, *Short Fiction in the "Spectator."* University, AL: University of Alabama Press, 1975. Kay demonstrates the variety and the sophistication of fictional devices used by Addison and Steele in their "essays." This book is essential to understanding the art which underlies the success and reputation of these periodicals.

Otten, Robert M. *Joseph Addison.* Boston: G. K. Hall, 1982. This bio-critical study traces Addison's development as a writer who brought art to journalism.

It emphasizes Addison's style and inventiveness rather than his contribution to reform or ideas.

Tuveson, Ernest Lee, *The Imagination as a Means of Grace.* Berkeley and Los Angeles: University of California Press, 1960. Tuveson's book complements Elioseff's study. Looking at the consequences rather than the sources of Addison's aesthetic, Tuveson credits Addison with profoundly shaping romantic attitudes toward literature.

Other Sources

Gay, Peter, "The Spectator as Actor: Addison in Perspective," *Encounter,* 29 (1967), 27–32. Re-evaluates Addison as a shaper of his age who helped to tame the religious, political, and social violence common to eighteenth-century England.

Lewis, C. S. "Addison," in *Eighteenth Century English Literature: Modern Essays in Criticism.* ed. James Clifford. New York: Oxford University Press, 1959, pp. 144–157. Attempts to define the importance and pleasures of reading Addison today.

Thorpe, Clarence DeWitt, "Addison's Contribution to Criticism," in *The Seventeenth Century: Studies by R. F. Jones and Others.* Stanford, CA: Stanford University Press, 1951, pp. 316–329. Surveys Addison's aesthetics and the impact of his literary criticism.

Selected Dictionaries and Encyclopedias

British Writers, Charles Scribner's Sons, 1980. Brief biography, literary analysis, and substantial bibliography.

Critical Survey of Short Fiction, Salem Press, 1982. Brief biography and short analysis of those *Spectator, Tatler,* and *Guardian* contributions that use fictional devices.

Dictionary of National Biography, Oxford University Press, 1953. Condensed biographical information.

Robert M. Otten
Indiana University-Purdue University at Fort Wayne

JAMES AGEE
1909–1955

Author's Chronology

Born November 27, 1909, Knoxville, Tennessee; *1916* father killed in automobile accident; *1919* enters St. Andrew's, Episcopalian school near Sewanee, Tennessee, and becomes lifelong friends with Father James H. Flye, teacher in school; *1925* enters Phillips Exeter Academy, Exeter, New Hampshire; *1927–1928* edits *Phillips Exeter Monthly,* school literary magazine; *1928* enters Harvard University; *1931–1932* edits *Harvard Advocate,* school literary magazine, and brings out special issue parodying *Time; 1932* graduates from Harvard; begins writing for *Fortune; 1933* marries Olivia Saunders ("Via"); *1936* studies Alabama tenant-farming families on assignment with photographer Walker Evans; *1938* divorced from Olivia Saunders, marries Alma Mailman; *1939* begins reviewing books for *Time; 1941* switches to reviewing films for *Time;* separated from Alma Mailman (later divorced); *1942* starts writing film column for *The Nation; 1944* marries Mia Fritsch; *1948* leaves *Time* and *The Nation;* begins writing film scripts in New York and Hollywood; *1955* dies of heart attack May 16 in New York; *1958* wins Pulitzer Prize posthumously for *A Death in the Family.*

Author's Bibliography (selected)

Permit Me Voyage, 1934 (poems); *Let Us Now Praise Famous Men,* 1941 (prose); *The Morning Watch,* 1951 (novella); *A Death in the Family,* 1957 (novel); *Agee on Film: Reviews and Comments,* 1958; *Agee on Film: Five Film Scripts,* 1960; *The Letters of James Agee to Father Flye,* 1962; *The Collected Short Prose of James Agee,* ed. Robert Fitzgerald, 1968; *The Collected Poems of James Agee,* ed. Robert Fitzgerald, 1968.

Overview of Biographical Sources

Because of his untimely death, James Agee left numerous friends and family members to comment on him in interviews and memoirs. Moreover, much of Agee's own writing is autobiographical in nature. Finally, Agee left letters, manuscripts, and papers which have since been published or housed in special collections. Despite such rich source material, most biographical commentary on Agee is disappointing—shallow appreciations or analyses distorted by biases, selectivity, and stereotypes. The grossest stereotypes occur in remarks on Agee's Appalachian family background and in attempts to fit him into Romantic myths of the artist. Other commentators offer glib explanations of Agee as a mass of contradictions or opposing impulses.

The friendly, selective memoirs of Agee must be considered source materials themselves rather than final statements, while much other biographical commentary—frequently inserted in critical articles and books—has simply been premature. The rich source material has required time to be collected, sorted out, and made available. Only recently has there been an attempt at a full, definitive biography.

Evaluation of Selected Biographies

Bergreen, Laurence, *James Agee: A Life.* New York: E. P. Dutton, 1984. Bergreen, a New York journalist and writer about television, has produced an extensively researched life of Agee. No other work comes close to the same detailed treatment, though even Bergreen is sketchy on Agee's Appalachian connections. Somewhat loosely documented by academic standards—Bergreen uses Agee's autobiographical fiction as fact, while sources of some other facts are not clearly noted—the biography is well written and highly readable, though the details can be tedious. In particular, the sordid details of Agee's sex life, drinking, self-pity, and general lack of discipline tend to obscure his idealistic qualities. The flawed Agee who emerges, however, is demythicized, rendered human in the contexts of his family life, social life, and work environment.

Doty, Mark A. *Tell Me Who I Am: James Agee's Search for Selfhood.* Baton Rouge: Louisiana State University Press, 1981. Drawing on studies of childhood bereavement and on Agee's own works, Doty concentrates on psychoanalyzing Agee. He finds Agee's life centered on the search for a father, for religion, and for death. In identifying these roots of Agee's creativity and psychological problems, Doty overemphasizes Agee's childhood experiences, and, by focusing on Agee's self-absorption, he neglects Agee's relationships and social life.

Madden, David, ed. *Remembering James Agee.* Baton Rouge: Louisiana State University Press, 1974. An uneven collection of reminiscences and appreciations of Agee by his friends, nine of the thirteen pieces appeared elsewhere before being collected here. All of the pieces are interesting and readable, but the most substantial are by Robert Fitzgerald, Dwight Macdonald, and Mia Agee.

Autobiographical Sources

The main source of autobiographical information on Agee is *The Letters of James Agee to Father Flye,* ed. James H. Flye (New York: Brazilier, 1962). A teacher of young Agee at St. Andrew's School, Father Flye remained Agee's friend and father-confessor figure throughout Agee's life. Spanning thirty years, from 1925 to 1955, the letters provide a running account of Agee's aspirations and failings, with comments on his reading, travel, projects, and theories. The second edition (Boston: Houghton Mifflin, 1971) includes a few responses from Father Flye.

Another autobiographical source is Agee's *Let Us Now Praise Famous Men* (Boston: Houghton Mifflin, 1941), the account of his experiences with Alabama share-cropping families in the summer of 1936. The account is especially important for its sense of Agee's compassion. Agee's autobiographical fiction, *The Morning Watch* (Boston: Houghton Mifflin, 1951) and *A Death in the Family* (New York: McDowell Obolensky, 1957), might also be included here, with some reservations. These works are obviously based on events in Agee's life, but Agee altered the facts as he pleased.

Overview of Critical Sources

Most of Agee's critics mix biographical commentary with literary analysis. Some, indeed, interpret Agee's work as his means of self-examination. Much early criticism revolved around the question of whether Agee wasted his talent. Noting his slim production of poetry and fiction, some critics saw Agee as exemplifying the horrible fate of the artist in America. Others, noting Agee's large production of journalism, reviews, and movie scripts, rushed to defend his achievement. All agreed on Agee's talent with language, and a few pointed out his originality, illustrated by his crossbreeding of genres and by his treatment of the movies as an important art form. Agee is now recognized as the dean of American movie critics, but his place in American literature is still to be properly evaluated.

Evaluation of Selected Criticism

Barson, Alfred, *A Way of Seeing: A Critical Study of James Agee.* Amherst: University of Massachusetts Press, 1972. Interweaving biography with analysis of Agee's development and major works, Barson makes some original and debatable—but well-supported—interpretations. He emphasizes the influence of James Joyce on Agee, sees *Let Us Now Praise Famous Men* as Agee's best work, and views Agee's last years as a decline in his talent.

Moreau, Geneviève, *The Restless Journey of James Agee.* trans. Miriam Kleiger with Morty Schiff. New York: William Morrow, 1977. Moreau, a French scholar, sometimes does not go into detail but nevertheless offers the most perceptive critical understanding of Agee, with insight into his symbolism, style, themes, and larger significance. Her book is actually a critical biography—not a full life but an account of Agee's career and the incidents most relevant to it.

Ohlin, Peter H. *Agee.* New York: Obolensky, 1966. The first major critical examination of Agee's works, and in some ways still the most useful, Ohlin's study was originally a doctoral dissertation. Its development is methodical and carefully documented, somewhat padded out with long quotations and explanations, but otherwise the writing is good. Ohlin is also an advocate for his subject.

Other Sources

Coles, Robert, *Irony in the Mind's Life: Essays on Novels by James Agee, Elizabeth Bowen, and George Eliot.* Charlottesville: University Press of Virginia, 1974. Appreciation of *A Death in the Family* by a psychiatrist and eminent sociologist.

Flanders, Mark Wilson, *Film Theory of James Agee.* New York: Arno, 1977. Reprint of a loosely organized dissertation which tries to piece together Agee's philosophy of film.

Frohock, W. M. "James Agee: The Question of Wasted Talent," in *The Novel of Violence in America.* Dallas: Southern Methodist University Press, 1957. Main statement of the view that Agee wasted his talent.

Kramer, Victor A. *James Agee.* Boston: Twayne, 1975. Introduction to Agee's life and works.

Larsen, Erling, *James Agee.* Minneapolis: University of Minnesota Press, 1971. Pamphlet giving a compact overview of Agee's work, with excellent summaries.

Seib, Kenneth, *James Agee: Promise and Fulfillment.* Pittsburgh: University of Pittsburgh Press, 1968. Another introduction to Agee's life and main works.

Snyder, John J. *James Agee: A Study of His Film Criticism.* New York: Arno, 1977. Reprint of a dissertation picturing Agee as a subjective film critic who had no systematic theory, who excelled partly because of his writing ability, and who valued film for its sense of immediacy and reality.

Selected Dictionaries and Encyclopedias

Great Writers of the English Language: Novelists and Prose Writers, St. Martin's Press, 1979. Bibliography and brief assessment.

Harold Branam

CONRAD AIKEN
1889–1973

Author's Chronology

Born August 5, 1889, the oldest child of Dr. William Ford and Anna Potter Aiken in Savannah, Georgia; *1901* Conrad's father kills his wife and then turns the gun on himself; Conrad, age eleven, discovers the murder-suicide; Aiken's younger sister and two brothers are adopted by a family in Philadelphia and Conrad goes to live in New Bedford, Massachusetts with relatives; *1903* enters Middlesex school in Concord, Massachusetts; *1907* enters Harvard University; at Harvard makes many friends including T. S. Eliot, Malcolm Cowley, and John Gould Fletcher; *1911* placed on probation at Harvard for irregularity in class attendance, goes to Europe in protest, but returns to Harvard to finish work on undergraduate degree; *1912* receives degree from Harvard and a few days later marries Jessie McDonald, who was attending school at Radcliffe College; *1913* first child, John Kempton, is born; *1914* first volume of poems published; *1915* moves from Cambridge to Boston in order to be near John Gould Fletcher; *1916* makes several trips abroad becoming acquainted with major poets Ezra Pound, Amy Lowell, and various literary critics both in England and in Massachusetts; *1917* begins career as critic and reviewer for various literary journals including *Dial* and various magazines and newspapers both in the United States and London; *1919* moves with his family to Cape Code; *1921* moves with family first to London, then to East Sussex; by this time he has published seven volumes of poetry, a volume of selected criticism, and almost seventy-five critical articles and reviews; *1924* moves to Jeake's House in Rye, East Sussex; another child, Joan Delano, is born same year; *1926* returns to United States on business trip and meets Clarissa Lorenz; *1927* with Clarissa goes to Harvard University where he becomes a tutor for one year; *1930,* divorces first wife and marries Clarissa; receives Pulitzer Prize for selected poems; in same year returns to Rye with Clarissa and Malcolm Lowry who has become close friend; *1934* receives Guggenheim fellowship and begins "London Letters" for the *New Yorker* magazine; *1936* travels to New York and to Savannah for the first time since *1901,* then returns to Boston, where he meets a young artist, Mary Hoover; *1937* divorces Clarissa and marries Mary; settles in Jeake's House in Rye; *1941* returns to the United States to settle in Cape Cod; *1950* accepts the Chair of Poetry with the title of Poetry Consultant at the Library of Congress; *1952* Conrad Aiken number of *Wake* Magazine printed, an important event in Aiken's literary career; *1953 Collected Poems* wins National Book Award; *1958* receives The Gold Medal in Poetry from the American Academy of Arts and Letters; *1960* returns to Savannah and occupies house next to old family home, staying in Savannah winters only; *1963* suffers heart attack; *1969* receives National Medal for Literature; *1973* named Poet Laureate of Georgia; dies the same year in Savannah.

Author's Bibliography (selected)

Earth Triumphant and Other Tales in Verse, 1914; *Turns and Movies and Other Tales in Verse,* 1916; *The Jig of Forslin: A Symphony,* 1916 (poems); *Nocturne of Remembered Spring and Other Poems,* 1917; *The Charnel Rose,* 1918 (poems); *Senlin: A Biography, and Other Poems,* 1918; *Scepticisms: Notes on Contemporary Poetry,* 1919 (essays); *The House of Dust: A Symphony,* 1920 (poems); *Punch: The Immortal Liar,* 1921 (poems); *Priapus and the Pool,* 1922 (poems); *The Pilgrimage of Festus,* 1923 (poems); *Bring! Bring! and Other Stories,* 1925; *Blue Voyage* 1927 (novel); *Costumes by Eros, Stories,* 1928; *Prelude,* 1929 (poems); *Selected Poems,* 1929; *John Deth, A Metaphysical Legend, and Other Poems,* 1930; *The Coming Forth by Day of Osiris Jones,* 1931 (poems); *Preludes for Memnon,* 1931 (poems); *Prelude: A Poem,* 1932; *And in the Hanging Gardens,* 1933 (poems); *Great Circle, a Novel,* 1933; *Among the Lost People* 1934 (stories); *Landscape West of Eden,* 1935 (poems); *King Coffin,* 1935 (novel); *Time in the Rock: Preludes to Definition,* 1936 (poems); *A Heart for the Gods of Mexico,* 1939 (novel); *Conversation: Or, Pilgrim's Progress,* 1940 (novel); *The Kid,* 1947 (poems); *Skylight One: Fifteen Poems,* 1949; *The Short Stories of Conrad Aiken,* 1950; *Ushant: An Essay,* 1952; *Collected Poems,* 1953; *A Letter from Li Po and Other Poems,* 1955; *A Reviewer's ABC,* 1958 (poems); *The Collected Short Stories of Conrad Aiken,* 1960; *Selected Poems,* 1961; *The Collected Novels of Conrad Aiken,* 1964; *A Seizure of Limericks,* 1964 (poems); *Cats and Bats and Things With Wings: Poems,* 1965; *Tom, Sue and the Clock,* 1966 (poems); *Collected Poems,* 1970; *A Little Who's Zoo of Mild Animals,* 1977 (poems).

Overview of Biographical Sources

Although Aiken insisted that everything he wrote was a reflection of himself, he was speaking more of Aiken the man as representative of modern men than of particulars of his work revealing specific details of personal life. Nevertheless, his novels, especially *Ushant; An Essay* (New York and Boston: Duell, Sloan, and Pearce, and Little, Brown, 1952) do reveal aspects of his personal life. Aiken himself makes the point that *Ushant* stands as a record of his stream-of-consciousness memory. *Loreli Two: My Life with Conrad Aiken* (1983) by Aiken's second wife Clarissa Lorenz, herself an author, provides a particularly vivid picture not only of Aiken but of their life together and of their many close friends. But even more vivid and revealing of Conrad Aiken from the time he was eleven to the time of his death is Joseph Killorin's *Selected Letters of Conrad Aiken* (1978). Aiken's voice coming through his letters to his relatives and close friends on a variety of subjects brings life to his biography.

Evaluation of Selected Biographies

Killorin, Joseph, ed. *Selected Letters of Conrad Aiken.* New Haven and London: Yale University Press, 1978. This volume, composed of two hundred and forty-five letters by Aiken, was selected from a representative collection of over three thousand. The volume was in preparation for eight years. Aiken's contribution to the volume was a list of his correspondents though, as Killorin says, Aiken seldom expected that his friends would have saved the letters that he wrote to them. Next to conversation, Killorin says, Aiken loved to receive and to write letters, and the letters are a dramatic record of Aiken's variety of interests and styles, as well as explanations of his works, influences upon him, and often what became the raw material for his art.

Lorenz, Clarissa M. *Lorelei Two: My Life with Conrad Aiken.* Athens: University of Georgia Press, 1983. Lorenz presents a dramatized account of her life with Aiken from the time of their courtship to the time of their breakup and divorce. This biography, based on personal experiences as well as diaries and letters, makes clear the guiding assumption on which Aiken rested his life and his writing—that the poet who finds the word for life not only makes life possible and coherent but also puts it within the reach of all.

Overview of Critical Sources

It has become a critical commonplace to make the point that although Aiken enjoys one of the most distinguished careers in his literary generation, he is also its most neglected figure. Besides receiving just about every distinguished prize his country could award him, he was the first of his generation to have a book-length study of his work published. *The Melody of Chaos* by Houston Petterson (New York, 1931), now long out of print, was published before Aiken's major works were produced. Frederick J. Hoffman's book, *Conrad Aiken* (1962) was the first serious attempt to come to terms with Aiken as an important figure in American Literature. Hoffman indicates that he wrote the book not simply as a matter of redressing balances, but because he finds that the development of Aiken's mind and its transference to art is, in itself, a fascinating story.

Jay Martin (1962) suggests that literary reviewers and critics did not bother to read Aiken as each new book was published but based their reviews and articles on initial impressions. Martin quotes Allen Tate who observed in his citation of Aiken for the Gold Medal of the Institute of Arts and Letters that Aiken has written "a formidable body of work with which we have not yet come to terms."

Evaluation of Selected Criticism

Hoffman, Frederick J. *Conrad Aiken.* New York: Twayne, 1962. Hoffman appears to be more at home handling Aiken's fiction than the poetry. Making the point that Aiken is a superb story teller, Hoffman suggests that Aiken's success occurs more often in the short story than in the novels. Hoffman seems to have a more difficult time coming to terms with the poetry because there is such a profusion of it, each succeeding volume adding freshness and different poetic devices. Hoffman concludes that the real issue of Aiken's poetry involves a "metaphysical" problem whereby intellectual and emotional difficulties and paradoxes cannot be indulged in or resolved. Consequently, Hoffman suggests that in Aiken's poetry there is a constant "forward-retreat-encircling motion," the language and the lines "moving ahead hesitantly towards statement, [but] never quite satisfactorily achieving it."

Martin, Jay, *Conrad Aiken: A Life of his Art.* Princeton: Princeton University Press, 1962. Martin does a better job with the poetry than Hoffman did. In looking to the corpus of the poetry, Martin makes the point that Aiken alternated between dramatic and lyrical themes and styles from the very beginning of his career to its end. With dramatic art, Martin believes that the ego of the poet explores itself by seeing what kind of characters it can create; in the lyric, this ego confronts and explores itself directly. Martin believes that Aiken developed consistently toward an image of the poet and writer as Emerson characterized him in *Representative Men.*

Martin's study was undertaken with Aiken's blessing and concluded with Aiken's mixed emotions. In a letter to Martin for whom Aiken had become both mentor and friend, Aiken takes Martin to task for insisting on the autobiographical nature of most of his writings. And in another letter, Aiken cautions Martin to pay particular attention in his next book to the role of the psyche in the creation of art and to the purely linguistic level of the art work. Nevertheless, despite Aiken's criticism, Martin's study is the most complete.

Other Sources

Beach, Joseph Warren, *Obsessive Images: Symbolism in Poetry of the Nineteen-Thirties and the Nineteen Forties.* Minneapolis: University of Minnesota Press, 1960, pp. 62–69. Beach comments on the psychological base of Aiken's work under the general heading of "Imagery of Terror."

Cowley, Malcolm, "Conrad Aiken: From Savannah to Emerson," *Southern Review,* XI, 1975, 245–59. Makes the point that after a rereading of Aiken's work one is impressed by the unity that underlies it's mass and diversity. Suggests that candor is close to being a central principle that evolved into a system of aesthetics and ethics that Aiken called the "Religion of Consciousness."

Schorer, Mark, "The Life and the Fiction," *Wake,* XI, 1952, 57–60. An excellent commentary on the short story "Life is Not a Short Story."

Mary Rohrberger
Oklahoma State University

RICHARD ALDINGTON
1892–1962

Author's Chronology

Born Edward Godfree Aldington, 8 July, 1892 at Portsmouth, England, son of a lawyer; *1910* enters University College, London; *1911* leaves University College and supports himself by writing sports journalism; *1912* becomes part of Imagist movement with Ezra Pound and H. D.; 18 October 1913 marries H. D.; *1914–1916* works as assistant editor of the *Egoist; 1915* publishes his first book; *1916* enlists in Royal Sussex Regiment as private; *1919* demobilized as captain, leaves H. D., lives with Dorothy Yorke, and finds work as critic for *Times Literary Supplement; 1922* works as assistant editor of *Criterion; 1928* begins affair with Brigit Patmore, leaves England to live on the Continent; *1929* achieves popularity as novelist with *Death of a Hero; 1938* divorces H. D.; leaves Brigit Patmore; marries Netta McCulloch Patmore; daughter Catherine is born; establishes residence in Connecticut; *1944* moves to Hollywood and works as script writer; *1946* establishes permanent residence in France; *1947* receives James Tait Black Memorial Prize for biography of the Duke of Wellington; *1950* separates from Netta; *1955* becomes target of abuse for his biography of Lawrence of Arabia; *1959* receives *Prix de Gratitude Mistralienne* for *Introduction to Mistral; 1962* visits Russia and is honored by Soviet Writers' Union on his 70th birthday; dies 27 July at Maison Sallé, Sury-en-Vaux.

Author's Bibliography (selected)

Images 1910–1915, 1915 (poems); *A Fool i' the Forest,* 1924 (poem); *Death of a Hero,* 1929 (novel); *A Dream in the Luxembourg,* 1930 (poem); *Roads to Glory,* 1930 (stories); *The Colonel's Daughter,* 1931 (novel); *Soft Answers,* 1932 (stories); *All Men Are Enemies,* 1933 (novel); *Women Must Work,* 1934 (novel); *Very Heaven,* 1937 (novel); *Seven Against Reeves,* 1938 (novel); *Rejected Guest,* 1939 (novel); *Life for Life's Sake,* 1941 (autobiography); *The Duke,* 1943 (biography); *The Complete Poems,* 1948; *Portrait of a Genius, But . . .,* 1950 (biography of D. H. Lawrence); *Pinorman,* 1954 (biography); *Lawrence of Arabia: A Biographical Enquiry,* 1955; *Richard Aldington: Selected Critical Writings, 1928–1960,* 1970 (ed. Alister Kershaw); *The Poetry of Richard Aldington: A Critical Evaluation and an Anthology of Uncollected Poems,* 1974.

Overview of Biographical Sources

Richard Aldington's public and private disputes with various literary and political figures have resulted in his virtual neglect. There exists no definitive biography, although Charles Doyle is completing the first full-length biography of Aldington. Some useful sources are available, but most memoirs, fiction, and biographies by and about D. H. Lawrence, H. D., Ezra Pound, Amy Lowell, T. S. Eliot, and others reflect the bias of those who resented Aldington or smarted from his satire. Aldington's biographies of D. H. Lawrence, Norman Douglas, and Lawrence of Arabia drew vehement and malicious abuse from the political and scholarly partisans of these figures.

Richard Aldington: An Intimate Portrait (1965), includes reminiscences of many people who knew or corresponded with Aldington at various times. Brigit Patmore's autobiography *My Friends When Young* (London: Heinemann, 1968), edited by her son Derek, presents a vivid and nostalgic account of her ten years with Aldington, omitting Aldington's leaving her for her daughter-in-law and the resulting alienation of affection suit the Patmores brought against Aldington. Norman T. Gates's introduction to *A Checklist of the Letters of Richard Aldington* (Carbondale, IL: Southern Illinois University Press, 1977) offers the most accurate biographical survey of Aldington's life. Barbara Guest's *Herself Defined: The Poet H. D. and Her World* (Garden City, NY: Doubleday, 1984) provides valuable and well-researched information on Aldington's marriage to H. D. and is usually objective.

Two collections of letters are also helpful biographical sources. *A Passionate Prodigality: Letters to Alan Bird From Richard Aldington, 1949–1962* (New York: Readex Books, 1975), edited by Miriam J. Benkovitz, includes 147 letters. Benkovitz describes Aldington and Bird's friendship, scrupulously annotates the letters, and provides invaluable information in her notes and biographical glossary. *Literary Lifelines: The Richard Aldington-Lawrence Durrell Correspondence* (London: Faber and Faber, 1981), edited by Ian S. MacNiven and Harry T. Moore, provides background material in the introduction, identifies obscure references, and includes the letters of both men.

Evaluation of Selected Biographies

Kershaw, Alister and F. J. Temple, ed. *Richard Aldington: An Intimate Portrait.* Carbondale: Southern Illinois University Press, 1965. This volume includes biographical essays by twenty-two people who knew or corresponded with Aldington. Entries range from a brief note of gratitude from Samuel Beckett to detailed accounts of various phases of Aldington's life by those who knew Aldington's warmth, generosity, and amiability first-hand.

Kittredge, Selwyn, "The Literary Career of Richard Aldington." Ph.D. dissertation, New York University, 1976. This 596-page work is particularly valuable for its wealth of previously unpublished correspondence and for Kittredge's interviews with others on their relationships with Aldington. Kittredge traces Aldington's literary career through all its phases and relies heavily on Aldington's autobiography for the early years and on the reminiscences of those he interviewed. He devotes only nine pages to the Lawrence of Arabia controversy, but he is extremely thorough on Aldington's involvement with Imagism and on Aldington's activities in the United States during World War II.

Autobiographical Sources

Aldington frequently used his experiences in his fiction with significant alteration. In *Pinorman,* his recollections of Norman Douglas, Pino Orioli, and Charles Prentice include his comments on his relationship with these men, and some of his satires (notably *Stepping Heavenward* and "Nobody's Baby," which lampoon Eliot and Pound), reveal his attitudes toward literary figures he knew. His only overtly autobiographical work, however, is *Life for Life's Sake: A Book of Reminiscences* (New York: Viking, 1941). He describes in a witty and engaging manner his development as an artist, his literary associations, his travels, and his observations from early childhood to the eve of World War II. He is vague about the identities of his companions during his European travels, electing not to discuss his personal relationships, and he is occasionally unclear about the dates of events he describes. As the subtitle suggests, these are less important than his development, his reactions to the literary figures he met, and his observations of the significant literary, political, and social trends of his time. The autobiography appeared before the controversies aroused by his later biographies, but it comments significantly on Aldington's involvement with Imagism and his career as a novelist.

Overview of Critical Sources

Since Aldington was significant as a poet, novelist, translator, critic, biographer, and essayist, many critics have focused on isolated aspects of his art rather than on his entire literary achievement. Ruth E. Galloway assesses Aldington's poetic achievement in "The Poetry of Richard Aldington: A Critical Introduction" (Ph.D. dissertation, Texas Tech University, 1972), and Sidney Rosenthal concentrates on Aldington's novels in "The Fiction of Richard Aldington" (Ph.D. dissertation, Harvard University, 1968), but these remain unpublished. Most criticism of Aldington appears in studies of literary movements and sub-genres, such as Imagism and war literature, emphasizing his historical rather than literary importance.

Evaluation of Selected Criticism

Gates, Norman T. *The Poetry of Richard Aldington: A Critical Evaluation and an Anthology of Uncollected Poems.* University Park, PA: Penn State University Press, 1974. The first half of this work is Gates's 161-page introduction, which summarizes critical views of the poetry, describes Aldington's editions of poetry, evaluates Aldington as a poet, and comments on "The Complete Poems."

McGreevy, Thomas, *Richard Aldington: An Englishman.* London: Chatto & Windus, 1931. McGreevy's study, the first full-length criticism of Aldington's work, traces his early poetry and fiction. Although the book appeared before Aldington's biographies and the later novels, it provides an extremely perceptive view of Aldington's literary merit.

Smith, Richard E. *Richard Aldington.* Boston: Twayne, 1977. Smith provides a chronology of Aldington's life and a biographical chapter, but he devotes most of his book to an examination of Aldington's work: three chapters on Aldington's poetry, three chapters on his novels, and one chapter on Aldington's biographies, translations, and criticisms. The book helps to place Aldington's art into its biographical context, and it provides a fully annotated bibliography of both primary and secondary sources, but it tends to summarize Aldington's texts rather than to explore them in the light of Aldington's passion for life and satiric intensity.

Other Sources

Gales, Norman T. ed. *New Canterbury Literary Society Newsletter.* Published quarterly by Gates since August 1973, the *NCLS Newsletter* provides biographical and bibliographical information for those interested in Aldington's life and work.

Gates, Norman T., "Richard Aldington in Russia," *Texas Quarterly* 21 (1978), 35-57. Describes Aldington's 1962 visit to Moscow.

Knightley, Phillip, "Aldington's Enquiry Concerning T. E. Lawrence," *Texas Quarterly* 16 (Winter 1973), 98-105. Describes the controversy and consequences to Aldington of his biography of Lawrence of Arabia.

Sims, George, "Richard Aldington at Home," *Antiquarian Book Monthly Review* (December 1982), 460-67; (January 1983), 4-11. View of Aldington during his later years.

Thompson, Michael B., "Richard Aldington and T. S. Eliot," *Yeats Eliot Review* 6 (1979), 3-9. Evaluation of the Aldington-Eliot relationship.

Selected Dictionaries and Encyclopedias

Dictionary of Literary Biography, Volume 20: British Poets, 1914-1945, Gale Research, 1983. Useful survey of Aldington's life and poetry.

Critical Survey of Long Fiction, Vol. 7, Salem Press, 1983. Excellent summary of Aldington's life and fiction.

Fred D. Crawford
University of Oregon

NELSON ALGREN
1909–1981

Author's Chronology

Born March 28, 1909, Nelson Ahlgren Abraham in Detroit, Michigan; *1912* Abraham family moves to Chicago; *1923–1928* attends Hibbard High School in Chicago; *1931* graduates from the University of Illinois with a Bachelor of Science degree in journalism; *1931–1933* seeks work in New Orleans and southwest Texas during which he spends four months in jail in Alpine, Texas; *1933* publishes first short story under name Nelson Algren; *1936* marries and divorces, works for WPA Illinois Writers' Project; *1942–1945* serves as private in U.S. Army in Wales, France, and Germany; *1945* legally changes name; *1948* takes two-month trip down the Mississippi and to Yucatan with Simone de Beauvoir; *1949* travels to Europe and meets the Jean-Paul Sartre circle of writers; *1950* receives first National Book Award for *The Man With the Golden Arm; 1962* travels to Far East; *1965* marries Betty Ann Jones; *1967* divorces; *1974* teaches creative writing at the University of Florida; moves to Paterson, New Jersey to investigate the murder conviction of black boxer Rubin "Hurricane" Carter; *1981* elected to the American Institute of Arts and Letters; dies in Southampton, New York on May 9; *1983* last novel, *The Devil's Stocking,* published in the United States.

Author's Bibliography (selected)

Somebody in Boots, 1935 (novel); *Never Come Morning,* 1942 (novel); *The Neon Wilderness,* 1947 (short stories); *The Man With the Golden Arm,* 1949 (novel); *A Walk on the Wild Side,* 1956 (novel); *Who Lost an American?,* 1963 (travel, autobiographical and satiric essays); *The Devil's Stocking,* 1983 (novel).

Overview of Biographical Sources

No definitive study of Algren's life exists. Critics and scholars have yet to reach a consensus concerning Algren's importance to American literature. As a result, interviews and memoirs by his acquaintances, subjective by nature, constitute the best information available on Algren. Martha Heasley Cox and Wayne Chatterton's bio-critical *Nelson Algren* (Boston: G.K. Hall, 1975), while focusing primarily on the fiction, does contain some valuable information about Algren's childhood and early years "on the road" in Texas and New Orleans. Cox and Chatterton's "Chronology" is especially useful. In 1964, H. E. F. Donohue published a book-length series of interviews with the novelist, *Conversations with Nelson Algren* (Hill and Wang). In *Conversations,* Algren speaks frankly about his complex attitude toward his parents, his four-month sojourn in the Alpine, Texas, jail, his army years, his bitter experiences in Hollywood, and his celebrated love affair with Simone de Beauvoir. De Beauvoir writes just as openly about the relationship in "An American Rendezvous: The Question of Fidelity," Part II, *Harper's,* CCXXIX (Dec., 1964), 111–122. Other significant interviews with Algren include the following: Alston Anderson and Terry Southern, "Nelson Algren," *Paris Review,* XI (Winter, 1955), 37–58. John William Corrington, "Nelson Algren Talks with *NOR*'s Editor-at-Large," *The New Orleans Review,* I (Winter, 1969), 130–132. David Ray, "Talk on the Wild Side: A Bowl of Coffee with Nelson Algren," *The Reporter,* XX (June 11, 1959), 31–33. W. J. Weatherby, "The Last Interview," included in Nelson Algren, *The Devil's Stocking* (Arbor House, 1983), pp. 7–12.

Autobiographical Sources

Algren fictionalized much of his personal experience; most memorably, the depression years "on the road" in New Orleans and Texas inspired his first novel, *Somebody in Boots.* While he never published an autobiography, he wrote directly about other periods of his life in *Who Lost an American?* (1963), *The Last Carousel* (1973), and *Notes from a Sea Diary: Hemingway All the Way* (1965). Among other things a travel book, a satire of the New York literary establishment and of America's *Playboy* mentality concerning sex, *Who Lost an American?* is a work which truly defies classification. It does contain some evocative, lyrical reminiscences of Algren's childhood in Chicago, emphasizing his family's "respectable" poverty, his father's inability to hold a job, and his own youthful struggles with religion. Along with the novels *Never Come Morning* and *The Man With the Golden Arm,* these reminiscences definitively establish Algren as a Chicago writer. *The Last Carousel,* a collection of stories and sketches, contains several autobiographical essays. "Previous Days" recounts many of the childhood experiences described in *Who Lost an American?.* "Otto Preminger's Strange Suspenjers" is a comic, yet embittered, narrative of Algren's disastrous attempt to work on the film version of *The Man With the Golden Arm.* "Go! Go! Go! Forty Years Ago" effectively dramatizes the 1919 Chicago Black Sox scandal as a symbol of Algren's loss of innocence and initiation into adulthood. Another group of essays describes Algren's travels to the Far East. His 1962 voyage to Korea, Bombay, Calcutta and other Asian ports was the inspiration for *Notes from a Sea Diary.*

Overview of Critical Sources

The lack of a critical consensus concerning Algren's importance as a writer is reflected in the scarcity of major critical assessments of his work. Much of the existing criticism is concerned with the question of Algren's relationship to the Dreiser-Crane-Norris school of American literary naturalism. On the basis of his first two novels, *Somebody in Boots* and *Never Come Morning,* he was instantly labeled a naturalist; and, as the validity of the naturalistic tradition came increasingly under attack in the post World War II area, his work was too often denounced as outdated or, worse, ignored.

Evaluation of Selected Criticism

Bluestone, George, "Nelson Algren," *Western Review,* XXII (Autumn, 1957), 27–44. Probably the best essay written about Algren, Bluestone argues that he "is not a naturalist, and to read him in the naturalist tradition is to misread him." He sees "the destruction of a love relationship" as the recurrent theme in Algren's novels and offers a defense of their seemingly episodic structure.

Cowley, Malcolm, *The Literary Situation.* New York: Viking, 1958. Cowley briefly, but perceptively, analyzes *The Man With the Golden Arm* as representative of a vital new direction for American literary naturalism.

Cox, Martha Heasley and Wayne Chatterton, *Nelson Algren.* Boston: G. K. Hall, 1975. The only book-length study of Algren is an exceptionally good one. Cox and Chatterton describe the evolution of Algren's fiction from the social protest of *Somebody in Boots* to the surrealist satire of *A Walk on the Wild Side.* They see Algren's heroes as being victimized by their own guilt as much as by environmental forces.

Eisinger, Chester E. "Nelson Algren: Naturalism as the Beat of the Iron Heart," *Fiction of the Forties.* Chicago: University of Chicago Press, 1963. Eisinger condemns Algren's "romanticism" and intellectual "indifference," but praises his "compassion." He asserts that "what gives Algren distinction is that he is a naturalist who cares about style, and who is linguistically adventuresome and aware, if not always successful."

Geismar, Maxwell, "Nelson Algren: The Iron Sanctuary," *College English* XIV (March, 1953), 311–315. Geismar praises Algren as one of the few American writers keeping alive the tradition of social protest. He perceives that the savage external environment and inner guilt in which Algren's characters exist cause them to seek jail as a refuge.

Gelfant, Blanche M. *The American City Novel.* Norman: University of Oklahoma Press, 1954. Gelfant credits Algren with perfecting "the ecological novel," which "is distinguished from both the portrait and the synoptic novels by its restriction to a small spatial unit within the city." Gelfant adds that "in very recent fiction, the most evocative and stirring use of urban imagery has been made by Nelson Algren."

James R. Giles
Northern Illinois University

KINGSLEY AMIS
1922

Author's Chronology

Born April 16, 1922, Clapham Commons, South London of William Robert and Rosa; *1934* wins scholarship to City of London School; *1941* enters St. John's College, Oxford; *1942–1945* serves in the Royal Corps of Signals; *1945* completes education at Oxford; *1947* publishes first volume of poetry, *Bright November; 1948* marries Hilary Ann Bardwell; *1949–1961* lecturer in English, University College, Swansea; *1954* publishes first novel, *Lucky Jim; 1955* wins Somerset Maugham Award for *Lucky Jim; 1958* film of *Lucky Jim; 1958–1959* Visiting Fellow in Creative Writing, Princeton; *1961–1963* Fellow and Director of Studies in English, Peterhouse, Cambridge; *1962* film of *That Uncertain Feeling; 1963* gives up university teaching to write full-time; *1965* divorces to marry Elizabeth Jane Howard; *1967–1968* Visiting Professor, Vanderbilt University; *1970* film of *Take A Girl Like You; 1976* wins John W. Campbell Memorial Award for *The Alteration,* made Honorary Fellow, St. John's, Oxford; *1983* divorces Elizabeth Jane Howard.

Author's Bibliography (selected)

Lucky Jim, 1954 (novel); *That Uncertain Feeling,* 1955 (novel); *I Like It Here,* 1958 (novel); *New Maps of Hell,* 1960 (criticism); *Take A Girl Like You,* 1960 (novel); *One Fat Englishman,* 1963 (novel); *The James Bond Dossier,* 1965 (criticism); *The Anti-Death League,* 1966 (novel); *I Want It Now,* 1968 (novel); *The Green Man,* 1969 (novel); *What Became of Jane Austen? And Other Questions,* 1970 (criticism, autobiography); *Girl, 20,* 1971 (novel); *Ending Up,* 1973 (novel); *Rudyard Kipling and His World,* 1975 (biography); *The Alteration,* 1976 (novel); *Jake's Thing,* 1978 (novel); *Collected Poems: 1944–1979,* 1979; *Russian Hide & Seek,* 1980 (novel); *Stanley and the Women,* 1984 (novel).

Overview of Biographical Sources

Although a definitive biography of Amis has not been written, several bio-critical books and two unpublished dissertations (which are readily available from University Microfilms) offer material useful to an understanding of the relationship between his life and work, as well as to pertinent literary influences upon his writing. The dissertations are Dale Salwak's "Kingsley Amis: Writer as Moralist" (University of Southern California, 1974) and Jack Benoit Gohn's "The Novels of Kingsley Amis: A Reading" (Johns Hopkins University, 1975). Salwak and Gohn quote heavily from interviews with the subject. Gohn is broadly informed in the facts of Amis' life, his work, and his place in Western literary tradition. He exhibits a range and perspective historically absent in much scholarship on Amis' life. Useful biographical material covers Amis' childhood, education, relationship to parents, education, military service, developing career, death of his father, re-marriage, and political views through to the writing of *Ending Up*. Philip Gardner's *Kingsley Amis* (Boston: Twayne, 1981) draws from already published sources as well as from interviews with some of Amis' contemporaries to sketch his life. Gardner presents a general bio-critical introduction to Amis' life and works. It does not discuss any material in great detail, and focuses more on Amis as novelist than as poet or critic. The catalogue of biographical information in the opening chapter is accurate, readable, and helpful, but distracts at times from the focus of his study.

Additional information pertaining to Amis' years at Oxford may be found in Philip Larkin's *Jill* (New York: St. Martin's, 1964), John Wain's *Sprightly Running: Part of an Autobiography* (New York and London: Macmillan, 1963), and Blake Morrison's *The Movement: English Poetry and Fiction of the 1950s* (Oxford and New York: Oxford, 1980). Finally, William Van O'Connor offers a brief overview of Amis' life and its relationship to his writings in his book, *The New University Wits, and the End of Modernism* (Carbondale: Southern Illinois University Press, 1963).

Autobiographical Sources

Amis' *What Became of Jane Austen? And Other Questions* is invaluable for what it reveals about his life. Of the thirty-one essays in the collection nine cover specific episodes that he considers important to his development as a writer, including the following: meeting with Dylan Thomas, early interest in horror films, childhood education, attitudes toward Cambridge and Oxford, memories of his father, politics, and Christianity. The essays are reprinted as they were published originally with only minor revisions and, in some cases, lengthy postscripts. Also, biographical details emerge from interviews conducted by Peter Firchow in *The Writer's Place* (Minneapolis: University of Minnesota Press, 1974); by James Clive in *The New Review* (1:4, July 1974, pp. 21–28); by Melvyn Bragg in *The Listener* (February 20, 1975, pp. 240–241); by Michael Blaber in *Paris Review* (16, Winter 1975, pp. 39–72); and by Dale Salwak in *Literary Voices* (San Bernardino: Borgo Press, 1984). For additional information, scholars should consult holdings of letters, manuscripts and notebooks at the following institutions: Humanities Research Center (University of Texas, Austin), Pennsylvania State University Library, Syracuse University Library, and Princeton University Library.

Overview of Critical Sources

Almost from the beginning of his career, Amis has enjoyed the attention of numerous and influential commentators. Because his works have been filled with innovations, surprises, and variations in technique and theme, it is not surprising that until recently critics and reviewers alike have found it difficult to make a definitive statement about his achievements. Of all his writings, however, his novels inspire the greatest amount of critical comment. This critical reception may be divided into four major areas of concern: (1) as an angry novelist protesting against the contemporary social, political, and economic scene in Britain; (2) as a comic novelist, an entertainer, an amiable satirist; (3) as a storyteller who antedates the great modernist writers; (4) as a moralist whose view of life grows increasingly pessimistic. Two bibliographies are particularly helpful in tracing the development of Amis' critical reception. Jack Benoit Gohn's *Kingsley Amis: A Checklist* (Kent, OH: Kent State University Press, 1976) covers primary and secondary materials through 1975 with occasional annotations. Dale Salwak's *Kingsley Amis: A Reference Guide* (Boston: G. K. Hall, 1978) offers an annotated listing of the judgments passed on Amis' literary endeavors from 1951 through 1977. A four-page introduction traces his career through an analysis of the critical reception of his work through the years.

Evaluation of Selected Criticism

Bergonzi, Bernard, *The Situation of the Novel.* London: Macmillan, 1970. Bergonzi evaluates Amis' comic spirit as having diminished over fifteen years of writing, to be replaced by an increasing sense of fear and irrationality. Bergonzi is particularly helpful in showing that Amis is more than just a comic social commentator; he is a serious writer with serious concerns.

Gardner, Philip, *Kingsley Amis.* Boston: Twayne, 1981. This is the first published introduction to the works of Amis. It includes an analysis of all of his novels through *Ending Up,* as well as a perceptive chapter on his poetry and a useful survey of the short stories. Missing is a real enjoyment of Amis' humor and a failure to capture the diversity of Amis' imagination.

Gindin, James, *Postwar British Fiction: New Accents and Attitudes.* Berkeley and Los Angeles: University of California Press, 1962. A useful, detailed survey of the comic world as it develops in Amis' first four novels.

Lodge, David, *Language of Fiction: Essays in Critical and Verbal Analysis of the English Novel.* London: Routledge and Kegan Paul; New York: Columbia University Press, 1966. Lodge is the first major critic to consider Amis in light of Stephen Spender's distinction between the "modern" and the "contemporary." He offers a close, perceptive examination of *Lucky Jim, I Like It Here,* and *Take A Girl Like You.*

Rabinovitz, Rubin, *The Reaction Against Experiment in the English Novel, 1950–1960.* New York and London: Columbia University Press, 1967. The first thorough study of Amis' dislike for experimentalism, Rabinovitz discusses Amis' preference for a direct, conventional style, similar to that found in both 18th century and early 19th century novels.

Other Sources

Colby, Winetta, "Kingsley Amis," in *Wilson Library Bulletin* 32 (May 1958), 618. Brief survey of Amis' early years, including his experiences as a student.

Holloway, David, "The Amis Family," London *Daily Telegraph,* August 9, 1957, pp. 10, 11. Fascinating insights into the writing lives of Amis, his former wife Elizabeth Jane Howard, and son Martin.

Selected Dictionaries and Encyclopedias

Contemporary Novelists, St. Martin's Press, 1980. Brief biography with short analysis of some of Amis' important novels.

Critical Survey of Long Fiction, Salem Press, 1983. Major events in Amis' life and their relation to four of his novels.

Dictionary of Literary Biography, Gale Research, 1983. Detailed overview of Amis' entire life up to 1980, and a discussion of major works.

Dale Salwak
Citrus College

SHERWOOD ANDERSON
1876–1941

Author's Chronology

Born September 13, 1876, in Camden, Ohio to Irwin M. and Emma S. Anderson; *1884* moves to Clyde, Ohio, attends public schools irregularly; *1896–1898* works as a laborer in Chicago; *1898–1899* in Spanish American War; *1900* completes senior year of high school at Wittenburg Academy, then takes job in a Chicago advertising agency; *1904* marries Cornelia Lane; *1906* moves to Cleveland to head United Factories Company (a mail-order firm); *1907* moves to Elyria, Ohio to head a mail-order paint business; *1912* suffers nervous collapse, apparently from tensions over incongruities between business demands and burgeoning literary interests; *1913* returns to Chicago and advertising business, but joins other artists of incipient "Chicago Literary Renaissance"; *1916* divorces Cornelia; marries Tennessee Mitchell 4 days later; publishes first novel, *Windy McPherson's Son; 1917* publishes second novel, *Marching Men; 1919* publishes *Winesburg, Ohio,* a montage-like novel consisting of short-story components; *1920* publishes *Poor White* (novel); *1921* publishes *Triumph of the Egg* (stories); wins *Dial* award for "service to letters;" *1923* publishes *Many Marriages* (novel) and *Horses and Men* (stories); *1924* makes first trip to Europe; divorces Tennessee Mitchell; marries Elizabeth Prall; publishes *A Story Teller's Story* (autobiography); *1925* spends summer in Troutdale, Virginia, near Marion; goes on lecture tour; publishes *Dark Laughter* (novel); *1926* purchases Ripshin Farm at Troutdale and starts to build a house there; *1926* leaves for second European trip; *1927* returns; settles at Ripshin but continues to lecture; purchases the two Marion weekly newspapers, *The Smyth County News* and *The Marion Democrat;* edits, manages, writes for the newspapers until the early 1930's; *1929* publishes *Hello Towns!,* (an anthology of his newspaper pieces); *1932* divorces Elizabeth Prall; attends Marxist peace conference in Amsterdam; *1933* marries Eleanor Copenhaver of Marion, a Y.W.C.A. executive; publishes *Death in the Woods* (final story collection); *1934* dramatization of *Winesburg, Ohio* at Hedgerow Theatre in Pennsylvania; *1934–1935* travels widely in America; writes mainly non-fiction; *1935 Puzzled America* (journalistic essays on the Depression and New Deal); *1936 Kit Brandon* (final novel); *1937–1940* more wide-ranging American travels; works sporadically on memoirs; *1941* begins trip with Eleanor to South America as a kind of unofficial ambassador; dies of peritonitis at Colon, Panama 8 March; is buried in Marion.

Author's Bibliography (selected)

Windy McPherson's Son, 1916 (novel), revised ed., 1921; *Marching Men,* 1917 (novel); *Mid-American Chants,* 1918 (poems); *Winesburg, Ohio,* 1919 (novel structured by means of individual story-sketches); *Poor White,* 1920 (novel); *The Triumph of the Egg,* 1921 (stories); *Many Marriages,* 1923 (novel); *Horses and Men,* 1923 (stories); *A Story Teller's Story,* 1924 (autobiography); *Dark Laughter,* 1925 (novel); *Tar: A Midwest Childhood,* 1926 (autobiographical novel); *Sherwood Anderson's Notebook,* 1926 (prose sketches); *A New Testament,* 1927 (poems); *Hello Towns!,* 1929 (newspaper pieces); *Perhaps Women,* 1931 (essays and sketches); *Beyond Desire,* 1932 (novel); *Death in the Woods,* 1933 (stories); *No Swank,* 1934 (biographical sketches); *Puzzled America,* 1935 (journalistic essays); *Kit Brandon,* 1936 (novel); *Plays: Winesburg and Others,* 1937; *Home Town,* 1940 (long essay in prose and photographs); *The Sherwood Anderson Reader,* edited by Paul Rosenfeld, 1947 (a miscellany).

Overview of Biographical Sources

Although the life of Sherwood Anderson has been a subject of much interest for both specialists and general readers, no full-scale biography exists. The nearest approximation is James Schevill's *Sherwood Anderson: His Life and Work* (1951). In the same year that Schevill's work appeared, Irving Howe published his *Sherwood Anderson* (1951) in the "American Men of Letters" series. Like Schevill's work, Howe's contains a full, though by no means definitive biographical account. Unlike Schevill, however, Howe focuses upon what he perceives as Anderson's limitations as a writer, giving him only scant and grudging credit for such aspects as his "lyrical and nostalgic feeling." An additional biographical source is particularly rich in material covering Anderson's background, his early years, and his career up to the publication of *Winesburg, Ohio* in 1919: William A. Sutton's *The Road to Winesburg* (1972). Although no study of comparable depth exists for Anderson's literary career following the publication of *Winesburg, Ohio*—twenty-two productive years remain—Walter B. Rideout has been working for more than two decades on what promises to be a definitive biography.

Evaluation of Selected Biographies

Howe, Irving, *Sherwood Anderson.* New York: William Sloane Associates, 1951. Though indispensable for both the biographical detail which it contains and for its discussion of some of the complicated questions regarding Anderson's life (e.g., his relationship with his parents), Howe's study tends to discount Anderson's career after the publication of the novel *Poor White* (1920) and to give little or no attention to several works of his last two decades.

Schevill, James, *Sherwood Anderson: His Life and Work.* Denver: University of Denver Press, 1951. Scion of a family with whom Anderson enjoyed an intimate friendship, James Schevill, himself a creative writer of note, brought to his critical biography special perceptions and skills. Schevill's critical evaluation, while on the whole positive, is very fair in that it addresses Anderson's shortcomings as well as his strengths.

Sutton, William A. *The Road to Winesburg.* Metuchen, N.J., The Scarecrow Press, 1972. Drawing upon living sources of information which have since disappeared and copiously documented, this study is widely accepted as being a full, reliable treatment of Anderson's evolution from obscure beginnings in rural Ohio to the publication of his masterpiece, *Winesburg, Ohio.*

Autobiographical Sources

Because he correctly recognized in his own life certain features that were either central to American life and values of his time (e.g., the artist versus an industrial society) or the basis for legendary treatment (e.g., his dramatic abandonment of business for a literary career), Sherwood Anderson's work is characterized by autobiography. Though many Anderson novels deal with personal adumbrations such as his Midwestern boyhood, his rise in business and the resulting disillusionment, several titles are professedly autobiographical. The earliest of these is *A Story Teller's Story.* Like most of Anderson's autobiographical writing, this book seems to occupy the grey area between fact and fiction, a distinction which Anderson was incapable of making. Rather, he was interested in getting the "essence" of a matter correct rather than the bare facts. Thus, *A Story Teller's Story,* like the later *Sherwood Anderson's Notebook* and *Memoirs,* is more an exercise in exploring for meanings than in relating basic details.

At his death, Anderson left some 3,000 unpublished pages of autobiography, which has subsequently resulted in two editions of memoirs. The first, *Sherwood Anderson's Memoirs* (New York: Harcourt, Brace, 1942), bears the heavy editorial imprint of Paul Rosenfeld, who rearranged, re-wrote, and generally regularized Anderson's chaotic manuscripts into a more polished form than Anderson likely would have achieved. The second, *Sherwood Anderson's Memoirs: A Critical Edition* (Chapel Hill: The University of North Carolina Press, 1969), edited by Anderson scholar Ray Lewis White, is far more complete than Rosenfeld's edition and closer to the structure outlined by Anderson but left incomplete at his death. In the opinion of most Anderson scholars, the second edition has supplanted the first.

In addition to the autobiographical writings, more than 6,000 letters written by Anderson are known to exist, only a fraction of which have been published, but with more publications anticipated in the near future. The two existing editions of letters, both of which cover a broad range of correspondents and subjects are: *Letters of Sherwood Anderson,* edited by Howard Mumford Jones in association with Walter B. Rideout (Boston: Little, Brown, 1953) and *Sherwood Anderson Selected Letters,* edited by Charles E. Modlin (Knoxville: University of Tennessee Press, 1984).

Overview of Critical Sources

The extent to which Anderson's early career attracted critical interest is suggested by the fact that in 1927 he was the subject of two monographs:

N. Bryllion Fagin's *The Phenomenon of Sherwood Anderson* (Baltimore: Rossi-Bryn) and Cleveland B. Chase's *Sherwood Anderson* (New York: Robert M. McBride & Company). Though obviously limited in scope and to some extent by critical approach, both studies reveal how Anderson was perceived by two contemporary critics while at the height of his popularity. No subsequent book-length studies of Anderson appeared until 1951, when the critical biographies of Schevill and Howe (qq.v.) appeared. By this time, a decade after his death, Anderson's place in American letters was by no means determined. While Schevill's study could be seen as a harbinger of future interest, Howe's could be seen as an attempt to discount Anderson's importance to a level where his permanent place would be obscure at best. But beginning in the 1960s and continuing to date, there has been a groundswell of critical activity the net result of which may be said to have enhanced Anderson's reputation and assured him a position among the influential American writers of the twentieth century.

Evaluation of Selected Criticism

Anderson, David D. *Sherwood Anderson: An Introduction and Interpretation.* New York: Holt, Rinehart and Winston, 1967. A salient feature of David Anderson's study is that it successfully treats the entire Anderson canon as "a chronological unit." In so doing, a consistent focus between the life and work is maintained. This study did much to further the interest in Anderson that has developed in the last two decades. It is also an appropriate place for the uninitiated reader to see the entire range of Anderson's prolific career closely analyzed.

Burbank, Rex, *Sherwood Anderson.* New York: Twayne, 1964. Though limited in scope by the requirements of the Twayne U.S. Authors Series, Burbank's well-written study reflects his own preferences for what he and other modern critics deem Anderson's most significant work. One particularly strong and welcome feature of the study is Burbank's tracing of the historical/cultural forces that shaped Anderson's art. This is an important contribution, as many former commentators had tended to see Anderson for the unique aspects of his life and work and not as part of a larger cultural milieu.

Weber, Brom, *Sherwood Anderson.* Minneapolis: University of Minnesota Press, 1964. Though a pamphlet-length study in the American Writers series, Weber's testament is surprisingly complete in identifying the major issues involved in understanding and assessing the scope of Anderson's achievement as a writer. His appraisal is well balanced in that he presents both positive and negative characteristics. This work serves well as an introduction for the general student as well as a summarizing statement for the reader with some prior knowledge.

Other Sources

Anderson, David D. ed. *Critical Essays on Sherwood Anderson.* Boston: G. K. Hall, 1981. The most recent and most comprehensive collection of essays on Anderson's life and work.

———, *Sherwood Anderson: Dimensions of His Literary Art.* East Lansing: Michigan State University Press, 1976. A collection of essays written by modern scholars, giving a good indication of the directions being taken in current studies.

Campbell, Hilbert H. and Charles E. Modlin, eds. *Sherwood Anderson Centennial Studies.* Troy, NY: Whitson Publishing Company, 1976. A collection of source materials and critical essays published on the centennial of Anderson's birth.

Rideout, Walter B. *Sherwood Anderson: A Collection of Critical Essays.* Englewood Cliffs, NJ: Prentice-Hall, Inc., 1974. Though some of the components of this collection are found in other similar sources, others are all but inaccessible for the average reader.

White, Ray Lewis, ed. *Sherwood Anderson: A Reference Guide.* Boston: G.K. Hall & Co., 1977. The most complete bibliography to date. Though containing annotated listings of works about, and not by Anderson, it is nevertheless the starting point for anyone seeking secondary materials. Covers the period 1916–1975 on a year-by-year basis.

Selected Dictionaries and Encyclopedias

Critical Survey of Long Fiction, Vol. 1, Salem Press, 1983. Short analysis of *Marching Men, Winesburg, Ohio, Many Marriages* and *Dark Laughter.*

Critical Survey of Short Fiction, Vol. 3, Salem Press, 1983. Analysis of the stories from *Winesburg, Ohio.*

Welford Dunaway Taylor
The University of Richmond

MATTHEW ARNOLD
1822–1888

Author's Chronology

Born December 24, 1822, Laleham, Middlesex, England, oldest son of Mary Penrose and Thomas Arnold (later famous headmaster of Rugby School); *1833* becomes close neighbor of William Wordsworth when family builds home, Fox How, in Lake District; *1836* enters Winchester College; *1837* enters fifth form of Rugby School; *1840* wins Rugby Poetry Prize for "Alaric at Rome"; *1841* enters Balliol College, Oxford; becomes close friends with Arthur Hugh Clough; *1843* wins Oxford's Newdigate Poetry Prize for "Cromwell"; *1844* takes B.A., second-class honors, *Litterae Humaniores; 1845* elected fellow of Oriel College, Oxford; *1847* becomes private secretary to Marquis of Lansdowne, influential government peer; *1848* has passion for Mary Claude ("Marguerite" in poems), French exile and authoress; *1849* publishes first work, *The Strayed Reveller, and Other Poems; 1851* begins long career as inspector of schools; marries Frances Lucy Wightman, daughter of Tory judge; *1857* elected Professor of Poetry at Oxford and begins long series of lectures covering two five-year terms; *1859* makes first of three official trips to study schools on Continent; *1870* awarded honorary degree, D.C.L., by Oxford University; *1883* awarded Civil List pension; *1883–1884* lectures in America; *1886* retires as inspector of schools; *1888* dies of heart attack in Liverpool, April 15.

Author's Bibliography (selected)

The Strayed Reveller, and Other Poems, 1849; *Empedocles on Etna, and Other Poems,* 1852; *Poems,* 1853; *Poems: Second Series,* 1855; *Merope,* 1858 (drama); *Popular Education in France,* 1861 (educational report); *On Translating Homer,* 1861 (criticism); *Last Words on Translating Homer,* 1862 (criticism); *A French Eton,* 1864; *Essays in Criticism: First Series,* 1865; *On the Study of Celtic Literature,* 1867 (criticism); *New Poems,* 1867; *Schools and Universities on the Continent,* 1868; *Culture and Anarchy,* 1869 (social criticism); *St. Paul and Protestantism,* 1870; *Friendship's Garland,* 1871 (social criticism); *Literature and Dogma,* 1873 (religious criticism); *God and the Bible,* 1875; *Last Essays on Church and Religion,* 1877; *Mixed Essays,* 1879; *Irish Essays and Others,* 1882; *Discourses in America,* 1885 (social and literary criticism); *Essays in Criticism: Second Series,* 1888; *Essays in Criticism: Third Series,* ed. E. J. O'Brien, 1910.

Overview of Biographical Sources

Matthew Arnold's express wish that no biography of him be written deterred would-be biographers during his life and for decades afterwards. Early published sources of information include Arthur Penrhyn Stanley's biography of his father, *The Life and Correspondence of Thomas Arnold, D.D.,* 2 vols. (London: Ward, Lock, 1844) and the memoirs of his brother and niece, Thomas Arnold the younger's *Passages in a Wandering Life* (London: Edward Arnold, 1900) and Mrs. Humphry Ward's *A Writer's Recollections,* 2 vols. (London: Collings, 1918). Otherwise, Arnold's surviving family respected his wish by withholding interviews and documents or by issuing only selected, censored information.

As a result, few biographies of Arnold exist, and much biographical commentary has been lodged in critical works. For a long time, commentary had to depend on the few public sources and on Arnold's own works; thus, the same quotations keep reappearing, sometimes supplemented by outright speculation (best illustrated by efforts to identify "Marguerite"). Early biographers reacted to the sketchy information in various ways. In *Matthew Arnold* (London: Longmans, Green, 1928), Hugh Kingsmill (pseud. of H. K. Lunn) imitated Lytton Strachey's idiosyncratic, debunking techniques, offering occasional humor and perception. Much more serious and perceptive is Louis Bonnerot's *Matthew Arnold, Poète: Essai de biographie psychologique* (Paris: Didier, 1947), a study of Arnold the man through close analysis of his poetry.

Only in recent decades has fuller biographical information on Arnold become available, mainly from the Clough family and Arnold's second-generation descendants. Some new material is still privately owned, but some has been published, including *The Correspondence of Arthur Hugh Clough,* 2 vols., ed. Frederick L. Mulhauser (London: Oxford University Press, 1957), and *New Zealand Letters of Thomas Arnold the Younger, with Further Letters from Van Diemen's Land, and Letters of Arthur Hugh Clough, 1847–1851,* ed. James Bertram (London: Oxford University Press, 1966). Other valuable documents are specially housed, notably in the Brotherton Collection of Leeds University, the Humanities Research Center at the University of Texas, and the Manuscript Collection at the University of Virginia. Articles based on the new material appeared throughout the 1960's and 1970's, and in 1981 Park Honan published *Matthew Arnold: A Life,* the definitive biography.

Evaluation of Selected Biographies

Chambers, E. K. *Matthew Arnold: A Study.* Oxford: Clarendon Press, 1947. Although written before recent information became available, Chambers' work is a concise critical biography giving the essential facts of Arnold's life and providing excellent summaries of his main work. The organization is slightly awkward, with Arnold's life treated sometimes chronologically, sometimes topically.

Honan, Park, *Matthew Arnold: A Life.* London: Weidenfeld and Nicholson, 1981. A superb example of literary biography, Honan's life of Arnold outdates every other work. Honan worked on the biography for ten years, enjoying the cooperation of Arnold's and Clough's descendants and of numerous other scholars, and he estimates that three-fourths of the information he presents is new. He fills in the details of Arnold's childhood and young manhood, identifies "Marguerite" as Mary Claude (a French exile, authoress, and Lake District neighbor), and shows the large roles several women played in Arnold's life. Arnold emerges as a real person, struggling and changing, and his works are shown to flow naturally out of the circumstances of his life. The writing is so good that the biography reads like a fat Victorian novel, and Honan's notes are a rich listing of sources.

McCarthy, Patrick J. *Matthew Arnold and the Three Classes.* New York: Columbia University Press, 1964. McCarthy's book is a specialized biography concentrating on Arnold's experiences with the three social classes treated in *Culture and Anarchy:* the Barbarians (aristocracy), the Populace (working class), and the Philistines (middle class). Well researched and well written, the study is interesting reading in itself aside from giving valuable background to Arnold's social theory and politics.

Autobiographical Sources

Autobiographical sources consist of Arnold's letters, notebooks, and diaries. George W. E. Russell edited *Letters of Matthew Arnold, 1848-1888,* 2 vols. (London: Macmillan, 1895), but only after Arnold's widow and sister Fanny heavily censored them: Russell himself called the resulting Arnold a "curious obscuration." Arnold's grandson, Arnold Whitridge, edited *Unpublished Letters of Matthew Arnold* (New Haven: Yale University Press, 1923). The most interesting picture of Arnold—young, smart-alecky, searching—emerges from *The Letters of Matthew Arnold to Arthur Hugh Clough,* ed. Howard Foster Lowry (London: Oxford University Press, 1932); unfortunately, Clough's replies are missing, but Lowry gives a good introduction and commentary. Lowry, Waldo H. Dunn, and Karl Young edited *The Notebooks of Matthew Arnold* (London: Oxford University Press, 1952), containing information on such matters as Arnold's reading, travel, finances, official appointments, and social engagements. William Bell Guthrie edited "Matthew Arnold's Diaries, the Unpublished Items: A Transcription and Commentary," 4 vols. (dissertation: University of Virginia, 1957).

Overview of Critical Sources

There are several good introductions to Arnold's work and numerous fine studies of special aspects. Generally scholars see Arnold as the Victorian most important to the modern period, as highly influential on literary studies in Britain and America, and as a better critic than poet. They also tend to see his career as an effort to resolve various conflicts in his personality—between detachment and engagement, Romanticism and Classicism, aesthetic temperament and ethical responsibility, poetry and criticism. An anthology of modern critical views is *Matthew Arnold: A Collection of Critical Essays,* ed. David J. DeLaura (Englewood Cliffs, NJ: Prentice-Hall, 1973), while reactions of Arnold's Victorian contemporaries are collected in *Matthew Arnold: The Poetry; the Critical Perspective,* ed. Carl Dawson (London: Routledge & Kegan Paul, 1973), and in *Matthew Arnold: Prose Writings; the Critical Perspective,* ed. Carl Dawson and John Pfordresher (London: Routledge & Kegan Paul, 1979).

Evaluation of Selected Criticism

Culler, A. Dwight, *Imaginative Reason: The Poetry of Matthew Arnold.* New Haven: Yale University Press, 1966. Culler maintains that Arnold's poetry is unified around patterns of imagery, particularly three symbolic landscapes which Culler calls the Forest Glade (the past, innocence, childhood), the Burning or Darkling Plain (the present, suffering, manhood), and the Wide-Glimmering Sea (the future, peace, old age or death). Though sometimes pushed too far, Culler's schematic interpretation is still the best study of Arnold's poetry.

Madden, William A. *Matthew Arnold: A Study of the Aesthetic Temperament in Victorian England.* Bloomington: Indiana University Press, 1967. Madden finds a conflict between Arnold's innate poetic temperament and the ethical sense of duty inculcated by his Victorian background. Arnold's poetry, says Madden, is an expression of this conflict and Arnold's criticism an attempt to resolve it.

Trilling, Lionel, *Matthew Arnold.* New York: Columbia University Press, 1939 (2nd ed. 1949). Long the standard critical treatment of Arnold and including some biography, Trilling's study is especially strong on Arnold's thought and its relation to the Victorian intellectual and social background. Though criticizing Arnold's vagueness, racial theories, and poor appreciation of comedy and the biological aspects of life, Trilling nevertheless sees Arnold as a great spokesman for the humanistic tradition of Western civilization, valuing intelligence, openness, tolerance, balance.

Other Sources (selected)

Anderson, Warren D. *Matthew Arnold and the Classical Tradition.* Ann Arbor: University of Michigan Press, 1965. A classicist explores the relationships of Arnold's work to his classical interests and sources.

apRoberts, Ruth, *Arnold and God.* Berkeley: University of California Press, 1983. Impressive study of Arnold's career from the perspective of his religious beliefs.

Brown, E. K. *Matthew Arnold: A Study in Conflict.* Chicago: University of Chicago Press, 1948. Treats conflict between the detached and the engaged, polemical Arnold.

Carroll, Joseph, *The Cultural Theory of Matthew Arnold.* Berkeley: University of California Press, 1982. Valuable, well-reasoned study.

Connell, W. F. *The Educational Thought and Influence of Matthew Arnold.* London: Routledge, 1950.

Eliot, T. S. "Matthew Arnold," in *The Use of Poetry and the Use of Criticism.* Cambridge: Harvard University Press, 1933. Eliot's somewhat rough handling of his critical mentor.

Gottfried, Leon, *Matthew Arnold and the Romantics.* London: Routledge & Kegan Paul, 1963. One of several good studies on Arnold's use of, reaction from, and sometimes rough treatment of his predecessors.

Jump, J. D. *Matthew Arnold.* London: Longmans, Green, 1955. Fine three-part introduction to Arnold's life, poetry, and prose.

Neiman, Fraser, *Matthew Arnold.* New York: Twayne, 1968. Another good introduction to Arnold's life and work.

Raleigh, John Henry, *Matthew Arnold and American Culture.* Berkeley: University of California Press, 1957. Studies Arnold's influence on American culture, literary criticism, and various literary figures.

Robbins, William, *The Ethical Idealism of Matthew Arnold: A Study of the Nature and Sources of His Moral Ideas.* Toronto: University of Toronto Press, 1959. Studies intellectual influences that turned Arnold into a strong moralist albeit unsystematic theologian.

Stange, G. Robert, *Matthew Arnold: The Poet as Humanist.* Princeton: Princeton University Press, 1967. Explores ideas of poetry, nature, the self, and love in Arnold's poetry.

Tinker, C. B. and H. F. Lowry. *The Poetry of Matthew Arnold: A Commentary.* London: Oxford University Press, 1950. Handbook of valuable notes on individual Arnold poems, their sources, and the circumstances of their composition.

Selected Dictionaries and Encyclopedias

Critical Survey of Poetry, Salem Press, 1982. Short biography and analysis of key Arnold poems.

Dictionary of Literary Biography, Gale Research, 1983. Concise treatment of Arnold's life and important works.

Harold Branam

W. H. AUDEN
1907–1973

Author's Chronology

Born Wystan Hugh Auden, February 21, 1907, York, England, third son of George Augustus, a medical officer, and Constance Rosalie, a nurse; *1925* enters Christ's Church College, Oxford; *1928* graduates, and spends a year in Berlin; *1930* publishes *Poems; 1930–1935* schoolmaster at various private schools; *1932* founds the Group Theatre; *1935* scriptwriter on films *Night Mail* and *Coal-Face;* travels to Iceland; collaborates with Christopher Isherwood on the play, *The Dog Beneath the Skin;* marries Ericka Mann; *1936* travels to Spain to support the loyalist cause during the Civil War; *1939* moves permanently to the United States, meets Chester Kallman, his lover and lifetime companion; *1941* a religious conversion shifts his poetic perspective dramatically; *1951* writes libretto, with Kallman, for Stravinsky's *The Rake's Progress; 1954* wins Bollingen Prize and is elected to the American Academy of Arts & Letters; *1956* wins National Book Award and serves as Professor of Poetry at Oxford; *1967* awarded the National Medal for Literature; *1972* returns to Oxford where he plans to spend half a year in residence and half at his new home in Kirchstetten, Austria; *1973* dies in Austria on September 29 from heart seizure; buried in Kirchstetten.

Author's Bibliography (selected)

Poems, 1930; *The Ascent of F6,* 1936 (with Isherwood, play); *Letters from Iceland,* 1937 (with Louis MacNeice); *Journey to a War,* 1939 (with Isherwood); *The Double Man* (British edition: *New Year Letter*), 1941 (poems); *For the Time Being* (including *The Sea and the Mirror*), 1944 (poems); *Collected Poetry,* 1945; *The Age of Anxiety,* 1947 (poems); *Nones,* 1951 (poems); *The Shield of Achilles,* 1955 (poems); *Homage to Clio,* 1960 (poems); *The Dyer's Nand* (essays), 1962; *Collected Shorter Poems, 1927–1957,* 1966; *Collected Longer Poems,* 1968; *City Without Walls,* 1969 (poems); *Thank You, Fog,* 1974 (poems); *Collected Poems,* edited by Edward Mendelson, 1976; *The English Auden,* edited by Edward Mendelson, 1977; *Selected Poems,* edited by Edward Mendelson, 1979.

Overview of Biographical Sources

Auden is one of the century's best-known poets, yet in his life-time there was no biography of him. To a great extent, one did not seem necessary. The poet's personality sounded so clearly in his works that the reader soon intuited an understanding of the man. Additionally, Auden discouraged the biographer, arguing on principle that the literary biography was superfluous, in bad taste, and usually a distraction from the poems themselves. Finally, Auden did wish to keep a life apart from the public: he was homosexual in an onerous time. As a result, biography took second place to critical analysis until 1974, a year after his death. Three studies, although limited in biographical range, are important. Richard Hoggart's monograph, *W. H. Auden* (originally published as a British Council Pamphlet in 1961, now available as a Bison Book, University of Nebraska Press, 1965) shrewdly weaves biographical data with a fine reading of Auden's British phase. George T. Wright's *W. H. Auden, revised edition* (Boston: Twayne, 1981), discusses the collected works with sensitivity, and with a sympathetic awareness of Auden's life. *Early Auden* (Cambridge, MA: Harvard University Press, 1983), written by the poet's executor, and although primarily a critical study, nevertheless uses the poet's private diaries and letters to clarify some mysteries of the life. After Auden's death, four considerations of the poet's life attempt in various ways to recreate and evaluate this much-liked yet evasive personality.

Evaluation of Selected Biographies

Carpenter, Humphrey, *W. H. Auden: A Biography.* Boston: Houghton Mifflin, 1981. This is the most definitive biography now available. The author had access to private and unpublished material, and it has helped him to focus upon the crucial periods in Auden's life, such as his decision to leave England for America, his religious rebirth, and his total dedication to Kallman. Carpenter stresses the intimate side of Auden's life, and this candor, while helpful in revealing the homosexual milieu in which the poet lived, also works against understanding the complexities of the artist. Consequently, the intense sophistication which belongs to the author of "The Sea and the Mirror" is rarely felt in these pages. On the other hand, Carpenter is quite sympathetic to the figure he knows, and does not hide his flaws or apologize for his bad behavior. This study is very readable and conscientious, and with its mass of detail, evokes a very unusual life.

Farnan, Dorothy J. *Auden in Love.* New York: Simon & Schuster, 1984. Although not as extensive a study as Carpenter's, Farnam's biography has the advantage of on-the-scene observation. She was a student at the University of Michigan in 1941 when Auden was a visiting professor. She became friendly with Chester Kallman who was also taking courses at Michigan, later followed him to New York and joined the satellite of friends surrounding Auden. Farnan eventually married Edward Kallman, Chester's father, and played a significant role in the Auden-Kallman relationship. She presents an account of their thirty-year-old "marriage" with fairness and perception, as well as vividly describing the very famous and talented people who made up their world. Farnan's history is psychologically revealing and gives the reader insight into the eccentric Auden—the occult believer, psychosomatic cures, and bizarre work habits.

Osborne, Charles, *W. H. Auden: The Life of a Poet.* New York: Harcourt, Brace, Jovanovich, 1979. This was the first biography written after Auden's death. Osborne was a friend of the poet's and therefore brings to his account a familiarity and understanding of personality and events which is valuable. Yet the author did not have access to all the material necessary to a study in depth, so he glides over Auden's life with anecdotes and a not-too-intense reading of the poems. However, the book has amusing stories about Auden and is a great deal of fun to read.

Spender, Stephen, ed. *W. H. Auden: A Tribute.* New York: Macmillan, 1974. Although clearly not a biography in the formal sense, this tribute by thirty-five friends, associates, admirers, and relations, has the cumulative sense of telling a life. Auden's brother, an early schoolteacher, and family friends testify to personal experiences and memories invoked by the poet's sudden death. All of them recognize different sides of the poet's personality, and collectively they merge into a portrait of an extraordinary figure. This is a highly recommended sourcebook for Auden's impact on several generations of strangers and brothers.

Overview of Critical Sources

There is no shortage of good and intelligent critical studies of Auden during all phases of his life and works. The general concern has been with explicating difficulties in some of the poetry, working on the chronology of the poems themselves, and attempting to place Auden's importance in perspective. Auden's own work continues to be published. There are plans for another volume of his critical essays as well as a volume of collected letters. However, the focus of study is concerned with the interrelationship between his life and work, the impact upon his work resulting from his move to America, the importance of his religious conversion upon his poetry, and the dispute over the relative importance of his later poetry in contrast to his early work in England and America.

Evaluation of Selected Criticism

Beach, Joseph Warren, *The Making of the Auden Canon.* Minneapolis: University of Minnesota Press, 1957. This study examines the many alterations in the various collections of Auden poems. Beach reveals that the poet eliminated many poems that conflicted with his later thought and style, and severely revised others which did not meet with present standards. All these changes, speculates Beach, make it difficult to recognize Auden as a specific identity.

Callen, Edward, *Auden: A Carnival of Intellect.* New York: Oxford University Press, 1983. Callen shows the development of Auden's poetry from its origins in 1930's romanticism to its final post-romantic, and neoclassical responses in the 1960's. A major theme that Callen emphasizes is Auden's fear of the inherent dangers in the romantic outlook, which the poet believed to be a corrupting force, leading to the political mania of Hitler, and distorting the later work of Yeats and Lawrence. Callen is particularly good on the intellectual influences behind the poetry, especially Kierkegaard, Jung, Sartre, and Niebuhr.

Fuller, John, *A Reader's Guide to W. H. Auden.* New York: Farrar, Straus & Giroux, 1970. A reliable and detailed guide to the works from the early *Paid on Both Sides* (1928) to *About the House* (1966). The commentary on the poetry is clear and precise, the difficult passages of the poems explored with sensitivity, and Fuller also traces many of the poet's sources and allusions. Fuller's guide is an invaluable tool for exploring many of Auden's poems.

Spears, Monroe K. *The Poetry of W. H. Auden: The Disenchanted Island.* New York: Oxford University Press, 1963. Spears' work stresses the influence of Auden's prose upon his poetry. He also pays more attention than most critics to Auden's theatre work and songs written in the 1930's. A fine section on Auden's work in opera and fugitive criticism adds to the value of this study.

Other Sources

Gingerich, Martin E. *W. H. Auden: A Reference Guide.* Boston: G. K. Hall, 1977. A useful annotated source for criticism of the major poems up to 1974.

Isherwood, Christopher, *Lions and Shadows.* London, 1938. A novelistic approach to autobiography in which the early Auden figures prominently as a character named Hugh Weston. It records the time both Isherwood and Auden spent in the public schools, and their stay in Berlin.

———, *Christopher and His Kind.* New York: Farrar, Straus, Giroux, 1976. A revisit to the same time period as *Lions and Shadows,* but now considered as a frank autobiography. Again, Auden plays a predominating role, and the writer sharply captures Auden's life in Nazi Germany, as well as his involvement with the Group theatre. The focus, however, is upon their homosexual adventures in Germany, and how their sexual proclivities influenced their decision to leave England for America.

Spender, Stephen, *World Within World.* London, 1951. A sensitive autobiography that throws light upon young Auden at Oxford, and how he became the artistic focus of his generation.

Selected Dictionaries and Encyclopedias

Dictionary of Literary Biography, Gale Research, 1983. A concise look at Auden's entire life with a brief discussion of the major works.

Edward Guereschi
St. John's University,
New York

JANE AUSTEN
1775–1817

Author's Chronology

Born December 16, 1775, Steventon, England to parents of the minor gentry; *1790* by this time has completed most of the witty literary parodies known as her juvenalia; *1796* begins *First Impressions,* the early version of *Pride and Prejudice; 1797 First Impressions* rejected, unread, by publisher; *1801* moves with her family from her beloved home to Bath; probably writes little in the next eight years; *1803* revises *Susan* (the original version of *Northanger Abbey*) which is sold to a publisher, advertised, but never published; *1805* death of her father leaves the family in straitened circumstances; *1809* moves to Chawton Cottage, owned by her wealthy older brother, and begins final creative phase with revisions of earlier work; *1811–1815* publishes four novels; *1816* revises her final completed novel, *Persuasion,* while in declining health; *1817* dies July 18.

Author's Bibliography (selected)

Sense and Sensibility, 1811 (novel); *Pride and Prejudice,* 1813 (novel); *Mansfield Park,* 1814 (novel); *Emma,* 1815 (1816 on the title page; novel); *Persuasion* and *Northanger Abbey,* 1818 (two novels published together posthumously).

Overview of Biographical Sources

Surviving records and accounts tell of a relatively uneventful life, one shaped largely by births and marriages, illnesses and deaths, financial gains and losses in her large and close-knit family. Practically the only record of her artistic and spiritual growth or of her personal triumphs and tragedies lies in her novels, no one of which is clearly autobiographical. Family members and their descendants wrote laudatory accounts which remain, along with her letters, the basis for all subsequent biographies. In 1870 her nephew, James Edward Austen-Leigh, wrote *A Memoir of Jane Austen* (R. W. Chapman, ed. Oxford: Clarendon Press, 1926) based on his own youthful recollections, some of her letters, and family traditions. His portrait of an unfailingly kind and gentle woman was echoed in a biography written by his son and grandson, William and Richard Arthur Austen-Leigh (*Jane Austen: Her Life and Letters; A Family Record.* London: Smith, Elder, and Co., 1913). Though the younger Austen-Leighs had access to additional letters and records, their account merely fleshes out the earlier biography. Most recent biographies follow the Austen-Leigh volumes with some modifications and also serve to set Austen in her historical and social context for the modern reader.

Evaluation of Selected Biographies

Chapman, R. W. *Jane Austen: Facts and Problems.* Oxford: Clarendon Press, 1948. Chapman, Austen's best modern editor, offers a brief survey of her life and literary career. He effectively describes her familial and social context but is very much an Austen partisan, intent on protecting her reputation as a paragon of quiet virtue from the least blemish. Still, Chapman's great knowledge of Austen and the brevity of this volume make it a good introduction.

Halperin, John, *The Life of Jane Austen.* Baltimore: Johns Hopkins University Press, 1984. Halperin has written what amounts to a revisionist biography, one which rejects the orthodox view of Austen as a serene, loving woman content in a retired life. While Hodge also counters that traditional view, Halperin goes much further in portraying Austen as anxious and bitter about her uncertain life as a dependent single woman. He sees her as an aloof woman frightened of emotions and frequently resentful of her family. Halperin relies on an unusually autobiographical reading of the novels and an often unsympathetic reading of the letters. Though speculative and at times unduly harsh, this is probably the most complete biography of Austen to date.

Hodge, Jane Aiken, *The Double Life of Jane Austen.* London: Hodder and Stoughton, 1972. Hodge's starting point is the discrepancy she senses between the orthodox view of Austen as a person—the loving woman innocent of any cruel deed or word—and what is emerging as the orthodox view of her as an artist—the keen ironist and frequently scathing social critic. Hodge suggests that the serene woman known by her family (and by most subsequent biographers) was a mask, a disguise that helped her to cope with the dilemma of being a gifted female artist in a stiflingly conventional, male-dominated society. Austen's writing, then, was her true life, which her social disguise freed her to live. Although Hodge frequently speculates beyond the available evidence, her challenge to the prevailing orthodoxy is interesting and often provocative.

Jenkins, Elizabeth, *Jane Austen.* London: Gollancz, 1938. Jenkins writes a detailed account of the traditional "gentle Jane." Jenkins is quite informative on Austen's family background, her social class, her reading, and her society as a whole. She makes extensive use of Austen's letters (and her own imagination) to produce an at times novelistic narrative of some episodes in Austen's adult life. Though Jenkins comments extensively on the novels, her remarks are more an appreciation than a critical discussion.

Autobiographical Sources

A deeply reticent woman, Austen published her novels anonymously and shunned publicity. Only her letters can be called autobiographical, and they have been severely expurgated. Cassandra, Austen's sister and her life-long confidante, chose to burn letters and excise passages that were too personal (or perhaps, as some scholars have speculated, were written in times of crisis or despair). The remaining letters, edited by R. W. Chapman (*Jane Austen's Letters to Her Sister Cassandra and Others.* 2nd ed. London: Oxford University

Press, 1952), do give information about the details of her day-to-day life, occasional comments on her reading and her artistic methods, and flashes of a wit more acerbic than she generally permitted herself in her published writings. But the letters rarely provide more than glimpses of an elusive artist.

Overview of Critical Sources

Austen's critical reputation has grown enormously since her death. She is now considered one of the greatest of English novelists. Early partisans praised her skill as a social miniaturist, a writer who portrayed a small part of society with remarkable fidelity and moral insight. Recent criticism (beginning especially with Marvin Mudrick's *Jane Austen: Irony as Defense and Discovery.* Princeton: Princeton University Press, 1952) has concentrated on her mastery of irony and her social satire. While there is now general agreement on her ironic perspective, critics disagree over whether she was a defender or a critic of the values of her society. Critics also differ on the question of her artistic "limitations"—some seeing an artist brilliant within narrow limits, others denying that her concerns are at all limited or provincial. Criticism has also paid attention to her style and narrative techniques, examining the complex and brilliant structure underlying apparent simplicity.

Evaluation of Selected Criticism

Brown, Julia Prewitt, *Jane Austen's Novels: Social Change and Literary Form.* Cambridge: Harvard University Press, 1979. Unlike those critics who praise Austen but insist on the narrowness of her vision, Brown argues that Austen's subjects—family life, courtship, and marriage—are indeed of universal human importance. Brown sees the novels as a revolutionary expression of a feminine tradition. Brown stresses Austen's artistry and her complex vision of the world, and she argues convincingly that *Mansfield Park* and *Persuasion* are profoundly, even brutally pessimistic novels of alienation and disillusionment.

Butler, Marilyn, *Jane Austen and the War of Ideas.* Oxford: Clarendon Press, 1975. Butler's study begins with a dense but fascinating essay in the history of ideas as she examines the literary and ideological context of Austen's novels. Butler argues that during the late eighteenth century certain novels were perceived as dangerously radical because of their emphasis on the individual's sensibility or reason as a better guide to conduct than society's traditional values. This movement provoked a reaction—the "anti jacobin" novel. Butler contends that Austen is a champion of conservative values and a satirist of the radicals. Butler's emphasis on Austen as ideologue often slights Austen the artist, but her argument is a significant challenge to Mudrick's position.

Lascelles, Mary, *Jane Austen and Her Art.* London: Oxford University Press, 1939. Lascelles's book was one of the first major Austen studies, and it remains a valuable introduction to the life and the novels. Lascelles is probably the best advocate for Austen as a social miniaturist, a gifted artist who chose to work within narrow limits. Lascelles's Austen is closer to the gentle sunny woman of the biographies than to Mudrick and Brown's embattled ironist or Butler's conservative ideologue, and her viewpoint provides an important contrast to those of more recent critics.

Mudrick, Marvin, *Jane Austen: Irony as Defense and Discovery.* Mudrick sees irony as the key to Austen. It is her defense against a conventional society he claims she must have scorned and her defense against the dangers of emotion. But it is also her means of discrimination and discovery. Mudrick traces a pattern of artistic growth as Austen moves from a largely destructive irony (*Sense and Sensibility*) through a momentary surrender to conventional values (*Mansfield Park*) to a discovery of irony as artistic form (*Emma*) and finally to a liberation of feeling (*Persuasion*). Though Mudrick is unrelentingly polemical and at times chastises Austen for failing to live up to his view of her, his arguments changed the way Austen is read and are still persuasive.

Other Sources

Fleishman, Avrom, *A Reading of Mansfield Park: An Essay in Critical Synthesis.* Minneapolis: University of Minnesota Press, 1967. A reading of Austen's "problem novel" from a variety of viewpoints, including historical, anthropological, and sociological.

Hardwick, Michael, *A Guide to Jane Austen.* New York: Charles Scribner's Sons, 1973. Includes a biographical sketch, a dictionary of characters, plot summaries, and brief evaluations.

Tave, Stuart M. *Some Words of Jane Austen.* Chicago: University of Chicago Press, 1973. Graceful criticism examining Austen's language as an index to her moral concerns.

Kevin P. Mulcahy
Rutgers University

JAMES BALDWIN
1924

Author's Chronology

Born August 2, 1924, Harlem Hospital, New York City, the oldest of nine children; *1927* Baldwin's mother Emma Berdis Jones marries David Baldwin, a manual laborer and storefront preacher; *1938–1941* undergoes conversion experience and preaches at the Fireside Pentecostal Assembly in Harlem; *1943–1948* lives and works in Greenwich Village; *1944* meets Richard Wright; *1945* receives Eugene F. Saxton Memorial Award; *1948* receives Rosenwald Fellowship; leaves United States for Paris to pursue writing career; *1948–1957* lives and writes primarily in Europe with brief visits to the United States in 1952 and 1954–1955; *1953* publishes *Go Tell It on the Mountain; 1954* receives Guggenheim Fellowship; *1957* first visit to the American South; *1957–1965* increasing involvement in the Civil Rights movement leads to emergence as "spokesman" in national media; *1963* meets with Attorney General Robert F. Kennedy; attends March on Washington; *1964 Blues for Mister Charlie* produced on Broadway; *1965–1985* divides time between France, Turkey and the United States; continues to write fiction and non-fiction and to speak publicly on various cultural and political issues.

Author's Bibliography (selected)

Go Tell It on the Mountain, 1953 (novel); *Notes of a Native Son,* 1955 (essays); *Giovanni's Room,* 1956 (novel); *Nobody Knows My Name,* 1961 (essays); *Another Country,* 1962 (novel); *The Fire Next Time,* 1963 (essays); *Blues for Mister Charlie,* 1964 (drama); *Going to Meet the Man,* 1965 (stories); *Tell Me How Long the Train's Been Gone,* 1968 (novel); *No Name in the Street,* 1971 (essays); *If Beale Street Could Talk,* 1974 (novel); *Just Above My Head,* 1979 (novel).

Overview of Biographical Sources

Despite Baldwin's richly varied public and private experience and his prominence as an Afro-American spokesman during the 1960s, no full scale biographical treatment exists. Fern Marja Eckman's *The Furious Passage of James Baldwin* (1966) provides a somewhat gossipy journalistic chronicle of Baldwin's career through 1964. Although she provides numerous anecdotes unavailable elsewhere, Eckman's reliance on autobiographical writings and interviews without adequate verification renders the book not altogether trustworthy. Similarly, W. J. Weatherly's *Squaring Off: Mailer vs. Baldwin* (New York: Mason/Charter, 1977) is an anecdotal volume focusing on a relatively narrow aspect of Baldwin's career. Generally more reliable, though less detailed, are the biographical sections of Carolyn Wedin Sylvander's *James Baldwin* (New York:

Frederick Ungar, 1980) and Keneth Kinnamon's essay on Baldwin in *American Writers: A Collection of Literary Biographies,* Supplement 1, Part 1 (New York: Charles Scribner's Sons, 1979). Clearly the most valuable guide to available biographical materials concerning Baldwin is Daryl Dance's overview of sources published in *Black American Writers: Bibliographical Essays,* Volume 2, eds. M. Thomas Inge, Maurice Duke, and Jackson Bryer (New York: St. Martin's Press, 1978).

Evaluation of Selected Biographies

Eckman, Fern Marja, *The Furious Passage of James Baldwin.* New York: M. Evans, 1966. Based primarily on Baldwin's autobiographical writings and journalistic reports of his activities, this book incorporates elements of literary biography into what is essentially a celebrity biography. The most valuable segments concern Baldwin's family background and his response to his growing public prominence during the early 1960's.

Autobiographical Sources

Throughout his career, Baldwin has recast his personal experience in a variety of forms ranging from explicitly autobiographical essays to fiction and drama. His first novel, *Go Tell It On the Mountain,* and play, *The Amen Corner,* draw heavily on his childhood experience in the storefront churches of Harlem where he and his stepfather preached. Nonetheless, like his later semi-autobiographical work in the genres, both are primarily literary works and neither can be safely used as a source of specific information concerning Baldwin's life. Similarly, Baldwin's autobiographical essays, in which he frequently reshapes events for rhetorical or thematic impact, must be approached with caution. Nonetheless, the "Autobiographical Notes" section of *Notes of a Native Son* and the "Down at the Cross" section of *The Firce Next Time* provide a fascinating overview of Baldwin's childhood and his growing involvement with the civil rights movement. Supplemented by the numerous autobiographical passages in *Nobody Knows My Name, No Name in the Street* and *The Devil Finds Work* (1976), these two volumes combine to provide a relatively full, if somewhat fragmented, autobiography. Of particular interest are the Baldwin's meditations on his relationships with Richard Wright ("Alas, Poor Richard") and Norman Mailer ("The Black Boy Looks at the White Boy"), both of which are included in *Nobody Knows My Name.*

Overview of Critical Sources

Although several cogent introductory studies of Baldwin have appeared, the vast majority of useful criticism of his work has taken the form of essays, many of which have been collected in *James Baldwin: A Critical Evaluation,* edited by Therman B. O'Daniel (Washington, DC: Howard University Press, 1977) and *James Baldwin: A Collection of Critical Essays,* edited by Keneth Kinnamon (Englewood Cliffs, NJ: Prentice-Hall, 1974). Much of the early commentary focused either on Baldwin's association with the "universalist" tendency in Afro-American writing of the 1950's or on the public positions he espoused during the 1960's. Increasingly, however, critics have emphasized the relationship between his political, psychological, moral, and technical concerns as they have developed during the distinct phases of his career. In addition, active debates continue concerning the significance of his sexual politics and his relation to both the Afro- and the Euro-American cultural traditions.

Evaluation of Selected Criticism

Kinnamon, Keneth, ed. *James Baldwin: A Collection of Critical Essays.* Englewood Cliffs, NJ: Prentice-Hall, 1974. This valuable collection brings together influential journalistic and polemical commentaries by Eldridge Cleaver, Langston Hughes, Calvin Hernton, Benjamin DeMott and Irving Howe; academic essays by Michel Fabre, John Reilly and Charles Newman; and the sections on Baldwin from standard studies of Afro-American letters including Robert Bone's *The Negro Novel in America* (New Haven: Yale University Press, 1966), George Kent's *Blackness and the Adventure of Western Culture* (Chicago: Third World Press, 1972), and Sherley Anne Williams' *Give Birth to Brightness* (New York: Dial Press, 1972).

Macebuh, Stanley, *James Baldwin: A Critical Study.* New York: Third Press-Joseph Okpaku, 1973. Written at the height of Baldwin's involvement with militant Afro-American politics, this introductory study emphasizes the historical and cultural backgrounds of the literary works, sometimes to the detriment of the textual analysis. Macebuh's thesis that Baldwin developed from a "personal" to a "radical" writer, while generally accurate at the time, stands in need of substantial revision in the light of subsequent works.

O'Daniel, Therman B. ed. *James Baldwin: A Critical Evaluation.* Washington, DC: Howard University Press, 1977. Divided into separate sections on Baldwin's novels, essays, short stories, plays, raps and dialogues, and movie scenarios, this collection of essays provides a comprehensive overview of Baldwin's literary achievement. Among the significant essays not included in the Kinnamon collection are those by Nick Aaron Ford, Donald Gibson and Darwin Turner.

Sylvander, Carolyn Wedin, *James Baldwin.* New York: Frederick Ungar, 1980. The best extended work on Baldwin to appear to date, Sylvander's study elaborates the connections between Baldwin's life and his writing. Neither the personal nor the political element of his work are underemphasized.

Other Sources

Cruse, Harold, *The Crisis of the Negro Intellectual.* New York: William Morrow, 1967. A generally hostile approach to Baldwin's position in Afro-American thought, including an extended discussion of his orientation to the debate between blacks and Jews.

Gayle, Addison, Jr. *The Way of the New World: The Black Novel in America.* Garden City, NY: Anchor Press/Doubleday, 1976. A reading of *Another Country* from an explicitly black nationalist perspective.

Harper, Howard, *Desperate Faith: A Study of Bellow, Salinger, Mailer, Baldwin, and Updike.* Chapel Hill: University of North Carolina Press, 1967. Concentrates on the tension between Baldwin's role as an artist and his role as a spokesman for political concerns.

Murray, Albert, *The Omni-Americans.* New York: Outerbridge & Dienstfrey, 1970. An extended comparison of Baldwin and Ralph Ellison in relation to their use of specifically Afro-American cultural materials.

Werner, Craig Hansen, *Paradoxical Resolutions: American Fiction since James Joyce.* Urbana: University of Illinois Press, 1982. Includes a discussion of *Go Tell It On the Mountain* emphasizing Baldwin's sophisticated use of the Euro-American modernist tradition.

Selected Dictionaries and Encyclopedias

American Writers: A Collection of Literary Biographies, Charles Scribner's Sons, 1979. Excellent overview of Baldwin's career, emphasizing the influence of church, self, city, and race.

Critical Survey of Long Fiction, Salem Press, 1983. Brief biography, and analysis of Baldwin's novels, including a lengthy discussion of *Just Above My Head.*

Dictionary of Literary Biography, Gale Research, 1978. Biographical overview with concise discussion of Baldwin's major works.

Craig Werner
University of Wisconsin

JOHN BARTH
1930

Author's Chronology

Born May 27, 1930, Cambridge, Maryland; *1947* graduates from high school and enrolls in music theory and composition at Julliard School of Music in New York; abandons studies at Julliard at the end of the summer and enters Johns Hopkins University, Department of Speech, Writing and Drama, on a scholarship; *1950* marries Harriette Anne Strickland; *1951* receives A.B. from Johns Hopkins; daughter Christine born; *1952* receives M.A. from Johns Hopkins; master's project is a novel, *The Shirt of Nessus* (unpublished); begins Ph.D. in literary aesthetics at Johns Hopkins; John, first son, born in October; *1953* financial constraints curtail Ph.D. studies; joins English faculty at Pennsylvania State University as an instructor; *1954* son David born; *1955* writes first two novels, *The Floating Opera* and *The End of the Road; 1957* assistant professor at Penn State; *1960* promoted to associate professor; *1963* tours Europe with his wife and children from January to June; *1965* joins the English department, State University of New York at Buffalo; *1965* awarded a "citation in fiction" by Brandeis University Arts Award Commission; *1969* receives Litt.D. from the University of Maryland; divorces Harriette Anne Strickland; *1970* marries Shelly Rosenberg; *1971* becomes Edward H. Butler Professor of English at State University of New York, Buffalo; *1972* visiting professor at Boston University; *Chimera,* 1973; co-winner of the National Book Award for *Chimera;* joins faculty of Johns Hopkins University Writing Seminars; *1985* currently Centennial Professor of English and Creative Writing at Johns Hopkins; resides with his wife, Shelly, in Baltimore and at Langford Creek on Maryland's Eastern Shore.

Author's Bibliography (selected)

The Floating Opera, 1956, revised edition 1967 (novel); *The End of the Road,* 1958, revised edition 1967 (novel); *The Sot-Weed Factor,* 1960, revised edition 1967 (novel); *Giles Goat-Boy,* 1966 (novel); *Lost in the Funhouse,* 1968 (short fiction); *Chimera,* 1972 (novellas); *LETTERS,* 1979 (novel); *Sabbatical,* 1982 (novel); *The Friday Book,* 1984 (prose).

Overview of Biographical Sources

An active writer still in his mid-fifties, Barth has not yet attracted the attention of biographers. Brief summaries of his life to date can be found in *Contemporary Authors* (Detroit: Gale Research, 1982), *Dictionary of Literary Biography* (Detroit: Gale Research, 1978), and *Contemporary Novelists* (New York: St. Martin's, 1982). The only major source for biographical details is David Morrell, *John Barth: An Introduction* (1976).

Evaluation of Biographical Sources

Morrell, David, *John Barth: An Introduction.* University Park: Pennsylvania State University Press, 1976. Though intended as a critical introduction to Barth's work, Morrell's study provides a fairly detailed account of the author's life up to 1969. Morrell enjoyed direct access to Barth and quotes at length both from his conversations with the author and from unpublished materials of biographical and critical interest. His examination of the sources for Barth's fiction and the circumstances surrounding the composition of each novel offers important background information for the literary critic. In the absence of any full biography, Morrell's sympathetic critical study provides the best introduction to both Barth's life and his work.

Autobiographical Sources

For *The New York Times Book Review* series, "The Making of a Writer," Barth wrote an autobiographical article in 1982, with the typically Barthian title, "Some Reasons Why I Tell Stories the Way I Tell Them Rather Than Some Other Sort of Stories Some Other Way," *The New York Times Book Review,* May 9, 1982. Barth discusses the influence upon his imagination of being an opposite-sex twin, his early life in Cambridge, the importance of his educational experiences at Julliard and Johns Hopkins, and his role as a university teacher. The details presented in Barth's account are accurate, but his article, written in anticipation of his then forthcoming novel, *Sabbatical,* is selective in emphasizing the significance of certain images and experiences in his life.

This essay is reprinted in *The Friday Book,* an important source for autobiographical material. Barth prefaces each piece in this volume with an introduction describing the personal circumstances that occasioned his original work. These range from a defense of his role as an "academic" writer to an account of his near experience with tear-gas, riot police and the National Guard during student disturbances at Buffalo in 1970. While autobiographical references also appear in some interviews with Barth, *The Friday Book* is the major autobiographical source.

Overview of Critical Sources

Though there is a growing body of critical commentary on Barth's fiction, his most recent work in *LETTERS* and *Sabbatical* has not yet been thoroughly examined. Most early criticism concentrates on *The Floating Opera* and *The End of the Road. Giles Goat-Boy,* a popular success when it was published, has also attracted considerable scholarly commentary. Book-length studies generally provide an adequate discussion of the individual novels up to *Chimera.* They focus on the links between Barth's work and his own speculative remarks on the nature of fiction, and the continuity in the thematic concerns that inform his work. There is, however, still a good deal of debate over the contemporary milieu in which Barth works. Barth's essays and his fiction are frequently cited in larger studies of contemporary literature, and these broader discussions are often the best source for insights into the cultural context of Barth's work and its significance in terms of literary history and theory.

Evaluation of Selected Criticism

Glaser-Wohrer, Evelyn, *An Analysis of John Barth's Weltanschauung: His View of Life and Literature.* Salzburg, Austria: Institut für Englische Sprache und Literatur, Universität Salzburg, 1977. Glaser-Wohrer considers Barth's work in light of the philosophical concepts that have shaped his world view. Her interpretation of the individual texts draws upon much previous criticism, and her book also includes a transcript of two interviews she conducted with Barth in 1975.

Harris, Charles B. *Passionate Virtuosity: The Fiction of John Barth.* Urbana: University of Illinois Press, 1983. This is the only book-length study to provide a critical commentary on *LETTERS.* Harris concentrates on the relationship between fiction and reality in Barth's work, and his discussion draws upon many of the recent trends in critical theory.

Joseph, Gerhard, *John Barth.* University of Minnesota Pamphlets on American Writers, No. 91. Minneapolis: University of Minnesota Press, 1970. In this early attempt to provide a critical overview of Barth's work, Joseph argues that Barth's fiction progresses from "realism to parodic fable." He examines Barth's work from *The Floating Opera* to *Chimera,* but he is most insightful in describing the moral concerns of Barth's first two novels.

Robinson, Douglas, *John Barth's* Giles Goat Boy: *A Study.* Jyväskylä, Finland: University of Jyväskylä, 1980. Though not widely available, Robinson's is the only book-length study of a single Barth novel. Robinson examines *Giles Goat-Boy* in terms of the relationship between metaphysics, metaphor and irony. Though he relies heavily upon Robert Scholes for his overall interpretation, Robinson provides a comprehensive and useful exegesis of the text.

Scholes, Robert, *The Fabulators.* New York: Oxford University Press, 1967. Scholes was an enthusiastic reviewer of *Giles Goat-Boy* when it appeared in 1966. In *The Fabulators,* he focuses on the allegorical dimension of this novel and identifies Barth's work with a type of contemporary fiction he calls "fabulation." This discussion is reprinted with his later comments on metafiction and *Lost in the Funhouse* in his *Fabulation and Metafiction.* Urbana: University of Illinois Press, 1979.

Tharpe, Jac, *John Barth: The Comic Sublimity of Paradox.* Carbondale: Southern Illinois University Press, 1974. Tharpe provides an overview of Barth's fiction from *The Floating Opera* to *Chimera.* His discussion focuses on the thematic importance of paradox in Barth's work and the notion that Barth's fiction seeks to "let what language creates be reality." Like Gerhard Joseph, Tharpe is perhaps most insightful in discussing Barth's earlier work.

Waldmeir, Joseph J., ed. *Critical Essays on John Barth.* Boston: G. K. Hall, 1980. This collection contains many important essays on both Barth's fiction generally and on the individual works from *The Floating Opera* to *Chimera.* It also contains Charles B. Harris's evaluation of the strengths and weaknesses of Barth scholarship to date.

Other Sources

McConnell, Frank D. *Four Postwar American Novelists.* Chicago: University of Chicago Press, 1977. McConnell's chapter on Barth is frequently cited in more recent studies. He argues that Barth's work moves toward "a mythic vision of the inauthentic condition of man."

Stark, John O. *The Literature of Exhaustion: Borges, Nabokov, and Barth.* Durham, North Carolina: Duke University Press, 1972. Though this book is not exclusively concerned with Barth, Stark bases his argument on his interpretation of Barth's 1967 essay, "The Literature of Exhaustion." Stark considers the importance of self-conscious techniques and the confusion of fiction and reality in Barth's work from *The Sot-Weed Factor* to *Chimera.*

Tanner, Tony. *City of Words: A Study of American Fiction in the Mid-Twentieth Century.* London: Jonathan Cape, 1971. Tanner is sharply critical of the "arbitrariness of invention" in Barth's work, but his chapter on Barth serves as a useful introduction.

Thomas Carmichael
Toronto, Canada

SAMUEL BECKETT
1906

Author's Chronology

Born April 13, 1906, Foxrock, County Dublin, Ireland, of middle-class, Protestant parents; *1920–1923* educated Portora Royal School, Co. Fermanagh; *1927* B.A. Modern Languages, Trinity College, Dublin; *1928* lectures at Ecole Normale Superieure, Paris, and meets James Joyce; *1930* first book, poem *Whoroscope,* published as winner of Hours Press competition; *1932* resigns lectureship in French at Trinity and begins period of short-term residences in London and on Continent; *1937* settles permanently in Paris; *1942–1945* aids French resistance, hides from Nazis in unoccupied France, and is awarded *Croix de Guerre; 1946–1950* returns to Paris apartment and writes trilogy of novels and *Waiting for Godot* in inspired "siege in the room"; *1953* gains worldwide fame with Paris production of *Waiting for Godot; 1961* marries long-time companion Suzanne Deschevaux-Dumesnil; *1964* visits New York City for filming of his screenplay *Film; 1969* awarded Nobel Prize for literature; *1985* continues to write and to supervise productions of his plays from residences in Paris and Ussy, France.

Author's Bibliography (selected)

More Pricks Than Kicks, 1934 (stories); *Murphy,* 1938 (novel); *Molloy,* 1951 (novel); *Malone Meurt* (*Malone Dies*), 1951 (novel); *En attendant Godot* (*Waiting for Godot*), 1952 (play); *L'Innommable* (*The Unnamable*), 1953 (novel); *Watt,* 1953 (novel); *Fin de partie* (*Endgame*), 1957 (play); *All That Fall,* 1957 (radio play); *Krapp's Last Tape,* 1958 (play); *Comment C'est* (*How It Is*), 1961 (novel); *Happy Days,* 1961 (play); *Poems in English,* 1961; *Words and Music,* 1962 (radio play); *Film,* 1965 (screenplay); *Eh Joe,* 1967 (television play); *Mercier et Camier* (Mercier and Camier), 1970 (novel); *Footfalls,* 1977 (play); *Collected Poems in English and French,* 1977; *Rockaby,* 1981 (play); *Company,* 1980 (novel); *Ohio Impromptu,* 1981 (play); *Worstward Ho,* 1983 (novel).

Overview of Biographical Sources

There is but a single important biographical study of Samuel Beckett, Deirdre Bair's *Samuel Beckett: A Biography* (1978). In an age congenial to biography of living authors, Beckett's life remains a private one, partly by design and partly by circumstance. He has cultivated privacy so successfully that critics who correspond regularly with him, and enjoy privileged access to his critical opinions, are hesitant to press personal inquiries. His life has also become reclusive and apparently uneventful. The decades of bohemian wanderlust and survival in war-torn France were unremarkable for literary productivity. Cloistered in his Parisian rooms, however, Beckett has produced a remarkable body of work that in its increasingly formalist premise discourages biographical interpretation.

Evaluation of Selected Biographies

Bair, Deirdre, *Samuel Beckett: A Biography.* New York: Harcourt Brace Jovanovich, 1978. Bair was a doctoral candidate in search of a thesis when she approached Beckett in 1971, and her biography is the product of exhaustive research through third parties launched when he ambivalently replied that he would neither help nor hinder her. Her portrait of Beckett, based largely on interviews with his friends and unpublished letters from Beckett to them, reinforces the popular image of Beckett as a passive pessimist burdened by metaphysical doubts and overwhelming depressions transferred intact to his characters. This is not an attempt at a critical biography, and its attention to the works themselves is cursory. Nor is it a satisfying psychological portrait, and its heavy reliance on the theory of a Travistock lecture by Carl Jung attended by Beckett seems facile. Nevertheless, Bair's readable, lengthy, and detailed chronology of Beckett's activities, literary and otherwise, should stand as the best factual account of his life until future biographers are in retrospect better able to place the man and his work in the context of his times.

Gluck, Barbara Reich, *Beckett and Joyce: Friendship and Fiction.* Lewisburg, PA: Bucknell University Press, 1979. There are numerous critical essays on connections between the work of Beckett and Joyce. Gluck's study begins with close attention to what is known about the personal friendship between the two Irish writers living in Paris, one portrayed as an elder statesman in search of a protege, and the other as an intellectually ambitious amateur eager to assume the role. Virtually all of the biographical information in this work is drawn from previously published sources. Gluck's presentation of the facts of one part of Beckett's life is conveniently compact, but her discussion of his works as emulations of Joyce's is misleadingly reductive.

Overview of Critical Sources

It is a commonplace to say that Beckett criticism has become prodigious while his own works have become minimal and infrequent. The truth of that statement, however, is apparent in every Beckett critic's reliance on Raymond Federman and John Fletcher's massive *Samuel Beckett: His works and his Critics: An Essay in Bibliography* (Berkeley: University of California Press, 1970). Moreover, updates from the *Journal of Beckett Studies* and other periodicals are essential to informed criticism.

The great bulk of studies of Beckett's work attempt to place it in a philosophical tradition, and this mainstream criticism differs most in which Beckett works it chooses to consider, with an immediate division being drawn in specialized criticism between studies of the plays and studies of the novels. The student approaching Beckett's works for the first time is best guided by the sort of general studies listed below. Although these are not among the most recent studies of a notoriously difficult author, they are likely to be more rewarding than the very specialized and self-referential sorts of critical discussions now in vogue in a field that calls itself "Beckett Studies."

Evaluation of Selected Criticism

Cohn, Ruby, *Samuel Beckett: The Comic Gamut.* New Brunswick, NJ: Rutgers University Press, 1962. A general survey of Beckett's works with emphasis on comic literary traditions. Its analyses ignore incidental humor for a broader intellectual background.

Fletcher, John, and John Spurling, *Beckett: A Study of His Plays.* New York: Hill and Wang, 1972. A student's guide to Beckett's plays, this study advantageously combines close attention to the texts with comments on contemporary dramatists with affinities to Beckett.

Harvey, Lawrence, *Samuel Beckett: Poet and Critic.* Princeton: Princeton University Press, 1970. Harvey concentrates on Beckett's early criticism and poetry, with an impressive side discussion of *Watt.* This is a definitive discussion of a small part of Beckett's work, one best approached with some facility in French.

Hesla, David H. *The Shape of Chaos: An Interpretation of the Art of Samuel Beckett.* Minneapolis: University of Minnesota Press, 1971. Heslea's often-cited study is a dense discussion of philosophical contexts for Beckett's works leading to an estimation of them as embodiments of a modern dissociated psyche.

Kenner, Hugh, *A Reader's Guide to Samuel Beckett.* New York: Farrar, Straus, and Giroux. 1973. An excellent introduction to the most frequently taught of Beckett's works. Kenner's criticism is eccentric and irreverent, but it effectively guides readers to problems in the works instead of toward traditions of thought ulterior to them.

Knowlson, James, and John Pilling, *Frescoes of the Skull: The Later Prose and Drama of Samuel Beckett.* New York: Grove Press, 1979. This study, with alternate chapters by each of the two co-authors, closely examines Beckett's work since the trilogy of novels and *Waiting for Godot.* It is an excellent introduction to some of Beckett's most perplexing fiction and drama.

Mercier, Vivian, *Beckett/Beckett.* New York: Oxford University Press, 1977. Mercier's focus is on antithetical themes in Beckett's work, such as gentleman/tramp or classicism/absurdism. It is distinct for a refreshing introductory chapter on Beckett and Ireland written by a compatriot.

Robinson, Michael, *The Long Sonata of the Dead: A Study of Samuel Beckett.* New York: Grove Press, 1969. Robinson's lucid discussion to all of Beckett's important works through the date of the study is a standard sourcebook for general readers. It has been influential in its examination of a "poetics of failure" in Beckett's work.

Other Sources

Alvarez, A. *Samuel Beckett.* New York: Viking Press, 1973. A volume in the Modern Masters series by a discriminating critic, though one with little personal relish for the problems of Beckett's works.

Calder, John, ed. *Beckett at 60: A Festschrift.* London: Calder and Boyars, 1967. A personal collection, including several biographical memoirs.

Driver, Tom F. "Beckett by the Madeleine," *Columbia University Forum,* IV (Summer 1961), 21–25. Driver's interview with Beckett was unprecedented, and he used the opportunity to glean some private revelations from an introspective man.

Graver, Lawrence, and Raymond Federman, eds. *Samuel Beckett: The Critical Heritage.* London: Routledge and Kegan Paul, 1979. This fine addition to an excellent series is the best compilation of a large number of commentaries, many of them early reviews.

John P. Harrington
Rutgers University

APHRA BEHN
1640(?)–1689

Author's Chronology

Place and date of birth disputed, but 1640 and Kent, England generally accepted; parentage obscure; *1663* sails to British colony of Surinam with parents; while in Surinam, first adopts penname "Astrea"; *1664* returns to London; *1664(?)* may have married merchant named Behn, who apparently dies shortly after; *1666–1667* commissioned as spy for Charles II, in Antwerp; *1668* imprisoned briefly, in London, for debt; *1670* first play, *The Forced Marriage,* performed in London; *1671–1687* sixteen plays (three of disputed authorship) performed in London; *1673(?)* begins long term love affair with Thomas Hoyle, lawyer of Gray's Inn; *1682* arrested for political epilogue to *Romulus and Hersilia; 1689* dies April 16; buried in cloisters, Westminster Abbey.

Author's Bibliography (selected)

Abdelazer, 1676 (play); *The Rover,* 1677 (play); *The Feigned Courtesans,* 1679 (play); *Poems Upon Several Occasions,* 1684 (poems); *Love Letters Between a Nobleman and His Sister,* 1684 (fiction); *The Lucky Chance,* 1686 (play); *Oroonoko,* 1688 (fiction, autobiography); *The Unfortunate Bride and Other Fiction,* 1698 (fiction); *The Works of Aphra Behn,* ed. Montague Summers, 1915, rpt. 1967.

Overview of Biographical Sources

Biographers have found little to agree on about Behn's life, due partly to scant evidence and largely to mixed attitudes to her explicitly sexual plays and openly unconventional life. The two brief biographies that appeared in 1696—"History of the Life and Memoirs of Mrs. Behn, by One of the Fair Sex" and Charles Gildon's "An Account of the Life of the Incomparable Mrs. Behn"—have remained, together with Behn's fictional/autobiographical *Oroonoko,* the main sources over which twentieth-century scholars have debated Behn's name, parentage, birthplace, love life, talent, and morality. While Vita Sackville-West's brief life, *Aphra Behn: The Incomparable Astrea* (New York: Viking, 1928), is chatty and condescending, Behn's first modern editor, Montague Summers, offers a balanced, researched, and supportive biographical analysis in his "Introduction" to *The Works of Aphra Behn,* 6 volumes (1915, rpt. 1967). Each of the three more recent book-length biographies offers a different approach to the problems of piecing together the fragments of Behn's poorly documented life. George Woodcock's *The Incomparable Aphra* (1948) offers a readable, concise, literary biography. Maureen Duffy's *The Passionate Shepherdess: Aphra Behn 1640–1689* (London: Jonathan Cape, 1977) adopts an informal tone and makes conjectures about Behn's relationships and activities that more cautious biographies avoid. And Angeline Goreau's *Reconstructing Aphra: A Social Biography* (1980) challenges some standard biographical assumptions through a feminist perspective and extensive research.

Evaluation of Selected Biographies

Goreau, Angeline, *Reconstructing Aphra: A Social Biography.* New York: Dial Press, 1980. Goreau has extensively researched not only the people and places directly connected to Behn but also the social, political, and psychological forces affecting her life, her works, and the contemporary response to both. Goreau's feminist scholarship brings into question heretofore unquestioned assumptions of previous biographers to shed new light on some of the paradoxes of Behn's work. Behn's plays and fiction are used as support for Goreau's contentions on biography, and Goreau quotes generously from unavailable primary documents like Behn's letters and poetry.

Summers, Montague, "Introduction: Memoir of Mrs. Behn," *The Works of Aphra Behn.* ed. Montague Summers. 6 vols. London: 1915; rpt. New York: Benjamin Blom, 1967. Like many others lured by the mystery of Behn's life, Summers feels he, too, has "the" answer to her puzzling life. But aside from an occasional certainty where one is not warranted, Summers provides a supportive reconstruction, especially helpful in its pithy analyses of prior biographies and critics.

Woodcock, George, *The Incomparable Aphra.* London: Boardman, 1948. Although more thoroughly researched works have followed, Woodcock's compact biography remains the best general introduction to Behn's life. He studies the clues to a life and makes reasonable deductions from them, but his work is most valuable because it is not mired in details and because his chapters on Behn's career serve as concise evaluations. The plays and novels are suitably summarized, and adequate background on the theatre and the times are provided.

Autobiographical Sources

Even critics who do not consider *Oroonoko* fully autobiographical mine the work for biographical material. Most scholars agree that the novel is based on Behn's 1663–1664 experience in Surinam, but because the novel was published (and presumably written) over twenty years after Behn's travels to the colony, the accuracy of her memory is questioned. In addition, Behn's statement in *Oroonoko,* as elsewhere, that the material is "true" must be seen as a convention of fiction as well as of autobiography. Many of the characters and events of *Oroonoko* can be historically documented. Yet in spite of many studies purporting to disentangle the two, the fiction and the history seem inextricably linked. The difficulty of separating fact from fiction in Behn's life is underscored by the extension of the debate, beyond *Oroonoko,* to other stories, to poetry, and even to the earliest biographies (several critics claim Behn wrote these too).

Overview of Critical Sources

Until very recently, much of the criticism about Behn focused on appraising her life, and attention to her writing was often no more than an afterthought. Recently, however, Behn's artistry has been taken more seriously. While a disproportionate amount of the criticism still focuses on the separation of fact from fiction in *Oroonoko,* there is less energy expended now in suppositions about whether and what Behn wrote and more expended on the way she wrote and the contexts she wrote in. Biographies by Goreau and Duffy offer critical readings of nearly all of Behn's writing, but the best (and only book-length) critical study is Frederick Link's *Aphra Behn.* Other valuable work usually concentrates on either fiction or drama, and some of the most probing studies have been done recently by feminist critics.

Evaluation of Selected Criticism

Cotton, Nancy, *Women Playwrights in England c.1363–1750.* Lewisburg: Bucknell University Press, 1980, pp. 55–80. Cotton's 25–page summary provides an overview of Behn's life and an evaluation of her work, including an analysis of the courtesan and the amazon in her plays and a comparison of her work with that of male Restoration writers.

Link, Frederick, *Aphra Behn.* New York: Twayne, 1968. In the only book-length study of Behn's work, Link studies the literature by genre (drama, poetry, fiction, translation) providing especially useful summaries of the drama (with plot outlines, production history, liberal quotations, and analysis). Since Behn's works can often be hard to come by, his information is useful for someone without access to the primary texts. Link even-handedly suggests Behn's strengths and weaknesses, and gives excellent structural analysis of her work. He shows that criticism of Behn need not get bogged down in debates over morality.

Other Sources

Armistead, J. M. *Four Restoration Playwrights: A Reference Guide to Thomas Shadwell, Aphra Behn, Nathaniel Lee, and Thomas Otway.* Boston: G. K. Hall, 1984. A thorough annotated bibliography, up to and including 1981; especially good for its listings of parts of books or surveys which include material on Behn.

Cameron, W. J. *New Light on Aphra Behn.* Auckland: University of Auckland Press, 1961. Presents, in full, documents and letters from Behn's spying in Antwerp, finding Behn a reliable source on her own life and suggesting that

"History of the Life and Memoirs of Mrs. Behn, by One of the Fair Sex" may largely be Behn's own work.

Carver, Larry, "Aphra Behn: The Poet's Heart in a Woman's Body," in *Papers on Language and Literature,* 14 (Fall 1978), 414–424. A feminist study which uncovers the ambivalence in Behn's attitude to women.

Guffey, George, "Aphra Behn's *Oroonoko:* Occasion and Accomplishment," in *Two English Novelists.* Los Angeles: William Andrews Clark Memorial Library, 1975, pp. 1–41. In suggesting a political basis for *Oroonoko,* Guffey calls into question the whole debate over the novel's autobiographical potential.

Susan L. Carlson
Iowa State University

SAUL BELLOW
1915

Author's Chronology

Born June 10, 1915, Lachine, Quebec, Canada of Jewish immigrant parents from Russia; *1924* moves with his family to Chicago; *1937* receives B.S. in anthropology and sociology from Northwestern University; breaks off graduate studies that same year in order to marry and become a writer; *1938–1944* earns a living as an instructor at a teachers college in Chicago and by publishing small writing assignments; *1944* publishes his first novel, *Dangling Man; 1944–1945* serves in the Merchant Marine; *1946–1959* teaches English and creative writing at the University of Minnesota, New York University, Princeton, and Bard College; *1947* is awarded Guggenheim Fellowship for his second novel, *The Victim; 1954* wins his first National Book Award for his next novel, *The Adventures of Augie March; 1960–1962* co-founds and co-edits *The Noble Savage; 1962* appointed Professor to the Committee on Social Thought at The University of Chicago; *1976* is awarded Pulitzer Prize for *Humboldt's Gift* and also receives Nobel Prize for Literature; continues to reside, now with his fourth wife, in Chicago.

Author's Bibliography (selected)

Dangling Man, 1944 (novel), *The Victim,* 1947 (novel); *The Adventures of Augie March,* 1953 (novel); *Seize the Day,* 1956 (novella); *Henderson the Rain King,* 1959 (novel); *Herzog,* 1964 (novel); *The Last Analysis,* 1965 (play); *Mosby's Memoirs and Other Stories,* 1968; *Mr. Sammler's Planet,* 1970 (novel); *Humboldt's Gift,* 1975 (novel); *To Jerusalem and Back: A Personal Account,* 1976; *The Dean's December,* 1982 (novel); *Him with His Foot in His Mouth and Other Stories,* 1984.

Overview of Biographical Sources

Suspicious of a public that would rather know the author than read his books, Bellow has consistently refused to dramatize his personality as part of his art. As a result, biographical information is not abundant and rarely provides more than the list of dates available in the latest edition of *Who's Who in America.* Over the years, nevertheless, a number of telling literary snapshots of Bellow have accumulated. Representative of these brief profiles are three comparatively accessible sketches by three of Bellow's long-standing friends and colleagues. Alfred Kazin's "My Friend Saul Bellow" (*Atlantic Monthly,* January 1965, 51–54) recollects an early meeting with the unpretentious but self-assured young Chicagoan in the New York of 1942; Joseph Epstein's "Saul Bellow of Chicago" (*New York Times Book Review,* May 9, 1971, 4, 12, 14) portrays the mature Bellow enjoying anonymity in Chicago, while ruminating on the fads of literary criticism; Richard Stern's "Bellow's Gift" (*New York Times Magazine,* November 21, 1976, 12, 43–44, 46, 48, 50) catches Bellow at the height of his fame, hours after he has learned about his having been awarded the Nobel Prize for Literature.

How unrelenting the American reader is about extorting information from the private lives of its public figures has again been shown by the publication of a remarkably eccentric biographical work on Bellow, Mark Harris' *Saul Bellow: Drumlin Woodchuck* (Athens: University of Georgia Press, 1980), a book-length account on how not to succeed in writing Bellow's biography. Taking his title from a Robert Frost poem on strategies of evasion, a self-depreciating Harris recounts his futile efforts to install himself as Bellow's Boswell. For about four years, from 1966–1970, Harris tried to extract Bellow's cooperation in this venture but found himself repeatedly sidestepped by the nimble-footed victim of his fawning admiration. Eager to recoup his emotional investment, Harris now describes the handful of meetings he had with Bellow in restaurants, at parties, at home, and on the lecture circuit. Harris captures a frequently sardonic, occasionally petulant and ill-tempered man in situations that simply look and sound accurate because they seem to stem from the pages of Bellow's novels as much as they are supposed to stem from Bellow's life.

Autobiographical Sources

It is not inconsistent with Bellow's disregard for personal publicity that his novels are filled with characters and scenes drawn from his own life's history. Herzog reminiscing on his childhood among Russian Jews in a poor section of Montreal clearly refracts recollections of Bellow's own boyhood in Lachine. Augie March's rough-and-tumble youth in depression-ravaged Chicago recalls the environment of Bellow's adolescence. The tragic fate of the avant-garde poet, Von Humboldt Fleischer, contains not only a portrait of Delmore Schwartz, a man Bellow once much respected, but also a retrospective of Bellow's own heady days in the Greenwich Village of the 1940's.

Apart from the many casually disguised autobiographical traces in his fiction, Bellow has volunteered several straight-forward vignettes from his life. In "Starting out in Chicago" (*American Scholar,* Winter 1974–1975, 71–77), he tells of his comic beginnings as a young, inexperienced writer. Bellow's "How I Wrote Augie March's Story" (*New York Times Book Review,* January 31, 1954, 3, 17) recounts his bohemian life-style while in Europe in 1949. Commemorative tributes to Isaac Rosenfeld (*Partisan Review,* 1956, 565–567), and to John Berryman (in John Berryman, *Recovery,* New York: Farrar, Straus and Giroux, 1973, ix–xiv) relive personal moments in Chicago, Greenwich Village, Princeton, and the University of Minnesota.

To Jerusalem and Back: A Personal Account, Bellow's appraisal of his stay in Israel during the latter half of 1975, shows a moderate, though not impartial, a gentle, though not defensive, writer who in the end feels saddened and overwhelmed by "the butcher problems of politics."

Overview of Critical Sources

Since the popular breakthrough of *Herzog* in 1964, it has become increasingly difficult to survey the growing bulk of critical and scholarly works on Bellow. By 1978, three comprehensive bibliographies had appeared: Francine Lercangée, *Saul Bellow: A Bibliography of Secondary Sources,* Brussels: Center for American Studies, 1977; Marianne Nault, *Saul Bellow: His Work and His Critics; An Annotated International Bibliography,* New York: Garland Publishers, 1977; and Robert G. Noreen, *Saul Bellow: A Reference Guide,* Boston: G. K. Hall, 1978. While criticism before *Herzog* often remained impressionistic in its approach, it became decidedly systematic after 1964, focusing its attention on psychological and metaphysical patterns in the development of the Bellowian hero as well as on Bellow's post-modern, anti-nihilistic philosophy of human worth. More recently, the stylistic means by which Bellow conveys his affirmative stance have also received greater attention.

Evaluation of Selected Criticism

Clayton, John Jacob, *Saul Bellow: In Defense of Man.* Second Edition. Bloomington: Indiana University Press, 1979. Bellow's work is analyzed as exhibiting an abiding contradiction between the author's affirmation of individual life in his non-fiction writings and the psychic patterns of alienation, masochism, and collective anonymity suffered through or espoused by his fictional protagonists. Clayton's second edition goes beyond these findings of 1968 by exploring a similar inconsistency in the political views of Bellow's later works. In spite of his reservations, Clayton is not unappreciative of Bellow's achievements. His study raises a number of constructive questions.

Dutton, Robert R. *Saul Bellow.* Revised Edition. Boston: Twayne, 1982. Dutton's study of Bellow's novels emphasizes the allegorical method by which the hero's search for integrity is depicted. While Dutton views the central figure as representing developing states of mind, the supporting cast of characters embodies for him a variety of literary, social, and philosophical forces which the hero encounters as temptations on his way to personal truth. Though this approach helps to probe the intellectual complexity of the narrative fabric, Dutton's hunt for historical and cultural analogues seems at times forced, his appreciation of Bellow's characters often too abstract.

Fuchs, Daniel, *Saul Bellow: Vision and Revision.* Durham: Duke University Press, 1984. This lengthy and demanding book is divided into two independent sections. The first two chapters locate Bellow within his cultural milieu by dealing with his reactions to two opposing literary traditions from the nineteenth century. In the following eight chapters, Fuchs, whom Bellow has granted sole access to his manuscripts, analyzes the compositional stages through which Bellow progressed to the final version of his novels. Definitely intended for the serious student of Bellow, Fuchs' study must be considered the most significant contribution to Bellow scholarship in many years.

Newman, Judie, *Saul Bellow and History.* New York: St. Martin's Press, 1984. Finding criticism surprisingly uniform in the assumption of an increasingly religious quest in Bellow's novels, Newman develops an alternate reading which stresses their historical specificity. In addition, she explores each novel for the theory of history which forms its intellectual content as well as its narrative form. Newman succeeds in redirecting attention.

Other Sources

Cohen, Sarah Blacher, *Saul Bellow's Enigmatic Laughter,* Urbana: University of Illinois Press, 1974. An Analysis of Bellow's increasingly complex use of comedy as a relief from pessimism.

Malin, Irving, ed. *Saul Bellow and the Critics.* New York: New York University Press, 1967. A collection of essays from the late 1950's and early 1960's together with Bellow's "Where Do We Go From Here: The Future of Fiction."

Modern Fiction Studies, 25, Spring 1979 (Special Bellow Issue). Eleven previously unpublished essays as well as a comprehensive bibliographical checklist.

Trachtenberg, Stanley, ed. *Critical Essays on Saul Bellow.* Boston: G.K. Hall, 1979. Reprints twelve influential reviews.

Selected Dictionaries and Encyclopedias

Critical Survey of Long Fiction, Salem Press, 1983. Brief biography, and short analysis of Bellow's novels.

Dictionary of Literary Biography, Volume II, Gale Research, 1978. Succinct biographical information and assessment of Bellow's works; also contains a helpful bibliography of Bellow's essays.

Joachim Scholz
Washington College

STEPHEN VINCENT BENÉT
1898–1943

Author's Chronology

Born July 22, 1898, into an Army family; *1899–1909* moves frequently as father is assigned to different posts; *1911–1915* attends school in Augusta, Georgia; *1915* enters Yale College; publishes first book of poetry; *1918* leaves Yale after junior year to enlist in Army; honorably discharged; *1919* re-admitted to Yale, graduates with B.A. degree, enters Yale Graduate School; *1920* receives A.M. from Yale, goes to France on traveling fellowship; *1921* returns to America, marries Rosemary Carr, honeymoons in Europe; *1922* returns to New York; *1926* receives Guggenheim Fellowship and moves to Paris; *1929* returns to United States, receives Pulitzer Prize for Poetry; *1929–1930* works in Hollywood with D. W. Griffith; *1930–1935* continues to write both fiction and poetry, *1936* receives O. Henry Memorial Prize for "The Devil and Daniel Webster;" *1938* elected to American Academy of Arts and Letters; *1939* hospitalized for overwork; *1940–1942* health deteriorates although begins to write speeches and radio plays on behalf of war effort; *1943* dies on March 13 of heart attack; *1944* awarded second Pulitzer Prize for Poetry.

Author's Bibliography (selected)

Five Men and Pompey, 1915 (poems); *Young Adventure,* 1918 (poems); *The Beginning of Wisdom,* 1921 (novel); *Young People's Pride,* (novel); *Jean Huguenot,* 1923 (novel); *Spanish Bayonet,* 1926 (novel); *John Brown's Body,* (poem); *James Shore's Daughter,* 1934 (novel); *Burning City,* 1936 (poems); *Thirteen O'Clock,* 1937 (stories); *Tales Before Midnight,* 1939 (stories); *Selected Works,* 1942 (compendium); *Western Star,* 1943 (poem); *America,* 1944 (history).

Overview of Biographical Sources

Interest in Benét has waned over the past two decades, and thus none of the major sources on Benét's life and work remain in print except the edition of his letters. Benét's full if relatively brief career paralleled those of many of his better remembered contemporaries: a youthful success in New York followed by several years of expatriate living in Paris in the 1920's, a mature career built on the need to write for commercial markets to support his family, and a premature death in his forties brought on in part by overwork. Benét's life is best documented in Charles Fenton's *Stephen Vincent Benét: The Life and Times of an American Man of Letters, 1989–1943* (1958). The only substantial additions to Fenton's portrait can be found in two volumes of sympathetic reminiscence. Laura Benét, herself a poet and biographer, wrote *When William Rose, Stephen Vincent and I Were Young* (New York: Dodd, Mead and Co., 1976), a memoir which contains several vivid scenes of her brother's childhood adventures on various Army bases. William Rose Benét's "My Brother, Steve" and John Farrar's "For the Record," which were published together in a slim volume titled *Stephen Vincent Benét: My Brother, Steve* (New York: *Saturday Review of Literature* and Farrar and Rinehart, 1943), both illuminate Benét's mature literary tastes and his dedication to his craft.

Evaluation of Selected Biographies

Fenton, Charles A. *Stephen Vincent Benét: The Life and Times of an American Man of Letters, 1898–1943.* New Haven: Yale University Press, 1958. This is the only full-length biography of Benét, and it is authoritative in that Fenton enjoyed complete access to the Benét papers at Yale as well as the cooperation of his widow and family. Fenton sensibly traces Benét's literary treatment of national and historic themes to his nomadic childhood as the son of a career Army officer; he reconstructs clearly Benét's precocious successes at Yale, and suggests how Benét's writing was permanently influenced by the poetic traditionalists on the Yale faculty; and he sympathetically documents Benét's struggle to support himself and his family as a writer in Depression-era America. Fenton's critical judgements are skimpy and generally conventional, and are focused on identifying Benét as essentially a poet who happened to write commercially in other genres. This biography, although stiff in style and written from an academic distance, succeeds in arguing that Benét was a man of character and one of the most successful and respected writers of his day; it fails when pleading the lasting merits of Benét's work beyond *John Brown's Body* and "The Devil and Daniel Webster."

Autobiographical Sources

Benét left no overt autobiography at the time of his sudden death in 1943, but he was a frequent, lively and informative letter writer with many correspondents, including many members of his family, his literary agent, and the publisher John Farrar. Thus his published correspondence, competently edited and annotated by Charles Fenton in *Selected Letters of Stephen Vincent Benét* (New Haven: Yale University Press, 1960), reveals much about Benét's personality, family life and literary concerns. Most of the letters Fenton selected were written between 1920 and 1940; Benét perforce wrote fewer letters during his childhood and during his last few years, when he was plagued by illness and overwork. Of special interest are the many letters concerning the composition and publication of *John Brown's Body,* written from France to agents and publishers in New York in the 1920's. This is a valuable companion volume to Fenton's biography of Benét.

Many of Benét's ideas about the art and vocation of writing are collected in his protegé George Abbe's *Stephen Vincent Benét on Writing: A Great Writer's Letters of Advice to a Young Beginer* (Brattleboro, VT: The Stephen Greene Press, 1964). Abbe divided his brief book into four parts: in a short introduction Abbe recounts his decade-long friendship with Benét; a second section arranges Benét's advice on the craft of writing under such topics as "Choosing the Theme," "Characterization," and "Revision;" a third presents Benét's advice on the vocation of writing, including choosing an agent and dealing with publishers; and finally, Abbe reprints thirty-one letters he received from Benét from 1935–1943. Abbe strains at times to prove the value of Benét's art as well as his advice, and his editorial tone is a bit too fawning, but Benét's own comments on the profession of authorship are sensible and astute.

Overview of Critical Sources

Although Benét enjoyed many literary honors during his lifetime, posterity has not been so kind. His poetry is not ironic, complex or ambiguous enough to have drawn much attention from academic critics, who most often dismiss him as working in an outmoded, "genteel" bardic tradition, a Whitman without the wit or vision. Thus Benét criticism is scant: only one book-length critical study exists—Parry Stroud's *Stephen Vincent Benét* (1962). Basil Davenport, in his brief "Introduction" to *Stephen Vincent Benét: Selected Poetry and Prose* (New York: Holt, Rinehart and Winston, 1960), stresses Benét's essential romanticism as well as his Americanism, and serves as a useful overview of Benét's work. Other critical articles have noted Benét's use of history and folklore, particularly in his long narrative poems. Critics generally agree that, while an admitted master of commercial short stories like "The Devil and Daniel Webster," whatever literary claim Benét might stake rests on his poetry, chiefly *John Brown's Body.*

Evaluation of Selected Criticism

Stroud, Parry, *Stephen Vincent Benét.* New York: Twayne, 1962. Stroud classified Benét as a national poet in the romantic Whitman tradition, but of considerably lesser achievement. Stroud's study is divided rather mechanically into separate chapters on Benét's minor poetry, his novels, his short stories, his propaganda work during World War II, *John Brown's Body,* and *Western Star.* He considers *John Brown's Body* to be Benét's greatest achievement. Stroud places Benét as a poet midway between the traditionalists and the modernists, and suggests that Benét's critical reputation has suffered because he was working against the modernist grain. Stroud makes a convincing case that Benét was an honest and interesting poet, but not a major figure in or influence on twentieth century poetry.

Other Sources

"As We Remember Him," *Saturday Review of Literature,* XXVI (March 27, 1943), 7–11. A series of short considerations of Benét written at the time of his death by fourteen contemporaries, including Henry Seidel Canby, Archibald

MacLeish and Thornton Wilder. These tributes are valuable biographically, and some contain critical appraisals of Benét's work.

Moffett, Judith, "Like Thistle-Seed: Stephen Vincent Benét's Narrative Poetry," Dissertation: University of Pennsylvania 1971. Moffett terms Benét a popular artist and a minor poet, but one who in *John Brown's Body,* despite technical lapses, succeeds in telling a good story.

———, "Some Corrections of Parry Stroud's *Stephen Vincent Benét," Notes and Queries,* XIII (Winter 1965), 420–421. Moffett points out minor errors in Stroud's reading of *John Brown's Body.*

Wiggins, Eugene, "Benét's Mountain Whippoorwill: Folklore atop Folklore," 41 (Fall 1975), 99–114. Wiggins demonstrates the great extent to which Benét drew upon American folklore in his poetry.

Wiley, Paul L. "The Phaeton Symbol in *John Brown's Body," American Literature,* 17 (November 1945), 231–42. Wiley provides a rare formalist reading of Benét's epic, and argues its symbolic richness.

Selected Dictionaries and Encyclopedias

Critical Survey of Poetry, Salem Press, 1982. Little biography, but brief discussions of Benét's poetic theories and works.

Dictionary of Literary Biography, Vol. 4, Gale Research, 1980. Brief discussion of Benét's expatriate years in Paris, focusing on his composition of *John Brown's Body.*

Richard Fine
Virginia Commonwealth University

ARNOLD BENNETT
1867–1931

Author's Chronology

Born Enoch Arnold Bennett, May 27, 1867, in Hanley, Staffordshire, the heart of England's "Pottery District," the eldest of six surviving children of the rigid Wesleyan Methodists Enoch Bennett, a solicitor in Hanley, and his wife Sarah Ann, daughter of a draper; *1877* begins formal education, entering the Burslem Endowed School; *1882* advances to the Middle School, Newcastle-on-Lyme; *1883* becomes clerk in father's law office; *1885* passes entrance examinations for London University, but does not matriculate because of his father's opposition; *1887–1888* twice fails law exams; *1889* moves to London to become solicitor's clerk; *1894–1900* consumed by numerous literary and journalistic enterprises; *1902* death of father; *1903* freed of parental onus, leaves London to reside in France for nearly ten years; *1906* temporarily engaged to a young American woman, Eleanor Green; *1907* marries a French woman, Marie Marguerite Soulié, in July, after a seven-month's acquaintance (no children); *1911* successful tour of the United States at the behest of his American publisher, George Doran; *1912* returns to live in England; *1914–1918* actively involved with several War Committees; *1915* visits the front in France to record his impressions; *1918* named Director of Propaganda for France, by Lord Beaverbrook; later succeeds Beaverbrook as Director of Ministry of Information; *1919* moves to London and circulates widely in society; *1921* separated from his wife Marguerite; *1922* meets Dorothy Cheston, with whom he was to live for the remainder of his life; *1924 Riceyman Steps* wins the James Tait Black Memorial Prize for fiction published in 1923; *1926* Bennett's only child, Virginia, born to Dorothy Cheston; *1931* dies March 27, from typhoid fever contracted following a trip to France.

Author's Bibliography (selected)

A Man from the North, 1898 (novel); *The Grand Babylon Hotel,* 1902 (novel); *Anna of the Five Towns,* 1902 (novel); *The Truth About an Author,* 1903 (autobiography); *The Old Wives' Tale,* 1908 (novel); *Buried Alive,* 1908 (novel); *Clayhanger,* 1910 (novel); *The Card,* 1911 (novel); *Hilda Lessways,* 1911 (novel); *These Twain,* 1915 (novel); *The Pretty Lady,* 1918 (novel); *Riceyman Steps,* 1923 (novel); *Lord Raingo,* 1926 (novel); *Imperial Palace,* 1930 (novel); *The Journals of Arnold Bennett, 1896–1928,* 3 vols., ed. Newman Flower, 1932–1933; *The Letters of Arnold Bennett,* 3 vols., ed. James G. Hepburn, 1966–1970; *"The Author's Craft" and Other Critical Writings of Arnold Bennett,* ed. Samuel Hynes, 1968; *Arnold Bennett in Love: Arnold Bennett and His Wife Marguerite Soulié: A Correspondence,* Ed. and trans. George and Jean Beardmore, 1972; *The "Evening Standard" Years: "Books and Persons,"* ed. Andrew Mylett, 1974 (essays); *Arnold Bennett: Sketches for Autobiography,* ed. James G. Hepburn, 1979.

Overview of Biographical Sources

The biographical literature on Bennett is greater in volume than in reliability. His wife and his mistress (who eventually took his name by deed poll), offer their predictably self-defensive biographical memoirs. Marguerite Bennett's two slim volumes: *Arnold Bennett* (New York: Adelphi, 1925) and *My Arnold Bennett* (New York: Dutton, 1932), were both written after he had left her and are tainted by her possessiveness and resentment. Dorothy Cheston Bennett's *Arnold Bennett: A Portrait Done at Home* (New York: Kendall and Sharp, 1935), is a more serene view of Bennett, but concerns only the last decade of his life. The three scholarly biographies are described below. The most valuable recent biographical works are Kinley E. Roby's *A Writer at War: Arnold Bennett, 1914–1918* (Baton Rouge: Louisiana State University Press, 1972), which intensively examines Bennett's wartime activities, finding the key to his creative resurgence in the twenties in his experiences during the war. Frank Swinnerton's *Arnold Bennett: A Last Word* (Garden City, NY: Doubleday, 1978), is an affectionate memoir of Swinnerton's close friendship with Bennett from 1909 to 1931.

Evaluation of Selected Biographies

Barker, Dudley, *Writer by Trade: A View of Arnold Bennett.* London: Allen and Unwin, 1966. The most readable of the biographies, Barker's account of Bennett's life differs little from Pound's (see below), except that he is able to deal more frankly with the break-up of Bennett's marriage to Marguerite, who was still alive when Pound had written his book. Barker's title indicates his primary view of Bennett as a "commercial" author, and an entrepreneurial businessman of letters. Yet he also offers the most insightful and generally most appreciative criticism of Bennett's fiction to be found in the biographies.

Drabble, Margaret, *Arnold Bennett: A Biography.* New York: Alfred A. Knopf, 1974. Bennett seems always to have commanded greater attention and appreciation from accomplished novelists (e.g., Somerset Maugham, Frank Swinnerton, H. G. Wells, Rebecca West), than from academic literary critics. His appeal to other professional writers is surely his masterly craftsmanship as well as his frankly pragmatic approach to his trade. Drabble continues this trend in her admiring biography of her fellow midlands novelist. She also shares with Bennett the lower-middle class, Wesleyan Methodist heritage: his "background, his childhood and origins . . . are very similar to my own."

Pound, Reginald, *Arnold Bennett: A Biography.* London: Heinemann, 1952. Pound's standard, scholarly biography of Bennett excellently describes the rise to fame and the public years of Bennett as journalist, social lion, and man of letters. His biography, however, is most valuable for its modification of

Bennett's self-created reputation as a methodical, businessman-novelist. Rather, Bennett is seen as a somewhat harried journalist, a driven man, of more psychological complexity than generally assumed.

Autobiographical Sources

Bennett was not given to introspection, by conviction. Rarely do his autobiographical writings reveal his own private thoughts and feelings. But they do provide a wealth of circumstantial details. His early autobiography, *The Truth About an Author* (Westminster: Constable, 1903), with its practical emphasis on Bennett's strategies for becoming a successful author, has done more to create his reputation as a literary entrepreneur than the criticisms of his worst detractors. (Pound's biography does much to correct this imbalanced view.) Bennett's voluminous *Journals,* ed. Newman Flower (3 vols., London: Cassell, 1932–1933), provide a virtually unbroken record of Bennett's activities for over thirty years. And a recent volume, *Arnold Bennett: Sketches for Autobiography,* ed. James G. Hepburn (London: Allen and Unwin, 1979), usefully gathers a number of Bennett's uncollected, though similarly impersonal autobiographical essays.

Overview of Critical Sources

Popular to this day with the general reader, Bennett has never been widely or enthusiastically received by academic literary critics. The reasons for Bennett's neglect by scholars are fairly easily summarized: many of his novels are "potboilers" that pretend to, and attain, no literary distinction; at the highpoint of his popular celebrity he was portrayed as a mere "commercial" writer (e.g., Ezra Pound's caricature in "Hugh Selwyn Mauberley," 1920), unable to portray the subtleties of human consciousness (e.g., Virginia Woolf's *Mr. Bennett and Mrs. Brown,* 1924—below); and, by the end of his life, he was displaced from academic attention by the generation of provocative, experimental, and complex writers (e.g., Pound, Woolf, James Joyce, and T. S. Eliot), who demanded critical exegesis. The most important exceptions to this pattern of critical neglect are included in the studies evaluated below.

Evaluation of Selected Criticism

Broomfield, Olga R. R. *Arnold Bennett.* Boston: Twayne, 1984. The most recently published study of Bennett, Broomfield's biographical and critical survey of his life and works is a competent and thorough account. Broomfield is able to devote only a few pages, at most, to the criticism of the major works; but she does have something useful to say about all the novels, in turn, and as much of the nonfiction and drama as space allows.

Hall, James, *Arnold Bennett: Primitivism and Taste.* Seattle: University of Washington Press, 1959. This fine study of Bennett's four most important novels, *The Old Wives' Tale* and the *Clayhanger* trilogy (*Clayhanger, Hilda Less-*

ways, and *These Twain*), concentrates on Bennett's technical and thematic balance of the opposed tensions of middle-class and aristocratic values.

Hepburn, James G. *The Art of Arnold Bennett.* Bloomington: Indiana University Press, 1963. In the best single study of the fiction, Hepburn argues persuasively against the received view of Bennett as exclusively a realist, seeing him as "equally a psychological realist, a symbolist, an allegorist . . . a discoverer of beauty" in his finest works. Hepburn also publishes a useful chronology for the composition of Bennett's numerous writings.

Lucas, John, *Arnold Bennett: A Study of His Fiction.* London: Methuen, 1974. Lucas offers intelligent, judicious, and often perceptive readings of eleven novels he finds most representative of Bennett's strengths as, by turns, a realist, formalist, naturalist, and symbolist writer.

Other Sources

Rice, Thomas Jackson, "Arnold Bennett," in *English Fiction, 1900–1950.* Detroit: Gale Research, 1979. Pp. 109–143. Rice's is the most current and most complete listing (with annotations) of books and articles written about Bennett and his works.

Woolf, Virginia, *Mr. Bennett and Mrs. Brown.* London: Hogarth, 1924. Woolf's essay, which stimulated a still unresolved and perhaps unresolvable debate between adherents of realist and non-representational theories of fiction, has been, by its distorted rejection of Bennett's documentary realism, the single most damaging influence on Bennett's academic critical reputation.

Selected Dictionaries and Encyclopedias

Dictionary of Literary Biography, Vol. 34, Gale Research, 1985, pp. 17–28. Concise biographical and critical overview, focusing on Bennett's career as a novelist.

Dictionary of Literary Biography, Vol. 10, Gale Research, 1982, pp. 55–60. Concise biography and overview of Bennett's largely forgotten plays.

Thomas J. Rice
University of South Carolina

THE *BEOWULF*-POET
before 1000

Author's Chronology

The anonymous *Beowulf*-poet, to whom scholars can confidently attribute only the single greatest Old English poem, shaped into its present, surviving form a story of people and events that date from the early sixth century A.D. in Denmark and southern Sweden. But although there is ample historical evidence for placing certain characters (e.g., Hrothgar and Hygelac) and actions (e.g., the Battle of Ravenswood) in this period, one should take full account of three additional sources. First, scholars have determined that *Beowulf,* whether itself a written composition or not, derives in some way from a vital oral tradition older than the Anglo-Saxons' tenure in Britain (thus, for instance, the subject of the poem). Because of these origins, it is necessary to consider the implications of oral tradition in the evolution of the story from an oral legend or set of legends to the sophisticated, elegant epic we find in the manuscript Cotton Vitellius A XV. Second, and complementarily, some elements in *Beowulf* (the monster-fights, Scyld Scefing, etc.) must be assigned not to any specific historical period but to the timeless world of mythology and folklore; indeed, critics have suggested Common Germanic or even Indo-European roots for some of these motifs and characters. Third, far at the other end of the spectrum, it is impossible to assess exactly how the originally pagan story reacted as it encountered the new world of Christian belief. Christian echoes and episodes can be located, of course, but in the end it is necessary to recognize that one is left with a single hybrid text that no doubt represents only one stage of the poem's ontogeny. In a real sense *Beowulf* was in a process of active evolution from the earliest stage of oral tradition onward, with a probably eighth- or ninth-century Anglian or Mercian poet providing the epitome encoded in the unique, tenth-century manuscript. *Beowulf* is a poem of all these ages, and each age contributed something of importance to it.

Author's Bibliography

Editions: Fr. Klaeber, *Beowulf and the Fight at Finnsburg,* 3rd ed.; Howell D. Chickering, *Beowulf: A Dual-Language Edition;* Donald K. Fry, *Finnsburh: Fragment and Episode.*

Translations: Michael Alexander, *Beowulf;* Stanley B. Greenfield, *A Readable Beowulf;* Burton Raffel, *Beowulf;* Joseph F. Tuso, ed., *Beowulf* (trans. by E. Talbot Donaldson).

Overview of Critical Sources

Early scholarship, particularly the German school of Higher Criticism, took as its primary goal the establishment of text and authorship, so that much of the nineteenth-century work on *Beowulf* consists of linguistic and narrative tests designed to characterize the style of its poet. In fact, for many years the Anglo-Saxon epic was seen as simply a philological or historical curiosity, either as a point of comparison with, for example, Old Norse saga or Middle High German narrative, or as a source for "mythologized" history that bore some faint resemblance to what survived in less literary formats. With J. R. R. Tolkien's *Beowulf: The Monsters and the Critics* (1936), the tide began to turn and critics started to treat *Beowulf* as a work of art. Soon books, monographs, and articles began to address questions not only of history, archaeology, and Germanic linguistics, but also of aesthetics and literary criticism. Within this latter category five areas of special activity may be distinguished: formalist readings, exegetical criticism, comparative approaches, literary history, and oral-formulaic scholarship. In all of these areas scholars recognize the contributions of the anonymous *Beowulf*-poet, who was responsible for the poem in its single surviving version, and also of the tradition and earlier individual poets who must share in his accomplishment.

Evaluation of Selected Criticism

Bede, *A History of the English Church and People.* trans. by Leo Sherley-Price; rev. ed. Harmondsworth: Penguin, 1968. The greatest of Anglo-Saxon scholars provides a firsthand, seventh-century view of contemporary England that complements latter-day literary and historical-social perspectives.

Bonjour, Adrien, *The Digressions in Beowulf.* Oxford: Basil Blackwell, 1970. Bonjour supplies much-needed background information about the fragmentarily described events of the poem, events with which the original audience of the poem would, of course, have been familiar.

Brodeur, Arthur G. *The Art of Beowulf.* Berkeley: University of California Press, 1959. A relatively early general study of the poem that emphasizes literary style.

Chambers, Raymond W. *Beowulf: An Introduction.* 3rd ed. Cambridge: Cambridge University Press, 1963. An invaluable source for background materials in other Germanic traditions.

Irving, Edward B., Jr. *A Reading of Beowulf.* New Haven: Yale University Press, 1968. The single most impressive and helpful general study of the poem, Irving's book includes remarks on the whole range of conventional literary subjects.

Lord, Albert B. *The Singer of Tales.* Cambridge, Ma: Harvard University Press, 1960. Lord provides the first comparative commentary on *Beowulf* and oral tradition (pp. 198–221).

Stenton, Frank M. *Anglo-Saxon England.* 3rd ed. Oxford: Clarendon Press, 1971. The standard history of the period.

Other Sources

Bruce-Mitford, Rupert L. *The Sutton Hoo Ship-Burial.* 3 vols. London: British Museum, 1975. The standard archeological record of the early seventh-century find that contained many of the objects mentioned in *Beowulf.*

Foley, John Miles, *Oral-Formulaic Theory and Research: An Introduction and Annotated Bibliography.* New York: Garland, 1985. Includes an introductory essay on oral literature (pp. 3–77) with numerous references to *Beowulf* and a bibliography of relevant works through 1982.

Fry, Donald K., Jr. *Beowulf and the Fight at Finnsburh.* Charlottesville: Bibliographical Society of the University of Virginia, 1969. An indexed and cross-referenced bibliography, with notes to reviews of major items.

Fry, Donald K., Jr. ed. *The Beowulf Poet.* Englewood Cliffs, NJ: Prentice-Hall, 1968. Collection of essays on a wide variety of topics.

Greenfield, Stanley B. and Fred C. Robinson, *A Bibliography of Publications on Old English Literature to the End of 1972.* Toronto: University of Toronto Press, 1980. A complete digest of literary criticism on *Beowulf* through 1972 (items 1628–3196A).

Malone, Kemp, ed. *The Nowell Codex.* Copenhagen: Rosenkilde and Bagger, 1963. Includes an extensive introduction to the manuscript as well as a photographic facsimile of the codex that contains *Beowulf.*

Nicholson, Lewis E. ed. *An Anthology of Beowulf Criticism.* Notre Dame: University of Notre Dame Press, 1963. A collection of essays that focuses primarily on Christian perspectives toward *Beowulf.*

Renoir, Alain, "*Beowulf:* A Contextual Introduction to Its Contents and Techniques," in Felix J. Oinas, ed. *Heroic Epic and Saga.* Bloomington: Indiana University Press, 1978. pp. 99–119. The best, most perceptive brief introduction to the poem.

Short, Douglas D. *Beowulf Scholarship: An Annotated Bibliography.* New York: Garland, 1980. Substantially annotated entries.

Whitelock, Dorothy, *The Beginnings of English Society.* rev. ed. Harmondsworth: Penguin, 1968. A brief introduction to the social institutions of the Anglo-Saxons.

John Miles Foley
University of Missouri/Columbia

JOHN BERRYMAN
1914–1972

Author's Chronology

Born October 25, 1914, McAlester, Oklahoma, the son of John Allyn Smith and Martha (Little) Smith; *1926* father commits suicide; mother marries John Angus McAlpin Berryman, whose surname John takes; *1932–1936* attends Columbia and graduates Phi Beta Kappa with A.B.; *1936–1938* wins scholarship to study at Clare College, Cambridge, England where he receives B.A.; *1940* appointed Instructor in English at Harvard; *1942* marries Eileen Patricia Mulligan (divorced 1956); *1945* records his poetry for the Library of Congress; *1946* teaches creative writing at Princeton University; *1947* has affair with 'Lise' and writes sonnet sequence later published as *Berryman's Sonnets* (1967); *1955* accepts position at University of Minnesota; *1956* marries Elizabeth Ann Levine (divorced 1959); *1961* marries Kathleen Donahue; *1964* publishes *77 Dream Songs,* which wins the Pulitzer Prize; *1968* publishes *His Toy, His Dream, His Rest* (the conclusion of *The Dream Songs*), which wins the National Book Award and the Bollingen Prize; *1970* treated for alcoholism at the Intensive Alcohol Treatment Center, St. Mary's Hospital, Minneapolis; *1971* awarded a Senior Fellowship by the National Endowment for the Humanities; *1972* commits suicide, 7 January.

Author's Bibliography (selected)

The Dispossessed, 1948 (poems); Stephen Crane, 1950 (critical biography); *Homage to Mistress Bradstreet,* 1956 (poetry); *Berryman's Sonnets,* 1968; *The Dream Songs* (complete edition of *77 Dream Songs* and *His Toy, His Dream, His Rest*), 1969 (poetry); *Delusions, Etc.,* 1969 (poems); *Love & Fame,* 1971 (poems); *Recovery,* 1973 (novel).

Overview of Biographical Sources

Since Berryman's life was usually the subject of his poetry, his poetry demands a knowledge of his biography. But until 1982 the only biographical material assembled on Berryman was J. M. Linebarger's ten page introduction to his critical work, *John Berryman* (1974), and Joel Conarroe's twenty-one page biographical sketch in his book, *John Berryman: An Introduction to the Poetry* (1977). Then in 1982 John Haffenden's authorized biography appeared. *The Life of John Berryman* is a thoroughly researched and essentially definitive work, with the exception that some facts, says Haffenden, were omitted to avoid offending persons still living. Given Berryman's reputation for having affairs and that all three of his former wives are still living, omissions were to be expected. Also in 1982 Berryman's first wife, Eileen Simpson, published her memoirs of the couple's marriage and their literary friendships. *Poets in Their*

Youth presents both an intimate look at Berryman's life and a portrait of a doomed generation of poets: Delmore Schwartz, Dylan Thomas, Randall Jarrell, Robert Lowell, and others.

Evaluation of Selected Biographies

Haffenden, John, *The Life of John Berryman.* London: Routledge & Kegan Paul, 1982. Haffenden compiled his biography using Berryman's papers stored at the University of Minnesota and from interviews with Berryman's relatives, friends, colleagues and students. It is a scholarly, extensively researched work that portrays Berryman, for the most part, as he portrayed himself in *The Dream Songs.* However, Berryman's wit and charm that is evident in *The Dream Songs* are overshadowed in Haffenden's biography due to Haffenden's over-reliance on accounts of Berryman's sexual adventures and bouts with alcohol. The biography has no sense of narrative, unfortunately, and is filled with awkward, roundabout sentences.

Simpson, Eileen, *Poets in Their Youth.* New York: Random House, 1982. Although Berryman is just one of many literary figures portrayed in Simpson's book, the central focus is on him. He is treated sympathetically, even affectionately by his ex-wife. His humor and loyalty to his friends get more emphasis here than in Haffenden's biography. Simpson, who is now a psychotherapist, lays the responsibility for Berryman's psychological problems not on Berryman's father's suicide as much as on Berryman's dominating, manipulative mother—a decidedly different perspective than the one Berryman presents in his poetry. Simpson controls her narrative masterfully. Her style is lucid and her descriptions, memorable.

Autobiographical Sources

While Berryman never wrote a formal autobiography, most of his poetry and his unfinished novel contain a wealth of autobiographical information. *Berryman's Sonnets* chronical Berryman's stormy affair with a woman he refers to as "Lise." He wrote the poems during the affair, which lasted from March to September 1947. But because of their potentially damaging effects, he refrained from publishing them for twenty years. Berryman claimed that he was not Henry in *The Dream Songs* but he also admitted that he and Henry did "fiendishly" resemble each other. Written over a thirteen year period (1955–1968), *The Dream Songs* explore the length and breadth of the poet's life, from the recounting of his father's suicide to his own breakdowns and contemplations of suicide. Berryman also protested that *Love & Fame* was not an autobiography in verse, but critics call these poems Berryman's most blatantly confessional. Covering a thirty-five year period, Berryman writes about his college career, loves, alcoholism, and spiritual struggles. *Recovery* is Berryman's uncompleted, posthumous, autobiographical novel. In 1971 Berryman entered the alcohol treatment facility at St. Mary's Hospital in Minneapolis. The novel records his struggle to overcome his addiction while he was there.

Overview of Critical Sources

Criticism is still divided on Berryman's place in twentieth century poetry. Admirers praise his originality of style and they point to his introduction into literature of a character they believe will be or should be as famous as Eliot's J. Alfred Prufrock. Their case is convincing that Henry is representative of at least the decade of the 1960's. Berryman's detractors, who claim that the poetry is unnecessarily obscure and that *The Dream Songs* lacks structure as a long poem, have not been satisfactorily answered. No agreement exists over the structure of his major work and few rigorous analyses of the poems are to be found—a condition that could change with Haffenden's recently published notes and biography.

Evaluation of Selected Criticism

Arpin, Gary Q. *The Poetry of John Berryman.* Port Washington, NY: Kennikat Press, 1978. Arpin comments briefly on each of Berryman's poetical works. His thesis is that Berryman, concerned with the question of how we should live in the world, created characters who rebel against life, then through suffering and self-examination find peace in love and work.

Bloom, James D. *The Stock of Available Reality: R. P. Blackmur and John Berryman.* London: Associated University Presses, 1984. Bloom discusses Blackmur's and Berryman's intellectual kinship, especially their reactions to major literary figures past and present, and their shared dissent with New Criticism, which Blackmur had earlier helped to found.

Conarroe, Joel, *John Berryman: An Introduction to the Poetry.* New York: Columbia University Press, 1977. Conarroe provides a good introduction to Berryman's work and is generally considered to have written some of the most illuminating criticism on the poetry. His approach is to point out the poetry's originality, provide glosses, describe themes and explain Berryman's technical achievements. His readings are usually convincing; however, he will probably continue to stand in the minority in his praise for Berryman's later works, *Recovery* and *Love & Fame.*

Haffenden, John, *John Berryman: A Critical Commentary.* New York: New York University Press, 1980. Having combed through Berryman's working drafts and personal papers, Haffenden attempts in the first part of his book to reveal the thematic structure and the genesis of Berryman's major poetical works. In the second half of his book, Haffenden includes extensive notes on *The Dream Songs* and *Delusions, Etc.,* and in an appendix he records the chronology of the dream songs' composition. This is a valuable resource book, with the weakest part by far being Haffenden's interpretations of thematic structures.

Linebarger, J. M. *John Berryman.* New York: Twayne, 1974. Linebarger traces Berryman's development as he moved away from the Academics's influence and toward the creation of Beat poetry. *The Dream Songs,* which embody a personal voice, are the apex of Berryman's achievement according to Linebarger, while *Homage to Mistress Bradstreet* is the "dead end of purely Academic verse for Berryman." Unfortunately, Berryman's publishers severely restricted Linebarger's use of the poems. He was forced, therefore, to rely on paraphrase and so his work suffers from overgeneralizations.

Other Sources

The Harvard Advocate, 103 (Spring, 1969). A special issue devoted to Berryman, including an interview, stories about Berryman, and criticism.

Linebarger, J. M. "A Commentary on Berryman's Sonnets," *John Berryman Studies* (January, 1975), pp. 13–24. Linebarger identifies literary, biographical, and historical allusions in *Berryman's Sonnets*—an invaluable aid.

Selected Dictionaries and Encyclopedias

Critical Survey of Poetry, Salem Press, 1982. Biographical summary, and an analysis of Berryman's poetry.

Great Writers of the English Language: Poets, St. Martin's Press, 1979. Brief critical review of Berryman's poetry.

Dennis Baeyen
Iowa State University

AMBROSE BIERCE
1842–1914?

Author's Chronology

Born June 24, 1842, in Meigs County, Ohio, of a farmer and a mother with aristocratic ancestry; *1861–1865* serves in Union Army; *1866* joins military expedition to West Coast; *1868* becomes editor of San Francisco *News-Letter; 1871* publishes first story in *Overland Monthly,* marries Mollie Day; *1872* leaves with Mollie for London and writes for *Fun* and *Figaro; 1875* returns to San Francisco and takes job in U.S. Mint; *1877* becomes associate editor of *Argonaut* and begins "Prattle" column; *1880* becomes agent for Black Hills Mining Company in Dakota Territory; *1881* returns to San Francisco and becomes editor of *Wasp; 1887* begins writing for William Randolph Hearst's *San Francisco Examiner; 1892* publishes *Tales of Soldiers and Civilians, Black Beetles in Amber; 1900* moves to Washington where he lives until his disappearance; *1908–1912* prepares *Collected Works; 1914* probably killed in a battle in Mexico in early January.

Author's Bibliography (selected)

The Fiend's Delight, 1873 (sketches); *Nuggets and Dust,* 1873 (sketches); *Cobwebs from an Empty Skull,* 1874 (sketches); *Tales of Soldiers and Civilians,* 1892, published in London as *In the Midst of Life,* 1892; *Black Beetles in Amber,* 1892 (verse); *Can Such Things Be?,* 1893 (stories); *Fantastic Fables,* 1899 (stories); (Shapes of Clay), 1903 (verse); *The Shadow on the Dial and Other Essays,* 1909; *The Collected works of Ambrose Bierce,* 1909–1912; *The Enlarged Devil's Dictionary of Ambrose Bierce,* 1967.

Overview of Biographical Sources

Four biographies of Ambrose Bierce appeared in 1929. Adolphe de Castro's *Portrait of Ambrose Bierce* and Walter Neale's *Life of Ambrose Bierce* are memoirs by men who knew Bierce—de Castro while Bierce was in San Francisco and Neale after he moved to Washington. Filled with admiring praise, they are often undependable. Grattan Hartley's *Bitter Bierce: A Mystery of American Letters* is sketchy, impressionistic, and poorly organized. However, Carey McWilliams's study, *Ambrose Bierce: A Biography,* is balanced, thoroughly researched, detailed and dependable. Of the modern biographers of Bierce, the most reliable, because the most thorough and the one most willing to go to original sources, is Paul Fatout. His *Ambrose Bierce: The Devil's Lexicographer* (1951) and *Ambrose Bierce and the Black Hills* (1956) are examples of careful scholarly research and well-supported hypotheses about Bierce's life and thought.

Evaluation of Selected Biographies

de Castro, Aldolphe, *Portrait of Ambrose Bierce.* New York: The Century Co., 1929. Written by Aldolphe Danziger, a German dentist who became a protégé of Bierce, this memoir contains many interesting anecdotes about Bierce's life in San Francisco and many recreated conversations which purport to reveal Bierce's thought; however it is less a biography than an extended eulogy by a man who was obviously flattered to be befriended by Bierce.

Fatout, Paul, *Ambrose Bierce and the Black Hills.* Norman: University of Oklahoma Press, 1956. The only detailed account of Bierce's experience as General Agent of the Black Hills Placer Mining Company, this study reveals a little-known aspect of Bierce's life. Fatout paints a well-documented picture of Bierce as a competent and honorable man in the midst of an inept muddle.

———, *Ambrose Bierce, The Devil's Lexicographer.* Norman: University of Oklahoma Press, 1951. This chronological account of Bierce's life based on original sources is the best recent biography. Fatout argues that Bierce's cynicism originates with his early childhood in a large Calvinistic family and that his social thinking was conditioned by his being torn between distaste for man's imperfect behavior and an equal distaste for attempts to improve it.

Grattan, C. Hartley, *Bitter Bierce: A Mystery of American Letters.* New York: Doubleday, Doran & Co., 1929. This book is divided into three parts: a biographical section, which is sketchy and disorganized; a section on Bierce's literary production, which is little more than plot summary and quotations; and a discussion of Bierce's ideas, which summarizes his attitudes toward economics, politics, religion, and "life in general."

McWilliams, Carey, *Ambrose Bierce: A Biography.* New York: Albert and Charles Boni, 1929; rpt. Hamden, CT: Archon Books, 1967, with a new introduction by the author. This is the best, most complete, and most dependable of the early biographies. Although an avid Bierce buff, McWilliams does a thorough job of researching Bierce's life from original sources and interviewing those who knew him, including Bierce's daughter. This is still the most detailed study of Bierce, particularly helpful on his literary and journalistic life in San Francisco.

Neale, Walter, *Life of Ambrose Bierce.* New York: Walter Neale, 1929. Neale was the publisher of Bierce's Collected Works and his friend in his later life. His book depends largely on recreated dialogues with Bierce, although one wonders how such extended conversations could be remembered so precisely. Because of his personal acquaintance with Bierce from 1901 until Bierce's death, Neale's memoir is the best account of the author's life after he left San Francisco.

Autobiographical Sources

The best source of autobiographical material is Volume I of the Collected Works (New York: Walter Neale, 1909–1912), which contains "Bits of Autobiography," mostly about Bierce's Civil War experiences. The only extensive collection of letters is *The Letters of Ambrose Bierce,* ed. Bertha Clark Pope. (San Francisco Book Club of California, 1922; rpt. 1967, The Gordian Press). The letters are in chronological order from 1892 to Bierce's last letter before he entered into Mexico. Most are to his protégé George Sterling. Volume X of The Collected Works contains many of Bierce's essays on literary matters. Bierce was a fierce opponent of the realistic school of William Dean Howells. His most powerful indictment of the realistic novel and his most eloquent defense of the romantic short story can be found here in his essays, "The Novel," "The Short Story," and "On Literary Criticism."

Overview of Critical Sources

Partially because the short story as a form has always been underrated by American critics, Ambrose Bierce has not, at least until recently, been subject to serious critical analysis of his work, in spite of the fact that his best-known story, "Occurrence at Owl Creek Bridge," is one of the most frequently anthologized stories in American literature. Early critics primarily dismissed him as a second-rate follower of Poe and a mechanical writer who manipulated fictional puppets for horrific effect. However, in the past twenty-five years, at least three book-length studies of Bierce's fiction have appeared, which may suggest that both the short story and Bierce's particular brand of grotesque and romantic fiction are at last being understood and appreciated.

Evaluation of Selected Criticism

Davidson, Cathy N. *The Experimental Fictions of Ambrose Bierce.* Lincoln: University of Nebraska Press, 1984. This study of Bierce makes use of the semiotic theory of Charles Sanders Pierce as well as contemporary reader-response theories to present Bierce as an impressionistic, surrealistic, postmodernist writer in the manner of Jorge Luis Borges and Julio Cortazar. Davidson's basic thesis is that Bierce structures his stories on characters who misperceive events or who misuse language. The book contains stimulating readings of several major Bierce stories, which Davidson presents as mimetic not of the external world, but rather of consciousness itself.

Grenander, M. E. *Ambrose Bierce.* New York: Twayne, 1971. The first half of this book is a condensed biographical sketch which makes use of primary sources such as previously unpublished letters. The four central chapters analyze a limited number of Bierce stories in terms of rhetorical categories. The approach is that of the so-called Neo-Aristotelian school of criticism of R. S.

Crane. Thus the focus is on types of plots that create certain kinds of emotional effects on the reader.

Woodruff, Stuart C. *The Short Stories of Ambrose Bierce: A Study in Polarity.* University of Pittsburgh Press, 1964. This is a valuable study in its effort to show that Bierce's stories need not be judged by realistic standards. Bierce's war stories are superior to his supernatural tales, says Woodruff, because in them the actions often serve as metaphors for psychological collapse. His war stories are fables of the essential movement of life toward disillusionment and disintegration.

Other Sources

O'Connor, Richard, *Ambrose Bierce: A Biography.* Boston: Little, Brown, 1967. A readable and detailed popular biography which mostly makes use of previous studies.

Wiggins, Robert A. *Ambrose Bierce.* Minneapolis: University of Minnesota, 1964. A pamphlet which summarizes Bierce's life and offers some helpful suggestions about Bierce's contribution to the tradition of the grotesque in American literature.

Selected Dictionaries and Encyclopedias

Concise Dictionary of American Literature, Philosophical Library, 1955. A short biographical sketch with brief criticism.

Critical Survey of Short Fiction, Salem Press, 1981. Brief discussion of Bierce's life and an analysis of his major stories.

Oxford Companion to American Literature, 4th ed. Oxford University Press, 1965. Brief summary of Bierce's work.

Charles E. May
California State University, Long Beach

EARLE BIRNEY
1904

Author's Chronology

Born Alfred Earle Birney May 13 in Calgary, in the Northwest Territories; lives early years on a farm near Lacombe; *1911* family moved to Banff, Alberta; *1916* family uprooted at the end of the Great War; settles on a fruit-farm near Creston, B.C.; works numerous menial jobs before entering University of British Columbia in 1922 to study chemistry; *1924* interests change to English; *1926* graduates with honours; continues education at University of Toronto; *1927* M.A.; attends graduate school at University of California; *1930* accepts lectureship at University of Utah; *1932* returns to Canada to begin his doctorial studies; becomes sympathetic to Leon Trotsky's views; *1936* marries Lydia Johnstone; marriage annulled the same year; *1935* receives fellowship to England; works for the British Independent Labour Party; *1938* receives Ph.D.; accepts teaching post at University of Toronto; begins to write seriously; *1942* publishes first book *David*; during World War II serves as a personnel selections officer; *1945* publishes second book, *Now is the Time; 1945–1947* editor of *The Canadian Poetry Magazine; 1948* accepts teaching post at the University of British Columbia; establishes the first creative writing department in Canada; *1974* moves to Toronto where he lives.

Author's Bibliography (selected)

David, 1942 (poems); *Strait of Anian,* 1948 (poems); *Turvey,* 1949 (novel); *Trail of a City,* 1952 (verse-play); *Down the Long Table,* 1955 (novel); *Ice cod bell and stone,* 1962 (poems); *November Walk Near False Creek Mouth,* 1964 (poems); *Selected Poems,* 1966; *The Creative Writer,* 1966 (criticism); *Pnomes, jukollages & other stunzas,* 1969 (concrete poems); *The poems of Earle Birney,* 1969; *Rag and Bone Shop,* 1971 (poems); *The Cow Jumped Over the Moon: the Writing and Reading of Poetry,* 1972 (criticism); *What's so big about green,* 1973 (poetry); *Collected Poems,* 1975; *The Rugged and the Moving Times* 1976, (poetry); *Alphbeings and other Seaysons,* 1976, (poetry); *Ghost in the Wheels: Selected Poems,* 1977; *Fall by Fury,* 1978 (poetry); *Big Bird in the Bush,* 1978 (poetry); *Spreading Time: Remarks on Canadian Writers, Book I, 1904–1949,* 1980 (criticism).

Overview of Biographical Sources

No extensive biography of Birney exists; only short commentaries on his public life are available to the reader. Part of the reason for this tremendous gap in Birney studies is due to the controversial nature of the man and his work. While he is living and writing, it would be extremely difficult to be objective about his eclectic use of poetic techniques, his politics, his influence, and his overall reputation. To many, although Birney is an undisputed leader in Canadian poetry, he seems a totally unpredictable figure and an extremely disturbing force in Canadian letters.

Evaluation of Selected Biographies

Aichinger, Peter, "Life and Times," in *Earle Birney.* Boston: Twayne, 1979, pp. 13–53. So far, this is the best and the most accurate account of Birney, his period, his influences and his achievements. Aichinger presents a bio-critical introduction to Birney's life and works. He offers a generally sound view of the man, his poetry, his fiction and his criticism. This book is the best introduction to Birney, particularly for the reader desiring the most complete and extended account of Birney available at this time in book form. One feature which makes this work particularly desirable is Aichinger's tracing of Birney's shift in social and political outlook, for knowledge of this aspect of Birney is often necessary to account for this writer's seemingly unexpected shifts in his themes, styles and poetic forms.

Davey, Frank, "The Career," in *Earle Birney.* Toronto: Copp Clark, 1971, pp. 1–27. An excellent short account of the main facts and accomplishments of Birney.

Robillard, Richard, "Introduction," in *Earle Birney.* Toronto: McClelland and Stewart, 1971, pp. 1–4. A brief yet remarkably concise account of Birney's life. The crucial aspect of this short biographical sketch is that it concentrates on the autobiographical elements of Birney's poems and novels.

Autobiographical Sources

Birney often attempted to use his life experience in his fiction and prose. Two of the most important works in this respect are *Turvey* and *Down the Long Table. Turvey* is a comic war novel based on his experiences in WW II. The book often reveals the folly of the Canadian involvement in the war. His second novel, *Down the Long Table* depicts the Trotskyist scene in which Birney participated in the 1930's. (Birney later rejected his political views of this time.) The semi-autobiographical works—*The Creative Writer* (Toronto, CBC publication, 1966); *The Cow Jumped Over the Moon: the Writing and Reading of Poetry* (Toronto: Holt, Rinehart and Winston, 1972); and *Spreading Time: Remarks on Canadian Writing and Reading, Book I, 1904–1949* (Montreal: Vehicule Press, 1980)—reveal how Birney uses events he participated in, actions he committed, and attitudes he developed in his own writing. These books, in particular, suggest that it would not be wrong to consider Birney, in part at least, an autobiographical poet who, like Robert Lowell, mythologizes his own life for aesthetic purposes.

Overview of Critical Sources

No single book offers a detailed and satisfactory account of Birney's art. Every time a critical study is published, it seems, Birney has changed technique, direction and emphasis. In the main, however, portions of his work have been critically assessed under four main headings: traditional narrative and lyric; symbolic and mythical archetypes; experimentalism (sound and concrete poetry); and travel poetry. The latter, in particular, deserves emphasis here. Birney is excellent at catching the shades and nuances of a culture in his travel poems. Birney's persistent shifts in forms, techniques and themes make it exceedingly difficult to come to terms with him as an artist.

Evaluation of Selected Criticism

Aichinger, Peter, *Earle Birney.* Boston: Twayne, 1979. This work emphasizes the thematic concerns of Earle Birney. Its strengths reside mainly in the work done on satiric and the political poetry, although the chapter on poetic technique deserves close attention. The weakness of the book resides in the critic's deliberate refusal to consider, even in passing, the numerous textual alterations evident in the various editions of Birney's poems.

Davey, Frank, *Earle Birney.* Toronto: Copp Clark, 1971. In this first full-length study of the novels, the lyrics and the major poems, Davey primarily explores textual details and ties them to the larger themes and concerns evident in Birney's writings. Davey's main contribution to Birney studies is his sensitive readings of many of the poems.

Nesbitt, Bruce, ed. *Earle Birney.* Toronto: McGraw-Hill Ryerson, 1974. Nesbitt has collected numerous essays and reviews dealing with various books by Birney. No single theme unifies these various selections, but on the whole it gives excellent representation to the variety of critical responses Birney has evoked in Canadian critical circles.

Robillard, Richard, *Earle Birney.* Toronto: McClelland and Stewart, 1971. Robillard's central concern is to illuminate the major trends in Birney's writing. He prefers to put material under key categories such as Nature, Love, War, Canadian Identity or World Travel. This critical approach is especially helpful for thematic studies.

Selected Dictionaries and Encyclopedias

Critical Survey of Poetry, Salem Press, 1983. Brief Biography, and short analysis of Birney's importance to Canadian poetry.

The Oxford Companion to Canadian Literature, Oxford University Press, 1983. Concise overview of Birney's life, and a discussion of the principle works.

Ed Jewinski
Wilfrid Laurier University

ELIZABETH BISHOP
1911–1979

Author's Chronology

Born February 8, 1911, Worcester, Massachusetts of Canadian-American parents; father dies when she is eight months old; *1916* mother, after several breakdowns, becomes permanently insane and daughter never sees her again; is raised by maternal grandparents in Nova Scotia and aunt in Boston; *1927* after being kept from school by various illnesses, enters Walnut Hill School; *1930* enters Vassar; *1934* meets Marianne Moore who becomes a life-long friend; mother dies; graduates from Vassar; *1935* first poems published in *Trial Balances* with introduction by Moore; *1935–1938* lives in New York and travels to France, England, North Africa, Spain and Italy using an inheritance; *1939* moves to Key West; *1946* receives Houghton Mifflin Poetry Award for first book, *North & South;* friendship with Robert Lowell; *1947* Guggenheim Fellowship; *1949–1950* Consultant in Poetry at the Library of Congress; *1951* settles in Brazil with Lota de Macedo Soares; *1955* second book, *Poems,* receives Pulitzer Prize; *1968* Lota de Macedo Soares dies; *1969 The Complete Poems* receives the National Book Award; *1970–1973* alternates fall terms at Harvard with seasons in Ouro Preto, Brazil; *1974* moves permanently to Boston waterfront with Alice Methfessel; begins teaching both terms at Harvard; *1976* wins *Books Abroad*/Neustadt International Prize; *1979* dies of a stroke at her Boston home.

Author's Bibliography (selected)

North & South, 1946 (poems); *Poems: North & South/A Cold Spring,* 1955; *The Diary of 'Helena Morley,'* 1957 (translation); *Brazil,* 1962 (travel); *Questions of Travel,* 1965 (poems); *The Complete Poems,* 1969; *Geography III,* 1976 (poems); *The Complete Poems 1927–1979,* 1983; *The Collected Prose,* 1984.

Overview of Biographical Sources

A reticent person who closely guarded her private life and who lived mostly abroad, Bishop has presented a difficult target for the biographer. As yet, there is no major biography. Anne Stevenson's primarily critical book, *Elizabeth Bishop* (Boston: Twayne, 1966), does contain biographical information, especially about Bishop's early life. It also benefits from Stevenson's extensive correspondence with the poet. Another sketch of her childhood may be found in the introduction to *Collected Prose* by her publisher, Robert Giroux. But if the basic facts of her childhood are available, and the influence of that painful period on the inwardness of her work is fairly well understood, the facts of her later life have been presented only in skeletal form. Some significant details may be gleaned from Ian Hamilton's *Robert Lowell: A Biography* (New York:

Random House, 1982), such as Bishop's literary influence on Lowell and her homosexuality. A definitive biography and the publication of her letters to such writers as Marianne Moore, Robert Lowell, Randall Jarrell and James Merrill are badly needed.

Autobiographical Sources

The autobiographical sources are richer than the biographical. Bishop wrote a series of brief memoirs (and short stories that are hard to tell from memoirs) which vividly recall her childhood in Nova Scotia. They are brought together in *Collected Prose.* Most important are the poetic "In the Village" which recreates the moment of her mother's final breakdown into madness and the breathtakingly matter-of-fact "The Country Mouse" (published after her death) which describes the poet's "kidnapping" away from her poor Nova Scotia (maternal) grandparents by her rich Boston (paternal) grandparents and her subsequent illness and near death. Separating fact from fiction cannot be certain in any of these memoir/stories, but they are the best sources for her pivotal early experiences. The whole of *Collected Prose* presents experience in crystal clear detail, but beyond the childhood stories there is little personal revelation. The poems of her childhood found in *Questions of Travel* and *Geography III* are also richly atmospheric, even magical.

Her literary opinions can be gleaned from a selection of letters published by Anne Stevenson, "Letters from Elizabeth Bishop," *Times Literary Supplement,* 7 March 1980, 261-262 and from interviews with Ashley Brown, *Shenandoah* 17 (1966), 3-19; George Starbuck, *Ploughshares,* 3 (1977), 11-29; Alexandra Johnson, *Christian Science Monitor* (23 March 1978), 20-21; and Elizabeth Spires, *Paris Review,* #80 (Summer 1981), 56-83. They reveal a precise, witty, proud, self-deprecating person whose firm commitment to clarity, freshness and restraint in artistic matters made her a shrewd critic of herself and others. Since she never published her critical theory, these interviews are the best source on that available.

Overview of Critical Sources

Bishop studies are still in a nearly fledgling state. Bishop's poetic career was slow in taking form, her most decisive work came latest, and it has yet to be thoroughly evaluated. Much of the early criticism on Bishop is in the form of reviews, often by fellow poets. Since her death in 1979, she has begun to attract more scholarly kinds of investigation. She has been appreciated as a brilliant and precise observer, but until recently, she was often billed simply as an objective recorder of surface detail. Now the curious inwardness and subtle subjectivity of her work is achieving greater recognition. Current criticism is attempting to define the underlying (and often unstated) themes that animate her elusive poems and give them importance. Her literary influence, more extensive than is yet understood, has yet to be adequately discussed.

Evaluation of Selected Criticism

Kalstone, David, *Five Temperaments: Elizabeth Bishop, Robert Lowell, James Merrill, Adrienne Rich, John Ashbery.* New York: Oxford University Press, 1977. Sensitive to Bishop's imagination and temperament, Kalstone shows a keen appreciation of Bishop's subtle subjectivity.

Stevenson, Anne, *Elizabeth Bishop.* Boston: Twayne, 1966. Still a good place to start, Stevenson's analysis is limited by having been written before much of Bishop's most decisive work had appeared. It asserts, wrongly, that Bishop's career shows no organic unity and attempts to establish a tenuous connection with the epistemology of Wittgenstein. But it contains information obtainable nowhere else.

Other Sources

Bloom, Harold, "Geography III by Elizabeth Bishop," *New Republic* (5 February 1977), 29–30. Places Bishop in the Romantic tradition.

Jarrell, Randall, *Poetry and the Age.* New York: Noonday, 1953. Contains an evaluation of Bishop's first book that shows shrewd understanding of her basic stoicism.

Schwartz, Lloyd and Sybil P. Estess, *Elizabeth Bishop and Her Art.* Foreward by Harold Bloom. Ann Arbor: University of Michigan Press, 1983. A rewarding potpourri. Contains analytical essays and reprints of reviews. Also includes excerpts from Bishop's rare and scattered essays and reviews.

Spiegelman, Willard, "Landscapes and Knowledge; The Poetry of Elizabeth Bishop," *Modern Poetry Studies,* 6 (Winter 1975), 203–224. Compares Bishop's landscape poetry to that of Wordsworth and Coleridge.

World Literature Today, Elizabeth Bishop Issue #51 (1977). Published in honor of her winning the Books Abroad/Neustadt International Prize. Contains essays by Ashbery, Octavio Paz, Frank Bidart, Howard Moss and others, as well as a detailed chronology and photographs.

Wyllie, Diana E. *Elizabeth Bishop and Howard Nemerov: A Reference Guide.* Boston: G. K. Hall, 1983. Provides a year-by-year, annotated listing of writings by and about Bishop.

Selected Dictionaries and Encyclopedias

Contemporary Poets, St. Martin's Press, 1970. A brief biographical sketch and critical assessment.

Thomas J. Travisano
Hartwick College

WILLIAM BLAKE
1757-1827

Author's Chronology

Born November 28, 1757, London, England, the third son of a moderately prosperous owner of a hosiery shop; *1767* enters a drawing school; *1772-1779* apprenticed to James Basire, engraver; *1779* becomes student at the Royal Academy and supports himself engraving on commission for novels and magazines; *1782* marries Catherine Boucher, daughter of a market-gardner; *1784-1785* unsuccessfully tries to run a printshop; *1785-1800* makes a modest living designing and engraving for other publishers; *1788* begins to print and decorate his own poetry; *1800* moves to Felpham, a village on the Sussex coast, at the invitation of the poet and biographer William Hayley; *1803* returns to London; *1804* acquitted of charges of assault and sedition stemming from a squabble with a drunken soldier at Felpham; *1809* holds an exhibition of sixteen of his own paintings; *1810-1817* lives in almost complete obscurity; *1818* begins to attract the attention of a group of younger painters; August 12, 1827 dies from the effects of gallstones.

Author's Bibliography (selected)

Songs of Innocence, 1789 (poems); *The Book of Thel,* 1789 (allegorical poem); *The Marriage of Heaven and Hell,* ca. 1790 (prose satires and aphorisms); *The French Revolution,* 1791 (incomplete historical poem); *Visions of the Daughters of Albion,* 1793 (the first in a series of increasingly complex mythical poems, as are most of his books after 1793); *America: A Prophecy,* 1793 (poem); *Songs of Experience,* 1794 (lyrical poems); *Europe: A Prophecy,* 1794 (poem); *The Book of Urizen,* 1794 (poem); *The Song of Los,* 1795 (poem); *The Book of Ahania,* 1795 (poem); *The Book of Los,* 1795 (poem); *The Four Zoas,* 1797-1807 (poem); *Milton: A Poem,* 1804-1808; *Jerusalem: The Emanation of the Giant Albion,* 1804-1820 (poem).

Overview of Biographical Sources

At the time of his death, Blake was generally judged a minor painter and engraver in whom a near-hallucinatory imagination had ruined the gifts of a talented craftsman. It was not until almost thirty years later that a young art critic, Alexander Gilchrist, chanced upon Blake's *Illustrations of the Book of Job* and decided to undertake a full-scale biography of the nearly forgotten artist. Laboring for over six years, the conscientious Gilchrist proceeded to write his *Life of William Blake, "Pictor Ignotus"* (London: Macmillan, 1863), a biography that was to remain unsurpassed for the next sixty years. Only when Geoffrey Keynes' critical edition of *The Writings of William Blake* (London: Nonesuch Press, 1925) made additional information accessible did biographical research move forward with the publication of Mona Wilson's *The Life of*

William Blake (London: Nonesuch Press, 1927). The outburst of interest in Blake during the last forty years has also generated several biographical studies. These works have set new accents, especially by paying closer attention to the political context of Blake's life and work, but have not been able to extend significantly the existing biographical data.

Evaluation of Selected Biographies

Gilchrist, Alexander, *Life of William Blake, with Selections from His Poems and Other Writings.* 2 Volumes. Reprint of the second, enlarged edition of 1880. New York: Phaeton Press, 1969. The first full-length biography of Blake, Gilchrist's work will always occupy a unique position, not only because it still bears the vivid stamp of the firsthand accounts that went into it, but also because from it sprang all serious interest in Blake. Nevertheless, after one hundred and twenty years, this venerable achievement must be read with considerable caution. Relying heavily on reminiscences supplied by the once young admirers of Blake's old age, Gilchrist draws the picture of a cheerful and child-like Blake who was completely oblivious of reality because he lived exclusively for and in the realm of the imagination. Gilchrist seriously underestimates the aspects of Blake's life which show him engaged in the politics of his time and trade. The selections from Blake's writings contain nothing of his prophetic books, and are only of historical interest.

Lindsay, Jack, *William Blake: His Life and Work.* New York: George Braziller, 1979. Lindsay views Blake as a total revolutionary who used a religious idiom only because it was the one language at that time not preempted by bourgeois expectations. Blake is credited with having achieved a symbolic version of an historical dialectic which ultimately foreshadows the thoughts of the early Marx. While Lindsay's forceful stance makes this a captivating book, the single-mindedness of its argument at times overwhelms the biographical purpose.

Wilson, Mona, *The Life of William Blake.* Edited and expanded by Geoffrey Keynes. New York: Oxford University Press, 1971. First published in 1927, since updated by scholarly notes, this work has not yet been superseded as the standard biography of Blake. Wilson chronicles Blake's life primarily through a meticulous account of Blake's contacts with friends, colleagues, and patrons. A certain defensiveness about the poet's excessive imagination gives evidence of the fact that the conception of this book belongs to a time when Blake scholars still felt the need to be apologetic about their subject.

Autobiographical Sources

Blake has drawn an amusing caricature of himself as a young man in the fragmentary prose satire, *An Island in the Moon* (c. 1784–1787). Employing the style of coarse burlesque, a self-confident and even rambunctious Blake pokes fun at the highbrow pretentions of a philistine culture as much as at the arrogant ambition and boastful disrespect displayed by him and his circle of boisterous friends. Blake never again spoke of himself with such levity. Where he incorporated episodes of his private life into the myths of his later works, the events tend to assume prophetic magnitude. Blake's quarrel with the officious Hayley is recounted in the opening section of *Milton: A Poem,* while Private Scofield, the false accuser at Blake's trial of 1804, repeatedly appears among the satanic forces in *Jerusalem: The Emanation of the Giant Albion.*

The Letters of William Blake, ed. Geoffrey Keynes (2nd Edition. Cambridge: Harvard University Press, 1970), shows Blake effusive in his gratitude to every sign of sincere encouragement but bristling with indignation at the slightest attempt to patronize him. His unorthodox creed as a painter and his notoriously impolitic forthrightness are expressed in exemplary fashion by *A Descriptive Catalogue* (1809), a prospectus written by Blake to advertise an exhibition of his paintings.

Overview of Critical Sources

The last forty years have seen a veritable apotheosis of virtually all aspects of Blake's work. In the process, Blake scholarship has assumed the proportions of a minor industry. Joseph P. Natoli's *Twentieth-Century Blake Criticism* (New York: Garland, 1982), a comprehensive bibliography of Blake scholarship since 1947, contains almost fourteen hundred references to works which over the years have analyzed Blake as, among others, a Freudian, a Jungian, a Neoplatonist, a Christian, a Marxist, a God-is-dead theologian, and an advocate of the sexual revolution.

Three scholarly approaches have, nevertheless, emerged as preeminent. Two of them can be traced to the very beginning of this bewildering maze. Mark Schorer in his *William Blake: The Politics of Vision* (New York: Holt, 1946) was one of the first to relate Blake's work closely to the political atmosphere of his time, considering the poet's symbolism the unavoidable disguise revolutionary ideas had to take under the impact of a repressive milieu. Northrop Frye's *Fearful Symmetry: A Study of William Blake* (1947), on the other hand, became the paradigm for those who focused on what Schorer regarded as mere paraphernalia, exploring instead Blake's symbols as elements of a sophisticated mythology within a vast literary and occult tradition. In addition, the last twenty years have seen a steady increase of research into the unique relationship between poetic text and pictorial context that exists for almost all of Blake's works. Study of this crucial interrelationship has been greatly facilitated by the meticulously prepared and very affordable edition of *The Illuminated Blake,* annotated by David V. Erdman (Garden City, NY: Anchor Books, 1974), which finally allows readers to view all of Blake's poems in their original form.

Evaluation of Selected Criticism

Bloom, Harold, *Blake's Apocalypse: A Study in Poetic Argument.* Garden City, NY: Doubleday, 1963; rpt. Ithaca, NY: Cornell University Press, 1970.

Considering Blake's poems, especially his epics, "the best poetry in English since Milton," Bloom wants to serve as an informed and sensitive guide to the poetic beauty of Blake's works. Often assuming the character of a running commentary, this is a most helpful introduction, particularly to those who for the first time take the often perturbing step from reading criticism on Blake to facing his poetry.

Erdman, David V. *Blake: Prophet Against Empire.* Revised Edition. Garden City, NY: Anchor Books, 1969. Of all the books that have attempted to place Blake's art within the social and political context of Blake's time, Erdman's is by far the most thorough and original. This prodigiously researched volume is generally convincing where it traces the symbolic transformation of contemporary events in Blake's poetry up to 1795. The same historical criticism, however, proves more conjectural for the later works and has not withstood the test of further evidence nearly as well. Erdman's study, immensely informative as it is, remains ultimately too narrow in its approach to allow a balanced assessment of Blake's poetic achievements.

Frye, Northrop, *Fearful Symmetry: A Study of William Blake.* Princeton: Princeton University Press, 1947; rpt. 1969. Frye's extended critical essay is still considered the single most important work on Blake. In his effort to unravel Blake's mythic symbolism, Frye finds that Blake's symbolic language exists within a tradition of archetypal motifs which has informed the great poetry of all ages. Frye's wide-ranging and demanding analysis begins with a discussion of Blake's argument against contemporary theories of knowledge, outlines Blake's religious, ethical, political, and aesthetic convictions, explores his basic myth and its refinements, and concludes with a spirited appeal for an allegorical reading of poetry. Frye succeeds, as probably no other interpreter has, in opening the reader's eyes to the kind of imaginative effort essential for an appropriate understanding of Blake's visionary universe.

Mitchell, W. J. T. *Blake's Composite Art: A Study of the Illuminated Poetry.* Princeton: Princeton University Press, 1978. In his research into the relationship between verbal and visual elements in Blake's illuminated books, Mitchell finds that Blake designed his illustrations as second, independent texts, rather than following the practice of his day by treating them as mere visual translations of the poetic word. Mitchell's intricate formalistic analysis is now widely considered to provide the most authoritative access to Blake's composite art.

Other Sources

Damon, S. Foster, *A Blake Dictionary.* Providence, RI: Brown University Press, 1965; rpt. New York: E. P. Dutton, 1971; rpt. Boulder, CO: Shambhala Press, 1979. Not always reliable and hardly complete, this dictionary still constitutes a helpful reference guide to a vast number of Blake's historical and mythological allusions.

Gleckner, Robert, *The Piper and the Bard.* Detroit: Wayne State University Press, 1959. A reading of Blake's earlier poems as developing key elements of the later prophecies.

Grant, John E. ed. *Discussions of William Blake.* Boston: D.C. Heath, 1961. Twelve essays from the 1950's, including seminal statements by Frye and Erdman on their differing approaches to Blake.

Nurmi, Martin K. *William Blake,* Kent, OH: Kent State University, 1976. Designed "to make Blake's poetry more easily accessible" and meeting this formidable challenge creditably.

Paley, Morton D. *Energy and the Imagination.* Oxford: Clarendon Press, 1970. Stresses development and change in Blake's thought.

Selected Dictionaries and Encyclopedias

Critical Survey of Poetry, Salem Press, 1982. Brief biography and short analysis of Blake's major poetry.

Encyclopaedia Britannica, 1984. Succinct introduction to Blake's life, his intellectual temperament, and his career as poet and artist.

Joachim Scholz
Washington College

LOUISE BOGAN
1897–1970

Author's Chronology

Born August 11, 1897, Livermore Falls, Maine of Irish-American parents; childhood in New Hampshire and Massachusetts; *1910* attends Girls Latin School, Boston; *1915* Boston University; *1916* marries Curt Alexander, soldier; lives in New York and Panama Canal Zone; *1917* birth of only child, Mathilde; *1919* separates from husband, who dies in 1920; *1921* first poems published in *Poetry* magazine; *1925* marries Raymond Holden, lives in Boston and Sante Fe, New Mexico; *1927* publishes first criticism; *1930* wins John Reed Memorial Prize in *Poetry* magazine; *1931* suffers nervous breakdown and is hospitalized; *1933* wins Guggenheim Fellowship, travels to Italy, France, Austria, Switzerland and suffers second breakdown; *1934* separates from Raymond Holden; *1937* wins Helen Haire Levinson Memorial Prize, *Poetry,* and a second Guggenheim Fellowship; *1944* Library of Congress Fellowship in American Letters; *1948* wins Harriet Monroe Poetry Award; *1952* elected National Institute of Arts and Letters; *1955* wins Bollingen Prize in Poetry; *1959* Academy of American Poets Fellowship; *1962* Brandeis University Creative Arts Award; *1967* National Endowment for Arts Award; *1968* elected American Academy of Arts and Letters; dies February 4, 1970, New York City.

Author's Bibliography

Body of This Death, 1923 (poems); *Dark Summer,* 1929 (poems); *The Sleeping Fury,* 1937 (poems); *Poems and New Poems,* 1941 (poems); *Achievement in American Poetry, 1900–1950,* 1951 (criticism); *Collected Poems 1923–1953,* 1954; *Selected Criticism: Poetry and Prose,* 1955; *The Golden Journey: Poems for Young People,* 1965 (anthology with William Jay Smith); *The Blue Estuaries: Poems 1923–1968; A Poet's Alphabet: Reflections on the Literary Art and Vocation,* 1970 (criticism); *What the Woman Lived,* 1973 (letters); *Journey Around My Room,* 1980 (autobiography); Translations—with Elizabeth Mayer, *The Glass Bees* by Ernst Juenger, 1960; *Elective Affinities* by Goethe, 1963; *The Sorrows of Young Werther* and *Novella* by Goethe, 1971; and with Elizabeth Roget, *The Journal of Jules Renard,* 1964.

Overview of Biographical Sources

For a woman of such distinguished literary accomplishment, relatively little scholarly attention has been paid Bogan. One biography has been completed and only several relatively short essays dealing with her life have been published. Part of the reason for this situation resulted from Bogan's own reluctance about self-revelation. In addition, her belief that knowledge of the private lives of artists was not necessary for public appreciation of art, a value she absorbed from the modern art doctrines prominent during her early career, influenced her own writing. Thus, she avoided political involvement and personal memoirs, and she studiously ignored most subjects other than literature. Like many other modern artists and writers, she confined her attention to the world of art and devoted her energies, when possible, to literature. In view of this, perhaps the best source of biographical information is simply the public record of her work, the books of poetry, criticism, and letters she left behind as testimony to her life in the twentieth century.

Two useful, though not definitive, bibliographies of her career are available. One, published by the Library of Congress, was accompanied by a fine essay about Bogan's life and poetry by a younger poet and friend, William Jay Smith, *Louise Bogan: A Woman's Words* (1970). A second traces Bogan's published writing alphabetically by subject and includes a chronology of major events in her life, Jane Couchman, *Louise Bogan: A Bibliography of Primary and Secondary Materials, 1915–1975,* (Bulletin of Bibliography, Vol. 3, 1976). Elizabeth Perlmutter's entry on Bogan in Harvard University's Belknap Press reference work, *Notable American Women: A Biographical Dictionary—The Modern Period* (1980), is a concise, informed essay providing a good overall summary of Bogan's life and career. Jean Gould has published a good biographical essay in *American Woman Poets,* (1980). Another short entry is Paul Christensen, "Louise Bogan" in *20th Century American Literature* (1980). There is biographical information contained in a number of book reviews, scattered over several decades, by both contemporary and younger writers who encountered Bogan and appreciated her quiet dedication and professionalism. The Couchman bibliography lists most of these to 1975, though they are not collected in an easily accessible single source.

Evaluation of Selected Biographies

Frank, Elizabeth, *Louise Bogan: A Portrait.* New York: Alfred A. Knopf, 1985. This book is the result of years of dedicated and sympathetic study and should be the definitive work on Bogan's life and the biographical sources of her art. By carefully utilizing the already published record of Bogan's work, and supplementing that data with interviews of friends, as well as providing astute psychological insight, Frank's book illuminates a career she sees as essentially tragic. Bogan's major work was accomplished in her early years Frank believes, even though Bogan had to overcome deep psychological problems resulting from family conflicts and economic hardship. Yet Bogan's own theory of poetic inspiration and her notion of the artist as an alien or exile from normal society akin to a criminal, ideas she absorbed from the French Symbolists, led to a later life increasingly marked by bitterness, resentment, and an inability to write poetry. Frank believes that Bogan was a woman of great achievement who nonetheless may have been her own worst enemy. Because Bogan's art remains difficult, and her entire personality and career reflect profound issues of American literary history, this book will remain the most important study of its subject for a long time.

Autobiographical Sources

Bogan was fortunate in her choice of literary executor, her friend Ruth Limmer. Though Bogan never intended for her private materials to be published, Limmer nonetheless put together a fine collection of Bogan's letters, mostly to her longtime friends of the New York publishing and literary community, with whom she felt most at ease. The volume of letters, titled *What the Woman Lived,* contains the most revealing documents available about Bogan's private values, reactions to experience, and friendships.

Limmer also arranged a number of published and unpublished Bogan writings for what she called an autobiographical "mosaic," *Journey Around My Room,* released ten years after Bogan's death. An autobiographical short story Bogan published in *The New Yorker* in 1933 served as the frame of, and title for, the mosaic. Limmer also edited the short, infrequent private journals Bogan kept at several crucial periods of her life, and published them in the January 30, 1978 *New Yorker.* This document forms a major part of *Journey Around My Room,* though in the book the journal is broken into sections and placed with other material. The editing causes the autobiography to seem, at points, disjointed and it thereby loses some of the full impact of Bogan's concentrated prose. *Journey Around My Room* is not, therefore, a complete, nor even wholly reliable, guide to Bogan's view of herself or life. Bogan's longtime friend and *New Yorker* colleague William Maxwell, writing in the November 29, 1980 *New Republic,* summarized this problem succinctly in a review which is also one of the finest tributes to Bogan's literary art, ". . . the simple truth is that you cannot rearrange any writer's work without in some way altering the effect, and if it is a writer of the first quality, is it yours to rearrange, morally speaking?" Nevertheless, *Journey Around My Room* is the only lengthy published document besides the *Letters* that reveals Bogan's personal perspective on her family and private history.

Overview of Critical Sources

No book length critical study of Bogan's poetry or criticism has yet been published. Except for reviews of her books through the years, Bogan received little critical attention until after her death. The rise of women's studies and the feminist political movement during the early 1970's sparked a renewed interest in her contribution to modern American literature. Early, though brief, discussions of Bogan included Babette Deutsch, *Poetry in Our Time* (1963), Allen Nevins, "American Civilization: 1922–1938," *Saturday Review of Literature,* XVIII (22 October 1938), and Theodore Roethke, "The Poetry of Louise Bogan," *Critical Quarterly,* III, No. 2 (Summer 1961).

Bogan's own major critical books reveal a great deal about her methods, aesthetics, and interpretation of modern cultural history. Her short book *Achievement in American Poetry: 1900–1950* is a remarkably lucid account of the complex social, stylistic, and political influences and history that motivated the rebellion (and renaissance) of American poets in the first half of the century. As poetry critic for the *New Yorker* for 38 years, she surveyed that history as closely as anyone. Her sympathy with the rebellion of modern American poets is clear in this book, and her own history parallels her subject to a remarkable degree.

Her volume of collected criticism, *A Poet's Alphabet,* is also filled with critical statements illuminating her poetics and philosophy, and again her sympathy with, and knowledge of, the long and complex history of Symbolist and modern art and literature. Her own formal, highly crafted, and lyric poetry was strongly influenced by her admiration for the English Elizabethan poets, who were prominent subjects of poetic scholarship in her early years and later promoted by T. S. Eliot, who also promoted another acknowledged influence on her, the French Symbolist poets of the late 19th century.

Other Sources

Kinzie, Mary, "Two Lives," *American Poetry Review,* X (Spring 1982), 20–21. Reviews *Journey Around My Room* and discusses it with respect to the *Notebooks* of Theodore Roethke, a friend and admirer of Bogan.

Moore, Patrick, "Symbol, Mask, and Meter in the Poetry of Louise Bogan," *Women and Literature,* Vol. I, 67–80. One of the few lengthy analytical treatments available of Bogan's poetry and poetic style.

Peterson, Douglas L. "The Poetry of Louise Bogan," *Southern Review,* 19 (Winter 1983), 73–87. An extensive treatment of the themes of stoicism, time, and death in Bogan's poetry, and one of the few serious treatments of her art.

Selected Dictionaries and Encyclopedias

Contemporary Authors, Gale Research, 1978. Contains full chronology and bibliography to 1977.

Critical Survey of Poetry, Salem Press, 1982. Contains good brief biography and analysis of the poetry.

James M. Kempf
Frostburg State College

JAMES BOSWELL
1740–1795

Author's Chronology

Born October 29, 1740 to an ancient and honorable Scottish family; his father, Alexander Boswell, a judge in the Court of Sessions at Edinburgh, against whom James rebelled all his life long; *1758*ff. studies civil law at university in Edinburgh, then Glasgow; writes verse and pamphlets while leading a gay life; after failing to get a commission in the Footguards, an honorable military appointment, spends time in London in indecision about a choice of career; *1763* (May 16) meets Samuel Johnson; to placate a critical father agrees to continue his study of law at Utrecht; travels through France, Italy, and Corsica, meeting famous men (Rousseau, Voltaire, and General Paoli); *1766* returns home shortly after his mother's death; admitted to practice law in Edinburgh, and begins to make a respectable living; *1767* writes *Account of Corsica,* published to widespread applause; spends the next years alternately practicing law, living unhappily in Scotland, and coming to London when court was not in session to enjoy himself in conversing, drinking, writing, and promiscuous sexual adventures; *1769* marries the sensible, patient Margaret Montgomerie on November 25; *1773* convinces Johnson to travel with him to Scotland and the Hebrides in fall, producing a journal of that tour (published in *1785*) having saved notes on conversations and encounters with Johnson since 1763; begins to assemble the materials for a *Life of Johnson,* which after much delay and help from Edmond Malone was printed in 1791 to great acclaim; health deteriorated slowly; dies on May 19, 1795.

Author's Bibliography (selected)

An Account of Corsica; the journal of a tour to that Island and memoirs of Pascal Paoli, 1768; modern edition ed. M. Bishop, London, 1951; *The Journal of a tour to the Hebrides with Samuel Johnson, LlD,* 1785; modern edition in Oxford Standard Authors Series; *The Life of Samuel Johnson, LlD,* 1791; modern edition in Oxford Standard Authors Series; *The Yale editions of the private papers of Boswell,* 11 volumes of journals printed as of 1981; *The Heart of Boswell,* 1981 (abridgement of journals).

Overview of Biographical Sources

As others' lives were fascinating to him, so Boswell's life has become fascinating to his posterity. Versions of his career have been appearing steadily for 200 years, but the definitive work is now done: F. A. Pottle's massive consideration of Boswell's youth, *James Boswell: the Early Years, 1740–1769* (1966), is complemented by Frank Brady's equally monumental companion text, *James Boswell: The Later Years, 1769–1795* (1984). These texts make the record of

Boswell's life available in full. Earlier biographers were not able to make full use of the astonishing mass of private papers that have become available in the twentieth century; even some written after the archives were uncovered at Malahide Castle and Fettercairn house do not pretend to do that material justice. Nonetheless, the most curious feature of twentieth-century biographies of Boswell is that they all refer to, and attempt to refute the essay by Macaulay in *The Edinburgh Review* in 1831, an interpretation of Boswell's life made without any reference to the store of recently discovered papers. Macaulay condemned Boswell as a foolish, unscrupulous, journey-man author who should not be credited for his accomplishments. To this day, the debate in the biographies continues, with Pottle and Brady on the defense.

Evaluation of Selected Biographies

Brady, Frank, *James Boswell: The Later Years, 1769–1795.* Brady, the author of another volume on Boswell's political career in this period, continues and incorporates much of Pottle's earlier work. He treats the events of Boswell's most productive period sympathetically, describing his vacillating career choices, his philandering and unpleasant treatment of his wife with restraint, and concentrates on the laborious and fitful process of producing *The Life of Samuel Johnson.* This biography is meticulously researched, with all the benefits of the industry at Yale University devoted to the task of ordering Boswell's papers, but it is rather too inclusive. The reader finds extensive consideration of minor court cases or entries from Boswell's journals that endlessly demonstrate his changeable temper.

Daiches, David, *James Boswell and his World.* New York: Charles Scribner's Sons, 1976. Daiches shares his subject's Scottish heritage and selects with unerring instinct the major developments of Boswell's life. This is a brief, easily read, fully illustrated biography that gives the student an alternative to the definitive editions of Pottle and Brady.

Lewis, Wyndham, *The Hooded Hawk.* New York: Longman's, 1947. Lewis produces a suggestive, imaginative recreation of scenes from Boswell's life, emphasizing the London *milieu* as a crucial determinant of Boswell's character. Whereas other biographies are full of quotations from Boswell's journal, Lewis prefers to depend on what *The Life of Samuel Johnson* tells the reader about its author, filling in the blanks with informed inference. This work is a pleasure to read, but will not be a sufficient basis for scholarly activity; it reveals a great deal about Lewis's attitudes towards the community of dons and the business of literature in mid-century Britain.

Pottle, Frederick A. *James Boswell: The Earlier Years, 1740–1769.* This biography shows Pottle's erudition and knowledge of the *minutiae* of Boswell's career in all its facets, taking into account those materials that are making their way into print in the Yale edition of the papers, and those which may never be included. Like his successor Brady, Pottle accepts Boswell's records of his own experience, values Boswell as a conscious artist in his style and organizing principles, and concludes that regardless of the irregularities in his personal life Boswell deserves respect. Pottle thoroughly details Boswell's relationship to his father, his career as a lawyer, and his mixed feelings about Scotland. This volume, like Brady's, is determined to include as much material and detail as possible, and therefore adopts the biographical principle that more is better, that to eliminate is to editorialize.

Autobiographical Sources

The journals currently being published in the Yale series, of which to date there are eleven, give all the information one could wish to have on Boswell's career from the early escapades in London to his careers as lawyer and laird. Boswell noted activities of all sorts: these journals reveal his daily activities, encounters with the famous men he sought so successfully, and nightly forays into the dark world of the London streets. They are an incomparable record of eighteenth-century life as well as a candid confession of his flawed character and various purposes in life. Of special use to a student beginning a consideration of this massive collection is *The Heart of Boswell: Highlights from the Journals of James Boswell* (New York: McGraw-Hill, 1981), selected by Mark Harris from the first six journals; this edition shows how brilliantly Boswell could evoke a scene in his notes.

Overview of Critical Sources

The scholarly community, devoted to interpreting his life, have spent proportionately less time with his literary output, with the exception, of course, of *The Life of Samuel Johnson.* Texts devoted to Johnson and his career frequently include mention of Boswell, and until recently it has been generally assumed that Boswell produced his famous life with no particular art; thus critical consideration was scattered. Now, as the following entries show, Boswell is getting more attention.

Evaluation of Selected Criticism

McAdam, E. L., Jr. *Johnson & Boswell: A Survey of their Writings.* Boston: Houghton Mifflin, 1969. The last section of this text is devoted to Boswell's life and work, and gives a summary of his literary accomplishments.

Schwartz, Richard B. *Boswell's Johnson: A Preface to the Life.* Madison: University of Wisconsin Press, 1978. Schwartz presents a brief, balanced argument detailing Boswell's artful intentions, without crediting him with every happy effect or every generous motive.

Siebenschuh, William, *Form and Purpose in Boswell's Biographical Works.* Berkeley: University of California Press, 1972. The three major texts of Boswell's literary career are discussed here and used to show a progression in his style, towards the mature art evident in *The Life of Samuel Johnson.*

Other Sources

Bronson, Bertrand, "Boswell's Boswell," in *Johnson Agonistes and Other Essays.* Berkeley: University of California Press, 1965. Bronson gives Boswell credit for critical self-scrutiny that made his scrutiny of others more accurate and insightful.

Buchanan, David, *The Treasure of Auchinleck.* New York: McGraw-Hill Book Company, 1974. The story of the discovery of the papers held for years by Boswell's family is meticulously told. To understand the vagaries of Boswell's reputation over the years one must know how these materials came to light.

Reid, B. L. "Johnson's Life of Boswell," *Kenyon Review* 18 (1956), 546–575. Reid advances the theory of Johnson's role for Boswell as the "Compleat Father."

Selected Dictionaries and Encyclopedias

Dictionary of National Biography, Oxford University Press, 1968, Vol. 2. Leslie Stephen summarizes the nineteenth-century view of Boswell.

Magill's Bibliography of Literary Criticism, Salem Press, 1979. A listing of critical sources of commentary on *The Life of Samuel Johnson.*

Survey of Contemporary Literature, Salem Press, 1977, Vol. 2. Brief essays on four of the journals in the Yale series.

John Chapman Ward
Kenyon College

ELIZABETH BOWEN
1899–1973

Author's Chronology

Born June 7, 1899, Dublin, Ireland, only child of Anglo-Irish parents; *1905* Henry Bowen's mental illness separates family, mother Florence and Elizabeth move to Kent, England; *1912* Florence dies, Elizabeth is raised by aunts at Harpenden, Herfordshire; *1914* attends Downe House, school near Orpington, Kent; *1918* Henry marries Mary Gwynn at Bowen's Court; *1923* publishes *Encounters* to good reviews; marries Alan Cameron; *1925* Alan named Secretary for Education, city of Oxford; *1926* publishes *Ann Lee's,* enjoys literary life of Oxford; *1927* first novel, *The Hotel,* appears; *1930* Henry dies, Elizabeth inherits Bowen's Court; meets Virginia Woolf; *1935* Alan appointed Secretary, Central Council of School Broadcasting, B.B.C.; the Camerons move to Regent's Park, London; *1937–38* theatre critic for Graham Greene's *Night and Day; 1941* London home bombed; Elizabeth increasingly involved in civil defense work; *1944* London home destroyed, dislocations influence style; *Demon Lover* appears; becomes journalist-reporter for B.B.C.; *1945* Alan's health deteriorates, resigns B.B.C.; Camerons retire to Bowen's Court; *1948* unpublished play, *Castle Anna* produced in London; broadcasts on English authors for B.B.C.; *1949* is appointed to Royal Commission on Capital Punishment; honorary doctor of literature, Trinity, Dublin; *1952* Alan dies August 26, Bowen's Court; *1956* honorary doctorate, Oxford; *1959* sells Bowen's Court; *1960* lectures at Vassar and other American colleges; settles at Hythe, Kent; *1969* begins *Pictures and Conversations; 1971* health declines; *1973* dies February 22 at Hythe.

Author's Bibliography (selected)

Encounters, 1923 (short stories); *Ann Lee's,* 1926 (short stories); *The Hotel,* 1927 (novel); *The Last September,* 1929 (novel); *To the North,* 1932 (novel); *The House in Paris,* 1935 (novel); *The Death of the Heart,* 1938 (novel); *Look At All Those Roses,* 1941 (short stories); *Bowen's Court,* 1942 (historical essay); *English Novelists,* 1942 (criticism); *Seven Winters: Memories of a Dublin Childhood,* 1942 (memoir); *The Demon Lover,* 1945 (short stories); *Anthony Trollope: A New Judgement,* 1946 (play); *Why Do I Write? An Exchange of Views between Elizabeth Bowen, Graham Greene, and V.S. Pritchett,* 1948 (*belles-lettres*); *The Heat of the Day,* 1949 (novel); *A Time in Rome,* 1960 (travel); *The Little Girls,* 1964 (novel); *A Day in the Dark,* 1965 (short stories); *The Good Tiger,* 1965 (novel); *Eva Trout,* 1968 (novel); *Pictures and Conversations,* 1975 (autobiography).

Overview of Biographical Sources

There is only one full-length biography, that by Victoria Glendinning, *Elizabeth Bowen: A Biography* (1978). Glendinning had cooperation of the estate, access to unpublished materials, and help from Bowen's friends. She is conservative since this is the approved biography. She notes, though she does not sensationalize, Bowen's difficult childhood, the history of mental illness in Bowen's family, the bland marriage to Alan Cameron, and the extra-marital affairs which followed. Jocelyn Brooke's *Elizabeth Bowen* (London: Longman's, 1952) is a pamphlet supplement to *British Book News* (No. 28). It was written as a popular appreciation. A. E. Austin's *Elizabeth Bowen* (New York: Twayne, 1971) is a short bio-critical study in the English Authors Series.

Evaluation of Selected Biographies

Glendinning, Victoria, *Elizabeth Bowen: A Biography*. New York: Alfred A. Knopf, 1978. Glendinning provides more information on Bowen's personal life than can be found in either the Brooke or the bio-critical Austin works cited above. It is conservative, the result of cooperation from the Bowen estate and friends, and it relies on biographical interpretations of Bowen's works to flesh out a life which had always been kept very private. These extended discussions and the family history drawn from *Bowen's Court* can become tedious for a general reader. The biography is at its best in its discussion of how Bowen saw herself in relation to English-Irish letters, formative sources such as Flaubert and James, Bowen's acquaintanceship with Virginia Woolf, and her relationship to contemporary writers such as Iris Murdoch and Muriel Spark.

Autobiographical Sources

Bowen was at work on her autobiography at the time of her death; it was published posthumously as *Pictures and Conversations* (Alfred A. Knopf: New York, 1975) and edited by Spencer Curtis Brown. It includes "The Move-In" (the first chapter of an unfinished novel) and *Nativity Play* (written for performance in an Irish cathedral), as well as an essay on Bergotte (one of Proust's characters), and "Notes on Writing a Novel" (an analysis of her own methods). *Pictures and Conversations* is an extension of the discreet and almost impersonal approach Bowen used in *Bowen's Court* (Longman's, Green: London, 1942) and *Seven Winters: Memories of a Dublin Childhood* (Cuala Press: Dublin, 1942; Longman's, Green: London, 1943). These latter works concern primarily family history. Her *Why Do I Write? An Exchange of Views between Elizabeth Bowen, Graham Greene, and V. S. Pritchett* (Percival Marshall: London, 1948) is bio-critical. Bowen has written that "however much simplified by distance of time no experience is to be vouched for as an author's own" ("Out of a Book," *Orion* III (1946) 10–14; also published in *Collected Impressions*. Toronto and London: Longman's Green, 1950). She believed that autobiography almost always adapts the truth to an author's perception of it, which sums up the way Bowen saw her relationship to autobiography, as essentially an outgrowth of her fiction.

Overview of Critical Sources

Bowen criticism ranges from far-fetched and vituperative to solid and quite good. Marxist critics often attack her work as *declassé* Bloomsbury, as "fussy," as "womanish," or as poor imitation of James (cf. Herbert Gold, "Random Dreams, True and False," *Hudson Review* VIII, 1955 150–155). Her "hypersensitive" world is Geoffrey Wagner's grounds for attack in "Elizabeth Bowen and the Artificial Novel," *Essays in Criticism* XIII (1963) 155–163. Angus Wilson parodies the "Woolf-Bowen style" in "Evil in the English Novel," *The Listener* XLIV (1950) 279–280, while John McCormick, *Catastrophe and Imagination* (London: Longman's, 1952, pp. 93), sees Bowen's post-war novels as parodies of her earlier style too much influenced by her love of Henry James. Still, more recent critics see Bowen's work where she herself would have liked it placed: incorporating the attention to scene found in Flaubert, the care for language of James, the intensity of Woolf.

Evaluation of Selected Criticism

Austin, A. E. *Elizabeth Bowen.* New York: Twayne, 1971. This is a solidly written analysis of the major works. It is bio-critical and conservative, though not the most scholarly text presently available. It is a good study for the general reader, presenting an encapsulated biography in the first chapter and analysis of the major works in the four which follow.

Blodgett, Harriet, *Patterns of Reality: Elizabeth Bowen's Novels.* The Hague: Mouton, 1975. This monograph considers Bowen's novels in the wake of Bloomsbury influence, and attempts to establish her independence citing the original elements of her work.

Brooke, Jocelyn, *Elizabeth Bowen.* (British Council Pamphlet; Supplement to *British Book News,* No. 28) London: Longman's, Green, 1952. This thirty page appreciation of Bowen enumerates her works to 1951, and provides straightforward discussion of key works rather than analysis.

Chessman, Harriet S. "Women and Language in the Fiction of Elizabeth Bowen," *Twentieth Century Literature* (1983) 69–85. This feminist view is interesting primarily because Bowen's work has almost never been considered along these lines. Indeed, Bowen has usually been seen as an apologist for British middle class society and values.

Lee, Hermione, *Elizabeth Bowen: An Estimation.* New York: Vision and Barnes and Noble, 1981. This is the best and most scholarly study of Bowen's works presently available. It uses information in the Glendinning biography, and presents a comprehensive study of the major works, giving notes, a complete bibliography of Bowen's works, and a complete index.

Other Sources

Hardwick, Elizabeth, "Elizabeth Bowen's Fiction," *Partisan Review* XVI (1949), 1114–1121. This is a scathing attack on Bowen's style and her middle class themes. Hardwick argues that beneath the outward elegance of her settings one can always perceive the decadence and moral intransigence which lies beneath them. She believes that the fault lies with Bowen's unquestioning acceptance of British conservatism.

Quinn, Antoinette, *Elizabeth Bowen's Irish Stories: 1939 to 1945.* Bonn: Bouvier, 1982. This is a needed discussion of the place of Ireland and Irish nationalism in Bowen's short fiction. Quinn argues that it has a more prominent place in the *corpus* than most critics have suggested.

Sellery, J'nan, "Elizabeth Bowen: A Check List," *Bulletin of the New York Public Library.* LXXIV (April 1970), 219–274. Sellery provides a complete list of works by and on Bowen, including reviews and articles, to 1969.

Sellery, J'nan, *Elizabeth Bowen: A Descriptive Bibliography.* Austin: Texas University Press, 1977. This is an expanded version of Sellery's earlier work with annotations. It is less readily available than the other list, though it is more complete and has been updated to 1976.

Selected Dictionaries and Encyclopedias

Contemporary Novelists, St. Martin's, 1972, pp. 132–136. This one-volume encyclopedia contains a brief biographical sketch, short discussions of several important works, and a selected bibliography.

Critical Survey of Long Fiction, Vol. 1, Salem Press, 1983. Presents a good biographical sketch, a brief analysis of several works, and a selected bibliography.

Encyclopedia of World Literature in the Twentieth Century, Frederick Ungar, 1981, pp. 309–310. Has a brief biographical sketch, a short chronology of events, and a list of selected works.

Robert J. Forman
St. John's University, New York

ANNE BRADSTREET
1612–1672

Author's Chronology

Born 1612, Northampton, England; father, Thomas Dudley, steward at Earl of Lincoln's estate; Anne educated by tutors and use of earl's extensive library; married Simon Bradstreet, also in earl's employ; *1628* sails to New World with first Puritan emigrants on the Arbella; *1630* settles in Boston, then Newtown, Ipswich and Andover; father and husband both governor of Massachusetts Bay Colony at different times; marriage produced eight children; family life and inner reflections became subjects for her poetry; first volume, *The Tenth Muse Lately Sprung Up in America,* published without Bradstreet's knowledge in London, *1650;* American edition, with author's revisions, published *1678,* six year's after Bradstreet's death.

Author's Bibliography (selected)

The Tenth Muse Lately Sprung Up in America, 1650; *Several Poems Compiled with great variety of Wit and Learning* . . . (2nd edition of 1650 publication, 1678; 3rd edition, 1758); *The Works of Anne Bradstreet, in Prose and Verse.* ed. J. Harvard, 1867; *Poems of Anne Bradstreet.* ed. R. Hutchinson, 1969.

Overview of Biographical Sources

The first lengthy treatments of Bradstreet's life which appeared in the latter portion of the nineteenth century leave much to be desired by modern standards. Helen Campbell's *Anne Bradstreet and Her Time* (1891) deals more with the period than with Bradstreet. Colonel Luther Caldwell's *An Account of Anne Bradstreet, the Puritan Poetess and Kindred Topics* (1898) deals with Bradstreet and her works, but more as a loving treatise than a scholarly account. Later biographical treatments often appear as part of larger studies. Moses Cort Tyler's *A History of American Literature During the Colonial Period* (1897) and Samuel Eliot Morison's *The Intellectual Life of New England* (1956) represent two significant examples. The only full-fledged biographies currently in print about Bradstreet are Josephine Piercy's *Anne Bradstreet* (1965) and Elizabeth Wade White's *Anne Bradstreet* (1971).

Evaluation of Selected Biographies

Piercy, Josephine K. *Anne Bradstreet.* New York: Twayne, 1965. Piercy divides this study into two sections: the author's spiritual growth amidst the Puritan Calvinism of Massachusetts Bay, and her maturation as a writer. Piercy feels that Calvinism in the New World was less strict than on the continent, which, together with the early settlers' emphasis on broad intellect, prompted

Bradstreet's verses. Piercy emphasizes the inner sense of rebellion that Bradstreet felt, and how her poems became a release for the pent-up rebelliousness.

Piercy details the poet's artistic progress, beginning with her quaternion writings. The poet reaches a fuller potential in her later elegies, domestic poems, and love poems to her husband. Her artistic peak appears in her "Contemplations," her nature poems which actually pre-date the English Romantics. Piercy punctuates documentation of her points with references to Bradstreet's prose writings.

White, Elizabeth W. *Anne Bradstreet.* New York: Oxford University Press, 1971. This is the most extensive and authoritative biography of Bradstreet. White emphasizes the Puritan upbringing Anne received and the politics of Anglican vs. Puritan England which affected her family. White's depiction of the New World details the hardships Bradstreet's group found.

Bradstreet's period of settlement and child-rearing also marks the beginning of her poetic career. White examines the private and public themes which appear in Bradstreet's works, as well as the influences of English poets such as Sidney and Spencer. White includes critical reaction, both early and more modern, to Bradstreet's verses, including a whole chapter devoted to *The Tenth Muse* (1650). She concludes her study of Bradstreet with the various deaths which occurred among Bradstreet's family in her later years, especially those of her young grandchildren, which caused her great anguish during those years and prompted some of her later elegies and reflective poems.

Autobiographical Sources

Although *The Tenth Muse* contains a significant number of Bradstreet's more personal poems, her complete works provide even greater insights into the feelings and attitudes of the poet. In these personal poems, two types dominate: those which deal with her family, and those which attest to the poet's religious convictions and faith.

Probably the most constant element in Bradstreet's life/art was the love and devotion she felt for her family. "To her Father with some verses" expresses the debt she feels she owes her father for his guidance in her upbringing; in "To my Dear and loving Husband" Bradstreet rates the latter's love as worth all the riches of the East. "In reference to her children, 23. June, 1659" surveys the poet's "eight birds hatcht in one nest," and how she dreads their leaving.

The other type of poetry which reveals much about Bradstreet personally is that which deals with religious matters. "The Flesh and Spirit" presents a dialogue which spells outs the pleasures and attractions of both elements, then leads to Bradstreet's recognition that earth's rewards pale in comparison to the rewards possible in the next life. However, Bradstreet's appreciation of the natural world did not diminish as a result. In her early "Four Seasons of the Yeare," she travels from season to season exploring their qualities and charm;

her "Contemplations" again reveals the great delight she finds in nature, and this becomes a vehicle for strengthening the poet's spiritual awareness and religious faith.

Overview of Critical Sources

Prior to the late nineteenth century, little criticism of Bradstreet's works exists, especially in book form. The 1678 and 1758 reprintings of *The Tenth Muse* produced no major critical responses. John Harvard Ellis's 1867 *Works of Anne Bradstreet* yielded the Charles Eliot Norton version in 1897, which criticized Ellis more than Bradstreet's verses. The major critical works on Bradstreet do not appear until the 1960's. From that decade on, the most significant assessments of her works have emerged, ranging from the overall structural and thematic evaluations, to the contextual analyses such as McElrath & Robb's *The Complete Works of Anne Bradstreet,* to the feminist approach in works such as Adelaide Amore's *A Woman's Inner World.*

Evaluation of Selected Criticism

Amore, Adelaide, *A Woman's Inner World.* Washington: University Press of America, 1982. Amore attempts to show here that many of Bradstreet's poems reflect her "inner feminist world." Beginning with brief biographical references, Amore shows how Bradstreet lived much in the shadows of her father and husband. Her removal to the New World intensified this as both her and her husband's families emigrated also. Amore points to Anne Hutchinson as an example of a woman who blatantly defied male convention and was banished from Massachusetts Bay as a result. This underscored the dilemma Bradstreet faced as a female poet in a male-dominated society. The poems Amore includes reflect how Bradstreet saw her poems *and* children in much the same light: both were created and nurtured by her. Other verses exemplify the frustration Bradstreet felt as wife-mother-poet. Early critics avoided these elements and concentrated on the imitative style of Bradstreet. Even some twentieth century critics have advocated assessing Bradstreet in a jocular vein rather than allowing for the feminist perspective which Amore sees.

Hensley, Jeanine, *The Works of Anne Bradstreet.* Cambridge: Harvard University Press, 1967. This volume reprints the poems from the first two editions of Bradstreet's poetry; it also contains two critical essays on the poet's works. Adrienne Rich touches on some early biography, then examines the strong Puritan beliefs which surrounded Bradstreet and became a central part of her writings. The theme of God's will and power persists in the poems, both personal and public. Rich also cites the important influence on Bradstreet of DuBartas, the French Calvinist poet. The second essay, by Jeanine Hensley, researches some of the scholarly and poetic aspects of Bradstreet's background, and the various members of her family who also versified. Hensley repeats the idea that Bradstreet's primary purpose in writing was not as personal release, but to reflect her Calvinist beliefs. The remainder of this essay comments on the various published versions of Bradstreet's poetry from the 1650 edition of *The Tenth Muse,* to the Ellis 1867 reprinting, and Piercy's 1965 facsimile.

Stanford, Ann, *Anne Bradstreet: The Worldly Puritan.* New York: Franklin & Co., 1974. Stanford sees Bradstreet's poetry as a statement of the poet's awareness of earthly pleasures such as love, family, learning, and her preference for those over possible other-worldly rewards. Stanford divides Bradstreet's works into two categories: "The Ipswich Poems" and "The Andover Poems." Bradstreet's early verses were written in the thriving town of Ipswich, and they reflect the growth of the town as well as that of the poet. Although this period produced some of the poet's most loving verses for her husband, it is characterized more by her public poems such as her quaternions and her commentaries on life in New England. The Bradstreets' move to Andover in the mid-1640s changed Anne's surroundings and her verses. A more rural and isolated Andover produced more personal, reflective poems, including Bradstreet's "Contemplations" and her later elegies. These poems reveal the poet's more mature years and style.

Other Sources

Berryman, John, *Homage to Mistress Bradstreet.* New York: Farrar, Straus, 1956. In fifty-seven stanzas of his own verse, Berryman creates Bradstreet as poetic persona, revealing her thoughts about the New World, her family, her art, her temporal life. Illustrated by Ben Shahn.

McElrath, Joseph and Allan Robb, *The Complete Works of Anne Bradstreet.* Boston: Twayne, 1981. A treatment of the textual elements in Bradstreet's works, including lengthy attention to the apparatus, errata and alterations found in her verses and the reprints.

Selected Dictionaries and Encyclopedias

American Writers Before 1800, Greenwood Press, 1983. A very brief biography and a one page summary of the criticism of Bradstreet and the "tensions" in her poetry.

American Women Writers, Vol. 1, Frederick Ungar, 1979. A three page survey of the poet's life, writings and reception. Complete listing of her publications and ensuing reprints, together with a selected bibliography of book and journal sources.

Kenneth A. Howe
Michigan State University

CHARLOTTE BRONTË
1816–1855

Author's Chronology

Born April 21, 1816, Thornton, England to Patrick Brontë, a minister and published poet, and Maria Branwell Brontë; *1820* family moves to parsonage in Haworth, West Yorkshire; *1821* mother dies; *1825* older sisters, Maria and Elizabeth, die after an outbreak of typhoid in their school; with younger children, Branwell, Emily, and Anne, Charlotte begins writing stories and plays about an imaginary world; *1831–1832* attends school at Roe Head; *1835* returns as teacher; *1836* writes Robert Southey to ask about her potential as a writer, receives discouraging response; *1838* leaves Roe Head School; *1839* becomes governess to Sidgwick family; *1842* travels to Brussels with Emily to study French at Pensionnat Heger; returns to Haworth in November to attend aunt's funeral; *1843* returns to Brussels as English teacher at the Heger's school, develops romantic feelings for Monsieur Heger; *1844* returns to Haworth to begin most productive period as novelist; *1845–1846* writes *The Professor* which is rejected by six publishers; *1846* uses pseudonym Currer Bell to publish poetry with sisters; takes father to Manchester for cataract operation; *1847* publishes *Jane Eyre; 1848* helplessly watches rapid deaths of Branwell and Emily; *1849* publishes *Shirley;* takes Anne to Scarborough where she succumbs to tuberculosis; travels to London, meets Thackeray; *1850* meets Elizabeth Gaskell, develops close friendship with her first biographer; *1853* publishes *Villette; 1854* marries Arthur Bell Nicholls, curate to Patrick Brontë for many years; takes wedding trip to Ireland; *1855* dies March 31, leaving fragment of last novel, *Emma.*

Author's Bibliography (selected)

Poems by Currer, Ellis and Acton Bell, 1846; *Jane Eyre; An Autobiography,* 1847 (novel); *Shirley,* 1849 (novel); *Villette,* 1853 (novel); *The Professor,* 1857 (novel); *Emma: A Fragment,* 1860 (novel); *The Poems of Charlotte Brontë and Patrick Branwell Brontë,* 1934; *The Miscellaneous and Unpublished Writings of Charlotte and Patrick Branwell Brontë,* 1934.

Overview of Biographical Sources

Because of the tragic circumstances surrounding the Brontë family, Charlotte's life has long appealed to biographers. For nearly one hundred years following her death, Charlotte was the subject of sentimental reminiscences and biographies which portrayed her as the romantic heroine of a Victorian tale of adversity. Of the latter group, Elizabeth Gaskell's *Life* (1857) was the first and most thorough. Many biographers tended to discuss Charlotte's work only in relation to her life, creating catalogs of correspondences between her own experiences and the experiences of her characters. Of these, Ellis Chadwick's *In the Footsteps of the Brontës* (London: Pitman, 1914) might be considered typical. A more constructive and recent trend in biographies of Charlotte reflects the awakened interest in her childhood and adolescent writing. Fannie Ratchford broke ground in this area with *The Brontës' Web of Childhood* (1941). Even more recent are the explicitly psychoanalytical approaches used by Charles Burkhart in *Charlotte Brontë: A Psychosexual Study of Her Novels* (London: Victor Gollancz, 1973) and Helene Moglen in *Charlotte Brontë: The Self Conceived* (New York: W. W. Norton, 1976). A Jungian analysis of Charlotte's life is contained in Barbara Hannah's *Striving Towards Wholeness* (New York: G. P. Putnam, 1971).

Evaluation of Selected Biographies

Gaskell, Elizabeth, *The Life of Charlotte Brontë.* London: Smith, Elder, 1857. Gaskell was friends with Charlotte Brontë and admired her for her courageous response to the rapid, successive deaths of Branwell, Emily, and Anne. She also appreciated Charlotte's novels, although she was occasionally bothered by what Victorian critics termed a "coarse" quality in the writing. A novelist herself, Gaskell was Patrick Brontë's choice as his daughter's biographer; at his request, she began the project less than three months after Charlotte's death. Gaskell collected information and copies of letters from many people who knew Charlotte very well: her schoolfriend Ellen Nussey (who published her own "Reminiscences" in 1871), her publisher George Smith and his associate W. S. Williams, her teacher at Roe Head Miss Wooler, her father, her husband. Despite this wealth of information, Gaskell's biography is biased because of her tendency to view Charlotte as a fictional heroine whose life should read like a novel. Charlotte is portrayed as a dutiful daughter to a somewhat tyrannical father, a silent sufferer who denied her own needs in order to make other's lives richer. Gaskell suppressed evidence she undoubtedly had about Charlotte's relationship with her teacher in Brussels, Clementin Heger. Charlotte's feelings for Heger were expressed in letters she wrote to him after leaving Brussels, but Heger, married, could not respond to her passion. Gaskell explains Charlotte's consequent depression as the result of her brother's affair with Mrs. Robinson. Although evidence of this relationship is present in both *The Professor* and *Villette,* Gaskell does not comment on it. Indeed, her discussion of Charlotte's writing is minimal; for Gaskell, Charlotte is interesting not because she was a novelist, but because she experienced family tragedy.

Gérin, Winifred, *Charlotte Brontë: The Evolution of Genius.* Oxford: Oxford University Press, 1967. Gérin's book is the most comprehensive recent biography of Charlotte Brontë. Gérin's work on the Brontës was extensive. She wrote biographies of the other Brontë children; in addition, she edited some of Charlotte's adolescent manuscripts, in a sense continuing the work of Fannie Ratchford. Gérin lived in Haworth herself, and enriches the biography with descriptions of the landscape and character of the Yorkshire people. She demonstrates that Charlotte grew into her genius, identifying as a pivotal point in Charlotte's artistic development the year 1839, when Charlotte vowed to stop writing about the imaginary world of Angria. In addition, Gérin provides a corrective to Gaskell's treatment of the Heger affair, analyzing Gaskell's motives for concealing information and including the texts of the letters in appendices.

Peters, Margot, *The Unquiet Soul: A Biography of Charlotte Brontë.* New York: Doubleday, 1975. In this biography, Peters uses a feminist approach to Charlotte's life and work. In a sense a corrective to Gaskell's portrayal of Charlotte as a submissive woman eager to recognize and fulfill her duty to others, this work examines the struggles that Charlotte engaged in to suppress her anger at her condition. Not an avowed feminist, Charlotte nonetheless rebelled against the role society imposed upon her by becoming a novelist (despite the advice of Robert Southey, then poet laureate of England). Peters identifies Charlotte's frustration at having so few opportunities to do anything she considered interesting, especially commenting on the wearisome tasks of teaching and governessing. This emphasis on Charlotte's geographical and intellectual isolation is then linked to her creation of characters who are alienated outsiders rebelling against their destinies.

Ratchford, Fannie, *The Brontës' Web of Childhood.* New York: Columbia University Press, 1941. This book was the first to examine the relationship of the childhood writings to the adult novels of the Brontë sisters. Ratchford examines the children's collaboration on the stories about Verdopolis, and explains how Branwell and Charlotte eventually developed the world of Angria while Emily and Anne created Gondal. The shortcoming of Ratchford's analysis is that in celebrating the genius of the children, she belittles the achievements of the adults, suggesting that the mature novels are little more than reworkings of plots and themes already developed in the early writing.

Overview of Critical Sources

Until the mid-1960's, most critical work on Charlotte Brontë could be divided into two categories: biographical criticism which assumed that a study of her novels was a study of her life and formal criticism which admitted that Charlotte produced literature in spite of technical incompetence. In the 1920's the interest in psychological analysis tended to reinforce the biographical approach while the early interest in narrative technique, stemming from work by Henry James and Percy Lubbock, reinforced the criticisms of Charlotte's craftsmanship. Only after an interest in narrative technique was fused with the idea of the integrity of a work as a whole were new directions explored in Brontë criticism.

Evaluation of Selected Criticism

Knies, Earl, *The Art of Charlotte Brontë.* Athens: Ohio University Press, 1969. An analysis of Charlotte's use of first-person narration, this study attempts to demonstrate her growth as an artist conscious of technical matters. In addition to explications of the four novels, Knies includes a chapter on the autobiographical nature of Charlotte's novels, showing that events from her own life are transformed dramatically to serve artistic purposes. He also tries to evaluate Charlotte's aesthetic sense, commenting on the sporadic theoretical comments to be found in her letters and notes to herself.

Martin, Robert Bernard, *The Accents of Persuasion: Charlotte Brontë's Novels.* New York: W. W. Norton, 1966. Martin was one of the first critics to separate a discussion of the novels from a discussion of Charlotte's life. This is a study of recurring themes in the novels and their relation to Victorian society.

Peters, Margot, *Charlotte Brontë: Style in the Novel.* Madison: University of Wisconsin Press, 1973. A linguistic analysis of Charlotte Brontë's prose style, this study identifies the tensions in Charlotte's language which reflect the cultural and psychological contexts in which she wrote. Of particular usefulness is the discussion of antithesis in language and structure which allows Brontë to express simultaneously public control and private rebellion. In this sense, the work supports feminist readings of Brontë's novels.

Other Sources

Alexander, Christine, *The Early Writings of Charlotte Brontë.* Oxford: Blackwell's, 1983. An examination and summary of Charlotte's childhood writing and the effect of her collaboration with Branwell.

Dessner, Lawrence Jay, *The Homely Web of Truth: A Study of Charlotte Brontë's Novels.* The Hague: Mouton, 1975. A study of narrative technique in Charlotte's novels, examining the influence of other writers on her work.

Eagleton, Terence, *Myths of Power.* London: Macmillan, 1975. A Marxist approach to works by all of the Brontë sisters.

Gilbert, Sandra and Susan Gubar, *The Madwoman in the Attic.* New Haven: Yale University Press, 1979. An important feminist reading of nineteenth-century women writers including excellent chapters on *Jane Eyre* and *Villette.*

Monahan, Melodie, ed. "*Ashworth:* An Unfinished Novel by Charlotte Brontë," *Studies in Philology* (Fall 1983). A reconstruction of a manuscript which follows Charlotte's last-known juvenile work but precedes *The Professor.*

Gweneth A. Dunleavy
University of Illinois

EMILY BRONTË
1818–1848

Author's Chronology

Born July 30, 1818, Thornton, Yorkshire, England; *1820* family moves to parsonage at Haworth; *1821* mother dies; *1822* Elizabeth Branwell, father's sister, moves in to take care of family; *1824–1825* resides with sisters at school for clergymen's daughters at Cowan's Bridge; *1825–1835* remains at Haworth working on imaginative world of Gondal; *1835* briefly attends Roe Head School, where her sister Charlotte was a teacher; *1835–1838* lives with family at Haworth; *1838* works as governess for six months and then returns to Haworth; *1842* attends school in Brussels with Charlotte from February to November and returns to Haworth when Elizabeth Branwell died; *1845–1846* composes *Wuthering Heights; 1846* publishes *Poems by Currer, Ellis, and Acton Bell,* with sisters Charlotte and Anne; *1847* publishes *Wuthering Heights* under pseudonym of Ellis Bell; December 19, 1848, dies of tuberculosis at Haworth.

Author's Bibliography

Poems by Currer, Ellis, and Acton Bell, 1846; *Wuthering Heights,* 1847 (novel).

Overview of Biographical Sources

Emily Brontë's life has always been surrounded by the air of mystery and romance. Although no primary materials have survived, many biographies and biographical novels have attempted to flesh out the picture of her short life. Most of these works combine Emily's story with that of the other Brontës, particularly Charlotte, about whom there is much more information. Indeed, Charlotte is the source of most material about Emily. Her "Biographical Notice of Ellis and Acton Bell," preface to *Wuthering Heights and Agnes Grey* (London: Smith, Elder, 1850), provided the first public view of Emily (Ellis Bell), and Elizabeth Gaskell's *The Life of Charlotte Brontë* (1857), remains the primary source for all biographies of the family. The earliest biography of Emily herself, based on Gaskell, appeared in *Galaxy* magazine (London), volume 15 (February 1873). This brief life is combined with analysis of the poems and the novel, as well as a comparison of the facts with the supposed portrayal of Emily in Charlotte's novels. Agnes M. F. Robinson Duclaux's *Emily Brontë* (London: W. H. Allen; Boston: Roberts Brothers, 1883), examines Emily's "character," especially by exploring the letters of Charlotte's friend Ellen Nussey. Using newly available letters, Clement K. Shorter added to and corrected Gaskell's version of the life of the Brontë family in three works: *Charlotte Brontë and Her Circle* (London: Hodder and Stoughton, 1896); *Charlotte Brontë and Her Sis-*

ters (London: Hodder and Stoughton; New York: Charles Scribner's Sons, 1905); *The Brontës Life and Letters,* two volumes (London: Hodder and Stoughton; New York: Charles Scribner's Sons, 1908). Another early biography is Ernest Dimnet's *Les Soeurs Brontë* (Paris: Bloud, 1910), translated by Louise Morgan Sill (London: Jonathan Cape, 1927). Romer Wilson's *All Alone: The Life and Private History of Emily Jane Brontë* (London: Chatto and Windus, 1928), corrects some factual errors in Charlotte's prefaces to the novels and examines Emily's character from the internal evidence of her poems. Other useful early biographies include May Sinclair's *The Three Brontës* (London: Hutchinson; New York and Boston: Houghton Mifflin, 1912; reprinted Port Washington, NY: Kennikat, 1967); Charles Simpson's *Emily Brontë* (London: Country Life; New York: Charles Scribner's Sons, 1929); Georges and Emilie Romieu's *Three Virgins of Haworth: Being an Account of the Brontë Sisters,* translated by Roberts Tapley (New York: Dutton, 1930); and Laura L. Hinckley's popularization, *The Brontës: Charlotte and Emily* (New York: Hastings House, 1945). Laurence and E. M. Hanson's *The Four Brontës: The Lives and Works of Charlotte, Branwell, Emily, and Anne Brontë* (London: Oxford University Press, 1949), emphasizes the interrelationships among family members, while Norma Crandall's *Emily Brontë: A Psychological Portrait* (Rindge, NH: R. R. Smith, 1957; rpt. 1978), offers suggestive analysis of Emily's personality. John Hewish's *Emily Brontë: A Critical and Biographical Study* (London: Macmillan; New York: St. Martin's, 1969), is an important work for scholars, combining criticism and biography. The most important recent study is Winnifred Gérin's *Emily Brontë* (1971). This study attempts to see the development in Emily's character from childhood to maturity. It offers a more detailed analysis of her childhood and adolescence than other biographies. Tom Winnifrith's *The Brontës and Their Background: Romance and Reality* (London: Macmillan, 1973), provides new information about the Brontës' views on religious and literary issues. Brian Wilks' *The Brontës* (New York: Viking, 1975), is a lavishly-illustrated biography for the general reader.

Evaluation of Selected Biographies

Gaskell, Elizabeth C. *The Life of Charlotte Brontë.* London: Smith, Elder, 1857. Although this work concentrates on Charlotte, it is the indispensible primary source of most information about Emily as well. Gaskell's view of Emily is, of course, Charlotte's view, but the biography gives a vivid picture of the life of the Brontë family.

Gérin, Winnifred, *Emily Brontë.* Oxford: Clarendon Press, 1971. This is the most widely-respected biography, by a writer who has also published studies of the other Brontës. Gérin carefully distinguishes between the facts and myths associated with Emily's life and provides the fullest narrative available, emphasizing especially the changes and developments in her character.

Simpson, Charles, *Emily Brontë.* London: Country Life; New York: Charles Scribner's Sons, 1929. Although superseded by Gérin, Simpson's biography is still a useful example of a carefully researched and eminently readable book. Written in the style of a novel, it will appeal to the general reader, but still offers the scholar an accurate picture of the life.

Autobiographical Sources

Although there has always been speculation about how much of *Wuthering Heights* and the poems comes directly from Emily Brontë's own experience, there is no autobiographical evidence to support any of these suppositions. Most of the juvenalia and all but three of Emily's letters have been lost.

Overview of Critical Sources

The earliest criticism of *Wuthering Heights* (the poems were ignored) focused on its inferiority to Charlotte Brontë's *Jane Eyre.* The passionate and morbid nature of the characters disturbed readers used to more genteel fiction. By the end of the nineteenth century, however, critical consensus was already shifting to consider *Wuthering Heights* as the finest of all the Brontës' works, a view widely held today. Contemporary readings of the novel stress psychological and mythical interpretation of character, analysis of narrators and narrative point-of-view, and studies of the relationship between the novel and Victorian society. Connections between the novel and the author's life are still an important part of Brontë studies, but the biographical emphasis has shifted to the poetry rather than the novel. Because the body of primary work is small (one novel and a selection of poems), most criticism is found in collections of larger studies or in journals.

Evaluation of Selected Criticism

Benvenuto, Richard, *Emily Brontë.* Boston: Twayne, 1982. A brief biography and general introduction to the works, fiction and poetry.

Cecil, David, "Emily Brontë and *Wuthering Heights,*" in *Early Victorian Novelists: Essays in Revaluation.* London: Constable, 1934, pp. 147–193. Cecil's early but still important study of the structure of the novel emphasizes its concern with the nature of cosmic harmony.

Craik, W. A. "*Wuthering Heights,*" in *The Brontë Novels.* London: Methuen, 1968, pp. 5–47. A study of the characters in the novel.

Dingle, Herbert, *The Mind of Emily Brontë.* London: Brian and O'Keefe, 1974. An attempt to construct the mind of the author from a close reading of the poems and the novel.

Ewbank, Inga-Stina, "Emily Brontë: The Woman Writer as Poet," in *Their Proper Sphere: A Study of the Brontë Sisters as Early-Victorian Female Novelists.*

Cambridge: Harvard University Press, 1966, pp. 86–155. An analysis of the characters and moral questions in *Wuthering Heights.*

Homan, Margaret, "Repression and Sublimation of Nature in *Wuthering Heights,*" in *PMLA,* 93 (1978), 9–19. A Freudian interpretation of the uses of external nature.

Kettle, Arnold, "Emily Brontë: *Wuthering Heights* (1847)," in *An Introduction to the English Novel.* London: Hutchinson House, 1951, pp. 139–155. An analysis of the use and importance of symbolism in the novel.

Miller, J. Hillis, "Emily Brontë," in *The Disappearance of God: Five Nineteenth-Century Women Writers.* Cambridge: Harvard University Press, 1963, pp. 157–211. An examination of the religious and moral philosophy behind the poetry and the novel.

Van Ghent, Dorothy, "On *Wuthering Heights,*" in *The English Novel, Form and Function.* New York: Rhinehart, 1953, pp. 153–170. An analysis that emphasizes mythic archetypes, the relationships of the narrators, and the importance of the passing of generations.

Visick, Mary, *The Genesis of Wuthering Heights.* Hong Kong: Hong Kong University Press, 1958; rpt. 1980. A study of the influence of the Gondal poems on *Wuthering Heights.*

Selected Dictionaries and Encyclopedias

Critical Survey of Long Fiction, Salem Press, 1983. Brief biography of the author and analysis of *Wuthering Heights.*

Dictionary of National Biography, Oxford University Press, 1917; rpt. 1973. Standard brief biography.

Lawrence F. Laban
Virginia Commonwealth University

RUPERT BROOKE
1887–1915

Author's Chronology

Born Rupert Chawner Brooke, August 3, 1887, Rugby, England, his father a master at Rugby School; *1901–1906* attends Rugby School; *1906* enters King's College, Cambridge; *1912* wins a fellowship at King's with a dissertation on John Webster; *1909* earns degree from Cambridge; *1909–1912* spends his days reading and bathing at the Old Vicarage, Grantchester; visits London, Munich, Berlin; *1910* serves a term as housemaster at Rugby; *1913* travels to New York, Boston, Canada, San Francisco, Hawaii, Samoa, Fiji, New Zealand, Tahiti; June *1914* returns to England with intent to settle at Cambridge; September *1914* commissioned in the Royal Navy Division; October *1914* participates in the Antwerp expedition; February *1915* sails for the Dardanelles; 23 April 1915 dies from bloodpoisoning and sunstroke; buried on Skyros.

Author's Bibliography (selected)

The Pyramids, 1904 (poems); *Poems,* 1911; *1914 and Other Poems,* 1915; *Lithuania,* 1915 (drama); *Collected Poems,* 1915; *War Poems,* 1915; *Poems,* 1916; *John Webster and the Elizabethan Drama,* 1916 (prose); *Letters from America,* 1916; *Selected Poems,* 1917; *Collected Poems,* 1918; *Poetical Works,* 1946; *Poems,* 1952; *The Prose of Rupert Brooke,* 1956; *Poetical Works,* 1970.

Overview of Biographical Sources

Biographical discussion really begins and ends with Christopher Hassall's *Rupert Brooke* (1964)—completed just before the author's death in April 1963 and seen through the press by Geoffrey Keynes. A number of other worthwhile biographical sketches do exist, including one by Edward Marsh (Brooke's literary executor) for the 1912–1921 *Dictionary of National Biography.* Prior to that, Margaret Lavington's "Biographical Note" had appeared at the end of George Edward Woodbury's *Collected Poems of Rupert Brooke* (New York: Dodd, Mead and Company, 1915), while Marsh appended a "Memoir" to his 1918 edition of Brooke's *Collected Poems.*

Evaluation of Selected Biographies

Hassall, Christopher, *Rupert Brooke, a Biography.* New York: Harcourt, Brace and World, 1964. Although instances when the merit of a biography rises above the reputation of its subject may be rare, Hassall's effort deserves consideration in just that context. He provides not only the narrative of the young poet's brief life, but captures the essence of all that Brooke symbolized: a transitional period when the world passed all too quickly from the superficial pastoralism of the second Georgian Age to the filth and disease of World War

I. The 539 pages of Hassall's text capture practically every detail of Brooke's twenty-seven years, eight months, and twenty days; more important, those pages identify the relationship between Brooke and his times. For Hassall, Brooke served to light the spirit of "the national mind" as it struggled to give meaning to the events of 1914–1915. ". . . on the eve of an historic and bloody campaign, when . . . the world was watching, one man died quietly in his bed, a young poet so eloquent of the hour, that it seemed almost inevitable that Death should single him out as the first installment of a holocaust."

If Hassall belonged in that long line of mourners for Brooke, he also mourned for the times, the spirit, and the values that died with the poet. The biographer paints for his readers, in the clearest of colors, life at Rugby School—on its cricket and football fields and in the house of his father, a master of Greek and Latin there—and King's College, Cambridge. He takes those same readers and guides them with Brooke on the poet's travels to Munich, Berlin, Boston, San Francisco, Hawaii, Tahiti. He introduces them to the poet's friends (Edward Marsh, Cathleen Nesbitt, James Strachey, Ka Cox, Noel Olivier, Frances Cornford), and to noted acquaintances (Henry James, Winston Churchill, Geoffrey Keynes, Edmund Gosse, H. G. Wells, Lytton Strachey, Harold Monro). More than a biography, Hassall's book constitutes the history of a brief literary age; more than a literary history, it identifies one of the many tragedies brought on by war. "He died before he had fulfilled his own hopes or ours," wrote Marsh three days after Brooke's burial on Skyros, "but either we believe in waste altogether or not at all. And if any seeming waste is not waste, there is none in a young life full of promise and joyfully laid down." Writing Brooke's biography almost half a century later, Hassall tried terribly hard to find that middle ground between fulfillment and waste.

Overview of Critical Sources

What little criticism there is of Brooke can easily be classified into three distinct categories: (1) focus upon "The Soldier" (or at least the opening sentence), particularly its rhetorical and political problems; (2) the pre-war sonnets and the idea of the Byronic hero being alive and well during the reign of George V, although transformed, slightly, into an early twentieth-century daydreamer; and (3) pure speculation that, had Brooke survived the voyage to Gallipoli, his Cambridge thesis on "John Webster and the Elizabethan Drama" in combination with the poetry would have given Cambridge and all of England one of its better scholar-poets.

Edmund Blunden (*War Poets, 1914–1918.* London: Longmans, Green, 1958, pp. 14–21) attempts to achieve a balance between Brooke, "the new poet living eagerly in the world as he walked it," and the poetry itself. Unfortunately, since he must discuss his subject in the same chapter that houses commentary upon Charles Hamilton Sorley, Julian Grenfell, and Arthur Graeme West, the result proves little beyond general observations and reactions. If nothing else, Blunden proves that the best of Brooke may well be outside (or, in this case, prior to) the war poems. He strives hard to build an argument for the collected *Poems* of 1911, particularly the love sonnets, as "premonitions" for the war poems and the ultimate demise of the poet. Again, unfortunately, the reader cannot see enough of the poetry or see enough of Blunden's specific reactions to specific pieces to agree with or challenge his position. Instead, that reader must rely on excerpts from Churchill and Dean Inge—in addition to Blunden's overgeneralized comparisons and contrasts of Brooke with Sorley, Grenfell and West—to form any concrete notion about the opportunity of poets and their poetry during times of war.

Geoffrey Bullough (*The Trends of Modern Poetry,* 3rd ed. Edinburgh: Oliver and Boyd, 1949, pp. 46–64, 243–245) briefly, but with acute critical specificity, places Brooke within the context of the Georgian tradition—a term that he defines and explains beyond the superficial terminology of literary history. Thus, the student of Brooke's poetry may see those pieces in relation to the Metaphysicals and other religious poets, to the romantic nostalgia of the pre-Raphaelites, to the realistic impressionists, to the early twentieth-century naturalists. Brooke's work, according to Bullough, ought to be discussed in the same critical breath with Abercrombie, Drinkwater, Flecker, Masefield, Monro, and Turner. He focuses upon the reawakening of "lyrical fervour" as it protested, once more in English social history, the pressure of social change. Brooke moved, according to Bullough, from an imitator of Yeats and the Decadents to a link with Pater and "the enchantment of being for a moment alive in a world of real matter and actual people." Most important, this critic shies away from the false fascination of Brooke's war poetry, leaving that genre for one or two comparative generalizations in his later chapter on the poets of World War II.

"Now that he is in love," writes Hoxie Neale Fairchild of Brooke's *The Call* (written 1905–1908), "what heaven-shattering poetry he can write!" Although a terribly shocking remark for those readers who think of Brooke only as a war poet Fairchild's comments, and the religio-poetic observations that follow, prove especially refreshing in terms of the stereotypes clamped upon Brooke's poetic reputation. Fairchild (*Religious Trends in English Poetry, V: 1880–1920. Gods of a Changing Poetry.* New York: Columbia University Press, 1962, pp. 355–358) notices a number of distinct periods—initiatory, idealistic, mature—and concludes that there exists, beneath Brooke's Byronic swagger and seeming anti-Puritanism, a vein of seriousness. His one complaint focuses upon Brooke's insincerity—or at least an inability to be convincing and consistent in his meandering attempts at self-judgment.

Other Sources

Enright, D. J. "The Literature of the First World War," in *The Modern Age. Volume 7 of the Pelican Guide to English Literature.* ed. Boris Ford. Harmondsworth, Middlesex: Penguin Books, 1961, pp. 154–169. Admittedly, Enright takes his cue from Blunden; yet, he offers a clear and concise outline of the war sonnets (1915).

Phelps, William Lyon, *The Advance of English Poetry in the Twentieth Century.* New York: Dodd, Mead and Company, 1917, pp. 124–130. If nothing else, the opening sentence of Phelps' fifth chapter bears memorization and repetition: "Rupert Brooke left the world in a chariot of fire." Beyond that, Phelps concisely surveys the relationship between the person and the personality, focusing upon those poems written prior to 1914.

Seymour-Smith, Martin, *Guide to Modern World Literature.* New York: Funk and Wagnalls, 1973, pp. 238. A negative view of Brooke as poet, admitting to his "proficiency" as a writer of verse, but also denouncing his "unoriginality" and characterizing, with frankness, "The Soldier" as a bad poem.

Selected Dictionaries and Encyclopedias

Great Writers of the English Language: Poets, St. Martin's Press, 1979. Brief biography and bibliography, in addition to an equally brief critical survey.

Who's Who in Twentieth-Century Literature, Holt, Rinehart and Winston, 1976, pp. 56–58. An objective but superficial discussion of Brooke's life and his poems.

Samuel J. Rogal
Illinois Valley Community College

GWENDOLYN BROOKS
1917

Author's Chronology

Born June 7, 1917, Topeka, Kansas; family settles in Chicago where father finds work as janitor; mother, a former school teacher, cares for Gwendolyn and younger brother Raymond and is active in church work; *1930* Brooks discovers *Writer's Digest,* realizes agonies of writing are widely shared; *1939* marries Henry Blakely; *1940* son, Henry Jr., born; *1941* joins writer's workshop taught by socialite Inez Cunningham Stark; *1943* wins Midwestern Writer's Conference Poetry Award; *1945* publishes *A Street in Bronzeville,* first book of poetry; *1948–1967* reviews books for *Chicago Daily News, Negro Digest* (now *Black World*), *New York Times; 1949* publishes second book of poetry *Annie Allen; 1950* wins Pulitzer Prize; *1951* daughter, Nora, born; *1963–1971* teaches writing at Chicago's Columbia College, Northeastern Illinois State University, University of Wisconsin-Madison; *1967* attends conference at Fisk University which sensitizes her to new militancy among young Blacks; *1968* succeeds Carl Sandburg as Poet Laureate of Illinois; *1969* separates from husband; *1971* heart attack forces resignation as Distinguished Professor at City College of New York; Black-owned Broadside Press, Detroit becomes her publisher; visits East Africa; friends honor her with anthology, *To Gwen with Love; 1972* publishes autobiographical *Report from Part One; 1974* reunites with husband.

Author's Bibliography (selected)

A Street in Bronzeville, 1945 (poems); *Annie Allen,* 1949 (poems); *Maud Martha,* 1953 (novel); *The Bean Eaters,* 1960 (poems); *Selected Poems,* 1963; *In the Mecca,* 1968 (poems); *Riot,* 1970 (poems); *Aloneness,* 1971 (poems); *Family Pictures,* 1971 (poems); *Report from Part One,* 1972 (autobiography); *The Tiger who Wore White Gloves,* 1974 (illustrated children's poem); *Beckonings,* 1975 (poems).

Overview of Biographical Sources

Though her work continues to grow in importance, Brooks has not yet been the subject of a book-length biography. Biographical information is available in standard reference works, in some of the articles and essays listed in R. Baxter Miller's annotated bibliography *Langston Hughes and Gwendolyn Brooks: A Reference Guide* (Boston: G. K. Hall, 1978), and in the prefaces and interviews in *Report from Part One* (Detroit: Broadside Press, 1972). In his critical study *Gwendolyn Brooks* (Boston: Twayne, 1980; see below) Harry B. Shaw devotes a chapter—"The Artist and the Person" (pp. 13–39)—to a survey of formative influences on Brooks' artistic life.

Autobiographical Sources

Brooks generously shares her life with her readers. The persona of such poems as "A Song of the Front Yard" has been identified with Brooks, and her novel *Maud Martha* contains obvious autobiographical elements. Like Brooks as a young girl, the heroine of *Maud Martha* suffers a certain social isolation because of her dark color, her exquisite dresses, and her interest in writing. Much of Brooks' poetry is autobiographical in the sense that it deals, before 1967, with the plight of Modern Urban Blacks and her effort to accommodate the dominant white culture and, after 1967, with the importance of black unity and black pride.

The most notable autobiographical source is *Report from Part One.* As the title suggests, Brooks sees her life as divided by the 1967 conference at Fisk University which awakened her to the current direction of the Black movement and prepared her for a "surprised queenship in the new Black sun." *Report From Part One* contains prefaces by Brooks' long-time associates Don L. Lee and George E. Kent commenting on Brooks' effort to "define one's self from a historically and culturally accurate base." In the title section Brooks identifies strengths she drew from her parents and grandparents, describes childhood activities which influence her life, comments on her marriage and motherhood, and reviews her career as student, teacher and poet. "African Fragment" is a selective journal of a 1971 trip Brooks took to East Africa. Thirty pages of photographs of family and friends and a section of three interviews printed between 1967–1971 comprise the remainder of the book. In an appendix Brooks offers a series of marginal comments on some of her poems and a brief section of personal reminiscences.

Overview of Critical Sources

Though numerous articles have been written about Brooks and she has frequently been considered in books on Black writers, to date Harry Bernard Shaws' *Gwendolyn Brooks* is the only book-length critical study. In *Black Poetry in America* (Baton Rouge: Louisiana State University Press, 1974) Blyden Jackson and Louis D. Rubin, Jr. praise her "universal insights and revelations" and commend her mastery of technique. Arthur P. Davis in *From the Dark Tower* (Washington, DC: Howard University Press, 1974) discusses her changing ideology and concomitant changes in technique. Houston P. Baker's often quoted "The Achievement of Gwendolyn Brooks" (*College Language Association Journal,* Fall, 1972, pp. 23–31) is reprinted in *Singers of Daybreak* (Washington, DC: Howard University Press, 1974). George E. Kent's two part appreciation "The Poetry of Gwendolyn Brooks" appears in *Black World,* Vol. 20 (September, 1971), 30–43 and (October, 1971), 36–48.

Evaluation of Selected Criticism

Shaw, Harry Bernard, *Gwendolyn Brooks.* Boston: Twayne, 1980. After two chapters in which he presents a biographical sketch of Brooks and comments on the physical context out of which her works have grown, Shaw devotes a chapter to each of four major themes in her poetry. In "Death" he discusses her use of both physical and spiritual death as consequences of the Black's oppression by a dominant white culture. In "Fall from Glory" he studies her description of the present life as a Hell which the Black suffers after the Fall. "The Labyrinth" analyzes Brooks' presentation of the Black person's struggle to find his way home, while "Survival" examines Brooks' treatment of the strategies her characters use to survive in an alien world. Shaw includes a separate chapter on the novel *Maud Martha.* The work is prefaced with a chronology and concludes with a selected bibliography. Though he sometimes seems to strain to make the material fit the themes he has chosen to analyze, Shaw's study is balanced overall and helpful. Because Brooks works consistently in shorter forms, Shaws' thematic approach offers a very helpful synthesizing and unifying framework.

Selected Dictionaries and Encyclopedias

American Women Writers, Frederick Ungar, 1979, I, 241–243. Brief evaluation of each major work with short bibliography.

Contemporary Authors, Gale Research, 1967, I, 121–122. A very brief biography and bibliography.

Contemporary Literary Criticism, Gale Research, Vol. I, 45–46, 1973. Short critical appraisals by four critics; Vol. II, 81–82, 1974. Short biography and one assessment of her work; Vol. IV, 78–79, 1975. Short reviews of *Report from Part One.* Vol. XV, 91–95. Excerpts from five anthologized shorter studies of Brooks.

Dictionary of Literary Biography, Gale Research, 1983, pp. 100–106. Concise account of her life with an overview of her works.

Twentieth Century Authors: First Supplement, H. W. Wilson, 1955. Very brief, but useful view of early opinions of Brooks' career.

Richard H. Beckham
University of Wisconsin-River Falls

CHARLES BROCKDEN BROWN
1771–1810

Author's Chronology

Born January 17, 1771, Philadelphia, to Quaker parents; *1781–1786* (or *1787*) attends Friends' Latin School; *1787–1792* studies law and is a member of the Belles Lettres Club; August *1789* publishes "The Rhapsodist," a manneristic collection of four essays; *1790* meets Elihu Hubbard Smith; *1793* yellow fever epidemic in Philadelphia; *1794* visits Smith, now a doctor of medicine, in New York; meets William Dunlap, a playwright and his later biographer, and members of the Friendly Club, an intellectual elite of America; *1795* begins a "Philadelphia novel," probably the first version of *Arthur Mervyn;* visits Dunlap in Perth Amboy; *1796* moves to New York in the summer to start a literary career; *1797* returns to Philadelphia where he completes *Skywalk,* his never published and now lost novel; *1797* arrives in New York in July; in September Smith dies of yellow fever while Brown recuperates from the disease at Dunlaps'; *1798–1801* publishes his major fiction; *1799–1800* serves as editor of *The Monthly Magazine; 1800* returns to Philadelphia; *1801* tours the Hudson; *1803–1806* publishes *The Literary Magazine;* turns to political writing; *1804* marries Elizabeth Linn; develops first symptoms of tuberculosis; *1807* starts *The American Register; 1810* dies on February 21 or 22 in Philadelphia.

Author's Bibliography (selected)

Alcuin (Part I and II), 1798 (fictional dialogue on the rights of women); *Wieland,* 1798 (novel); *Ormond,* 1799 (novel); *Arthur Mervyn* (Part I), 1799 (novel); *Edgar Huntly,* 1799 (novel); *Arthur Mervyn* (Part II), 1800 (novel); *Clara Howard,* 1801 (novel); *Jane Talbot,* 1801 (novel); *Memoirs of Stephen Calvert* (unfinished novel) and "Memoirs of Carwin, the Biloquist" (unfinished sequel to *Wieland*) first appeared in Brown's magazines and were posthumously published in 1815 in Paul Allen and William Dunlap's *The Life of Charles Brockden Brown.*

Overview of Biographical Sources

The primary biographical source for the study of Brown's life and literary career is Paul Allen and William Dunlap's *The Life of Charles Brockden Brown* (Philadelphia, 1815) in two volumes. The first volume was written and compiled by Paul Allen and remained in manuscript form until it was discovered and then published in 1975 under the editorship of Charles E. Bennett (Delmar, NY: Scholars' Facsimiles & Reprints). Dunlap revised and rearranged Allen's first volume and supplied the second one. Dunlap's biography is available on microfilm in major American university libraries. It includes reprints of Brown's writings from literary magazines, his unpublished manuscripts, and much of his correspondence. The biography offers little authorial comment or criticism, however. Allen's introduction and conclusion, on the other hand, provide first serious critical commentary on Brown's work. There are two modern biographies of Brown—Harry Warfel's *Charles Brockden Brown: American Gothic Novelist* (1949) and David Lee Clark's *Charles Brockden Brown: Pioneer Voice of America* (Durham, NC: Duke University Press, 1952). Of the two, Warfel's is more selective and more readable. It offers general descriptions of the themes and plots of Brown's novels to demonstrate the diversity of Brown's interests and the scope of his achievement. Clark's, in a sense, is more important for biographers as it relies extensively on Brown's original materials, including his unpublished letters, but, unfortunately, is unimaginatively written, avoids analysis, and treats Brown's fiction very marginally.

Evaluation of Selected Biographies

Warfel, Harry R. *Charles Brockden Brown: American Gothic Novelist.* Gainesville: University of Florida Press, 1949. Using sources such as Dunlap's *The Life of Charles Brockden Brown,* Elihu Hubbard Smith's *Diary,* and Brown's correspondence, Warfel traces the important stages and incidents of Brown's life to demonstrate the intellectual growth of the first major American novelist. In parts that deal with the description of Brown's fiction, Warfel does not, however, go beyond general and superficial comments. Brown's "gothicism" is not convincingly addressed. Warfel's style lacks vigour and his approach is traditional. Still, unlike Clark's, Warfel's biography has clear coherence, easy-to-follow development, and well-defined purpose.

Overview of Critical Sources

Except for a few early nineteenth-century reviews, Brown's art was largely neglected by critics until the last thirty years, although it was greatly admired by Godwin, the Shelleys, Keats, Poe, and Walter Scott. The revival of interest in Brown's work began in the 1950's and reached its peak in the recent years. Critics, such as Leslie Fiedler, R. W. B. Lewis, and Richard Chase, incorporated a discussion of selected aspects of Brown's work in their studies of American literature. The existing four modern, book-length studies of Brown's art and dozens of articles represent a wide spectrum of critical approaches and testify to the richness and complexity of the novelist's achievement.

Evaluation of Selected Criticism

Axelrod, Alan, *Charles Brockden Brown. An American Tale.* Austin: University of Texas Press, 1983. This is a very well-documented study of Brown. Axelrod draws from many different historical and literary sources as well as from modern ideas and critical methodology to place both Brown's work and personality in a rich cultural, social, historical, and moral climate of America at the turn of the century. The author's arguments, although sometimes speculative, are very forcefully presented and in all cases help us further appreciate Brown's art.

Grabo, Norman S. *The Coincidental Art of Charles Brockden Brown.* Chapel Hill: University of North Carolina Press, 1981. Grabo thoroughly investigates, through a close reading and analysis of the novels, the narrative, structural, and thematic aspects of Brown's fiction to reveal the recurrent motifs, patterns, techniques, and their respective significance. Grabo concentrates especially on the function of Brown's "coincidental doubling" of events, characters, and motifs. Grabo's style is lively and lucid, his observations and conclusions are convincingly substantiated by Brown's texts. The book is addressed to a patient and careful reader of Brown.

Ringe, Donald A. *Charles Brockden Brown.* New York: Twayne, 1966. Ringe introduces the modern reader to the scope and quality of Brown's artistic achievement. Brown's four major novels are discussed in separate chapters. The book also includes a brief examination of Brown's minor fiction and his uncompleted works. The restrained objectivity, non-commitment to any particular methodological bias invite the reader to explore the potential inherent in Brown's fiction.

Other Sources

Berthoff, Warner B. " 'A Lesson on Concealment': Brockden Brown's Method in Fiction," *Philological Quarterly,* 37 (1958), 45-57. Berthoff uses Brown's short story to demonstrate that the novelist treated his fiction as "an instrument for discovering ideas, for exploring and testing them out."

Brancaccio, Patrick, "Studied Ambiguities: *Arthur Mervyn* and the Problem of the Unreliable Narrator," *American Literature,* 42 (1970), 18-27. Brancaccio shows how in *Arthur Mervyn,* Brown effectively employs multiple points of view and "nested" narration to portray the entrance of his ambiguous protagonist into a complex, fluid, and deceptive world.

Kimball, Arthur G. *Rational Fictions: A Study of Charles Brockden Brown.* McMinnville, OR: Linfield Research Institute, 1968. Brown's four major novels are discussed as a reflection of the ideological confrontation between the forces of Enlightenment and early Romanticism.

Hedges, William, "Charles Brockden Brown and the Culture of Contradictions," *Early American Literature,* 9 (1974), 107-142. Hedges argues that Brown's fictional world and his characters reflect the struggle of the new American society to define its cultural and national identity.

Hume, Robert D. "Charles Brockden Brown and the Uses of Gothicism: A Reassessment," *ESQ,* 66 (1972), 10–18. A very lucid and convincing demonstration that Brown's art stands on its own and escapes labels and easy definition.

Manly, William M. "The Importance of Point of View in Brockden Brown's *Wieland,*" *American Literature,* 35 (1963), 311-321. Manly sees Clara Wieland's narration as a reflection of the conflict between Brown's rational mind and his fascination with the Gothic and the sentimental.

Parker, Patricia, *Charles Brockden Brown: A Reference Guide.* Boston: G. K. Hall, 1980. An annotated guide to biography and criticism on Brown from early reviews through the 1970's.

Ringe, Donald A. *American Gothic.* Lexington: University Press of Kentucky, 1982. Ringe demonstrates Brown's originality as a creator of a serious, psychological type of the Gothic.

Rosenthal, Bernard, ed. *Critical Essays on Charles Brockden Brown.* Boston: G. K. Hall, 1981. A collection of early and modern critical essays on Brown followed by a selective bibliography.

Selected Dictionaries

American Writers Before 1800: A Biographical and Critical Dictionary, 1983. A brief biography and a critical appraisal by Donald Ringe.

American Writers: A Collection of Literary Biographies, 1979. A twenty-page biographical and critical essay by Emory Elliott. Very useful introductory material.

Tomasz Warchol
Georgia Southern College

SIR THOMAS BROWNE
1605–1682

Author's Chronology

Born October 19, 1605, London; *1613* Browne's father dies; *1614* his mother marries Sir Thomas Dutton; *1616–1623* attends Winchester College; *1623* matriculated at Broadgates Hall, Oxford; *1624* delivers Latin oration in ceremonies inaugurating Broadgates Hall as Pembroke College; *1626* admitted to the degree of Master of Arts; visits Ireland; *1629–1633* pursues medical studies at Montpellier, Padua, and Leyden; *1633* admitted to the M.D. at Leyden; *1635–1637* performs medical apprenticeship at Oxfordshire; *1637* admitted to M.D. degree at Oxford; settles at Norwich and remains till the end of his life; *1641* marries Dorothy Mileham, who bears him twelve children; *1664* elected Fellow of the Royal College of Physicians; testifies at Bury St. Edmunds in witchcraft trial; *1667* knighted by Charles II at Norwich; *1682* dies October 19, on his 77th birthday.

Author's Bibliography

Religio Medici, 1642 (autobiographical essay); *Pseudodoxia Epidemica,* 1646 (scientific essay); *Hydriotaphia* (*Urn Burial*) (essay) and *The Garden of Cyrus,* 1658 (essay); *Letter To A Friend,* 1690; *Christian Morals.* ed. J. Jeffery, 1916 (aphorisms); *Selected Writings.* ed. Geoffrey Keynes. Chicago: University of Chicago Press, 1964; *Religio Medici and Other Works.* ed. L. C. Martin. Oxford: Oxford University Press, 1964; *Works.* ed. Sir Geoffrey Keynes, 2nd ed. 4 vols. Chicago: University of Chicago Press, 1964; *The Major Works.* ed. C. A. Patrides. Hammondsworth: Penguin, 1977.

Overview of Biographical Sources

Biographies of Browne are scarce. The only full-length biographical study is Jeremiah S. Finch's *Sir Thomas Browne,* 1950. Prior to this solid, readable account of Browne's life, readers had to settle for the often superficial and inaccurate volume by Edmund Gosse: *Sir Thomas Browne* (London: Macmillan, 1905) which, like most subsequent books on Browne, mixes biography with criticism. An accurate chapter-length account of Browne's life can be found in the opening chapter of Joan Bennett's *Sir Thomas Browne* (Cambridge: Cambridge University Press, 1962). Similar in length but more analytical in approach is Peter Green's *Sir Thomas Browne* in the Writers and Their Work Series (1959). For a slightly fuller portrait there is the first part of F. L. Huntley's *Sir Thomas Browne* (1962). Of these three overviews, Bennett's sticks closest to a chronicle of Browne's life, while Green and Huntley better convey the intellectual climate in which he lived and wrote. Emphasizing the scientific and philosophical cast of Browne's mind, Green sees him as "a quintessential Englishman: ironic, melancholy, learned, humorous, eccentric." Less concerned with identifying Browne's cast of mind, like Green, or with rehearsing the bare facts of his life, like Bennett, Huntley illuminates the world in which he lived, depicting especially the relationship between science and religion in England and on the continent.

Evaluation of Selected Biographies

Finch, Jeremiah S. *Sir Thomas Browne.* New York: Henry Schuman, 1950. Although this work cannot be considered the definitive study of Browne's life, largely because of its lack of psychological analysis, it does present a useful portrait of Browne. Equally important is its presentation of background information on the state of medical practice in Browne's day along with an informed discussion of the significance of Browne's antiquarianism. Photographs of the medical schools at Padua and Leyden, of a manuscript fragment from *Urn Burial,* of Browne's places of worship, of his contemporaries, and of his exhumed skull complement the text.

Green, Peter, *Sir Thomas Browne.* London: Longmans, Green, 1959. This economical account surveys the main outlines of Browne's career while illuminating simultaneously both his philosophy of life and his scientific method. Unlike Finch's book, which emphasizes the external life, Green sheds light on Browne's inner life in its eclecticism and paradoxes.

Huntley, Frank Livingstone, *Sir Thomas Browne: A Biographical and Critical Study.* Ann Arbor: University of Michigan Press, 1962. A good scholar with a lively readable style, F. L. Huntley examines Browne's life, education, religious beliefs, and scientific views. Especially useful are Huntley's concise chapters on the religious and scientific milieu. Addressed to a general audience as well as to students and scholars, Huntley's work is the best introduction to Browne's life and work.

Autobiographical Sources

Browne never wrote a work either entitled "Autobiography" or primarily intended as a life history. The essential features of his autobiography, however, are available in the *Religio Medici* and his correspondences. The letters to his family depict an intimate knowledge of his domestic relationships. They also provide a striking contrast in style, tone, and structure with his published writings like the *Religio Medici.* Rich in self-revelation and strewn with odd bits of biography, the *Religio Medici* is fundamentally a spiritual testament, an *apologia* for Browne's way of reconciling science and religion, faith and imagination. It is one of the great personal documents and one of the true monuments of English prose.

Overview of Critical Sources

Critical books about Browne's work focus more on his mind than his art. Nearly all treat Browne as a figure in intellectual history—a natural philosopher, antiquarian, or physician rather than as a literary artist. Such volumes include W. P. Dunn's *Sir Thomas Browne: A Study in Religious Philosophy* (Minneapolis, 1950). This incisive work compares favorably with another often inaccurate study, *Outflying Philosophy* (London, 1923), by R. Sencourt. Another excellent little volume is E. S. Merton's *Science and Imagination in Sir Thomas Browne* (New York: Kings Crown Press, 1949), which includes engaging observations on Browne's scientific, philosophical, and artistic imagination.

Two books that approach Browne more fully as a writer while also doing justice to his thought are the two single most important works for a study of his mind and art: the previously mentioned critical biography by F. L. Huntley, *Sir Thomas Browne,* 1962, and Leonard Nathanson's perceptive and learned *The Strategy of Truth,* 1967. Also important, though of much briefer scope, is the graceful introduction to C. A. Patrides's edition of Browne's *Major Works,* 1977. Entitled " 'Above Atlas His Shoulders': An Introduction to Sir Thomas Browne," Patrides's essay is the best brief approach to Browne's writings, impeccable in its scholarship and richly suggestive in relating Browne's writing to his precursors and his contemporaries. Patrides's introduction is handsomely complemented by an appendix which includes the first important criticism on Browne, Samuel Johnson's *The Life of Sir Thomas Browne,* first published in 1756 when it was prefixed to an edition of *Christian Morals.* Aside from its historical value as the first and one of the best analyses of Browne's prose style, Johnson's brief critical biography sheds light on both writer and subject as prose stylists and as Christian moralists.

Evaluation of Selected Criticism

Huntley, Frank Livingstone, *Sir Thomas Browne: A Biographical and Critical Study.* Ann Arbor: University of Michigan Press, 1962. More critically analytical than biographically informative, Huntley's book includes influential discussions of *Religio Medici, Urn Burial* and *The Garden of Cyrus.* In an important contribution to the study of *Urn Burial* and *Cyrus,* Huntley argues convincingly that any analysis of one must include the other since they stand together by design. An additional attractive feature of Huntley's book is his sensible discussion of *A Letter To a Friend,* a charming piece too often overlooked in favor of Browne's more famous and ambitious works.

Patrides, C. A. ed. *Approaches to Sir Thomas Browne.* Columbia: University of Missouri Press, 1982. This recent collection of fifteen essays offers a range of informed criticism both literary and intellectual-historical. Including some of the best analysis in nearly two decades, this volume re-establishes Browne's position as an important seventeenth-century artist.

Wise, James N. *Sir Thomas Browne's Religio Medici and Two Seventeenth-Century Critics.* Columbia: University of Missouri Press, 1973. This unusual book contains a summary of controversial issues in the *Religio* along with an analysis of two critical responses from critics of Browne's own time, Sir Kenelm Digby and Alexander Ross. Wise reconstructs the arguments, quoting liberally from all three, thus enriching the reader's understanding of Browne's work while opening a window on the intellectual currents in seventeenth-century England.

Other Sources

Fish, Stanley, "Sir Thomas Browne: The Bad Physician," in *Self-Consuming Artifacts: The Experience of Seventeenth-Century Literature.* Berkeley: University of California Press, 1973. An ingenious and engaging misreading of *Religio Medici* that focuses on style, especially on the reader's responses to the emerging text.

Keynes, Sir Geoffrey, *A Bibliography of Sir Thomas Browne.* Oxford: Clarendon, 1968. A scholarly comprehensive bibliography that requires only slight updating.

Miller, Edmund, "The Browne Doublet: *Religio Medici* in the History of English Prose Style," in *Bulletin of Research in the Humanities,* 82 (Summer 1979), 213-221. A perceptive analysis of the epistemological implications of one of Browne's most notorious stylistic habits.

Warren, Austen, "The Styles of Sir Thomas Browne," in *Connections.* Ann Arbor: University of Michigan Press, 1970. A good introduction to Browne's varied styles, high, middle, and low, but oversimplifies the way these styles are deployed in the works.

Robert DiYanni
Pace University

ELIZABETH BARRETT BROWNING
1806–1861

Author's Chronology

Born March 6, 1806 near Durham, England; *1809* the Barretts move to Hope End, in Herefordshire; Elizabeth is educated at home; *1821* and for many years after experiences a series of illnesses; *1826* publishes *An Essay on Mind, with Other Poems; 1835* after financial reverses the Barretts move to London, where she publishes widely in periodicals; *1838* leaves London for Torquay, where it is hoped the sea air will be beneficial to her diseased lungs; *1840* her brother Edward is drowned in a boating accident at Torquay; Elizabeth returns to London and lives in seclusion, rarely leaving her room in the family home at 50 Wimpole Street; her popular volume *Poems* (1844) brings about a correspondence with Robert Browning, then an obscure poet; after a secret courtship of nearly a year and a half, she secretly marries Robert on September 12, 1846, at Saint Marylebone Parish Church; a week later the couple leaves for Italy; *1849* a son, Robert Wiedeman Barrett Browning, is born; travels extensively during the next ten years in Venice, Paris, and England; never sees her father again; *1855* publication of her "novel in verse," *Aurora Leigh,* makes her a celebrity; dies in Florence June 29, 1861.

Author's Bibliography (selected)

An Essay on Mind, with Other Poems, 1826; *Prometheus Bound, Translated from the Greek of Aeschylus: And Miscellaneous Poems,* 1833; *Poems,* 1844 (two volumes); *Poems,* new edition (containing *Sonnets from the Portugese),* 1850; *Casa Guidi Windows. A Poem,* 1851; *Aurora Leigh,* 1857 (poem); *Poems before Congress,* 1860.

Overview of Biographical Sources

The life of Elizabeth Barrett Browning was fascinating to the public almost from the very beginning. However, the "Browning legend" tended to overshadow or even obscure the literary achievements. Gardner Taplin's 1957 biography was therefore a landmark in treating both the life and the literary works thoroughly. The 1960's saw a number of previously unavailable letters and diaries published, providing additional sources for biographical treatment, and the 1970's saw a feminist turn to the interpretation of both the poet and the poetry. The student should be aware, too, of the importance of biographical material concerning Robert Browning to the study of Barrett Browning. One such source is Betty Bergson Miller's *Robert Browning: A Portrait* (New York: Charles Scribner's Sons, 1953, rpt. 1973). Not to be overlooked is Virginia Woolf's delightful *Flush, A Biography* (New York: Harcourt Brace and World, 1933), which describes the Browning/Barrett affair through the eyes of her dog.

Evaluation of Selected Biographies

Grebanier, Frances, *Immortal Lovers: Elizabeth Barrett and Robert Browning.* New York: Harper and Brothers, 1950. Written in popular style, this account of the Browning love affair and marriage is highly romanticized, although it is written from a solid basis in fact. It is, however, of little use to scholars.

Hewlett, Dorothy, *Elizabeth Barrett Browning: A Life.* New York: Octagon Books, 1952, 1972. Hewlett wrote this book to change the public image of Barrett Browning from that of the wife of Robert Browning, heroine of a romantic love story, to that of a poet in her own right. In doing so she hoped to create an interest in reading the poetry. Hewlett's book is good reading, but sparsely documented.

Lupton, Mary J. *Elizabeth Barrett Browning.* Long Island, NY: Feminist Press, 1972. Part of a series published to "rediscover and recreate the history and achievements of women," this brief (103 page) biography not only reinterprets the life of the poet, but attempts to provide the reader with tools for doing such reinterpretation. It is written at a fairly basic level, and is not extensively documented.

McAleer, Edward C. *The Brownings of Casa Guidi.* New York: The Browning Institute, 1979. This book, dealing with the Florence years of Robert Browning and Barrett Browning, provides a chronological ordering of events there, but also adds a wealth of detail concerning the local scene and relationships with other expatriots. It includes photographs and other material of interest, but provides little in the way of documentation that would enhance follow-up for the student.

Radley, Virginia L. *Elizabeth Barrett Browning.* New York: Twayne, 1972. Radley has tried to respond to a 1968 call by Michael Timko for more critical assessments of Barrett Browning's work, both as a whole and as studies of individual works. As a result, this book is useful both as a brief, readable biography and as a critical guide to the poetry. Radley hopes that the book will be useful in suggesting future critical directions. There is an annotated bibliography.

Taplin, Gardner B. *The Life of Elizabeth Barrett Browning.* New Haven: Yale University Press, 1957, and Hamden, CT: Archon, 1970. Many years in the making, this biography is still one of the most important. Since it made use of much previously unavailable material, it provided, at the time of its first appearance, some new approaches to Barrett Browning. Taplin's final chapter summarizes the history of Barrett Browning criticism.

Autobiographical Sources

Two important diary sources are *The Barretts at Hope End: The Early Diary of Elizabeth Barrett Browning* (Elizabeth Berridge, ed. London: J. Murray,

1974) and *Diary by EBB: The Unpublished Diary of Elizabeth Barrett Browning, 1831–1832* (Philip Kelley and Ronald Hudson, eds. Athens: Ohio University Press, 1969). The latter includes psychoanalytic observations by Robert Coles. Collections of letters abound, for Barrett Browning was a prolific letter writer, and moreover, was inclined to include in these letters important discussions of her philosophy concerning her art and its meaning. Naturally, the love letters are of popular interest. A selection of these is found in *How Do I Love Thee? The Love Letters of Robert Browning and Elizabeth Barrett* (selected and with an introduction by V. E. Stack, New York: P. G. Putnam, 1969). Another collection is the two-volume set edited by Elvan Kintner, *The Letters of Robert Browning and Elizabeth Barrett Browning, 1845–1846* (Cambridge: Harvard University Press, 1969). Including a thorough introduction, this work is a revision of an 1899 text which had many inaccuracies. Other letter collections include *Letters to Mrs. David Ogilvy, 1849–1861, with Recollections by Mrs. Ogilvy* (Peter N. Heydon and Philip Kelley, eds. New York: Quadrangle, 1973).

Overview of Critical Sources

As a subject for critical study, Elizabeth Browning was not widely regarded until the 1960's when Taplin called for more critical attention, and then the 1970's when a feminist re-evaluation of her prompted another approach. It is to be expected, then, that her poem *Aurora Leigh,* dealing as it does with the problem of the female artist in the 19th-century society, would receive attention. One important essay pre-dating those revaluations was Virginia Woolf's essay "Aurora Leigh," published in *The Common Reader, Second Series* (New York: Harcourt, Brace and World, 1932), which calls the book one that "still lives and can be read." Two important works of feminist criticism that deal with Barrett Browning (although neither devotes a whole chapter to her) are Ellen Moers' *Literary Women* (Garden City, NY: Doubleday, 1976) and Sandra Gilbert and Susan Gubar's *The Madwoman in the Attic: The Woman Writer and the Nineteenth-Century Literary Imagination* (New Haven: Yale University Press, 1979). Virginia Radley's biography (see *Evaluation of Selected Biographies*) also serves as a fine introduction to the criticism and a suggestion for further study.

Three recent articles, all appearing in *Victorian Poetry,* provide excellent examples of a feminist re-evaluation of Barrett Browning. Two of these deal with *Aurora Leigh:* Barbara Charlesworth Gelpi's "*Aurora Leigh:* The Vocation of the Woman Poet," Vol. 19 (Spring 1981), 35–48, and Virginia V. Steinmetz's "Images of 'Mother-Want' in Elizabeth Barrett Browning's *Aurora Leigh,*" Vol. 21 (Winter 1983), 351–367. Gelpi's article is significant in showing the interaction of that work with other Victorian writers. Steinmetz interprets the work as revealing a sense of maternal abandonment. Sandra Donaldson's article " 'Motherhood's Advent in Power': Elizabeth Barrett Browning's Poems about

Motherhood," Vol. 18, 51–60, compares her poems written before and after the birth of her child.

Evaluation of Selected Criticism

Hayter, Alethea, *Mrs. Browning: A Poet's Work and Its Setting.* London: Faber and Faber, 1962. This harbinger of renewed critical interest in Barrett Browning's poetry traces the development of her theory and practice. Most discussions, however, are descriptive rather than evaluative.

Other Sources

Barnes, Warner, *A Bibliography of Elizabeth Barrett Browning.* Austin: University of Texas and Baylor University, 1967. Only descriptive bibliography of Barrett Browning's work.

Hudson, Gladys W. *An Elizabeth Barrett Browning Concordance.* Detroit: Gale Research, 1973.

Selected Dictionaries and Encyclopedias

Critical Survey of Poetry, Salem Press, 1982. Good brief biography and overview of her work.

Moulton's Library of Literary Criticism, Vol. 3, Frederick Ungar. Excerpts from early assessments of her work.

Linda Yoder
West Virginia University

ROBERT BROWNING
1812–1889

Author's Chronology

Born May 7, 1812, in Chamberwell, a London suburb, of middle-class parents; *1826* discovers Shelley's poetry; temporarily becomes a vegetarian and atheist; *1833* anonymously publishes first poem, *Pauline; 1834* travels to Russia with his father; *1834* makes first trip to Italy: *1840* publishes *Sordello* under his name to detriment of his literary reputation; *1841–1846* attempts to write for theatre and produces several unsuccessful dramas; *1846* secretly marries Elizabeth Barrett and elopes to the continent; *1847* settles in Florence, Italy, at the Casa Guidi, his residence for seventeen years; *1855* publishes *Men and Women,* a critical and popular success; *1861* Elizabeth dies and Browning returns to London; *1869* proposes marriage, unsuccessfully, to Lady Ashburton; *1870–1879* leads an active social life, becoming a "literary lion" in upper-class London society; *1880* Browning Societies are formed; *1887* supervises the 16-volume complete edition of his poems; *1889* dies in Venice, Italy, on December 12, and is buried on December 31 in "Poet's Corner" in Westminster Abbey.

Author's Bibliography (selected)

Pauline, 1833 (poem); *Strafford,* 1837 (verse play); *Sordello,* 1940 (poem); *Dramatic Lyrics,* 1842 (poems); *Christmas Eve and Easter Day,* 1849 (poem); *Men and Women,* 1855 (poems); *Dramatic Personae,* 1864 (poems); *The Ring and the Book,* 1869 (poem); *Dramatic Idyls,* 1879 (poems); *Parleyings with Certain People of Importance,* 1887 (poems); *Asolando,* 1889 (poem).

Overview of Biographical Sources

Robert Browning was a man of anomalous character, a trait noticed by Henry James who wrote a novelette entitled *The Private Life* (1892) that is a thinly disguised story about Browning's dual personality. While not a full-scale biography, James's fictional treatment is a suggestive approach to Browning's life. His interpretation of Browning is that he was two people—a bourgeois social climber on one hand and on the other a poet of genius. The gap between Browning the public figure and Browning the private man is a problem taken up by more orthodox biographers. One of the earliest efforts to understand Browning's life was Edmund Gosse's *Robert Browning: Personalia* (London: Fisher and Unwin, 1890), which is more a tribute to Browning by a close acquaintance than an interpretative biography. A more interesting early life is Mrs. Sutherland Orr's two-volume *Life and Letters of Robert Browning* (London: Bell & Sons, 1891), which is the nearest to being an "official" biography, since she knew Browning personally and had access to some of his private papers and correspondences. The early biographers of Browning tend toward sympathy or else blandness, as is the case with the first full-scale biography, *The Life of Robert Browning* by W. H. Griffin and H. C. Minchin (1910, revised 1938), the standard life for decades. In the 1950's there was a turn to more interpretative approaches to Browning's life, such as Betty Miller's *Robert Browning: A Portrait* (1952), which relies on Freudian analysis, and J. M. Cohen's *Robert Browning* (1952), a brief revisionary study that focuses more on the poems than the life, cutting Browning away from the Victorian view of the poet as prophet. Maisie Ward's *Robert Browning and His World,* 2 vols. (1967), is a "big-book" biography that develops even further the "Two Brownings" theory that James originated. The most complete and balanced account of Browning's life yet to appear is by William Irvine and Park Honan, *The Book, the Ring, and the Poet* (1974), which supersedes Griffin and Minchin as the definitive biography. It is a judicious blend of the factual and interpretative, a major reassessment of Browning's life and works. In addition to the scholarly and academic accounts of Browning's life, there have been several overly romanticized books about the famous courtship and elopement with Elizabeth Barrett. Some studies which focus on this phase of Browning's life are Rudolf Besier's *The Barretts of Wimpole Street* (Boston: Little Brown, 1930) and Frances Winwar's *The Immortal Lovers* (New York: Harper, 1950).

Selective Evaluation of Major Biographies

Griffin, W. H. and H. C. Minchin, *The Life of Robert Browning With Notices of His Writing, His Family, and His Friends.* New York: Macmillan, 1910, revised 1938. Long the standard "life," this biography provides a factual and full account of the early life of Browning, but is extremely bland and very reticent about the last part of his career, judiciously omitting mention of his relationships with Julia Wedgwood and Isabella Blagden. Even the 1938 revision leaves large gaps in the record, either out of politeness or lack of knowledge.

Irvin, William and Park Honan, *The Book, the Ring, and the Poet: A Biography of Robert Browning.* New York: McGraw Hill, 1974. A good example of modern biographical scholarship, this is a meticulous, detailed account of Browning's life that goes beyond earlier "official" biographies. The poetry is put accurately against the events of the poet's life, which is told so as to make a good story. While not as successful in explaining Browning's psychological and intellectual positions, the authors are good in tracing his dependence on his mother's religious conceptions and the Shelleyan influence on his ideas about the function of poetry.

Miller, Betty, *Robert Browning: A Portrait.* New York: Charles Scribner's Sons, 1952. A well-written biography that employs Freudian analysis, this book offers the thesis that Browning was psychologically dependent upon his mother well into his adult life, and that he was conditioned by her to need women who would dictate to him. Mrs. Miller's was the first interpretative biography and offered many new—and sometimes forced—psychoanalytical views. This is an enjoyable book to read, but one should be wary of its conclusions.

Ward, Maisie, *Robert Browning and His World.* 2 vols. New York: Holt, Rinehart and Winston, 1967, 1969. Providing a more restrained reading of Robert Browning's life than Miller, Ward tends to theorize where she does not always have facts. Ward tries to reconcile the simple character of Browning with his complex intellect, but is not totally convincing. Nevertheless, this biography makes an attempt at a comprehensive, factual reconstruction of Browning's life against the background of his times.

Autobiography

Browning did not write an autobiography and so the main source of autobiographical materials is his letters. There is no collected edition of his letters at present, though one has long been projected. Until it appears, it is necessary to use editions of letters to various individuals distributed among several volumes, such as *Dearest Isa: Robert Browning's Letters to Isabella Blagden* (Austin: University of Texas, 1951), or *Learned Lady: Letters from Robert Browning to Mrs. Thomas Fitzgerald,* ed. E. C. McAleer (Cambridge: Harvard University Press, 1966), an inconvenient and distracting process for the casual reader and the researcher alike. Of the 5,000 extant letters by Browning, some 3,000 have never been printed; this is because much of his correspondence is dull. Browning tended to destroy his letters and most of those that have survived are mundane. The exception is his famous love letters that fully reveal the state of his emotions. These important letters are collected in the two-volume *Letters of Robert Browning and Elizabeth Barrett 1845–46,* Elvan Kinter, ed. (Cambridge: Harvard University Press, 1969).

Although Robert Browning published no literary criticism during his lifetime, he did write an essay on Shelley in 1851 which was to have introduced a volume of letters but was withdrawn when they were discovered to be forgeries. Donald Smalley's edition of *Browning's Essay on Shelley* (Cambridge: Harvard University Press, 1948) is the best edition, containing an insightful introduction by W. C. DeVane.

Overview of Critical Sources

In the Victorian period the critical emphasis was on Browning's role as a philosophical sage or a religious teacher. During the course of Browning's career he went from being censured for obscurity to being praised for being an optimistic prophet. His early admirers who formed the Browning societies tried to promote the understanding and appreciation of his poetry. The objections to Browning's "difficulties" were overcome as he was turned into an oracle. Most of the writing done on Browning was not analytical in the modern critical sense, and it was not until the middle of the 20th century that Browning's criticism showed any sophistication. Critics and scholars revealed parts or aspects of Browning's canon, but there was no full-length study. The nearest thing to such a book was Clyde DeVane's justly famous *Browning Handbook* (1935), which provided useful commentary on all of the verse and summarized the scholarship on each poem.

In general, modern critics have found Browning's technique more interesting than his message and see in his poetry an experimental quality that anticipated modern verse, making him seem more contemporary than other Victorian poets. Recent critical approaches to Browning are represented by E. D. H. Johnson's *The Alien Vision of Victorian Poetry* (Princeton: Princeton University Press, 1952), Roma King's *The Bow and the Lyre* (1957), and Park Honan's *Browning's Characters* (New Haven: Yale University Press, 1961). Each of these books offers a detailed examination of Browning's poetry. Johnson and Langbaum use theoretical and historical approaches while King and Honan apply the technique of close textual analysis favored by the New Criticism to illuminate Browning's technical achievements as a poet. More recently, critics have attempted to evaluate and to explicate Browning's individual poems. Several long studies have been done on *The Ring and the Book,* the *magnum opus* among the dramatic monologues which has been most fully dealt with by Richard Altick in *Browning's Roman Murder Story* (1968). Perhaps the most extreme case of narrow critical focus is R. J. Berman's *Browning's Duke* (New York: Rogess Press, 1972) where a book of 135 pages is devoted to the fifty-six lines of "My Last Duchess," tracing its historical sources and summarizing much of the previous criticism and scholarship on this famous dramatic monologue.

Evaluation of Selected Criticism

DeVane, W. C. *A Browning Handbook.* New York: Crofts, 1935, rev. 1955. Long the standard handbook, DeVane's has been called the "most useful single commentary on Browning ever written." It contains much valuable information on the sources, influences, and composition dates of all of Browning's poems. More scholarly than critical in nature, DeVane's handbook occasionally offers useful judgments on poems and makes sensible conjectures about the meaning of lines. Norton B. Crowell's *A Browning Guide,* University of New Mexico Press, 1972, supplements and modifies some of DeVane's views.

Drew, Philip, *The Poetry of Browning: A Critical Introduction.* London: Methuen, 1970. In this study the author argues for Browning's critical acceptance despite his overlay of Victorian views, easy optimism and muscular Christianity. This is a good book to help understand both Browning and his age. Drew also refutes Langbaum's view that Browning was morally a relativist.

Jack, Ian, *Browning's Major Poetry.* Oxford: Clarendon Press, 1973. This is a scholarly treatment that provides satisfactory discussions of individual works but is best for locating Browning's poetry in the main tradition of English poetry. Jack shows the variety and richness of Browning's poetic techniques, and traces the sources of and influences on various poems.

King, Roma A. *The Bow and the Lyre: The Art of Robert Browning.* Ann Arbor: University of Michigan Press, 1957. Providing a close analysis of some of Browning's most famous dramatic monologues, King uses textual criticism to show the technical, emotional, and intellectual features of "Andrea del Sarto," "Fra Lippo Lippi," "The Bishop Orders His Tomb," "Bishop Blougham" and "Saul." Another study by the same author is *The Focusing Artifice* (Athens, OH: Ohio University Press, 1968) that concentrates on four poems: *Sordello, The Ring and the Book, Fifine at the Fair,* and *Parleyings with Certain People of Importance.*

Ryals, Clyde, *Becoming Browning: The Poems and Plays of Robert Browning, 1833–1884.* Columbus: Ohio State University Press, 1984. Providing a careful reading of Browning's poems and plays between 1833 and 1846, Ryals completes his earlier examination of Browning's *Later Poetry* (Ithaca: Cornell University Press, 1976), 1876–1889. Ryals holds the view that Robert Browning's development as a poet was congruent with a growing sense of irony which enabled him to subdue a tendency toward Victorian didactics.

Other Sources

Peterson, William, ed. *Browning Institute Studies.* 12 vols. College Park: University of Maryland. Begun in 1973 as the yearbook of the Institute, this scholarly periodical published longer articles about the Brownings as well as other aspects of Victorian literary and cultural history. While academic in nature, the journal is written for the non-specialist, too, with emphasis on bibliographic and historical rather than analytical articles.

Woolford, John, ed. *Browning Society Notes.* 14 vols. London: Browning Society. In 1970 this magazine was started as the organ of the New Browning Society. An attractive quarterly, it carries short items on particular topics concerning Robert and Elizabeth Browning for the purpose of educating the public to appreciate the Brownings.

Selected Dictionaries and Encyclopedias

Critical Survey of Poetry, Salem Press, 1983. Contains a twelve-page essay that summarizes Browning's achievements, his life, and gives a brief analysis of selected major poems.

Hallman B. Bryant
Clemson University

JOHN BUCHAN
1875–1940

Author's Chronology

Born August 26, 1875, Perth, Scotland, the son of a Free Church minister; *1895* enters Brasenose College, Oxford; *1899–1901* studies for the Bar in London and writes for the *Spectator; 1901–1903* secretary to Lord Milner in South Africa; *1906* joins the publishing firm of Thomas Nelson and Sons; *1907* marries Susan Grosvenor; *1915* reports on the Western Front for the *Times; 1916* becomes a major in the Intelligence Corps; has a serious duodenal attack; *1918* made a Director in the Ministry of Information; *1919* becomes Director of Reuters news agency; buys Elsfield Manor; *1927–1935* elected MP for the Scottish Universities; *1933, 1934* appointed High Commissioner to the General Assembly of the Church of Scotland; *1935* created Baron Tweedsmuir of Elsfield and made Governor-General of Canada; *1940* dies in Ottawa of cerebral thrombosis.

Author's Bibliography (selected)

Nelson's History of the War, 1915–1919 (history); *The Thirty-Nine Steps,* 1915 (novel); *Midwinter,* 1923 (novel); *Witch Wood,* 1927 (novel); *Montrose,* 1928 (biography); *Sir Walter Scott,* 1932 (biography); *Memory Hold-the-Door* (American title, *Pilgrim's Way*), 1940 (autobiography); *Sick Heart River* (American title, *Mountain Meadow*), 1941 (novel).

Overview of Biographical Sources

Although the facts of John Buchan's life are fairly clear, his accomplishments as novelist, historian, statesman, barrister, journalist, and publisher, as well as the many facets of his personality, have provided material for several biographies. Much of the work is in the form of personal reminiscences by family and friends giving perceptive but limited views of Buchan. Only Janet Adam Smith's biography takes a broad overview of Buchan's life, yet she misses much of the personal side of Buchan. Some of the later biographies defend Buchan against charges of racism, jingoism, snobbery, and related matters that have been made against him by liberal critics.

Evaluation of Selected Biographies

Adam Smith, Janet, *John Buchan.* London: Rupert Hart-Davis, 1965. This detailed and comprehensive study is the definitive Buchan biography. Adam Smith, a friend of Buchan and his family, covers all phases of Buchan's career with accuracy and sympathy, using documents, letters, private papers, and interviews. The book includes lengthy chapters on Buchan's fiction and historical writings. Buchan's private life, however, is covered with less depth and

Adam Smith avoids deep psychological probing. Though cumbersome, this book is indispensible for serious students of Buchan's life. Adam Smith's later biography, *John Buchan and his World* (New York: Charles Scribner's Sons, 1979), a shorter and lavishly illustrated work incorporating some newly discovered documents, might be better for the casual reader.

Buchan, Susan, *John Buchan by his Wife and Friends.* London: Hodder and Stroughton, 1947. Lady Tweedsmuir gives an account of Buchan's life and brings together writings on Buchan by Stanley Baldwin, Catherine Carswell, A. L. Rowse, Janet Adam Smith, Alastair Buchan, and others. The book also includes portraits of some of Buchan's friends not discussed in his autobiography. Though unsystematic, this biography sheds light on several phases of Buchan's life by those who knew them best. Thus, Charles Dick, an old friend, writes of Buchan's childhood, Walter Elliot of his parliamentary career, and so on. Its value lies in these special insights rather than a comprehensive view of Buchan's life and work.

Buchan, William, *John Buchan: a Memoir.* London: Buchan and Enright, 1982. Buchan's third son gives an engaging account of the private side of his father's life. Though William Buchan writes of his father with sympathy and respect, he also reveals Buchan's limitations and failings. Buchan thus comes across as a more human and approachable figure than in the earlier biographies. William Buchan provides little analysis or background information on Buchan's writings, but he does complain of modern critical coldness to Buchan, based, he feels, on the critical shift away from the well told story to more experimental fictional techniques and the unfashionableness of Buchan's conservative values. This book is enjoyable and perceptive, but does not radically alter previous views of Buchan's life.

Autobiographical Sources

Buchan's autobiography, *Memory Hold-the-Door,* was begun near the end of his life and finished shortly before his death. It is less a strict history of his life than a series of carefully selected reminiscences. Buchan refers to it in his introduction as a record of the impressions made upon him by the world. Though Buchan does tell the main events of his life, much of the book deals with detailed portraits of the people Buchan had known including Raymond Asquith, T. E. Lawrence, and King George V; loving descriptions of landscapes like the Scottish countryside and the South African veldt; and the development of Buchan's beliefs. The book contains little treatment of any of his friends who were still living or his wife and children. There is only a cursory description of his writings, but Buchan does provide some background material to his novels. *Memory Hold-the-Door* is an excellent introduction to Buchan's mind. It sets forth in serviceable prose Buchan's principles, his wide sympathies, and his habit of tying complex ideas to sensitive renderings of landscape, all of which form the bases of his novels.

Several Buchan scholars consider his last novel *Sick Heart River* to contain autobiographical elements. Written at the same time as *Memory Hold-the-Door,* it is more introspective than his other novels, concerning the lawyer Edward Leithen who achieves a spiritual rebirth near the end of his life. The descriptions of Leithen's illness are similar to Buchan's, as are the memories of which Leithen reflects for much of the novel. A reader may agree with Janet Adam Smith that Buchan put many of his doubts and fears into the mind of Leithen though it is possible to read too much into the novel.

Overview of Critical Sources

Though Buchan produced over seventy books including historical romances, biographies, poetry, essays, short stories, political treatises, and histories, he is known today primarily for his spy novels especially those featuring Richard Hannay, like *The Thirty-Nine Steps.* In addition to this neglect of much of his best work, Buchan suffers from the hostility of liberal critics who see him as an anti-semite, snob and success worshipper. Thus Buchan has a reputation today as an entertaining thriller writer with outmoded values. Much of the recent criticism on Buchan has tried to rescue his literary status by viewing the entire range of his work; putting him in the tradition of earlier Scottish writers like James Boswell, Sir Walter Scott, and Robert Louis Stevenson; and examining the serious themes in his works.

Evaluation of Selected Criticism

Brown, Barbara B. "John Buchan and Twentieth Century Biography," *Biography,* II (Fall, 1979), 328–341. Brown surveys Buchan's biographies of Montrose, Cromwell, Scott, and Augustus, which Buchan and several other critics consider to be his best work. She sees Buchan as writing sympathetic but balanced life-studies in the tradition of Boswell rather than the more subjective New Biography of Lytton Strachey.

Daniell, David, *The Interpreter's House: A Critical Assessment of John Buchan.* London: Thomas Nelson and Sons, 1975. Daniell, in the only book length critical treatment of Buchan's work, surveys all of Buchan's writings to trace his major themes of spiritual development through conflict with evil. He makes a close study of the early novels to show the development of this theme. Though he tends to overrate Buchan's talents, Daniell mounts a powerful argument for regarding Buchan as a serious writer of sympathy, wit, and honesty who deserves better critical treatment. He effectively disposes of the view of Buchan as a jingoist and success-worshipper. A flawed but perceptive study of Buchan.

Ridley, M. R. "A Misrated Author?" in *Second Thoughts.* London: J. M. Dent, 1965. The theme of soul-making is analyzed in Buchan's fiction along with his style in light of Buchan's essay "The Novel and the Fairy Tale" (1931). Ridley sees Buchan as a romancer in the Stevenson tradition.

Usborne, Richard, *Clubland Heroes.* London: Barrie and Jenkins, 1953. In this "nostalgic study" of early thriller writers, Buchan's work is linked with the crude, racist, and sometimes sadistic fictions of Sapper (H. C. McNeile) and Dornford Yates. Usborne thinks Buchan an excellent writer but finds his too successful heroes repelling, except for Leithen. A witty but superficial reading of Buchan.

Other Sources

Buchan, Anna (O. Douglas), *Unforgettable, Unforgotten.* London: Hodder and Stroughton, 1945. Buchan's sister's autobiography gives much information on their family.

Hanna, Archibald, *John Buchan, a Bibliography.* Hamden, CT: Shoe String Press, 1953. A useful primary bibliography.

Selected Dictionaries and Encyclopedias

Critical Survey of Long Fiction, Salem Press, 1983. Short biography and brief overview of Buchan's novels.

Dictionary of National Biography, 1931-1940, Oxford University Press, 1949. A concise biography of Buchan's life.

Anthony J. Bernardo Jr.
University of Delaware

PEARL BUCK
1892–1973

Author's Chronology

Born Pearl Comfort Sydenstricker on June 26, 1892, at Hillsboro, West Virginia, while Presbyterian missionary parents were home on leave; *1892–1910* lives in China (primarily Chinkiang); studies with mother and with Confucian tutor; contributes to children's page of *Shanghai Mercury; 1910* enters Randolph-Macon Women's College; *1914* teaches psychology at Randolph-Macon, then returns to China to nurse her ill mother; *1917* marries American agricultural missionary John Lossing Buck; *1920* daughter Carol is born; *1921* begins teaching English Literature at University of Nanking; *1922* starts to write articles and short stories about China; *1924–1925* adopts daughter Janice, learns that Carol is severely retarded, earns an M.A. in English from Cornell, then returns to China to teach in Nanking; *1932* wins Pulitzer Prize for *The Good Earth; 1934* comes to live in United States; *1935* divorces Buck and marries Richard J. Walsh, her publisher; *1936* receives the first two children of the eight children adopted during her second marriage; *1938* wins Nobel Prize in Literature; *1949* founds Welcome House, an adoption agency for racially-mixed children; *1958–1965* serves as president of Authors' Guild; *1964* establishes Pearl S. Buck Foundation to care for Amerasian children left behind by U.S. servicemen; dies March 6, *1973,* in Danby, Vermont.

Author's Bibliography (selected)

East Wind: West Wind, 1930 (novel); *The Good Earth,* 1931 (novel); *Sons,* 1932 (novel); *The Mother,* 1934 (novel); *A House Divided,* 1935 (novel); *The Exile,* 1936 (biography of mother); *Fighting Angel,* 1936 (biography of father); *The Townsman,* 1945 (novel under pseudonym John Sedges); *Pavilion of Women,* 1946 (novel); *The Child Who Never Grew,* 1950 (autobiography); *My Several Worlds,* 1954 (autobiography); *Command the Morning,* 1959 (novel); *A Bridge for Passing,* 1962 (autobiography); *The Time is Noon,* 1967 (novel).

Overview of Biographical Sources

Most biographies of Pearl Buck were written by family and friends or depend heavily on her autobiographies. They tend to be laudatory about her public accomplishments, silent about personal matters, and weak on evaluation. Only Nora Stirling's *Pearl Buck: A Woman in Conflict* (1983) uses interviews and secondary sources to develop controversial material. Besides the adult biographies, there are several for young readers. Irvin Block's *The Lives of Pearl Buck: A Tale of China and America* (New York: Thomas Y. Crowell, 1973) presents the standard information soundly and emphasizes Buck's humanitarian accomplishments.

Evaluation of Selected Biographies

Harris, Theodore F. *Pearl S. Buck: A Biography.* 2 volumes. London: Methuen, 1969–1971. Largely based on tape-recorded conversations with Buck, the first volume has lively anecdotes, a generous selection of reviews, and an adulatory tone. The second volume contains many of Buck's letters and speeches on public topics and on the craft of writing.

Spencer, Cornelia, *The Exile's Daughter: A Biography of Pearl S. Buck.* New York: Coward McCann, 1944. Buck's sister, Grace Sydenstricker Yaukey, writes under the pseudonym Cornelia Spencer and supplies detailed information about Buck's childhood, college years, and early adult life in China.

Stirling, Nora, *Pearl Buck: A Woman in Conflict.* Piscataway, NJ: New Century, 1983. Written in a lively narrative style attractive to general readers, Stirling's book is also the most researched biography to date. It includes information about the Chinese man Buck loved in the 1920's, commentary on other emotional involvements, and some evaluation of her character.

Autobiographical Sources

Buck's primary autobiography, *My Several Worlds* (New York: Day, 1954), was written twenty years before her death and is a thoughtful memoir which interprets the interplay of Asia and America in her life, traces the origin of her humanitarian ideals, and describes the scenes and people that gave rise to some of her fiction. The book is, however, very reticent about personal information and private feelings. *A Bridge for Passing* (New York: Day, 1962) is a similar but more limited memoir which tells of her return to Asia. In *The Child Who Never Grew* (New York: Day, 1950), Buck tells the history of her daughter Carol and pleads for better understanding of retarded people.

In addition, Buck used personal observation and experience to explain her support for various causes. Articles about race relations, the United States' presence in Asia, mental retardation, transracial adoption, colonialism, women's issues, nuclear war, pacifism, and other subjects can be located in magazine files by using the Zinn bibliography (listed below). Some of Buck's fiction is thinly veiled autobiography. *The Time is Noon* (New York: Day, 1967) was written and set in type in the late 1930's and then withdrawn because Buck's advisers felt that the story would damage her reputation.

Overview of Critical Sources

Although Buck produced over a hundred books, remains very popular in other parts of the world, and is the sole American woman among winners of the Nobel Prize for Literature, only one critical study devoted to her has been published in the United States. Among the reasons for academic neglect of Buck are her gender, her popularity, the Chinese subject matter of her best books, and her use of fiction to support humanitarian causes.

Given the scarcity of criticism in books, the excerpts reprinted in *Contemporary Literary Criticism* (Detroit: Gale Research) are useful. Volume 7 (1977) has a number of brief passages from contemporary reviews of Buck's works. Volume 11 (1979) supplies substantial excerpts from an essay by Malcolm Cowley and from Phyllis Bentley's article "The Art of Pearl Buck" in *English Journal,* XXIV (December 1935) and summarizes Paul Doyle's evaluations of the major works from the first edition of *Pearl S. Buck* (1965). Volume 18 (1981) includes some of the 1938 controversy over the awarding of the Nobel Prize and excerpts from articles by Walter Langlois and G. A. Cevasco on the Chinese tradition in Buck's work.

Evaluation of Selected Criticism

Doyle, Paul A. *Pearl S. Buck.* Boston: Twayne, 1980. The revised and updated edition of a study first published in 1965 supplies analysis and criticism of Buck's important books, describes many of her other works, and comments on her critical reputation.

Thompson, Dody Weston, "Pearl Buck," in *American Winners of the Nobel Literary Prize,* ed. Warren G. French and Walter F. Kidd. Norman: University of Oklahoma Press, 1968. An analysis of Buck's career discusses the conflict between European and Asian literary traditions and contends that Buck was influenced by both but mastered neither.

Other Sources

Zinn, Lucille S. "The Works of Pearl S. Buck: A Bibliography," *Bulletin of Bibliography,* XXXVI (October-December 1979), 194–208. Detailed list of Buck's novels, stories, biographies, juveniles, articles, essays, plays, screenplays and radio scripts. Also lists selected reviews and interviews.

Selected Dictionaries and Encyclopedias

American Women Writers: A Critical Reference Guide from Colonial Times to the Present, Frederick Ungar, 1979. Short factual account of Buck's life and evaluation of her work.

Dictionary of Literary Biography, Gale Research, 1981. Brief biography, one-sentence summaries of major works, and overview of Buck's literary development and reputation.

Notable American Women: The Modern Period, Belknap, 1980. Excellent factual biography with accurate dates, summary of literary career, and recording of the ideals and causes that Buck supported.

Sally Mitchell
Temple University

ANTHONY BURGESS
1917

Author's Chronology

Born John Anthony Burgess Wilson February 25, 1917, Manchester, England of Irish-English parents; *1940* is graduated with a B.A. in English from Manchester University; *1942* marries Llewela Isherwood Jones, a Welsh student at the university; she is assaulted by American deserters and her unborn child is killed; *1943–1946* serves on Gibraltar as a training college lecturer; *1946–1954* teaches English literature and music at English universities and grammar schools; *1954–1957* lectures in English in Kahta Baru, Malaya with the Colonial Service; *1956* publishes his first novel; *1957–1959* lectures in English in Brunei, Borneo; *1959* possible brain tumor discovered, returns to England; *1960–1963* publishes nine novels including *A Clockwork Orange* (*1962*); *1968* his wife dies; he marries Liliana Macellari; *1969* teaches in the United States; continues to live and write in Monaco.

Author's Bibliography (selected)

Time for a Tiger, 1956 (novel); *The Enemy in the Blanket,* 1958 (novel); *Beds in the East,* 1959 (novel); *The Right to an Answer,* 1960 (novel); *A Clockwork Orange,* 1962 (novel); *The Wanting Seed,* 1962 (novel); *Inside Mr. Enderby,* 1963 (novel); *Nothing Like the Sun,* 1964 (fictional biography); *ReJoyce,* 1965 (criticism); *Tremor of Intent,* 1966 (novel); *The Novel Now,* 1967 (criticism); *Skakespeare,* 1970 (criticism); *MF,* 1971 (novel); *Napoleon Symphony,* 1974 (novel); *The Clockwork Treatment or Enderby's End,* 1975 (novel); *Beard's Roman Women,* 1976 (novel); *Abba Abba,* 1977 (novel); *1985,* 1978 (novel); *Man of Nazareth,* 1979 (novel); *Earthly Powers,* 1980 (novel); *The End of the World News,* 1983 (novel).

Overview of Biographical Sources

No biographies of Anthony Burgess currently exist. Most biographical information can be found in the first chapters of the critical works about his fiction and in various interviews in various journals.

Evaluation of Selected Biographies

Aggeler, Geoffrey, *Anthony Burgess: The Artist as Novelist.* University, AL: University of Alabama Press, 1979. Aggeler presents a general overview of Burgess's life up to 1978. His account is detailed, elegantly written and offers perceptive comments on Burgess's first marriage, his various moves from country to country, his intellectual background, and his life in the army and as a teacher. He discusses Burgess's work with films, with the musical stage, and with his own music. He describes in detail Burgess's Manichean theories, his ideas about art, the poet's role in contemporary times, and his views of western and eastern cultures.

Coale, Samuel, *Anthony Burgess.* New York: Frederick Ungar, 1981. Coale describes Burgess as a Catholic exile in love with what language as language can do. The chronological pattern of his life reveals the basic events without great detail. Coale focuses on Burgess's Medieval Manichean vision, the clash of eastern and western cultures, and the basic theme in several of the novels of the individual in confrontation with the State. He examines Burgess's love of ritual, James Joyce, and art as an ultimate game.

DeVitis, A. A. *Anthony Burgess.* New York: Twayne, 1972. DeVitis's account of Burgess's life is straightforward and general. He does not discuss any material in great detail but presents a chronological portrait of the events in Burgess's life. He focuses on Burgess primarily as a novelist and describes the plots of the novels in detail.

Overview of Critical Sources

Besides the three critical books above, which concentrate on Burgess as writer and novelist, two other monographs that examine the vision of his fiction include Richard Mathews' *The Clockwork Universe of Anthony Burgess* (Popular Writers of Today, 1978) and Robert K. Morris's *The Consolation of Ambiguity: An Essay on the Novels of Anthony Burgess,* 1971.

Evaluation of Selected Criticism

Mathews, Richard, *The Clockwork Universe of Anthony Burgess.* San Bernardino, CA: The Borgo Press, 1978. Mathews' title accurately describes his attitude towards Burgess's vision of the world in his fiction. Within such a universe the individual must struggle against mighty odds and may reach an awareness only of that universe's ultimate demonic and mechanical designs. This book offers an interesting and informed introduction to Burgess's fiction.

Morris, Robert K. *The Consolation of Ambiguity: An Essay on the Novels of Anthony Burgess.* Columbia, MO: University of Missouri Press, 1971. In this philosophical and well-written account of Burgess's vision of the modern world, Morris argues perceptively for Burgess's belief in the ultimate ambiguities of existence. Good and evil are inextricably mixed in a "duoverse" of actual experience rather than completely separate and differentiated in a "universe." Consolation lies in the fact that life is far more complex than Burgess's villains, who see the world in only black and white or good and evil terms, will admit. Burgess's heroes act from the knowledge of life's ambiguities and the mysterious workings of God's—or the Devil's—dark designs.

Other Sources

Coale, Samuel, "The Ludic Loves of Anthony Burgess," *Modern Fiction Studies,* 27 (Autumn 1981), 453-463. Describes Burgess's vision of life and religion as necessary games to be played, aware of man's self-conscious fictionalizing of all his experience.

Jeutonne, Brewer, *Anthony Burgess: A Bibliography.* Metuchen, NJ: Scarecrow Press, 1980. Most recent and detailed bibliography of critical sources for Burgess's work.

LeClair, Thomas, "Essential Opposition: The Novels of Anthony Burgess," *Critique: Studies in Modern Fiction,* 12 (1971), 77–94. A solid overview of the clash of good and evil, East and West, free will and predestination in Burgess's fiction.

Pritchard, William H. "The Novels of Anthony Burgess," *The Massachusetts Review,* 7 (1966), 525–539. Excellent overview of the major themes in Burgess's fiction.

Stinson, John J. "The Manichee World of Anthony Burgess," *Renascence,* 26 (1973), 38–47. "Better to Be Hot or Cold: *1985* and the Dynamic or the Manichean Duoverse," *Modern Fiction Studies,* 27 (Autumn 1981), 505–516. Excellent discussion of the Manichean vision at the heart of Burgess's novels.

Selected Dictionaries and Encyclopedias

Critical Survey of Long Fiction, Salem Press, 1983. Brief biography and short critical analysis of Burgess's most important novels.

Encyclopedia of World Literature in the Twentieth Century, Frederick Ungar, 1981. Concise description of Burgess's major novels.

Encyclopedia of World Literature in the Twentieth Century, Vol. 4, Supplement and Index, Frederick Ungar, 1975. Contains selections from six different critics on Burgess's art and methods.

Contemporary Literary Criticism, Vols. 1–2, Gale Research, 1975. Selected criticism of Burgess's works and achievements.

Dictionary of Literary Biography, Gale Research, 1983. Concise overview of Burgess's life and a discussion of the principal works.

Samuel Coale
Wheaton College
Massachusetts

FANNY BURNEY
1752–1840

Author's Chronology

Born June 13, 1752, fourth child of Esther Sleepe and Charles Burney at King's Lynn, England: *1760* family moves to London; *1762* mother dies; *1767* father remarries; burns own early writing including first novel *The History of Carolyn Evelyn;* begins diary; *1778* publishes *Evelina; 1778* becomes an intimate of Dr. Johnson and the Thrales; *1779* finishes comedy, *The Witlings,* but does not publish it; *1782* publishes *Cecilia; 1786* becomes Second Keeper of the Robes to Queen Charlotte, wife of George III, lives at court; *1793* marries Alexandre d'Arblay, penniless French emigré; writes *Brief Reflections relative to the Emigrant French Clergy; 1794* gives birth to son Alexander; *1796* publishes *Camilla; 1802* moves to France; *1812* returns to London; *1814* publishes *The Wanderer;* travels to France; *1815* is in Brussels at Napoleon's defeat at Waterloo; returns to England; *1832* publishes *The Memoirs of Dr. Burney; 1840* dies on January 6.

Author's Bibliography (selected)

Evelina, 1778 (novel); *Cecilia,* 1782 (novel); *Edwy and Elgiva,* 1791 (tragedy); *Camilla,* 1796 (novel); *The Wanderer,* 1814 (novel); *The Memoirs of Dr. Burney,* 1832 (biography of father); *Diary and Letters of Madame d'Arblay,* 1843, rpt. 1906, 1972 (journal and letters); *The Early Diary of Francis Burney,* 1889; included in *The Journals and Letters of Francis Burney,* ed. Joyce Hemlow *et al.* 1972 (journal).

Overview of Biographical Sources

Possibly because she led a long life, meeting so many well-known political and literary figures and possibly because she herself left a rich store of letters and journals, there are several biographies of Fanny Burney. The early ones, however, are outdated and one or two later ones are thoroughly unsympathetic. Averyl Edward's *Fanny Burney 1752–1840: A Biography* (London: Staples Press, Ltd., 1948) is a fine, brief biography. Edwards supplements the information given in the journals and letters with material from the papers of other family members and friends. *Fanny Burney* by Sarah Kilpatrick (1980) is an excellent biography written from a feminist point of view. The definitive biography, however, remains Joyce Hemlow's *The History of Fanny Burney* (1958).

Evaluation of Selected Biographies

Hemlow, Joyce, *The History of Fanny Burney.* London: Clarendon Press, 1958. Hemlow, who has been studying Burney's life and work for many years, is now engaged in assembling a multi-volume edition of her letters and journal.

The History of Fanny Burney is a distillation of this material supplemented by the letters and journals of Burney's contemporaries. She begins her history with a glance at the courtship and marriage of Charles and Esther Burney, then discusses Fanny's childhood. There is little criticism of the novels or the plays but Hemlow discusses the circumstances under which they were written and their reception. Hemlow gives a full description of Burney's life at court including her experiences during the King's bouts of insanity. She also gives a full account of (1) the Burney family's opposition to her marriage to d'Arblay, and the happiness of her marriage despite financial worries (2) Burney's experiences in Europe, her return home after many years, and her problems as the loving parent of a son who never quite fulfilled his early promise (3) the sadness of her old age during which she lost her father, sisters, husband and son. Hemlow paints the picture of an age as well as the life of one woman.

Kilpatrick, Sarah, *Fanny Burney*. London: David & Charles, 1980. Kilpatrick discusses Burney as a member of a lively family whose lives may have provided her with material for her novels. Kilpatrick describes Burney's life at court, supplying details about the royal family that are omitted from Burney's journals and letters. Although she does not offer any critical discussion of the works, she does describe their reception, including the disastrous performance of Burney's tragedy, *Edwy and Elgiva,* which was laughed off the stage. Kilpatrick's biography is sympathetic, readable and very informative.

Autobiographical Sources

The definitive source is *The Journals and Letters of Fanny Burney* (*Madame d'Arblay*), Joyce Hemlow *et al.* (London: Oxford University Press, 1972). Volumes I-VIII covering the years 1792 to 1815 are now available. This set supersedes the six volume *The Diary and Letters of Madame d'Arblay* edited by Charlotte Barrett, Burney's niece, with a preface and notes by Austin Dobson (London: MacMillan, 1904–1905). It also supersedes *The Early Diary of Fanny Burney 1768–1778* edited by Annie Raine Ellis (London: G. Bell, 1913). There also exists *A Catalogue of the Burney Family Correspondence* edited by Joyce Hemlow (New York: New York Public Library, 1971). A far less exhaustive study is *The Famous Miss Burney: The Diary and Letters of Fanny Burney* edited by Barbara G. Schrank and David J. Supino (New York: The John Day Company, 1976). Schrank notes that Burney's diary is the only record of a young girl written by herself published in the eighteenth century and as such is valuable as a historical record. She admits that Burney may have seemed somewhat narrow-minded and naive but notes that her behavior in becoming a professional writer and her views on marriage were unconventional, even daring, for that era. She attributes the decline in the quality of her novels not only to a heightened elevation of style but to her loss of pleasure in writing.

Overview of Critical Sources

The most recent book-length study is Michael Adelstein's *Fanny Burney* (1968). He discusses the later novels as well as *Evelina* and even provides an analysis not only of *Edwy and Elgiva,* Burney's one published play, but also of the unpublished tragedies and comedies. He explains the suppression of *The Witlings* and *A Busy Day;* which he considers a masterpiece. He believes the diaries provide excellent characterizations, and dramatic representations of the scenes they portray, but he also notes Burney's deletions from them and their limitations. He sees *Evelina* as a comedy of manners enlivened by Burney's portrayal of middle class manners which he believes is much more accurate than her depiction of aristocratic behavior.

Two other books, Cecil David's *Poets and Story-Tellers* (1949) and Frank Bradbrook's *Jane Austen and Her Predecessors* (1966) address Burney's influence on literature. James Foster's *History of the Pre-Romantic Novel in England* (1940) also traces influences, and links her works to Fielding and Smollett, while Janet Todd explores the relationship of women within the novels from a feminist perspective.

Evaluation of Selected Criticism

Adelstein, Michael E. *Fanny Burney.* New York: Twayne, 1968. This is the most complete study of Burney's work to date. Adelstein comments on the diaries, novels and plays. As he examines Burney's record of court life, he supplies the negative information about the royal family that she omits. He also comments on her marriage, her travels and her old age. Finally, he assesses her contributions as a novelist and a diarist, insisting that whatever her limitations, she succeeded in presenting an entertaining picture of her world.

Bradbrook, Frank, *Jane Austen and Her Predecessors.* Cambridge: University Press, 1966. Bradbrook is primarily concerned with influences; he discusses Burney's use of Johnsonian language, characters drawn from Richardson, and scenes reminiscent of Fielding. He also believes that *Cecilia* influenced Jane Austen's early novels, but he points out that Burney's heroines, unlike those of Jane Austen, are passive and require the protection of parents or the hero.

Cecil, David, *Poets and Story-Tellers: A Book of Critical Essays.* New York: Macmillan, 1949. In his chapter on Burney, Cecil points out the influence of Smollett, as well as that of Fielding, on the novels. He characterizes the writer herself as an English lady, civilized, lively and keenly sensitive to social distinctions, but limited by prudery and narrow-mindedness.

Foster, James R. *History of the Pre-Romantic Novel in England.* New York: The Modern Language Association of America, 1949; rpt. 1966. Foster points out that Burney's novels blend satire with sentiment. He links her work with the novels of Prevost, Marivaux and Sterne as well as with those of Fielding and Smollett by showing how her heroines are innocent, tender-hearted and extremely emotional while her heroes are too prudent to be considered genuine men of feeling.

Montague, Edwine and Louis L. Martz, "Fanny Burney's *Evelina,* "*The Age of Johnson: Essays Presented to Chauncey Brewster Tinker.* ed. Frederick W. Hilles. New Haven: Yale University Press, 1949; rpt. 1964. In dialogue form, Montague and Martz discuss the careful construction of *Evelina.* They see the characters as stock figures deriving from restoration comedy and Evelina herself as a central consciousness providing a point of view.

Steeves, Harrison J. *Before Jane Austen: The Shaping of the English Novel in the Eighteenth Century.* New York: Holt, Rinehart and Winston, 1965. Summarizes the novels and quotes extensively from *Evelina.*

Todd, Janet, *Women's Friendship in Literature.* New York: Columbia University Press, 1980. Janet Todd is one of the few critics who discuss *Cecilia* and *The Wanderer* in any detail; she writes from a feminist stance. In these two novels she focuses on the heroine's intense relationship with another woman.

Other Sources

Lonsdale, Roger H. *Dr. Charles Burney: A Literary Biography.* Oxford: Clarendon Press, 1965. The biography of Charles Burney, musician, writer, friend to the great and father of Fanny Burney.

Selected Dictionaries and Encyclopedias

English Fiction, 1660–1800: A Guide to Information Sources, Gale Research, 1978. Very brief biography and list of works by and about Burney.

Barbara Horwitz
C.W. Post Center of Long Island University

ROBERT BURNS
1759–1796

Author's Chronology

Born January 25, 1759, Alloway near Ayr in Ayrshire, Scotland; *1765* educated at a school in Alloway under John Murdoch and at home; *1774* works on a farm in Mount Oliphant near Alloway; begins writing verse. *1783 The First Commonplace Book* begun; *1785* begins to write his major poetry; meets Jean Armour; *1786* copy from *Poems, Chiefly in the Scots Dialect* sent to printer; plans to emigrate to Jamaica; *1787 Second Commonplace Book* begun, publication of an enlarged edition of *Poems in Edinburgh; 1788* marries Jean Armour; appointed as an officer of His Majesty's Excise (customs officer) in the area of Dunfries; *1791 Tam o' Shanter* published in Grose's *Antiquities;* death of his patron, the Earl of Glencairn; *1792* four of the *Scots Musical Museum* appeared; sixty of the hundred songs written or collected with some revision by Burns; *1793* second Edinburgh edition of *Poems, Chiefly in the Scots Dialect* appeared with nineteen additional poems; *1794* sends forty-one songs to Johnson, the publisher of *The Scots Musical Museum;* final edition during Burns' lifetime of the *Poems, Chiefly in the Scots Dialect* appears; *1795* severely ill with rheumatic fever; *1796* dies and is buried on July 25, the day his son Maxwell is born; fifth volume of *The Scots Musical Museum* is published.

Author's Bibliography (selected)

Poems, Chiefly in the Scots Dialect, 1786 (forty-four poems and songs); *Poems, Chiefly in the Scots Dialect,* 1787 (contains twenty-two additional poems); *Poems, Chiefly in the Scots Dialect,* 1793 (contains nineteen additional poems); *The Scots Musical Musem,* ed. James Johnson, six volumes, 1787, 1788, 1790, 1792, 1796, 1803 (contains about 200 songs written, revised or collected by Burns); *A Select Collection of Original Scotish [sic] Airs for the Voice,* ed. George Thompson (published in eight parts, 1793, 1798, 1799, n.d. [1799?], 1802, 1803, 1805, 1818; it includes more than seventy songs by Burns); *The Poems and Songs of Robert Burns,* ed. James Kingsley, three volumes (Oxford: Clarendon Press, 1968). The definitive edition; volumes one and two contain the poems and songs; volume three, a commentary.

Overview of Biographical Sources

Burns' conspicuous love of wine, women and song, his cultivated image of the uneducated ploughman-poet, and his reputation as the national poet of Scotland have attracted well over fifty biographers. Most of the modern biographies give criticism of the poems as well as an account of his life. The first major biography of the twentieth century, written by Hans Hecht in 1919, was not published in English until 1936 (London: William Hodge). It views him against the broad background of eighteenth-century culture and views Burns as a poet of universal appeal. Franklin B. Snyder's *The Life of Robert Burns* (New York: Macmillan, 1932), presents a particularized, thorough, and judicious view of the poet. Cyril Pear's *Bawdy Burns: The Christian Rebel* (London: Muller, 1958), puts Burns' love of the girls and the grog in the context of the times and shows him to be no worse than many of his contemporaries. It is polemical in tone. For an overview of the era see Alan Dent in *Burns in His Time* (London: Nelson, 1966). He also quotes from contemporary critics to J. B. Priestly. John DeLancey Ferguson's *Pride and Passion: Robert Burns* (New York: Russell and Russell, 1964) focuses on Burns' mature years where more reliable documentation is available. The tone is amiable and the style scholarly. An interesting account of the genesis of the poems and songs is found in Robert T. Fitzhugh's *Robert Burns: The Man and the Poet* (1970), a well-researched book that quotes copiously from Burns' works. Hugh Douglas gives an intimate account of the Burns' country in *Robert Burns: A Life* (London: Robert Hale, 1976). A valuable reader's tool to biographical information about Burns is Maurice Lindsay's *The Burns' Encyclopedia* (New York: St. Martin's, 1980). People and places alluded to in Burns' works are sketched. It is amply illustrated. Helpful for biography are Burns' *Glenriddle Manuscripts,* ed. Desmond Donaldson (Hamden, CT: Archon, 1973). It contains letters and poems assembled for Robert Riddell. Robert Burns' *Tour of the Borders,* ed. Raymond Lamont Brown (Totowa, NJ: Rowman and Littlefield, 1973) and the *Tour of the Highlands and Sterlingshire,* ed. Raymond Lamont Brown (Ipswich: Boydell Press, 1973) give us the poet's candid and sometimes sarcastic view of people and events. For an intimate view of Burns' feelings about people and places, life and art his *Commonplace Book 1783–1785,* ed. James Cameron Ewing and Davidson Cook (Glasgow: Gowan's and Gray, 1938) is valuable. Impressions of the poet by twelve people who knew him are to be found in W. L. Renwick, ed. *Burns as Others Saw Him* (Edinburgh: Saltire Society 1960). An abundance of biographical information is to be found in the standard edition of the *Letters,* ed. by John DeLancey Ferguson, 2 vols. (Oxford: Clarendon Press, 1931).

Evaluation of Selected Biographies

Daiches, David, *Robert Burns and His World.* New York: Viking, 1972. Daiches has provided a short, reliable, and readable life of the poet. Daiches writes with the easy erudition of a scholar steeped with knowledge of his subject. It is copiously illustrated to give a visual sense of the time.

Fitzhugh, Robert T. *Robert Burns: The Man and the Poet.* Boston: Houghton Mifflin, 1970. This is the fullest and most accurate biography to date. The author gives detailed accounts of the poems and quotes extensively from the letters. The book is carefully researched and renders an unbiased view of the poet's life and work. It contains several appendices that are noteworthy. One contains Scots vernacular poetry that influenced Burns; another suggesting that Burns died, as was originally diagnosed, of rheumatic fever and not of alcoholism or venereal disease as has been alleged by some biographers.

Lindsay, Maurice, *Robert Burns: The Man, His Work, the Legend.* London: MacGibbon and Kee, 1954. Lindsay provides an excellent, readable life of the poet. Lindsay maintains a judicious balance between criticism and biography. He concludes with a special plea to keep Scots, the language of Burns alive as Hugh MacDiarmid (C. M. Grieve) and others have attempted to do.

Autobiographical Sources

Burns' autobiographical material is to be found in his commonplace books, his travel journals, his letters and to some extent his poetry as discussed above.

Overview of Critical Sources

There has been relatively little critical material on Burns since most biographies have combined commentary of the poems along with an account of his life. *A Complete Word and Phrase Concordance to The Poems and Songs of Robert Burns,* compiled and edited by J. B. Reid (New York: Burt Franklin, 1969) is a valuable tool for stylistic and thematic studies. Two essays contained in *From Sensibility to Romanticism* (New York: Oxford University Press, 1965) are useful. John Butt's "The Revival of Vernacular Scottish Poetry in the Eighteenth Century" shows Burns working in a tradition established by Allan Ramsay and Robert Fergusson. In "Burns's Use of Scottish Diction," Raymond Bentman suggests that while Burns wrote some poems in pure English, he wrote none in pure Scottish vernacular. Burns' indebtedness to the tradition of Ramsay and Fergusson is also treated in L. M. Angus's *Robert Burns and the Eighteenth Century Revival in Scottish,* but the bulk of the book is concerned with various aspects of Burns' career. A useful survey of critical reactions to Burns from his contemporaries to the late romantic writer is found in Donald A. Low, ed. *Robert Burns: The Critical Heritage* (London: Routlege and Kegan Paul, 1974).

Evaluation of Selected Criticism

Daiches, David, *Robert Burns.* Edinburgh: Spurbooks, 1981. Daiches gives a detailed reading of the poems. It is a book that is scholarly, perceptive, and readable. It will be the standard critical work for some time to come.

Jack, R. D. S. and Andrew Noble, eds. *The Art of Robert Burns.* Totowa, NJ: Barnes and Noble, 1982. A collection of essays by nine critics on various aspects of Burns' work ranging from his letters to his bawdy verse. It is a uniformly well-researched, readable collection of criticism.

Selected Dictionaries and Encyclopedias

British Writers, Vol. 3. Charles Scribner's Sons, 1980. Well-written, accurate sketch of Burns' life and criticism with a bibliography.

Encyclopedia Britannica, Vol. 4. William Benton, 1970. Contains an excellent sketch of Burns' career with a bibliography.

Great Writers of the English Language: Poets, St. Martin's Press, 1979. Gives a brief but scholarly life of Burns with a criticism of selected poems with a bibliography.

John J. Dunn
St. John's University

ROBERT BURTON
1577–1640

Author's Chronology

Born February 8, 1577, into a genteel family at Lindley Hall, in Leicestershire, the fourth of nine children; his parents, Ralph Burton Esq. and Dorothy Faunt; attends elementary schools at Nuneaton and Sutton Coldfield, Warwickshire; *1593* enters Brasenose College, Oxford; *1599* elected a student of Christ Church, Oxford; *1602* graduates with a B.A.; *1605* awarded an M.A.; lives the remainder of his life at Christ Church, serving as tutor and college librarian; *1614* receives a Bachelor of Divinity; *1616* becomes Vicar of St. Thomas's Church, Oxford; *1633–1634* receives, as patronage, a position as Vicar at Seagrave in his home county of Leicestershire; death on January 25, 1640; buried in Christ Church Cathedral.

Author's Bibliography

Poemata, some 19 poems (in Latin) contributed to various Oxford University anthologies, 1603–1638; 1606 composed *Philosophaster* (Latin comedy), revised in 1615, not published until 1862; 1612, Preface (in Latin) to John Rider's *Dictionarie;* 1621, first edition of *The Anatomy of Melancholy* (prose); 2nd to 6th editions, in 1624, 1628, 1632, 1638, 1651–1652 (contain extensive revisions and broad expansions of the text by the author).

Overview of Biographical Sources

Burton's life was obscure, with few details about his life recorded. A congenial but retiring scholar at Oxford, he seemed to be, as his own Latin epitaph explained, *paucis notus,* little-known. Much of his life and his motivations remain a mystery. As a result, no book-length biographies whatsoever have been written about him. Quoting men who knew Burton, Anthony à Wood devoted two pages to him in his *Athenae Oxonienses,* 1691–1692, and other brief notes about his life have been supplied from time to time by authors such as Thomas Hearne (in 1703) and John Nichols (in 1795–1815). In our own century, Chapters I and IV of a dissertation by Richard Leonard Nochimson, "Robert Burton: A Study of the Man, His Work, and His Critics," Columbia University, 1967, attempts to explore his life and ideas. The difficulty is, simply, that too little precise information is available.

Autobiographical Sources

Burton's *Anatomy of Melancholy* is a monumental treatise and encyclopedic compendium, both solemn and witty, that studies madness, its causes and symptoms, its types, its effects, and its possible cures. Supposedly written by Burton's *persona,* "Democritus, Junior," the work is obviously comic and satiric as well as serious, in the tradition of Cynic philosophers, of medical doctors, and of Rabelais, yet it is frequently self-revelatory. Eccentric, bachelor, bookworm, and recluse, Burton openly confesses, here and there, that his attention to *melancholia* was caused by his own propensities to suffer from the disease, and he freely concedes that his writing of the book (literally a life-long task) helped to assuage the illness. The writing of this book similarly provided a vicarious travel exercise as Burton imaginatively roamed all over geography and history, compensating for his own cloistered and confined life. Furthermore, the *Anatomy of Melancholy* takes us just as surely upon an extended autobiographical tour of Burton's reading. A polymath, Burton quotes thousands of authors, ancient, medieval, and modern (most commonly in Latin), and his book is a vast, loping pachyderm of quotations, citations, and learned allusions. Burton's own quaint mixture of seriousness and humor, of formidable and formal learning with one of the most relaxed and informal of styles reflects a paradoxical dichotomy that he appears to bear with ease. For discussion of Burton's self-reference and self-revelation in his book, see especially Sir William Osler, "Robert Burton: The Man, His Book, His Library," *Oxford Bibliographical Society Proceedings and Papers,* I (1922–1926), 185–198; and Bridget Gellert Lyons, *Voices of Melancholy: Studies in Literary Treatments of Melancholy in Renaissance England.* 1971. New York: W. W. Norton, 1975, Chapter V, esp. pp. 121–141. A psychologically oriented exploration of Burton's personality may be found in Bergen Evans, *The Psychiatry of Robert Burton.* New York: Columbia University Press, 1944, esp. Chapter I.

Overview of Critical Sources

Because of its elephantine learning, borrowings, and citations, the *Anatomy of Melancholy* has largely enticed most scholars to compile bibliographies of this work's many editions, and of relevant learned volumes and source studies of the works and authors Burton drew upon. A related group of studies has surveyed Burton's influence upon later authors: upon the Jacobean playwright John Ford, Laurence Sterne, Charles Lamb, and John Keats. Other studies, less numerous, have scrutinized the "form" and "structure" of the *Anatomy.* Such critical works are intent upon demonstrating the *Anatomy*'s "unity" and coherent organization—a considerable task, given the work's relaxed style, its vast digressions, its ambling pace, and the slow process of its creation, from edition to edition, by accretion. A new trend, in recent books, has been concerned with demonstrating that the *Anatomy* is itself paradoxical and even disorderly. See, for instance, Rosalie L. Colie, *Paradoxia Epidemica: The Renaissance Tradition of Paradox.* Princeton: Princeton University Press, 1966, Chapter 14.

Evaluation of Selected Criticism

Babb, Lawrence, *Sanity in Bedlam: A Study of Robert Burton's "Anatomy of Melancholy."* East Lansing: Michigan State University Press, 1959. Though brief, this is one of the first full-length volumes to be devoted to the *Anatomy of Melancholy,* treating its editions, its vast contents, its composition, the biography, seventeenth-century melancholy, and a final four chapters on the *Anatomy* itself, its sources and its chief ideas.

Fox, Ruth A. *The Tangled Chain. The Structure of Disorder in the "Anatomy of Melancholy."* Berkeley, Los Angeles, London: University of California Press, 1976. The most thorough literary study of the *Anatomy* to date. Fox is concerned primarily with the *Anatomy*'s meaning, artistry, and structure. It argues extensively that the *Anatomy*'s order is designed chiefly to describe the disorder of Burton's world. Fox offers some good analyses of sections of Burton's work.

Simon, Jean Robert, *Robert Burton (1577–1640) et l'Anatomie de Mélancolie.* Paris: Didier, 1964. This is the first full treatment, in a large study, of Burton and his work. In eighteen chapters, it methodically presents much of the cultural, medical, historical, and intellectual background of the *Anatomy,* with studies of its author's biography, and the sources, references, organization, and style of his masterwork. It is rich in factual details.

Other Sources

Donovan, Dennis G. *Sir Thomas Browne and Robert Burton; A Reference Guide.* Boston: G. K. Hall, 1981. An updating of earlier bibliographical (1924–1966) material through 1978 by Ann E. Imbrie. Lists editions, commentaries, and criticism.

Nochimson, Richard L. "Studies in the Life of Robert Burton," *Yearbook of English Studies,* 4 (1974), 85–111. Detailed review of facts of Burton's life, with corrections of common biographical errors propagated by historians and critics.

Selected Dictionaries and Encyclopedias

The Dictionary of National Biography, Oxford University Press, 1959–1960. Three pages of biography and historical information.

Great Writers of the English Language, St. Martin's Press, 1979. Brief bibliography, dates of life, and critical survey of the *Anatomy.*

John R. Clark
University of South Florida

SAMUEL BUTLER
1612–1680

Author's Chronology

Born February 8, 1612, Strensham, England of a learned and well-to-do farmer; during his childhood, he probably attended King's school in Worcester; *1626* father dies, leaving him a share in the family property and his father's books; as a young man, he may have studied at Oxford; *1630's* loses or sells his share of the family property; works as aide and secretary for various nobility and government personages; *1640's* may study law at Grey's Inn; also *1640's,* writes essays, may already have begun *Hudibras;* to *1661,* in spite of royalist sentiments, serves government dignitaries; *1661–1662* steward to Richard Vaughn, Earl of Carbery; *1662 Hudibras,* Part I, appears; *1663 Hudibras,* Part II, appears; *1660's* may have married wealthy woman; *1670's,* after hiatus in *1660's,* he returns to work as secretary for George Villiers, Duke of Buckingham; *1677* King Charles may have granted him a pension; *1678 Hudibras,* Part III, appears; dies September 25, 1680, London, England in abject poverty.

Author's Bibliography (selected)

Hudibras, Parts I-III, 1663, 1664, and 1678 (satirical epic poem); *The Genuine Remains in Verse and Prose of Samuel Butler* (edited by Robert Thyer), 1759; *Characters, Observations, and Reflexions from the Notebooks* (edited by A. R. Waller), 1908 (prose sketches); *Samuel Butler: Satires and Miscellaneous Poetry and Prose* (edited by René Lamar), 1928; *Samuel Butler, 1612–1680: Characters* (edited by Charles W. Daves), 1970 (prose sketches); *Samuel Butler: Prose Observations* (edited by Hugh de Quehen), 1979.

Overview of Biographical Sources

Much of Samuel Butler's life is obscure, and biographers have had to rely on traditional accounts, which they have supplemented with historical documents such as letters and court records. The difficulties associated with researching Butler's life have led to two distinct kinds of biographies about him: the traditional and the historical. Those biographers who have relied on the traditions about the poet's life have based their accounts primarily on the writings of John Aubrey and Anthony à Wood. In his *Brief Lives* (edited by Andrew Clark. 2 volumes. Oxford: Clarendon, 1898), Aubrey provides notes on his personal acquaintance with Butler. Although a contemporary of Butler, Wood relies on the accounts of others for his biography in his *Athenae Oxoniensis* (edited by Philip Bliss. 5 volumes. London: F. G. and J. Rivington, 1813–1820; circa 1691–1692). Both Aubrey, Wood, and most subsequent biographers based their work on an oral tradition of Butler's life that is unreliable.

The historical approach to Butler's life has only recently begun to supplant the traditional approach, although as far back as Samuel Johnson's *Lives of the English Poets* (1779), the historical approach has been evident. The historical approach relies on documentary evidence; most of the historical biographers have used such evidence to supplement traditional accounts because records of Butler are scarce. George R. Wasserman mixes traditional accounts and historical data in his brief biographical discussion in *Samuel "Hudibras" Butler* (1976), as does Edward Ames Richards in *Hudibras in the Burlesque Tradition* (1937). Richards' discussion is particularly useful for its insights into Butler's character.

Evaluation of Selected Biographies

Johnson, Samuel, "Butler," in *Lives of the English Poets,* 1779. This short biography retains its value as much because it is the work of a major author as for its account of Butler's life. Johnson relied on the biography by Wood and the notes of Aubrey, as well as eighteenth-century biographies such as that found in the *General Dictionary* of 1734–1741. He also used the notes of William Longueville, Butler's literary executor, and may have used some of Butler's autobiographical notes, as well. Johnson admits the shortcomings of his sources and still creates a credible portrait of a highly intelligent man who believed in the supremacy of reason over man's other faculties. Johnson's criticism of the poetry is incisive.

Autobiographical Sources

Much of Butler's life was spent during the English Revolution, during which his Royalist sympathies could have cost him employment or even his life. Therefore, it is not surprising that he left fewer notes about himself than biographers would wish. The Waller (1908), Lamar (1928), and de Quehen (1979) editions of his prose include some autobiographical materials.

Overview of Critical Sources

Critics have taken three basic approaches to Butler: Butler as satirist, Butler's influence on satire, and Butler's work as a reflection of its time. Although his prose "characters" have received some attention in recent years, his great poem *Hudibras* has been the focus of most criticism. In general, critics agree that *Hudibras* is one of the best satires in English; most also agree that its topicality has made much of its wit inaccessible to modern audiences, although its rollicking plot still has appeal.

Evaluation of Selected Criticism

Richards, Edward Ames, *Hudibras in the Burlesque Tradition.* New York: Columbia University Press, 1937. Richards emphasizes the burlesque aspects of

Hudibras, notably its distortion of its subject for humorous effect. He views the poem as Butler's expression of the triumph of Royalist and rational sentiments over Puritan and irrational ones. In tracing the imitations of the poem and its verse, Richards draws parallels between the popularity of Hudibrastic satire and the rise and fall of political and religious philosophies. He includes a useful bibliography of imitations of the poem.

Wasserman, George R. *Samuel "Hudibras" Butler.* Boston: Twayne, 1976. Wasserman provides an evenhanded overview of Butler's achievement, with comments on the prose "characters" as well as *Hudibras.* He emphasizes the integrity of Butler's vision in *Hudibras* and discusses the poem's organization and imagery. This book includes a short but helpful annotated bibliography.

Other Sources

Jack, Ian, "Low Satire: *Hudibras,*" *Augustan Satire: Intention and Idiom in English Poetry, 1600–1750.* Oxford: Clarendon, 1952. Overview of the distinguishing qualities of the poem.

Quintana, Ricardo, "Samuel Butler: A Restoration Figure in a Modern Light," *English Literary History,* 18 (March 1951), 7-31. Places the poem in historical perspective.

Selected Dictionaries and Encyclopedias

Critical Survey of Poetry, Salem Press, 1982. Brief biography, critical analysis, and short bibliography.

Kirk H. Beetz
National University, Sacramento

WILLIAM BYRD II
1674–1744

Author's Chronology

Born March 28, 1674, first son of William Byrd I, an important colonial businessman; *1681–1696* enters school in England, trains for business in Holland, and studies law in London; *1696* elected to the Royal Society, returns to Virginia and is elected to House of Burgesses; *1697–1705* serves as agent for Virginia in London; *1705* returns to Virginia following death of father (*1704*); *1706* marries Lucy Parke, with whom he was to have four children; *1708* became member of the Council of State; *1715* returns to London as colonial agent, where his wife dies the following year; *1724* after numerous courtships marries Maria Taylor; *1726* returns to Virginia to remain; *1728* leads crew surveying border between North Carolina and Virginia; *1730–1731(?)* rebuilds home at Westover, Virginia; *1732* and *1733* makes investigative trips into frontier; *1737* laid out future city of Richmond; *1743* becomes president of Council; *1744* dies August 26.

Author's Bibliography (selected)

The Secret Diary of William Byrd of Westover, 1709–1712, 1941; *The London Diary (1717–1721) and Other Writings,* 1958; *The History of the Dividing Line, 1728,* 1966 (diary); *The Secret History of the Line, 1728,* 1966 (diary); *A Progress to the Mines, 1732,* 1966 (diary); *A Journey to the Land of Eden, 1733,* 1966 (diary); *Another Secret Diary of William Byrd of Westover, 1739–1741,* 1942 (diary, letters and literary exercises); *The Correspondence of the Three William Byrds of Westover, Virginia, 1684–1776,* 1977.

Overview of Biographical Sources

The major primary sources for Byrd biographical materials are his diaries. Most of his major writing chronicled events of his daily life or important trips he took through Virginia; these works, not published in his own day but now available, are the foundation of Byrd biographical scholarship. Several useful secondary biographical studies were written before the publication of all the autobiographical materials and are, therefore, incomplete. These works, however, remain important because they demonstrate the growth of the recognition of Byrd's place in American letters. The most important book-length study to appear after publication of the diaries is Pierre Marambaud's *William Byrd of Westover, 1674–1744.* This excellent study contains much biographical information, but since it also is the major critical study of Byrd, it will be discussed below under Critical Sources. It should be noted that most essays on Byrd contain both biography and criticism.

Evaluation of Selected Biographies

Beatty, Richard Croom, *William Byrd of Westover,* ed. by M. Thomas Inge. Hamden, CT: Archon Books, 1970. This book, which first came out in 1932, was the major biography until the publication of all the diaries and literary exercises. In 1970 Inge edited the book and included a preface which compared Beatty's scholarship with the later evidence, which updates Beatty's work but does not contradict his conclusions.

Bruce, Philip Alexander, *The Virginia Plutarch.* Chapel Hill: University of North Carolina Press, 1929. Bruce's biographical essay on Byrd, while romantic and sentimental, discovers themes in Byrd's life which remain important, such as his gardens and slaves.

Hatch, Alden, *The Byrds of Virginia: An American Dynasty.* New York: Holt, Rinehart and Winston, 1969. In this readable biography of the entire family from 1670 to the present, Hatch devotes about twenty-five percent of his book to William Byrd II. This study presents an ordinary view of Byrd which perpetuates the myth of him as the Black Swan of Virginia, a popular but uncritical view.

Wright, Louis B. *The First Gentlemen of Virginia: Intellectual Qualities of the Early Colonial Ruling Class.* Charlottesville: University Press of Virginia, 1964. This important book by one of America's premiere colonial scholars discusses the cultural lives of numerous early Virginia intellectuals, including the first two William Byrds. In placing them in the tradition of the Virginia gentleman, Wright discusses the character of William Byrd II as a man of letters, with special emphasis on his library.

Autobiographical Sources

For most of his adult life Byrd kept daily diaries in shorthand. Those which survived remained unpublished during his lifetime, but have now been transcribed and published. His diaries document his life and times in a manner reminiscent of Pepys. He normally would describe his reading and studying, his devotions, his care for his plantation or affairs of state, and his diversions, including his sexual activity. Three volumes of the daily diaries have been published, covering the years 1709–1712, which deals with Virginia; 1717–1721, which deals with Byrd's stay in London; and 1739–1741, which covers his later years in the colony.

In addition, four journals kept while Byrd was on tour of Virginia provide readers with detailed descriptions of colonial life. Again, none was published during his day, but latter-day publication has given modern readers one of the fullest portraits of rural eighteenth-century life. In 1728 while leading a group of surveyors as they established the boundary line between North Carolina and Virginia, Byrd maintained a diary. *The Secret History of the Line* was apparently circulated among his friends and included descriptions of the arguments among the supervisors and of their sexual escapades. In addition, he seems to have prepared some of his notes for publication but never saw the project through to publication; this manuscript has now been published as *The History of the Dividing Line,* described by Louis B. Wright as a classic of early American literature. This narrative gives a detailed view of life on the frontier. Byrd was to make two other trips into the frontier in 1732 and 1733. The journals of these trips, *A Progress to the Mines* and *A Journey to the Land of Eden,* record the events.

Marion Tinling has edited *The Correspondence of the Three William Byrds of Westover, Virginia, 1684–1776.* The letters of William Byrd II included here provide additional insights.

Overview of Critical Sources

Although most criticism of Byrd's works focuses on his life, attention has also been paid to his literary abilities and place in colonial history and society. Only two books have thus far been published of Byrd criticism, and one of these is a dissertation (Henry A. Robertson, Jr. *A Critical Analysis of William Byrd II and His Literary Technique in "The History of the Dividing Line" and "The Secret History of the Line,"* The University of Delaware, 1966). Therefore, those looking for criticism must find it in shorter form—either articles or chapters in books. In addition, scholars should not overlook the useful introductions in collections of Byrd's writings, such as John Spenser Bassett, *The Writings of Colonel William Byrd of Westover in Virginia* (New York: Burt Franklin, 1901, 1970); William K. Boyd, *William Byrd's Histories of the Dividing Line betwixt Virginia and North Carolina* (New York: Dover, 1929, 1967); and Louis B. Wright, *The Prose Works of William Byrd of Westover: Narratives of a Colonial Virginian* (Cambridge: Harvard University Press, 1966).

Evaluation of Selected Criticism

Marambaud, Pierre, *William Byrd of Westover, 1674–1744.* Charlottesville: University Press of Virginia, 1971. This French scholar has written the major scholarly book on Byrd, a mixture of history and literary criticism. Marambaud sees Byrd as essentially a talented literary amateur and believes that Byrd's strongest claim to literary fame rests with his *History of the Dividing Line.* Among the valuable sections of this book are chapters on Byrd's personality and on the plantation legend which has influenced Southern literature. It is Marambaud's judgment that Byrd was the first Southern writer of any real value.

Other Sources

Cutting, Rose Marie, *John and William Bartram, William Byrd II and St. John de Crèvecoeur: A Reference Guide.* Boston: G. K. Hall, 1976. Cutting provides a detailed annotated bibliography to works about Byrd.

Davis, Richard Beale, "William Byrd: Taste and Tolerance," in Everett Emerson, ed. *Major Writers of Early American Literature.* Madison: University of Wisconsin Press, 1972. This review of Byrd's writings places him in Southern culture and literature.

Lynn, Kenneth S. *Mark Twain and Southwestern Humor.* Westport, CT: Greenwood, 1959, 1972. Lynn demonstrates Byrd's contributions to American humor.

Masterson, James R. "William Byrd in Lubberland," *American Literature,* IX (1937-1938), 153-168. This article documents Byrd's view of the poor in North Carolina.

McIlwaine, Shields, *The Southern Poor-White from Lubberland to Tobacco Road.* New York: Cooper Square, 1939, 1970. A chapter discusses Byrd's view of the poor.

Siebert, Donald T., Jr. "William Byrd's *Histories of the Line:* The Fashioning of a Hero," *American Literature,* XIVL (1975-1976), 535-551. Siebert shows Byrd's English sources.

Simpson, Lewis P. *The Dispossessed Garden: Pastoral and History in Southern Literature.* Athens: University of Georgia Press, 1975. A chapter discusses the garden as metaphor in writings by Byrd and Robert Beverley.

Weathers, Willie T. "William Byrd: Satirist," *William and Mary Quarterly,* IV (1947), 27-41. This article describes the English roots and American subjects of Byrd's satire.

Robert A. Armour
Virginia Commonwealth University

GEORGE GORDON, LORD BYRON
1788–1824

Author's Chronology

Born George Gordon Byron, January 22, 1788, London, England; his right foot deformed from birth; *1791* his father dies in France; until *1798,* raised in Aberdeen; possibly molested by his nurse; *1798* inherits title, moves to Newstead Abbey, Nottinghamshire; *1801* in school at Harrow; *1805* enters Trinity College, Cambridge; friendship with John Edelston; *1809* takes seat in House of Lords; travels to Spain, Turkey, Greece; *1811* returns to England; *1812–1816* years of fame and liaisons; *1815* marries Annabella Milbanke; *1816* separates; leaves England forever (15 April); lives with the Shelleys near Geneva, then Italy; *1817* affairs in Venice; *1819* relationship with Teresa Guiccioli begins; moves to Ravenna; *1822* moves to Pisa to join the Pisan Circle with Shelley, who dies, 8 July; then lives in Leghorn and Albaro, near Genoa; *1823* sails for Greece to take part in the Greek war for independence; *1824* dies at Missolonghi, 19 April.

Author's Bibliography (selected)

Fugitive Pieces, 1806 (destroyed poems); *Hours of Idleness,* 1807; "English Bards and Scotch Reviewers," 1809 (verse satire); *Childe Harold's Pilgrimage,* cantos I and II, 1812; III, 1816; IV, 1818 (poem); "The Giaour" and other poetic tales, 1813–1814; "The Prisoner of Chillon," 1816 (poem); *Manfred,* 1817 (verse drama); "Beppo," 1818 (poem); *Don Juan,* 1818–1824 (poem); "A Vision of Judgment," 1822 (poem); *Cain* and other plays, 1821–1822.

Overview of Biographical Sources

Few literary figures, if any, have received more biographical attention. Between 1824 (his death) and 1830, Robert C. Dallas, Thomas Medwin, Leigh Hunt, Pietro Gamba, Leicester Stanhope, William Parry, and James Kennedy all wrote books recalling their associations with Byron. Thomas Moore's *Letters and Journals of Lord Byron, with Notice of His Life* (1830) was the first full biography. Further anecdotes and observations then appeared in books by Lady Blessington, Teresa Guiccioli, and Edward J. Trelawney (the last being colorful but not always reliable). A large number of other associates, including Percy and Mary Shelley, Claire Claremont, Thomas Moore, Samuel Rogers, Walter Scott, John Cam Hobhouse, Lady Caroline Lamb, John William Polidori, and Edward E. Williams also described Byron in letters and journals. Ernest J. Lovell's *His Very Self and Voice: Collected Conversations of Lord Byron* (1954) is a very useful source.

Modern psychoanalytical approaches to Byron began in 1905 with Lord Lovelace's *Astarte* (privately printed), which endorsed a controversial revelation by Lady Byron on her deathbed in 1869 (and reported by Harriet Beecher Stowe the next year) that Byron's relationship with his half-sister Augusta had been incestuous. Ethel C. Mayne, in *Byron* (1912; rev. 1924) and Sir John C. Fox, *The Byron Mystery* (1924) accepted the incest theory, which was disputed the next year by John Drinkwater in *The Pilgrim of Eternity* (1925). Its truth is now generally assumed. Important biographies since the centennial of Byron's birth include Andre Maurois, *Byron* (1930); Harold Nicolson, *Byron: The Last Journey, 1823–1824* (1924; 1940); Peter C. Quennell, *Byron: The Years of Fame* (1935) and *Byron in Italy* (1941); C. L. Clim, *Byron, Shelley, and Their Pisan Circle* (1952), and John Buxton, *Byron and Shelley: The History of a Friendship* (1968). Utilizing a copy of Moore's *Life* annotated by John Cam Hobhouse, Nicolson (1940) and Quennell discovered Byron's bisexuality, since stressed by Bernard Grebanier in *The Uninhibited Byron: An Account of His Sexual Confusion* (1970). The longest, fullest, and most respected biography of Byron currently available, however, is Leslie A. Marchand, *Byron: A Biography* (3 vols., 1957). His *Byron: A Portrait* (1970) both abridges and amends the longer work.

Evaluation of Selected Biographies

Drinkwater, John, *The Pilgrim of Eternity*. New York: Doran, 1925. Though unable to refute their charge of incest, Drinkwater briskly calumniated both Stowe and Lovelace for sensationalism and folly; a useful corrective to muckrakers before and since. His Byron, unfortunately, is unlikely to have been the real one.

Marchand, Leslie A. *Byron: A Biography*. 3 vols. New York: Alfred A. Knopf, 1957. This is the fullest, most objective, and best documented life of Byron presently available. Marchand, who edited the twelve volume edition of Byron's letters, brings to his biography full erudition and scholarship required to sort Byron's legend from the facts of his life. Covering the entire scope of Byron's life, Marchand acknowledges the full-spirited, adventuresome Byron without being overly impressed with the rhetoric and self-image Byron depicts in his letters. For all of its careful scholarship, however, Marchand is limited by the wealth of materials about Byron recorded and distorted by his admirers and critics.

Mayne, Ethel Colburn, *Byron*. Second edition. New York: Barnes and Noble, 1924; rpt. 1969. Significantly more rigorous than Moore, and the first full biography since his, Mayne effectively began the modern analysis of Byron.

Moore, Thomas, *Letters and Journals of Lord Byron, with Notice of His Life*. London: John Murray, 1830 (with many later editions). As scholarship, Moore's work has been superseded, with his versions of Byron's letters being particularly unreliable. Still valuable, however, are Moore's personal recollections and others contributed anonymously by Mary Shelley.

Origo, Iris, *The Last Attachment: The Story of Byron and Teresa Guiccioli.* New York: Charles Scribner's Sons, 1949. Of all recent books detailing a portion of Byron's life, this is the most important, covering Byron's years 1819–1824. Based in part on Guiccioli's published recollections, it utilized her extensive private archives as well and is indispensable for this relationship and Byron's Italian years.

Autobiographical Sources

Byron's literary works have often been read as veiled autobiography. A standard critical problem in approaching both *Childe Harold's Pilgrimage* and *Don Juan,* especially, is to ascertain what role, if any, Byron himself is taking in the poem.

Between 1818 and 1821 Byron also drafted a lengthy autobiography which dealt mostly with his years in England. Written in Italy, the manuscript was transmitted to Thomas Moore. When news of Byron's death arrived in England (May 1824), elaborate consultations were held among Moore, John Murray, and others regarding proper disposal of the shocking document. At the instigation of Murray, it was burned in his fireplace on the 17th. Moore was then commissioned to write an acceptable life of Byron, which presumably reflects Moore's knowledge of the private revelations in the destroyed manuscript.

Byron is almost universally recognized as one of the very finest letter writers in English. The first substantial collection of his letters, by Moore in 1830, was superseded by Roland E. Prothero's in *The Works of Lord Byron . . . Letters and Journals* (6 vols., 1898–1901). This edition, still available in many libraries, includes elaborate annotations useful even now. But the edition one should consult and cite is Leslie A. Marchand, ed. *Byron's Letters and Journals,* 12 vols. Cambridge, MA: Harvard University Press, 1973–1982. No biography of Byron presently incorporates the new material fully.

Overview of Critical Sources

While many good books deal with aspects of Byron's life, or with his life as a whole, it is hard to say as much about those commenting on his art. As is now generally recognized, Byron's poetry is of a popular sort. Techniques of close literary analysis developed within the twentieth century have firmly distinguished Byron's from more sophisticated work, but have only partially defined its unique qualities.

Except for a loyal defense of Alexander Pope, Byron remained relatively uninterested in either literary criticism or theory. His earliest works, through 1812, derive primarily from eighteenth-century poets; the ensuing tales are best analyzed in terms of contemporary prose fiction. Through the influence of Shelley in 1816, Byron attempted to infuse his work (notably *Childe Harold's Pilgrimage,* canto III) with metaphysical depth. This experiment failing, he then returned to the tradition of eighteenth-century satire he had first utilized in "English Bards and Scotch Reviewers" (1809) but now augmented with models from Italian literature, as became apparent in "Beppo" (1818). Semi-dramatic works like *Manfred* (1817) and *Cain* (1821) were influenced by still other models. *Don Juan* (1819–1824) is often regarded as his finest and most original work.

Evaluation of Selected Criticism

Marchand, Leslie A. *Byron's Poetry: A Critical Introduction.* Boston: Houghton Mifflin, 1965. In contrast to Rutherford Marchand's survey is predictably more concerned with Byron's life. Descriptive rather than evaluative, it is particularly helpful in its summaries of longer works, in its awareness of dramatic details, and of structure imposed by the chronology of events.

Rutherford, Andrew, *Byron: A Critical Study.* Stanford, CA: Stanford University Press, 1961. Remarkably free of biographical controversy, this is probably the best introduction to Byron's poems. Regarding the poems solely as literature, Rutherford ignores the sensational social elements which made Byron the most "read" poet of his time.

Thorslev, Peter L. *The Byronic Hero: Types and Prototypes.* Minneapolis: University of Minnesota Press, 1962. One of the two or three most helpful commentaries, this one deals with the important subject of Byron's characterization. Summing up a good deal of earlier criticism, Thorslev finds many Byronic protagonists anticipated in Romantic prose fiction, and explains how a "character type" was transformed into a "prototype" which embodied the fears and desires of an age.

Trueblood, Paul G. *Lord Byron.* New York: Twayne, 1969. A basic survey for students, Trueblood's is biographically up to date while emphasizing twentieth-century critical opinion.

Other Sources

Gleckner, Robert F. *Byron and the Ruins of Paradise.* Baltimore: Johns Hopkins University Press, 1967. Concerned primarily with the Romantic Byron, Gleckner concentrates upon works written before 1816.

McGann, Jerome, *Fiery Dust: Byron's Poetic Development.* Chicago: University of Chicago Press, 1968. Emphasizing *Childe Harold's Pilgrimage,* McGann's book is often considered the finest critical study of Byron.

Ridenour, George M. *The Style of Don Juan.* New Haven: Yale University Press, 1960. A major study of Byron as satirist.

Dennis R. Dean
University of Wisconsin-Parkside

GEORGE WASHINGTON CABLE
1844–1925

Author's Chronology

Born October 12, 1844, New Orleans; *1859* father dies; assumes father's position in custom house; *1863* enlists in Confederate Army; *1869* begins "Drop Shot" column in New Orleans *Picayune; 1873* publishes " 'Sieur George"; other stories follow over next three years; *1877* H. H. Boyesen initiates correspondence of crucial importance to literary career; *1879* publishes *Old Creole Days;* first installments of *The Grandissimes; 1881* publishes *Madame Delphine;* becomes full-time writer; *1883* first public readings from works; *1884* pieces on Creoles and slavery bring resentment from Southerners and Creoles; reading tour with Mark Twain; *1885* publishes *The Silent South* thereby becoming notorious as a champion of Negro rights; moves to Northampton, Massachusetts; *1886* begins Home Culture Clubs; *1889* begins twenty year association with Adelene Moffat; *1889* Moffat becomes general secretary of the Home Culture Clubs; *1892* last essay on Southern problems; *1898* makes triumphant reading tour of England; *1907* Adelene Moffat fired; rumors bring Home Culture Clubs under public scrutiny; *1909* Home Culture Clubs renamed "The People's Institute"; *1925* dies January 31 in St. Petersburg, Florida.

Author's Bibliography (selected)

Old Creole Days, 1879 (short stories); *The Grandissimes: A Story of Creole Life,* 1880 (novel); *Madame Delphine,* 1881 (novelette—included in subsequent editions of *Old Creole Days*); *The Creoles of Louisiana,* 1884 (essays); *Dr. Sevier,* 1884 (novel); *The Silent South,* 1885 (essays); *The Cavalier,* 1901 (novel).

Overview of Biographical Sources

Cable, long considered primarily as a member of the "Local Color" movement, was both immensely popular and deeply reviled during most of his life; he is currently receiving a level of critical attention appropriate to his rightful place in American letters. The earliest biography of merit is daughter Lucy Leffingwell (Cable) Biklé's *George W. Cable: His Life and Letters* (New York: Charles Scribner's Sons, 1928; rpt. New York: Russell and Russell, 1967). Mrs. Biklé sympathetically tells the story of her father's life, omitting much of the controversy surrounding his writings on behalf of Negro rights. She quotes extensively from Cable's correspondence. The standard biography continues to be Arlin Turner's *George Washington Cable: A Biography* (1966). A *précis* of Turner's longer work is his *George W. Cable* (Austin, Texas: Steck-Vaughan Co. Southern Writers Series no. 1, 1969). The forty-four page biographical and critical study discusses both the fiction and non-fiction, with short appraisals of major works. A third effort by Turner is *Mark Twain and George W. Cable: The Record of a Literary Friendship* (East Lansing: Michigan State University Press, 1960), the most detailed examination of the Twain-Cable relationship during their celebrated reading tour. It makes heavy use of Cable's letters to his wife and of Twain's letters to his manager. Philip Butcher, another major Cable scholar, has contributed two significant studies: *George W. Cable* (1962), and *George W. Cable: The Northampton Years* (New York: Columbia University Press, 1959). The latter is the best work on Cable's career as social and civic reformer, especially his activity on behalf of Negro rights, the Open Letter Club, and Home Culture Clubs. His relationship with Adelene Moffat is explored in depth, aided by extensive materials she provided. Louis D. Rubin, Jr.'s *George W. Cable: The Life and Times of a Southern Heretic* (1969) is a critical biography placing Cable's work in the "Genteel Tradition," in relationship to the overall growth and development of Southern writing.

Evaluation of Selected Biographies

Butcher, Philip, *George W. Cable.* New York: Twayne, 1964. This is probably the best biography for undergraduate readers. Chronologically arranged, the narrative of Cable's life is interrupted by discussions of important fictional and social writing in light of the life and times of their author. While sympathetic, Butcher is not a blind apologist for all of Cable's work; some of his evaluations are acerbic, albeit well-informed and often deserving. The biography lacks the detail of Turner's work but does not contradict it in any significant way. The endnotes are frequently expository, and the book contains an annotated selected bibliography.

Rubin, Louis D., Jr. *George Washington Cable: The Life and Times of a Southern Heretic.* New York: Western Publishing Co., 1969. This survey of Cable's career is novelistically written and thus extremely readable. It emphasizes the socially relevant aspects of Cable's life and work, and cogently analyzes both the fiction and non-fiction. Rubin makes extensive use of Cable's correspondence, typescripts of Cable's works, and his early "Drop Shot" columns. Rubin's thesis that Cable's growing social concerns strangled his artistic abilities is one with which Butcher, to an extent, disagrees.

Turner, Arlin, *George Washington Cable: A Biography.* Durham, NC: Duke University Press, 1956; rpt. LSU Press, 1966. Turner's massive biography remains definitive, heavily cited by all subsequent biographers. Ideally suited for graduate students and scholars, it meticulously details Cable's life; the style is pedestrian—a deficiency compensated for by the rich detail and documentation. The work is particularly useful for its discussion of the New Orleans *milieu* and Cable's relationships with Twain and Moffat. There are extensive footnotes—many of them usefully expository.

Overview of Critical Sources

Because Cable's career spanned so many areas, and because he aroused deep and widespread feelings of both admiration and condemnation, there is a vast amount of critical material dating from the earliest phases of his career, and continuing unabated to this day in scholarly studies, theses, and dissertation. Discussions of Cable focus on politics, education, social history, race relations, southern literature, American fiction, and other topics with which Cable concerned himself over an amazingly productive and long career.

Evaluation of Selected Criticism

Robertson, William H. *George Washington Cable: An Annotated Bibliography.* Metuchen, NJ: The Scarecrow Press, 1982. This is an indispensable book for anyone intending to do research on Cable. It is a complete listing of writings by and about Cable through 1980 in a format elegantly designed and impeccably executed. Writings by Cable include every known essay, column, letter, and book that this amazingly prolific writer published. Writings about Cable (both as central subject, and peripherally) include books and pamphlets, articles, parts of books, recordings, reviews, and dissertations and theses. In an appendix, Robertson gives a complete catalogue of special collections of Cable source materials and their locations. The annotations are precise, concise, and informative. The volume is the first place to go before undertaking any project on any aspect on Cable's life, career, or thought.

Turner, Arlin, *Critical Essays on George W. Cable.* Boston: G. K. Hall, 1980. This collection, with a superb introduction tracing Cable's literary career and discussing the development of Cable scholarship, is a compilation of sixty-three items many of which are of a critical nature, including several previously unpublished Cable letters. They include both contemporaneous and modern appraisals of Cable's fiction and non-fiction. The selections are somewhat arbitrary if representative, serving as an excellent sourcebook.

Other Sources

Southern Quarterly, 18 (Summer 1980), 1–73. In this special Cable issue, Theodore J. Richardson discusses the critical history of Cable scholarship, especially as it relates to *The Grandissimes.* It contains six articles representing a cross section of current thought and approaches to Cable's finest and most famous novel.

Selected Dictionaries and Encyclopedias

Critical Survey of Long Fiction, Salem Press, 1983. Brief biography, and short analyses of *The Grandissimes* and *Madame Delphine.*

The Literary History of the United States, 3rd ed., The Macmillan Company, 1963. Carlos Baker provides a brief biography and appraisal in context of the Local Color movement; special attention to *The Grandissimes.*

David Sadkin
Niagara University

CAEDMON
600's

Author's Chronology

Born during the early seventh century in Yorkshire, England; lived a secular life as a herdsman until advanced age; sometime between *658* and *680* left a dinner early to avoid being called upon to sing to the harp; that night composed "Caedmon's Hymn" to praise the Creator as ordered to by a figure in a dream; was received by Abbess Hild into the Monastery of Streaneshalch, now Whitby, where he spent the rest of his life turning scriptural history into poetry.

Author's Bibliography

"Caedmon's Hymn," (poem).

Overview of Biographical Sources

It was only through the interest of the eighth-century historian Bede in the story of the first Christian poet that any information was preserved about the poet Caedmon. Although scholars have been able to verify parts of the story, Bede's account of Caedmon's life is still the only authoritative source of information: *Bede's Ecclesiastical History of the English People,* eds. B. Colgrave and R. A. B. Mynors (1969). However, translations of and commentaries on the events can also be found in critical discussions of "Caedmon's Hymn," such as Bernard F. Huppé's chapter "Caedmon's Hymn," in *Doctrine and Poetry: Augustine's Influence on Old English Poetry* (1959), pp. 99–130, and the introduction to A. H. Smith's edition, *Three Northumbrian Poems: Caedmon's Hymn, Bede's Death Song and the Leiden Riddle* (New York: Appleton-Century-Crofts, 1968).

Evaluation of Selected Biographies

Colgrave, B. and R. A. B. Mynors, eds. *Bede's Ecclesiastical History of the English People.* Oxford: Clarendon Press, 1969, pp. 415–421. In this standard edition of the text, Colgrave and Mynors give both the Latin version and a clear and readable English translation of Bede's account. The introduction to the edition and explanatory notes are helpful in understanding Bede's methods and reliability as a historian.

Huppé, Bernard F. "Caedmon's Hymn," *Doctrine and Poetry: Augustine's Influence on Old English Poetry.* New York: SUNY, 1959, pp. 99–130. Huppé's paraphrase of the paragraphs from Bede precedes an excellent critical analysis explaining Bede's reaction to the poem in terms of Augustinian aesthetics.

Magoun, Francis P. "Bede's Story of Caedmon: The Case History of an Anglo-Saxon Oral Singer," *Speculum,* 30 (1955), 49–63. After translating Bede's

Caedmon story, Magoun discusses the date of the hymn, the poet's age, and the literary background. Magoun concludes the hymn must have developed from earlier Christian poetry.

Smith, A. H. *Three Northumbrian Poems: Caedmon's Hymn, Bede's Death Song and the Leiden Riddle.* New York: Appleton-Century-Crofts, 1968. Smith recounts Bede's version of Caedmon's life and argues for its historical authenticity. A thorough analysis of the orthography, language, and variants among the texts is also included.

Overview of Critical Sources

Although many early critical studies argued for including as Caedmon's works the biblical paraphrases and poems found in the Junius Manuscript, modern critics now agree that of the works previously attributed to Caedmon only the hymn is his. Predominantly articles or chapters in books, much current scholarship focuses on the cultural and religious traditions that may have influenced "Caedmon's Hymn," including Augustinian, Celtic, patristic, and prophetic elements. Several studies trace the textual history of the manuscripts, and still other scholars have noted the many analogues in world literature to the story of the divinely inspired poet. Only one book-length study of Caedmon's poem is widely available: C. L. Wrenn, *The Poetry of Caedmon* (1947; rpt. 1969).

Evaluation of Selected Criticism

Dobbie, Elliott Van Kirk, *The Manuscripts of Caedmon's Hymn and Bede's Death Song.* New York: Columbia University Press, 1937. Dobbie's excellent study of the historical descent and distribution of the manuscripts containing the poem corrects misreadings in earlier editions.

Schwab, Ute, *Caedmon.* University of Messina: Istituto di Lingue e Letterature Germaniche, 1972; printed in abbreviated and revised form as "The Miracles of Caedmon," *English Studies,* 64 (February 1983), 1–17. Schwab notes that it was in the monastery at the hands of learned monks that oral poetry like "Caedmon's Hymn" became literature. The hymn is not an improvisation, with its sophisticated vocabulary, order, and rhythm.

Wrenn, C. L. *The Poetry of Caedmon.* 1947; rpt. Folcroft, PA.: The Folcroft Press, 1969. Wrenn summarizes the critical history of "Caedmon's Hymn" from Alfred's time on. He also notes the evidence of an oral tradition in the poem.

Other Sources

Bloomfield, Morton W. "Patristics and Old English Literature: Notes on Some Poems." *Studies in Old English Literature in Honor of Arthur G. Brodeur.*

ed. Stanley B. Greenfield. New York: Russell & Russell, 1973, pp. 36–43. Bloomfield uses a study of the early Christian Fathers to illuminate the hymn.

Frampton, M. G. "Cadmon's Hymn," *Modern Philology,* 22 (August 1924), 1–15. This detailed study of the seventeen manuscripts of the poem finds the Moore Manuscript to be the oldest and most authoritative.

Henry, P. L. "The Origin of *Caedmon's Hymn," The Early English and Celtic Lyric.* New York: Barnes and Noble, 1967, pp. 209–215. Through a diction and meter analysis, Henry traces the Celtic influence on "Caedmon's Hymn."

Shepherd, G. "The Prophetic Caedmon," *Review of English Studies,* NS 5 (1954), 113–122. Citing examples of other early English Christians who could prophesy, Shepherd places Caedmon in the English prophetic tradition.

Selected Dictionaries and Encyclopedias

Dictionary of National Biography, Macmillan & Co., 1886. Complete overview of the events of Caedmon's life and the early scholarship on his poem.

Encyclopaedia Britannica, 1973. Full review of Bede's account of Caedmon and the poetry attributed to him.

The Oxford Companion to English Literature, Clarendon Press, 1967. Brief account of Caedmon and his work.

The Reader's Encyclopedia, Thomas Y. Crowell, 1948. Brief mention of Caedmon as a poet.

Marilyn S. Butler
Iowa State University

ERSKINE CALDWELL
1903

Author's Chronology

Born December 17, 1903, White Oak, Coweta County, Georgia; parents are the Reverend Ira Sylvester Caldwell (Presbyterian minister) and Caroline Bell Caldwell of Staunton, Virginia; September *1920* enters Erskine College in Due West, South Carolina; also attends the University of Virginia on a DAR scholarship and the University of Pennsylvania; does not graduate from either college; *1925* marries Helen Lannegan; fathers three children; *1926* publishes first piece, "The Georgia Cracker;" *1933–1943* works as a journalist, Hollywood writer, and foreign correspondent in Europe and Mexico; *1938* divorces Lannegan; *1939* marries photographer Margaret Bourke-White; *1940* travels to China, Mongolia, and Turkestan; collaborates with Bourke-White on four books between *1937* and *1942; 1942* divorces; marries June Johnson and fathers a son; *1957* divorces Johnson; marries Virginia Moffat Fletcher; tours Europe in the *1960's* for the United States State Department; continues to write and live in Florida.

Author's Bibliography (selected)

The Bastard, 1929 (novel); *American Earth,* 1930 (novel); *Tobacco Road,* 1932 (novel); *God's Little Acre,* 1933 (novel); *Journeyman,* 1935 (novel); *Kneel to the Rising Sun,* 1935 (short stories); *You Have Seen Their Faces* with Margaret Bourke-White, 1937 (picture-text book); *Trouble in July,* 1940 (novel); *Say! Is This the U.S.A.* with Margaret Bourke-White, 1941 (picture-text); *Georgia Boy,* 1943 (novel); *Tragic Ground,* 1944 (novel); *The Sure Hand of God,* 1947 (novel); *Call It Experience,* 1951 (autobiography); *Deep South,* 1968 (non-fiction).

Overview of Biographical Sources

Biographical sources in English on Erskine Caldwell are generally limited to those in such standard references as *Authors Today and Yesterday* (1933), *Current Biography* (1940), *Twentieth Century Authors* (1942, 1955), and *Southern Writers: A Biographical Dictionary* (1979). Articles dealing with aspects of his life, especially his career, are available in such periodicals as *The Nation, The New Republic, Atlantic Monthly, Esquire,* and *Life.* Many are interviews with Caldwell. William A. Sutton's article in *The Courier* (1973), "Margaret Bourke-White and Erskine Caldwell: A Personal Album," details his most famous marriage. A recent biographical piece is Donald Noble's "Erskine Caldwell: A Biographical Sketch," *Pembroke* Magazine (1979).

Autobiographical Sources

Two autobiographical books, written nearly twenty years apart, can provide some of the biographical details missing from the scanty chronologies listed above. *Call It Experience: The Years of Learning to Write* (1951) concerns Caldwell's life as a writer from the "humble beginnings" to his ultimate successes as one of America's best-selling writers. Anecdotal, reportorial in style, it contains many verifiable facts and is highly readable. *Deep South: Memory and Observation* (1966) concerns in the main Caldwell's observations about his preacher father and the presence of religion in his youth. Anecdotes about the people he met travelling about the South with his father and in the various parishes where his father was assigned give insights into the life that produced the characters and events of some of his writings.

Overview of Critical Sources

Many articles and book chapters have been devoted to Caldwell's prodigious output. A few doctoral dissertations are available as well. These sources treat the author as a delineator of grotesqueries, black humor, primitivism, naturalism, and pornography, and as a chronicler of Southern poverty and social, economic, and racial problems. Except for mention in the Korges source (below), little critical attention has been paid to the documentary picture-texts done with Bourke-White although these works are judged by some critics to be excellent for the genre. The works most often discussed are his novels written in the 1930s and 1940s.

Evaluation of Selected Criticism

Beach, Joseph Warren, *American Fiction 1920–1940.* New York: Macmillan, 1941. Two chapters are devoted to Caldwell's early novels, from *Tobacco Road* to *Trouble in July.* They look at the author's sociological aims, his commentary on the poverty of Southern whites, his use of comic effect to make the "moral seriousness" of his work more imaginative and palatable. It analyzes some of his most memorable characters.

Curley, Dorothy N. and others, *Modern American Literature.* Vol. I. New York: Frederick Ungar, 1973. This is a useful source of brief excerpts from some of the most-often cited critical materials on Caldwell. It contains commentaries on him as a writer, on the most affecting literary trends, his themes, creative aims, style, and critical rank as a writer. It serves as a good preliminary bibliographical source.

Jacobs, Robert D. "The Humor of *Tobacco Road,*" in Louis D. Rubin, ed. *The Comic Imagination in American Literature.* New Brunswick, NJ: Rutgers University Press, 1973. This chapter addresses the comic elements in *Tobacco*

Road, Caldwell's intent in using them and the prototypes that earlier American humorists had developed that Caldwell modernizes.

Korges, James, *Erskine Caldwell.* University of Minnesota Pamphlets on American Writers No. 78. Minneapolis: University of Minnesota Press, 1969. A highly readable, brief critique of Caldwell's work, including his *Call It Experience* (1951) and the non-fiction *In Search of Bisco* (1965). It contains a rare examination of early novels *The Sacrilege of Alan Kent* (1936), *The Bastard* (1929) and *Poor Fool* (1930). There is a brief discussion of the picture-texts done with Bourke-White and of some of his short stories. The perceptive analyses of *Tobacco Road, God's Little Acre, Journeyman, Trouble in July, Georgia Boy,* and *Miss Mamma Aimee* reveal Caldwell's strengths and weaknesses and some of the not-so-apparent values in his best work.

MacDonald, Scott, *Critical Essays on Erskine Caldwell.* Boston: G. K. Hall, 1981. This is a collection of reviews and essays on Caldwell. Some are written by Caldwell.

Other Sources

Pembroke Magazine, 11 (1979). The entire issue is devoted to Caldwell and contains 26 articles, biographical and critical.

White, William, "About Erskine Caldwell: A Checklist, 1933–1980," *Bulletin of Bibliography,* 39 (March 1982), 9—16, and an addendum in the December 1982 issue, pp. 224–226. This bibliography lists mostly periodical articles and book chapters dealing with Caldwell's life and work, arranged chronologically from 1933 to 1979 (the addendum includes works published in 1982). Many foreign language works are included.

Selected Dictionaries and Encyclopedias

Contemporary Authors, Gale Research, 1967. Succinct discussion of biographical and career highlights, bibliography of his works from 1930 to 1967 and of biographical and critical sources. An overview of his critical reception.

Southern Writers: A Biographical Dictionary, Louisiana State University Press, 1979. More biographical detail about his parents and his early life than in most references. Personal insights, such as Caldwell's children's names and the possible source of the rumor of his Communist leanings, are touched on.

Jane L. Ball
Wilberforce University

MORLEY CALLAGHAN
1903

Author's Chronology

Born February 22, 1903, Toronto, Canada, of Roman Catholic parents; *1921* enters St. Michael's College at the University of Toronto; participates in boxing, debating, and hockey; *1923* works for *Toronto Star* four summers; befriended and encouraged by Ernest Hemingway at *Star; 1925* graduates with B.A.; same year enrolls in Osgoode Hall law school; *1926* first story, "A Girl With Ambition" published in *This Quarter,* Paris, France; visits Nathan Asch, Ford Madox Ford, Katherine Anne Porter, Allen Tate, William Carlos Williams in New York; *1928* graduates from Osgoode and admitted to Ontario, Canada bar; for a period of fourteen years accepted in J. Edward O'Brien's *Best Short Stories; 1929* marries Loretto Dee; writes in Paris and meets Hemingway, F. Scott Fitzgerald, James Joyce, and other literary expatriates; *1940* monthly commentaries commissioned for *New World Magazine; 1943* appears on radio for Canadian Broadcasting Company (CBC); *1950* becomes regular panelist on CBC show *Fighting Words; 1952* wins Canada's major literary prize, the Governor General's Award; *1960* Lorne Pierce Medal for Literature from Royal Society of Canada; *1965* receives honorary Doctor of Letters, University of Western Ontario; *1966* Canada Council Medal; *1970* Molson Award; Royal Bank of Canada Award.

Author's Bibliography (selected)

Strange Fugitive, 1928 (novel); *A Native Argosy,* 1929 (stories); *It's Never Over,* 1930 (novel); *Such Is My Beloved,* 1934 (novel); *Now That April's Here and Other Stories,* 1936; *More Joy in Heaven,* 1937 (novel); *Luke Baldwin's Vow,* 1948 (children's literature); *The Loved and the Lost,* 1951 (novel); *Morley Callaghan's Stories,* 1959; *A Passion in Rome,* 1961 (novel); *That Summer in Paris,* 1963 (autobiography); *A Fine and Private Place,* 1975 (novel); *Close to the Sun Again,* 1977 (novel); *A Time for Judas,* 1983 (novel); *Our Lady of the Snows,* 1985 (novel).

Overview of Biographical Sources

In his 1965 book, *O Canada: An American's Notes on Canadian Culture,* Edmund Wilson declares Morley Callaghan the "most unjustly neglected novelist in the English speaking world." Although this statement is not as true today as it was then, as Callaghan's awards prove, the lack of biographical work can be judged as scandalous. No major biography has been done at all, which is even more puzzling considering the longevity of his career and the distinction of his work. Cursory treatments of his life have been included in the lengthy critical evaluations, but they offer few insights into the complex nature of his thought.

Evaluation of Selected Biographies

Conron, Brandon, *Morley Callaghan.* New York: Twayne, 1966. Conron, himself, comments that his book is the first comprehensive study of Callaghan's writings. Although the focus is mainly critical, Conron provides a short biography which outlines the central events in Callaghan's life. He suggests that Callaghan's early apprenticeship for the *Toronto Star* newspaper led him to adopt a reportorial style for his fiction. Some of Callaghan's influences, Sherwood Anderson, Hemingway, and Jacques Maritain, are noted but not analyzed in depth. Often superficial and hackneyed, this is still valuable as an introduction to Callaghan's work.

Sutherland, Fraser, *The Style of Innocence: A Study of Hemingway and Callaghan.* Toronto: Clarke, Irwin, 1972. A lively, opinionated examination of both writers, especially Hemingway's effect on Callaghan, which, Sutherland argues, is greater than most critics believe. His interpretation of the writing is intelligent and probing, but Sutherland relies much too heavily on John Glassco's *Memoirs of Montparnasse* (Toronto: Oxford, 1970) and Callaghan's *That Summer in Paris* for his biographical material.

Autobiographical Sources

That Summer in Paris (New York: Coward-McCann and Toronto: Macmillan, 1963) is a calculated and dramatic memoir of Callaghan's literary life in 1929. He presents both attractive and critical portraits of Sherwood Anderson, Sinclair Lewis, Robert McAlmon, Sylvia Beach, James Joyce and others of a jealous, transient, and creative community. In the most compelling vignette, Callaghan recounts his legendary boxing knockdown of Hemingway with Fitzgerald as time-keeper. The book is not wholly anecdotal, however, with Callaghan articulating the developing literary perceptions which informed much of his fictional style. Unfortunately, this incomplete record must remain the major published source of information on Callaghan's life.

Overview of Critical Sources

In his autobiographical novel *A Fine and Private Place,* Callaghan uses the persona of neglected novelist, Eugene Shore, to promote his reputation as a significant author. He indulges in attacks on critics who ignore, dismiss, or misinterpret his contribution to literature. This bitterness is understandable, but Callaghan has always been well thought of by his peers, and over the last twenty-five years more frequent and sympathetic critical analysis has tended to right the balance.

Evaluation of Selected Criticism

Conron, Brandon, ed. *Morley Callaghan.* Toronto: McGraw-Hill, Ryerson Limited, 1975. Conron compiles twenty-two articles by figures such as Sinclair

Lewis, R. P. Blackmur, Maxwell Perkins, Wyndom Lewis, and William Saroyan. These are largely positive pictures of various aspects of Callaghan's work, verifying the wide appeal of Callaghan among international writers.

Hoar, Victor, *Morley Callaghan.* Toronto: Copp Clarke, 1969. In a short book with two long sections, Hoar explores Callaghan's technique and important themes. Hoar's approach is interesting, but he underestimates the symbolic value and the passion of Callaghan's prose.

Morley, Patricia, *Morley Callaghan.* Toronto: McClelland and Stewart, 1978. Unlike many critics, Morley finds Callaghan's novels superior to his short stories. In this brief monograph, she censures Callaghan for his dated views on women, but values his comic perspective and his unifying cosmic vision.

Staines, David, ed. *The Callaghan Symposium.* Ottawa: University of Ottawa Press, 1981. Staines includes a panel discussion and seven lengthy and penetrating articles by Canadian critics on a wide range of topics.

Other Sources

Cameron, Donald, "There are Gurus in the Woodwork," *Conversations With Canadian Novelists.* 2. Toronto: Macmillan, 1973. A witty and sometimes abrasive interview essential to studies of Callaghan.

Dooley, D. J. *Moral Vision in the Canadian Novel.* Clarke, Irwin, 1979. Contains an excellent, tough-minded essay on the critical problems inherent in the work of an author so often inclined to moral ambiguity.

Wilson, Edmund, *O Canada: An American's Notes on Canadian Culture.* New York: Farrar, Straus, Giroux, 1965. Famous essay on Callaghan which tries to rescue him from critical obscurity.

Selected Dictionaries and Encyclopedias

Contemporary Novelists, 3rd ed. St. Martin's Press, 1982. Short entry by William Walsh provides a biography, bibliography, and commentary.

Critical Survey of Long Fiction, Salem Press, 1983. Biography, influences, and analysis of Callaghan's major works before *A Time for Judas.*

James C. MacDonald
Humber College

THOMAS CAMPION
1567-1620

Author's Chronology

Born February 12, 1567 in London; *1581* enters Peterhouse, Cambridge; *1584* leaves Cambridge, apparently without a degree; *1586* admitted to Gray's Inn to study law; *1591* five songs by Campion under the pseudonym "Content" appear appended to surreptitious edition of Sidney's *Astrophil and Stella; 1591-1592* probably serves under Sir Robert Carey in Essex Norman expedition sent to aid Henri IV against the Catholic League; *1594* composes at least one song for *Gesta Grayorum,* a revels presented at court; *1595* publishes *Thomas Campiani Poemata; 1601* publishes *A Book of Ayres* with lutenist Philip Rosseter; *1602* publishes *Observations in the Art of English Poesie; 1603* Samuel Daniel publishes *A Defense of Ryme* to answer Campion's *Observations; 1605* receives medical degree from the University of Caen in France; probably returns to London to practice medicine; perhaps converts to Roman Catholicism while on the Continent; *1607 The Lord Hay's Masque* performed at court; *1613(?) Two Bookes of Ayres* published; *1613 Songs of Mourning* on the death of Prince Henry (d. November 6, 1612) published; music by Coperario, words by Campion; *1613 The Lords' Masque, The Caversham Entertainment, The Somerset Masque* all performed at Court; *1613-1614(?)* publishes *A New Way of Making Fowre Parts in Counter-point; 1615* Campion examined and cleared of complicity in the murder of Sir Thomas Overbury; *1617(?) The Third and Fourth Booke of Ayres* published; *1617 The Ayres That Were Sung and Played at Brougham Castle* by George Mason and John Earsden, perhaps with words by Campion, performed for James I's return from Scotland; *1618* publishes *Ayres; 1619* publishes *Tho. Campiani Epigrammatum Libri II;* 1620 dies and is buried in London.

Author's Bibliography

Campion's Works. The standard editions of Campion's works are: Percival Vivian, ed. 1909; rpt. Oxford: Clarendon Press, 1966. *The Workes of Thomas Campion: Complete Songs, Masques, and Treatises, with a Selection of Latin Verse.* Walter R. Davis, ed. 1967; rpt. New York: W. W. Norton, 1970.

Biographical Sources

No full biography is available, due to paucity of information; most authorities rely on the forty-page biography in Vivian's edition of *Campion's Works.* Davis' edition of Campion's *Works,* as well as the critical studies cited below, repeat the biographical information found in Vivian.

Overview of Critical Sources

Campion has long been considered a minor poet, but acknowledged as an important figure for understanding the English Renaissance. He draws heavily from the poetic commonplaces then current, so that his work exemplifies the major themes and conventions of the late sixteenth and early seventeenth century; Campion gives stock poetic ideas their loveliest poetic expression. He chooses not to write sonnets, composing instead unrhymed verse and experimenting with metres imitating Greek and Latin lyric; his work includes poems based on translations of Catullus, Horace, Ovid, and Propertius. Like Dowland, Daniel, and Alfonso Ferrabosco, Campion also composed "airs," songs for the solo voice, accompanied perhaps by the lute or the viol. Since Campion wrote both words and music, the central problem he has posed for modern critics of literature is assessment of his work. For Campion's original audience, no problem existed; his lyrics were appreciated with or without their musical settings. Most critics, however, either attempt analysis of the poems as songs, or feel that they must justify their study of lyrics divorced from musical settings.

Campion's critics also study his *Observations in the Arte of English Poesie* (1602) as a statement of Campion's theories of prosody, and also as the key to the metrics of his poems. Critics are divided on the significance of the essay. Focusing on the application of Campion's theories to his own poetry, some critics find the essay irrelevant; others find evidence in the poems that Campion was able to practice his own prosodic principles. Current criticism continues to focus on Campion's musicality, either metrically or in studies of lyrics together with their musical settings.

Evaluation of Selected Criticism

Davis, Walter R. ed. *The Works of Thomas Campion.* 1967; rpt. New York: W. W. Norton, 1970. In a brief introduction to his edition, Davis, like Kastendieck, finds Campion's prosodic theory in *Observations in the Arte of English Poesie* "gave rise to his metrical effects in the songs." Davis discusses selected works to illustrate Campion's strength as a "poet of the auditory imagination"—both because of his use of aural, rather than visual description, and because of his practice of "word painting," using the movements of a melodic line to reinforce poetic meaning.

Ing, Catherine, *Elizabethan Lyrics.* London: Chatto and Windus, 1968. In a book on the relationship between Elizabethan music and poetry, Ing's chapter on Campion points out that Campion's words were available to contemporary audiences without their musical settings. Ing finds that Campion's metrical theory makes no significant contribution to his poetic practice, but that his poetic success is attributable to an ear finely tuned to the cadences of English speech.

Kastendieck, Miles M. *England's Musical Poet: Thomas Campion.* 1938; rpt. New York: Russell and Russell, 1963. This early study shaped much subsequent work, since Kastendieck studies Campion as a "poet-musician" and the airs as inseparable from their musical settings. Kastendieck also clarifies Campion's *Observations in the Arte of English Poesie* by substituting modern vocabulary, and finds little or no disparity between his poetry and his prosodic theory.

Lowbury, Edward, Timothy Salter, and Alison Young. *Thomas Campion: Poet, Composer, Physician.* London: Chatto and Windus, 1970; New York: Barnes and Noble, 1970. This study traces Campion's reputation during and after his lifetime, attempting a "multilateral survey" of Campion's work, and considers music and poetry separately. Included is a technical analysis of the music, and studies of the masques.

Mellers, Wilfrid, *Harmonious Meeting: A Study of the Relationship between English Music, Poetry, and Theatre, 1600–1900.* London: Dobson, 1965. This is a general study that includes a discussion of Campion's *Lord Hayes Masque* as an example of the form's becoming a "ritual apotheosis of humanism." In Campion's masque, as in Jonson's, "marriage-concord becomes equated with public concord," exemplifying the aspects of the masque that reinforce celebration of public virtue.

Pattison, Bruce, *Music and Poetry of the English Renaissance.* 1948; rpt. New York: Da Capo Press, 1971. Like Ing, Pattison gives an overview of the relationship of music and poetry in the English Renaissance in his discussions of the madrigal, the air, and Continental influences, Campion is only one example of many Renaissance poet-musicians. Pattison does not analyze individual poems by Campion, but does discuss his prosodic theories, finding, as Ing does, that Campion achieved in his poetry what he was unable to articulate satisfactorily in his theory.

Ratcliffe, Stephen, *Campion: On Song.* Boston: Routledge & Kegan Paul, 1981. Ratcliffe chooses "Now winter nights enlarge" as a representative Campion song. He analyzes it exhaustively, describing syntax, phonetic structures, prosody, and music, in order to arrive at a preliminary "aesthetics of song," a description of what the listener or reader experiences.

Other Sources

Bryan, Margaret B. "Recent Studies in Campion," *English Literary Renaissance* 4 (1974), 404–411. An exhaustive annotated bibliography of Campion's works and secondary sources aimed primarily at specialists.

Irwin, John T. "Thomas Campion and the Musical Emblem," *Studies in English Literature* 10 (1970), 121–141. Argues that Campion's poetry has been underestimated because of the "musical qualification" associated with him; explicates "Now winter nights enlarge" to show that music-related components—phonemic patterns, musical thematic structure, and the symbol of music—produce the complexity of Campion's poetry.

Peltz, Catherine W. "Thomas Campion, An Elizabethan Neo-Classicist," *Modern Language Quarterly* 11 (1950), 3–6. Peltz believes that Campion's insistence on form makes him basically neo-classical; his influence was weaker than Jonson's because of the latter's prestige as a dramatist.

Thompson, John, *The Founding of English Metre.* New York: Columbia University Press, 1966. Standard history of English prosody. Campion is not discussed specifically, but Thompson's chapter on English experiments with classical metres is pertinent to background study for Campion's *Observations in the Arte of English Poesie.*

Selected Dictionaries and Encyclopedias

The Concise Encyclopedia of English and American Poets and Poetry, Hawthorn Books, 1963, 1967. Brief biography, evaluation of Campion's relative importance in the literary canon, and concise summary of criticism of his poems, masques, and *Observations in the Arte of English Poesie.*

English Literature in the Sixteenth Century Excluding Drama, Clarendon Press, 1954–1968. Brief biography, survey of Campion's canon, excellent introduction to his masques. Brief discussion of *Observations;* C. S. Lewis concludes that "when all is said his theory has very little to do with English practice, even his own."

Carmela Pinto McIntire
Florida International University

THOMAS CAREW
1594(?)–1640

Author's Chronology

Born 1594 or 1595 in Kent, England; *1608* enters Merton College, Oxford; *1610* enters Cambridge; *1612* receives degree from Cambridge; *1613* employed by Sir Dudley Carleton, English ambassador to Italy; *1616* released from Carleton's employment after publicly casting doubt on Lady Carleton's fidelity; *1619* attends Sir Edward Herbert on his embassy to Paris; *1624* recalled to England; *1624* begins serious writing and circulates his poetry; *1630* appointed to a court position; *1634 Coelum Britannicum* presented at court; *1639/1640 The Workes of Thomas Carew, Esquire* published; *1640* dies after accompanying Charles I on his first Scottish mission, later referred to as the First Bishops' War.

Bibliography

The Workes of Thomas Carew, Esquire, 1639/1640; *Poems,* 1642; *Poems, with a Masque, by Thomas Carew Esquire,* 1650; *Poems, Songs, and Sonnets, Together with a Masque,* 1670; *The Poems of Thomas Carew with His Masque Coelum Britannicum,* 1949.

Overview of Biographical Sources

Only two book-length studies of Thomas Carew present detailed biographical information, and neither of these is primarily interested in biography. Rhodes Dunlap's *The Poems of Thomas Carew with His Masque Coelum Britannicum* (1949) is the standard edition of Carew's poetry. Moreover, it provides the most detailed treatment of Carew's life available. The primary focus of this biographical sketch is to trace Carew's involvements with important persons in political and literary circles. Dunlap's record is in agreement with the only other book-length study which provides biographical information, Lynn Sadler's *Thomas Carew* (1979).

Evaluation of Selected Biographies

Dunlap, Rhodes, ed. *The Poems of Thomas Carew with His Masque Coelum Britannicum.* Oxford: At the Clarendon Press, 1949. Although the style is encyclopedic, and therefore requires close reading, Dunlap's introduction is the major source of information on Carew's life. He details the numerous difficulties between Carew and his father Mathew Carew and the elder Carew's efforts to help his son progress in political circles. Moreover, he deals with the younger Carew's misspent youth which caused him difficulties with his employers. Dunlap relies heavily on Mathew Carew's letters for his information; however, he tends to speculate excessively about Carew's life after the death of his father when little information is available. The most helpful part of Dunlap's study is his discussion of Carew's reputation as a poet.

Sadler, Lynn, *Thomas Carew.* Boston: Twayne Publishers, 1979. Sadler provides only a brief biographical sketch. As does Dunlap, Sadler tends to emphasize the period of Carew's life between his matriculation from Cambridge and his court appointment, also relying heavily on the letters of Mathew Carew for information. She does not, however, try to fill in the gaps through excessive speculation. Sadler does note the two anecdotes commonly repeated, first about Carew's death-bed conversion and second about his saving Queen Henrietta from being discovered by the King with a court favorite.

Autobiographical Sources

There are technically no autobiographical sources from Thomas Carew. However, much speculation has suggested that his love poems, especially the Celia poems—Celia being a pseudonym—, have an autobiographical element. Specific titles include "Upon some Alterations in my Mistress, after my Departure into France," "Song, To my inconstant Mistress," and "Disdaine returned."

Overview of Critical Sources

In addition to the two studies of Thomas Carew already mentioned, a third, Edward I. Selig's *The Flourishing Wreath: A Study of Thomas Carew's Poetry* (1958), is a major critical study of Carew's poetry. These three are, in fact, the only book-length studies of Carew. Each, however, takes a distinctly different approach to the analysis of Carew's canon.

Evaluation of Selected Criticism

Sadler, Lynn, *Thomas Carew.* Boston: Twayne Publishers, 1979. Sadler's approach to the study of Carew is that popularized by the new critics. Therefore, a student working to develop a detailed understanding of specific titles will find her line by line analysis extremely helpful. The brief biographical sketch is followed by chapters on the Celia poems, the love poems, the poetry which details Carew's aesthetics, the social and court poems, and the masque. Most notable is the chapter which views Carew as a critic, for it investigates in excellent detail Carew's masterpiece, "An Elegie upon the Death of the Deane of Pauls, Dr. John Donne." By scrutinizing the poem's praise of Donne's use of language and imagery, Sadler draws appropriate conclusions about Carew's own ideas about poetry writing.

Selig, Edward I. *The Flourishing Wreath: A Study of Thomas Carew's Poetry.* New Haven: Yale University Press, 1958. In his introduction, Selig establishes the purpose of his study through the query, "Is Carew a witty, elegant, and creatively representative poet, or is he superficial and unoriginal?" The book clearly establishes that Carew's negative reputation is unjustified and that it has been created by serious misunderstandings of his technique. To establish the validity of his own positive assessment of Carew's abilities, Selig discusses Carew's court verse—the verse compliment in particular—, songs, and "golden verse," to use the term popularized by C.S. Lewis. The especial value of Selig's study is not, however, his correction of misunderstandings, but rather his clear analysis of selected poems from the Carew canon.

Selected Dictionaries and Encyclopedias

British Authors Before 1800, H.W. Wilson, 1952. Brief biographical sketch.

British Writers, Charles Scribner's Sons, 1979. General biographical and critical discussion.

Critical Survey of Poetry, Salem Press, 1983. Brief biography and analysis of selected poems.

Dictionary of National Biography, Oxford University Press, 1917. Excellent biographical sketch.

Gerald William Morton
Auburn University at Montgomery

THOMAS CARLYLE
1795-1881

Author's Chronology

Born December 4, 1795, Ecclefechan, Scotland, the son of a stonemason; *1809* enters the University of Edinburgh; *1821* discovers German literature; begins writing reviews, translations, articles, essays, with which he supports himself for sixteen years; meets Jane Welsh; *1826* marries Jane Welsh; *1828* moves to Craigenputtoch, Scotland; *1833* is visited by Ralph Waldo Emerson; *1833-1834* publishes *Sartor Resartus* in *Fraser's* magazine; *1834* moves to Cheyne Row, London; *1837* publishes *The French Revolution,* which establishes him as a major literary figure in England; begins career as a lecturer; *1842* begins visting Lady Harriet Baring, fostering a relationship that strained his marriage; *1850* publishes *Latter-Day Pamphlets,* a series of controversial, reactionary essays that cause many to reject his ideas; *1866* while away from London, learns of Jane's death; begins writing memoir of her; *1881* dies in London, and is buried in Ecclefechan.

Author's Bibliography (selected)

Life of Schiller, 1825 (biography); *Sartor Resartus,* 1834 (prose); *The French Revolution,* 1837 (history); *Critical and Miscellaneous Essays,* 1839 (prose); *Chartism,* 1840 (prose); *On Heroes and Hero-Worship,* 1841 (essays); *Past and Present,* 1843 (historical commentary); *Oliver Cromwell's Letters and Speeches,* 1845 (history); *Latter-Day Pamphlets,* 1850 (essays); *Life of John Sterling,* 1851 (biography); *History of Frederick the Great,* 6 vols., 1858-1865; *Reminiscences,* 1881 (biography, autobiography); *The Works of Thomas Carlyle,* Centenary Edition, ed. H.D. Traill, 30 vols. (1897-1901).

Overview of Biographical Sources

Like most major literary figures of the nineteenth century, Carlyle was the subject of several biographies almost immediately after he died. Between 1882 and 1884, James Anthony Froude, working with Carlyle's personal papers, produced a four-volume biography that scandalized many readers by hinting at Carlyle's psychological and sexual irregularities. Froude's study prompted at least a dozen other biographies of Carlyle, and spawned a literary exchange between pro- and anti-Froude forces who defended or attacked both Carlyle and Froude's treatment of him. The final "answer" to Froude's work appeared during the 1920's and 1930's: David Alec Wilson's six-volume life of Carlyle, which reports almost every scrap of information about both Thomas and Jane. Carlyle's relationship with his wife has also been the subject of several book-length studies. More detached, objective portraits have appeared in the past thirty years, beginning with Julian Symons' *Thomas Carlyle: The Life and Ideas of a Prophet* (New York: Oxford University Press, 1952). Ian Campbell's *Carlyle* (New York: Charles Scribner's Sons, 1974) is a similar, modest biographical study. The major modern biography is Fred Kaplan's *Thomas Carlyle: A Biography* (1983).

Evaluation of Selected Biographies

Froude, James Anthony, *Thomas Carlyle: A History of the First Forty Years of His Life, 1795-1835.* 2 vols. London: Longman's, 1882; *Thomas Carlyle: A History of His Life in London, 1834-1881.* 2 vols., London: Longman's, 1884. Froude was a young historian with whom Carlyle became impressed during the early 1870's. At about the same time, Carlyle grew concerned when unauthorized, inaccurate accounts of his life began appearing. He decided to make Froude his literary executor, and entrusted him with a large volume of his own and his wife Jane's personal papers. From these, Froude constructed one of the major biographies of the Victorian period. For contemporaries accustomed to thinking of Carlyle as a moral arbiter, these volumes were shocking. They revealed a mean-spirited, selfish man given to ignoring his wife; further, they suggested that the Carlyles had sexual difficulties, and that Carlyle had been enamored with Harriet Baring in the years before her death. While Froude's analysis of Carlyle's character is not particularly penetrating, his work is still important as a source for other biographical studies.

Kaplan, Fred, *Thomas Carlyle: A Biography.* Ithaca, NY: Cornell University Press, 1983. Kaplan's biography is a fine blend of historical analysis and critical narrative, a sound scholarly study that does not suffer as some works do from an overbearing apparatus of notes and digressions. Kaplan focuses on the man at the expense of the works, but provides sufficient commentary on Carlyle's writings to afford readers an insight into the way that events in his life helped to determine what and how he wrote. Carlyle is presented as a man of varied moods, a many-sided personality who was much more human than previous biographers have made him out to be. The strange relationship he had with his wife is examined with great care; Kaplan offers a fair assessment of why both partners were at fault for their marital difficulties. This study also provides valuable assessments of Carlyle's relationships with numerous other prominent figures of the period. Throughout, Kaplan is careful to base his judgments on available evidence, avoiding the temptation to speculate about Carlyle's psychological makeup.

Autobiographical Sources

Almost every work Carlyle wrote provides some autobiographical information. Those generally considered to be directly based on his own life are his unpublished novel *Wotton Reinfred* and *Sartor Resartus,* his spiritual autobiography. His *Reminiscences,* published posthumously, also provide valuable insight into his life. Carlyle left behind a wealth of autobiographical material, especially letters, many of which have been edited and published. *Early Letters of Thomas Carlyle* and *Letters of Thomas Carlyle,* ed. C. E. Norton (London: Macmillan, 1886, 1889), and *New Letters of Thomas Carlyle,* ed. Alexander Carlyle (London: J. Lane, 1904) have been supplemented by several specialized editions of Carlyle's correspondence with family members and important literary figures such as Emerson, Johann Wolfgang von Goethe, and John Ruskin.

Overview of Critical Sources

Carlyle's writings touch on many disciplines: history, biography, social criticism, religion, literature. For this reason, systematic criticism has been difficult, and most scholars have chosen to study Carlyle from a particular perspective. Several books and dozens of articles explore his development and influence as an intellectual and cultural historian, usually focusing on his ideas of heroism, work, and duty. Detailed critical studies of Carlyle's aesthetic principles, and of individual works, especially *Sartor Resartus,* are also available. Carlyle's relationship to modern fascism has been studied in essays and in two monographs.

Evaluation of Selected Criticism

Fielding, K. J. and R. L. Tarr, eds. *Carlyle Past & Present.* New York: Barnes & Noble, 1976. This collection of eleven essays by noted scholars offers an excellent introduction to Carlyle's works. G.B. Tennyson's "Carlyle Today" surveys scholarship on Carlyle and summarizes the evolution of his reputation. Included are essays on *Frederick the Great* and *Latter-Day Pamphlets,* as well as assessments of Carlyle's relationship with Dickens and Arnold.

Holloway, John, *The Victorian Sage.* London: Macmillan, 1953. In his chapters on Carlyle, Holloway provides a systematic introduction to Carlyle's antimaterialistic philosophy. He outlines the basic tenets of Carlyle's beliefs and explains how the confusing and seemingly anarchic style of the works is actually a conscious device used to elucidate a philosophical stance. Further, Holloway shows how Carlyle shares with certain other Victorian writers the characteristics of the Sage: a modern prophet who uses literature to lead men to understand life by appealing to a sense higher than mere reason.

LaValley, Albert J. *Carlyle and the Idea of the Modern.* New Haven: Yale University Press, 1968. LaValley's study focuses on Carlyle's modernity, showing how his method and his concerns place him as a member of a tradition that includes Blake, Nietzsche, and Marx. Carlyle's career illustrates the problem of the modern artist, straining to break the bonds of materialism while simultaneously rejecting extremist notions of unbridled liberty. LaValley examines Carlyle's aesthetic development, showing how his early writings illustrate attempts to find a proper mode of expression. The final "voice" that Carlyle adopts in *Sartor Resartus* and carries through in future writings is that of the prophet, but throughout the canon of his works two tendencies emerge: the autobiographical (an exploration of the self) and the public voice (the need to speak about social ills). Carlyle saw literature, rather than religion, as the best means of reforming society; that underlying motive for his writings helps explain both the rhetoric and emphasis of his prose. LaValley provides careful analyses of the major works, especially *Sartor Resartus, The French Revolution, Past and Present,* and the *Life of Sterling.*

Other Sources

Harris, Kenneth M. *Carlyle and Emerson.* Cambridge: Harvard University Press, 1978. An analysis of the relationship between two figures who had significant impact on their contemporaries.

Harrold, Frederick C. *Carlyle and German Thought: 1819–1834.* New Haven: Yale University Press, 1934. The best of earlier scholarly studies of Carlyle's intellectual development.

Ikeler, A.A. *Puritan Temper and Transcendental Faith: Carlyle's Literary Vision.* Columbus: Ohio State University Press, 1972. A brief study of Carlyle's method for presenting religious ideas.

Levine, George, *The Boundaries of Fiction.* Princeton: Princeton University Press, 1968. Levine's chapter on *Sartor Resartus* offers insight into Carlyle's literary method and main themes.

Tennyson, G.B. *Sartor Called Resartus.* Princeton: Princeton University Press, 1965. An important study of Carlyle's literary method, focusing on the early works and *Sartor Resartus.*

Selected Dictionaries and Encyclopedias

British Writers, Charles Scribner's Sons, 1981, IV: 238–250. An excellent short biographical and critical sketch.

Dictionary of National Biography, Oxford University Press, 1959, III: 1019–1036. A biographical sketch with brief assessments of major works.

Laurence W. Mazzeno
Annapolis, Maryland

JOYCE CARY
1888–1957

Author's Chronology

Born Arthur Joyce Lunel Cary, December 7, 1888, Londonderry, Northern Ireland; *1903* enters Clifton College near Bristol; *1906–1907* studies painting in Paris; *1907* enrolls in School of Art, Edinburgh; *1908* publishes first work, *Verse,* privately, and enrolls in Oxford; *1912* joins Red Cross in the Balkans; *1913* enters Nigerian Service; *1915* sent to northern frontier with Southwest African Field Force; *1916* marries Gertrude Ogilvie; *1919* sells first story to the *Saturday Evening Post; 1932* publishes first of his African novels, *Aissa Saved;* follows with *An American Visitor, 1933; 1941–1944* publishes first trilogy; *1941* expresses political views on Africa in *The Case for African Freedom; 1949* Book-of-the-Month Club chooses American edition of *The Horse's Mouth* as a reserve selection; wife dies the same year; *1951* hospitalized with an illness later diagnosed as amyotrophic lateral sclerosis; *1952–1955* publishes second trilogy; *1956* stage adaptation of *Mr. Johnson* well-received in New York; *1957* dies on March 29 at Oxford; *1958* posthumous publication of *Art and Reality.*

Author's Bibliography

Verses by Arthur Cary, 1908; *Aissa Saved,* 1932 (novel); *An American Visitor,* 1933 (novel); *The African Witch,* 1936 (novel); *Castle Corner,* 1938 (novel); *Mister Johnson,* 1939 (novel); *Power in Men,* 1939 (essays); *Charley Is My Darling,* 1940 (novel); *The Case for African Freedom,* 1941 (essays); *A House of Children,* 1941 (novel); *Herself Surprised,* 1941 (novel); *To Be a Pilgrim,* 1942 (novel); *The Process of Real Freedom,* 1943 (essays); *The Horse's Mouth,* 1944 (novel); *Marching Soldier,* 1945 (novel); *The Moonlight,* 1946 (novel); *Britain and West Africa,* 1946 (essays); *The Drunken Sailor,* 1947 (novel); *A Fearful Joy,* 1949 (novel); *Prisoner of Grace,* 1952 (novel); *Except the Lord,* 1953 (novel); *Not Honour More,* 1955 (novel); *Art and Reality,* 1958 (essays); *The Captive and the Free,* 1959 (novel); *Spring Song and Other Stories,* 1960; *Memoirs of the Bobotes,* 1960; *Cock Jarvis,* 1974 (incomplete novel); *Selected Essays,* 1976.

Overview of Biographical Sources

Despite recent growth in the number and scope of book-length critical studies of his writing, no full-length biography of Cary has been produced since 1968, when Malcolm Foster published *Joyce Cary: A Biography.* Two earlier studies by Walter Allen and Andrew Wright are useful today mainly as a general overview of Cary's life and work. Most of the criticism of Cary's work contains some elements of biography, tied always to the writer's particular critical stance, and should be read with this in mind.

Evaluation of Selected Biographies

Allen, Walter E. *Joyce Cary,* No. 41 in the *Writers and Their Work* series. London: Longmans, Green, rev. ed. 1963. This brief, early monograph on Cary is regarded as an excellent short appreciation of the life and works. It is still useful today for the reader who needs only a brief acquaintance with the author.

Foster, Malcolm, *Joyce Cary: A Biography.* Boston: Houghton Mifflin, 1968. The current "standard" biography of Cary, Foster's comprehensive work is the source to which most students of Cary refer. It is well documented and quite readable.

Noble, R. W. *Joyce Cary.* New York: Barnes and Noble, 1973. Another brief introduction to the "life and works," Noble's study traces the development of Cary's personal philosophy—especially his aesthetic and political theory—and shows how they are reflected implicitly and explicitly in his writing. Noble contends that for Cary creative activity is the reason for and the fulfillment of life, and that moral and political freedom form the necessary milieu for creativity.

Roby, Kinley E. *Joyce Cary.* Boston: Twayne, 1974. In the first chapter of this study, Roby outlines the basic facts of Cary's life as a prologue to his discussion of Cary's works. The chapter notes indicate that Kinley relied on Foster for much of the biographical information.

Starkie, Enid, "Joyce Cary: A Portrait," in *Essays by Divers Hands.* ed. Joanna Richardson. London: Oxford University Press, 1963, pp. 124–144. In this long essay, English novelist Starkie recalls aspects of her personal friendship with Cary. She stresses Cary's concern with injustice and contends that he has more in common with his conservative character Tom Wilcher than he does with the ebullient Gulley Jimson.

Wright, Andrew, *Joyce Cary: A Preface to His Novels.* London: Chatto and Windus, 1958. Though now more than a quarter-century old, this early introductory study provides useful insights into Cary the person as well as the novelist. It would be of special interest to the student who wants to trace the development of Cary's reputation.

Autobiographical Sources

Although Cary wrote no autobiography, some of his significant personal experiences are revealed in several of his novels, a memoir, and his essays dealing with his political convictions and aesthetic theories. *Castle Corner,* set in northern Ireland, is generally regarded as drawn directly from Cary's childhood in Donegal, Ulster. His African novels—*Aissa Saved, An American Visitor, The African Witch,* and *Mr. Johnson*—are all derived from his experiences in colonial Nigeria. In *Memoirs of the Bobotes,* Cary reflects on his experiences in 1912 with the Red Cross in the Balkan/Turkish wars.

Cary has revealed a great deal about himself in his nonfiction, his essays on political themes and aesthetics. *Power in Men* is the earliest expression of his political theory. In *The Process of Real Freedom,* Cary presents a defense of democracy written in the midst of World War II. *The Case for African Freedom,* the most detailed presentation of Cary's views on African colonialism as they developed during and after his experiences in Nigeria, expresses his pragmatic plan for gradual independence for the African colonies, which is based on his belief that national security depends on national freedom. In *Britain and West Africa,* Cary continues his case for freedom for Africa, stressing that men are born free and require freedom for development. *Art and Reality,* published posthumously, is a collection of essays that set forth Cary's aesthetic theories. They were originally part of the series of Clark Lectures Cary delivered while he was coping with his terminal illness.

Finally, several of the very few interviews Cary granted contain insights into his character and works: "The Novelist at Work: A Conversation Between Joyce Cary and Lord David Cecil," *Adam International Review* 18 (the whole November-December 1950 issue is devoted to Cary); and "Conversation with Joyce Cary," *Tamarack Review* 3 (Spring 1957).

Overview of Critical Sources

Although increasing attention has been focused on Joyce Cary in the 1970's and 1980's, many critics maintain that he is still underrated and undervalued. His writing—both his fiction and his essays—has prompted an extraordinarily broad range of response. There are books of criticism and individual articles dealing with his works as they express his political and social views, his aesthetics and philosophy, his attitudes toward African and human freedom, his "place" in modern literature, his mythology and use of archetypes, his existentialism and views on organized religion, his attitudes toward women. Other studies have focused on his technique and style, particularly his experimentation with characterization, point of view, and richly detailed storytelling, as well as on his important contributions to the form of the trilogy.

Evaluation of Selected Criticism

Adams, Hazard, *Joyce Cary's Trilogies: Pursuit of the Particular Real.* Tallahassee: University Presses of Florida, 1983. In this study of Cary's trilogies, Adams focuses on his narrative technique, especially his use of the "unrealiable" narrator. In contrast to many other critics of Cary, Adams maintains that there has been an overemphasis on the abstract ideas Cary expresses in his nonfiction as a means for comprehending his novels. Instead, he concludes, a more productive and meaningful way to approach the trilogies is to focus on the specifics, the particularities with which each of the six novels deals.

Bloom, Robert, *The Indeterminate World: A Study of the Novels of Joyce Cary.* Philadelphia: University of Pennsylvania Press, 1962. Bloom's study, though written over two decades ago when Cary was still "neglected," is still readable and influential. For Bloom, Cary's novels are evidence of his "indeterminateness"—his unshakable openness before the possibilities and contradictions of life.

Fisher, Barbara, *Joyce Cary: The Writer and His Theme.* Gerrards Cross: Smythe, 1980. Fisher contends that Cary's novels constitute a "spiritual autobiography" that reveals his basic theme to be embedded in the concepts of freedom and grace. She also maintains that Cary used his characters symbolically, an assessment with which many other critics would disagree.

Hoffman, Charles G. *Joyce Cary: The Comedy of Freedom.* Pittsburgh: University of Pittsburgh Press, 1964. In this relatively early study of Cary, Hoffman concludes that the novels express Cary's view of the world as a place of perpetual change, and of the condition of man as one of freedom within this flux.

Larsen, Golden, *The Dark Descent: Social Change and Moral Responsibility in the Novels of Joyce Cary.* London: Michael Joseph, 1965. Larsen discerns two major themes in Cary's work—the fundamental injustice of life and the role of the free and creative mind. He contends that the novels show how Cary stressed the necessity for personal commitment and self-sacrifice, and the importance of the exercise of imagination.

Mahood, Molly, *Joyce Cary's Africa.* Boston: Houghton Mifflin, 1965. Mahood provides an extended description of Cary's experiences in Africa as a basis for her analysis of his African novels.

Other Sources

Adam International Review, special Cary issue, 18 (November-December 1950). The entire issue is devoted to Cary and includes a revealing interview.

Burrows, John, and Alexander Hamilton, "An Interview with Joyce Cary," in *Writers at Work: The Paris Review Interviews.* ed. Malcolm Cowley. London: Secker and Warburg, 1958, pp. 47-62. Cary discusses his novels and his philosophy.

Modern Fiction Studies, special Cary issue, 9 (Autumn 1963). Essays on a variety of topics related to his individual works, politics, and aesthetics.

Patricia A. Farrant
Coe College

WILLA CATHER
1873-1947

Author's Chronology

Born December 7, 1873 in Back Creek Valley near Winchester Virginia; *1883* with family moves to Webster County, Nebraska; *1890* enters University of Nebraska at Lincoln; *1893* begins writing reviews for *Nebraska State Journal; 1896* becomes editor of the *Home Monthly* in Pittsburgh; *1901* accepts high school teaching position in Pittsburgh; *1903* publishes first volume of poetry, *April Twilights; 1905* publishes first collection of short stories, *The Troll Garden; 1906* becomes an editor for *McClure's* magazine in New York City; *1908* meets Sarah Orne Jewett who was to become an important influence; *1912* publishes first novel, *Alexander's Bridge,* and visits the American Southwest; *1923* wins Pulitzer Prize for *One of Ours (1922); 1930* receives Howells medal for fiction from the Academy of the National Institute of Arts and Letters; *1933* is awarded the Prix Femina Américain for *Shadows on the Rock; 1944* receives the gold medal of the National Institute of Arts and Letters; *1947* dies April 24 in New York City.

Author's Bibliography (selected)

April Twilights, 1903 (poems); *The Troll Garden,* 1905 (stories); *Alexander's Bridge,* 1912 (novel); *O Pioneers!,* 1913 (novel); *The Song of the Lark,* 1915 (novel); *My Ántonia,* 1918 (novel); *Youth and the Bright Medusa,* 1920 (stories); *One of Ours,* 1922 (novel); *A Lost Lady,* 1923 (novel); *The Professor's House,* 1927 (novel); *Shadows on the Rock,* 1931 (novel); *Obscure Destinies,* 1932 (stories); *Lucy Gayheart,* 1935 (novel); *Not Under Forty,* 1936 (essays); *Sapphira and the Slave Girl,* 1940 (novel); *The Old Beauty and Others,* 1948 (stories).

Overview of Biographical Sources

For many years biographical accounts of Willa Cather were full of misinformation and myth, at least partly because she guarded her personal life and discouraged biographical inquiry. It was not until 1953, with the publication of E. K. Brown's *Willa Cather: A Critical Biography* that any sort of "official" biography was available. However, a good deal of biographical material could be gleaned from published interviews, and from sketches and reminiscences by people who knew Cather. One such piece is Elizabeth Shepley Sergeant's "Willa Cather," in *Fire Under the Andes* (New York: Alfred A. Knopf, 1927). Others are George Seibel's "Miss Willa Cather from Nebraska" (*New Colophon,* September, 1949), Elizabeth Moorhead's (Vermorcken's) "The Novelist: Willa Cather" in *These Too Were Here* (Pittsburgh: University of Pittsburgh Press, 1950), and Fanny Butcher's chapter on Cather in *Many Lives—One Love* (New York: Harper and Row, 1972). Brown's valuable study was prepared with the blessing and assistance of Cather's long-time friend and companion, Edith Lewis. Later biographers, however, would have materials unavailable to Brown. Two other biographical works were published on Cather in 1953, both by friends. Edith Lewis's *Willa Cather Living: A Personal Record* (New York: Alfred A. Knopf) and Elizabeth Shepley Sergeant's *Willa Cather: A Memoir* (Lincoln: University of Nebraska Press) add interesting personal insights and details. Other helpful biographical-critical works, in addition to those below, include Philip L. Gerber's *Willa Cather* (New York: Twayne, 1975) and Dorothy Van Ghent's *Willa Cather* (Minneapolis: University of Minnesota Press, 1964).

Evaluation of Selected Biographies

Bennett, Mildred R. *The World of Willa Cather.* New York: Dodd, Mead & Company, 1951; rpt. Lincoln: University of Nebraska Press, 1961, with notes and index. This is an important account of the Nebraska influences on Cather's work, gathered from scores of sources—people who knew Cather, letters, clippings, family papers, and the like. The book is full of Cather lore, and it points to numerous models and actual incidents that Cather translated into fiction.

Brown, E. K. *Willa Cather: A Critical Biography.* Completed by Leon Edel. New York: Alfred A. Knopf, 1953. Brown had the benefit of Edith Lewis's cooperation in the preparation of his biography, and thus saw materials unavailable to others at the time. Still, he was limited by what a protective friend was willing to give him. His portrayal of the woman and his interpretation of her work are sound and insightful.

Robinson, Phyllis C. *Willa: The Life of Willa Cather.* Garden City, New York: Doubleday, 1983. The least reliable of the major Cather biographies, Robinson's book is written for a popular rather than an academic audience. Readers should be aware that Robinson often treats speculation as fact and invents attitudes she presumes Cather to have held.

Woodress, James, *Willa Cather: Her Life and Art.* New York: Pegasus, 1970. Bison Book edition, Lincoln: University of Nebraska Press, 1974. Regarded by Woodress as an interim rather than a definitive biography (he is now working on a more ambitious study), this book is nevertheless the most objective and accurate biography currently available. Woodress places Cather in a direct line of descent from such American romantics as Emerson and Whitman.

Autobiographical Sources

Cather wrote no autobiography, contending that her biography was in her books. In some sense this is true, for most of her books are based on her own experience, though she freely altered facts to serve the purposes of her art.

Critics have called *The Professor's House* her "spiritual autobiography," while regarding *The Song of the Lark* as a fictional representation of her youth in Red Cloud.

Cather spoke often of the function of art and the artist, in her fiction as well as in essays, interviews, and countless newspaper columns. Her early critical pronouncements, including drama, music, and literary criticism, show a preference for the romantic over the realistic mode. Many of her more than 500 newspaper articles and reviews are collected in *The Kingdom of Art: Willa Cather's First Principles and Critical Statements 1893–1896,* edited by Bernice Slote (Lincoln: University of Nebraska Press, 1966), and *The World and the Parish: Willa Cather's Articles and Reviews, 1893–1902,* edited by William M. Curtin, 2 vols. (Lincoln: University of Nebraska Press, 1970). Her most important critical pronouncement is probably an essay titled "The Novel Démeuble" in which she argues for the simplification, or "unfurnishing," of the novel.

Overview of Critical Sources

There are hundreds of essays and a number of full-length critical treatments of Cather's work, most of which concentrate on her novels. Criticism over the years has ranged from adoration to dismissal, depending on the decade and the bias of the critic. Typically, Cather's detractors regard her as nostalgic and escapist, while her adulators praise her commitment to values and to fineness in both life and art. Detractors and adulators alike, however, admire her lucid, classical style.

Evaluation of Selected Criticism

Arnold, Marilyn, *Willa Cather's Short Fiction.* Athens: Ohio University Press, 1984. This is the only major treatment of the whole body of Cather's short fiction.

Bloom, Edward A. and Lillian D. Bloom, *Willa Cather's Gift of Sympathy.* Carbondale: Southern Illinois University Press, 1962. This is a useful, though sometimes oversimplified, discussion of Cather's principal themes and methods.

Giannone, Richard, *Music in Willa Cather's Fiction.* Lincoln: University of Nebraska Press, 1968. Giannone discusses this specialized but very important aspect of Cather's work.

Randall, John H., III. *The Landscape and the Looking Glass: Willa Cather's Search for Value.* Boston: Houghton Mifflin, 1960. Although it has predecessors, this is the first substantial full-length critical study of Cather's work. Randall admits to some of Cather's strengths, but dogmatically attacks her work as the product of a querulous and nostalgic personality.

Stouck, David, *Willa Cather's Imagination.* Lincoln: University of Nebraska Press, 1975. Stouck intelligently interprets Cather's fiction in terms of various artistic forms and modes.

Other Sources

Gelfant, Blanche H. "The Forgotten Reaping-hook: Sex in *My Ántonia,*" in *American Literature,* 43 (March 1971), 60–82. Gelfant probably overstates her case in arguing that *My Ántonia* forms a pattern of sexual aversion, but her contention that Jim Burden's role must be re-evaluated is persuasive.

Jones, Howard Mumford, *The Bright Medusa.* Urbana: University of Illinois Press, 1952. Jones studies Cather's portrayal of the youthful artist, suggesting that the art she depicts is Dionysian rather than Appollonian.

Slote, Bernice, ed. Introduction to *The Kingdom of Art: Willa Cather's First Principles and Critical Statements 1893–1896.* Lincoln: University of Nebraska Press, 1966. This exceptionally valuable essay by a leading Cather scholar argues that Cather's early journalistic writings reveal her to be a primitive and a romantic.

Whipple, T. K. *Spokesmen: Modern Writers and American Life.* New York: D. Appleton & Company, 1928. In one of the better early estimates, Whipple describes Cather's artistic development and her principal theme: the conflict between a superior person and an inferior social environment.

Selected Dictionaries and Encyclopedias

Critical Survey of Long Fiction, Salem Press, 1983. Brief biography and analysis of selected Cather novels.

Critical Survey of Short Fiction, Salem Press, 1981. An overview of Cather's contribution as a writer of short fiction.

Dictionary of Literary Biography, Documentary Series. Gale Research, 1982. Provides a variety of materials by and about Cather, including bibliography, locations of archives containing Cather material, and selected articles, reviews, and illustrations.

Marilyn Arnold
Brigham Young University

MARGARET CAVENDISH, DUCHESS OF NEWCASTLE 1623–1673

Author's Chronology

Born in 1623 in Essex, daughter of Sir Thomas Lucas; serves as lady in waiting to Queen Henrietta-Maria *1643–1645;* accompanies her into exile at Paris; meets William Cavendish, marquis and later Duke of Newcastle, and marries him in *1645; 1653* briefly in England, she publishes *Philosophical Fancies* and *Poems and Fancies* before rejoining her husband on the continent; at the Restoration returns to England and spends the rest of her life writing, serving as a patroness of the arts and gaining a reputation for eccentricity; dies in London on January 7, 1673 and is buried in Westminster Abbey.

Author's Bibliography (selected)

Philosophical Fancies, 1653 (essays); *Poems and Fancies,* 1653; *Natures Pictures,* 1656 (essays); *Playes,* 1662; *Sociable Letters,* 1664; *The Lives of William Cavendish . . . and His Wife,* 1667; *Orations of Diverse Sorts,* 1668.

Overview of Biographical Sources

Because she was the wife of one of the great men of England, an eccentric famous in her own right, and a prodigious writer of autobiographical materials, Margaret Cavendish's is one of the best documented lives of any woman of her century. Her name and anecdotes about her strange behavior appear in the writings of Samuel Pepys, Christian Huygens, Samuel Johnson and many others. Henry T. Perry's *The First Duchess of Newcastle and Her Husband as Figures in Literary History* (1918) was the first book-length study of the Newcastles. Douglas Grant's *Margaret the First* (1957) is the definitive biography.

Evaluation of Selected Biographies

Grant, Douglas, *Margaret the First.* London: Rupert Hart-Davis, 1957. This is a fine popular biography, well illustrated with reproductions of portraits and sketches of the Duchess, her husband, and her home. Grant clearly loves his subject but just as clearly recognizes her many faults, and he manages to convey with great deftness her simultaneous eccentricity and wisdom. He is particularly good on Cavendish's scientific studies and on her feminism.

Perry, Henry T. *The First Duchess of Newcastle and Her Husband as Figures in Literary History.* Boston: Ginn, 1918. Basically a double biography of Cavendish and her husband, this work concentrates on their life together and thus skimps on Cavendish's early years. The book is a bit dated in its approach, but Perry is particularly strong in his discussion of the author's biography of her husband and on the Duke and Duchess's joint role as patrons of the arts.

Turberville, A. S. *A History of Welbeck Abbey and Its Owners,* Vol. 1. London: Faber and Faber, 1938. Turberville is a historian and he is as much interested in the Abbey as in its owners, but nearly half his first volume involves the Duke and Duchess and a full chapter is devoted to Cavendish's writing.

Autobiographical Sources

Although Samuel Pepys, writing in the year after its publication, termed the book "ridiculous", and its author "a mad, conceited, ridiculous woman," Margaret Cavendish's *The Lives of William Cavendish . . . and His Wife* is widely considered to be one of the finest and most important examples of early biography and autobiography in Europe. The work was very popular in its day and saw several editions. Cavendish adored her husband, however, and was perhaps not entirely objective about either him or herself. The work, as Perry points out, may thus best be taken "as a literary product as well as an authentic history." Also extant, though not so readily available, are Cavendish's *Sociable Letters* and numerous other works containing autobiographical material.

Overview of Critical Sources

Until recently little serious criticism of Margaret Cavendish's work existed and what there was was devoted primarily to her *Lives of William Cavendish . . . and His Wife.* This situation has been remedied over the past decade by the increasing interest in her as a feminist and as a woman writer. Perry's is still the most extensive examination of her work, with Grant and Turberville also containing critical material of interest. There are no full-length critical studies.

Evaluation of Selected Criticism

Davis, Natalie Z. "Gender and Genre: Women as Historical Writers, 1400–1820," *Beyond Their Sex: Learned Women of the European Past.* ed. Patricia H. Labalme. New York: New York University Press, 1979. Exploring the role of gender in the interpretation of history with emphasis on Cavendish, this is an interesting and useful piece of feminist criticism.

Gagen, Jean, "Honor and Fame in the Works of the Duchess of Newcastle," *Studies in Philology,* 56 (1959), 519–538. Gagen sees the Duchess as obsessed with the acquisition of Honor and Fame. Barred by her sex from obtaining them on the field of battle, she sought them through her literary productions.

Levy, Michael, "The Transformations of Oberon: The Use of Fairies in Seventeenth-Century Literature." Dissertation: University of Minnesota, 1982. Containing a long chapter on Cavendish's poetry about fairies, Levy's dissertation postulates her use of them as directly tied to both her obsession with fame and her self-concept as a woman.

Paloma, Dolores, "Margaret Cavendish: Defining the Female Self," *Women's Studies,* 7 (1980), 55–66. Paloma discusses Cavendish's attitude toward women and her attempt to come to terms with her role in a male-dominated society.

Woolf, Virginia, "The Duchess of Newcastle," *The Common Reader.* New York: Harcourt, Brace & Co., 1925. Although barely a dozen pages long and over sixty years old, Woolf's essay remains the single most engaging piece written about the Duchess. Woolf shows great insight into Cavendish's eccentric intellectualism and portrays her as an Everywoman figure, daring to step outside of Woman's role and condemned for doing so.

Selected Dictionaries and Encyclopedias

British Authors Before 1800, H. W. Wilson, 1952. Brief biography and a discussion of the principle works.

Dictionary of National Biography, Oxford, 1968. Detailed biographical essay.

Michael M. Levy
University of Wisconsin—Stout

GEORGE CHAPMAN
1559(?)-1634

Author's Chronology

Born 1559 or 1560, Hitchin, Herfordshire, England, second son of prosperous parents; ca. *1574* enrolls in Oxford for an uncertain period of time; ca. *1583* enters into the service of Sir Ralph Sadler, a wealthy aristocrat; *1591* takes part in a military campaign on the continent, probably in the Low Countries; *1594* publishes first long poem, *The Shadow of Night; 1595–1600* writes several plays for the theatrical company called the Lord Admiral's Men, all of which are performed at the Rose, an outdoor public theater; *1598* publishes a partial translation of Book XVIII of the *Iliad,* called *Archilles Shield,* with seven other books of the *Iliad,* seeking royal patronage for the enterprise; *1598* enhances reputation as poet by publishing four sestiads completing Christopher Marlowe's popular but unfinished narrative poem, *Hero and Leander; 1599* cedes to a relative all of his rights to the family estate; *1600* arrested for debt to a usurer, John Wolfall; *1601–1609* writes several plays for a company of child actors known as Children of the Chapel, who perform at the private indoor Blackfriars Theater; *1605* imprisoned together with Ben Jonson for certain comical passages in the play *Eastward Ho* which King James I finds offensive; *1608* narrowly escapes being imprisoned again, this time for scenes in *The Conspiracy and Tragedy of Charles Duke of Byron* which are insulting to the Queen of France; *1609* publishes translation of twelve books of the *Iliad; 1610–1614* writes several plays for the company of child actors called the Queens Revels, all of which are performed at the new Whitefriars Theater; publishes the completed translation of the *Iliad;* left destitute by the sudden, unexpected death of his young patron, Prince Henry, who had promised to subsidize his translations of the Homeric epics; ca *1612* imprisoned for debt; *1613* writes a masque for the royal wedding of the King's daughter Elizabeth; *1614* honors his new patron, Lord Somerset, with a poem celebrating his marriage; *1614–1615* publishes his translation of the *Odyssey; 1616* publishes his translation of both epics in a single volume *The Whole Works of Homer; 1621* acquitted of the debt charge which had sent him to prison; ca. *1624* publishes his translation of the minor poems of Homer, completing his life work on that enterprise; *1634* dies on May 12, is buried with a monument in his honor made by noted stage designer Inigo Jones.

Author's Bibliography (selected)

The Shadow of Night, 1594 (poems); *Ovid's Banquet of Sense,* 1595 (poem); *Hero and Leander,* 1598 (poem); *The Iliad,* 1598, 1611 (translation); *Euthymiae Raptus: Or, The Tears of Peace,* 1609; *Petrarch's Seven Penitential Psalms,* 1612 (poems); *The Odyssey,* 1614 (translation); *Eugenia,* 1614; *Andromeda Liberata,* 1614 (poem); *Pro Vere,* 1622 (poems); *The Whole Works of Homer,* 1624 (translation).

Overview of Biographical Sources

The available biographical information about George Chapman is very limited, as is the case with many poets and playwrights of the sixteenth and seventeenth centuries. Much less is known about the details of his life than is known about Ben Jonson, but much more than about John Webster. Apart from brief statements in standard dictionaries and encyclopedias, there are only three biographical treatments, none of them extensive: Allardyce Nicoll, "The Dramatic Portrait of George Chapman" (1962); Millar MacLure, *George Chapman: A Critical Study* (1966); and Charlotte Spivack, *George Chapman* (1967). In the absence of primary materials, it is unlikely that a definitive biography will ever be possible.

Evaluation of Selected Biographies

MacLure, Millar, *George Chapman: A Critical Study.* Toronto: University of Toronto, 1966. MacLure's opening chapter, "The Poet in the World" (pp. 3–31), offers a useful summary of the poet's life. He sees Chapman's lifelong struggle with debt as emblematic of a popular Renaissance theme, the feud between Virtue and Fortune. Although Chapman was recognized and admired by his contemporaries, he was unlucky in his patrons and unfortunate in his timing, never quite achieving the success he felt he deserved. MacLure also infers some interesting features of Chapman's personality from the facts known about his life and from comments by his contemporaries.

Nicoll, Allardyce, "The Dramatic Portrait of George Chapman," in *Philological Quarterly* XLI (1962), 215–228. Nicoll interprets the character of Bellamont in the play *Northward Ho* as a portrayal of Chapman. There is much evidence from the time to support this reading, and Bellamont is generally acknowledged as a good-natured parody of the poet. Nicoll's analysis is both scholarly and imaginative, resulting in an authentic and sympathetic image of the poet as a man.

Spivack, Charlotte, *George Chapman.* New York: Twayne, 1967. Spivack's first chapter, "George Chapman, Second Son" (pp. 13–29), surveys the known facts about the poet's life, with emphasis in his financial frustrations, ultimately deriving from his status as second son in a time when the eldest son by law inherited the entire estate. In this solid introduction to Chapman's life, the information is presented straight forwardly, indicating the relevance of biographical details to the poet's works.

Autobiographical Sources

Although there is no autobiography, there are two direct sources of first-person information. First, scattered throughout Chapman's prefaces to his poems are many references to his own life. Second, the Folger Shakespeare Library has a collection of unsigned letters in manuscript, some of which have been attributed to Chapman.

Overview of Critical Sources

Although contemporary critics have been more interested in Chapman as a playwright than as a poet or translator, there is one major study of his poetry, two works dealing with his entire *oeuvre,* and articles concerned with facets of individual poems. There is no full-length study of the Homeric translations.

Evaluation of Selected Criticism

MacLure, Millar, *George Chapman: A Critical Study.* Toronto: University of Toronto, 1966. Half of this comprehensive study of Chapman's works is devoted to his poetry and translations. The author gives a close and careful analysis of the arcane early poems, *The Shadow of Night* and *Ovid's Banquet of Sense,* as well as of the later, also difficult *Andromeda Liberata* and *Euthymiae Raptus: Or, The Tears of Peace.* In the fullest study to date, he assesses the Homeric translation as a flawed masterpiece. Although the author's own style is highly metaphorical, he succeeds in illuminating Chapman's often obscure verse. He deals effectively with both ideas and language.

Spivack, Charlotte, *George Chapman.* New York: Twayne, 1967. One chapter of this bio-critical introduction to Chapman's works is devoted to the poems, "The Beyond-Sea Muse" (pp. 30–58). The author first discusses Chapman's theory of poetics, then deals with the poems in groups: the metaphysical, the neo-classical and satirical, the allegorical, and the translations. The aim is placing the poems in their literary and historical context rather than giving close line by line reading.

Waddington, Raymond B. *The Mind's Empire: Myth and Form in George Chapman's Narrative Poems.* Baltimore: Johns Hopkins University Press, 1974. Waddington analyzes Chapman's poetic achievement in the light of Renaissance platonism, with attention to the poet's persona as prophet or oracle, revealing truth only to the select few, and to his language and structure as primarily allegorical. He offers full and detailed readings of all the narrative poems, stressing their mythic or inner form in contrast to their outer or generic form. He develops the significance of form as central to Chapman's poetic mode. The only book-length study of Chapman's poetry, this work is intellectually demanding but clear and lucidly written, not only the best book on its subject but a contribution to scholarship on the Renaissance.

Other Sources

Huntington, John, "Condemnation and Pity in Chapman's Hero and Leander." *ELR* VII (1977), 307–323. A reading of the narrative poem as delicately balanced between moral condemnation of and genuine sympathy for the guilty lovers.

Ide, Richard S. "Exemplary Heroism in Chapman's Odysses," *SEL* XXII (1982), 121–136. A consideration of Chapman's Odysseus in the light of Renaissance humanism and concepts of heroism.

Ribner, Rhoda M. "The Compass of This Curious Frame: Chapman's Ovid's Banquet of Sense and the Emblematic Tradition," *Studies in the Renaissance* XVII (1969), 233–258. A learned treatment of the emblematic traditions informing the imagery of the poem.

Waddington, Raymond B. "Visual Rhetoric: Chapman and the Extended Poem," *ELR* XIII (1983), 36–57. Chapman's use of symbolic typographical features in his published poetry as a way of extending the meaning of the verbal text.

Selected Dictionaries and Encyclopedias

Critical Survey of Poetry, Salem Press, 1983. Brief biography and short analysis of Chapman's major poems.

Charlotte Spivack
University of Massachusetts

THOMAS CHATTERTON
1752–1770

Author's Chronology

Born November 20, 1752, his father deceased, in Bristol, England, where he will spend all but the last four months of his life; *1760* enters Colston's, a charity school; *1764* writes first extant poem "Apostate Will"; *1767* indentured to an attorney, John Lambert, as a scrivener apprentice; *1768* published spurious history of old Bristol bridge, duping local antiquarians; writes the first of many "Rowley Poems," the pseudo-medieval epic "Bristol Tragedy," pretending it was written by the non-existent fifteenth-century poet-cleric Thomas Rowley; it extols the deeds of his munificent patron, the actual Mayor of Bristol and merchant prince William Canynge; writes his masterpiece "Aella, a Tragical Interlude," also claiming it to be by Rowley; *1769* attempts futile correspondence with Horace Walpole seeking patronage; *1770* indenture cancelled as result of suicide threat; leaves Bristol for London, attempting to write contemporary satire in the popular mode; competes last Rowley poem "Ballad of Charity;" kills himself August 24, 1770; buried in Shoe Lane workhouse burial ground in London; *1777* first publication of Rowley Poems by Thomas Tyrwhitt; *1777–1778* years of continual controversy begin by public exposure as literary forger; *1780* publication of Herbert Croft's *Love and Madness* including section on Chatterton; *1803* first publication of collected works.

Author's Bibliography (selected)

Poems, supposed to have been written at Bristol, by Thomas Rowley and Others in the Fifteenth Century, edited by Thomas Tyrwhitt, 1777; *The Works of Thomas Chatterton,* three volumes, edited by Robert Southey and Joseph Cottle, 1803. Between 1803 and 1971 the numerous collections of Chatterton's work were generally derivative and textually unauthentic, the possible exception being that edited by Walter W. Skeat published in 1871 which recognized this tendency and is prefaced by the editor's assertion that "The present edition of Chatterton's Poetical Works is no mere reprint." In 1971 a Bicentenary Edition in two volumes was published, *The Complete Works of Thomas Chatterton,* edited by Donald S. Taylor and Benjamin B. Hoover. This collection which includes not only the poetry and prose but also the sequence of their composition and major sources, is now the definitive edition.

Overview of Biographical Sources

The years following the brief life of Thomas Chatterton witnessed a heated debate about the legitimacy of the Rowleyan poems, and as the controversy raged, little attention was paid to the life of the poet other than how the known facts supported or refuted the arguments of the Rowleians or the anti-Rowleians. Added complications arose from Chatterton's emergence as a mythic martyr figure to major Romantic poets—William Blake, William Wordsworth, Samuel Taylor Coleridge, Percy Bysshe Shelley, and John Keats primarily—who saw the boy-poet as a like victim of an indifferent and insensitive world that little valued imaginative genius. The many derivative editions of Chatterton's works that appeared for almost two hundred years prefixed an introductory biography, often only a thinly veiled moralizing treatise pointing out the fate of misdirected genius and duplicity. It is not surprising, considering these circumstances, that a balanced objective biography had not appeared; not until 1930 was the "definitive" biography published, E. H. W. Meyerstein's *A Life of Thomas Chatterton* (1930).

Evaluation of Selected Biographies

Ellinger, Esther P. *Thomas Chatterton, the Marvellous Boy.* Philadelphia: The University of Pennsylvania Press, 1930. Ellinger's is the first major example of psychoanalytic criticism of Chatterton's life as it might illuminate his work. A follower of Alfred Adler, Ellinger discovered a pattern of neurotic behavior that justified both his creation of and identification with the fictitious Rowley as well as rationalized his compulsion to forge manuscripts.

Gregory, George, *The Life of Thomas Chatterton, with Criticism on his Genius and Writings, and a Concise View of the Controversy Concerning Rowley's Poems.* London: G. Kearsley, 1789, reprinted in "The Life of Thomas Chatterton" prefixed to the 1803 edition edited by Southey and Cottle. Although relatively brief, Gregory's balanced, unadorned record of Chatterton's life is significant in that it is an eighteenth century unsympathetic and austere view that avoids the excessively sentimental versions that would follow to fuel Chatterton's image as a martyr to genius. In Gregory's opinion the fate of the youth provided "a strong dissuasive" for those who veered from the straight and narrow path of Truth.

Meyerstein, E. H. W. *A Life of Thomas Chatterton.* London: Igpen and Grant, 1930. Meyerstein's is the indispensable standard biography, a thorough, comprehensive and objective documentation and acute analysis of both the life and work of Chatterton set against the shaping background of his environment. The Walpole controversy is revalued as well as the mystery of the poet's final resting place. A poet himself, Meyerstein successfully sought to rid Chatterton's life of the sentimental excesses by which it had for so long been distorted. His almost obsessive devotion to this cause erases forever the maudlin image of Chatterton as boy-victim, freeing readers to evaluate his works on their own merits. His is a monumental work, thoroughly dependable.

Russell, Charles E. *Thomas Chatterton, the Marvelous Boy: The Story of a Strange Life.* New York: Moffat, Yard and Co., 1908. Continuing in the characteristic nineteenth-century Romantic "poor boy" portrayal of Chatterton, Russell sustains an excessively commiserating tone in fulfilling his prefatory vow to attempt "to clear from calumny and undeserved reproach the memory of one of the greatest minds and sweetest souls that ever dwelt upon this earth." Evoking Russell's wrath in particular was Horace Walpole, branded "a spiteful old man" for his denial of Chatterton's request for assistance and his alleged persecution. Russell pays tribute to the earlier biographies of Bell and Wilson as "the most accurate" and sympathetic to the maligned youth.

Autobiographical Sources

Chatterton's creation of the fictitious fifteenth-century cleric-poet Thomas Rowley assumes autobiographical significance strong enough to convince his major biographer and critic Meyerstein to assert that "Chatterton is Rowley, and so far as literature is concerned, nothing else." This premise challenges the reader of the Rowley Poems to seek revealing keys toward understanding Chatterton beneath the guise of his alter-ego. In Rowley's devotion to his patron Canynge many critics have discerned Chatterton's yearning for a surrogate father and supporting protector; in his plaintive "Ballad of Charity" an anguished plea for succor in his final desperate weeks of life.

Overview of Critical Sources

Opinion of Chatterton and his work has irrevocably been colored by the troubling aspect of forgery as well as his apotheosis into a Romantic hero and proto-martyr. Although Chatterton continues to inspire plays, operas, poetry, and paintings, very little attention has been directed toward the prosody, diction, narrative structure, or imagery in his work separate from fascination with events of his life. Major biographies, both competent and fictionalized, combine factual data with criticism, and therefore should be consulted. Re-assessment of his work from a New Critical position has been gradual, stimulated greatly by Meyerstein's competent biography and the bicentennial critical edition of the canon.

Evaluation of Selected Criticism

Bronson, Bertrand H. "Thomas Chatterton" in *The Age of Johnson.* New Haven: Yale University Press, 1949. This comprehensive chapter placing Chatterton within the larger frame of a literary era not only marks his significant and unique contributions, but also deals with more specific critical problems, most particularly the enigmatic figure of Rowley as he influenced Chatterton's life and inspired his finest work.

Taylor, Donald S. *Thomas Chatterton's Art: Experiments in Imagined History.* Princeton: Princeton University Press, 1978. This is the only full-length systematic critical study of Chatterton's work that focuses on his artistic achievements, the new and radical poetry that broke with eighteenth-century tradition, and what Dante Gabriel Rossetti claimed was the dawning of modern romantic poetry. Described by its author as dealing with "the peculiar problems of a sequential critical history of Chatterton's writings," he sees them as resulting from disproportional emphasis on the melodramatic myth of his life to the exclusion of the individual works, his fragmentary mode of composition, and the distorting tendency to treat his work on terms other than his own, such as its influence on his successors.

Other Sources

Browning, Robert, *Essay on Chatterton.* ed. Donald Smalley. Cambridge: Harvard University Press, 1948. In both the essay itself and Smalley's introduction the point is evident that although Browning intended to write a study in criticism and biography for a serious journal (it first appeared anonymously in *Foreign Quarterly Review* for 1842), correcting earlier misrepresentations and taking a new approach, the essayist, as Smalley sees it, "wrote as a creative artist." Browning's future work, especially his dramatic monologues, is adumbrated in the handling of his Chatterton material, "a remarkable example of ingenious plotting, special-pleading, and case-making," as he defends his fellow-poet against the biases and distortions of his past biographers. Even though the essay ultimately reveals more about its author than its idealized subject, it is nevertheless valuable as an example of Victorian opinion.

Croft, Herbert, *Love and Madness.* London: G. Kearsly, 1780. This is a curious epistolary novel including an extensive central section on the life of Chatterton, purported to be verified by letters and testimony of his family and friends, when in fact much of the data is fictionalized and sensationalized. For all its eccentricities, this work remains the first biography of Chatterton. Taking no sides in the then raging Rowley controversy, Croft, at a critical time in the formation of the Romantic ethos, presented a sentimental and hyperbolic portrayal of Chatterton as a heroic martyred genius that became fixed permanently in the consciousness of generations to come. Seven editions of this best-seller were published.

Maryhelen C. Harmon
University of South Florida

GEOFFREY CHAUCER
1343?–1400

Author's Chronology

No birth record, 1343 surmised from life-records: family wealthy wine importers and wholesalers; *1356–1359* is attendant, as a page, to a daughter-in-law of Edward III; *1360* is captured by French and ransomed, in part by the King, for 13s 4d, less than for a nobleman's horse ransomed at the same time; *1360–1366* perhaps studies at Inns of Chancery and Court; marries Philippa Roet, sister of the future wife of John of Gaunt, fourth son of Edward III; *1365* Philippa is granted a royal annuity; *1368* upon death of Blanche, wife of Gaunt, writes *The Book of the Duchess; 1369* enters Gaunt's service; *1372* visits Florence while Boccaccio is there lecturing; *1374* receives royal grant, leases Aldgate house, is appointed London customs' comptroller for wool, skins and hides; enjoys financial security; *1377* accession of Richard II at age ten makes Gaunt power behind throne; *1379–1381?* writes *House of Fame* and translates Boethius; *1380* is released from suit for "raptus" of Cecily Champain; *1380–1386?* writes *Parliament of Fowls* and "Palamon;" begins *Troilus and Criseyde,* "To Adam the Scrivener," and *Legend of Good Women; 1383–1389* loses positions and falls into debt, probably because of Gaunt's increasing difficulties; *1387–1400?* writes poems later incorporated into *The Canterbury Tales; 1389* becomes clerk of the King's works after Richard comes to power; *1391* not reappointed clerk of the works; *1399* writes "A Complaint of Chaucer to his Purse;" royal annuity is doubled when Henry IV, Gaunt's son, deposes Richard; October 25, 1400 dies.

Author's Bibliography (selected)

Dates and order of composition surmised: *Romance of the Rose,* ?1361–1367 (translation); *Book of the Duchess,* ?1368–1369 (poem); "St. Cecelia," later incorporated into *Canterbury Tales,* ?1373–1377 (poem); Monk's tragedies and *Anelida and Arcite,* ?1376–1377 (poems); *House of Fame,* ?1378–1381 (poem); *Consolation of Philosophy,* ?1378–1381 (translation); *Troilus and Criseyde,* "Palamon," "To Adam the Scrivener," a *Parliament of Fowls,* and *Legend of Good Women,* ?1380–1386 (poems); *The Canterbury Tales* (The General Prologue, the Knight's Tale and Fragment VII), ?1387 (poems); *The Canterbury Tales* (Miller's and Reeve's Tales), ?1388–1389 (poems); *The Canterbury Tales* (so-called marriage group), ?1390–1394 (poems); "Complaint of Chaucer to His Purse," ?1399 (poem).

Overview of Biographical Sources

Because not one of the nearly five hundred records in the *Chaucer Life-Records* (ed. Martin M. Crow and Clair C. Olson. Oxford: Clarendon, 1966) mentions Geoffrey Chaucer's poetry, biographers have had problems in establishing from the surviving manuscripts the dates and order of his poetry and translations, and even the canon. Moreover, not one poem has survived in Chaucer's holograph, and the one work which might be in the author's hand is an equitorie, a geometric device for calculating the position of the planets in relation to one another, recently edited by its discoverer, D. J. Price in *The Equatorie of the Planits* (Cambridge: Cambridge University Press, 1955). Finally, further difficulties arose because at various stages of auctorial revision copies were made, each of which spawned offspring which produced sometimes profound variation among manuscripts of the same work.

The earliest "biography," in Thomas Speght's, *Works* (1598), surmised from the poems themselves a prosperous upper middle class background for Chaucer, one which provided enough leisure for education, travel, reading and writing, but it was not until 1876 when F. J. Furnivall discovered a deed of conveyance of a house on Thames Street, in which Chaucer identified his parentage, that this bourgeois upbringing was confirmed. Working with scraps of evidence found in unlikely places—such as among the stuffings of a manuscript cover—modern scholarship has rounded out the picture of a busy diplomat often on the continent on royal missions, and a civil servant who managed to survive the always shifting power struggles that plagued England in the latter half of the fourteenth century. Because of this lack of contemporary evidence about his writings, a "definitive" biography has not emerged, although John Gardner's *The Life and Times of Chaucer* (New York: Alfred A. Knopf, 1977) attempts, sometimes inaccurately, to be one.

Despite the difficulties caused by the lack of evidence about Chaucer's writing, several treatments of his historical, cultural and literary backgrounds are useful: Edith Rickert's *Chaucer's World* (New York: Columbia University Press, 1948) recreates Chaucer's world through a collection of fourteenth century writings in modern English; George G. Coulton's *Chaucer and His England* (London: Methuen, 1930) uses literature and history to illuminate each other; Robert D. French's *A Chaucer Handbook* (New York: Crofts, 1927) presents much valuable material, including summaries of important works Chaucer used, analogues to his works, and a commentary on Chaucer's use of these materials; Derek Brewer's *Chaucer in His time* (London: Nelson, 1963) gives much that is illuminating about the society in which Chaucer lived; and a "popular" biography reprinted in paperback in 1958 is Marchette Chute's *Geoffrey Chaucer of England* (New York: E. P. Dutton, 1946). Recent studies tend to stress historical and cultural data which support a particular interest of the writer, such as D. W. Robertson's *Chaucer's London* (New York: John Wiley and Sons, 1968), emphasizing the timeliness of Chaucer's interest in Boethius, antimendicant propaganda, and the immorality of the newly acquisitive city.

Overview of Critical Sources

By the end of the nineteenth century, historical grammar and the efforts of the Early English Texts Society and the Chaucer Society had solved many of the problems in the pronunciation and grammar of Chaucer's language, had made accessible the texts of his contemporaries, and had gathered much of the factual data of his biography. Autobiographical readings of his works were common at the beginning of this century, and scholars attempted to identify the narrator of the poems with the author, and to identify the fictitious characters in the works, especially in *The Canterbury Tales,* with real-life prototypes. Typical of such work, and perhaps the best, is John M. Manly's *Some New Light on Chaucer* (New York: Holt, 1926) in which Manly tries to find historical persons who served as the bases for the portraits of the pilgrims in the General Prologue to *The Canterbury Tales.* Although Manly's work was expanded and interpreted by Muriel Bowden in *A Commentary on the General Prologue to the Canterbury Tales* (New York: Macmillan, 1948), autobiographical readings since have fallen into disfavor in, for instance, George Kane's *The Autobiographical Fallacy in Chaucer and Langland* (London: H. K. Lewis for University College, London, 1965).

At the beginning of this century, the emphasis in criticism was on identifying Chaucer's sources and explaining the historical precedents for the characters and situations in his writings. This factual and historical criticism, which tended to read poems autobiographically, was brought to an end by C. S. Lewis in *Allegory of Love* (Oxford: Oxford University Press, 1936). Lewis claimed that Chaucer was far more abstruse and conceptual than had been hitherto recognized. Distinguishing between allegory and symbolism in a way which has been modified significantly since, this landmark work coincided with the rejection of autobiographical and historical studies by the "new critics" such as I. A. Richards in England and Robert Penn Warren and Cleanth Brooks in the United States.

Since then, Chaucer criticism has emphasized close textual analysis, tension, paradox, symbolism and structure. A large share of the work of *The Canterbury Tales* continues to study such issues as the background of the pilgrimage; the order and unity of the tales; appropriateness of tale to teller; dramatic interplay among pilgrims; and sources and analogues of the framework and of the tales themselves. Early in this century, studies of *Troilus and Criseyde* were concerned with the genuineness of the moral rejection of earthly love at the end of the poem, with attacks and defenses of Criseyde, with the use of Boethius and *II Filostrato,* and with other developments of the story in the Middle Ages. Recent studies have been more interested in establishing Chaucer's attitude to the love affair—whether "courtly" love, human love, or spiritual love. Reaction to the readings given by the "new critics" appeared with the emergence of the so-called patristic exegesis school, exemplified by the work of D. W. Robertson and Bernard F. Huppé. Reaction to this approach was quick and vehement, providing a lively controversy throughout the 1960's and 1970's.

Evaluation of Selected Criticism

Ackerman, Robert, *Backgrounds to Medieval English Literature.* New York: Random House, 1966. This book presents clear, thoughtful and precise summaries of aspects of medieval literature which puzzle modern readers. Included are descriptions of the geocentric universe, astronomy, the humors, Christianity in the Middle Ages and the reasons for the antagonism between the ecclesiastics, the monks and the friars.

Bryan, William, and Germaine Dempster, eds. *Sources and Analogues of Chaucer's Canterbury Tales.* Chicago: Chicago University Press, 1941. Comprehensive and indispensible, this work contains possible sources and analogues of the Prologue and the individual tales in separate chapters.

David, Alfred, *The Strumpet Muse.* Bloomington: Indiana University Press, 1976. Presenting a stimulating and provocative new critical analysis of Chaucer's work, David articulately shows the tension between aesthetics and morality in Chaucer's works.

Donaldson, E. Talbot, *Speaking of Chaucer.* New York: W. W. Norton, 1970. This valuable collection of essays, many of which had appeared earlier, includes the differentiation between Chaucer the poet and Chaucer the pilgrim in *The Canterbury Tales,* and a statement of opposition to the use of patristic exegesis in the interpretation of medieval poetry.

———, *The Swan at the Well: Shakespeare Reading Chaucer.* New Haven: Yale University Press, 1985. Focusing on the plays most indebted to Chaucer, *Troilus and Cressida, Romeo and Juliet* and *A Midsummer's Night's Dream,* Donaldson goes beyond the details Shakespeare uses from Chaucer to demonstrate the similarity of the two poets' basic approach to their heroines, of their sad celebrations of romantic love and of their triumphant, if unsavory, celebrations of human vitality.

Elbow, Peter, *Oppositions in Chaucer.* Middletown, CT: Wesleyan University Press, 1975. Typical of a critical trend to see "tensions" between the sacred and the profane in medieval poets, Elbow argues that Chaucer, like Boethius and certain other medieval writers, often thought in terms of opposites and expressed ideas by affirming both sides of the opposition.

Fyler, John, *Chaucer and Ovid.* New Haven: Yale University Press, 1979. Fyler presents a fascinating theory that Chaucer and Ovid shared a skeptical view of human understanding in their subversion of Dante and Vergil. The author argues that neither Chaucer nor Ovid resolved the problem that man's limited understanding and perception might prevent effective action in the world.

Huppé, Bernard F. *A Reading of the Canterbury Tales.* Albany, NY: SUNY Press, 1964. Writing for undergraduates, Huppé presents the theory behind the patristic school of interpretation of medieval texts and explains many of the tales in terms of this approach. Despite the depth into which this work delves, it is never difficult to understand and manages to provide stimulating insights, careful textual analysis and enough historical background of medieval controversies to clarify the disputes between the pilgrims.

———, and D. W. Robertson, *Fruyt and Chaf: Studies in Chaucer's Allegories.* Princeton: Princeton University Press, 1963. Interpreting *The Book of the Duchess* and *The Parliament of Foules* in light of medieval literary theory, the authors present important details of conventional iconography and traditional imagery, chiefly Scriptural, which clarify what these early poems would mean to Chaucer's audience.

Jones, Terry, *Chaucer's Knight: The Portrait of a Medieval Mercenary.* Baton Rouge: Louisiana State University Press, 1980. Challenging the conventional pious attitude toward the Knight, the humane British satirist Terry Jones claims that Chaucer's "first audience" would have seen the Knight as a rapacious brigand, "crusading" against Christians as well as non-Christians, who participated in campaigns which were infamous and much criticized by contemporaries.

Kittredge, George L. *Chaucer and His Poetry.* Cambridge: Cambridge University Press, 1915. Although Kittredge's work has not been in favor for some time, these essays are significant because of the famous suggestion of the "Marriage Group" theme in *The Canterbury Tales.*

Lumiansky, Robert M. *Of Sondry Folk: The Dramatic Principle in the Canterbury Tales.* Austin: University of Texas Press, 1955. Lumiansky shows the suitability of tales to tellers in *The Canterbury Tales* and three stages of dramatic development of this relationship.

Meech, Sanford B. *Design in Chaucer's Troilus.* Syracuse: Syracuse University Press, 1959. Along with detailed comparison with Boccaccio's *II Filostrato* which reveals the complex transformation Chaucer achieved, Meech steers a careful course between those who believe that *Troilus* ultimately praises courtly love, such as C. S. Lewis in *The Allegory of Love* (see above), and those who believe that the poem condemns courtly love, such as Father Denomy in *The Heresy of Courtly Love* (New York: Macmillan, 1947).

Robertson, D. W. *A Preface to Chaucer.* Princeton: Princeton University Press, 1962. This important and provocative work sets forth the principles of patristic exegesis of medieval texts, analyzes major themes such as love, medieval aesthetics, and typology; and applies medieval moral philosophy to Chaucer's sources and works. Exegetical criticism as developed by Huppé and Robertson has been the most important and controversial issue in Chaucer criticism for the last twenty-five years.

Rose, Donald L. ed. *New Perspectives in Chaucer Criticism.* Norman, OK: University of Oklahoma Press, 1981. These essays include applications and discussions of current trends in Chaucer criticism, semiotic, comparative and structuralist literary theory, the influence of the French tradition and a treatment of visual arts in Chaucer's time.

Rowland, Beryl, ed. *Companion to Chaucer Studies.* New York: Oxford, 1968. Each author in this significant collection of twenty-two essays is an acknowledged expert in the field about which Rowland asked him to write, as for example Robert O. Payne on the art of rhetoric, Mustanoja on prosody, Jordan on narrative, Chauncey Wood on astrology, Charles Owen on the design of the *Tales,* Robertson on *The Book of the Duchess* and John McCall on *Troilus and Criseyde.*

Schoeck, Richard, and Jerome Taylor, eds. *Chaucer Criticism.* Notre Dame, IN: University of Notre Dame Press, 1960. Volume I deals with *The Canterbury Tales* and Volume II with *Troilus and Criseyde.* This important anthology contains significant essays which reflect a wide range of approaches to Chaucer.

Selected Dictionaries and Encyclopedias

Critical Survey of Poetry, Salem Press, 1982. Brief biography and short analyses of some of Chaucer's major works.

Dictionary of the Middle Ages, Charles Scribner's Sons, 1983—in progress. See "Chaucer" for biography, analysis of his canon, works and criticism with a selected bibliography.

Middle English Dictionary, eds. Sherman M. Kuhn, John Reidy, *et al.,* Ann Arbor, MI.: University of Michigan Press, 1956—in progress.

Spurgeon, Carolyn, *Five Hundred Years of Chaucer Criticism and Allusion, 1357-1900,* (1914-1925), Chaucer Society, Cambridge University Press, 1925. A fascinating collection of what was written about Chaucer from the fourteenth century to the twentieth, this work contains the famous remarks about Chaucer by Dryden, Coleridge and others.

Judith Weise
State University College-Potsdam, NY

JOHN CHEEVER
1912–1982

Author's Chronology

Born May 27, 1912, Quincy, Massachusetts; *1929* expelled from Thayer Academy, Braintree, Massachusetts, and for the next three years lives with his brother Frederick; *1930* publishes his first short story, "Expelled," in *New Republic; 1932* moves to New York City, where he earns barely enough to survive; *1934* spends his first summer at the Yaddo artists' colony in Saratoga Springs, New York; *1935* begins his long association with the *New Yorker; 1941* marries Mary Winternitz; *1941–1945* serves in United States Army; *1951* receives a Guggenheim fellowship; *1954* Benjamin Franklin Award for his story "The Five-Forty-Eight"; *1956* O. Henry Award for "The Country Husband"; *1957–1958* spends year in Italy; *1958* National Book Award for *The Wapshot Chronicle; 1961* moves to Ossining, New York; *1964* O. Henry Award for "The Embarkment for Cythera;" cover story in *Time; 1965* Howells Medal for *The Wapshot Scandal; 1973* elected to American Academy of Arts and Letters; *1974–1976* period of severe depression and illness ending with successful treatment for alcoholism; *1977 Falconer* hailed as "Cheever's Triumph;" *Newsweek* cover story; *1978* Pulitzer Prize and National Book Critics Circle Award for *The Stories of John Cheever;* honorary doctorate from Harvard University; *1979* MacDowell Medal for "outstanding contribution to the arts;" *1980* television adaptations of three short stories aired on Public Broadcasting System; American Book Award for paperback edition of *The Short Stories of John Cheever; 1982* Cheever's original screenplay, *The Shady Hill Kidnapping,* aired on Public Broadcasting System; awarded National Medal for Literature; dies June 18 of cancer.

Author's Bibliography (selected)

The Way Some People Live, 1943 (stories); *The Enormous Radio and Other Stories,* 1953; *The Wapshot Chronicle,* 1954 (novel); *The Housebreaker of Shady Hill and Other Stories,* 1958; *Some People, Places, and Things That Will Not Appear in My Next Novel,* 1961 (stories); *The Brigadier and the Golf Widow,* 1964 (stories); *Bullet Park,* 1969 (novel); *The World of Apples,* 1973 (stories); *Falconer,* 1977 (novel); *The Stories of John Cheever,* 1978; *Oh What a Paradise It Seems,* 1982 (novel).

Overview of Biographical Sources

The publication of Susan Cheever's memoir, *Home Before Dark* (Boston: Houghton Mifflin, 1984), radically alters and deepens Cheever's biography, which had previously been little more than a series of dates fleshed out by the subject's own versions of his past. Susan Cheever divides her father's life into two parts: the first, and longest, involved a "struggle for stability" as a writer and as a husband during which he fashioned his public persona, the genial country squire; the second, lasting about twenty years, saw Cheever desperately trying to escape from the middle-class security he had tried so hard to attain. In exhaustively detailing his alcoholism, financial difficulties, marital problems, long-repressed homosexuality, and terrifying sense of homelessness, she makes abundantly clear the autobiographical underpinnings of the fiction. However, in documenting the man she often misses the art, which becomes grist for the biographer's mill, as in her failure to distinguish personal revelations from drafts of stories and novels when quoting from her father's unpublished journals.

Autobiographical Sources

Cheever's protestations to the contrary, his fiction may be considered, at least in part, "crypto-autobiography." The best autobiographical sources, however, are the journal excerpts published in *Home Before Dark* and the many interviews that the usually reticent Cheever began to give during the last six years of his life. Of these the most revealing are Annette Grant, "The Art of Fiction," *Paris Review,* 17 (Fall 1976), 39–66 (rpt. in *Writers at Work,* 5th series [New York: Viking, 1981]); John Hersey, "Talk with John Cheever," *New York Times Book Review,* March 6, 1977, pp. 1, 24, 26–28; Susan Cheever, "A Duet of Cheevers," *Newsweek,* March 14, 1977, pp. 68–70, 73; and Jesse Kornbluth, "The Cheever Chronicle," *New York Times Magazine,* October 21, 1979, pp. 26–29, 102–105. (The Grant and Hersey interviews are reprinted in *Critical Essays on John Cheever,* ed. R. G. Collins [Boston: G. K. Hall, 1982]). Fifteen of Cheever's letters (1933–1956) to Elizabeth Ames, director of the Yaddo artists' colony, have been published in *Vanity Fair,* May 1984, pp. 60–65.

Overview of Critical Sources

Although Cheever was the subject of a 1964 *Time* cover story, it was not until the publication of *Falconer* in 1977 that he began to receive serious critical attention. Although he is now recognized as a master of the short story, many critics continue to question his achievement as a novelist, in part because he first made his reputation as a short story writer and in part because he continues to be judged as a novelist of manners. Anyone wishing to survey the critical commentary should consult Francis Bosha's *John Cheever: A Reference Guide* (Boston: G. K. Hall, 1981), which lists and annotates writings about Cheever, 1943–1979, and also includes a list of Cheever's book publications (including translations) and articles as well as adaptations of his work. Deno Trakas's "John Cheever: An Annotated Secondary Bibliography (1943–1978)," *Resources for American Literary Study,* 9 (1979), 181–199, though more limited in scope, includes a number of items missed by Bosha. Dennis Coates's "John

Cheever: A Checklist, 1930–1978," *Bulletin of Biography,* 36 (1979), 1–13, 49 is useful for its very thorough listing of all of Cheever's shorter publications.

Evaluation of Selected Criticism

Coale, Samuel, *John Cheever.* New York: Frederick Ungar, 1977. In this, the first book-length study of Cheever's work, Coale emphasizes the author's concern for the moral matters which lie behind the suburban facade. His characters are alienated yet hopeful; they lose their various paradises but eventually regain them in lyrically rendered moments of "mystical illumination." He includes a biographical chapter and analysis of eleven stories and the first four novels.

Collins, R. G. ed. *Critical Essays on John Cheever.* Boston: G. K. Hall, 1982. Reprints many of the most important reviews, interviews, and critical essays, including Clinton S. Burhans, Jr. "John Cheever and the Grave of Social Coherence" (1966); Eugene Chesnick, "The Domesticated Stroke of John Cheever" (1971); and John Gardner, "Witchcraft in *Bullet Park*" (1971). Burhans sees Cheever as a moralist concerned with the chaotic nature of contemporary American life. Chesnick makes a similar point, reading Cheever as a modern Transcendentalist "struggling to make his fictional meanings clear in an increasingly absurd world." Gardner analyzes the poetic logic of *Bullet Park* and its relation to Cheever's theme, that chance may rule the world. Of the items published here for the first time, three are especially noteworthy: Collins' introduction, in which he surveys Cheever's life and the critical response to his fiction; Dennis Coates's updating of his 1979 bibliography, and Samuel Coale's "Cheever and Hawthorne: The Romancer's Art," the best essay yet published on Cheever. According to Coale, Cheever is a romancer (like Hawthorne), not a realist, and as such is concerned with manichean doubleness: good and evil, light and dark, reality and dream/nightmare. This manichean strain is most obvious in the stories of brothers, but it also manifests itself in the conflict between Cheever's episodic plots and decorous, nearly neoclassical style.

Hunt, George W. *John Cheever: The Hobgoblin Company of Love.* Grand Rapids, MI: William B. Eerdmans, 1983. A far-ranging study in which Cheever emerges as an essentially religious writer who abandoned his earlier Hemingway style for a lyricism more appropriate to his affirmative and compassionate vision. Hunt emphasizes the development of Cheever's distinctive voice and the unity of the novels. Many readers will undoubtedly be troubled by Hunt's ability to find affirmation everywhere in Cheever's fiction.

Waldeland, Lynne, *John Cheever.* Boston: Twayne, 1979. Like Coale's, this is a useful introduction to Cheever's work. Waldeland covers more ground than Coale and takes greater notice of previous criticism. Her general thesis, however, that Cheever is a romantic and a moralist whose stories concern "the relationships between the inner person and the outer world, the present and the past, the best we dream of being and the compromises we continually make," adds little that is new.

Other Sources

Collins, R. G. "Fugitive Time: Dissolving Experience in the Later Fiction of Cheever," *Studies in American Fiction,* 12 (Autumn 1984), 175–188. At the midpoint of his career, Cheever began to see the present moment as unstable; it became an ocean in which his characters found themselves adrift.

Cowley, Malcolm, "John Cheever: The Novelist's Life as a Dream," *Sewannee Review,* 91 (Winter 1983), 1–16. Discusses his fifty-year friendship with Cheever.

Morace, Robert A. "The Religious Experience and the 'Mystery of Imprisonment' in *Falconer,*" in *Cithara,* 20 (November 1980), 44–53. Discusses Cheever's use of the prison metaphor and the growth of the protagonist and the structure of the novel in terms of this metaphor.

Selected Dictionaries and Encyclopedias

American Writers: A Collection of Literary Biographies, Charles Scribner's Sons, 1979. Combines biography and literary analysis.

Critical Survey of Long Fiction, Salem Press, 1983. Analyzes all five novels.

Critical Survey of Short Fiction, Salem Press, 1981. Analyzes several of the stories in depth.

Dictionary of Literary Biography, Gale Research, 1978. Biographical material interwoven with analysis of all the novels and story collections through 1977. Emphasizes narrative experiments and development.

Robert A. Morace
Daemen College

CHARLES WADDELL CHESNUTT
1858–1932

Author's Chronology

Born June 20, 1858, in Cleveland, Ohio; *1866* moves to Fayetteville, North Carolina; attends Howard School; *1872* becomes student teacher at Howard School; *1878* marries Susan Perry, a teacher at Howard; *1880* assumes principalship of Fayetteville State Normal School; *1883* resigns as principal and moves to New York, taking work as a court reporter and stenographer; moves to Cleveland six months later and works as an accountant with the Nickel Plate Railroad Company; *1887* passes the Ohio Bar Examination and admitted to bar; publishes first story "The Goophered Grapevine" in *The Atlantic Monthly; 1899* gives up work as attorney, court reporter and stenographer to set up literary office; publishes a biography and short story collection; *1900* publishes first novel; *1928* receives the Spingarn Medal of the NAACP for distinguished achievement; *1932* dies in Cleveland.

Author's Bibliography (full-length works)

Frederick Douglass, 1899 (biography); *The Wife Of His Youth and Other Stories Of The Color Line,* 1899; *The Conjure Woman,* 1899 (stories); *The House Behind The Cedars,* 1900 (novel); *The Marrow Of Tradition,* 1901 (novel); *The Colonel's Dream,* 1905 (novel).

Overview of Biographical Sources

Three full-length biographies, significant portions of bio-critical works, and several shorter sources furnish biographical information that explain Chesnutt's background, social and political milieu, and his motivation for writing. Chesnutt's daughter Helen, with the assistance of her family, assembled her father's correspondence and journal entries to write *Charles Waddell Chesnutt: Pioneer Of The Color Line* (1952), a biography that contains the richest published source of his journal entries and correspondence. Sympathetic, but less adulatory than Helen Chesnutt's biography of her father, is *An American Crusade: The Life Of Charles Waddell Chesnutt* (1978) by Frances Richardson Keller. Although Keller's work analyzes more thoroughly the historical and social realities attendant upon the man and his works, Helen Chesnutt's biography often contains the full text of letters and journal entries only alluded to by Keller. Discrepancies between some portions of the text of the letters, particularly letters from Chesnutt to Booker T. Washington and George Washington Cable, are noted by Keller, who attributes the discrepancies to either Helen Chesnutt's deliberate editing of her father's letters, errors or oversights, or simply different drafts of the same letter. J. Noel Heermance's *Charles W. Chesnutt: America's First Great Black Novelist* (1974) emphasizes more substantially than the other biographies the historical context in which Chesnutt lived and worked, devoting the last two chapters of his biography to an outline of the scope of Chesnutt's works and an analysis of craftsmanship, themes and purposes. Heermance's work also includes a complete bibliography of Chesnutt's works. Of some value to researchers seeking a brief overview of Chesnutt's life and works are the introduction to Sylvia Lyon Render's *The Short Fiction of Charles W. Chesnutt* (1974) and Chapter 6 of *The Negro in Literature and Art: In the United States* (1930) by Benjamin Brawley. Chesnutt's letters and journals were turned over to Fisk University, but Frances Richardson Keller notes that many of the letters in Helen Chesnutt's biography are not included in the Chesnutt Collection at Fisk.

Evaluation of Selected Biographies

Chesnutt, Helen M. *Charles W. Chesnutt.* Chapel Hill: University of North Carolina Press, 1952. Helen Chesnutt's biography of her father offers a comprehensive chronology in the two biographies of Chesnutt's life and the influences on his writings. Presenting numerous entries from the journal and personal correspondence of Chesnutt, the biographer organizes her work around particular phases of the subject's life or a literary work and follows that presentation with relevant personal correspondence or journal entries. Although she refrains from a critical evaluation of literary works, her presentation includes reviews of the literary works as well as Chesnutt's correspondence with publishers and literary figures. Particularly instructive to readers interested in Chesnutt's social and political ideology are the letters written to Booker T. Washington, a dominant Black political leader, and George W. Cable, a prominent literary figure. The chronological presentation of the correspondence is essentially reliable through 1900, with some reversals in chronology between 1901 and 1908; the volume of correspondence also decreases during these years. After 1908, the reliable chronology is resumed, but the volume of the correspondence remains considerably below that of the earlier years.

Heermance, J. Noel, *Charles W. Chesnutt: America's First Great Black Novelist.* Hamden, CT: Archon Books, 1974. Heermance analyzes rather thoroughly the historical and sociological implications of Chesnutt's milieu. This work is bio-critical, with the preponderance of emphasis placed on the historical and biographical. Of the three biographies, Heermance's research extends more often and more systematically into resources outside the Chesnutt Collection. This work should be particularly helpful to researchers interested in a sociohistorical analysis of the literature. One of the two final chapters reviews the scope of Chesnutt's writing and the last chapter analyzes the literary components of the works. The critical section is ultimately less analytical than descriptive.

Keller, Frances Richardson, *An American Crusade: The Life of Charles Waddell Chesnutt.* Provo, UT: Brigham Young University Press, 1978. Keller's biography is essentially literary narrative without sacrificing essential factual, biographical information. She presents a section of photographs showing Chesnutt at various ages along with photographs of other family members and the Howard School where he was educated and later worked as a student teacher. Although this biography devotes some coverage to a critical evaluation of Chesnutt's work and his ideological stance relative to national issues, the primary thrust is biographical, and the political/social milieu seems to be depicted accurately. She relies quite heavily on Helen Chesnutt's biography, without adding substantially to Chesnutt scholarship. The narrative flow and transitional markers, however, place many events in clearer perspective and justify the publication of this later biography.

Overview of Critical Sources

A considerable body of Chesnutt criticism is available. The biographies by Keller and Heermance contain interpretive and critical evaluations of Chesnutt's works. Two widely available journals have published articles addressing a variety of critical issues; these publications are *Phylon,* published quarterly from Atlanta University and the *College Language Association Journal.* The richer source of Chesnutt criticism is the *CLAJ,* with volumes 4 (1960), 5 (1962), and 10 (1966), carrying substantial critical articles. Among the criticism in *Phylon* is an essay by Hugh M. Gloster, author of *Negro Voices In American Fiction* (1948), "Charles W. Chesnutt—Pioneer In The Fiction of Negro Life", *Phylon* 2 (1941), 57–66. A full-length book of criticism, *The Literary Career of Charles W. Chesnutt* (1980), by William L. Andrews places Chesnutt's works in a sociohistorical framework but invokes the sociohistorical emphasis only to the extent that it impinges on the literary achievement.

Evaluation of Selected Criticism

Andrews, William L. *The Literary Career of Charles W. Chesnutt.* Baton Rouge: Louisiana State University Press, 1980. This source offers interpretive and critical assessments of Chesnutt's works. Andrews presents a systematic categorization of periods or phases in the subject's life with corresponding descriptions, summaries, and analyses of the literature. Chesnutt's three novels, the dialect stories, the color-line stories, and one short story, "Baxter's Procrustes," occupy one chapter each. Also examined are the sociological and ideological implications of the literature. Andrew's work concludes with a complete bibliography of Chesnutt's publications.

Render, Sylvia Lyons, ed. *The Short Fiction of Charles W. Chesnutt.* Washington, DC: Howard University Press, 1974. This collection which includes Chesnutt's short stories, tales, and anecdotes, has a well-organized, comprehensive bio-critical introduction. The 50-page introduction is bio-critical and gives an overview of Chesnutt's life as well as commentary on the literary aspects of his works. The source is valuable in that it apprises the reader of the major themes in Chesnutt's writing, his writing style, and the critical reception of his works.

Other Sources

Bone, Robert, *The Negro Novel in America.* New Haven: Yale University Press, 1958 (pp. 35–38). Critical analyses of Chesnutt's novels which evoked considerable controversy relative to Bone's critical perspective.

Loggins, Vernon, *The Negro Author.* Port Washington, NY: Kennikat Press, 1964 (pp. 310–331) a comparative analysis of Chesnutt's and Paul Laurence Dunbar's approaches to fiction and treatment of the race problem.

Selected Dictionaries and Encyclopedias

Afro-American Fiction 1853–1976, Gale Research, 1979. Excellent list of secondary sources.

Black American Writers: Bibliographic Essays, Vol. 1, St. Martin's Press, 1978. Annotated list of biographical and critical sources.

Black American Writers Past and Present, Vol. 1, Scarecrow Press, 1975. Brief biographical sketch, bibliography of Chesnutt's works, and list of secondary sources.

Index to Black American Writers in Collective Biographies, Libraries Unlimited, 1983. Listing of collective biographies that include Chesnutt.

Modern Black Writers: A Library of Literary Criticism, Frederick Ungar, 1978. Short summaries of selected critical articles.

Twentieth Century Authors: A Biographical Dictionary, H. W. Wilson, 1942. Brief biographical sketch and descriptions of Chesnutt's major works.

Robbie Jean Walker
Auburn University at Montgomery

G. K. CHESTERTON
1874–1936

Author's Chronology

Born Gilbert Keith Chesterton, May 29, 1874, Campden Hill in the Kensington section of London; *1887* enters as a day student St. Paul's Preparatory School; *1892* begins his study of art at Slade School and experiences a traumatic period of personal and religious problems; *1895* begins his work as a journalist on Fleet Street; *1900* publishes his first books: *Graybeards at Play* and *The Wild Knight,* also gains attention as opponent of the Boer War; *1901* marries Frances Blogg and that winter settles in Battersea; *1908* publishes *The Man Who Was Thursday, All Things Considered,* and *Orthodoxy; 1909* moves to Beaconsfield; *1914* has mental and physical collapse and remains in a coma from Christmas eve until almost Easter; *1918* Cecil Chesterton dies in the War and G. K. C. is obliged to edit his brother's *New Witness; 1920* takes his first trip to the United States; *1922* becomes a Roman Catholic on July 30; *1925* starts *G. K.'s Weekly; 1930* makes his second trip to the United States and lectures at the University of Notre Dame; *1932* begins series of talks on BBC; *1936* dies; *Autobiography* published.

Author's Bibliography (selected)

Graybeards at Play, 1900 (nonsense verse); *The Wild Knight,* 1900 (verse play); *The Napoleon of Notting Hill,* 1904 (novel); *Heretics,* 1905 (criticism); *Charles Dickens,* 1906 (criticism); *The Man Who Was Thursday,* 1908 (novel); *Orthodoxy,* 1908 (theology); *George Bernard Shaw,* 1909 (criticism); *The Innocence of Father Brown,* 1911 (fiction); *The Victorian Age in Literature,* 1913 (criticism); *Collected Poems,* 1927; *The Thing,* 1929 (criticism); *St. Thomas Aquinas,* 1933 (biography); *Autobiography,* 1936.

Overview of Biographical Sources

The earliest biography of Chesterton was that written by his friend and assistant editor at the *New Witness* the year Chesterton died: W. R. Titterton's *G. K. Chesterton: A Portrait* (London: Alexander Ousley Ltd., 1936). It is frankly eulogistic. In 1945 F. A. Lea's *The Wild Knight of Battersea: G. K. Chesterton* (1945) took a quite different tack, identifying Chesterton's two great limitations as his embracing the Roman Catholic Church and his failing to embrace pacifism. Maisie Ward's *Gilbert Keith Chesterton* (1943) and her *Return to Chesterton* (1952) remain the closest accounts to a "definitive" biography and the sources where other biographers begin. One of those biographers, and the best since Ward, is Dudley Barker *G. K. Chesterton* (1973).

Evaluation of Selected Biographies

Barker, Dudley, *G. K. Chesterton.* New York: Stein and Day, 1973. Though Barker's biography must rely heavily on Ward's since hers is so complete and in some cases the only source of Chesterton's papers destroyed in World War II, his work is immensely readable and not so peppered with documents as is Ward's. He is among the few non-Catholic writers on Chesterton, but offers a sympathetic account of Chesterton's spiritual journey. His only pique—an understandable one—is with Catholics glorying in Chesterton's "conversion" from Anglo-Catholicism to Roman Catholicism. Barker is the place to start a study of Chesterton.

Lea, F. R. *The Wild Knight of Battersea: G. K. Chesterton.* London: James Clarke & Co, 1945. While Chesterton has been sometimes ill served by enthusiastic Catholic writers, Lea's anti-Catholic biases clearly hurt this short biography. Had Chesterton's development not led beyond his fondness for Whitman, Lea would have been content with him. As it is, he finds in Chesterton a clarity of vision in assessing other's beliefs but a failure to see the lasting virtues of Whitman's pantheism. Lea believes Roman Catholicism led this otherwise perceptive critic to perverse judgments, as in his enthusiasm about Mussolini's early fascism.

Ward, Maisie, *Gilbert Keith Chesterton.* New York: Sheed and Ward, 1943, and *Return to Chesterton.* New York: Sheed and Ward, 1952. Ward offers a full and very sympathetic biography of Chesterton in the first and larger of these works. She relies heavily on Chesterton's own writings and on correspondence with such friendly opponents as Bernard Shaw and H. G. Wells. The reader is given a clear picture of how independent a thinker Chesterton was, how—unlike Shaw—he was not in tune with the *zeitgeist* but arrived at philosophical and theological positions such as those of *Orthodoxy* alone. Likewise, she makes clear the extent to which Belloc later learned from Chesterton and he from Belloc. Ward defends Chesterton even on issues where he has received little defense; e.g., his factual inaccuracy or his opposition to woman's suffrage. The latter defense is qualified in the *Return,* where Ward asserts Chesterton generalized too much about women on the basis of his wife.

Autobiographical Sources

Chesterton's *Autobiography* appeared posthumously. A delightful work, it is not always as helpful for detail as the biographies. Chesterton is amusing, for example, when he reluctantly confesses he has no fashionable tale to tell of cruel and misunderstanding parents. However, what did depress young Chesterton in his years at Slade School is not clear and must be gleaned from other sources like his *Robert Louis Stevenson.*

Overview of Critical Sources

Chesterton's writings represent virtually every literary genre. He was poet, fiction writer, dramatist, critic, apologist, biographer, and prophet. He shows glaring weaknesses in all of these modes; yet he somehow transcends his limitations and makes his genius felt. Thus some of the more successful critics of

Chesterton have, like Hugh Kenner in *Paradox in Chesterton* (1947), focused on the general topic of Chesterton's style. Others, like Gary Wills in *Chesterton: Man and Mask* (New York: Sheed and Ward, 1961) have fixed on his "existentialist" mind set or like Christopher Hollis in *The Mind of Chesterton* (1970) on his overall philosophy. Even more specialized studies such as Ian Boyd's *The Novels of G. K. Chesterton* (London: Paul Elek, 1975) study the novels as much for Chesterton's political and social thought as for their artistic merit. A book that successfully argues for Chesterton's permanence on the basis of his imaginative success in any literary form has yet to be written.

Evaluation of Selected Criticism

Belloc, Hilaire, *On the Place of G. K. Chesterton in English Letters.* New York: Sheed and Ward, 1940. This historian and man of letters, who struggled together with Chesterton for a distributist state, shows that their political aim was the restoration of property, the struggle against Communism, and against the Capitalism whence Communism springs. Chesterton's chief value and his chief effect, believes Belloc, lay in his recognition that only a philosophy can produce political action, and that such a philosophy is vital only when it is the soul of a religion.

Clipper, Lawrence J. *G. K. Chesterton.* New York: Twayne, 1974. Clipper lays to rest the romanticized image of Chesterton the jolly giant, drinking wine and laughing uproariously as he writes down his latest paradoxes in a London pub. He depicts a more serious Chesterton, a writer growing ever more depressed with world events and reflecting this depression in his work. However, Clipper misses much of Chesterton's gusto and quibbles with every favorable evaluation of his works. Nonetheless, he provides an appraisal of many of Chesterton's writings that is critical, not eulogistic.

Hollis, Christopher, *The Mind of Chesterton.* London: Hollis and Carter, 1970. A generally objective and balanced account of Chesterton's intellectual growth, the work is less effective when Hollis discusses "Chesterton and His Survival." He feels the need to reconcile Chesterton with Teilhard de Chardin, a thinker whose ideas are more closely akin to those of Chesterton's adversary, Bernard Shaw.

Kenner, Hugh, *Paradox in Chesterton.* New York: Sheed and Ward, 1947. Kenner's study argues that Chesterton was a natural philosopher in the Thomist tradition from the beginning. Chesterton's style was functionally suited to convey the paradoxical and analogical, and not meant to attract attention to itself. However, Kenner dismisses him as an artist, holding that he did not strongly *feel* the insight in the manner of Hopkins, just strongly *meant* it. Insight came to Chesterton too easily to make his attempt at conveying it anything but primarily intellectual.

Sullivan, John, ed. *G. K. Chesterton: A Centenary Appraisal.* New York: Barnes & Noble, 1974. Unlike Clipper, Sullivan supplies a good deal that is of interest about the man. The essays vary in quality, and Sullivan's own attack on academe is too lengthy and tiresome.

Other Sources

Donaghy, Henry J. "Chesterton on Shaw's Idea of Catholicism," X, 3 in *Shaw Review* (September 1967), 108–116. Chesterton argued Shaw did not understand Catholicism. Article asserts he might have understood *de facto* Catholicism better than Chesterton.

Furlong, William, *GBS/GKC: Shaw and Chesterton: The Metaphysical Jesters.* University Park: Pennsylvania State University Press, 1970. Studies the life-long, friendly debate between Shaw and Chesterton.

Mason, Michael, *Center of Hilarity.* New York: Sheed and Ward, 1959. A philosophico-historical treatise of changes in literature from the Middle Ages to the present. Places GKC in Christian comic tradition.

Maurois, Andre, "G. K. Chesterton" in *Prophets and Poets.* New York: Harpers, 1935. Finds Shaw and Wells essentially aristocrats but Chesterton a democrat more interested in the common man.

Shaw, Bernard, *Pen Portraits and Reviews.* London: Constable and Co. Ltd, 1932. Contains four essays on Chesterton by his life-long, philosophical antithesis.

Sullivan, John, *G. K. Chesterton. A Bibliography.* London: University of London Press, 1958. Indispensable bibliography.

———. *Chesterton Continued: A Bibliographical Supplement.* London: University of London Press, 1968.

Henry J. Donaghy
Kansas State University

KATE CHOPIN
1850–1904

Author's Chronology

Born July 12, 1850, St. Louis, Missouri, to a French Creole mother and an Irish father; Katherine O'Flaherty (later Kate Chopin) grows up knowing both French and English; *1868* graduates from the Academy of the Sacred Heart in St. Louis; *1870* marries Oscar Chopin, a cotton factor (broker) and moves to New Orleans; *1879* Oscar Chopin's business fails and the family moves to Natchitoches, Louisiana, where he manages the Chopin family plantation; *1882* Oscar Chopin dies, and Kate manages the plantation for a year before moving back to St. Louis; *1885* she is left alone by her mother's death; *1888* Chopin begins to write poetry and short stories, followed by three novels and more short stories; August 22, *1904* Chopin dies in St. Louis, five years after the publication of her major work, *The Awakening* (*1899*).

Author's Bibliography

In her brief career, Kate Chopin published two novels and two collections of short stories; a number of stories remained unpublished at her death, and some of them are included in *The Complete Works.* A third novel, *Young Doctor Gosse,* was never published, and the manuscript is no longer extant. *At Fault,* 1890 (novel); *Bayou Folk,* 1894 (stories); *A Night in Acadie,* 1897 (stories); *The Awakening,* 1899 (novel); *The Complete Works of Kate Chopin,* 2 vols. ed. Per Seyersted, 1969 (includes the novels and stories, essays, and poems).

Overview of Biographical Sources

Only two full-length biographies of Kate Chopin have been published in the almost one hundred years since she began her career. The first, Daniel S. Rankin's *Kate Chopin and Her Creole Stories* (1932), is a critical biography concentrating primarily on her short stories. Per Seyersted's much more comprehensive biography, *Kate Chopin: A Critical Biography* (1969) has yet to be supplanted, though at least two additional biographies are in progress. Brief biographical sketches are to be found in a number of standard biographical dictionaries.

Evaluation of Selected Biographies

Rankin, Daniel S. *Kate Chopin and Her Creole Stories.* Philadelphia: University of Pennsylvania Press, 1932. Rankin's biography is valuable for the material on how Chopin was regarded by those who knew her; yet, as the title indicates, the author views Chopin primarily as a writer of "local color" stories, and does not treat her as a novelist. The book contains eleven of Chopin's short stories, and has a bibliography and illustrations.

Schuyler, William, "Kate Chopin," *The Writer,* VII (August 1894), 115–117. Published shortly after Chopin's *Bayou Folk* was first published, this brief biographical sketch is based on an interview with Chopin, and thus offers insight into the attitudes toward her of her contemporaries. Schuyler also comments on Chopin's unpublished novel, *Young Doctor Gosse.*

Seyersted, Per, *Kate Chopin: A Critical Biography.* Baton Rouge: Louisiana State University Press, 1969. The work of a Norwegian scholar who also edited Chopin's complete works, this is to date the standard biography. Seyersted provides analyses of her stylistic methods and the critical reception of her work, and includes a detailed study of *The Awakening.* The book includes a selected bibliography.

Overview of Critical Sources

Although Chopin was known during her lifetime as a writer of stories about the Creole and Cajun cultures of Louisiana, the storm of adverse critical reaction provoked by her second published novel, *The Awakening,* in 1899 caused her to be generally ignored by critics for many years, or, at best, to be regarded as a minor writer of "local color" stories—stories that primarily capture the folkways of people in distinct regions of the country. It was not until the middle of the twentieth century that critics reassessed her longer works and found *The Awakening* to be an important part of the tradition of women's literature in America. There is as yet no book-length study of her work as a whole, though it has been the subject of several doctoral dissertations.

Evaluation of Selected Criticism

Eble, Kenneth, "A Forgotten Novel: Kate Chopin's *The Awakening,*" *Western Humanities Review,* X (Summer 1956), 261–269. One of the first major critics to urge reappraisal of *The Awakening,* Eble admires it for its artistry, especially Chopin's use of metaphor, and compares Chopin's skill to that of Stephen Crane. A slightly revised version of this article formed Eble's introduction to the Capricorn reprinting of *The Awakening* in 1964.

Ringe, Donald A. "Romantic Imagery in Kate Chopin's *The Awakening,*" *American Literature,* XLII (Jan. 1972), 580–588. Ringe approaches the novel as a romantic work in the sense that it details a person's awakening to a concept of self and a recognition of the essential isolation of human beings.

Taylor, Helen, Introduction to *Kate Chopin: Portraits* (London: The Women's Press, 1979), pp. vii-xix. Taylor provides a good introductory survey of Chopin's life, literary influences, and place in literary history, concentrating particularly on the short stories, of which the volume is a selection.

Walker, Nancy, "Feminist or Naturalist: Kate Chopin's *The Awakening,*" *The Southern Quarterly,* XVII, no. 2 (Winter 1979), 95–103. Walker explores the question of whether Edna "awakens" to a consciousness of women's subjugation in society or whether hers is a naturalistic character, doomed by forces beyond her control.

Wolff, Cynthia Griffin, "Thanatos and Eros: Kate Chopin's *The Awakening,*" *American Quarterly,* XXV (Oct. 1973), 449–471. Wolff's study is a psychological analysis, drawing upon the theories of Freud and Laing to propose that the story of Edna Pontellier is a description of the disintegration of personality.

Other Sources

Kate Chopin Newsletter, ed. Emily Toth. Pennsylvania State University, University Park, PA. 1975–1977.

Springer, Marlene, *Edith Wharton and Kate Chopin: A Reference Guide.* Boston: G. K. Hall, 1976. An annotated list of biographical and critical sources from 1890–1973.

———. "Kate Chopin: A Reference Guide Updated," *Resources for American Literary Study,* 11, no. 2 (Autumn 1981), 280–281.

Nancy Walker
Stephens College

AGATHA CHRISTIE
1890–1976

Author's Chronology

Born September 15, 1890, Torquay, of Anglo-American parents; *1914* marries Lt. (later Col.) Archibald Christie; *1916* writes her first detective novel, *The Mysterious Affair at Styles,* during time off from volunteer work in hospital dispensary; *1926* following death of mother, leaves Christie and disappears for ten days, registering in Yorkshire spa under last name of Christie's mistress; *1928* divorces Christie; *1930* meets Max Mallowan on her second visit to Iraq, marries him in Edinburgh; *1933–1938* spends winters on Mallowan's excavations in Iraq and Syria, summers in Torquay; *1940–1945* works in dispensary in Torquay; *1947–1960* continues to spend winters on excavations in Middle East; *1952* her play *The Mousetrap* opens in London; *1956* receives Order of the British Empire; *1971* named Dame Commander, O.B.E.; dies January 12, 1976, Berkshire, Wallingford.

Author's Bibliography (selected)

The Murder on the Links, 1923 (novel); *The Murder of Roger Ackroyd,* 1926 (novel); *Murder on the Orient Express,* 1934 (novel); *The ABC Murders,* 1935 (novel); *Cards on the Table,* 1936 (novel); *Death on the Nile,* 1937 (novel); *Ten Little Niggers* (American title: *Ten Little Indians* or *And Then There Were None*), 1939 (novel); *Five Little Pigs* (American title: *Murder in Retrospect*), 1943 (novel); *Towards Zero,* 1944 (novel); *Death Comes as the End,* 1944 (novel); *A Pocket Full of Rye,* 1953 (novel); *4:50 from Paddington* (American title: *What Mrs. McGillicuddy Saw!*), 1957 (novel); *At Bertram's Hotel,* 1965 (novel); *Endless Night,* 1967; *Poems,* 1973.

Overview of Biographical Sources

Agatha Christie's shyness and diffidence about public statements and public appearances, which led her to refuse interviews and to reveal little about herself during her lifetime, have limited most biographical accounts to a relatively superficial recitation of the public facts of her life. Her biographers have typically concentrated on either Christie's theatrical career, which is well-documented by her colleagues, or her mysterious disappearance from her first husband's home in 1926, which in later life she declined to explain. Since most biographers approach her within the context of the detective fiction in which she excelled, their tone is uniformly respectful. Earlier biographical studies, based most often on speculations about Christie's autobiographical novels (written under the pseudonym Mary Westmacott), were superseded by Christie's own *Autobiography* (New York: Dodd, Mead, 1977), which, for all its reticence, should remain the definitive account of Christie's life for the forseeable future.

Evaluation of Selected Biographies

Murdoch, Derrick, *The Agatha Christie Mystery.* Toronto: Pagurian Press, 1976. The first half of Murdock's book, the most substantial account of her life predating the *Autobiography,* based principally on the characters in her Mary Westmacott novel *Unfinished Portrait* (1934), is more original and valuable than the second, a historical survey of detective fiction with special reference to Christie's work.

Osborne, Charles, *The Life and Crimes of Agatha Christie.* London: Collins, 1982. Osborne integrates the study of Christie's life and works into a single narrative proceeding year by year. Although it follows the *Autobiography,* which it occasionally corrects on minor points, it is more tightly organized and more useful as a reference to specific dates, places, and events. Osborne devotes considerably more space to Christie's books than to the events of her life, but is less incisive on them; his critical remarks are often limited to identifications of dedicatees, indications of factual inconsistencies within or between novels, and remarks on anti-Semitic references in Christie's early work. Nonetheless, this is in many ways the single best book on Christie.

Robyns, Gwen, *The Mystery of Agatha Christie.* Garden City, NY: Doubleday, 1978. Robyns is most useful as a supplement to the *Autobiography,* for she spends over half her biography on Christie's life since World War II, which Christie herself describes only briefly. Robyns's own writing, however, is more facile and melodramatic than Christie's.

Autobiographical Sources

Considering her resistance to public appearances and public revelations, Christie left a surprisingly rich store of autobiographical materials. The fullest of these is *An Autobiography,* written between 1950 and 1965, and dealing most fully and illuminatingly with Christie's childhood. Christie is quite capable of telling an anecdote about the source for one of her stories without naming the story. Despite its richness in incident and summarizing aphorism, therefore, the *Autobiography* is of limited use as a reference. Its structure is digressive and marked by striking lacunae—for example, Christie never refers to her disappearance in 1926. Equally anecdotal and noncommittal about the author is *Come, Tell Me How You Live* (London: Collins, 1946), an account of Christie's life with Max Mallowan in the Middle East from 1933 to 1938. Christie is far more introspective and revealing in her Westmacott novels, particularly *Unfinished Portrait* (London: Collins, 1934), which all biographers, including Mallowan, have taken as a fictionalized account of the breakup of her first marriage, and *Absent in the Spring* (London: Collins, 1944), an analysis of the midlife crisis of a woman who resembles Christie in many particulars.

Overview of Critical Sources

Criticism on Christie falls into three categories: trivial or ephemeral books which present quizzes, plot summaries, or lists of character names; competent surveys of her work which repeat the same information; and unusually perceptive or original studies. The first, and by far the largest, category includes Andy East, *The Agatha Christie Quizbook* (New York: Drake, 1975); Dick Riley and Pam McAllister, editors, *The Bedside, Bathtub, and Armchair Companion to Agatha Christie* (New York: Frederick Ungar, 1979); Dennis Sanders and Len Lovallo, *The Agatha Christie Companion* (New York: Delacorte Press, 1984); Randall Toye, *The Agatha Christie Who's Who* (New York: Holt, Rinehart, Winston, 1980); and Nancy B. Wynne, *An Agatha Christie Chronology* (New York: Ace Books, 1976). The second group includes Jeffrey Feinman, *The Mysterious World of Agatha Christie* (New York: Grosset & Dunlap, 1975); Russell H. Fitzgibbon, *The Agatha Christie Companion* (Bowling Green, OH: Bowling Green State University Popular Press, 1980); and Gordon C. Ramsey, *Agatha Christie: Mistress of Mystery* (New York: Dodd, Mead, 1967). Studies in the third group generally take the form of short essays, with three principal exceptions.

Evaluation of Selected Criticism

Bargainnier, Earl F. *The Gentle Art of Murder: The Detective Fiction of Agatha Christie.* Bowling Green, OH: Bowling Green University Popular Press, 1980. Despite covering the same topics—setting, characters, plot, theme, and so on—which other critics adopt, and which seldom take account of Christie's strengths, Bargainnier is more sophisticated and more thorough in pursuing his observations. Without being at all original in its methods or arguments, his is perhaps the best general study of Christie's fiction.

Barnard, Robert, *A Talent to Deceive: An Appreciation of Agatha Christie.* London: Collins, 1980. Barnard focuses on the problem of Christie's popularity, which he ascribes to her ability to create characters and situations which are universal in appeal without being vividly particular. He compares her work favorably to that of such self-consciously literary writers of detective fiction as Dorothy L. Sayers and Margery Allingham whose work has proved less enduringly popular.

Maida, Patricia D. and Nicholas B. Spornick, *Murder She Wrote: A Study of Agatha Christie's Detective Fiction.* Bowling Green, OH: Bowling Green State University Popular Press, 1982. Like Barnard, Maida and Spornick treat Christie's popularity as a critical problem, but their discussion is more wide-ranging and correspondingly more diffuse. They attempt, with varying success, to trace the influence of earlier detectives and the detective-story conventions, of social and cultural beliefs, and of the events of Christie's life on her work. Their style is distinctly less readable than that of Barnard.

Other Sources

Cawelti, John G. *Adventure, Mystery, and Romance.* Chicago: University of Chicago Press, 1976. Contains the best close examinations of any of Christie's works (*One, Two, Buckle My Shoe* and *Third Girl*).

Gregg, Hubert, *Agatha Christie and All That Mousetrap.* London: Kimber, 1980. Despite its self-aggrandizing tone, this account of Christie's theatrical career by her sometimes director, who remembers her as vain, insensible, and domineering, offers a useful corrective to the generally devotional tone of Christie's biographers.

Keating, H. R. F. ed. *Agatha Christie: First Lady of Crime.* New York: Holt, Rinehart, Winston, 1977. A memorial volume of essays on a wide range of subjects. The most significant are by Julian Symons, on Christie's plot construction, and Dorothy B. Hughes, on the Westmacott novels.

Mallowan, Max, *Nallowan's Memoirs.* London: Collins, 1977. Several valuable chapters on Christie's personality by her second husband, whose discussion of her books is uncritical.

Panek, LeRoy, *Watteau's Shepherds: The Detective Novel in Britain 1914–1940.* Bowling Green, OH: Bowling Green University Popular Press, 1979. Emphasizes the importance of Christie's early thrillers in establishing the world of her formal detective novels.

Saunders, Peter, *The Mousetrap Man.* London: Collins, 1972. Memoirs of the producer of all Christie's plays since 1951, including *The Mousetrap* and *Witness for the Prosecution.*

Selected Dictionaries and Encyclopedias

Encyclopedia of Mystery and Detection, McGraw-Hill, 1976. Surveys Christie's career and those of her two most famous detectives, Hercule Poirot and Jane Marple.

Twentieth Century Crime and Mystery Writers, Macmillan, 1980. A concise appreciation by H. R. F. Keating, and a comprehensive bibliography.

Thomas M. Leitch
University of Delaware

JOHN CLARE
1793–1864

Author's Chronology

Born July 13, 1793 at Helpston, Northamptonshire to rural laborers, Parker and Anne Clare; *1800–1805* attends day school; *1806* probably first read Thomson's *The Seasons,* which stimulated him to compose his first poem, "The Morning Walk"; *1820* publishes first volume, *Poems Descriptive of Rural Life and Scenery;* enjoys period of popular fame; first trip to London, where he meets Samuel Coleridge, Charles Lamb, and Thomas De Quincey; marries Martha (Patty) Turner; *1821* publishes *The Village Minstrel, and Other Poems; 1827* publishes *The Shepherd's Calendar, with Village Stories, and Other Poems; 1835* publishes *The Rural Muse; 1837* is committed to asylum at High Beech, Essex; *1841* escapes from the High Beech asylum and walks eighty miles home; *1842* is committed to Northampton General Lunatic Asylum, where he writes some of his greatest poetry; *1864* dies May 20 at the Northampton Asylum.

Author's Bibliography (selected posthumous editions)

The Poems of John Clare, ed. J. W. Tibble, 1935; *The Midsummer Cushion,* eds. Anne Tibble and R. K. R. Thornton, 1979 (poems); *John Clare: The Journals, Essays and The Journey from Essex,* ed. Anne Tibble, 1980; *The Natural History Prose Writings of John Clare,* ed. Margaret Grainger, 1983; *The Later Poems of John Clare, 1837–1864,* 2 vols., eds. Eric Robinson and David Powell, 1984; *John Clare,* eds. Eric Robinson and David Powell, 1984 (best collection of poems and prose).

Overview of Biographical Sources

Attracted by the pathos of his poverty and ultimate insanity, several biographers have recorded Clare's life story. Frederick Martin published the first biography, *The Life of John Clare* (1865). Martin's sympathetic and emotional biography focused on the scandalous poverty which he believed fostered Clare's madness. J. L. Cherry published a more scholarly, though less vivid biography, *The Life and Remains of John Clare* (London: Frederick Warne, 1873). Cherry contributed to a deeper understanding of Clare because he published some of Clare's letters and a number of his asylum poems. He discounts Martin's correct belief that Clare's father was illegitimate, and disagrees with him on various other relatively minor points. The first major twentieth century biography, *John Clare: A Life* (1932), was written by J. W. and Anne Tibble. They combine the enthusiasm for Clare shown by Martin with quotations from his poems, prose, and letters, thus providing a detailed and vivid picture of Clare's life. As with both of Clare's previous biographers, the Tibbles are sometimes inaccurate, and they print Clare's poetry only after standardizing his erratic spelling and punctuation. Anne Tibble later corrected these errors and published a revised version in 1972. June Wilson's 1951 biography of Clare, *Green Shadows: A Life of John Clare* (London: Hodder and Stoughton, 1951), tells the story of Clare's life in a readable style, but its intended audience is primarily general rather than scholarly. The most recent biography, by Edward Storey, is *A Right to Song: The Life of John Clare* (London: Methuen, 1982). Storey's well written biography benefits from the extensive manuscript work done on Clare in recent years. He publishes Clare's letters to his children written from the asylum, and thus reveals Clare to be a loving father. Despite the number of biographies, there is still no definitive critical biography of Clare.

Evaluation of Selected Biographies

Martin, Frederick, *The Life of John Clare.* eds. Eric Robinson and Geoffrey Summerfield. London: Macmillan, 1865; rpt; London: Frank Cass, 1964. Martin's biography aroused a great deal of irritation, most notably from Charles Dickens, both because he made large claims for a poet generally considered merely another "peasant poet," and because he accused the London literary world, especially John Taylor, of negligence towards Clare. But through the efforts of modern Clare scholars, Robinson and Summerfield, Martin's biography was reprinted in 1964. In their introduction to his work, Robinson and Summerfield argue that Martin offers the freshest version of Clare's life. Nevertheless, Martin is not an entirely satisfactory biographer because he does not present a critical understanding of Clare's poetry, and because he frequently records in novelistic detail what he imagines his subject must have felt or thought.

Tibble, J. W. and Anne Tibble, *John Clare: A Life.* London: Cobden-Sanderson, 1932; rev. Anne Tibble. London: Michael Joseph, 1972. The Tibble's biography, divided into the four seasons to emphasize Clare's unity with nature, is the best introduction to Clare's life. The revised 1972 edition represents an acceptance of the importance of printing Clare's original style. The Tibble's greatest achievement is their understanding of the social and economic forces—enclosure and the trials of the London publishing world—which so strongly affected Clare's fate. They are most often criticized for their weaknesses in understanding his poetry. The Tibbles tend to use Clare's poems to elucidate his life instead of providing a coherent theory of his poetic vision.

Autobiographical Sources

At the request of John Taylor, his publisher, Clare began to write his autobiography in 1821, but his haphazard method of composition resulted in a mass of notes which were never published as a formal autobiography. In 1931

Edmund Blunden edited these notes and published *Sketches in the Life of John Clare Written by Himself.* Blunden's work has been largely superseded by later editions of Clare's autobiographical prose published by Anne Tibble and Eric Robinson. Anne Tibble's 1980 edition, *John Clare: The Journal, Essays and The Journey from Essex,* publishes his journal entries from 1824–1825 and provides vivid insight into Clare's daily life—his reading, family events, and his observations of nature. "The Journey from Essex," Clare's fascinating account of his long walk back to Helpston after his escape from the High Beech asylum, reveals both Clare's emotional instability and the acuity of his narrative ability. Eric Robinson's *John Clare's Autobiographical Writings* (1983) includes the "Sketches in the Life of John Clare" as well as the autobiographical fragments and "Journey out of Essex" with some slight variations from Tibble's edition. The autobiographical fragments record Clare's impressions of his visits to London and of the people he met there, including Hazlitt, Lamb, Coleridge, and De Quincey. Robinson's excellent introduction argues that biographers have tended to take Clare's autobiography at face value, being insufficiently aware of the artist's power of shaping material to suit himself. *The Letters of John Clare,* edited by J. W. and Anne Tibble, published in 1951 and reprinted in 1970, contains only about half of Clare's letters, but provides a good selection from throughout his life. Overall, these editions acquaint the reader with Clare's prose, which speaks almost aloud in a direct, original voice shaped both by his wide reading and his expressive Northamptonshire dialect.

Overview of Critical Sources

Before the extensive textual criticism of Eric Robinson, Geoffrey Summerfield, and David Powell, Clare's poems were read in context of their "improved" state. Clare wrote without regarding grammar, spelling, or punctuation rules, and his first editor, John Taylor, altered the poems to suit convention, even though Clare protested these corrections. Taylor set a precedent which was followed, until recently, by all of Clare's subsequent editors, including J. W. Tibble. Thus, Tibble's 1935 edition of *The Poems of John Clare,* though valuable in its efforts to establish a complete Clare text, is nevertheless corrupt. Working from Clare's manuscripts, Eric Robinson and his co-editors have sought to publish Clare's poetry as he originally intended. The first two volumes of what should be the definitive Clare text, *The Later Poems of John Clare, 1837–1864,* edited by Robinson and Powell, were published by the Clarendon Press of Oxford University in 1984. In emphasizing careful attention to Clare's manuscripts, scholars have not only corrected inaccuracies in editions of Clare's poetry, but they have also routed the critical attitude that Clare's poetry needs improvement before it is acceptable. As a result of this textual work, recent studies of Clare, though still relatively few in number, reveal an increasingly unapologetic and sophisticated interest in the vision and originality of his poetry.

Evaluation of Selected Criticism

Barrell, John, *The Idea of Landscape and the Sense of Place, 1730–1840.* Cambridge: Cambridge University Press, 1972. Barrell's study of Clare's landscape descriptions and sense of place is especially valuable because he discusses Clare's differences from Thomson, who was a major influence on him. He emphasizes the pre-Asylum poetry in contrast to many recent critics who have focused their attention on Clare's later poems.

Storey, Mark, *The Poetry of John Clare: A Critical Introduction.* London: Macmillan, 1974. Storey's work provides an intelligent introduction to Clare's poetry. He focuses on Clare as a nature poet and on the development of his vision of nature into an emotionally complex understanding of human alienation from innocence and freedom.

Other Sources

Brownlow, Timothy, *John Clare and Picturesque Landscape.* Oxford: Clarendon Press, 1983. Seeks to identify Clare's uniqueness by placing him in the Picturesque tradition.

Howard, William, *John Clare.* Boston: Twayne, 1981. A general introduction with a brief biography.

Storey, Mark, ed. *Clare: The Critical Heritage.* London: Routledge and Kegan Paul, 1973. A well edited collection of reviews from 1820–1964.

Tibble, J. W. and Anne Tibble, *John Clare: His Life and Poetry.* London: William Heinemann, Ltd., 1956. A short biography with critical commentary on the poems.

Selected Dictionaries and Encyclopedias

Critical Survey of Poetry: English Language Series, Vol. 2, Salem Press, 1982. A substantial summary of Clare's life and poetic achievements.

Great Writers of the English Language: Poets, St. Martin's Press, 1979. A short but pithy essay which includes biographical, bibliographical, and critical information.

Barbara T. Allen
The Citadel

ARTHUR HUGH CLOUGH
1819–1861

Author's Chronology

Born in Liverpool on New Year's Day, 1819, to a family of the gentry who had recently turned to commerce; *1822* the Cloughs move to Charleston, South Carolina; *1828* Arthur returns to England for his preparatory schooling at Chester; *1829* enters Rugby, where he befriends headmaster Thomas Arnold's sons Tom and Matthew; *1837* enters Balliol College, Oxford on a scholarship and takes his degree four years later; *1842* elected to a fellowship at Oriel College, having been denied at Balliol; resigns fellowship in *1848* as an act of conscience (reflecting his inability to endorse the Thirty-Nine Articles of the Anglican Church); during the same year he publishes *The Bothie of Tober-na-Vuolich* and, in *1849, Ambarvalia;* accepts position at University Hall, London and writes *Amours de Voyage* (also in 1849); *1850* begins *Dipsychus* while visiting in Venice; *1851* resigns from University Hall; *1852* in America; *1853* returns to England, takes position with the Education Office; marries Blanche Smith during the following year; undertakes clerical duties for Florence Nightingale (Blanche's cousin) in 1857; *1858 Amours de Voyage* published in *Atlantic Monthly; 1860* after an attack of scarlatina, Clough is sent abroad by his physician; *1861* travels extensively on the continent alone and begins *Mari Magno;* joined by Blanche at Paris; they travel to Florence where Clough dies on 13 November.

Author's Bibliography (selected)

The Bothie of Tober-na-Vuolich, 1848 (long poem); *Ambarvalia,* 1849 (poems); *Amours de Voyage,* 1858 (poems); *The Poems and Prose Remains of Arthur Hugh Clough,* 1862 (posthumous).

Overview of Biographical Sources

Biographies of Arthur Hugh Clough fall into two groups. The first consists of early books which depend heavily on the memoir written by Clough's wife, Blanche, for *The Poems and Prose Remains of Arthur Hugh Clough* (London: Macmillan, 1869). It includes Samuel Waddington's *Arthur Hugh Clough* (London: Bell, 1883), and Goldie Levy's book by the same name (London: Sigdwick and Jackson, 1938). Mrs. Clough's uneasiness over Arthur's skepticism apparently caused her to suppress some materials. Her interpretation that Clough was just beginning to reach his powers at the time of his death is a direct reply to various acquaintances who believed that Clough's life was somehow a failure. He had attended the "best schools," and had been widely acknowledged as the brightest among his circle. But his life seemed a continual decline. He resigned a fellowship at Oxford, resigned as Principal of University Hall,

London, and was thereafter never able to recover an academic post or an effective post in government. He ended his days "running errands" for Florence Nightingale. The question, why did Clough "fail," and Blanche's reply dominated biographies up to the 1950's.

Following the appearance of a new, scholarly edition of *The Poems of Arthur Hugh Clough,* edited by H. F. Lowry, F. L. Mulhauser, and A. L. P. Norrington (Oxford: Clarendon Press, 1951) and *The Correspondence of Arthur Hugh Clough,* edited by Mulhauser (Oxford: Clarendon Press, 1957), a second group of biographies began to appear—grounded in primary sources and more objective in viewpoint. Katherine Chorley's *Arthur Hugh Clough, The Uncommitted Mind: A Study of His Life and Poetry* (1962) turned attention away from the question of Clough's "failure" and was the first of a group of books attempting Freudian and Jungian psychoanalyses of his complex personality, his ambiguity toward religion and his stern sense of duty. More recently Evelyn Greenberger in *Arthur Hugh Clough: The Growth of a Poet's Mind* (Cambridge: Harvard University Press, 1970) rejects the psychoanalytic interpretations in favor of a history of his developing thought.

Evaluation of Selected Biographies

Biswas, R. K. *Arthur Hugh Clough: Towards a Reconsideration.* Oxford: Clarendon Press, 1972. Perhaps the most thorough biography to date, this work extends Chorley's psychoanalytic approach. Blanche became for Clough the Beatific Woman, and he allowed her commonplace conception of the world to blur the crisply honest skepticism of his earlier days. Rather than revealing some new horizon (as Blanche thought), Clough's last work, *Mari Magno,* is merely conventional, a decline from his earlier, more searching work.

Chorley, Katherine, *Arthur Hugh Clough, The Uncommitted Mind: A Study of His Life and Poetry.* Oxford: Clarendon Press, 1962. This work puts Clough's biography on a more scholarly level than earlier attempts. Clough suffers an Oedipal conflict from having been too early depended on by his fond mother. Later withdrawals from positions of responsibility are withdrawals toward the womb. The argument is only as strong as Freudian method. The causal link between Clough's youth and his later withdrawals is only inferential.

Greenberger, Evelyn, *Arthur Hugh Clough: The Growth of a Poet's Mind.* Cambridge: Harvard University Press, 1970. Greenberger rejects the notion that Clough was an "Oedipal quietist" and stresses the development of his thought as the proper focus of a biography. His mind moved from "naiveté to polemics to disappointment to greater wisdom." The topics of earlier poems were increasingly absorbed by a morality that addresses the essentials: wholeness and intellectual honesty.

Williams, David, *Too Quick Despairer: A Life of Arthur Hugh Clough.* London: Hart-Davis, 1969. Williams's method is also largely Freudian. Clough needed some strong father figure—a Thomas Arnold—to guide him. The lack of such a figure in later life explains the lessening force of his work. This book generally fails to give sources of quotations.

Overview of Critical Sources

Critical sources, like the biographies (and for similar reasons), also fall into two groups. Among early critics, Clough's friend Matthew Arnold was perhaps the most stern. Arnold believed that Clough's modern characters and situations constituted a surrender to the tasteless, overheated inwardness of modernity. A technical issue raised by early critics is whether the hexameters, which Clough often uses, are apt for English. George Saintsbury described Clough's meter as "intolerable."

Since the 1950's, however, critics have tried to look at the whole of the work—its symbols, development, and thought. Walter Houghton in *The Poetry of Clough: An Essay in Revaluation* (1963) and Michael Timko in *Innocent Victorian: The Satiric Poetry of Arthur Hugh Clough* (Athens: Ohio University Press, 1963) are largely responsible for this refocusing of critical attention. These books have been followed by articles and other books which examine individual works and image patterns. As a result, Clough's poetic reputation has continued to increase.

Evaluation of Selected Criticism

Houghton, Walter E. *The Poetry of Clough: An Essay in Revaluation.* New Haven: Yale University Press, 1963. Houghton believes that Clough belongs among the best of the Victorian poets—Tennyson, Browning, Arnold, and Hopkins. He "is not only one of the best of Victorian poets, he is also perhaps the most modern." Houghton replies to the claims that Clough is more accurately a footnote to Victorian literature, by saying that if he is a footnote, it is one "that is crucial . . . the kind . . . which challenges the main text."

Timko, Michael, *Innocent Victorian: The Satiric Poetry of Arthur Hugh Clough.* Athens: Ohio University Press, 1963. Clough's lyrical poetry fails to achieve the complexity of his satirical poems, where the ironic discrepancy between human ideals and conduct is more fully explored. Clough did not lack a coherent view after turning skeptical. Rather, he developed a "positive naturalism" which is affirmative but makes no appeal to the supernatural.

Other Sources

Gollin, Richard, Walter Houghton, and Michael Timko. *Arthur Hugh Clough: A Descriptive Catalogue.* New York, 1967. A description of the Clough materials now available to scholars.

McGrail, John, "Three Image Motifs in Arthur Hugh Clough's *The Bothie of Tober-na-Vuolich,*" *Victorian Poetry* 13 (1975), 75–78. Images of water, trees, and the keystone give more artistic coherence to the poem than previously supposed.

Ryals, Clyde Del, "An Interpretation of Clough's *Dipsychus,*" *Victorian Poetry,* I (August, 1963), 182–188. Typical of the numerous recent articles which concentrate on specific works. Argues that Dipsychus and Spirit (sometimes seen as antagonists) are complements to one another which give wholeness to experience.

Thorpe, Michael, *Clough: The Critical Heritage.* London: Critical Heritage Series, 1972. A historical survey of the fall and rise of Clough's artistic reputation.

Veyriras, Paul, *Arthur Hugh Clough.* Paris: Diderot, 1964. A critical biography in French. Gives close attention to the relation between Clough's texts and his personal experiences.

Selected Dictionaries and Encyclopedias

Critical Survey of Poetry, Salem Press, 1983. Brief biography and analysis of Clough's poems.

The Victorian Poets: A Guide to Research, Harvard University Press, 1956. Brief analysis of the criticism up to the time of the reassessment.

L. Robert Stevens
North Texas State University

SAMUEL TAYLOR COLERIDGE
1772–1834

Author's Chronology

Born October 21, 1772, at Ottery St. Mary, Devonshire; *1782* enters Christ's Hospital School, London; *1791* enters Jesus College, Cambridge; *1792* writes prize-winning Greek Sapphic *Ode on the Slave Trade; 1793* publishes first poem in *Morning Chronicle;* enlists in Light Dragoons as Silas Tomkyn Comberbache; *1794* discharged from Light Dragoons; meets Robert Southey at Oxford; leaves Cambridge; *1795* lectures on politics and religion in Bristol; marries Sara Fricker; *1797* in daily contact with William and Dorothy Wordsworth; *1798* accepts an annuity from the Wedgewood family of £150; publishes *Lyrical Ballads* with William Wordsworth; travels to Germany with Wordsworth; *1799* death of son Hartley; returns to England; *1800* reporter and leader-writer for *Morning Post* in London; superintends second printing of *Lyrical Ballads; 1801–1803* works in London; has severe domestic discord; takes walking tours and visits friends in Wales, Scotland, and the Lake district; *1804–1805* journies to Malta and Italy; *1806* returns to England and separates from Sara Coleridge; *1807–1810* plans and publishes *The Friend;* lectures at Royal Institution on Poetry and Criticism; quarrels with Wordsworth; *1813 Remorse* opens at Drury Lane; *1814* lectures at Bristol on literature, education, and politics; is under care of Dr. Daniel for opium addiction and suicidal depression; *1815* dictates *Biographia Literaria; 1816* accepted as patient and housemate by Dr. Gillman; *1817* publishes *Second Lay Sermon, Biographia Literaria,* and *Sibylline Leaves; 1818* lectures on poetry and drama; *1823* moves with Gillman to 3, The Grove, Highgate; *1824–1834* increasing fame; publishes *Aids to Reflection* and *On the Constitution of the Church and State; 1833* suffers a series of serious illnesses; *1834* dies at Highgate, July 25.

Author's bibliography (selected)

The Fall of Robespierre, with Robert Southey, 1794 (drama); *Poems on Various Subjects,* 1796; *The Watchman,* 1796 (journalistic essays and poems); *Lyrical Ballads,* with William Wordsworth, 1798 (poetry); *Lyrical Ballads, 2nd ed,* with William Wordsworth, 1801 (poetry); *The Friend,* 1809 (journalistic essays); *Christabel,* 1816 (poem), *Statesman's Manual,* 1816 (political essay); *Biographia Literaria,* 1818 (literary criticism); *Second Lay Sermon,* 1817 (political essay), *Sibylline Leaves,* 1817 (poetry); *Aids to Reflection,* 1825 (theological essays); *Poetical Works,* 1828 (collected poetry); *On Constitution of Church and State,* 1829 (political essay).

Overview of Biographical Sources

The difficulties in a successful biography of Coleridge are legendary. His psychological complexities as well as the extraordinary range and convolutions of his intellectual interests make him a tempting, yet illusive subject. Until the 1960's there were four major biographies: James Gillman's *Life* (London, 1838); James Dyker Campbell's *Coleridge* (London, 1894); Lawrence Hanson's *Life* (London, 1938); and E. K. Chamber's *Coleridge* (Oxford, 1938). Campbell's *Coleridge* is accurate and full, but sheds little light on Coleridge's tormented psychological complexity and his intellectual development. Hanson's *Life* goes only to 1800, but is interesting and well documented. Chamber's biography is well organized, but turns into a caricature due to its author's lack of sympathy.

A great deal of information has become available since these early biographies. The massive *Collected Letters of Samuel Taylor Coleridge,* edited by Earl Leslie Griggs, 6 vols. (Oxford: Clarendon Press, 1956–1971) and the excellent editions of *The Notebooks of Samuel Taylor Coleridge,* edited by Kathleen Coburn, 3 vols. (Princeton: Princeton University Press, 1957–present) helped clarify the shape and structure of Coleridge's "peculiar and majestic intellect" and psychology. The publication of *The Collected Works of Samuel Taylor Coleridge* by Princeton University Press (1969–present) under the general editorship of Kathleen Coburn, continues to make available accurate texts of all of Coleridge's published and unpublished writing for the first time. Despite the voluminous amount of material now available, there is still no "definitive biography" of Coleridge. Oswald Doughty's *Perturbed Spirit: The Life and Personality of Samuel Taylor Coleridge* (1981) is the most comprehensive life of Coleridge, but falls short in its treatment of Coleridge's intellectual and psychological complexity. The most useful book is Walter Jackson Bate's *Coleridge* (1968) combining, in a brief study, biography and intellectual assessment.

The problem of balancing a treatment of Coleridge's poetic and critical gifts with a recognition of the darker aspects of his tormented life is demonstrated in two other recent biographies, Norman Fruman's *Coleridge: The Damaged Archangel* (1971) and Molly Lefebure's *Samuel Taylor Coleridge: A Bondage of Opium* (1974). Both are antagonistic biographies: Freeman argues that Coleridge was an entrepreneur of other men's images and ideas and Lefebure argues that he was a "junkie."

Evaluation of Selected Biographies

Bate, Walter Jackson, *Coleridge.* New York: Macmillan, 1964. An excellent bio-critical introduction to Coleridge's life and work, this is especially valuable on Coleridge's criticism and his development as a poet. While evading some of the psychological complexity of the writer, Bate's thesis is that mental activity and biography are inseparable in any analysis of Coleridge. Coleridge's politics and journalism are not discussed in any detail.

Doughty, Oswald, *Perturbed Spirit: The Life and Personality of Samuel Taylor Coleridge.* East Brunswick, NJ: Associated University Press, 1981. Because

Doughty died before the footnotes and bibliography were completed, it is often difficult to trace the sources of the author's interpretation of texts and events. Although there is an attempt at a balanced and comprehensive presentation of the facts of Coleridge's life, one must conclude that Doughty had not studied the recent secondary literature on Coleridge's poetry and thought.

Fruman, Norman, *Coleridge, The Damaged Archangel.* New York: George Braziller, 1971. Fruman's is an antagonistic biography which concentrates on the psychological and literary sources of Coleridge's plagarism. The information is accurate and, while the interpretation of Coleridge's work yields some interesting insights, this biography focuses too exclusively on the relationship of Coleridge's emotional life to the form and meaning of his poems.

Lefebure, Molly, *Samuel Taylor Coleridge: A Bondage of Opium.* New York: Stein and Day, 1974. A biography which concentrates much of its attention on Coleridge's morphine reliance, Lefebure's style is melodramatic and often the information is shaped to fit a theory. Readers should be aware of the writer's biases, and her attempt to be vivid rather than accurate.

Autobiographical Sources

As a result of a plan for an autobiographical introduction to a new edition of his poems, Coleridge produced, in July 1817, two volumes of what he called the *Biographia Literaria, or biographical sketches of my literary life and opinion.* These two volumes are not, in a strict sense, an autobiography. They are, in Coleridge's own words, "an unmethodical miscellany" whose purpose is "to defend myself (not indeed to my own conscience;) but as far as others are concerned, from the often and public denunciation of having wasted my time in idleness . . . to state my own principles of taste, but to settle, if possible . . . the controversy concerning the nature and claims of poetic Diction." The focus of the *Biographia* is the evolution and development of Coleridge's theories of poetry and criticism, and therefore the evaluation and development of his own mind. It is an obscure but magnificent work of literary and self criticism.

Overview of Critical Sources

There have been several attempts to survey Coleridge's total achievement in recent years; however, most of these have been hampered by the sheer magnitude of the project and by the lack, until quite recently, of reliable texts of his writing, both public and private. Most critical writing on Coleridge has focused on either his poetry, his political and religious thought, his philosophic and aesthetic criticism, or, more recently, the development of this prose style. A number of contemporary critics have used theories of composition and reading, and discourse analysis to situate Coleridge's own poetics and his theories of composition. The secondary literature on Coleridge's poetry and prose is voluminous; much of it is expository and explicative, rather than critical. However, more recently writers are stressing the inseparable link between mental activity and biography, and between exposition and analysis in any assessment of Coleridge.

Evaluation of Selected Criticism

Abrams, M. H. *The Mirror and the Lamp.* New York: Oxford University Press, 1953. One of the classic critical studies Abrams places Coleridge's aesthetics within the wider context of critics and critical assumptions in the Romantic period. Abrams clearly develops Coleridge's aesthetic of the "organic" relationship of man to nature, and the importance of seeing the "universal" in the particular.

Beer, John, *Coleridge the Visionary.* London, Chatto and Windus, 1959. Studying Coleridge's use of occult and mythological material in the poems, Beer argues that the myth of the Fall and of redemption provide an organizing frame for the poems. He concentrates on "The Rime of the Ancient Mariner," "Christabel," and "Kubla Khan."

Calleo, David P. *Coleridge and the Idea of the Modern State.* New Haven: Yale University Press, 1966. Written by a political scientist, this book is a useful and accurate assessment of Coleridge's "conservatism with a strong radical impulse." The concluding chapters on the relevance of Coleridge's ideas to European federation after the French Revolution, and to the modern national state are oversimplified.

Colmer, John, *Coleridge, Critic of Society.* Oxford, Clarendon Press, 1959. Clear, chronological account of Coleridge's social and political writing. This is not an analysis so much as a running commentary. A sympathetic, plodding, and somewhat somber book.

Cooke, Katharine, *Coleridge.* London: Routledge and Kegan Paul, 1979. A valuable brief critical survey which includes all aspects of Coleridge's work: poetry, plays, political journalism, and philosophy.

Fogle, R. H. *The Idea of Coleridge's Criticism.* Berkeley: University of California Press, 1962. A clear and complete treatment of Coleridge's critical theory. At times the attempt to create a unified theory denies the fragmentation and contradictions of the writer.

Harding, Anthony, *Coleridge and the Idea of Love.* Cambridge: Cambridge University Press, 1974. A useful analysis of Coleridge's work as it deals with human relationships. The book aims to explain Coleridge's ideas through biography, textual criticism, and a contextual chapter on the history of ideas.

Lowes, John Livingston, *The Road to Xanadu.* New York: Houghton Mifflin, 1927. This is a classic study of Coleridge's literary sources in "The Rime of the

Ancient Mariner" and "Kubla Khan." Although the psychological speculations in the book should be treated with caution, Lowes traces the symbolic and imagistic sources which form the mythological basis for the poems. In some ways, this book is as much about Coleridge's creative process and poetic genius as it is about the poems.

McFarland, Thomas, *Coleridge and the Pantheist Tradition.* Oxford: Clarendon Press, 1969. Analyzing one of the key elements of the Romantic philosophy, McFarland examines all aspects of Coleridge's thoughts which demonstrate a systematic unity. McFarland takes Abrams work on Coleridge's "organicism" even further by documenting Coleridge's relationship to other European philosophers in the eighteenth century, and to the main figures in the history of philosophy.

Schulz, Max, *The Poetic Voices of Coleridge.* Detroit, Wayne State University, 1963. A comprehensive treatment of all of Coleridge's poetry. A finely argued and close reading of the poems.

Wheeler, Kathern M. *Sources, Processes and Methods in Coleridge's "Biographia Literaria."* Cambridge: Cambridge University Press, 1980. An informative and useful study of the structure, as well poetics and rhetoric, of the *Biographia.*

Willey, Basil, *Nineteenth Century Studies. Coleridge to Matthew Arnold.* New York: Columbia University Press, 1949. A good general essay examining Coleridge's entire *oeuvre* for its religious ideas and prose.

Woodring, Carl, *Politics in the Poetry of Coleridge.* Madison: University of Wisconsin Press, 1961. Useful introductory study.

Stephen F. Wolfe
Linfield College

WILKIE COLLINS
1824–1889

Author's Chronology

Born January 8, 1824, Borough of St. Marylebone, England of Anglo-Scottish parents; *1830's* attends Maida Hill Academy; *1836–1838* lives in Italy; *1841* apprenticed to a tea merchant; *1843* first known publication, a short story; *1846* begins study of law at Lincoln's Inn; *1847* father dies; *1848* first book published, *The Memoirs of the Life of William Collins, Esq., R.A.,* a biography of his father, a notable landscape painter; *1849* exhibits a painting of his own at the Royal Academy; *1850* publishes first novel, *Antonina: or, The Fall of Rome; 1851* meets Charles Dickens and forms a close friendship; *1855* first play produced, *The Lighthouse; 1856* joins editorial staff of Dickens's magazine *Household Words; 1856* publication of first of several collaborations with Dickens, *The Wreck of the Golden Mary* (a Christmas book); late *1850's* Mrs. Caroline Elizabeth Graves becomes his mistress, which she remains except for the years *1868–1872; 1860 The Woman in White* finishes its serialization and appears in book form, making him an international celebrity; *1868* begins affair with Martha Rudd (they have three children); also, *1868* mother dies; *1873* only sibling Charles dies; *1873–1874* gives public readings in the United States; dies September 23, 1889 in London.

Author's Bibliography (selected)

Basil: A Story of Modern Life, 1852 (novel); *The Frozen Deep,* 1857 (drama); *The Queen of Hearts,* 1859 (short stories); *The Woman in White,* 1860 (novel); *No Name,* 1862 (novel); *Armadale,* 1866 (novel); *The Moonstone,* 1868 (novel); *Man and Wife,* 1870 (novel); *The New Magdalen,* 1873 (novel); *The Haunted Hotel* and *My Lady's Money,* 1878 (novellas); *Heart and Science,* 1883 (novel); *Little Novels,* 1887 (novellas).

Overview of Biographical Sources

Until the publication of Kenneth Robinson's biography in 1951, those interested in Collins's life had to rely on the memoirs of his acquaintances and a small number of Collins's letters published in scholarly journals. The most valuable of the early memoirs are Hall Caine's "Wilkie Collins" in *My Story* (London: Heinemann, 1908; New York: Appleton, 1909) and William Winter's "Wilkie Collins" in *Old Friends: Being Literary Recollections of Other Days* (New York: Moffat, Yard, 1909). Caine was one of the many young writers that Collins had helped, and Winter was a popular American writer with whom he corresponded extensively. These memoirs and others by actors, artists and friends gave an incomplete and contradictory picture of Collins. Winter made

Collins seem like a saint; some who were jealous of his close friendship with Charles Dickens made him seem like an incompetent egomaniac.

Some scholars tried to get at the truth of Collins's life and character. Malcolm Elwin's "Wallflower the Sixth: Wilkie Collins" in *Victorian Wallflowers: A Panoramic Survey of the Popular Literary Periodicals* (London: Jonathan Cape, 1934) presented a speculative but balanced account of Collins's life that caught the interest of other researchers. A significant breakthrough in the study of Collins was made when Clyde K. Hyder revealed hitherto thought undiscoverable aspects of Collins's personal life in "Wilkie Collins and *The Woman in White*" (*PMLA*, 54 [March 1939], 297–303); his revelations about Collins's mistress, Mrs. Graves, were surprising at the time.

Robinson's biography established the basic outlines of Collins's life, and since 1951 scholars have tried to fill in the gaps in what was known of Collins's life and to clear up the many mysteries about his career and character that still remain. Alethea Hayter's "Wilkie Collins" in *Opium and the Romantic Imagination* (London: Faber and Faber, 1968; Berkeley: University of California Press, 1968) is the best discussion of Collins's drug addiction. Sue Lonoff's "Charles Dickens and Wilkie Collins" (*Nineteenth-Century Fiction,* 35 [September 1980], 150–170) is the most recent elaboration on the information on the Collins-Dickens friendship first developed by Robert Ashley in the 1950's. Kirk H. Beetz's "Wilkie Collins and *The Leader*" (*Victorian Periodicals Review,* 15 [Spring 1982], 20–29) explains much of Collins's early career.

Evaluation of Selected Biographies

Davis, Nuel Pharr, *The Life of Wilkie Collins.* Urbana: University of Illinois Press, 1956. Davis attempts to penetrate the mysteries of Collins's life by combining the known facts of the author's life with materials from previously unstudied letters in library manuscript collections, notably those at the University of Illinois, and with his speculations about the possible autobiographical nature of some of Collins's fiction. Although Davis presents previously unknown biographical materials, his purely speculative remarks on what he suspects are autobiographical passages in the novels are not distinguished from his verifiable information, thus making his book confusing for those who are unfamiliar with Collins. Of interest is Davis's portrait of Collins as a cruel, selfish, and unpleasant man; this view runs contrary to most modern portraits of Collins.

Robinson, Kenneth, *Wilkie Collins: A Biography.* London: John Lane, 1951; New York: Macmillan, 1952. This remains the standard biography of Collins. Although the book has some gaps in the history of Collins's life, it assembles the basic reference materials and presents the most coherent biography available. Robinson presents Collins as a man with slightly above average talent who overcame great obstacles to make an important contribution to literature.

The portrait of Collins is sympathetic without ignoring the flaws in his character. Also presented is some sensible criticism of the major works.

Autobiographical Sources

Few autobiographical materials of Collins have as yet been published, although a collection of his letters is in the offing. Although Collins himself does not seem to have been overly secretive about the details of his unusual family life, his friends seem to have made an effort to suppress those details, including those that could be revealed by diaries and letters. What materials have been published have appeared in small articles in journals and book-collectors' magazines. The dearth of published autobiographical materials has prompted some scholars, such as Nuel Pharr Davis, to try to detect autobiographical passages in Collins's fiction. Such speculations have value when they reveal important sources for Collins's works, but unfortunately have little biographical merit when not corroborated by outside references, such as letters.

Overview of Critical Sources

Collins's first novels met with general critical approval, but he seemed to go out of his way to antagonize the critics of his day, and by the end of his life many critics dismissed him as an old, out-of-touch writer whose work featured good plots but was deficient in all other ways. From the late Victorian critics derived the myth that Collins could not create good fictional characters; many recent critics have shown that Collins's characters so defied Victorian stereotypes as to antagonize his contemporary critics. His female characters were often accused of being too masculine; to modern readers, the female characters seem realistic and fully developed. Collins did have admirers, however, including Edmund Yates, who in 1857 (two years before the serialization of the first of Collins's great novels) ranked Collins fourth among British novelists, after Charles Dickens, William Makepeace Thackeray, and Charlotte Brontë ("W. Wilkie Collins," *The Train* [June 1857], pp. iii and 352–357); Harry Quilter's "Wilkie Collins" in *Preferences in Art, Life, and Literature* (London: Swan Sonnenschein, 1892, pp. 247–280) is among the best early surveys of Collins's work, along with Algernon Charles Swinburne's often cited "Wilkie Collins" in *Studies in Prose and Poetry* (London: Chatto and Windus, 1894, pp. 110–128).

Since the 1950's, critics have increasingly found literary merit in Collins's writings. His sensational novels—which often hinge on mysteries—have had a particular appeal to people interested in mystery fiction. For instance, U. C. Knoepflmacher's "The Counterworld of Victorian Fiction and *The Woman in White*" in *The Worlds of Victorian Fiction* (ed. Jerome H. Buckley. Cambridge, Massachusetts: Harvard University Press, 1975, pp. 351–369) discusses how the mysterious aspects of Collins's fiction make significant statements about people and society.

Evaluation of Selected Criticism

Andrews, R. V. *Wilkie Collins: A Critical Survey of His Prose Fiction with a Bibliography.* New York: Garland, 1979 (dissertation, 1959). This is a strikingly intelligent overview of the complicated issues related to Collins's fiction; it presents astute observations on Collins's style and his characterizations. Its bibliography is enormously useful.

Marshall, William H. *Wilkie Collins.* New York: Twayne, 1970. Although a little sketchy in places, this book presents the best overview of Collins's achievements and features insightful commentary on both the fiction and drama. Marshall views Collins as a minor novelist who wrote five major novels, *The Woman in White, No Name, Armadale, The Moonstone,* and *Man and Wife.*

Other Sources

Ashley, Robert, *Wilkie Collins.* New York: Roy, 1952. A bio-critical study of his entire corpus. About 25% biographical, 75% critical. The first book-length critical study. Tries to rehabilitate Collins from modern criticism.

Beetz, Kirk H. *Wilkie Collins: An Annotated Bibliography, 1889–1976.* Metuchen, NJ: Scarecrow, 1978.

Lonoff, Sue, *Wilkie Collins and His Victorian Readers: A Study in the Rhetoric of Authorship.* New York: AMS, 1982. Sometimes confusing but up-to-date; explores relationship of Collins to his Victorian audience.

Page, Norman, ed. *Wilkie Collins: The Critical Heritage.* London: Routledge and Kegan Paul, 1974. Collection of about 80 early reviews and essays.

Selected Dictionaries and Encyclopedias

Dictionary of Literary Biography: Victorian Novelists After 1885, Gale Research, 1983, pp. 61–77. The best short introduction.

Kirk H. Beetz
National University, Sacramento

WILLIAM COLLINS
1721–1759

Author's Chronology

1721 born at Chichester; of William Collins, a hatter and mayor, and Elizabeth Martin; *1734* admitted as a scholar of Winchester; father dies; *1739* publishes poems in *Gentleman's Magazine* of January and October; *1740* enters Queens College, Oxford: *1741* elected to a demyship at Magdalene College; *1742 Persian Ecloques* published; *1743* receives his B.A.; publishes *Verses Humbly Submitted to Sir Thomas Hanmer on his Edition of Shakespeare by a Gentleman of Oxford; 1744* mother dies on July 6, leaving the poet a small inheritance which he dissipates; applies to the Duke of Richmond for patronage; is offered a curacy at Birdham which he rejects; *1745* has developed acquaintance with Johnson, Quin, Garrick, Foote, Davies and other literary and theatrical figures; his uncle Charles leaves him property in Chichester, which he sells the following year; *1746* project to publish a volume of odes with Joseph Warton set aside and each publishes his own; publishes *Odes on Several Descriptive and Allegoric Subjects* (dated *1747*) to a disappointing reception; *1748* publishes three poems in Dodsley's *Collection; 1749* his uncle, Colonel Martin, leaves him one-third of his estate, estimated at 2000 pounds; *1750 The Passions* set to music by William Hayes and performed at Encaenia at Oxford; printed as a pamphlet; *1751–1754* declining health; travels in France; visits Bath; meets Johnson at Islington; *1754* reported temporarily in a madhouse; visits Oxford; lives at Chichester with his sister, Anne; *1759* dies on 12 June and is buried at St. Andrews Church.

Author's Bibliography (selected)

Persian Ecloques, 1742 (poetry); *Verses Humbly Addressed to Sir Thomas Hamner,* 1743 (poetry); *An Epistle: Addressed to Sir Thomas Hamner,* 1744 (poetry, a revised version of the preceding); *Odes on Several Descriptive and Allegoric Subjects,* 1746 (poetry); *Ode Occasioned by the Death of Mr. Thomson,* 1749 (poetry); *The Passions, an Ode,* 1750 (poetry set to music by William Hayes); *Oriental Ecloques,* 1757 (poetry, re-issue of *Persian Ecloques*); *An Ode on the Popular Superstitions of the Highlands of Scotland,* 1788 (poetry).

Overview of Biographical Sources

A study of Collins' biography is hampered by the absence of extensive comments on his life by his contemporaries. Although he was a schoolmate of Joseph Warton at Winchester and their friendship persisted, there is no correspondence to record that portion of his life. He knew Samuel Johnson and other literary personalities of his day, but all that remains of substance is the brief biography written by Johnson, included in his *Lives of the English Poets.* A biographical memoir is included in *The Poetical Works . . . with Memoirs of the*

Author: and Observations on his Genius and Writings, ed. by John Langhorne (London: Becket and Denhondt, 1765). *The Poetical Works of William Collins,* ed. Alexander Dyce (London: William Pickering and Oxford: D. A. Talboys, 1827) contains biographical and critical notes by Dyce. Two letters by Collins are extant, one to John Gilbert Cooper, dated London, November 10, 1747 has been published by H. O. White in "Letters of William Collins," *Review of English Studies,* January 1927, Vol. III (Number 9), 12–21; the other to Dr. William Hayes, dated Chichester, Sussex, November 8, 1750, is included in the fine biographical preface to the *Poetical Works,* ed. William Moy Thomas (London: Bell and Daldy 1858). Two letters about Collins, one by Thomas Warton and the other by John Ragsdale were printed in an essay by Thomas Maude in "The Reaper" #26 in the *York Chronicle* (16 February 1797). Extensive modern research has added little to what was known of Collins's life in the period shortly after his death. *Poor Collins, His Life, His Art, and His Influences* by Edward Gay Ainsworth, Jr. (1937) places his life within the framework of his work as artist. The introduction and notes to *Drafts and Fragments of Verse* ed. J. S. Cunningham (1956) contain useful biographical material. A recent biographical study is that of P. L. Carver, *William Collins: The Life of a Poet* (1967).

Evaluation of Selected Biographies

Ainsworth, Edward Gay, Jr. *Poor Collins: His Life, His Art and His Influence.* Ithaca, NY: Cornell University Press, and London: Oxford University Press, 1937. Ainsworth's study is both biographical and critical. He provides a summary that includes the limited biographical data available. His major effort in the first part of the book is to study the relationship between the man and his art. He tries to see both the merits and limitations of Collins as a poet within the context of his life. The remainder of the work is essentially literary criticism.

Carver, P. L. *William Collins: The Life of a Poet.* New York: Horizon Press, 1967. Carver's biography of Collins is based on the author's earlier studies of the poet's life, some of which were published in "Notes on the life of William Collins," *Notes and Queries,* CLXXVII (August-October 1939). It is a meticulous study of sources, providing both an updating of information previously known about Collins and adding new material.

Cunningham, J. S. ed. *Drafts and Fragments of Verse.* Oxford: Clarendon Press, 1956. In both the introduction and notes, Cunningham provides significant material of value to the biographer. The fragments are in the British Library, and have come down to modern times through the hands of Collins's contemporary, Joseph Warton. They include four stanzaic poems, a fragment of an "Ode for Music," and five drafts of epistolary poems in couplet form. Of the other fragments, of particular interest to the biographer is a Latin oration written by Collins at Winchester as a school exercise.

Johnson, Samuel, "William Collins" in *Prefaces, Biographical and Critical, to the Works of the English Poets,* 10 volumes (London, 1779). In its many modern editions it is known as *The Lives of the Poets.* Johnson's life of Collins is the starting point of all modern biographical studies. Johnson knew Collins personally and, although written a good number of years after their acquaintance, Johnson's recollections are both strong and compassionate. He offers a useful picture of the Collins' indecisiveness as a literary planner, and provides testimony regarding the nature of Collins's final deterioration.

Overview of Critical Sources

Considering the slender body of Collins's work, there has been considerable interest in him in modern critical and scholarly studies. Much of this interest has centered on the relationship of his work to the Romantic movement, the Miltonic tradition, and the pastoral. In these areas, individual articles are important, for example the study by A. S. P. Woodhouse, "The Poetry of Collins Reconsidered" in *From Sensibility to Romanticism* ed. Frederick Hilles and Harold Bloom (New York: Oxford University Press, 1965, pp. 93–137); and that of Richard Eversole, "Collins and the End of the Shepherd Pastoral," in *Survival of Pastorals* (Lawrence: University of Kansas Humanistic Studies, 1979, #52, pp. 19–32). The Miltonic tradition is studied by Paul S. Sherwin in *Precious Bane: Collins and the Miltonic Legacy* (1977). Other significant studies have been Ricardo Quintana, "The Scheme of Collins' *Odes on Several . . . Subjects,*" *Restoration and Eighteenth-Century Literature* (Chicago: University of Chicago Press, 1963); Patricia Meyer Spacks, "Collins Imagery," *Studies in Philology,* LXII, 719–736; and Janice Haney-Peritz, "In Quest of Mistaken Beauties: Allegorical Indeterminancey in Collins's Poetry," *English Literary History,* XLVIII, #4 (Winter 1981), 732–756.

Evaluation of Selected Criticism

Ainsworth, Edward Gay, Jr. *Poor Collins; His Life, His Art, and His Influences.* Ithaca, NY: Cornell University Press and London: Oxford University Press, 1937. In addition to his study of Collins as man and poet in the first part of the book, which is primarily of biographical interest, the second part of the volume discusses literary sources, concentrating on the classics, Milton, Dryden, Pope, the Elizabethans, and Collins's contemporaries. The third section of his study attempts to demonstrate that Collins was popular in the Romantic period and that he exerted a major influence on poets of that era.

Doughty, Oswald, *William Collins,* London: Longman's, 1964. This is a valuable short study of Collins. Doughty provides a knowledgeable summary of Collin's life in the light of modern scholarship, and studies in detail many of the poet's individual works. Most of the directions modern critical studies, including the influence of Milton on Collins and of Collins on the Romantics, have admirably informed Doughty's own reading, which is both personal and modern.

Sherwin, Paul S. *Precious Bane: Collins and the Miltonic Legacy.* Austin and London: University of Texas Press, 1977. Noting the vitality and originality of Collins's genius, Sherwin undertakes a study of the relationship of that genius to his historical past. He sees Collins as a precursor of the sensibility poets and of the Romantics. He considers the force of Milton's personality as well as his poetry on Collins, arguing that he could not have made his major contributions as a poet without the influence of "Milton's overshadowing presence." He concludes that none of the sensibility poets were as greatly influenced by Milton as was Collins. His detailed study of individual works of Collins include the "Ode on the Poetical Character," the "Ode to Fear," and the "Popular Superstitions Ode."

Sigworth, Oliver, *William Collins.* New York: Twayne, 1965. Sigworth's study is primarily critical, while providing enough biographical material to set the poetry in context. The work has value in providing an analysis of the individual works of Collins that is useful to both graduate and undergraduate students.

Other Sources

Garrod, Heathcote William, *Collins.* Oxford: Clarendon Press, 1928. A commentary on the poetry of Collins that stresses extensive analysis of Collins's texts, emphasizing the poet's use of faulty figures of speech, errors in learned allusions and similar shortcomings.

Williams, Iolo Aneurin, *Seven XVIIIth Century Bibliographies.* London: Dulau and Company, 1924. This bibliography of seven eighteenth-century writers includes one on Collins. It also includes an essay on the poet prefixed to the bibliography.

Selected Dictionary

Dictionary of National Biography, Volume IV, Oxford University Press, 1919. The biographical account of Collins in this standard biographical source supplies most of the known facts about the poet and contains detailed information about biographical sources.

Richard J. Dircks
St. John's University

JOSEPH CONRAD
1857–1924

Author's Chronology

Born Josef Teodor Konrad Nalecz Korzeniowski December 3, 1857, near Berdyczew, Poland; *1862* moves to Vologda, Russia, with politically exiled parents; *1867* returns to Poland; *1869* attends St. Anne's School, Cracow; *1874* arrives in Marseilles and begins seafaring life; *1878* signs on British ship *Mavis* and enters British Merchant service; *1880* passes Third Mate's examination; *1886* becomes naturalized British citizen and passes Master Mariner's examination; *1889* begins writing *Almayer's Folly,* first novel (published *1895*); *1890* tours Belgian Congo; *1896* marries Jessie George; *1898* birth of first son, Borys; *1906* birth of second son, John; *1913* publishes first best-seller, *Chance; 1914* visits Poland; *1923* visits United States; August 3, 1924 dies at home near Bishopsbourne, Kent.

Author's Bibliography (selected)

Almayer's Folly, 1895 (novel); *An Outcast of the Islands,* 1896 (novel); *The Nigger of the "Narcissus",* 1897 (novel); *Tales of Unrest,* 1898 (stories); *Lord Jim,* 1900 (novel); *Youth, A Narrative, and two Other Stories,* 1902; *Typhoon, and Other Stories,* 1903; *Nostromo, A Tale of the Seabord,* 1904 (novel); *The Mirror of the Sea,* 1906 (memoirs); *The Secret Agent, A Simple Tale,* 1907 (novel); *A Set of Six,* 1908 (stories), *Under Western Eyes,* 1911 (novel); *A Personal Record,* 1912 (memoir); *Chance,* 1913 (novel); *Victory, An Island Tale,* 1915 (novel); *Within the Tides, Tales,* 1915; *The Shadow-Line, A Confession,* 1917 (novel); *The Arrow of Gold, A Story Between Two Notes,* 1919 (novel); *The Rescue, A Romance of the Shallows,* 1920 (novel); *Notes on Life and Letters,* 1921 (essays); *The Rover,* 1923, (novel); *Suspense: A Napoleonic Novel,* 1925; *Tales of Hearsay,* 1925 (stories); *Last Essays,* 1926; *The Congo Diary,* 1926 (travel diary).

Overview of Biographical Sources

Although Conrad had few biographers in the first thirty-five years after his death, he has been the subject of several important biographical studies in the past quarter century. The first full biographical study, Georges Jean-Aubry's *Joseph Conrad: Life and Letters* (Garden City, NY: Doubleday, 1927), remains a valuable resource and was, for many years, the standard; it was complemented by Jean-Aubry's *The Sea Dreamer: A Definitive Biography of Joseph Conrad* (Garden City, NY: Doubleday, 1947). Several reminiscences of Conrad focus on the domestic life of a writer, among them Jessie Conrad's *Joseph Conrad as I Knew Him* (Garden City, NY: Doubleday, 1926), Borys Conrad's *My Father: Joseph Conrad* (London: Calder and Boyars, 1970), John Conrad's *Joseph Conrad: Times Remembered* (Cambridge: Cambridge University Press,

1981), and Richard Curle's *The Last Twelve Years of Joseph Conrad* (Garden City, NY: Doubleday, 1928). The first modern biography, Jocelyn Bains's *Joseph Conrad: A Critical Biography* (1960), presents a clear, readable detailed account of most of Conrad's life. Jerry Allen's *The Sea Years of Joseph Conrad* (Garden City, NY: Doubleday, 1965) illustrates his premise that much in Conrad's fiction is based on personal fact, characters on actual acquaintances, locations on places Conrad had visited. Bernard C. Meyer's *Joseph Conrad: A Psychoanalytic Portrait* (Princeton: Princeton University Press, 1967) is a Freudian quest after the man behind the writer's mask that discovers Conrad, his preoccupations, fears, anxieties, and fantasies in his fiction. In *The Three Lives of Joseph Conrad* (Boston: Houghton Mifflin, 1972) Olivia Coolidge provides a good, brief overview of Conrad's life for the general reader. Frederick R. Karl's *Joseph Conrad: The Three Lives* (1979) mixes biography and criticism in a monumental work that is not without long, novelistic passages of its own. Roger Tennant's *Joseph Conrad: A Biography* (London: Sheldon Press, 1981) does not attempt literary criticism but presents a straightforward, psychologically credible portrait of its subject. The most recent and important biography is Zdislaw Najder's *Joseph Conrad: A Chronicle* (1983) which is a chronological treatment of Conrad's life based on painstaking research into letters and private papers Najder published elsewhere as *Conrad under Familial Eyes* (Cambridge: Cambridge University Press, 1983).

Evaluation of Selected Biographies

Baines, Jocelyn, *Joseph Conrad: A Critical Biography*. New York: McGraw-Hill, 1960. Baines provides full and helpful analysis of some of the varied political backgrounds against which Conrad lived and wrote, draws heavily upon Conrad's correspondence to get at his own process of composition and sense of his works, and provides a good entry to Conrad's circle of friends by using their reminiscences, letters and published statements. Among those whose impressions and words she gathers are H. G. Wells, John Galsworthy, Arthur Symons and Ford Madox Ford. This is a good, standard work that is readable and clear, although it does not adequately address the issue of Poland in Conrad's life and consciousness. It is also insufficiently concerned with his opinions on social and political issues apart from those he writes about in his fiction.

Karl, Frederick R. *Joseph Conrad: The Three Lives*. New York: Farrar, Straus and Giroux, 1979. Karl's massive thousand-page study incorporates criticism of Conrad's fiction, largely as autobiographical, with a well-researched and well-documented examination of Conrad's lives as a youth in Poland, a global sailor, and a writer. Karl makes extensive and appropriate use of the major works on Conrad that precede his and considerably expands upon the interplay between his life and works.

Najder, Zdislaw, *Joseph Conrad: A Chronicle.* Halina Carroll-Najder, trans. New Brunswick, NJ: Rutgers University Press, 1983. This major scholarly biography of Conrad draws upon the facts of his life and times to present a full picture of the man and his career. Najder, more than any biographer, writes authoritatively about Conrad's Polish years and draws upon a wealth of Conradiana to reinterpret the life of Conrad in several new ways. Najder is especially convincing as he examines Conrad's attempts to re-shape his own past and to transform it into literature in a therapeutic attempt to create a fable of his identity.

Autobiographical Sources

Conrad's fiction contains innumerable autobiographical references to his travels, acquaintances, and impressions, more or less veiled by his frequent narrator, Marlow. One notable study of the interplay of fiction and self-revelation is Edward W. Said's *Joseph Conrad and the Fiction of Autobiography* (Cambridge, MA: Harvard University Press, 1966). His overtly autobiographical accounts, *The Mirror of the Sea* (1906) and *A Personal Record* (1912) are complemented by the semi-autobiographical novel, *The Arrow of Gold* (1919). His brief diaries of the Congo trip have been edited by Zdislaw Najder in Joseph Conrad, *Congo Diary and Other Uncollected Pieces* (Garden City, NY: Doubleday, 1979) and form the autobiographical base of his novella *Heart of Darkness* (1899). Many of Conrad's letters have been published between 1925 and the present, notably in Jean-Aulrey's *Joseph Conrad: Life and Letters,* in Richard Curle's *Conrad to a Friend* (Garden City, NY: Doubleday, 1928), in Zdislaw Najder's *Conrad's Polish Background: Letters to and from Polish Friends* (London: Oxford University Press, 1964), and in six other volumes. Frederick Karl and Lawrence Davies have begun publication of an eight-volume edition of *The Collected Letters of Joseph Conrad* (Cambridge: Cambridge University Press); the first volume (1861–1897) appeared in 1983 and the entire series will contain over 3,500 letters, nearly 1,500 of which have not been previously published.

Overview of Critical Sources

Conrad's literary reputation, never great in his lifetime until he published *Chance* (1913) declined in the 1930's, gradually increased by mid-century and has continued to grow since then to such an extent that Conrad is now considered among the greatest of England's modern writers. One journal, *Conradiana,* is devoted entirely to the study of Conrad and his works; his works and reviews of Conrad studies find a place in the journal *English Literature in Transition: 1880–1920* and in numerous other journals. In the past twenty-five years dozens of monographs and scholarly studies and hundreds of essays have dealt with the varied aspects of his fiction.

Evaluation of Selected Criticism

Guerard, Albert J. *Conrad the Novelist.* Cambridge, MA: Harvard University Press, 1966. Guerard views Conrad's work as exemplary of the progress of the novel from 1875 to 1925 and focuses on the artist at work in his short stories and novels in a thorough examination of Conrad's fiction. The work foreshadows many later studies devoted to individual works, especially in its treatment of *Heart of Darkness* and *Nostromo* and of *Lord Jim* as an impressionist novel.

Moser, Thomas, *Joseph Conrad: Achievement and Decline.* Cambridge, MA: Harvard University Press, 1957. This pioneering critical work treats much of Conrad's fiction as the product of a psychologist, political observer, artist, and moralist whose power declined once he had achieved both public recognition and greatness. Moser's work remains among the few indispensable critical works on Conrad and contains close textual readings that have provoked controversy.

Watt, Ian, *Conrad in Nineteenth Century.* Berkeley: University of California Press, 1979. Watt's outstanding analysis of four of Conrad's works (*Almayer's Folly, The Nigger of the "Narcissus," Heart of Darkness,* and *Lord Jim*) fixes Conrad firmly in the nineteenth century, examines sources, techniques, ideological, and critical perspectives in his fiction in a thoroughly scholarly volume.

Watts, Cedric, *A Preface to Conrad.* London: Longmans Green, 1982. Watts provides a fine, general introduction to Conrad's work by focusing on the "homo duplex," the double man, in the fiction as reflecting Conrad himself. The work contains a major essay on *Nostromo* as the ultimate product of Conrad's varied experiences, influences, and concerns. This is a first-rate introduction to Conrad for the undergraduate and general reader.

Other Sources

Megroz, Rodolphe, *Joseph Conrad's Mind and Method.* London: Faber & Faber, 1931. Though dated and superseded by later works, it remains a valuable analysis of the artist at work in his fiction.

Said, Edward, *Joseph Conrad and the Fiction of Autobiography.* Cambridge, MA: Harvard University Press, 1966. Said examines Conrad's letters as they reflect his concerns and illuminate his fiction.

Stallman, R. W. *The Art of Joseph Conrad: A Critical Symposium.* Athens, OH: Ohio University Press, 1982. A collection of thirty-five essays on Conrad's works.

Sherry, Norman, ed. *Conrad: The Critical Heritage.* London: Routledge and Keegan Paul, 1973. A collection of early reviews and essays on Conrad's work.

———, *Conrad's Eastern World.* Cambridge: Cambridge University Press, 1966. An examination of the people and places Conrad transformed in his Eastern fiction.

———, *Conrad's Western World.* Cambridge: Cambridge University Press, 1971. An examination of the people and places of Africa and the Gulf of Mexico Conrad wrote of in his western fiction.

Teets, Bruce E. and Helmut E. Gerber. *Joseph Conrad: An Annotated Bibliography of Writings About Him.* DeKalb: Northern Illinois University Press, 1971. Contains 1,977 entries on Conrad dated between 1895 and 1966.

Selected Dictionaries and Encyclopedias

Critical Survey of Short Fiction, Salem Press, 1981. Brief biography and an analysis of short stories.

Critical Survey of Long Fiction, Salem Press, 1983. Biref biography and concise analysis of the novels.

John J. Conlon
The University of Massachusetts at Boston

JAMES FENIMORE COOPER
1789–1851

Author's Chronology

Born September 15, 1789, Burlington, New Jersey; *1790* family moves to Cooperstown, New York, founded by the novelist's father; *1803–1805* student at Yale College; *1806* apprentice on the merchant vessel *Stirling; 1808* becomes a midshipman in the United States Navy; *1809* father killed by political opponent; *1810* leaves Navy; *1811* marries Susan DeLancey; *1820* publishes first book, *Precaution; 1821* publishes *The Spy,* the first thoroughly American novel; *1823* publishes *The Pioneers,* first of the Leatherstocking Tales; *1824* publishes *The Pilot,* the first sea novel; *1826* sails for Europe, where he will remain to write and travel until 1833; *1839* publishes his *History of the Navy of the United States of America; 1841* publishes *The Deerslayer,* last of five Leatherstocking Tales, amid growing controversy and legal action over reviews of his writing; *1850* publishes *The Ways of the Hour,* the last of over thirty novels; *1851* dies September 14.

Author's Bibliography (selected)

Precaution, 1820 (novel); *The Spy,* 1821 (novel); *The Pioneers,* 1823 (novel); *The Pilot,* 1824 (novel); *The Last of the Mohicans,* 1826 (novel); *The Prairie,* 1827 (novel); *The Red Rover,* 1827 (novel); *Notions of the Americans,* 1828 (social criticism); *The Bravo,* 1831 (novel); *The Monikins,* 1835 (novel); *Sketches of Switzerland,* 1836 (first of five travel books); *The American Democrat,* 1838 (political theory); *Homeward Bound,* 1838 (novel); *The History of the Navy of the United States of America,* 1839 (prose); *The Pathfinder,* 1840 (novel); *The Deerslayer,* 1841 (novel); *Ned Myers,* 1843 (biography); *Afloat and Ashore,* 1844 (novel); *Satanstoe,* 1845 (first of the fictional "Littlepage Manuscripts"); *Lives of Distinguished American Naval Officers,* 1846 (biography); *The Crater,* 1847 (novel); *The Sea Lions,* 1849 (novel).

Overview of Biographical Sources

The first and in many ways still the most influential biography is Thomas R. Lounsbury's *James Fenimore Cooper* (1882). W. B. Shubrick Clymer's brief *James Fenimore Cooper* (Boston: Small, Maynard, & Company, 1900) is more personal. Though not so detailed as Lounsbury's work, Donald A. Ringe's *James Fenimore Cooper* (1962) and Warren S. Walker's *James Fenimore Cooper: An Introduction and Interpretation* (New York: Barnes & Noble, 1962) benefit from modern scholarship. Robert E. Spiller explored the social and political context of Cooper's life and writings in *Fenimore Cooper: Critic of His Times* (1931) and Ethel R. Outland followed the sinuous course of Cooper's legal struggles of the 1840's in *The "Effingham" Libels on Cooper* (1929). George Dekker, in *James Fenimore Cooper: The Novelist* (London: Routledge

& Kegan Paul, 1967), emphasizes Cooper's place in the tradition of the historical novel as established by Sir Walter Scott, while Stephen Railton, in *Fenimore Cooper: A Study of His Life and Imagination* (Princeton: Princeton University Press, 1978), uses Cooper's life psychoanalytically to interpret the writings. Cooper's daughter, Susan Fenimore Cooper, provides charming but largely unreliable personal glimpses of the novelist's life in "Small Family Memories" (1883) published by the grandson, James Fenimore Cooper, in *Correspondence of James Fenimore-Cooper* (New Haven: Yale University Press, 1922). Susan had much earlier published her anecdotes on the composition of her father's books in *Pages and Pictures, from the Writings of James Fenimore Cooper* (New York: W. A. Townsend and Company, 1861).

Evaluation of Selected Biographies

Lounsbury, Thomas R. *James Fenimore Cooper.* Boston: Houghton Mifflin and Company, 1882. Lounsbury's contribution to the American Men of Letters series must have been a difficult biography to write: even thirty years after the novelist's death, no information was forthcoming from the family. Lounsbury's dependence on outside sources sometimes forces a one-sided view of Cooper; this most especially seems to be the case in regard to the novelist's personal life and character. Despite this handicap, the biography is important as being the first full-length treatment of Cooper. Lounsbury's critical response to Cooper's writing is also refreshingly direct.

Outland, Ethel R. *The "Effingham" Libels on Cooper.* University of Wisconsin Studies in Language and Literature, Number 28 (1929). Outland focuses on Cooper's legal activities from 1837–1845. In many ways this period was Cooper's most productive and most diverse, but reading the works of this period does not convey fully Cooper's intellectual development—nor can the works themselves be fully understood without the record of Cooper's libel suits.

Ringe, Donald A. *James Fenimore Cooper.* New Haven: College and University Press, 1962. Ringe's biography "intends quite frankly to state the case for James Fenimore Cooper." Ringe limits the amount of biographical material to just enough to provide continuity. Instead, the work focuses on Cooper's development as a writer of fiction. Ringe identifies several different areas of focus in Cooper's art: the American Past, Europe and the United States, Values in Conflict, and the Decay of Principle. Ringe puts particular emphasis on the later works of Cooper.

Spiller, Robert E. *Fenimore Cooper: Critic of His Times.* New York: Minton, Balch, & Company, 1931. Spiller's work concentrates on Cooper's response to European society and his evaluation of American society. The emphasis in this book thus falls on Cooper's European travels and their after-effects. Spiller revolutionized the study of Cooper: his studies revealed Cooper as an able social critic, an approach still largely followed.

Autobiographical Sources

The reading of Cooper's fictions as autobiography, particularly the New York novels (*Pioneers, Homeward Bound, Home As Found,* and the "Littlepage Manuscripts"), has often led biographers astray. There is no doubt that descriptions of scenery and many characterizations find their basis in Cooper's own experience, but recent work shows equally certainly that those same landscapes and characters have strong infusions of pure fiction. The major autobiographical documents extant are included in the six volumes of *The Letters and Journals of James Fenimore Cooper,* edited by James Franklin Beard (Cambridge: The Belknap Press of Harvard University Press, 1960–1968). These six volumes, with their notes and section headings, are essential to serious study of Cooper. Most of the journal materials refer to journeys and may be considered primary material for the travel books collectively known as "Gleanings in Europe." It is probable that Cooper kept other journals; if any more are extant, none has been brought to general notice. Cooper's *Ned Myers; or, A Life Before the Mast* (1843) contains some descriptions of Cooper's voyage in the *Stirling,* and his sketch "Melancthon Taylor Woolsey" in *Lives of Distinguished American Naval Officers* (1846) reveals some of Cooper's activities as a young midshipman. "The Eclipse," published posthumously in *Putnam's Magazine* (September 1869), describes a visit of Cooper to his parents in Cooperstown in 1806.

Overview of Critical Sources

Known in his own day as the master of the Indian novel and the inventor of the sea novel, Cooper was soon recognized by his contemporaries—to the detriment of the sales of his novels—as a strong critic of the young American republic. Cooper's works were widely imitated but themselves fell into the category of juvenile books in the years following the Civil War. Serious recognition throughout the remainder of the nineteenth century was sporadic. The 1920's and 1930's restored Cooper to the canon of major writers with the work of Spiller on Cooper as social critic and with D. H. Lawrence's seminal—if controversial—*Studies in Classic American Literature* (1923). Since then Cooper has been the subject of most phases of scholarship and trends in criticism.

Evaluation of Selected Criticism

McWilliams, John P., Jr. *Political Justice in a Republic: James Fenimore Cooper's America.* Berkeley: University of California Press, 1972. McWilliams gives a more modern and textually relevant discussion of many of the political and social themes treated biographically by Spiller. Nearly every work by

Cooper, whatever its genre or other themes, shows Cooper's concern for natural and legal justice in an America still defining its Constitution.

Philbrick, Thomas, *James Fenimore Cooper and the Development of American Sea Fiction.* Cambridge: Harvard University Press, 1961. The only full-length study of Cooper's sea novels, Philbrick's book shows the context and influence of Cooper's dozen sea novels. Included in his survey are detailed analyses of three representative novels: *The Red Rover, Afloat and Ashore,* and *The Sea Lions.*

Ringe, Donald A. *Space & Time in the Art of Bryant, Irving & Cooper.* Lexington: The University Press of Kentucky, 1971. Ringe's book provides by far the best study of Cooper's style and is the most detailed of the studies linking Cooper to his contemporaries in the fine arts. Most works concentrate on Cooper as a thinker; this one concentrates on Cooper as an artist. While other critics have felt they needed to apologize for Cooper's style while praising his themes, Ringe shows how the style is part of the literary intent—and how well it actually works.

Other Sources

Beard, James Franklin, ed. *The Writings of James Fenimore Cooper.* Albany: State University of New York Press, 1980- . Besides providing a rigorously edited text, each volume in this series provides a historical introduction which covers the inception, composition, publication, and reception of the work.

Spiller, Robert E. and Philip C. Blackburn, *A Descriptive Bibliography of the Writings of James Fenimore Cooper,* 1934; rpt. New York: Burt Franklin, 1968. This is the standard list of Cooper's own writings, although a few additions and many minor corrections need to be made.

Walker, Warren S. *Plots and Characters in the Fiction of James Fenimore Cooper.* Hamden, CT: Archon Books, 1978. This work contains, along with the summaries of plots and list of characters, chronologies of Cooper's life and his fiction.

R. D. Madison
United States Naval Academy

JAMES GOULD COZZENS
1903–1978

Author's Chronology

Born August 19, 1903, Chicago, Illinois to Henry and Bertha (Wood) Cozzens; *1916* enters Kent School, Kent, Connecticut; *1920* "A Democratic School" appears in *Atlantic Monthly; 1922* enters Harvard University; *1924* publishes first novel, *Confusion,* as Harvard sophomore; *1924* takes leave of absence from Harvard, does not return; *1925–1926* teaches at Tuinucú, Cuba; goes to France with mother; tutors in Europe; *1927* returns to United States; marries Sylvia Bernice Baumgarten; *1928* employed by advertising firm of M.P. Gould & Company; *1933* purchases Carrs Farm, Lambertville, New Jersey; *1938* works on *Fortune* staff; *1942* enlists in Air Force, Officer's Training School; assigned to Training Aids Directorate; *1943* transferred to Office of Technical Information, Air Force Headquarters; *1945* discharged from Air Force with rank of major; *1949* wins Pulitzer Prize for *Guard of Honor; 1952* awarded honorary doctor of letters degree by Harvard; *1957* featured as *Time* cover story; *1958* purchases "Shadowbrook," Williamstown, Massachusetts; *1971* moves to Florida; *1978* wife, Bernice, dies; August 9 James Gould Cozzens dies in Stuart, Florida.

Author's Bibliography (selected)

Confusion, 1924 (novel); *Michael Scarlett,* 1925 (novel); *Cock Pit,* 1928 (novel); *The Son of Perdition,* 1929 (novel); *S.S. San Pedro,* 1931 (novel); *The Last Adam,* 1933 (novel); *Castaway,* 1934 (novel); *Men and Brethren,* 1936 (novel); *Ask Me Tomorrow,* 1940 (novel); *The Just and the Unjust,* 1942 (novel); *Guard of Honor,* 1948 (novel); *By Love Possessed,* 1957 (novel); *Children and Others,* 1964 (stories); *Morning Noon and Night,* 1968 (novel).

Overview of Biographical Sources

Despite compiling a canon of thirteen novels and numerous short stories, Cozzens has received scant attention and remains one of the least read and least regarded major American novelists. Few biographical treatments exist, and these are comparatively brief. Based on interviews, "The Hermit of Lambertville" (*Time,* 2 September 1957) provides valuable biographical information, including a number of quotations, some ironically intended, and various pronouncements on other noted writers. Robert Van Gelder's interview, "James Gould Cozzens at Work" (*New York Times Book Review,* 23 June 1940), presents Cozzens's comments on his style and his life. Following his death, two additional biographical sources were published. *James Gould Cozzens: Selected Notebooks 1960–1967,* edited by Matthew J. Bruccoli (Columbia and Bloomfield Hills: Bruccoli Clark, 1984), is a collection of journal entries focusing on a wide range of personal and literary matters. *A Time of War: Air*

Force Diaries and Pentagon Memos 1943–1945, edited by Matthew J. Bruccoli (Columbia and Bloomfield Hills: Bruccoli Clark, 1984), contains the selected entries of Cozzens during his years in the Air Force and offers important insights into the personalities and events that shaped his mature thinking and his later works, particularly *Guard of Honor.*

Evaluation of Selected Biographies

Bruccoli, Matthew J. *James Gould Cozzens: A Life Apart.* San Diego, New York, London: Harcourt Brace Jovanovich, 1983. Bruccoli worked with Cozzens in preparing *Just Representations: A James Gould Cozzens Reader* (Carbondale and Edwardsville: Southern Illinois University Press/New York and London: Harcourt Brace Jovanovich, 1978) and with Fannie Baumgarten Collins with the biography. Written in an informal, readable style, Bruccoli's work is detailed and accurate, objectively tracing Cozzens's life and presenting the development of his novels and stories as well as their financial and critical reception. Bruccoli's attitude is respectful but infused with a desire to accelerate the reassessment of Cozzens's overlooked career.

Michel, Pierre, *James Gould Cozzens.* New York: Twayne, 1974. Michel presents a general bio-critical introduction to Cozzens's life and works. He views Cozzens's fiction chronologically and devotes separate chapters to the short stories and the author's "conservatism." Michel's primary focus is on the thematic continuity and artistic evolution of Cozzens's fiction. Each novel is critically assessed.

Autobiographical Sources

Though Cozzens did not write what can strictly be called an autobiography, he did fictionalize his experiences in two personal novels, *Ask Me Tomorrow* and *Morning Noon and Night.* The former can be viewed as Cozzens's attempt to understand the defensive pride that characterized the antisocial attitudes and behavior of his early years. The novel focuses on the events of a young writer in Europe with his mother. Finding himself in reduced circumstances, he accepts employment as a traveling tutor. Like Cozzens too, he loves an American girl also touring Europe, and his inability to spend time with her frustrates him. Suggestions of Cozzens's strong, religious education as a child are also discernible. *Morning Noon and Night* features the first-person recollections of a narrator who at age sixty-five is seeking to put his life into perspective. (Cozzens was also sixty-five when the novel was published.) The book inventories all the things Cozzens valued (Puritan ethic, intelligence, reason) as well as those he deprecated (emotion, youth, the literary life), and in the course of the memoir presents the summation of his broodings on success, reputation, luck, power, love, sex, marriage, and the process of aging. Because Cozzens was primarily concerned with advancing certain themes, readers should be wary of any declaration that the author's personal involvement was baldly autobiographical.

Overview of Critical Sources

Critics have generally ignored Cozzens, a fact that hardly mattered to Cozzens himself. He insisted that he did not care either for literary fame or any posthumous reputation. Those critics who have focused on his novels have concerned themselves with Cozzens's artistic technique and his often difficult style—inverted syntax with heavy subordination, varied allusions (both open and concealed), and parenthetical constructions. They have overlooked Cozzens's attempt to achieve "just representations of general nature," and in so doing provide "a new acquist of true experience" for the reader, by accommodating form with content.

Evaluation of Selected Criticism

Bracher, Frederick, *The Novels of James Gould Cozzens.* New York: Harcourt, Brace, 1959. In this first, book-length study of Cozzens's themes and techniques, Bracher discusses all the novels except *Morning Noon and Night* but does not deal with the short stories. Though sometimes drawing incautious conclusions about Cozzens's intent, Bracher's study discusses the furor over his style. He remains critically objective, and does not mention at all Cozzens's supposed prejudices.

Hicks, Granville, *James Gould Cozzens.* University of Minnesota Pamphlets on American Writers, no. 58. Minneapolis: University of Minnesota, 1966. Hicks provides a concise, chronological introduction of Cozzens's work through *Children and Others,* including a discussion of the artist's style and thematic threads. In the course of his overview, Hicks also offers biographical information, occasionally relating Cozzens's experiences to the novels themselves. The last third of the book is devoted to comparing Cozzens to his contemporaries and noting that he has stayed within the limits of the traditional social novel.

Maxwell, D. E. S. *Cozzens.* Edinburgh and London: Oliver and Boyd, 1964. Maxwell chronologically treats Cozzens's novels from *Cock Pit* to *By Love Possessed,* arguing that his technique displays a classical temperament and a highly intellectual disposition. The article also discusses Cozzens's "philosophy."

Mooney, Harry J. *James Gould Cozzens: Novelist of Intellect.* Pittsburgh: University of Pittsburgh Press, 1963. Noting that few systematic interpretations of Cozzens's novels presently exist, Mooney undertakes to present not only Cozzens's capacity for continual development and his command of complex technique, but also his intellectual ability to depict modern man's condition.

Mooney examines eight novels, *S.S. San Pedro* through *By Love Possessed,* analyzing the major characters and correctly stating one of Cozzens's major themes—the individual has little control over chance occurrences that shape his life. The book's last chapter is devoted to the critics and their understanding and treatment of Cozzens.

Other Sources

Bracher, Frederick, "James Gould Cozzens: Humanist," *Critique,* 1, No. 3 (Winter 1958), 10-29. Notes Cozzens's refusal to accept new intellectual fads and declares that avoidance of literary fashion may explain critical neglect of his works. Bracher perceptively discusses also Cozzens's heroes and his complex, ornate style.

Coxe, Louis, "The Complex World of James Gould Cozzens," *American Literature,* 27, No. 2 (May 1955), 157-171. Perceptive, intellectual article arguing that the denseness of Cozzens's method owes to his attempt to portray the double vision of modern man—the central paradox of action and contemplation, of understanding and conduct.

Ward, John William, "James Gould Cozzens: The Condition of Modern Man," *James Gould Cozzens.* Carbondale and Edwardsville: Southern Illinois University Press, 1979. Readable article showing that in Cozzens's world man is limited by time and his own nature. Dignity resides in acting in the full awareness of the ironic conditions within which he must act.

Selected Dictionaries and Encyclopedias

Contemporary Authors, Gale Research, 1974. Brief treatments of Cozzens's life, career, and writings but, more importantly, an analysis of the attitudes of various critics toward him and statements by Cozzens himself.

Dictionary of Literary Biography, Gale Research, 1981. Concise overview of Cozzens's entire life, together with a thorough analysis of his novels and a discussion of his controversial style.

A. Gordon Van Ness
University of South Carolina

GEORGE CRABBE
1754–1832

Author's Chronology

Born December 24, 1754, Aldborough, Suffolk, England, eldest son of local collector of salt duties; *1763–1767* attends grammar schools in Bungay and Stowmarket; *1768–1775* studies medicine as surgical apprentice; *1775* publishes first significant poem, "Inebriety"; *1775–1780* works as common laborer; practices medicine in Aldborough; *1780* abandons medical practice; moves to London to pursue career as poet; *1781* finds patron in statesman Edmund Burke; *1782* ordained as Anglican clergyman; *1783* marries Sarah Elmy; *1785–1807* series of domestic tragedies and health problems contribute to suspension of poetic activity; *1807–1819* publishes major collections of narrative poetry; February 3, 1832 dies in the rectory at Trowbridge, Wiltshire.

Author's Bibliography (principal poetic works)

"Inebriety," 1775; "The Candidate," 1780; "The Library," 1781; "The Village," 1783; "The News-Paper," 1785; *Poems,* 1807; *The Borough,* 1810; *Tales in Verse,* 1812; *Tales of the Hall,* 1819.

Overview of Biographical Sources

Shortly after the poet's death appeared what to many still remains the seminal work in Crabbe biography, *The Life of the Rev. George Crabbe, LL.B. by his son the Rev. George Crabbe, A.M.* (1834). A number of reprinted editions make this work generally accessible. Two subsequent efforts, T. E. Kebbel's *Life of George Crabbe* (London: Walter Scott, 1888) and Alfred Ainger's *Crabbe* (London: Macmillan, 1903) offer little that is new, although the latter is not without value. The most ambitious, and still most generally useful, study of Crabbe's life is René Huchon's *George Crabbe and his Times, 1754–1832* (1907). More recently, Neville Blackburne's *The Restless Ocean: The Story of George Crabbe the Aldeburgh Poet, 1754–1832* (1972) has provided a welcome supplement to the earlier works. Finally, it might be noted that biographical analysis forms an integral part of certain of the better critical overviews of Crabbe's work; e.g. Robert L. Chamberlain's *George Crabbe* (1965) and Terrence Bareham's *George Crabbe* (1977).

Evaluation of Selected Biographies

Bareham, Terrence, *George Crabbe.* New York: Barnes & Noble, 1977. The strength of this study lies in the manner in which Bareham elucidates the inseparable correlation between Crabbe the poet and Crabbe the Anglican clergyman. The result is a bio-critical commentary which examines Crabbe's work as the natural outgrowth of a man imbued with strong religious, moral and political sensitivities and which allows for the interpretation of certain peculiar elements, such as the recurring theme of madness, which mark the poet's work.

Blackburne, Neville, *The Restless Ocean: The Story of George Crabbe the Aldeburgh Poet, 1754–1832.* Lavenham: Terrence Dalton, 1972. Perhaps the most readable of the purely biographical studies of Crabbe, and the only one to provide a number of helpful illustrations, Blackburne's work is of value in providing some new biographical information not available to earlier writers. Though the author proclaims that he is not attempting a critical analysis of Crabbe's poetry, one must be wary of certain superficial judgements, such as the assertion that "Crabbe's persistently sombre view of human nature" is "the distinctive element in his work."

Chamberlain, Robert L. *George Crabbe.* New York: Twayne, 1965. An effective synthesis of biographical and critical analysis, Chamberlain's book provides what in many respects is the most accessible short work on Crabbe for the non-specialist. Though at times a bit overenthusiastic in its claims for Crabbe's literary stature, it provides a sound, thorough summary of the man and his work.

Crabbe, George (son), *The Life of the Rev. George Crabbe, LL.B. by his son the Rev. George Crabbe, A.M.* London: John Murray, 1834. This, the cornerstone of Crabbe biography, is still well worth the modern reader's attention, not only for the value of the light it sheds on Crabbe but in a more general sense as an excellent example of 19th century biography. Among its many virtues are the insights it provides into the twenty-two year period of Crabbe's life during which he published no poetry, though he is known to have written, and subsequently destroyed, an enormous number of poems as well as three novels and an extensive prose treatise on botany.

Huchon, René, *George Crabbe and his Times, 1754–1832.* trans. Frederick Clarke. London: John Murray, 1907. Despite its age, Huchon's work remains the standard source for those wishing a painstakingly thorough examination of Crabbe's life. Included is a great deal of information not available to Crabbe's son. Though the work is excellent as biography, the reader is cautioned to be wary of its somewhat diminished value as literary criticism.

Autobiographical Sources

What passes for autobiographical source material on Crabbe is scant indeed. On January 1, 1816, there appeared in *The New Monthly Magazine* a short entry entitled "Biographical account of the Rev. George Crabbe, LL.B." Though it cannot be proven, it has always been assumed that Crabbe himself was the anonymous author. Much of the material contained in the sketch was later incorporated by the younger Crabbe within his biography of his father. A number of Crabbe's letters, appearing in isolated sources, have surfaced in the years since his death, but to date no comprehensive edition of the collected letters has appeared. A somewhat eccentric and unreliable examination of the postal flirtations which took place between Crabbe and various women in his later years is provided by A. M. Broadley and Walter Jerrold in *The Romance of an Elderly Poet: A Hitherto Unknown Chapter in the Life of George Crabbe Revealed by his Ten Years Correspondence with Elizabeth Charter from 1815–1825* (London: Stanley Paul, 1913).

Overview of Critical Sources

Crabbe, in the opinion of many, has not received the amount of critical attention he deserves. It was not, in fact, until the middle of the 20th century that the first full-scale critical analysis of the poet appeared with Lilian Haddakin's *The Poetry of Crabbe* (1955). Since then, however, and particularly in the decade of the 1970's, a number of very useful and diversified studies have appeared.

Evaluation of Selected Criticism

Haddakin, Lilian, *The Poetry of Crabbe.* London: Chatto & Windus, 1955. Haddakin was the first to break from a long-prevailing pattern of viewing Crabbe as a sort of pre-realistic verbal photographer and to lead her readers to a finer appreciation of his talents as a narrative poet. While its emphasis is more upon the technical features of Crabbe's poetry than upon thematic concerns, the book amply demonstrates the poet's use of life experiences in shaping his craft.

Hatch, Ronald B. *Crabbe's Arabesque: Social Drama in the Poetry of George Crabbe.* Montreal: McGill-Queen's University Press, 1976. More than any other work on Crabbe, this study focuses its energies upon an examination of the social criticism embedded within the poet's narratives and upon the manner in which the dramatic structures of these narratives enhance their didactic purposes.

Nelson, Beth, *George Crabbe and the Progress of Eighteenth-Century Narrative Verse.* Lewisburg, PA: Bucknell University Press, 1976. Nelson's valuable study places Crabbe within the context of evolving literary styles and demonstrates the manner in which his work relates to such seemingly diverse elements as Augustan satire, the 18th century novel, and the emerging narrative patterns of Romanticism.

New, Peter, *George Crabbe's Poetry.* New York: St. Martin's, 1976. In what may well be the most effective general critical study of Crabbe to appear thus far, New strikes an effective balance between the examination of broad literary/historical influences on Crabbe's canon as a whole and the close explication of individual poems.

Other Sources

Bareham, T. and S. Gatrell, *A Bibliography of George Crabbe.* Hamden, CT: Archon Books, 1978. A relatively complete listing, with brief descriptions, of primary and secondary materials pertaining to Crabbe.

McGann, Jerome J. "The Anachronism of George Crabbe," in *ELH,* 48 (Fall 1981), 555–572. An examination of the Romantics' critical hostility towards Crabbe.

Pollard, Arthur, ed. *Crabbe: The Critical Heritage.* London: Routledge & Kegan Paul, 1972. Useful collection of contemporary reviews and other criticisms of Crabbe.

Sale, A. "The Development of Crabbe's Narrative Art," in *The Cambridge Journal,* 5 (May 1952), 480–498. Seminal article on the evolution of Crabbe's narrative techniques.

Sigworth, Oliver F. *Nature's Sternest Poet.* Tucson: University of Arizona Press, 1965. Five essays on Crabbe's work, ranging from broad literary/historical contexts to examinations of theme and technique.

Selected Dictionaries and Encyclopedias

British Writers, Vol. III, Charles Scribner's Sons, 1980. Brief biography and overview of literary accomplishments; selective bibliography.

Critical Survey of Poetry, Vol. 2, Salem Press, 1982. Brief biography and descriptive analysis of major works.

Richard E. Meyer
Western Oregon State College

HART CRANE
1899–1932

Author's Chronology

Born July 21, 1899, Garrettsville, Ohio to Clarence and Grace Hart Crane; *1908* father founds Crane Company, a candy chain, in Cleveland; *1916* first poem published, moves to New York after parents divorce; *1918* associate editor of *The Pagan,* reporter for *Cleveland Plain Dealer; 1919* works for father's company and for *The Little Review; 1920–1923* works in advertising in Cleveland; *1923* returns to New York, publishes "For the Marriage of Helen and Faustus;" *1924* begins "Voyages;" *1925–1926* works on *The Bridge,* publishes *White Buildings; 1928–1929* travels in Europe; *1930* publishes *The Bridge; 1931* resides in Mexico; *1932* dies by jumping from ship returning to New York from Mexico (April 27); *1933 Collected Poems* published.

Author's Bibliography

White Buildings, 1926 (poems); *The Bridge,* 1930 (poetic sequence); *The Collected Poems of Hart Crane,* 1933; *The Letters of Hart Crane 1916–1932,* 1952; *The Complete Poems and Selected Letters and Prose of Hart Crane,* 1966.

Overview of Biographical Sources

Until recently, Crane's short, tragic life was viewed as an allegory of the creative artist in America. Misunderstood and too frail of spirit to fully exploit his gifts and reach his goals, the thwarted, undernourished genius was led to take his own life. By paying so much attention to Crane's personal frustrations and making him a case in point for gloomy romantic notions about America's inhospitable treatment of artists, biographers and critics have had to see failure in Crane's accomplishments, albeit magnificent failure. More objective approaches have allowed Crane some degree of personal satisfaction and much in the way of original and fully realized artistic success. The three biographies by Horton, Weber, and Unterecker can be approached as points along this continuum, though Weber's is the one most attentive to Crane's career as a poet.

Students of Crane will want to make independent assessments of the man revealed in *The Letters of Hart Crane 1916–1932,* edited by Brom Weber (Berkeley: University of California Press, 1965). Crane's relationships with members of his family, his confidences to close friends, and his active literary correspondence reveal a colorful, alert, moody, and esthetically principled young man. *Robber Rocks: Letters and Memories of Hart Crane,* edited by Susan Jenkins Brown (Middletown, CT: Wesleyan University Press, 1969) is a collage of letters and impressions that conveys some sense of Crane's literary milieu. Other specialized collections include Thomas Parkinson's *Hart Crane and Yvor Winters: Their Literary Correspondence* (Berkeley: University of California Press, 1978) and *Letters of Hart Crane and His Family,* edited by Thomas S. W. Lewis (New York: Columbia University Press, 1974).

Evaluation of Selected Biographies

Horton, Philip, *Hart Crane: The Life of an American Poet.* New York: W. W. Norton, 1937. Based to a great extent on interviews with the poet's mother, this treatment over-emphasizes Crane's victimhood. As the title suggests, Crane's life becomes a paradigm of the artist oppressed by a materialistic society and (in this case) an unsympathetic father. Easily the most readable of the full-length biographies, Horton's is also the most imaginative. Extrapolating from minimal and biased sources, Horton has fleshed out the myth of the suffering romantic hero and perpetuated that myth in a compelling fashion.

Unterecker, John, *Voyager: A Life of Hart Crane.* New York: Farrar, Straus, and Giroux, 1969. *Voyager* lacks a clear guiding principle, a vision of Crane strong enough to shape the voluminous materials that Unterecker has gathered. This is by far the most comprehensive biography; factual thoroughness and reliability make it indispensable. Still, a meaningful, coherent portrait of Crane does not emerge. Perhaps no such portrait is possible.

Weber, Brom, *Hart Crane: A Biographical and Critical Study.* New York: The Bodley Press, 1948; rpt. New York: Russell and Russell, 1970. This book has more of a critical emphasis than those by Horton and Unterecker. Crane's friendships and his reading are presented in detail in order to trace the intellectual and esthetic development of the poet. Weber gives the best picture of the emerging artistic personality and of the poet at work. Elaborate appendices offer previously uncollected Crane material. Weber devotes 130 pages to the making of *The Bridge* and to a careful analysis of it.

Overview of Autobiographical Sources

Beyond the revelations in Crane's correspondence (discussed above), readers can find examples of his critical thinking in part four of *The Complete Poems and Selected Letters and Prose of Hart Crane,* edited by Brom Weber (New York: Liveright, 1966). A number of reviews are collected, as well as such credo pieces as "General Aims and Theories" and "Modern Poetry."

Overview of Critical Sources

From the beginning, Crane's work has provoked a range of agitated and enthusiastic responses. Because he was on the cutting edge of American modernism, and because the corpus of his work is manageably small, Crane has been the subject of countless notes, articles, chapters in books, and full-length studies. Few writers have had so much comment on such a small body of work. Among Crane's contemporaries, critics like Yvor Winters, Allen Tate, and Malcolm Cowley had important and controversial things to say. The basic tendency of the criticism is to elevate Crane from the status of intriguing, ambitious, talented, but psychologically crippled minor poet to that of a controlled, purposeful craftsman who carved out a fresh idiom and experimented boldly with both old and new forms to leave a small body of major poetry. Early critics praised Crane's lyrics at the expense of *The Bridge;* Lawrence S. Dembo anchored the group of critics who brought the long poem to great acclaim in the 1950's; most recently, critics have felt *The Bridge* unduly praised at the expense of the lyrics.

Evaluation of Selected Criticism

Butterfield, R. W. *The Broken Arc: A Study of Hart Crane.* Edinburgh: Oliver and Boyd, 1969. Butterfield argues that the terms of Crane's personal and artistic disintegration are linked in ways that make him a "crucial figure in American cultural and intellectual history." Emphasis falls on Crane's enormous daring and its inherent risks. Butterfield provides an appendix on work by Samuel Greenberg that Crane drew upon.

Clark, David R. *Critical Essays on Hart Crane.* Boston: G. K. Hall, 1982. Clark represents the most important critical documents in Crane's shifting reputation. His introduction is a precise, dependable guide through Crane studies: "bibliographies, editions, biographies, concordances, and criticism." Anyone needing more than the present survey should turn to Clark.

Dembo, Lawrence S. *Hart Crane's Sanskrit Charge: A Study of "The Bridge."* Ithaca, NY: Cornell University Press, 1960. This is the major critical document in the shift of fortunes for Crane's long poem. Avoiding biographical traps, Dembo locates and persuasively argues for the sources and terms of the poem's unity and success.

Leibowitz, Herbert A. *Hart Crane: An Introduction to the Poetry.* New York: Columbia University Press, 1968. This unique approach emphasizes Crane's craft rather than individual works. Leibowitz considers diction, imagery, syntax, verse forms, and metrics after giving extended treatments of "Faustus and Helen" and "Voyages." Crane's fusion of romantic and modernist practices is stressed. Leibowitz provides an instructive alternative to the work-by-work approach.

Lewis, R. W. B. *The Poetry of Hart Crane: A Critical Study.* Princeton: Princeton University Press, 1967. This comprehensive look at Crane's career provides clear, compelling readings of most of Crane's poems. Concerned with Crane's growth as a poet, Lewis determines various phases of Crane's development and marks out certain poems as touchstones of the poet's sensibility and mastery. Lewis provides a rich sense of Crane's cultural environment in this very readable, sympathetic study.

Nilsen, Helge Normann, *Hart Crane's Divided Vision: An Analysis of "The Bridge."* Oslo: Universitetsforlaget, 1980. Nilsen's close readings of the poem's nine sections are prefaced by a careful summary of earlier criticism and by a fine discussion of the influence of Walt Whitman and Waldo Frank. Nilsen argues for a redefinition of myth relevant to Crane's intentions. Of particular note are Nilsen's fruitful excursions into American Indian lore.

Paul, Sherman, *Hart's Bridge.* Urbana: University of Illinois Press, 1973. An inventive and sometimes dazzling study, Paul's complex meditation attempts, with intermittent success, to enter the world and mind of the poet as the poems reflect, express, and transform that world. Paul calls himself a qualified phenomenological critic.

Sugg, Richard P. *Hart Crane's "The Bridge": A Description of Its Life.* University: The University of Alabama Press, 1976. Sugg argues that Crane's long sequence "is about the poetic act rather than the action of the poet as a person in the world, about the life of the imagination trying to realize its 'dream of act' by giving form, and thereby meaning, to itself." Sugg's readings are often highly individualistic. Early chapters treat Crane's modernist esthetics, structure, and style.

Other Sources

Hart Crane Newsletter, which published four issues, has been continued and broadened as *The Visionary Company: A Magazine of the Twenties.* Published at Mercy College, Dobbs Ferry, New York.

Schwartz, Joseph, *Hart Crane: A Reference Guide.* Boston: G. K. Hall, 1983. The authoritative guide to Crane criticism.

Schwartz, Joseph and Robert C. Schweik, *Hart Crane: A Descriptive Bibliography.* Pittsburgh: University of Pittsburgh Press, 1972. All of Crane's own publications are listed here.

Selected Dictionaries and Encyclopedias

Critical Survey of Poetry, Salem Press, 1982. Brief biography, assessment of achievement, and analyses of representative poems.

Philip K. Jason
United States Naval Academy

STEPHEN CRANE
1871–1900

Author's Chronology

Born November 1, 1871, Newark, New Jersey, 14th child of the Reverend Jonathan Townley and Mary Helen Peck Crane; *1878* family moves to Port Jervis, New York; *1880* death of Reverend Crane; *1883* Mrs. Crane moves family to Asbury Park, New Jersey, where Stephen earns good grades in public school; *1885* Crane pens his first story, "Uncle Jake and the Bell-Handle," unpublished during his lifetime; enrolls at Pennington Seminary, Pennington, New Jersey; *1887* leaves Pennington; *1888* transfers to Hudson River Institute, Claverack, New York; *1890* leaves Claverack, enrolls at Lafayette College, Easton, Pennsylvania; leaves at end of year; *1891* transfers to Syracuse University, and writes pieces for New York *Tribune;* leaves college finally at end of year; *1891–1894* lives in New York and vicinity, freelancing; *1893* first novel, *Maggie: A Girl of the Streets* published privately (under the pseudonym Johnston Smith); *1894 The Red Badge of Courage,* Crane's most famous novel, published in serial form for Bacheller syndicate; *1895* under contract for Bacheller, travels to the West and Mexico, and returns to Port Jervis to write; *Red Badge of Courage* becomes best seller; *1896* novel, *George's Mother,* published in London; Crane appears as character witness for chorus girl Dora Clark, and is declared *persona non grata* by New York Police, then leaves for Florida to cover Cuban insurrection; meets Cora Steward (Cora Taylor) in Florida; *1897* survives shipwreck of the *Commodore,* permanently impairing his health; this experience becomes basis for story "The Open Boat"; travels to Greece to cover Greco-Turkish war, and is joined there by Cora, herself a correspondent; couple returns to live together in England; *1898* covers Spanish-American war on Cuban front, later Puerto Rican front; *1899* returns to England, where the Cranes move into Brede Place, unrestored mansion; several further publications; *1900* dies June 5 at sanitarium in Badenweiler, Germany. Cora brings the body home for burial in Hillside, New Jersey.

Author's Bibliography (selected)

Maggie: A Girl of the Streets, 1893 (novel; first edition privately printed) 1896 revised edition; *The Black Riders,* 1895 (poems); *The Red Badge of Courage,* 1895 (novel); *George's Mother,* 1896 (novel); *The Little Regiment,* 1896 (short stories); *The Third Violet,* 1897 (novel); *The Open Boat,* 1898 (short stories); *War is Kind,* 1899 (poems); *Active Service,* 1899 (novel); *The Monster,* 1899 (short stories), 1901 enlarged edition; *Whilomville Stories,* 1900 (short stories); *Wounds in the Rain,* 1901 (reportage); *Great Battles of the World,* 1901 (history); *The O'Ruddy,* by Crane and Robert Barr, 1904 (novel).

Overview of Biographical Sources

The definitive biography of Stephen Crane has yet to be written. For a modern author who has just been celebrated in a centenary (1971), Crane's life remains enigmatic. The problems of lost or widely dispersed materials, as well as Crane's own enigmatic personality have persisted through the years. At some future date, perhaps enough of the lost materials and different collections can be synthesized into some definitive statement, but the future will tell. To date, three different valuable works lead the slender field of Crane biography: R. W. Stallman's *Stephen Crane: A Biography* (1968), John Berryman's *Stephen Crane* (1950), and Thomas Beer's *Stephen Crane: A Study in American Letters* (1923). Beer's work remains an important and quite entertaining first source. Berryman's work is largely indebted to Beer for dates and a number of letters, though he includes a Freudian analysis of Crane's life and perceptive readings of some of the major corpus. Stallman's work is elaborately documented and indexed, and it is the closest to definitive. All three biographers, interestingly, make references to private sources they cannot disclose. Future letters and memorabilia coming to light should bring further possibilities for a definitive biography.

Evaluation of Selected Biographies

Beer, Thomas, *Stephen Crane: A Study in American Letters.* New York: Alfred A. Knopf, 1923; rpt. New York: Farrar, Straus & Giroux, 1972. Drawing on some first-hand interviews and materials, some now irreplaceable, Beer writes a very impressionistic, more literary than scholarly biography. Beer's work is a primary biographical source, informed by interviews from Crane's contemporaries (including Joseph Conrad, who writes the introduction). Many of Beer's dates and quotes have been shown to be inaccurate, but at its best his book conveys a set of insightful feelings, impressions about Crane and his era. Without documentation or scholarly apparatus, *Stephen Crane: A Study in American Letters* is a set of vignettes and highlights from its subject's life. Beer emphasizes Crane's cynical, ironic and brash public personality; many of his stories have been retold in subsequent biography and criticism.

Berryman, John, *Stephen Crane.* New York: William Sloane Associates, 1950. Berryman's biography is more elaborate than Beer's though largely based on Beer's facts. Berryman writes the best literary biography of Crane to date, offering perceptive readings of some of Crane's major works. Berryman, as would many a Crane critic subsequently, sees Crane as a primitive impressionist, not primarily a Naturalist writer such as Frank Norris. In his final chapter, Berryman offers a classic Freudian analysis of the main patterns of Crane's life—an interpretation that has proven quite controversial. Crane's life is traced back to a mother-complex and this complex is seen to account for his interest in prostitutes or other women in a discredited social position. Berryman's poetic and insightful imagination makes this biography of Crane an important source to consult.

Stallman, R. W. *Stephen Crane: A Biography.* New York: George Braziller, 1968. Voluminous and scholarly, Stallman's work is the closest to definitive of Crane's biographies to date, but has not been received as the final word. Large numbers of unacknowledged sources and inaccuracies in the record have been cited as problems with Stallman's text. Stallman's book, still and all, is solid and thorough, and though it does not offer the first-hand quality of Beer's biography nor the imaginative flights of Berryman's study, the treatment offered is useful, readable, and above all, detailed.

Autobiographical Sources

Many letters and papers have been lost, or repose in widely scattered collections, or are in private hands, a situation which presumably could be rectified in the future with increased public access and diligent scholarly research. The two Crane correspondence editions perhaps to be consulted first are R. W. Stallman and Lillian Gilkes, editors, *Stephen Crane: Letters* (New York: New York University Press, 1960) and Edwin H. Cady and Lester G. Wells, *Stephen Crane's Love Letters to Nellie Crouse* (Syracuse: Syracuse University Press, 1954). Crane's letters are often delightful, though his secretive personality has provided the most formidable problem for students of Crane's psyche. A number of Crane letters also were published in the helpful *Stephen Crane Newsletter,* edited by Joseph Katz (University of South Carolina, 1966–1970). Some of the most recent Crane scholarship has been concerned with verification and recovery of primary materials such as these valuable letters.

Overview of Critical Sources

A perennial favorite with readers of American and world literature, Crane has an assured place in literary history, though Crane criticism has seen fluctuations of interest. After a flurry in the 1920's, the criticism and scholarship on Crane's works began in earnest in the 1950's and 1960's, spurred on by Berryman's influential biography. Works by major Crane scholars like Cady, Stallman, Pizer, Katz, Fryckstedt, Gullason and others broadened and deepened the body of scholarly publication.

Crane's relationship to the literary movements of his day, notably Realism and Naturalism, was the first set of questions exclusive of biographical or textual matters which critics addressed. His influence on the development of modern literature, especially on the styles of writers like Fitzgerald or Hemingway, also received a good deal of treatment. As a writer of perhaps the finest war novel in American history, and as a famous war correspondent, Crane's relationship to war and war reporting also has concerned a number of critics. By now, Crane has been approached from a great number of angles, and analyzed in relationship to many modern and nineteenth-century trends.

Evaluation of Selected Criticism

Hoffman, Daniel, *The Poetry of Stephen Crane.* New York: Columbia University Press, 1957. The first book-length treatment of Crane's poetry, Hoffman's analysis of the poems traces backgrounds and provides interesting insights on a number of the favorites from the Crane canon.

Holton, Milne, *Cylinder of Vision: The Fiction and Journalistic Writing of Stephen Crane.* Baton Rouge: Lousiana State University Press, 1972. In a subtle study of Crane's literary technique, Holton moves through the corpus of Crane's prose to show how the author balanced impressionism, with its subjective view of reality, and naturalism, with its emphasis on objective reality and in fact the power of the environment. He sees Crane as an early, nihilistic modern author.

Solomon, Eric, *Stephen Crane: From Parody to Realism.* Cambridge: Harvard University Press, 1966. The first book-length treatment of Crane's prose, Solomon's study approaches Crane as a parodist and satirist, showing how the sentimental conventions of nineteenth-century popular writing are deflated by Crane's art. At its best, Solomon shows, Crane's writing manages to be both realistic and parodic at once.

Other Sources

Gilkes, Lillian, *Cora Crane: A Biography of Mrs. Stephen Crane.* Bloomington: Indiana University Press, 1960. A well-written biography of Cora Crane.

Linson, Corwin K. *My Stephen Crane.* edited by Edwin H. Cady. Linson's well-written memories of his friend Stephen Crane.

Stallman, R. W. *Stephen Crane: A Critical Bibliography.* Ames: Iowa State University Press, 1972. An invaluable bibliography, thorough and exemplary. The bibliography to consult first.

The Works of Stephen Crane, 10 volumes. edited by F. Bowers. Charlottesville: University Press of Virginia, 1969–1976. Despite some major scholarly controversy, the definitive edition of Crane's works. Ample and helpful commentary on the texts and their analysis.

Ray Miller, Jr.
University of Delaware

RICHARD CRASHAW
c. 1612–1649

Author's Chronology

Born c. 1612, London, England; mother dies during his infancy; father, William Crashaw, is Anglican divine and major Low Church, anti-Roman Catholic preacher whose writings and sermons are in sharp contrast to the eventual Roman Catholicism of the son; attends Charterhouse School two years; *1631* enters Pembroke College, Cambridge; BA *1634;* MA *1638; 1634* publishes *Epigrammatum Sacrorum Liber* (only work he personally sees through printing); *1635* appointed to fellowship, Peterhouse College; shortly thereafter ordained to Anglican priesthood; *1635–1643* moves in Laudian circles and becomes involved in liturgical reform; learns Spanish and Italian, reads Italian mystics including Teresa of Avila and John of the Cross, makes acquaintance with Nicholas Ferrar and the Little Gidding movement; *1640* censured for "popish doctrines;" early in Civil Wars expelled from fellowship and flees to Continent; *1643–1649* travels on Continent, converts to Roman Catholicism; works on *Steps to the Temple* and *Carmen Deo Nostro;* visits Rome and Paris; c. late *1648* appointed to staff of a Roman Cardinal and sent to Loreto; dies at Marian shrine there August 21, 1649.

Author's Bibliography

Epigrammatum Sacrorum Liber, 1634 (poems); *Steps to the Temple,* 1646, 1648 (poems); *Carmen Deo Nostro,* 1652 (poems).

Overview of Biographical Sources

Except for the brief materials noted above, little is known of Crashaw's life and virtually nothing of the years in which students of the poetry are most interested, the period of Crashaw's travels on the Continent and conversion to Roman Catholicism. Much more is known about his father, William Crashaw, and this information is helpful for the light it sheds upon the son's development. The main biographical material is contained in several books which, after early sections on the poet, go on to treat of the poetry; these works, which will be cited in this section, are also helpful for anyone wishing to study the poetry in more depth. The closest thing to a definitive biography is L. C. Martin's *The Poems, English, Latin, and Greek, of Richard Crashaw* (Oxford: Clarendon, 1927, 1957). Crashaw's lack of appeal for the restoration and eighteenth-century reader probably accounts for the fact that there is little in the way of early biographical material; not until the twentieth century did some major writings appear.

Evaluation of Selected Biographies

Parrish, Paul A. *Richard Crashaw.* Twayne, 1980. This is an excellent introduction to the life of the poet, beginning with a good section on the historical backgrounds and treating Crashaw's early and college years with references to all of the extant material, and continuing with a very readable explanation of the Little Gidding movement which so influenced Crashaw will help any reader. The section on Crashaw's later life stays close to the known materials. A chapter entitled "Backgrounds: The Life and the Art" is indispensable for anyone discovering this poet for the first time.

Wallerstein, Ruth C. *Richard Crashaw: A Study in Style and Poetic Development.* Madison: University of Wisconsin Press, 1935. This is one of the first major early works on the poet and an invaluable source for both biography and poetry. Chapter II, "Crashaw's Life and Inner Growth," explores the spiritual development of the poet with sensitive insight.

Warren, Austin, *Richard Crashaw: A Study in Baroque Sensibility.* Ann Arbor: University of Michigan, 1939. Warren's is another classic not to be missed, once again for treatment of poetry as well as poet. Chapters I and II, "The Laudian Movement and the Counter-Reformation" and "The Man," contain rich biographical material. Warren, who is responsible for the association of the term "Baroque" with Crashaw, argues the thesis that Crashaw exemplified baroque movement in art, poetry and spirituality.

White, Helen C. *The Metaphysical Poets.* New York: Macmillan, 1936. This is the last of three major books published in the 1930's which remain touchstones for criticism of the poet. Interested in treating the major poets in relation to one another, White nicely emphasizes the differences in Crashaw's background and spirituality. Excellent treatment of the movement at Little Gidding.

Autobiographical Sources

Quite literally the only autobiographical material about Richard Crashaw, aside from a few references in the early poems, is contained in the single piece of English prose written in his hand, usually termed "The Letter Written at Leyden," which is reprinted in full in L. C. Martin's *The Poems, English, Latin, and Greek, of Richard Crashaw* (Oxford: Clarendon, 1927, 1957). The original is at University Library, Cambridge. Writing possibly to John Ferrar (brother to Nicholas of Little Gidding) or to the father of Mary Collet (she is termed the "mother" of the community at Leyden, where Crashaw was apparently in residence), the poet makes some proposals about regaining his lost fellowship in order to restore needed income. More important for the biographer, the letter shows Crashaw attempting to reassure his reader and friends about the anxiety which he attributes to them. It seems likely that the poet is referring to his pending or already accomplished move toward Roman Catholicism; since the letter is dated February 20, 1643, scholars are able to trace Crashaw's spiritual development with more certainty.

Overview of Critical Sources

Critical studies of Crashaw tend to take one of several perspectives: some study him as part of the metaphysical school of Donne and Marvell; some treat him as a baroque poet, following Warren's lead; some explore his spiritual growth and the religious imagery in his poetry. Martin's 1927 edition of the poems inspired a rush of Crashaw criticism in the 1930's, of which major examples have been cited above. Criticism after 1940 was rather more sporadic, although the major works by Louis Martz (cited below) gave important new direction to Crashaw studies. The past fifteen years have seen a resurgence in criticism and indicate perhaps a new appreciation of this poet. There is as yet no single study of Crashaw which integrates the spiritual, artistic, and poetic approaches to his work.

Evaluation of Selected Criticism

Bertonasco, Marc F. *Crashaw and the Baroque.* Tuscaloosa: University of Alabama Press, 1971. Bertonasco attempts to re-focus attention on Crashaw's artistry after a period of some neglect with a full treatment of the context out of which Crashaw writes. Chapters on "Crashaw and the Emblem" and "The Influence of St. Francis de Sales" prepare for a full-scale treatment of "The Weeper," considered by some to be Crashaw's best poem. An appendix surveys Crashaw scholarship in the twentieth century.

Low, Anthony, *Love's Architecture: Devotional Modes in Seventeenth-Century English Poetry.* New York: New York University Press, 1978. After a survey of the several devotional modes employed by seventeenth-century poets (among them vocal, meditative, affective, and contemplative prayer), Low moves, in Chapter 5, to study Crashaw as an example of "sensible affection." Less inclined to focus on Crashaw's baroque attributes and more attuned to the devotional styles of the day, Low gives special treatment to "The Weeper" and the St. Teresa poems.

Martz, Louis, *The Wit of Love: Donne, Carew, Crashaw, Marvell.* Notre Dame, IN: University of Notre Dame Press, 1969. In his classic *Poetry of Meditation* (New Haven: Yale University Press, 1954) Martz explored the meditative structure of much seventeenth-century religious poetry. In this work he continues his sensitive readings, here giving attention to the love, sacred and secular, which informs the works by the poets named in the title. "Love's Architecture," the Crashaw chapter, treats the baroque traits of the poet and proposes the Gerhard Seghers painting of St. Teresa as a possible inspiration for "The Flaming Heart" (rather than, as many have suggested, the Bernini sculpture).

Williams, George Walton, *Image and Symbol in the Sacred Poetry of Richard Crashaw.* Columbia: University of South Carolina Press, 1963. This is a full and highly readable exploration of the principal images and themes in Crashaw's poetry with complete citations of the passages under discussion. Williams categorizes the images in groups such as white and red, light and dark, liquidity, animals, and fire. A helpful index provides references to any mention of each poem.

Selected Dictionaries and Encyclopedias

Critical Survey of Poetry, Salem Press, 1982; Vol. II. Brief biography and short analysis of some of Crashaw's most important poems.

Moulton's Library of Literary Criticism, Frederick Ungar, 1966; Volume I, pp. 407–411. Brief selections from eighteenth and nineteenth-century criticism.

Katherine Hanley, CSJ
The College of Saint Rose

COUNTÉE CULLEN
1903–1946

Author's Chronology

Born Countée Porter May 30, 1903, New York City; early childhood shrouded in mystery, difficult to pin down exact dates of Cullen's life until age 15; reared by maternal grandmother until the age of eleven; *1918* adopted by the Rev. and Mrs. Frederick A. Cullen, pastor of the influential Salem Methodist Episcopal Church in Harlem; educated at De Witt Clinton High School, recipient of many honors including the editorship of the *Clinton News,* the school's weekly paper, chairman of the senior publications committee, and editor of the Senior edition of *The Magpie,* the school's literary magazine, which publishes in January 1921 issue, "I Have a Rendezvous with Life," and brings Cullen wide acclaim; *1922* enters New York University; *1923–1924* twice won second prize in the Witter Bynner undergraduate poetry contest; works as bus boy at the Traymore Hotel in Atlantic City during the summers, a short distance from the Cullen's summer place in Pleasantville, N.J.; *1925* wins first prize in the Witter Bynner poetry contest; wins the John Reed Memorial Prize; wins second prize in the *Opportunity* Literary Contest; publishes *Color,* his first and perhaps most important collection of verse; elected to Phi Beta Kappa; graduates with his B.A. from NYU; *1926* earns his M.A. from Harvard; serves as assistant editor of *Opportunity, a Journal of Negro Life* (under Charles S. Johnson); tours Europe and the Holy Land; *1927* first recipient of the Harmon Foundation Literary Award; publishes *Copper Sun,* second major collection of poems; *1928* awarded Guggenheim Fellowship; marries Nina Yolande Du Bois, daughter of the distinguished W. E. B. Du Bois; sails for Paris to work on Guggenheim project; *1930* divorces Yolande in Paris, returns to America; *1932* to the surprise of many, Cullen, a Republican, joins the Foster and Ford Committee, a group of prominent writers pledged to support the Communist ticket; *1934–1946* teaches French and English at Frederick Douglass Junior High School in Harlem; *1940* marries Ida Mae Roberson; resides in Tuckahoe, New York; dies January 9, 1946 in New York City.

Author's Bibliography

Color, 1925 (poems); *Copper Sun,* 1927 (poems); *Caroling Dusk,* 1927 (anthology); *The Ballad of the Brown Girl: An Old Ballad Retold,* 1927 (poem); *The Black Christ and Other Poems,* 1929; *One Way to Heaven,* 1932 (novel); *The Medea and Some Poems,* 1935; *The Lost Zoo* (*A Rhyme for the Young, But Not Too Young*), 1940 (poems for children); *On These I Stand: An Anthology of the Best Poems of Countée Cullen,* 1947 (posthumously published selections made by the poet).

Overview of Biographical Sources

As a result of the historical moment in which he lived, the Harlem Renaissance (1915–1935), Cullen exemplified Du Bois' Talented Tenth philosophy of promoting racial uplift through culture, achievement, and example. His life was a struggle to emancipate himself from the label "Negro poet" and follow in the footsteps of his poetic forefather, John Keats (1795–1821). Never able to resolve this tension of being both an American and a Black man, Cullen's life is a study in paradox. Though preeminently a lyric poet and a Romantic in thematic content, Cullen is best remembered for those poems that treat black themes.

There is no "definitive" biography on the life of Cullen. Blanche E. Ferguson's *Countée Cullen and the Negro Renaissance* (1966), the first and only full-length biography, makes no pretense of being a scholarly study. Sophomoric in approach, it lifts its artistic voice and sings the praises of Cullen. He emerges not as a distinct individual but rather as the exemplary role model. Three shorter treatments of his life are to be found in Margaret Perry's *A Bio-Bibliography of Countée P. Cullen, 1903–1946* (Westport, CT: Greenwood Publishing, 1971); Jean Wagner's (trans. Kenneth Douglass) *Black Poets of the United States: From Paul Laurence Dunbar to Langston Hughes* (Urbana: University of Illinois Press, 1973); and Arthur P. Davis, *From the Dark Tower: Afro-American Writers, 1900–1960* (Washington: Howard University Press, 1974). Perry's is a pamphlet-length study of Cullen's life, description of his poetic interests and influences, and a narrative concerning contemporary reviews of Cullen's work. Wagner, a Frenchman, combines selected biographical material with criticism. It is the most provocative interpretation of Cullen's life. Many details about Cullen's mysterious childhood emerge in this uncompromising analysis. Davis presents a very readable, and perhaps the best, bio-critical introduction for the student new to Cullen.

Evaluation of Selected Biographies

Ferguson, Blanche E. *Countée Cullen.* New York: Dodd, Mead & Co., 1966. Ferguson presents a general biographical introduction to Cullen's life with very little critical comment. It does not discuss any material in great detail and focuses on his achievements rather than on his struggle to be "known as a poet, not as a Negro poet." It suggests that Cullen used his creativity to resolve his internal conflicts, yet it raises few critical questions about the sudden demise of his early promise. Ferguson relies on fictionalized passages which are not supported by the historical record in her reconstruction of Cullen's life. Though Cullen's life is treated sympathetically, some of the information is inaccurate.

Autobiographical Sources

The little autobiographical materials that Cullen left for posterity is in the form of a few interviews and letters. Several of his Harlem Renaissance contemporaries have left their impression of him.

Overview of Critical Sources

Although Cullen is a widely read, popular poet, enjoyed for his mastery of poetic forms and for being inherently a romantic at heart, there is still no single book-length critical study that gives a detailed and systematic treatment of the entire *oeuvre.*

Evaluation of Selected Criticism

Baker, Houston A., Jr. *A Many-Colored Coat of Dreams: The Poetry of Countée Cullen.* Detroit: Broadside Press, 1974. In this biocritical pamphlet length study of Cullen, Baker chides critics for their parochialism in evaluating Cullen's poetry for its lack of fidelity to black aesthetics rather than judging it on its merits.

Bronz, Stephen H. *Roots of Negro Racial Consciousness The 1920's: Three Harlem Renaissance Authors.* New York: Libra Publishers, 1964. Overall this is not a sympathetic treatment of Cullen. Bronz makes the point that Cullen approached race theoretically rather than racially; his poetry is characterized by indirectness rather than fire and passion.

Turner, Darwin T. *In a Minor Chord: Three Afro-American Writers and Their Search for Identity.* Carbondale: Southern Illinois University Press, 1971. Turner sees Cullen as one who wore blackness like a mask. He breaks no new ground on Cullen scholarship.

Wagner, Jean, *Black Poets of the United States: From Paul Laurence Dunbar to Langston Hughes.* Urbana: University of Illinois Press, 1973. Wagner's is the most controversial and comprehensive documented study of Cullen as poet yet published. Wagner sees Cullen as a tortured and unstable person, and he traces this to Cullen's childhood. Cullen's sense of abandonment, inferiority, conflicts about his sexuality, tension between his racial and religious self, and his fascination with death are treated in detail in Wagner's often brilliant analysis. These pressures, Wagner contends, cause Cullen to retreat into himself; therefore, he never intellectually develops beyond his early promise.

Other Sources

Canaday, Nicholas, Jr. "Major Themes in the Poetry of Countée Cullen," in *The Harlem Renaissance Remembered,* ed. Arna Bontemps. New York: Dodd, Mead & Co., 1972, pp. 103–125. Canady believes that most of Cullen's themes are found in his greatest poem, "Heritage."

Davis, Arthur P. "The Alien-and-Exile Theme in Countée Cullen's Racial Poems," in *Phylon,* 14, No. 4 (Fourth Quarter 1953), 390–400. Examining only the poems dealing with race, Davis believes that Cullen felt that blacks are both in a state of geographical and spiritual exile.

Huggins, Nathan Irvin, *Harlem Renaissance.* Oxford University Press, 1971. This cultural historian places Cullen within the context of the social ambience of the 1920's. Huggins' analysis of Cullen's poetry is weak.

Lewis, David Levering, *When Harlem Was in Vogue.* New York: Vintage Books, 1982. Lewis, a social historian, unravels Cullen's mysterious childhood but his documentation is weak.

Perry, Margaret, *The Harlem Renaissance: An Annotated Bibliography.* New York: Garland Publishing, 1982. Perry has updated her previous bibliography on Cullen.

Singh, Amritjit, *The Novels of The Harlem Renaissance: Twelve Black Writers, 1923-1933.* University Park: Pennsylvania State University Press, 1976. Singh analyzes Cullen's only novel, *One Way to Heaven,* a romantic social comedy about lower-class blacks and the upper bourgeoisie in New York City. Cullen gently satirizes the world of the black church.

Woodruff, Bertram L. "The Poetic Philosophy of Countée Cullen," in *Phylon,* 1, No. 3 (Third Quarter 1940), 213–223. Woodruff presents a detailed study of Cullen's romanticism.

Selected Dictionaries and Encyclopedias

Dictionary of American Biography, Supplement #4, Charles Scribner's Sons, 1974. Brief biography with useful bibliography.

Dictionary of American Negro Biography, Four, 1946–1950, W.W. Norton, 1982. Concise overview of Cullen's entire life, and a discussion of the principal works.

Dolan Hubbard
University of Illinois
at Urbana-Champaign

E. E. CUMMINGS
1894–1962

Author's Chronology

Born Edward Estlin Cummings, October 14, 1894, Cambridge, Massachusetts; *1911* enters Harvard; *1912* publishes first poems in *Harvard Monthly; 1915* graduates from Harvard *magna cum laude* and delivers Commencement Address entitled "The New Art;" *1916* receives M.A. from Harvard; *1917* sails for France and joins Norton Harjes Ambulance Corps, American Red Cross; September-December; *1917* imprisoned by French authorities on suspicion of disloyalty; *1918* released on New Year's Day from prison and returns to New York City; summer *1918* drafted into Army, Camp Devens, Massachusetts, until Armistice; *1920* publishes in the *Dial; 1921–1923* lives in Paris where he resides intermittently during the *1920's; 1923* returns to New York City and lives in Greenwich Village, his permanent home, and at Joy Farm, a summer place in Silver Lake, New Hampshire; *1924* marries Elaine Orr, divorces soon after; *1925* receives the Dial Award; *1925–1927* writes essays for *Vanity Fair* and other journals; *1927* marries Anne Barton, divorces later; *1931* travels to Russia; first major showing of paintings at the Painters and Sculptors Gallery, New York City; marries Marion Morehouse, famous model, actress, and photographer; *1933* awarded Guggenheim Fellowship; *1950* receives Fellowship of American Academy of Poets; *1951* receives Guggenheim Fellowship; *1952–1953* serves as Charles Eliot Norton Professor at Harvard; *1955* awarded special citation by National Arts Festival Award; September 2, 1962 dies in North Conway, New Hampshire.

Author's Bibliography (selected)

The Enormous Room, 1922 (autobiography); *Tulips and Chimneys,* 1923 (poems); *Him,* 1927 (play); *No Title,* 1930 (burlesque sketches and drawings); *Anthropos: the Future of Art,* 1933 (play); *Eimi,* 1933 (autobiography); *Tom,* 1935 (play); *Santa Claus,* 1946 (play); *i: Six Nonlectures,* 1953 (Charles Eliot Norton lectures); *Poems 1923–1954,* 1954; *95 poems,* 1958; *73 poems,* 1963; *Adventures in Value* (with Marion Morehouse), 1962 (Morehouse's photographs and cummings' commentaries); *Fairy Tales,* 1965; *Selected Letters of E. E. Cummings,* 1969; *Complete Poems: 1913–1962,* 1972.

Overview of Biographical Sources

Though only two important books are specifically biographical, many other critical works include information about cummings' life, sometimes interspersing the material in chapters about particular works, sometimes introducing the information in a chapter that precedes critical analyses of cummings' art. Rushworth M. Kidder's *E. E. Cummings: An Introduction to the Poetry* (New York:

Columbia University Press, 1979) is an example of the first approach, with its allusions to specific events in cummings' life, such as his marriage to and divorce from Elaine Orr, and its suggestion that knowledge of these events affects interpretation of cummings' poetry. Bethany Dumas' *E. E. Cummings: A Remembrance of Miracles* (New York: Barnes and Noble, 1974) reflects the latter approach, with its excellent introductory chapter entitled "Life and Times."

Evaluation of Selected Biographies

Kennedy, Richard S. *Dreams in the Mirror: A Biography of E. E. Cummings.* New York: Liveright, 1980. Kennedy's biography is considered definitive. It is a carefully researched work, using the cummings' materials at Houghton Library, at the Humanities Research Center of The University of Texas, and elsewhere. Detailing significant events of cummings' life, the biography also examines the literary works, with thoughtful attention to the development of cummings' style.

Norman, Charles. *E. E. Cummings: A Biography,* 2d ed. New York: E. P. Dutton, 1967. Norman's book is not particularly scholarly or critical, but it includes a wealth of facts, anecdotes, and details about cummings' life and works. It was written with cummings' approval and cooperation.

Autobiographical Sources

Cummings' autobiographies are frequently labeled something else. *The Enormous Room* is typically viewed as a war book, and *Eimi* is often examined as a prose experiment. Both books, however, are self-portraits, focusing on specific experiences in cummings' life.

The Enormous Room (1922) deals with cummings' imprisonment in La Ferté Macé during the First World War. During this three-month captivity in 1917, cummings met prisoners and captors whom he describes in poetic prose. He also explores the horrors of war, the limitations of bureaucracies, and the restrictions of educational and religious institutions. *Eimi* (1933) is, as cummings wrote in the 1934 edition, "a more complex individual, a more enormous room." This autobiography uses the framework of a diary to trace cummings' experiences during a visit to Russia in 1931. Less structured than the previous self-portrait, *Eimi* explores many of the same ideas, particularly the inhumanity and drabness of bureaucracies, this time as they appear in Russia.

i: six Nonlectures (1953), delivered during 1952–1953 when cummings was the Charles Eliot Norton Professor at Harvard, also contains autobiographical material. After telling his audience that he did not have "the remotest intention of posing as a lecturer," cummings discussed—and subsequently wrote down—ideas about his life and his commitment to love, beauty, and individuality.

Overview of Critical Sources

Criticism of e. e. cummings' work is frequently extremist—people tend to praise his art, elevating cummings to the position of major writer, or object to it, demoting him to the lowly status of "minor." This extremism is especially evident in a decade-by-decade examination of the critical work on cummings.

In the 1920's, critics cited cummings as either a significant modernist or a rigid antimodernist. A similar split occurred in the 1930's when cummings was either criticized for being anti-rational and anti-political—and thus a threat to anti-modernism and leftist criticism—or praised for that anti-intellectualism, a quality some saw as cummings' ability to respond to life in both social and artistic ways. The New Critics, spearheaded by R. P. Blackmur, embodied some of both positions, praising cummings' experimentation but concerned with his romantic vagueness.

In subsequent decades, particularly the 1940's and 1950's, the divided opinion focused on cummings' vision: deep, clear, anarchic vs. merely fresh, direct, and immediate. The New Critics could not find the kinds of irony, paradox, and ambivalence for which they were looking, while others found virtues in what they perceived as cummings' concepts of transcendence, mysticism and timelessness.

In the 1950's and 1960's critics continued to debate cummings' position in the annals of American literary history, the only difference being the increased seriousness with which they approached his work. Parts of books, bibliographies, and book-length studies were published for the first time, ushering in a new period of critical attention.

During the past two and a half decades, this serious and divided evaluation has continued. Debating his status as major or minor artist, critics have generally focused on his modernist style and traditional themes, concerning themselves primarily with his poetry, while also considering his drama, prose, visual art, as well as the relationship between his work and his life.

Evaluation of Selected Criticism

Baum, S. V. ed. *ΕΣΤΙ: eec: E. E. Cummings and the Critics.* East Lansing: Michigan State University Press, 1962. This collection reprints reviews and essays and includes an introductory essay and primary and secondary bibliographies. An "Index of General Names" is a useful way to find references in this volume to a diverse group of people ranging from Ralph Waldo Emerson to Nicolai Lenin.

Dumas, Bethany K. *E. E. Cummings: A Remembrance of Miracles.* New York: Barnes and Noble, 1974. This book includes chapters on cummings' life, early poems, later poems, prose, and drama. Dumas is helpful in understanding cummings' autobiographies, especially when she says that *Eimi* is a deciphering of what the author [cummings] has called 'on-the-spot-scribbled hieroglyphics.'

This gives the book, she notes, "a sense of immediacy that the earlier book lacks. That is its happiest virtue; it is also responsible for its difficulty."

Friedman, Norman, *e. e. cummings: the art of his poetry.* Baltimore: The Johns Hopkins Press, 1960. An overview of cummings' poetry through *95 Poems,* this book deals with cummings' major themes and techniques as well as his growth as a writer. A second edition of the book, published in 1967, includes a lengthy listing of critical responses to cummings published from 1922 to 1965.

———, ed. *E. E. Cummings: A Collection of Critical Essays.* Englewood Cliffs, NJ: Prentice-Hall, 1972. In addition to fourteen important essays by distinguished critics like R. P. Blackmur, Paul Rosenfeld, and Alfred Kazin, this volume includes an introductory piece by Friedman, a chronology of important dates in cummings' life, and a selected bibliography. A particular value of this book is its essays on virtually all of cummings' major works. Allen Tate and R. P. Blackmur examine *ViVa* and *50 Poems;* David E. Smith, Robert E. Maurer, Paul Rosenfeld, Alfred Kazin, and Robert Graves review the autobiographical works *The Enormous Room, Eimi,* and *i: Six Nonlectures;* and Barbara Watson and others look at cummings' attitudes and themes as they are reflected in the artist's canon as a whole.

Kidder, Rushworth M. *E. E. Cummings: An Introduction to the Poetry.* New York: Columbia University Press, 1979. A volume in the Columbia Introductions to Twentieth-Century Poetry series, this book provides careful analyses of numerous poems and supplemental information about sources and allusions.

Rotella, Guy, ed. *Critical Essays on E. E. Cummings.* Boston: G. K. Hall, 1984. This collection is divided into three sections: an introduction which surveys the critical work on cummings, reviews of cummings' work, and essays on cummings. Among the important essays in the collection is L. S. Dembo's "E. E. Cummings: The Now Man"—reprinted from Dembo's book *Conceptions of Reality in Modern American Poetry*—which examines the problem of perception and response in selected poems. Another significant article, reprinted from the *Georgia Review,* is Rushworth Kidder's "Twin Obsessions': The Poetry and Paintings of E. E. Cummings."

Other Sources

Firmage, George, *E. E. Cummings: A Bibliography.* Middletown, CT: Wesleyan University Press, 1969. The authoritative bibliographic study, this is a descriptive bibliography of primary works, including cummings' contributions to periodicals, translations of his writings, musical settings of poems, and recorded readings.

Kennedy, Richard S. ed. E. E. Cummings Special Number, *Journal of Modern Literature,* 7 (1979), 175–393. Among several significant essays in this issue is Norman Friedman's "Cummings Posthumous," a detailed study of cummings' works published since his death. This essay completes the survey Friedman began in *e. e. cummings: The Growth of a Writer* (Carbondale: Southern Illinois University Press, 1964). Rushworth M. Kidder's article, "Cummings and Cubism: The Influence of the Visual Arts on Cummings' Early Poetry," is another important study.

Lauter, Paul, *E. E. Cummings' Index to First Lines and Bibliography of Works By and About the Poet.* Denver: Alan Swallow, 1955. This is a primary and secondary bibliography.

Rotella, Guy, *E. E. Cummings: A Reference Guide.* Boston: G. K. Hall, 1979. This is the most complete and accurate list of criticism. It summarizes each important item clearly and concisely.

Triem, Eve, *E. E. Cummings.* University of Minnesota Pamphlet of American Writers, No. 87. Minneapolis: University of Minnesota Press, 1969. This is a brief but useful pamphlet.

Selected Dictionaries and Encyclopedias

Makers of Modern Culture, Facts on File, 1981. Concise biography, overview of cummings' work, and brief bibliography of primary and secondary materials.

The Oxford Companion to American Literature, fifth edition, Oxford University Press, 1965. Brief biography with concise analysis of major characteristics of cummings' work.

Marjorie Smelstor
The University of Texas at San Antonio

CYNEWULF
775–825(?)

Author's Chronology

Recent commentators place Cynewulf in the period 775–825 A.D., assuming, largely on the basis of linguistic evidence and historical context, that he was of Mercian or Northumbrian origin. Not only is there no further information about his identity (the most educated guess is that Cynewulf is the bishop of Lindisfarne who died 783), but scholars are also uncertain about the extent of his actual poetic corpus. The safest course, and one ratified by the latest research, is to attribute to Cynewulf only those poems which bear his famous signature in runes, the ancient Germanic alphabet used for secret encoding and divining throughout the Anglo-Saxon period. Cynewulf stands at a crossroads in the evolution of Old English poetry: while he was almost surely a literate and educated ecclesiastic, he also had inherited the native Germanic oral tradition, which he would convert to his own special hagiographic purposes. Like the earlier Caedmon, himself probably an illiterate singer who was the first to use the traditional Germanic idiom to tell Christian stories, Cynewulf straddled two worlds—that of oral tradition and that of Christian Latin learning—and spoke in a new poetic voice that drew from the best of each.

Author's Bibliography

Signed Poems: "Elene," "Juliana," "Christ II" or "The Ascension," "The Fates of the Apostles." Unsigned Poems (so-called Cynewulf Group): "Andreas," "The Dream of the Rood," "Christ I" or the "Advent Lyrics," "Guthlac A" and "B," "The Phoenix," the "Riddles," "Christ III" or "Doomsday." Translations: R. K. Gordon, *Anglo-Saxon Poetry;* Charles W. Kennedy, *The Poems of Cynewulf;* Burton Raffel, *Poems from the Old English.*

Overview of Critical Sources

Most older studies of Cynewulf's poems are highly technical and usually written in German, concerned mainly with the then current philological practice of establishing the texts and canon through metrical, phraseological, and narrative tests for authorship. A modern derivative of such lexical studies is Klaus Faiss' monograph on the semantics of expressions for "mercy," *"Gnade" bei Cynewulf und seiner Schule.* After the initial discoveries of the runic signatures in "Elene," "Christ II," and "Juliana" by Jakob Grimm and J. M. Kemble (independently) in 1840, the tendency was to attribute to this newly emergent figure more and more of the surviving Old English poetic corpus. Heinrich Leo epitomized this tendency in 1857 by finding a Cynewulfian "hidden signature" in the poem "Wulf and Eadwacer" and arguing for his authorship not only of that poem but of all of the ninety-five riddles that follow it in the Exeter Book manuscript. Not even *Beowulf* escaped being attributed to Cynewulf; in fact, F. Charitius' claim that this greatest of Anglo-Saxon poems should be assigned to Cynewulf prompted a long and intense debate that led to many interesting discoveries about early English poetry. As the opening surge of enthusiasm over the appearance of a semi-identifiable author in an almost completely anonymous period abated, scholars began to look more closely at possible sources and analogs for the signed poems and to inquire about the aesthetics of Cynewulf's *oeuvre.* Modern criticism has focused on illuminating the early ninth-century historical context in which the poems were written, with emphasis on the author's obvious close knowledge of liturgy, of Latin rhetorical practices, of the voluminous commentaries of the Church fathers and their bearing on his poems, and not least of the Germanic oral tradition that provided his poetic idiom. Today scholars view Cynewulf as a rather complex and innovative poet, a man both of his and of our times.

Evaluation of Selected Criticism

Calder, Daniel G. *Cynewulf.* Boston: Twayne, 1981. This book contains a fine evaluative summary of previous scholarship on the various problems associated with the author and his canon, but its real importance is as a closely worked manual on the poet's style.

Schaar, Claes, *Critical Studies in the Cynewulf Group.* 1949; rpt. New York: Haskell House, 1967. Schaar provides the first thorough investigation of style as a method for both determining probable authorship and characterizing the poet Cynewulf. Although later scholars have disagreed with points in his analysis, his methods and conclusions remain influential. (Caution: he includes the unsigned poems as part of the Cynewulfian canon.)

Sisam, Kenneth, *Cynewulf and His Poetry.* Proceedings of the British Academy, 1933. Sisam concludes that Cynewulf "was a ninth-century ecclesiastic of cultured taste; very devout in his old age and probably always of a devotional caste of mind; not a great scholar like Bede, but well versed in the Latin works that the educated clergy of those days used; not boldly original, but unusually sensitive and pliant to the influence of Christian Latin models; and, perhaps one may say, a man of letters, the first in English whose name and works are known" (p. 22).

Other Sources

Calder, Daniel G. and M. J. B. Allen, eds. *Sources and Analogues of Old English Poetry.* Cambridge and Totowa, NJ: D.S. Brewer and Rowman & Littlefield, 1976. This useful volume presents the major Latin sources and analogues for Cynewulf's poems, in modern English translation.

Diamond, Robert E. "The Diction of the Signed Poems of Cynewulf," in *Philological Quarterly,* XXXVIII (1959), 228–241. Diamond explains and illustrates the oral traditional diction employed by Cynewulf.

Foley, John Miles, *Oral-Formulaic Theory and Research: An Introduction and Annotated Bibliography.* New York: Garland, 1985. Contains an introductory essay on oral literature (pp. 3–77) with references to Cynewulf and a bibliographical record of relevant works through 1982.

Greenfield, Stanley B. and Fred C. Robinson, *A Bibliography of Publications on Old English Literature to the End of 1972.* Toronto: University of Toronto Press, 1980. A complete digest of literary criticism on Cynewulf through 1972 (items 3368–3408).

Old English Newsletter. The annual bibliography of literary criticism on Old English poetry (to supplement Greenfield and Robinson after 1972).

Selected Dictionaries and Encyclopedias

Critical Survey of Poetry, Vol. 2, Salem Press, 1983. Evaluation of Cynewulf's contributions to the development of English poetry, and an analysis of several poems.

John Miles Foley
University of Missouri/Columbia

SAMUEL DANIEL
1562?-1619

Author's Chronology

Born in 1562 or 1563 in Somersetshire, England; *1581* matriculates on 17 November at Magdalen Hall, Oxford; *1581-1584* meets John Florio, Giordano Bruno, Matthew Gwinne, and Robert Ashley, all formative influences on his later work; *1584* receives the patronage of Sir Edward Dymoke, the King's Champion; *1585-1586* travels to France and may have been in the employ of the diplomatic service while in Paris; *1590* travels to Italy with Sir Edward Dymoke and meets Battista Guarini; *1592* probably becomes tutor to William Herbert and receives patronage of Mary, Countess of Pembroke; *1593-1594* earns the patronage of his new friend Charles Blount, Lord Mountjoy; *1597* lives in the house of Lady Margaret, Countess of Cumberland; *1601* probably receives patronage of Sir Thomas Egerton; *1608* lives on a farm in Wiltshire, but still maintains ties with London and the court; *1619* makes out a will dated 4 September and probably dies near the end of the month; buried in Beckington, 14 October.

Author's Bibliography (selected)

Delia, 1592 (sonnet sequence); *Complaint of Rosamond,* 1592 (Ovidian love poem); *Cleopatra,* 1594 (Senecan tragedy); *Civil Wars,* 1595 (historical epic in verse); *Musophilus,* 1599 (philosophical dialogue in verse); *Defence of Rhyme,* 1603 (literary criticism); *Civil Wars,* 1609 (revised and augmented); *First Part of the History of England,* 1612 (prose history); *Collection of the History of England,* 1618 (prose history).

Overview of Biographical Sources

A truly "definitive" biography of Daniel does not exist and probably never will. The necessary sources are lost in the interstices of history. However, two early biographical accounts remain fairly accessible and suprisingly readable: Thomas Fullers's essay in *The History of the Worthies of England,* Vol. 1, ed. P. Austin Nuttall (London: T. Tegg, 1840), and Anthony Wood's "Samuel Daniel" in *Athenae Oxonienses,* ed. Philip Bliss (London: F. C. and J. Rivington, 1813). Both essays contain some information as yet unsubstantiated, but together they constitute the primary sources for later biographical accounts. More modern and more scholarly are the short biographical sketches in Arthur Colby Sprague's "Introduction" to *Samuel Daniel: Poems and A Defence of Rhyme* (Cambridge: Harvard University Press, 1930), and Raymond Himelick's "Daniel's Life and Works," in *Samuel Daniel's Musophilus* (West Lafayette: Purdue University Studies, 1965). Sprague and Himelick also offer balanced and judicious appraisals of Daniel's work and his "place" in Renaissance literature.

Evaluation of Selected Biographies

Rees, Joan, *Samuel Daniel: A Critical and Biographical Study.* Liverpool: Liverpool University Press, 1964. Rees interweaves Daniel's life and work and presents new biographical information. Her attempt to parallel Daniel's life and literary development largely succeeds, although a few of her biographical inferences appear farfetched.

Seronsky, Cecil C. *Samuel Daniel.* New York: Twayne, 1967. The pre-eminent modern scholar and critic of Daniel, Seronsky offers a bio-critical evaluation of Daniel's work that is insightful and sympathetic. The final chapter, "Poet and Thinker," presents a fine analysis of Daniel's poetic skills and a needed emphasis on Daniel's sense of history.

Spriet, Pierre, *Samuel Daniel (1563-1619): Sa vie—son oeuvre.* Paris: Didier, 1968. Part 1 provides the most detailed biography yet of Daniel. Spriet is particularly helpful in discussing Daniel's many friendships and his complex relations with several patrons. The author also identifies and examines earlier writers who helped shape Daniel's thought. Part 2 closely evaluates Daniel's work, especially his notions of—and contributions to—the writing of history. No English translation of Spriet's study has yet appeared.

Autobiographical Sources

Daniel's scattered autobiographical references and his few extant letters are generally well treated, with full references, by Joan Rees in *Samuel Daniel,* listed above.

Overview of Critical Sources

Samuel Daniel's *oeuvre* consistently splits critics into two diametrically opposed camps. Some commentators, like Samuel Taylor Coleridge, find Daniel "one of the golden writers of our golden Elizabethan age, now most causelessly neglected," while other readers agree with Edmund Gosse that "we are tempted to call him a Polonius among poets." Before 1960, modern critics emphasized Shakespeare's use of Daniel as a source; in recent years, however, the Coleridgean view has begun to dominate and highly appreciative studies of Daniel's poetry and historical thought have begun to appear.

Evaluations of Selected Criticism

Kelly, Henry Ansgar, "Daniel's *Civil Wars,*" in *Divine Providence in the England of Shakespeare's Histories.* Cambridge: Harvard University Press, 1970. Chapter Eight demonstrates that the Tudor Myth and Divine Providence were *not* the center of Daniel's thought in constructing the *Civil Wars.* Indeed, whatever interest Daniel had in such theories waned as the work grew.

La Branche, Anthony S. "Samuel Daniel: A Voice of Thoughtfulness," in *The Rhetoric of Renaissance Poetry: From Wyatt to Milton.* eds. Thomas O. Sloan and Raymond B. Waddington. Berkeley: University of California Press, 1974. La Branche emphasizes Daniel's poetic craftsmanship by analyzing the rhetorical strategies he used. The author demonstrates that Daniel employs a "rhetoric of thoughtfulness," not ornament, and that the thought process itself informs and structures Daniel's poetry.

Levy, F. J. "Political History," in *Tutor Historical Thought.* San Marino: Huntington Library, 1967. Levy examines Daniel's sophisticated views on politics and the writing of history, with special attention to the *History of England.*

Spencer, Theodore, "Two Classic Elizabethans: Samuel Daniel and Sir John Davies," in *Theodore Spencer: Selected Essays.* ed. Alan C. Purves. New Brunswick: Rutgers University Press, 1966. Spencer's richly appreciative essay surveys Daniel's work and finds its author "unsurpassed" among his contemporaries for contemplative, reflective, and distanced poetry.

Other Sources

Hotson, Leslie, "Marigold of the Poets," *Essays by Divers Hands,* 17 (January, 1938), 47–68. Reconstructs an exciting series of events in Daniel's life.

Michel, Laurence A. and Cecil C. Seronsky. "Shakespeare's History Plays and Daniel: An Assessment," *Studies in Philology,* 52 (October, 1955), 549–577.

Selected Dictionaries and Encyclopedias

Dictionary of Literary Biography, Gale Research, 1983. Short discussion of Daniel's life and major works.

The New Cambridge Bibliography of English Literature, Vol. 1. Cambridge University Press, 1974. Lists bibliographies, collections, published works, and selected criticism, through 1971.

Edmund M. Taft, IV
Iowa State University

SIR WILLIAM DAVENANT
1606–1668

Author's Chronology

Born February 1606, Oxford, England, the son of a vintner and mayor of Oxford; *1622* intended for apprenticeship to a merchant, but instead preferred to the Duchess of Richmond as a page; *1624* takes service with Fulke Greville, Lord Brooke; *1627* his tragedy *The Cruel Brother* is licensed; *1630* very ill, possibly syphilis; *1638* gains reputation as a poet and named Poet Laureate; *1640* serves in the Bishops War and is implicated in the First Army Plot against Parliament; serves in the Royalist army in the Civil War; knighted in *1642;* flees to France after the war; with Thomas Hobbes develops neo-classical theory and, in 1650, publishes *The Preface to Gondibert with An Answer by Mr. Hobbes; 1652* captured while enroute to America and imprisoned by Parliament; *1656* stages musical drama ancestral to both John Dryden's heroic drama and opera; gains popular success as playwright and theater manager; dies April 7, 1668.

Author's Bibliography (selected)

The Wits, 1633 (play); *Madagascar: With Other Poems,* 1638; *Salmacidia Spolia,* 1640 (masque); *The Preface to Gondibert with An Answer by Mr. Hobbes,* 1650 (essay); *Gondibert,* 1651, 1971 (unfinished epic poem); *The Siege of Rhodes,* 1656 (musical drama); *Works,* 1673; *The Shorter Poems and Songs from the Plays and Masques,* 1972.

Overview of Biographical Sources

Davenant's life is better documented than that of many seventeenth-century poets because he spent so much of it in the public eye. Though his exact birthdate is unknown, the rest of his life can be outlined from baptismal records, legal documents, the papers of his patrons and military commanders, and the records of the theaters he wrote for and managed. An early biographical essay can be found in John Aubrey's gossipy *Brief Lives* (1669). The best short introduction to Davenant's life is the "Biographical Introduction" to A. M. Gibbs' edition of *The Shorter Poems and Songs from the Plays and Masques* (Oxford: Clarendon, 1972). Alfred Harbage's *Sir William Davenant: Poet Venturer* (1935) and A. H. Nethercot's *Sir William D'Avenant: Poet Laureate and Playwright-Manager* (1938) are both solid, full-scale biographies.

Evaluation of Selected Biographies

Harbage, Alfred, *Sir William Davenant: Poet Venturer.* Philadelphia: University of Pennsylvania Press, 1935. Harbage is a fine stylist and an excellent critic. His book is a pleasure to read but very partisan. For Harbage, Davenant can do very little wrong. He is, to quote the biographer, a man at once "courageous, loyal, sincere, rather naive, but withal shrewd and resourceful." The book covers Davenant's life in six chapters. The next four chapters concentrate on the poet-playwright's major achievements, *Gondibert,* his comedies, his masques and musical dramas, and his adaptations of Shakespeare. A final chapter discusses Davenant's literary reputation.

Nethercott, A. H. *Sir William D'Avenant: Poet Laureate and Playwright-Manager.* Chicago: University of Chicago Press, 1938. Nethercot defends the legitimacy of a new Davenant biography so soon after Harbage's by stating that he puts more stress on narrative and biographical features. This book contains much less literary criticism than does Harbage's but devotes twice as much space to Davenant's life. Nethercot's prose is flowery but adequate. He is not quite so enamored of Davenant as is Harbage, but seems to treat him fairly. The book is particularly strong on Davenant's theatrical career.

Autobiographical Sources

Davenant left no specifically autobiographical work and few personal letters, but his shorter poems, particularly those written to friends such as Henry Jarmin and Endimion Poerter, contain numerous autobiographical references, as does the *Preface to Gondibert.*

Overview of Critical Sources

Harbage's biography, the introductory material to Gibbs' *The Shorter Poems and Songs from the Plays and Masques* and to David F. Gladish's edition of *Gondibert* (Oxford: Clarendon Press, 1971), and Philip Bordinat and Sophia B. Blaydes' *Sir William Davenant* (1981) are the best basic sources of criticism. Most critical material concentrates on Davenant's *Gondibert* and on his late dramas. His shorter poetry, for the most part, receives only passing mention in various surveys of the seventeenth-century lyric.

Evaluation of Selected Criticism

Bordinat, Philip and Sophia E. Blaydes, *Sir William Davenant.* Boston: Twayne, 1981. This brief, basic discussion of Davenant's life and works had little original research, but the material is accurate and well presented. This is a solid introduction to Davenant's life and to his part in the creation of neoclassical literary theory.

Collins, Howard, *The Comedy of Sir William Davenant.* The Hague: Mouton, 1967. A detailed study of Davenant's plays, translations, and adaptations, this is a sensible, straight-forward piece of work, very probably a rewritten dissertation. It includes a brief biographical essay, a general essay on seventeenth-century comedy, and a short bibliography.

Dowlin, Cornell March, "Sir William Davenant's *Gondibert,* Its Preface and Hobbes Answer, A Study in English Neoclassicism." Dissertation: University of Pennsylvania, 1934. This dissertation, designed originally as the introduction to an edition of *Gondibert* which never appeared, remains the most detailed study of that poem and the theory behind it. Dowlin is particularly good on the influences on Davenant's theories, both continental and English. He sees Davenant's greatest originality as lying in his rejection of the doctrines of authority and imitation which so dominated seventeenth-century poetry.

Other Sources

Davies, H. Neville, "Davenant, Dryden, Lee and Otway," in *English Drama (excluding Shakespeare) Selected Bibliographical Guide.* ed. Stanley Wells. London: Oxford University Press, 1975. Excellent, brief, and readily available discussion of Davenant's plays and his importance as a stage innovator. Contains a complete list of his plays.

McCarthy, William, "Davenant's Prefatory Rhetoric," in *Criticism,* 20 (1978), 128–143. The most recent word on Davenant's neoclassicism and on *Gondibert.*

Selected Dictionaries and Encyclopedias

Critical Survey of Poetry, Salem Press, 1983. Brief biography and analysis of Davenant's major poems.

Dictionary of National Biography, Oxford, 1968. Good brief biographical essay with some critical material.

Michael M. Levy
University of Wisconsin—Stout

ROBERTSON DAVIES
1913

Author's Chronology

1913 born August 28, Thamesville, Ontario, Canada; *1935* attends Queen's University, Kingston; *1938* completes education, Balliol College, Oxford (B. Litt.); *1939* Dent publishes thesis: *Shakespeare's Boy Actors; 1938–1940* joins Old Vic theatre under Tyrone Guthrie, where directs and teaches; marries Brenda Matthews February 2, 1940; returns to Canada as literary editor of *Saturday Night,* Toronto; *1942* writes for, edits, subsequently publishes *Peterborough Examiner;* maintains this affiliation twenty years; *1947* publishes *Diary of Samuel Marchbanks,* witty observations from *Examiner* column; *1951* publishes *Tempest Tost,* first Salterton novel; *Leaven of Malice* (*1955*), *Mixture of Frailties* (*1958*) complete trilogy; *1954* play *A Jig for the Gipsy* successfully produced, Crest Theatre, Toronto: *1957* awarded L.L.D., University of Alberta, Edmonton; *1960 Love and Libel,* stage adaptation of *Leaven of Malice,* produced on Broadway at Martin Beck Theatre, closes after six performances; *1960* appointed Professor of English, University of Toronto; *1962* L.L.D., Queen's University, Kingston; resigns from *Examiner;* appointed master Massey College, graduate unit of University of Toronto; *1962–1981* serves as member, Board of Governors, Stratford Ontario Shakespeare Festival; *1970* publishes *Fifth Business,* first Deptford novel; *The Manticore* (*1972*), *World of Wonders* (*1975*) complete trilogy.

Author's Bibliography (selected)

Shakespeare's Boy Actors, 1939 (thesis); *Diary of Samuel Marchbanks,* 1947 (fiction); *Table Talk of Samuel Marchbanks,* 1949 (fiction); *Eros at Breakfast, and Other Plays,* 1949 (drama); *Tempest Tost,* 1951 (fiction); (with Tyrone Guthrie) *Renown at Stratford: A Record of the Shakespeare Festival in Canada,* 1953 (history of drama); (with Guthrie) *Twice the Trumpets Sounded,* 1954 (history of drama); (with Guthrie) *Thrice the Brinded Cat Hath Mew'd,* 1955 (history of drama); *Leaven of Malice,* 1955 (novel); *A Mixture of Frailties,* 1958 (novel); *A Voice from the Attic,* 1960 (essays); *Samuel Marchbanks' Almanack,* 1967 (fiction); *Fifth Business,* 1970 (novel); *The Manticore,* 1972 (novel); *Hunting Stuart and Other Plays,* 1972 (drama); *World of Wonders,* 1975 (novel); *Feast of Stephen: A Study of Stephen Leacock,* 1976 (monograph); *One Half of Robertson Davies,* 1977 (essays); *The Rebel Angels,* 1981 (novel); *The Mirror of Nature: The Alexander Lectures, 1982,* 1983 (essays); *High Spirits,* 1983 (stories).

Overview of Biographical Sources

No full-length biography exists, though much information is available from the increasing critical attention being paid to Davies' works. *Current Biography*

(1975), 105–108 provides biographical information up to the year of publication of *World of Wonders.* Donald Cameron, *Conversations with Canadian Novelists* (Toronto: Macmillan, 1973) offers background concerning Davies' interest in Jungian psychology. John Kenneth Galbraith provides information about Davies' early years in Canada, at Oxford and the Old Vic in a review of *The Rebel Angels* (*New York Times Book Review,* February 14, 1982, p. 7).

Autobiographical Sources

Davies' Marchbanks' columns for the Peterborough *Examiner,* dating from 1942 and written with the mask of a fictional personna, reveal the author's whimsical personality. Many of these were republished in the first two Marchbanks collections cited above. *Samuel Marchbanks' Almanack* contains previously unpublished pieces. *A Voice from the Attic* provides information on Davies' approach to writing and the authors he particularly enjoys. Each essay in *One Half of Robinson Davies* (Viking: New York, 1978) is prefaced by information concerning the event in the author's life which elicited the piece. These essays were originally speeches, stories read to an audience, or lectures given to literary or academic audiences. They often touch on interesting personal episodes or acquaintanceships. *High Spirits* (New York: Viking, 1983), a collection of ghost stories set in Davies' own Massey College, provides an introductory autobiographical essay on Davies' affinity for the genre acquired during his childhood and student years. Davies has discussed his eclectic influences in "A Rake at Reading," *Mosaic: A Journal for the Interdisciplinary Study of Literature* 14.2 (1981), 1–19. Cf. also Geoffrey James, "Mystic of Massey College," *Time* (21 May 1973), 9 and Gordon Jocelyn, "The Manticore," *Canadian Forum* 52 (February 1973), 44–45.

Overview of Critical Sources

Criticism on Davies' works has become so substantial in recent years that an annotated list is now available: "Robertson Davies: An Annotated Bibliography," *The Annotated Bibliography of Canada's Major Authors,* Vol. 3 Downsview: ECW, 1981.

Evaluation of Selected Criticism

Lawrence, Robert G. and Samuel L. Macey, eds. *Studies in Robertson Davies' Deptford Trilogy* (*English Literary Studies,* Monograph Series No. 20). British Columbia: University of Victoria, 1980. This impressive collection of essays by academic authors contains an introduction by Davies on how he came to write the trilogy and how themes of transmitted evil and contingency have always fascinated him. Worthwhile essays in the collection include R. F. Radford's on the earlier Salterton novels and the great mother theme in *Fifth Business,* and Lawrence's own essay on Canadian theatre in *World of Wonders.*

Monk, Patricia, *The Smaller Infinity: The Jungian Self in the Novels of Robertson Davies.* Toronto: University of Toronto Press, 1982. The author prepared this book with Davies' advice and encouragement. It incorporates several articles previously published, and presents a serious readable study which traces Jung's influence in Davies' major works, not just the most obviously Jungian, *The Manticore.*

Other Sources

Bligh, John, "The Spiritual Climacteric of Dunstan Ramsay," *World Literature Written in English* 21.3 (1982), 575–593. Bligh discusses the protagonist of *Fifth Business* and Davies' use of Jung.

Cude, Wilfred, "The College Occasion as Rabelaisian Feast," *Studies in Canadian Literature* 7.2 (1982), 184–189. This article discusses the cynically witty view of academic life and Davies' use of Rabelais in *The Rebel Angels.*

Dawson, Anthony B. "Davies, His Critics, and the Canadian Canon," *Canadian Literature* 92 (1982), 154–159. This brief survey discusses Davies' place in Canadian fiction, and cites available criticism on the novels.

Harris, John, "A Voice from the Priggery," *Journal of Canadian Fiction* 33 (1981-82), 112–117. Harris discusses Davies' fascination with contingency and evil in the context of *The Rebel Angels.*

Hoy, Helen, "Poetry in the Dunghill: The Romance of the Ordinary in Robertson Davies' Fiction," *Ariel: A Review of International English Literature* 10.3 (1970), 69–98. Hoy focuses on Davies' provincial settings, his dispassionate character descriptions, and his use of the grotesque in the Deptford books.

Radford, F. L. and R. R. Wilson, "Some Phases of the Jungian Moon," *English Studies in Canada* 8.3 (1982), 311–332. This is a survey of Jungian influence on modern writers which features Canadian authors, many of whom are not widely known outside of Canada. Davies figures prominently in the analysis.

Wood, Barry, "In Search of Sainthood: Magic, Myth, and Metaphor in Robertson Davies' *Fifth Business,*" in *Critique: Studies in Modern Fiction* 19.2 (1977), 23–32. Wood's article is a discussion of Davies' ability to synthesize disparate elements and traditions in the first of the Deptford novels.

Robert J. Forman
St. John's University, New York

SIR JOHN DAVIES
1569–1626

Author's Chronology

Baptized on April 16, 1569 at Chicksgrove in the hamlet of Tisbury, Wiltshire, the third son of Edward Davies, a Wiltshire tanner; after attending Winchester College, enters Oxford and then the Middle Temple on February 10, 1588; *1592–1593* visits University of Leiden; *1596* publishes first version of *Orchestra* with a dedication to Richard Martin; satirized for calling himself Erophilus, in imitation of Essex, during the Middle Temple Christmas Revels of 1597–1598; *1598* expelled from the Middle Temple on February 10 for breaking a bastinado over Richard Martin's head; *1601* readmitted to the Middle Temple; appointed Solicitor General of Ireland in *1603* and Attorney General in *1606; 1609* marries Eleanor, Lady Audley; *1613* elected Speaker of Irish Parliament; *1623* marries daughter and sole heir, Lucy, to Ferdinando Hastings, the Earl of Huntingdon's heir; appointed Lord Chief Justice, but dies December 7, 1626 before taking office.

Author's Bibliography (selected)

Poetry published during Davies' life includes *Epigrams,* which appeared in an undated edition with Christopher Marlowe's translation of Ovid's *Elegies; Orchestra* (1596), reprinted with a new dedication and different ending in the 1622 collection of the major poems; *Nosce Teipsum* (1599), reprinted five times during Davies' life, and *Hymnes of Astraea* (1599), both of which also appear in the 1622 collected edition. The unpublished works, an "Epithalamion," series of "Gulling Sonnets," and miscellaneous occasional poems, have been collected in the standard edition *The Poems of Sir John Davies,* ed. Robert Krueger (Oxford: Clarendon Press, 1975). Because unresolved bibliographical problems still exist with identifying the canon and the texts of Davies' major works, it would be wise also to consult a facsimile edition, *The Poems of Sir John Davies,* ed. Clare Howard (New York: Columbia University Press, 1941). Most of Davies' historical and legal essays and treatises have been collected in *The Works in Verse and Prose of Sir John Davies,* ed. Alexander B. Grosart, Fuller Worthies Library. 3 vols. (Blackburn: Printed for private circulation, 1869–1876).

Overview of Biographical Sources

There is no book-length biography of Davies. As with many biographies of Elizabethan and Jacobean writers, there are numerous factual gaps in the life of Sir John Davies. This lack of information has prompted biographers to fill in the blank spaces with conjecture. In Rev. Alexander Grosart's nineteenth-century edition of Davies' works, *The Works in Verse and Prose of Sir John Davies,*

Davies is depicted as the typical Victorian gentleman who metamorphoses from a youthful gay blade, who writes witty and salacious epigrams and who publicly breaks a bastinado over the head of a close friend, to a repentant young man, author of the long philosophical poem *Nosce Teipsum,* to a lawyer and judge, who stops writing verse to devote himself to public service.

Robert Krueger, twentieth-century editor of the standard edition, *The Poems of Sir John Davies* (1975), accepts the bibliographical and biographical facts outlined by Grosart: that Davies began his career writing epigrams and *Orchestra,* a poem in praise of dance, was sobered by his expulsion from the Middle Temple, wrote *Nosce Teipsum* after being expelled, and concluded his career by giving up poetry for prose. Krueger, however, supplies a less Victorian interpretation of these facts, suggesting that Davies wrote poetry in order to win advancement, was appointed Solicitor General of Ireland for writing *Nosce Teipsum,* and once he had achieved success, abandoned his muse. J. R. Brink, in "The Composition Date of Sir John Davies' *Nosce Teipsum*" (*Huntington Library Quarterly,* XXXVII (1973), 19–32), has presented evidence that Davies probably wrote *Nosce Teipsum* while he was writing his epigrams and that his appointment in Ireland was not a reward, but very likely a punishment for being too outspoken in parliament.

Evaluation of Selected Biographies

Finkelpearl, Philip J. *John Marston of the Middle Temple: An Elizabethan Dramatist in His Social Setting.* Cambridge: Harvard University Press, 1969. Finkelpearl provides a general discussion of the literary life and revels at the Inns of Court, the four major law schools in London. Although Finkelpearl concentrates on John Marston, a student at the Middle Temple and later an important seventeenth-century dramatist, he presents a detailed description of the 1597–1598 Christmas revels at the Middle Temple and of the "Prince D'Amour" pageant in which Davies participated. Finkelpearl identifies Davies as *Stradilax* who called himself "Erophilus, in saucy imitation of the great Earle [Earl of Essex] of the time" and who is ridiculed by his companions for his social pretensions (p. 53). Finkelpearl's identification of Davies as Stradilax is well supported, but his attempt to connect Davies' possible embarrassment during the revels with his attack on Richard Martin is less convincing.

Grosart, Rev. Alexander B. ed. *The Works in Verse and Prose of Sir John Davies.* Lancashire: Blackburn, 1869–1876 (collected in 3 vols. at Fuller Worthies Library). Although a moralized biography, based on an inaccurate chronology of the major poems, Grosart's biographical introduction prints a number of letters from manuscripts and remains the most complete description of Davies' political career in Ireland.

Krueger, Robert, ed. *The Poems of Sir John Davies.* Oxford: Clarendon Press, 1975. Krueger's biography, although important because it appears in the standard edition, is not factually reliable. Krueger mistakenly gives Davies' death date as March 8, 1626; his daughter had December 7, 1626 inscribed on his tombstone. The biography is also flawed by highly speculative commentary on Davies' motives and behavior.

Sanderson, James L. *Sir John Davies.* New York: Twayne, 1975. Sanderson largely accepts the factual summary and the chronology of the poems first put forward by Grosart, but his presentation is judicious. He resists speculation and offers the best biographical treatment available in book form.

Overview of Critical Sources

Davies' work became well-known because of E. M. W. Tillyard's *The Elizabethan World Picture* (1943), a study in the history of ideas which describes Davies' *Orchestra* as the typical Elizabethan poem. Tillyard praises *Orchestra*'s exuberant celebration of dance as a principle of cosmic order. Beginning with G. A. Wilkes' article entitled "The Poetry of Sir John Davies" (*Huntington Library Quarterly,* XXV (1962), 283–298) critics such as Krueger and Sanderson have argued that Tillyard takes too solemn a view of *Orchestra,* and that Davies intended the poem as a *jeu d'esprit.* Looking more favorably on Tillyard's interpretation and using bibliographical as well as textual evidence, J. R. Brink, in "Sir John Davies' *Orchestra:* Political Symbolism and Textual Revision" (*Durham University Journal,* LXXII (1980), 195–201) and in "The 1622 Edition of Sir John Davies' *Orchestra*" (*The Library,* XXX (1975), 25–33), has argued that Davies' witty celebration of dance as cosmic order conceals an exhortation to the Queen to determine a successor to the throne and so insure the future order of England. The best brief critical study of Davies' poetry and of *Nosce Teipsum* in particular is T. S. Eliot's "Sir John Davies" (1926). It is also worth noting that selections from *Orchestra* have been reprinted in *High Adventure: A Treasury for Young Adults,* ed. S. Manley and G. Lewis (New York: Funk & Wagnall, 1968).

Evaluation of Selected Criticism

Eliot, T. S. "Sir John Davies" (originally published in *The Times Literary Supplement,* 1926). Essay collected in *On Poetry and Poets.* New York: Farrar, Straus and Cudahy, 1957, and in *Elizabethan Poetry.* ed. Paul J. Alpers. London: Oxford University Press, 1967. Describing *Orchestra* as a masterpiece of versification, Eliot pays special attention to *Nosce Teipsum,* Davies' long philosophical poem. Comparing Davies' success with that of Dante in the *Purgatorio,* Eliot praises him for keeping *Nosce Teipsum* consistently on the level of poetry, finding the merit of the poem in the "perfection of the instrument to the end."

Krueger, Robert, *The Poems of Sir John Davies.* Oxford: Clarendon Press, 1975. Krueger's critical assessment of Davies is unsympathetic. Claiming that

Davies' poems will never again be read for either profit or pleasure, Krueger reveals his own "romantic" bias when he censures them for lack of feeling.

Sanderson, James L. *Sir John Davies.* Boston: Twayne, 1975. In addition to assessing Davies' poems as expressions of the period in which they were written, Sanderson identifies the genres and literary conventions with which Davies was working. This sound approach results in the best book-length examination of the poems as works of continuing literary interest.

Tillyard, E. M. W. *The Elizabethan World Picture.* London: Chatto & Windus, 1943, and *Five Poems, 1470–1870.* London: Chatto & Windus, 1948. Both works contain perceptive and appreciative critical commentary on the poetry. Tillyard also provides important examinations of Davies' poems as reflections of the philosophical and cultural world in which they were written.

Selected Dictionaries and Encyclopedias

Critical Survey of Poetry, Vol. 2, Salem Press, 1982. Biographical summary and analysis of the major poems.

Dictionary of National Biography, 1885–1886; rpt. Oxford University Press, 1921–1922, Vol. V, 590–594. Biography with summaries from manuscript correspondence.

The Reader's Encyclopedia, Thomas Y. Crowell, 1965, pp. 253. Concise biographical summary.

Jeanie R. Brink
Arizona State University

CECIL DAY-LEWIS
1904–1972

Author's Chronology

Born April 27, 1904, Ballintubbert, Ireland of Anglo-Irish parents; *1908,* mother dies; is raised by aunt and father; *1917* enters Sherburne School in Dorset; becomes head boy in his house but has to stay an extra year to win scholarship to Oxford; *1925* publishes first volume of verse *Beechen Vigil and Other Poems* and two poems in *Oxford Poetry 1925,* convincing him of his vocation as a poet; *1926* meets W. H. Auden whose influence on the style and subject matter of Day-Lewis' early poetry is considerable; *1927* B.A., Wadham College, Oxford; *1927–1928* teaches at Summer Fields, a preparatory school near Oxford; marries Mary King; *1930* teaches at Cheltenham Junior School; *1935* publishes detective novel under pseudonym Nicholas Blake, accepts contract to write novels giving him financial independence and allowing him to leave teaching and join the Communist Party; *1935* first American publication of work; *1938* leaves Communist Party, abandons political activity, moves to Musbury, a small village in Devon, engages in an affair with Billie Currall; *1940* begins translation of Vergil's *Georgics,* commands a unit of the Home Guard; *1941* edits propaganda for Ministry of Information, begins affair with novelist Rosamund Lehmann; broadcasts for BBC, becomes London celebrity; *1946* gives Clark Lectures at Cambridge; *1947* becomes reader at publishers Chatto and Windus; *1950* awarded CBE, active in London literary life; *1951* divorces Mary, ends affair with Rosamund Lehmann and marries Jill Balson, a young actress; elected Professor of Poetry at Oxford; *1952* travels to Italy; *1957* lectures in the United States; *1960* publishes autobiography *The Buried Day; 1961* named chairman of poetry panel of Arts Council of Great Britain; *1964* lectures at Harvard; *1968* appointed Poet Laureate of England; contracts cancer; *1972* dies.

Author's Bibliography (selected)

A Hope for Poetry 1934 (criticism); *The Georgics of Vergil,* 1940 (translation); *The Poetic Image,* 1947 (criticism); *The Poet's Task,* 1951 (criticism); *Collected Poems,* 1954 (poems); *The Poet's Way of Knowledge,* 1957 (criticism); *Pegasus and other Poems,* 1958 (poems); *The Buried Day,* 1960 (autobiography); *Requiem for Living,* 1964 (poems); *The Lyric Impulse,* 1965 (criticism); *Selected Poems,* 1965 (poems); *The Whispering Roots and Other Poems,* 1970 (poems); *Poems of C. Day-Lewis, 1925–1972,* edited by Ian Parsons, 1977 (poems).

Overview of Biographical Sources

Possibly because of a lack of critical interest in him in recent years, only one book-length biography of Cecil Day-Lewis exists. Written by his son Sean Day-

Lewis, it is *C. Day-Lewis: An English Literary Life* (1980). It does not pretend to be totally objective, but is a very complete treatment of his life and his work, including the detective novels and his serious novels, as well as his poetry and criticism.

Evaluation of Selected Biographies

Day-Lewis, Sean, *C. Day-Lewis: An English Literary Life.* London: Weidenfeld and Nicholson, 1980. Sean Day-Lewis tells the story of his father's life in great detail and gives a general introduction to the writings. He accuses his father of misleading readers of *The Buried Day,* maintaining that the real cause of his father's divided mind was his attempt to balance the demands of a wife and family against the demands of a mistress. Indeed, while Day-Lewis' best known poetry is about the necessity for revolution, the poems written after 1943 often focus on love and its difficulties.

Since his son was thoroughly involved in his father's marital problems, he may not be totally objective about them. On the other hand, he has benefited from having access to Cecil's letters and from the cooperation of those who knew his father, most of whom were still living when the book was written.

The book ties the events of Day-Lewis' life to particular works, not only to the poetry but to the novels. His political ideas, his wartime experiences and the progress of his marriage are also traced.

This book is particularly valuable as the picture of a life of a literary celebrity, who was acquainted with all the important writers and thinkers of his day, a lecturer at home on radio and television, a poet whose later work may have been ignored by critics and anthologizers but whose poetry was admired by the general reader.

Autobiographical Sources

The autobiography, Cecil Day-Lewis, *The Buried Day* (New York: Harper and Row, 1960) discusses the author's life only until 1940 with a brief glance at his situation in 1955, as a well-known writer with a new wife and two young children. It does, however, give a fairly complete picture of Day-Lewis' childhood, his school days, his association with Auden at Oxford, his decision to join the Communist Party and his decision to leave the party. He describes, too, his courtship, marriage, and the birth of his children. At first he wished to use his poetry to help incite revolution but then he gave up political activity because he believed it was harming his poetry. Eventually he focused his poetry on almost purely private concerns.

The autobiography also comments on the relation between the poet's life and work. He believes his politics initially strengthened his imagery as it influenced his choice of subject matter, but ultimately caused his writing to degenerate. In addition, he found his public life took too much time away from his writing. He sees his mind as a divided one, torn between the comfort and security of the past, a love of nature and private life, and the wish for a revolutionary future devoted to the common good and communal relationships.

The autobiography also explains how he happened to write the still popular detective novels which appear under the name Nicholas Blake; he simply needed the money.

Overview of Selected Criticism

Critics have focused their attention almost exclusively on C. Day-Lewis' poetry and criticism written between 1925–1943 when he was considered a member of the Auden school, which included W. H. Auden, Stephen Spender, and Louis MacNeice. Although Day-Lewis admits being strongly influenced by Auden, he denies they were ever a school. He maintains they were never in the same room together until well after the period in question. At any rate, they did share the same intense concern with left wing politics and the belief that poetry must reflect political concerns. To these writers, unemployment, social inequality and decaying cities seemed evidence of the imminent collapse of western civilization. They hoped their poetry would spur a revolution which would free men's energy, promote economic progress, encourage human brotherhood, freedom and honesty, and spawn a renaissance in art and literature.

Evaluation of Selected Criticism

Dyment, Clifford, *C. Day Lewis.* London: Longmans, Green, 1955, revised 1969. In this pamphlet Dyment discusses Day-Lewis' poetry and criticism as the product of a conscience at war with itself. Day-Lewis rejects the evils of the past but does not wish to reject its respect for the individual. He also experiences a dual loyalty, both to the public good and to his own private vision. In this, Dyment sees Day-Lewis as the paradigm of modern man. Although Dyment emphasizes the poetry of the 1920's and 1930's, he also writes about some of the later poetry, demonstrating that Day-Lewis' poetry has followed a consistent line of development in technique and in thought, his work becoming more musical and more compassionate.

Riddel, J. N. *C. Day Lewis.* New York: Twayne, 1971. Riddel's discusses both Day-Lewis' poetry and his criticism, emphasizing the 1930's period. He gives just enough biographical information to understand the poems, and offers close and sympathetic readings of the more important poetry. He demonstrates that the changes in Day-Lewis' poetry, emphasizing the personal rather than the political, the lyric rather than the argumentative.

Smith, Elton Edward, *The Angry Young Men of the Thirties.* Carbondale, Southern Illinois University Press, 1975. Smith places the 1930's poets in the context of the events of the Great Depression. He notes C. Day-Lewis' acceptance of Marxism, but finds that by 1943 Day-Lewis has changed his focus from the need for revolution to the difficulty of living in the world as it is.

Tolley, A. T. *The Poetry of the Thirties.* New York: St. Martin's Press, 1975. Tolley comments on over twenty poems written by Day-Lewis from 1925 to 1943. He also discusses the relationship of the Auden group to modernism in literature as well as to economic and social problems.

Other Sources

Handley-Taylor, Geoffrey and D'Arch-Smith, Timothy, *Day-Lewis, the Poet Laureate: A Bibliography.* Chicago: St. James Press, 1968.

Maxwell, D. E. S. *Poets of the Thirties,* London: Routledge and Kegan Paul, 1969. Maxwell relates the poetry of the 1930's to violent revolution. He also demonstrates Day-Lewis' desire to appear scientific in not only the subject matter but the style of his poetry. This, Maxwell believes, gives the early poetry some freshness. Maxwell also discusses Day-Lewis' criticism and his novels.

Stanford, Derek, *Stephen Spender, Louis MacNeice, C. Day-Lewis: A Critical Essay.* Grand Rapids, MI: Eerdman's, 1969. This brief pamphlet discusses not only the political ideas but the poetic techniques used by the poets in question. Stanford finds a continuity of development in Day-Lewis' poetry marked by the use of traditional form even when his subject was revolution.

Selected Dictionaries

Dictionary of Literary Biography, Gale Research, 1983. A discussion of Day-Lewis' life and the principal works, illustrations.

Barbara Horwitz
C. W. Post Center of Long Island University

WALTER DE LA MARE
1873–1956

Author's Chronology

Born April 25, 1873, Charleton, England of French and Scottish ancestry; *1890* becomes clerk for Anglo-American Oil Company; *1899* marries Constance Elfrida Igpen (they will have four children); *1902* publishes first book, *Songs of Childhood,* poetry (under the pseudonym Walter Ramal); *1904* publishes first novel, *Henry Brocken; 1908* British government awards him an annual Civil List pension of one hundred pounds and he becomes a full-time author; *1910 The Return,* a novel, receives the de Polignac Prize; *1928* publishes *At First Sight,* his last work of long fiction; *1943* his wife dies; *1948* made a Companion of Honour; *1953* awarded the Order of Merit; dies June 22, 1956, Twickenham, Middlesex, England.

Author's Bibliography (selected)

Henry Brocken, 1904 (novel); *The Three Mulla-Mulgars,* 1910, reprinted as *The Three Royal Monkeys: Or, The Three Mulla-Mulgars,* 1935 (children's novel); *Rupert Brooke and the Intellectual Imagination,* 1919 (criticism); *Memoirs of a Midget,* 1921 (novel); *Behold, This Dreamer!,* 1939 (anthology); *Pleasures and Speculations,* 1940 (essays); *The Best Short Stories of Walter de la Mare,* 1942; *Collected Stories for Children,* 1947; *Ghost Stories,* 1956; *The Complete Poems,* 1969.

Overview of Biographical Sources

Walter de la Mare preferred to keep his personal life private—a desire that friends and family generally respected. Thus, little of substance has been published about his life. What little is publicly known about de la Mare's biography has been inferred from some of his nonfiction writings or derived from the publications of his friends. The two most significant biographical publications are R. L. Mégroz's *Walter de la Mare: A Biographical and Critical Study* (1924) and Russell Brain's *Tea with Walter de la Mare* (1957). The former was published in the middle of de la Mare's career and therefore only provides information on the early years. The latter, while having the advantage of appearing after de la Mare's death, is more concerned with the author's ideas than biographical details.

Evaluation of Selected Biographies

Brain, Russell, *Tea with Walter de la Mare.* London: Faber and Faber, 1957. Brain presents conversations that he had with de la Mare, emphasizing the author's later years. This account is useful for the insights it provides into de la Mare's thinking on metaphysical subjects, as well as literature, but it provides few details about de la Mare's personal life.

Mégroz, R. L. *Walter de la Mare: A Biographical and Critical Study.* London: Hodder and Stoughton, 1924. This book is the principal source for the facts of de la Mare's early life. Mégroz was de la Mare's friend and had the advantage of being able to get his information firsthand; also as de la Mare's friend, he had to respect the author's desire that certain matters be kept private.

Autobiographical Sources

Although de la Mare was virtually silent about his adult life, he seems to have often drawn on his childhood experiences for many of his writings. *Early One Morning in the Spring* (London: Faber, 1935) is an anthology of writings about early childhood and includes indications of what de la Mare's own childhood was like. *Behold, This Dreamer!* (London: Faber, 1939) is another anthology, this time emphasizing mysticism and imagination. It indicates some of the mystical experiences that de la Mare had during his life.

Overview of Critical Sources

Criticism of de la Mare's works is fragmentary, usually focusing on a single work or just a part of a work. Mégroz's criticism is now out of date in his *Walter de la Mare: A Biographical and Critical Study,* but still provides some helpful hints about the major issues of de la Mare's writings. The best early critical study is G. K. Chesterton's "Walter de la Mare" (*Fortnightly Review,* July 1932, pp. 47–53). In de la Mare's own day, his poetry was held in higher esteem than his fiction by most critics, with the notable exception of Edward Wagenknecht, who in *Cavalcade of the English Novel* (New York: Holt, Rinehart and Winston, 1954) ranked de la Mare as one of the twentieth century's greatest novelists. Since de la Mare's death, critics have tended to emphasize his fiction at the expense of his poetry.

Evaluation of Selected Criticism

Duffin, Henry Charles, *Walter de la Mare: A Study of His Poetry.* London: Sedgwick and Jackson, 1949. This is the standard study of de la Mare's poetry, in spite of its having been written several year's before the poet's death. It provides an overview of de la Mare's poetic achievement, but its wordiness can irritate readers.

McCrosson, Doris Ross, *Walter de la Mare.* New York: Twayne, 1966. This book leans too heavily toward the novels at the expense of the poetry and short stories to be a satisfactory introduction to de la Mare's total literary achievement, but it provides the best commentary on the novels that is available.

Other Sources

Atkins, John, *Walter de la Mare: An Exploration.* London: C. and J. Temple, 1947. Short but insightful analysis of the major themes of de la Mare's fiction and poetry.

Hopkins, Kenneth, *Walter de la Mare.* London: Longmans, Green, 1953. Good, short study of de la Mare's literary career and major works. A general introduction that would be useful for anyone interested in de la Mare.

Reid, Forrest, *Walter de la Mare: A Critical Study.* London: Faber and Faber, 1929. A thoughtful study of de la Mare's early writings, including all the novels. Written in a scholarly manner that is best suited to advanced readers.

Thomas, Dylan, "Walter de la Mare as a Prose Writer," *Quite Early One Morning.* London: Dent, 1954. New York: New Directions, 1954. Thomas provides a general evaluation of de la Mare's merits as a prose writer. His comments are balanced and thoughtful and are a good introduction to a neglected subject.

Selected Dictionaries and Encyclopedias

Critical Survey of Long Fiction, Salem Press, 1983. Brief biography, critical introduction, and bibliography.

Critical Survey of Poetry, Salem Press, 1982. Brief biography, critical introduction, and bibliography.

Kirk H. Beetz
National University, Sacramento

THOMAS DE QUINCEY
1785-1859

Author's Chronology

Born August 15, 1785, Manchester, England to a successful merchant; *1793* father dies; *1793-1796* tutored by Reverend Samuel Hall; *1796-1799* attends Bath Grammar School; *1800-1802* attends Manchester Grammar School; *1803-1808* attends Worcester College, Oxford, but does not take a degree; *1804* first takes opium to relieve facial pain; *1804* or *1805* meets Charles Lamb; *1807* meets Samuel Taylor Coleridge, William Wordsworth, and Robert Southey; *1808-1809* lives with Wordsworth; *1813* addicted to opium; *1816* inheritance runs out; *1817* marries Margaret Simpson (they have eight children); *1818-1819* edits *Westmorland Gazette; 1821 The Confessions of an Opium-Eater* appears in *London Magazine,* in book form in 1822; *1826* becomes regular writer for *Blackwood's Edinburgh Magazine; 1830* moves to Edinburgh; *1832* imprisoned for debt; *1833* bankrupt; *1837* wife dies; *1846* mother dies; *1847* achieves financial security; *1848* overcomes opium addiction; *1851* publication of collected works begins in United States; *1853* publication of collected works begins in Edinburgh; dies December 8, 1859, Edinburgh, Scotland.

Author's Bibliography (selected)

The Confessions of an English Opium-Eater, 1822 (autobiography); *Klosterheim,* 1832 (novel); *The Logic of Political Economy,* 1844 (nonfiction); *Suspiria de Profundis,* 1845-1849 (autobiography); *The Confessions of an English Opium-Eater,* 1856, revised and expanded; *Posthumous Works,* edited by A. H. Japp, 1891; *De Quincey as Critic,* edited by John E. Jordan, 1973 (essays).

Overview of Biographical Sources

Much of Thomas De Quincey's literary reputation rests on his autobiographical writings; therefore, biographers have had to sort fact from fancy in De Quincey's accounts of himself, as well as assemble information from other sources, such as memoirs by his acquaintances. Although many critics from his day to the present have been hostile in their accounts of his personality, De Quincey has fared well at the hands of his biographers. His *Confessions of an English Opium-Eater* in particular has captured the imagination of many readers and has inspired popular biographies.

David Masson's *De Quincey* (New York: Harper and Brothers, 1901) is one such biography. Masson follows H. A. Page's *Thomas De Quincey: His Life and Writings* (London: J. Hogg, 1877), but his book is more elegantly written, though less substantial, than is Page's. Malcolm Elwin shares Masson's admiration of De Quincey in *De Quincey* (London: Duckworth, 1935), a short overview of the author's life that makes for pleasant reading. Another unpretentious effort is John Calvin Metcalf's *De Quincey: A Portrait* (Cambridge, Massachusetts: Harvard University Press, 1940). Metcalf's book is among the best written of the biographies, although it contributes little new information about De Quincey's life. *De Quincey and Friends,* edited by James Hogg (London: Sampson Low, Marston, 1895), is a gathering of firsthand accounts of De Quincey that these and other biographers have often used for reference.

Evaluation of Selected Biographies

Eaton, Horace A. *Thomas De Quincey: A Biography.* New York: Oxford University Press, 1936. This remains the most complete of the biographies. Generally avoiding interpretation of his materials, Eaton presents the facts of De Quincey's life in an orderly manner. No other biography makes as full use of letters and legal documents to fill out details of De Quincey's activities. Eaton's dating is sometimes misleading, and he admits that there are gaps in his account. He portrays De Quincey as a tragic hero in a lifelong drama.

Lindop, Grevel, *The Opium-Eater: A Life of Thomas De Quincey.* London: J. M. Dent and Sons, 1981. In his "Epilogue," Lindop asserts that "De Quincey's life is a strange one, and studying it we become strongly aware of how far the external events of a life may really be determined by inner, psychological factors." This sensational account of De Quincey's life emphasizes that weaknesses in the author's character were responsible for many of the miseries that dominate the biography. Lindop provides the fullest discussion of De Quincey's opium addiction, asserting that it was a reflection of De Quincey's character. This biography uses materials that were unavailable to Eaton and Sackville-West, but as Lindop notes, family papers available to Eaton are now dispersed and hard to find. Lindop's focus is on De Quincey's character, as opposed to the straightforward factual presentation found in Eaton's book and the criticism found in that of Sackville-West.

Sackville-West, Edward, *Thomas De Quincey: His Life and Work.* New Haven: Yale University Press, 1936. (British title, *A Flame in Sunlight).* This critical biography is not as detailed as that of Eaton but offers more insight into De Quincey's motivations. Sackville-West does not portray De Quincey as quite the tragic hero that Eaton presents him to be, but he does perceive the author's life as a triumph over great adversity. Far more willing to examine De Quincey's faults than other biographers, Sackville-West's account nonetheless sometimes seems unbalanced by psychoanalytic speculations. With its combination of sound criticism of De Quincey's writings and thoughtful examination of the author's character, this is probably the most helpful reference for both student and scholar.

Autobiographical Sources

Although a prolific author on a wide variety of subjects, De Quincey is best known for his autobiographical writings, particularly *The Confessions of an*

English Opium-Eater. Some critics now argue that another autobiographical work, the incomplete *Suspira de Profundis,* is De Quincey's greatest literary achievement. The autobiographical writings emphasize a Romantic view of life, highlighting deep emotional responses to events, as well as revelatory insights into the meanings of events. Critics are divided over the merits of the autobiographical writings as literature, although most agree that they are important to the history of literature.

Overview of Critical Sources

Critics have always been uncertain of how to regard De Quincey's writings. At once mystical and factual, the writings persistently imply genius that is never quite realized. De Quincey's contemporary critics were sometimes furious with him for his prose that read like poetry and his habit of discussing even trivial topics in elevated language. To those who disliked his work, his efforts seemed overblown and full of mystical nonsense. His admirers thought of him as a brilliant scholar whose wealth of learning helped to reveal the relationships between seemingly small events and the great worlds of society and nature. To them, *The Confessions of an Opium-Eater* gave not only De Quincey's problems, but the seemingly small problems of all people a cosmic significance.

After his death, De Quincey's popularity increased. Victorians tended to view him as a great Romantic figure whose genius was thwarted by the afflictions imposed on him by society and his greedy, overdemanding editors. They defended his poetic prose as the product of a Romantic mind that saw the poetry in life. So confusing is much of De Quincey's writing that even his admirers have consistently felt the need to defend, rather than simply praise, him. In the early twentieth century, many critics were prepared to dismiss him as a self-indulgent opium addict who lacked any real insight into his literary topics. Some, notably Sackville-West in his critical biography, sought to formulate balanced appraisals of De Quincey's achievements. That effort to even-handedly evaluate De Quincey's works continues to this day. Most modern critics seem willing to acknowledge De Quincey's historical importance, but they still are puzzled by his unusual prose style.

Evaluation of Selected Criticism

De Luca, V. A. *Thomas De Quincey: The Prose of Vision.* Toronto: University of Toronto Press, 1980. This is the best study of De Quincey's literary art published to date. De Luca asserts that De Quincey's best work is marked by "a prose of vision, a prose marked by pervasive transcendental concerns, by an aggrandized inwardness, and by conspicuous renderings of dreams and hallucinatory states." Emphasizing De Quincey's mysticism, De Luca presents a full evaluation of De Quincey's literary achievement. He believes that De Quincey's idea of *imagination* is the key to understanding the author's works. Clearly an admirer of De Quincey, De Luca nonetheless notes the faults in De Quincey's writings and is able to conclude with justifiable conviction that De Quincey is something more than a minor author, although he is unwilling to apply the word *major.*

Devlin, D. D. *De Quincey, Wordsworth and the Art of Prose.* London: Macmillan, 1983. Many critics have viewed De Quincey as a transitional figure, neither wholly Romantic nor wholly Victorian. Devlin uses the relationship between De Quincey and Wordsworth to place De Quincey in the Romantic tradition. He notes in detail how De Quincey's imaginative prose reflects Wordsworth's concepts of art. This book is an interesting way to become acquainted with the intricacies of De Quincey's style.

Proctor, Sigmund K. *Thomas De Quincey's Theory of Literature.* Ann Arbor: University of Michigan Press, 1943. Proctor sees De Quincey's work as divided between mystical and intellectual views of the world and believes that the conflict between the two views creates the ambiguity typical of much of De Quincey's writings. This book provides a good analysis of the background for De Quincey's style.

Other Sources

Jordan, John E. *Thomas De Quincey, Literary Critic: His Method and Achievement.* Berkeley: University of California Press, 1952. Thoroughly evaluates De Quincey's merits as a literary critic.

Lyon, Judson S. *Thomas De Quincey.* New York: Twayne, 1969. A general introduction to the life and work of De Quincey intended for college students. Perceives him as an important author of limited appeal because of the complexities of his style.

Whale, John C. *Thomas De Quincey's Reluctant Autobiography.* London: Croom Helm, 1984. Totowa, NJ: Barnes and Noble, 1984. Discusses how De Quincey had to discipline his talent for the literary tastes of his day.

Kirk H. Beetz
National University, Sacramento

DANIEL DEFOE
1660(?)-1731

Author's Chronology

Born 1660(?) London, England; *1674(?)-1679(?)* attends Reverend Charles Morton's Presbyterian academy; *1684* marries Mary Tuffley; *1685* participates in Monmouth's Rebellion; *1685–1692* establishes himself as a merchant, publishes some political tracts; *1692* goes bankrupt—for the rest of his life plagued by recurring financial problems; *1697–1702* serves William III as pamphleteer, adviser, and friend; *1702* death of William involves him in political difficulties; *1703* imprisoned and pilloried for *The Shortest Way with the Dissenters,* an ironic attack on Tory extremists; *1704–1714* after making his peace with the moderate Tory government, serves it as writer, editor, and secret agent; *1714–1730* serves various Whig governments as writer and agent; *1719–1724* publishes all his major novels; *1731* dies "of a lethargy," perhaps while hiding from creditors.

Author's Bibliography (selected)

The True-Born Englishman, 1701 (satiric poem); *The Shortest Way with the Dissenters,* 1702 (satire); *The Review,* 1704–1713 (journal); *Robinson Crusoe,* 1719 (novel); *Colonel Jack,* 1722 (novel); *A Journal of the Plague Year,* 1722 (novel); *Moll Flanders,* 1722 (novel); *Roxana, or the Fortunate Mistress,* 1724 (novel); *A Tour Thro' The Whole Island of Great Britain,* 1724–1727 (travel).

Overview of Biographical Sources

Merchant and bankrupt, prisoner for debt and for libel, adviser to King and Minister, secret agent, author of more than five hundred works of history, politics, economics, religion, and virtually every other subject of interest to his age, and one of the fathers of the English novel, Daniel Defoe played a variety of parts with a protean zest that makes him at once an attractive and an elusive figure for biographers. Defoe was a secretive man, hiding so successfully behind pseudonyms and ironic personas that scholars are still laboring to determine which works he actually wrote. Many biographers did valuable work on Defoe throughout the 19th and early 20th centuries, but that work has been summed up and built upon by more recent writers. James Sutherland's *Defoe* (1950) is a succinct, balanced, and highly readable account. John Robert Moore's *Daniel Defoe: Citizen of the Modern World* (1958) is enthusiastic and informative, but often incautious in its claims for Defoe. F. Bastian's *Defoe's Early Life* (1981) is an exhaustive account of Defoe's first forty-three years. While all three are fine works, they pay relatively little attention to the novels. A biography still in progress, by Maximillian Novak and Paula Backscheider, promises to be definitive.

Evaluation of Selected Biographies

Bastian, F. *Defoe's Early Life.* Totowa, NJ: Barnes and Noble, 1981. Bastian's scope is narrow but deep as he attempts to glean as much information as possible about Defoe's life up until 1703, the year he was pilloried for political libel. Since this period predates more than ninety percent of his writings, Bastian ignores both Defoe's precarious life as a political provocateur (first for the Tories and then for the Whigs) and his career as a novelist. Despite his focus on the less well documented and less interesting part of Defoe's life, Bastian's account is rewarding. His approach is frankly speculative. He mines the novels and the journalism for passages which might be autobiographical and uses the information thus gathered to fill in gaps in the early years. Bastian's methods demand a reader's caution, but his conclusions usually merit respect. This is, however, a work better suited for the specialist than for the general reader.

Moore, John Robert, *Daniel Defoe: Citizen of the Modern World.* Chicago: University of Chicago Press, 1958. Moore's biography is probably the most ambitious yet available. His approach is not purely chronological; instead he groups his chapters around different phases of Defoe's career—traveler, merchant, reporter, economist, etc. (writing the novels receives no more attention than any other activity). Moore sees Defoe as one of the first modern men, and though the study is frequently illuminating, it is marred by the thesis. Moore presents Defoe as a man whose every word and action must be seen in the best light. Looking for the hero, he often overlooks or oversimplifies the complex, contradictory, and appealingly human man.

Sutherland, James, *Defoe.* London: Methuen, 2nd ed., 1950. Sutherland has spent a lifetime studying Defoe, and his biography is probably the best to date. While not so ambitious as Moore's biography, Sutherland's study presents a more judicious interpretation of the man and his work. Sutherland explicitly avoids taking sides, and his refusal to see Defoe as either hero or villain leads to a well rounded portrait of a fascinating character. Sutherland spends little time on the fiction but provides a wonderfully lucid account of Defoe's tangled political career.

Autobiographical Sources

Defoe left behind no sustained autobiographical record like Jean Jacques Rousseau's *Confessions* or James Boswell's *Journals.* His most extensive autobiographical work is a 1715 pamphlet, *An Appeal to Honour and Justice,* although it is not a candid memoir so much as an attempt to justify his political behavior to his former Whig allies who viewed him as a traitor to the party. It is more disguise than revelation. George Healey's edition of *The Letters of Daniel Defoe* (Oxford: Clarendon Press, 1955) is an invaluable source, but most of the letters concern his career as an agent for the Tory minister Robert Harley; not one refers to the composition, publication, or reception of the novels, and little is revealed of the private man. While autobiographical passages can be found throughout his voluminous writings, the clues Defoe left to his life and character are disappointingly few.

Overview of Critical Sources

Defoe's critical reputation has grown steadily over the last four decades with no sign of a recession. Though critics were once inclined to apologize for his supposed artistic deficiencies or to regard him as a hack who somehow wrote one masterpiece (*Robinson Crusoe*), most now see him as an artist who contributed greatly to the form and themes of the novel. While some critics still see him as an "unconscious" writer, one who created great books almost despite himself, more see a skilled and deliberate artist exercising considerable control over his materials. A growing body of criticism traces the connections between Defoe's novels and the intellectual traditions and developments in his time. Recent critics have begun to explore a strikingly modern Defoe, one obsessed with the alienation and fragmentation of personality in a world suddenly devoid of traditional values.

Evaluation of Selected Criticism

Blewett, David, *Defoe's Art of Fiction.* Toronto: University of Toronto Press, 1979. Among the strengths of this fine study is Blewett's concise summary of the major debates in Defoe criticism, including the question of Defoe's artistic consciousness. Blewett traces a growth in Defoe's artistry and a darkening in his vision of society. He identifies structural patterns common to the novels—imprisonment and deliverance, disaster followed by slow recovery, success through disguise. For Blewett, *Roxana, or the Fortunate Mistress* is the culmination of Defoe's artistic development and of his increasingly bleak perception of the moral decline of an age.

Starr, G. A. *Defoe and Casuistry.* Princeton: Princeton University Press, 1971. Starr examines Defoe's novels in light of the discipline of casuistry, the study of how particular circumstances may alter general moral precepts. Starr shows how Defoe drew upon the casuistical tradition in his presentation of characters who at the same time confess and try to justify themselves for their violations of a moral code they profess to respect. Casuistry, with its emphasis on particular "cases of conscience," also contributes to the episodic form of the novels. This study is one of the finest critical works on Defoe. Also noteworthy is Starr's *Defoe and Spiritual Autobiography.* Princeton: Princeton University Press, 1965.

Sutherland, James, *Daniel Defoe: A Critical Study.* Cambridge: Harvard University Press, 1971. Sutherland offers perhaps the best introduction to Defoe. A biographical chapter (nicely summing up his full length biography) is followed by chapters on the poetry and journalism and a long chapter on the fiction.

Sutherland's readings of the novels are clear and sensible, he is quite informative on the sources, and he identifies most of the major critical issues.

Other Sources

Earle, Peter, *The World of Defoe.* London: Weidenfeld and Nicolson, 1976. An informative survey of Defoe's political, economic, religious, and philosophical ideas.

Novak, Maximillian, *Defoe and the Nature of Man.* London: Oxford University Press, 1963. One of several valuable works in which Novak demonstrates Defoe's debts to, and place in, the intellectual currents of his time.

Richetti, John, *Defoe's Narratives: Situations and Structures.* Oxford: Clarendon Press, 1975. Difficult but rewarding criticism, focusing on the protagonists' powerful self assertion in the face of external restraints.

Watt, Ian, *The Rise of the Novel: Studies in Defoe, Richardson and Fielding.* Berkeley: University of California Press, 1957. One of the most important studies of 18th century fiction. Much subsequent criticism has been a response to Watt's excellent chapters on Defoe.

Selected Dictionaries and Encyclopedias

British Writers, Charles Scribner's, Sons, 1980. Concise overview of the life and principal works.

Kevin P. Mulcahy
Rutgers University

THOMAS DELONEY
1543?–1600

Author's Chronology

No firm evidence exists to establish a date of birth, but most scholars list his birth date as around 1543, probably in Norwich, England; *1583* publishes translations of two Latin pieces; *1586–1592* publishes eight street ballads in broadside form; *1593* publishes *Garland of Good Will; 1595* is sent to jail for distributing a printed complaint against foreign weavers; *1596* publishes "Ballad on the Want of Corn," for which he is sought by the law for having published "foolish and disorderly matter"; *1597* March 7, *Jack of Newbury* entered in Stationers' Register; *1597* October 19, *The Gentle Craft* entered in the Stationers' Register; *1597* probably publishes *Thomas of Reading* during the summer; *1598* probably publishes *The Gentle Craft, Part 2; 1598* January 5, *Canaans Calamitie* entered in the Stationers' Register; *1600* "Died poorly . . . and was honestly buried."

Author's Bibliography (selected)

How many poems Deloney wrote during his lifetime cannot be known because the broadside publication is by its nature impermanent, but most of his extant poems were collected into three books. *The Garland of Good Will,* the earliest extant edition dated 1631, contains twenty-seven ballads, most of which were published originally as broadsides. *Strange Histories,* the earliest extant edition dated 1602, contains eleven ballads and a prose dialogue. *Canaans Calamitie, or the dolefull destruction of faire Ierusalem,* entered in the Stationers' Register in January 1598, is not a collection, but a single poem of 1278 lines. Deloney's four prose romances are early forms of the novel. *Jack of Newbury* (1596) portrays hard-working clothiers in tune with the moral and ethical order of the universe and valuable members of society. *Thomas of Reading* (1597) praises the clothing industry and shows its importance to the prosperity and general well-being of England. *The Gentle Craft, Part 1* (1597) and *The Gentle Craft, Part 2* (1598) glorify the members of England's gentle craft, the shoemakers.

Overview of Biographical Sources

Less is known about the life of Thomas Deloney than any other significant writer of the period: he has remained obscure, partly because he was a member of the merchant class, about whom contemporary historians wrote little. J. W. Ebbsworth contributed a brief biographical sketch on Deloney to the *Dictionary of National Biography,* and several later dictionaries and encyclopedias have followed Ebbsworth's pronouncements on dates of birth, death, and publications. In his *The Works of Thomas Deloney* (1912), Francis Oscar Mann offers in his introduction the first attempt to present a thorough scholarly presentation of Deloney's biography. In the introduction of *The Novels of Thomas Deloney* (1961), Merritt E. Lawlis sketches Deloney's life, updating Mann's work in the light of more recent scholarship; but both Mann and Lawlis have as their primary purposes the editing of the works of Deloney. The only book dealing with analysis, criticism, and biography of Deloney is *Thomas Deloney* (1981) by Eugene P. Wright. Wright's biographical purpose is to pull together the few pieces of evidence concerning the life of Deloney, to fill in the gaps with what is known about the social, political, economic, and religious life of the middle-class Elizabethan, and to formulate as complete a picture of Thomas Deloney as the facts and reasonable extrapolation will allow.

Evaluation of Selected Biographies

Lawlis, Merritt E. *The Novels of Thomas Deloney.* Bloomington: Indiana University Press, 1961. A reprinting of the earliest extant editions of Deloney's four novels, all collated with other editions. The result is a copy of all the best texts, with significant emendations recorded in the notes. The introduction sketches Deloney's life using F. O. Mann's book on Deloney as the basis, but correcting Mann in light of more recent scholarship.

Mann, Francis Oscar, *The Works of Thomas Deloney.* Oxford: The Clarendon Press, 1912. Mann includes extant prose and poetry, copious notes, explanations, and an introduction. Although succeeding scholars have found extant copies of editions missed by Mann, this collection remains a solid scholarly effort and the only complete collection of Deloney's works. The introduction uses contemporaneous public documents and literary works to put together the major facts of Deloney's life.

Wright, Eugene P. *Thomas Deloney.* Boston: Twayne, 1981. This book uses recent scholarship and a rereading of contemporaneous documents to update Deloney's biography in a chapter entitled "The Balletting Silke Weaver." It also uses studies on middle-class life in Elizabethan England and on economic problems of the time to explain the themes of Deloney's works and many of the events in his life. The book deals with Deloney's life, poetry, prose, and his literary reputation in separate chapters. It is the only book available on Deloney which has as its purpose biography, analysis, and criticism.

Overview of Critical Sources

Thomas Deloney is known to most students of literature only as the author of *The Gentle Craft,* a prose work Thomas Dekker used as his source for his dramatic comedy *The Shoemakers' Holiday.* Some few others know him as one of a group of Elizabethan writers who experimented with prose fiction before there was anything generally called a novel. Only scholars who specialize in the English Renaissance will have read his ballads and novels; and as a result, few readers are aware of Deloney's considerable talents as a literary craftsman, his contemporary popularity, and his role of innovator in the genre of prose fiction.

Since the publication of F. O. Mann's *The Works of Thomas Deloney* (*supra*), however, scholars in growing numbers have paid attention to Deloney. Modern scholars now recognize Deloney as a middle-class Englishman who had a good education, spent a period of apprenticeship writing ballads, and finally wrote four significant prose works which altered the course of English prose fiction.

Evaluation of Selected Criticism

Chevalley, Abel, *Thomas Deloney: le Roman des Métiers au temps de Shakespeare.* Paris: Librairie Gillimard, 1926. Chevalley discusses Deloney's novels as both for and about middle-class merchants, unlike all other prose fiction up to his time. Included is a discussion of the economic problems in Elizabethan England which influenced Deloney's works. This is a major study, but has not been translated.

Hablützel, Margrit Elisabeth, *Die Bildwelt Thomas Deloneys.* Bern: Verlag A. Francke Ag., 1946. This is a detailed listing of Deloney's use of imagery in his prose compared and contrasted with the use of imagery by other writers of his time. Tables are included to show the types of images used and their frequency. No translation exists.

Lawlis, Merritt E. *Apology for the Middle Class.* Bloomington: Indiana University Press, 1960. A thorough but elementary discussion of the realistic dialogue, the plot structure, and characterization of Deloney's novels. Lawlis includes plot summaries of the four novels.

Other Sources

Baker, Ernest A. *The History of the English Novel.* Volume II, "The Elizabethan Age and After." New York: Barnes and Noble, 1936. A fair, if somewhat limited, discussion of Deloney's novels as occupying "a foremost place in the history of Elizabethan fiction."

Davis, Walter R. *Idea and Art in Elizabethan Fiction.* Princeton: Princeton University Press, 1969. Davis says that Deloney describes factual details accurately, but that his view of life is romantic, not realistic. Davis is not always accurate in reporting plot details.

Pätzold, Kurt-Michael, "Thomas Deloney and the English Jest-Book Tradition," *English Studies,* 53 (1972), 172–180. Discusses Deloney's close proximity to the jest books in terms of narrative details and events.

Powys, Llewelyn, "Thomas Deloney," *Virginia Quarterly Review,* (1933), 578–594. An encomium to Deloney outlining "the astonishing genius of this great Elizabethan novelist." Powys does not discuss the poetry.

Reuter, Ole, "Some Aspects of Thomas Deloney's Prose Style," *Neuphilologische Mitteilungen,* 49 (1939), 23–72. A thorough review of Deloney's reputation, along with an analysis of his prose works.

Sievers, Richard, "Thomas Deloney: Eine Studie über Balladenlitteratur der Shakespere Zeit. Nebst Neudruck von Deloney's Roman *Jack of Newbury,*" *Palaestra,* 36 (1904), 1–146. A sketch of Deloney's life and brief summaries of his novels precede a classification and discussion of the ballads. Not translated.

Selected Dictionaries and Encyclopedias

Critical Survey of Poetry, Salem Press, 1982, pp. 782–791. Brief biography and a short analysis of Deloney's poetry.

Dictionary of Literary Biography, J. M. Dent, 1962. A brief sketch of Deloney's life and works.

Dictionary of National Biography, Smith, Elder & Co., 1896. A concise discussion of Deloney's life. J. W. Ebbsworth, the contributor on Deloney, does not always explain how he arrives at the details of Deloney's biography.

Eugene P. Wright
North Texas State University

CHARLES DICKENS
1812–1870

Author's Chronology

Born February 7, 1812, Landport, Portsea, England; *1824* works in blacking factory, father imprisoned for debt, attends Wellington House Academy, London; *1827* works as clerk in law office, learns shorthand; *1829–1832* works as a court reporter for various journals; *1836* publishes *Sketches by Boz,* marries Catherine Hogarth, meets John Forster; *1842* makes first trip to America; *1844* travels in Italy with family; *1850* founds and edits *Household Words; 1851* acts in amateur theatrical productions; *1856* collaborates with Wilkie Collins on *The Frozen Deep; 1858* separates from his wife, gives first public readings from his works; *1859* begins *All the Year Round; 1860* moves into Gad's Hill, the house he admired as a child; *1867* makes second trip to America, gives public readings; *1870* suffers a stroke at Gad's Hill on June 8, dies the evening of June 9, is buried in Westminster Abbey on June 14.

Author's Bibliography (selected novels)

Posthumous Papers of the Pickwick Club, 1837; *Oliver Twist, or the Parish Boy's Progress,* 1838; *The Life and Adventures of Nicholas Nickleby,* 1839; *The Old Curiosity Shop,* 1841; *Barnaby Rudge: A Tale of the Riots of 'Eighty,* 1841; *The Life and Adventures of Martin Chuzzlewit,* 1844; *Dealings with the Firm of Dombey and Son,* 1848; *The Personal History of David Copperfield,* 1850; *Bleak House,* 1853; *Hard Times: For These Times,* 1854; *Little Dorrit,* 1857; *A Tale of Two Cities,* 1859; *Great Expectations,* 1861; *Our Mutual Friend,* 1865; *The Mystery of Edwin Drood,* 1870.

Overview of Biographical Sources

Because of his fame, popularity among general readers, and prolific output, biographies of Charles Dickens exist in abundance—there are no fewer than fifty—but none approach the level of scholarship or the significance of the major biographies discussed below. Most deal both with Dickens's life and with his work. Among the useful shorter studies are Andre Maurois's *Dickens* (New York: Ungar, 1967) which seeks to correct the "rather unpleasing light" in which Dickens has been presented; G. K. Chesterton's *Charles Dickens* (New York: Schocken, 1965), which, though stylistically eccentric, is, according to Steven Marcus ("Introduction") "one of the first important modern estimates"; Wolf Mankowitz's *Dickens of London* (New York: Macmillan, 1976), an unscholarly but lively and profusely illustrated biography; and K. J. Fielding's *Charles Dickens: A Critical Introduction* (New York: David McKay, 1958), which is often mentioned as the best introduction to Dickens's life and works. An especially impressive bio-critical study is Angus Wilson's *The World of*

Charles Dickens (New York: Viking, 1970), which attempts to demonstrate the relationship between Dickens's public and private life and his novels. A controversial aspect of Dickens's life is treated in Ada Nisbet's *Dickens and Ellen Ternan* (Berkeley: University of California Press, 1952), which examines Dickens's relationship with the actress with whom he is thought to have been romantically involved. In addition, a good deal of biographical material is available in journal articles, particularly those published in *The Dickensian,* a scholarly periodical devoted to Dickens. Of course, a wealth of biographical detail can be found in Dickens's letters, which have been published in several editions. When completed, the definitive collection will be *The Letters of Charles Dickens,* Pilgrim Edition, eds. Madeline House, Graham Storey, and Kathleen Tillotson (Oxford: The Clarendon Press, 1965–); other editions include *The Letters of Charles Dickens,* ed. Walter Dexter, 3 vols. (Bloomsbury: Nonesuch Press, 1938), and *The Heart of Charles Dickens as Revealed in His Letters to Angela Burdett-Coutts,* ed. Edgar Johnson (Boston: Little, Brown, 1952), which contains the correspondence between Dickens and this long-time associate with whom he collaborated in advancing various social causes.

Evaluation of Selected Biographies

Forster, John, *The Life of Charles Dickens.* 3 vols. London: Chapman and Hall, 1872–1874. The most widely available edition of this work is that edited by A. J. Hoppé, 2 vols., Everyman's Library (London: Dent, 1966). Written by a close friend, this biography of Dickens was the definitive study until the publication of Johnson's book (see below). Forster utilizes an autobiographical fragment given to him by Dickens in 1847 to explain Dickens's traumatic childhood experience of having to work in a blacking factory to aid his financially troubled family. Although it contains much valuable and detailed information, Edgar Johnson (*One Mighty Torrent,* New York: Stackpole, 1937) has criticized the book for being "unsatisfyingly vague about Dickens's troubled marriage," and its author has been judged as having unduly emphasized his relationship with Dickens.

Johnson, Edgar, *Charles Dickens: His Tragedy and Triumph.* 2 vols. New York: Simon and Schuster, 1952. Revised and Abridged. New York: Viking, 1977. Superseding Forster's book, Johnson's is now the standard biography. Based upon an enormous amount of new material—the author consulted 3500 unpublished documents—the facts contained in the book are scrupulously researched and presented in a prose style which is lucid and highly readable. Johnson's emphasis is on Dickens as "a penetrating commentator on life and modern society," and he also presents new evidence confirming Dickens's relationship with Ellen Ternan. This definitive biography also contains some of the best criticism of Dickens's works, making it one of the most highly regarded bio-critical sources both for the general reader and for the serious student. For readers who do not require the critical analyses, the revised and abridged edition, which contains new material, eliminates the criticism and careful bibliographical documentation of the original.

Mackenzie, Norman and Jeanne, *Dickens: A Life.* New York: Oxford University Press, 1979. Despite the fact that the authors of this book acknowledge their "great debt to the Pilgrim Edition of the Dickens Letters," reviewers generally agree that the book reveals nothing substantially new about Dickens's life. The focus of this biography is on Dickens as "a man of paradoxes." A good book for the general reader, this biography contains a thorough and competently presented account of the existing evidence. However, those in need of critical analyses of Dickens's works will not find this book useful.

Autobiographical Sources

Dickens's autobiographical fragment has already been discussed (see Forster above). Many details from Dickens's early life—including the blacking factory incident—are present, though in embellished, fictionalized form, in the novel, *David Copperfield.* However, readers are cautioned against drawing parallels between the author's life and that of the novel's main character, except in the most general sense, for in the book Dickens subordinates reality to the requirements of art. From the narrow perspective of autobiography, the novel is significant chiefly as a psychological document, revealing Dickens's submerged resentments and desires.

Overview of Critical Sources

Perhaps the most useful works to the student who does not have access to a large research library are the collections of important journal articles available in book form. Among the most useful are those edited by Martin Price, *Dickens: A Collection of Critical Essays* (Englewood Cliffs, NJ: Prentice-Hall, 1967); A. E. Dyson, *Dickens: Modern Judgements* (London: Macmillan, 1969); Michael Slater, *Dickens, 1970* (New York: Stein and Day, 1970); John Gross and Gabriel Pearson, *Dickens and the Twentieth Century* (Toronto: University of Toronto Press, 1962); Ada Nisbet and Blake Nevius, *Dickens Centennial Essays* (Berkeley: University of California Press, 1971); and Jerome H. Buckley, *The Worlds of Victorian Fiction* (Cambridge and London: Harvard University Press, 1979, pp. 1–71). These books contain a broad range of essays on Dickens and his works from a variety of critical perspectives.

Also useful, though more general than the collections cited above, are treatments of Dickens in books which survey the literature of the period or the novel. Among the best are the sections devoted to Dickens in Walter Allen's *The English Novel* (New York: E. P. Dutton, 1954); Annette T. Rubinstein's

The Great Tradition in Literature: From Shakespeare to Shaw, vol. 2. (New York: Modern Reader Paperbacks, 1953); and Frederick Karl's *A Reader's Guide to the Nineteenth Century Novel* (New York: The Noonday Press, 1964).

The following two books are devoted entirely to critical appraisal of one of Dickens's most widely discussed novels: A. E. Dyson, ed., *Dickens: Bleak House* (London: Macmillan, 1969); and Jacob Korg, ed., *Twentieth Century Interpretations of Bleak House* (Englewood Cliffs, NJ: Prentice-Hall, 1968). Dyson's book contains sections on background and early reviews and comment.

A study which every reader of Dickens should be familiar with is Edmund Wilson's "Dickens: The Two Scrooges," in *The Wound and the Bow: Seven Studies in Literature* (New York: Farrar, Straus, and Giroux, 1978). In this, the latest reprint of his classic essay first published in 1941, Wilson discusses Dickens's "complexity" and "depth" as he traces the development of his social criticism. This essay has been credited with stimulating much subsequent scholarship.

There are many full-length studies of Dickens written from the perspectives of specific critical points-of-view and purposes. Among the most significant are Sylvere Monod's *Dickens the Novelist* (Norman: University of Oklahoma Press, 1967), a revision of *Dickens Romancier* (1953) in which the author defends Dickens's style while discussing how the novels were written; John Butt's and Kathleen Tillotson's *Dickens at Work* (London: Methuen, 1957) which examines the effect of serial publication on Dickens's novels; Humphrey House's *The Dickens World* (London: Oxford University Press, 1941), which treats the novels from the perspective of literary history; and T. A. Jackson's *Charles Dickens: The Progress of a Radical* (New York: International Publishers, 1938) which advances a Marxist interpretation of Dickens's works. An important recent study is Michael Slater's *Dickens and Women* (Stanford: Stanford University Press, 1983), which traces Dickens's "response to the presentation of . . . femaleness and its myriad interrelationships with maleness." Two other important books of the "Dickens and . . ." variety are Philip Collins's *Dickens and Crime* (Bloomington: Indiana University Press, 1968); and *Dickens and Education* (London: Macmillan, 1963). Collins treats these special topics in a thorough, scholarly manner.

Evaluation of Selected Criticism

Daleski, H. M. *Dickens and the Art of Analogy.* London: Faber and Faber, 1970. The author traces Dickens's development as a novelist through a discussion of representative novels and argues that Dickens's use of analogy illuminates both the focus and structure of each work. Daleski identifies money and love as Dickens's dominant themes.

Ford, George H. *Dickens and His Readers: Aspects of Novel-Criticism Since 1836.* Princeton: Princeton University Press, 1955; rpt. New York: Gordian

Press, 1974. This is a classic study of Dickens's reputation as a novelist, based upon "reviews . . . diaries, autobiographies, letters, memoirs, and critical essays."

Hobsbaum, Philip, *A Reader's Guide to Charles Dickens.* New York: Farrar, Straus, and Giroux, 1973. Typical of the series, this book is an extremely useful introductory work-by-work critique, and contains a good bibliography.

Marcus, Steven, *Dickens: From Pickwick to Dombey.* New York: Simon and Schuster, 1965. An important study of Dickens's early works which relates the novels to his "vision of society." Marcus also treats the ways in which the changes in English society during Dickens's lifetime affected his works.

Miller, J. Hillis, *Charles Dickens: The World of His Novels.* Cambridge: Harvard University Press, 1958. Miller's important study attempts to reveal Dickens's unified imaginative vision. His thesis is that Dickens's novels are more than reflections of his age. Rather, the world in which he lived becomes the basis of the unique and consistent imaginative universe which is given "form and substance" in his novels.

Other Sources

Nelson, Harland S. *Charles Dickens.* Boston: Twayne, 1981. A very useful comprehensive treatment of Dickens's work. Contains annotated bibliography.

Smith, Grahame, *Dickens, Money, and Society.* Berkeley: University of California Press, 1968. Treats the theme of money as central to an understanding of Dickens.

Stoehr, Taylor, *Dickens: The Dreamer's Stance.* Ithaca: Cornell University Press, 1965. Advances the theory that Dickens's novels are like dreams. Contains analyses of his "dark" novels.

Selected Dictionaries and Encyclopedias

British Writers, Vol. 5. New York: Charles Scribner's Sons, 1982. Excellent bio-critical survey with bibliography.

Dictionary of Literary Biography, Vol. 21. Detroit: Gale Research, 1983. Good general biography. Contains unannotated bibliography.

Eugene Zasadinski
St. John's University

JAMES DICKEY
1923

Author's Chronology

Born February 2, 1923, Atlanta, Georgia to Eugene and Maibelle (Swift) Dickey; *1942* graduates from North Fulton High School where he stars in football and track; attends Clemson A & M College but leaves before end of first semester to join Army Air Force; *1942–1945* flies approximately 100 missions in South Pacific for 418th Night Fighters and participates in firebombing of major Japanese cities; *1948* marries Maxine Syerson; *1949* obtains B.A. degree from Vanderbilt University; *1950* takes M.A. degree from Vanderbilt and teaches at Rice Institute before being recalled by Air Force for Korean War; *1951* son, Christopher Swift, born; *1952–1954* teaches again at Rice; wins *Sewanee Review* Fellowship; lives, travels, writes in Europe; *1955–1956* teaches at University of Florida; begins advertising career with firms in New York and Atlanta; *1958* son, Kevin Webster, born; *1961* awarded Guggenheim Fellowship; *1962* travels and writes in Europe; *1963* Poet-in-Residence at Reed College; *1964* Poet-in-Residence at San Fernando Valley State College; *1966* wins National Book Award for *Buckdancer's Choice;* Poet-in-Residence at University of Wisconsin, Madison; becomes Consultant in Poetry for Library of Congress; *1969* named Carolina Professor of English and Writer-in-Residence at University of South Carolina; *1976* wife, Maxine, dies; marries Deborah Dodson; *1977* reads his poem "The Strength of Fields" at President Carter's inauguration; *1981* daughter, Bronwen, born; *1985* continues to live in Columbia, South Carolina.

Author's Bibliography (selected)

Into the Stone, 1960 (poems); *Drowning with Others,* 1962 (poems); *Helmets,* 1964 (poems); *The Suspect in Poetry,* 1964 (criticism); *Buckdancer's Choice,* 1965 (poems); *Poems 1957–1967,* 1967 (poems); *Babel to Byzantium,* 1968 (criticism); *Deliverance,* 1970 (novel); *The Eye-Beaters, Blood, Victory, Madness, Buckhead and Mercy,* 1970 (poems); *Self-Interviews,* 1970 (autobiography); *Sorties,* 1971 (prose); *The Zodiac,* 1976 (poem); *The Strength of Fields,* 1979 (poems); *Puella,* 1982 (poems); *Night Hurdling,* 1983 (criticism, prose, poems).

Overview of Biographical Sources

Because of his past notoriety and his refusal to authorize or cooperate with any biography, James Dickey's life presents an unusual problem. Most of what is known derives from Dickey himself in the form of conversations, interviews, and various autobiographical essays. No substantial biography presently exists, and none is likely until after his death. Certain comparatively brief glances at

Dickey's life are available, though almost all of these focus on one aspect of his life. Geoffrey Norman's "The Stuff of Poetry" (*Playboy,* May 1971) relates a canoe trip taken with Dickey in which the events related are typical of those which have helped establish the poet's popular image. Much biographical information is included. Richard Calhoun's "After a Long Silence: James Dickey As South Carolina Writer" (*South Carolina Review,* November 1976) explores Dickey as a Southerner. R. V. Cassill's "The Most Dangerous Game of the Poet James Dickey" (*South Carolina Review,* April 1978) relates anecdotes about Dickey's life and speculates on his reputation. Both writers know Dickey personally. "The Poet as Journalist" (*Time,* 13 December 1968) discusses Dickey's years as pilot and journalist. Sheldon Kelly's "James Dickey—'Poet of Survival and Hope' " (*Reader's Digest,* November 1979) offers a more intimate look at Dickey the man.

Evaluation of Selected Biographies

Calhoun, Richard and Robert Hill, *James Dickey.* Boston: Twayne, 1983. The authors present a general bio-critical introduction to Dickey's life and works. None of the poet's works is thoroughly discussed, but the information is accurate and the analysis does provide a reader's guide to Dickey's poetic philosophy and his various thematic concerns, images, and symbols. The authors' treatment of the man and his achievements is objective but favorable.

Autobiographical Sources

In interviews and personal essays, Dickey has presented a full picture of himself and created the Dickey myth of a man for whom "the dance at the edge" constitutes life's value. "The Poet Turns on Himself" (*Babel to Byzantium*) shows how he "eased into poetry" in high school and the South Pacific, and what he attempted to accomplish in his early writings. *Self-Interviews* also presents a look at Dickey's early life, examining his college years, his marriage to Maxine Syerson and subsequent advertising career, and the various influences on his life. The book is the closest thing to an autobiography available. *Sorties* is a collection of prose ramblings—almost an undated journal—in which the poet comments on a wide range of topics and concerns. Dickey presents a thorough overview of his life in an interview that recounts his college years up through his present endeavors (*Conversations with Writers,* Detroit: Gale Research, 1977). In *The Starry Place Between the Antlers: Why I Live in South Carolina* (Bloomfield Hills, Michigan and Columbia, South Carolina: Bruccoli Clark, 1981), Dickey offers an intimate and sometimes amusing look at his Southern heritage. *Night Hurdling,* particularly the section called "Some Personal Things," displays various aspects—and moments—in Dickey's life and, taken as a whole, quite likely represents a portrait of how the poet wishes himself seen.

Overview of Critical Sources

Although the reading public knows Dickey primarily for his novel *Deliverance,* critics have judiciously viewed not only his prose but his poetry and criticism as well. Dickey considers himself principally a poet and has experimented throughout his career with new poetic forms, in particular the "open poem." A large body of criticism exists that analyzes the various aspects of his work, but this assessment is generally found in the form of essays, many of the best now collected in edited books. The existing criticism on Dickey's poetry acknowledges the poet's concern with the connection that can occur between an individual and the external world, leading to a new and heightened sense of reality and an awareness of human possibilities.

Evaluation of Selected Criticism

Lensing, George, "James Dickey and the Movements of Imagination," *James Dickey: The Expansive Imagination.* Deland, FL: Everett/Edwards, 1973. Lensing states that Dickey's intense subjectivity constitutes a new post-modern romanticism. Subjectivity and objectivity become fused, such that the external world becomes identified with—and psychically remade through—the imagination. Lensing's intellectual article shows that Dickey's poems begin with an undistorted view of reality and, after the setting is emotionally recreated, conclude with a return to normalcy.

Lieberman, Laurence, "The Worldly Mystic," *Unassigned Frequencies: American Poetry in Review, 1964–1977.* Urbana and Chicago: University of Illinois Press, 1977. Lieberman claims that Dickey deliberately traps his persona in moral predicaments to dramatize the conflict between modern worldly-mindedness and the spirit's inner life. The poems show the existential self making lifesaving connections with its own hidden resources. Lieberman's well-known essay argues that Dickey's purpose is to resurrect the individual's imagination.

Oates, Joyce Carol, "Out of Stone, into Flesh: The Imagination of James Dickey 1960–1970," *The Imagination as Glory.* Urbana and Chicago: University of Illinois Press, 1984. This illuminating essay argues that Dickey's poetry is characterized by a concern with the poet's "personality" as it relates to nature and experience. Oates's psychological study shows that Dickey's endless questioning of the self has resulted in a movement from a poetry of Being, which can effect a passive resolution into some "other," to a poetry of anguished Becoming, which fails to reconcile any opposites.

Weatherby, H. L. "The Way of Exchange in James Dickey's Poetry," *James Dickey: The Expansive Imagination.* This early essay shows that Dickey's poetry portrays an act of "transmission," a mysterious process of exchange between a man and his opposites, in which both participants enter into each other to present a composite vision. Weatherby warns that such situations sometimes seem staged and affected. Though acclaimed by critics, Dickey has faulted the essay.

Other Sources

Calhoun, Richard, "Whatever Happened to the Poet-Critic?" *Southern Literary Journal,* 1 (Autumn 1968), 75–88. Stresses the importance of the "I" in poetry and its infinite capacity for extension. Wants Dickey to write more criticism since he demands poetic honesty.

Howard, Richard, "On James Dickey," *Partisan Review,* 33 (Summer 1966), 414–428, 479–486. Analysis of the various themes, images, and symbols that characterize Dickey's early poetry. Praises the poet's "yearning to transcend."

Mills, Ralph, "The Poetry of James Dickey," *Triquarterly,* 11 (Winter, 1968), 231–242. Notes Dickey's evocative capacity for imaginative extension but warns that his poems should proceed from inner necessity and not from the external demands of his reputation.

Selected Dictionaries and Encyclopedias

Contemporary Poets, St. Martin's Press, 1980. Brief biography, together with a listing of Dickey's publications, commentary from the poet himself, and a brief critical examination of his poetry.

Dictionary of Literary Biography, Gale Research, 1980. Concise overview of Dickey's life and a detailed analysis of his work.

A. Gordon Van Ness
University of South Carolina

EMILY DICKINSON
1830–1886

Author's Chronology

Born December 10, 1830, Amherst, Massachusetts, to Edward and Emily Norcross Dickinson; attends local primary school and Amherst Academy (forerunner of Amherst College); *1847–1848* attends Mount Holyoke College; *1850* publishes a Valentine poem in Amherst College *Indicator* (atypical poem and the first of only a few published poems during her lifetime); *1855* Dickinson family moves to the "Homestead," where Dickinson lived the rest of her life; *1856* Dickinson's brother, Austin, marries Susan Gilbert, Emily's childhood friend; *1862* writes letter to Thomas Wentworth Higginson, asking advice about her poetry; *1874* father dies; *1875* mother becomes invalid; *1882* mother dies; May 15, 1886, Emily Dickinson dies, virtually unpublished and unknown as a poet.

Author's Bibliography

Because Emily Dickinson rarely sought publication of her poetry and was largely unappreciated as an artist by critics during her lifetime, fewer than a dozen of the more than 1770 poems now credited to her were published before her death. Thomas Wentworth Higginson and Mabel Loomis Todd edited a selection, *Poems,* in 1890; 1891 *Poems,* Second Series, ed. T. W. Higginson and Mabel Loomis Todd; 1896 *Poems,* Third Series, ed. Mabel Loomis Todd; 1924 *The Complete Poems of Emily Dickinson* (incomplete); 1931 *Letters of Emily Dickinson* (a selection); 1955 *The Poems of Emily Dickinson,* 3 vols., ed. Thomas H. Johnson; 1958 *The Letters of Emily Dickinson,* 3 vols., ed. Thomas H. Johnson.

Overview of Biographical Sources

Emily Dickinson's reclusiveness and the consequent mystery and mythology surrounding her life, coupled with the earnest efforts of friends and relatives to guard her reputation shortly after her death, have led to great scholarly interest in her biography, much of it speculative. Curiosity about the life of a poet whose life was outwardly almost without event has caused most critics to incorporate biographical matter, real or assumed, into readings of the poetry, making the line between biography and criticism unusually blurred in Dickinson study. The earliest full-length biographical study, Martha Dickinson Bianchi's *The Life and Letters of Emily Dickinson* (Boston: Houghton Mifflin, 1924) is colored by the author's relationship to Dickinson: Bianchi was Dickinson's niece, the daughter of her brother Austin, and was influenced by the dramatic "legend" of Emily Dickinson. George F. Whicher's *This Was a Poet: A Critical Biography of Emily Dickinson* (New York: Charles Scribner's Sons, 1938) is therefore in some sense the first "real" biography of the poet. A turning point in Dickinson biography was reached with the publication of Thomas H. Johnson's *Emily Dickinson: An Interpretive Biography* (1955). Johnson, who edited the definitive collections of Dickinson's poems and letters, had access to a wealth of information and produced the most reliable biography to that date. The most controversial biographical study is John Cody's *After Great Pain: The Inner Life of Emily Dickinson* (1971), a psychoanalytic study that has been severely attacked by recent feminist critics. The most definitive biography to date is the massive *The Life of Emily Dickinson* by Richard B. Sewall (1974).

Evaluation of Selected Biographies

Cody, John, *After Great Pain: The Inner Life of Emily Dickinson.* Cambridge: Harvard University Press, 1971. Cody's approach to Dickinson is psychoanalytic, and he sees the poetry as a response to and even the direct result of Dickinson's emotional turmoil. Had Emily Dickinson developed as a "normal" woman, with a positive image of her own mother after which to model herself, she would not have devoted herself to poetry, which was a means of coping with severe emotional problems. Though an admirer of Dickinson's art, Cody views it in a biographical context that emphasizes supposed abnormalities in Dickinson's psychic development.

Johnson, Thomas H. *Emily Dickinson: An Interpretive Biography.* Cambridge: Harvard University Press, 1955. As a major scholar and editor of Dickinson's work, Johnson is able in this work to blend biography and criticism in a manner that illuminates Dickinson's life and poetry without following a narrow critical approach. The biography is of manageable size, and Johnson's style is clear and readable.

Sewall, Richard B. *The Life of Emily Dickinson.* New York: Farrar, Straus, Giroux, 1974. 2 vols. This comprehensive biography, later issued in a one-volume paperback edition by Farrar, Straus in 1980, places Dickinson in the context of her time, place, and family, and draws upon all available sources of information to present a thorough and objectively sympathetic portrait of the poet and her times. The book includes a chronology of Dickinson's life, extensive references and bibliography, and an index of the first lines of the poems mentioned or examined in the text. Sewall's style is scholarly, but not abstruse.

Autobiographical Sources

Dickinson's letters, her only autobiographical writing (other than what can be surmised from the poetry) are almost equally enigmatic. Although she lived in a culture that valued letters as an important form of communication, and more than a thousand of her letters are extant, she observes here the maxim that also seems to inform her poetry: "Tell all the Truth but tell it slant—/ Success in circuit lies" (from poem #1129, written about 1868). Her penchant for cryptic, circuitous self-description was made famous by Thomas Wentworth Higginson, who was fond of quoting her response to his request for a picture of her, a response that reads in part, "Could you believe me—without?" Dickinson's refusal to be categorized by camera or direct self-revelation in words makes her letters—especially later in her life—nearly as metaphoric as her poetry, and therefore just as challenging. Thomas H. Johnson's three-volume edition of Dickinson's letters, *The Letters of Emily Dickinson* (1958) is the most comprehensive source of autobiographical information. Johnson's one-volume *Selected Letters* (Cambridge: Harvard University Press, 1971) includes a useful selection of the most significant ones. These volumes have been supplemented by the publication of *The Lyman Letters: New Light on Emily Dickinson and her Family.* ed. Richard B. Sewall (Amherst: University of Massachusetts Press, 1965).

Overview of Critical Sources

Dickinson scholarship is voluminous; her poetry has been studied seriously since shortly after her death, and her work has been the object of most of the major approaches of twentieth-century literary criticism. The publication of *The Poems of Emily Dickinson* in 1955 made her poetry readily available to scholars in one volume, and thus spurred renewed interest in her work. The development of feminist literary theory in the 1970's has created yet another spate of Dickinson criticism, much of it revisionist. There is now no question that she is a major figure in American letters, and the following is only a sampling of the myriad critical approaches to her work.

Evaluation of Selected Criticism

Anderson, Charles R. *Emily Dickinson's Poetry: Stairway of Surprise.* New York: Holt, Rinehart, 1960. One of the first critics to benefit from access to the complete works of Dickinson after their publication in 1955, Anderson takes Dickinson seriously as a poet who delighted in the possibilities of language, and provides a good overview of style and themes in her work. The book is organized by poetic themes, and is a good introductory study.

Juhasz, Suzanne, *Feminist Critics Read Emily Dickinson.* Bloomington: Indiana University Press, 1983. This is a collection of eight essays by leading scholars of Dickinson's work, preceded by an introduction in which Juhasz outlines some tenets of feminist literary scholarship. The essays are clear analyses of Dickinson's work as a female poet in a culture that has defined the woman's role in anti-intellectual ways. The approaches to Dickinson's work include the linguistic, the thematic, and the biographical.

———, *The Undiscovered Continent.* Bloomington: Indiana University Press, 1983. Juhasz rejects the persistent notion that Dickinson's self-imposed solitude was the result of neurosis or rejection by a lover. She examines the poetry for evidence that Dickinson found her own mind the most interesting and fulfilling place to inhabit and that her isolation from society was a conscious, positive choice rather than a retreat from "reality."

Keller, Karl, *The Only Kangaroo Among the Beauty: Emily Dickinson and America.* Baltimore: Johns Hopkins University Press, 1979. An interesting mixture of casual style and significant insight, this book explores the relationship of Dickinson's poetry and her response to American values to those of other major American writers, including Anne Bradstreet, Edward Taylor, Harriet Beecher Stowe, Walt Whitman, and Robert Frost. Keller emphasizes affinities rather than influences, and attempts to place Dickinson within the continuum of American literary thought, including the popular literature of her time.

Miller, Ruth, *The Poetry of Emily Dickinson.* Middletown, CT: Wesleyan University Press, 1968. Using the poetry, the letters, and biography, Miller explores Dickinson's publication history, her relationship with critic T. W. Higginson, the enigmatic "Master" letters, Dickinson's "fascicles" (hand-sewn volumes) of poetry, and the contents of the Dickinson family library. Miller's style is clear and the book offers useful information that aids in understanding Dickinson's work.

Mossberg, Barbara Antonina Clarke, *Emily Dickinson: When a Writer is a Daughter.* Bloomington: Indiana University Press, 1982. Mossberg takes seriously Dickinson's familial context as a source of the multiple *personae* in her poetry. Identifying with neither her conventionally passive mother nor her traditionally authoritarian father, Mossberg argues, Dickinson developed an individuality that defined her own relation to the world as an artist. The author is inclusive in her study of the poetry, examining "minor" as well as "major" poems.

Other Sources

Bingham, Millicent Todd, *Ancestors' Brocades: The Literary Debut of Emily Dickinson.* New York: Harper & Row, 1945. Written by the daughter of a family friend, this account of the publishing of Dickinson's work is far from objective, but interesting as part of Dickinson lore.

Buckingham, Willis J., ed. *Emily Dickinson: An Annotated Bibliography.* Bloomington: Indiana University Press, 1970. Out of date but useful for locating criticism to 1970.

Capps, Jack Lee, *Emily Dickinson's Reading 1836–1886.* Cambridge: Harvard University Press, 1966. A comprehensive study of the books and periodicals Dickinson did read or could have read during her lifetime.

Lilliedahl, Ann, *Emily Dickinson in Europe.* Washington, D.C.: University Press of America, 1981. A study of the reception and critical valuation of

Dickinson's work in Scandinavia, Switzerland, France, and Germany from 1886 to 1977.

Longsworth, Polly, *Austin and Mabel.* New York: Farrar, Straus, Giroux, 1984. An account of the thirteen-year affair between Dickinson's brother, Austin, and Mabel Loomis Todd, who later edited the first volumes of Dickinson's poems. Includes the correspondence of the lovers.

Martin, Wendy, *An American Triptych.* Chapel Hill: University of North Carolina Press, 1984. A study of Anne Bradstreet, Emily Dickinson, and Adrienne Rich as American women poets with strong affinities.

Rosenbaum, S. P., ed. *A Concordance to the Poems of Emily Dickinson.* Ithaca, NY: Cornell University Press, 1964.

Shurr, William H. *The Marriage of Emily Dickinson.* Lexington: University Press of Kentucky, 1983. An attempt to prove that Dickinson imagined a "spiritual marriage" to the Rev. Charles Wadsworth, and that most of the poetry is addressed to him.

Taggard, Genevieve, *The Life and Mind of Emily Dickinson.* New York: Alfred A. Knopf, 1930. An early biographical/critical study.

Wylder, Edith Perry Stamm, *The Last Face: Emily Dickinson's Manuscripts.* Albuquerque, NM: University of New Mexico Press, 1971. A study of Dickinson's handwritten manuscripts, analyzing composition, handwriting, and punctuation.

Nancy Walker
Stephens College

JOAN DIDION
1934

Author's Chronology

Born December 5, 1934, Sacramento, California; *1952–1956* attends the University of California at Berkeley and graduates; *1956* wins *Vogue's* Prix de Paris and moves to New York to work for *Vogue; 1963* publishes first novel, *Run River; 1964* marries John Gregory Dunne, leaves *Vogue,* and moves to Los Angeles area; *1967–1969* shares "Points West" column in *The Saturday Evening Post* with Dunne; *1968* publishes first collection of essays, *Slouching Towards Bethlehem; Los Angeles Times* names her "Woman of the Year"; *1969–1970* writes columns for *Life; 1971–1972* collaborates with Dunne on screenplays for *The Panic in Needle Park* and *Play It As It Lays; 1972–1979* publishes review articles in such periodicals as *The New York Review of Books* and *The New York Times Book Review; 1975* is a Regents Lecturer at the University of California at Berkeley; *1976–1977* writes "The Coast" column for *Esquire; 1979–1980* writes alternate "Didion & Dunne" columns for *New West; 1983* publishes first book-length nonfiction, *Salvador.*

Author's Bibliography (selected)

Run River, 1963 (novel); *Slouching Towards Bethlehem,* 1968 (essays); *Play It As It Lays,* 1970 (novel); *A Book of Common Prayer,* 1977 (novel); *Telling Stories,* 1978; *Salvador,* 1983 (book-length nonfiction); *Democracy,* 1984 (novel).

Overview of Biographical Sources

Perhaps because she is a living writer and her literary career is so relatively short, biographical sources on Didion are limited, and none yet can be considered definitive. Two general, one-chapter biographies are available in book-length, introductory studies of Didion and her work: Katherine Usher Henderson's *Joan Didion* and Mark Royden Winchell's *Joan Didion.* A particularly good source is Michiko Kakutani's "Joan Didion: Staking Out California," in Ellen G. Friedman's *Joan Didion: Essays and Conversations.*

Evaluation of Selected Biographies

Henderson, Katherine Usher, *Joan Didion.* New York: Frederick Ungar, 1981. This book contains a one-chapter general biography preceded by a chronology.

Kakutani, Michiko, "Joan Didion: Staking Out California," *Joan Didion: Essays and Conversations.* Princeton: Ontario Review Press, 1984. A combination of biography, criticism, and interview, this article contains one of the most comprehensive and well-formed biographical essays on Didion. It is an excellent synthesis of material from published interviews of Didion and from her essays.

Winchell, Mark Royden, *Joan Didion.* Boston: Twayne, 1980. While not so well-synthesized as Kakutani's piece, the one-chapter biographical essay in this book does clearly identify its interview and essay sources, and so is more useful for someone wishing to track down more primary material. It is also preceded by a chronology.

Autobiographical Sources

Most of Joan Didion's autobiographical material is scattered through her essays and in interviews with her. Some of the collected essays richest in autobiographical material include the following: from *Slouching Towards Bethlehem,* "On Keeping a Notebook," "On Self-Respect," "On Going Home," "Notes from a Native Daughter," "Letter from Paradise, 21° 19' N., 157° 52' W.," and "Goodbye to All That"; from *The White Album,* "The White Album," "In the Islands: 1969," "In Bed," "On the Road," "On the Mall," "On the Morning After the Sixties," and "Quiet Days in Malibu." Good autobiographical sources among the uncollected essays include the following: "On Being Unchosen by the College of One's Choice," in the April 6, 1968 *Saturday Evening Post;* "A Death in the Family," in the September 10, 1979 *New West;* and "Mothers and Daughters," in the December 31, 1979 *New West.*

Overview of Critical Sources

The major recurring concerns in criticism of Joan Didion's writing include how her sensibility influences her writing, the recurring themes of disorder and how people cope with it, how ideals can mislead us, the supposed frailty of her female characters, how she uses history in her fiction, her use of carefully chosen details, how she fits into the tradition of "new journalism," and the influences of the works of Ernest Hemingway on her writing. Much criticism of her work is in the form of contemporaneous articles, some of which have been collected into Ellen G. Friedman's *Joan Didion: Essay and Conversations.* Book-length studies of her work are primarily introductory volumes.

Evaluation of Selected Criticism

Henderson, Katherine Usher, *Joan Didion.* New York: Frederick Ungar, 1981. With one chapter devoted to each of Didion's books up through *The White Album,* Henderson's book focuses on Didion's concern with how people who hang on to traditional American dreams fare in an increasingly chaotic world.

Friedman, Ellen G. *Joan Didion: Essays and Conversations.* Princeton: Ontario Review Press, 1984. This is a collection of one Didion essay, three interviews with Didion, and fourteen critical essays on Didion's work. Most of the critical articles are reprints of pieces previously published in periodicals, but one is excerpted from a work in progress. Friedman's book is a milestone in the study of Didion's work because it is the first to bring together much of a previously scattered body of critical works.

Winchell, Mark Royden, *Joan Didion.* Boston: Twayne, 1980. This introductory study's chapters are organized theme-by-theme rather than book-by-book. It deals first with the major themes of her essays—chaos, illusions of order, American dreams—and then examines her fiction in light of these themes.

Other Sources

Kuehl, Linda, "Joan Didion," in *The Paris Review Interviews: Writers at Work, Fifth Series.* New York: Viking Press, 1981. First published in *Paris Review,* 20, No. 74 (Fall-Winter 1978). In this interview, Linda Kuehl draws Didion into an unusually open discussion of the craft of writing, thereby providing an uncommonly direct insight into the processes by which she produces her work.

Jacobs, Fred Rue, *Joan Didion—Bibliography.* Keene, CA: The Loop Press, 1977. This is the most nearly complete bibliography of works by and about Joan Didion through 1977.

Barbara A. King
California State University, Sacramento

JOHN DONNE
1572–1631

Author's Chronology

Born between January 24 and June 19, 1572, London; *1584* ff. studies at Oxford and possibly at Cambridge; *1589–1591* possibly travels abroad; *1591* begins legal studies; *1596–1597* sails on Cadiz and Azores expeditions; *1597* or early *1598* becomes secretary to Lord Keeper Egerton; *1601* serves in Parliament; in December secretly marries Ann More, daughter of Egerton's brother-in-law; *1602* confesses his marriage, is imprisoned, then dismissed from Egerton's service; takes refuge at Pyrford, estate of Francis Wolley; *1603* daughter Constance born; eleven more children (including two stillbirths) born over the next fourteen years; *1605–1606* probably travels to France and Italy; *1606* settles in Mitcham; *1608–1609* unsuccessfully seeks posts in Ireland and with the Virginia Company; *1610* receives honorary Oxford M.A.; *1611–1612* travels in Europe with Sir Robert Drury; *1612* moves with his family into a house on the Drury estate; *1614* serves in Parliament; fails in pursuit of state post; *1615* ordained Anglican deacon and priest; appointed a royal chaplain; *1616* granted church posts; *1617* wife dies; *1619* serves as chaplain during Doncaster's embassy to Germany; *1621* elected Dean of St. Paul's; *1622* becomes rector of Blunham and Justice of the Peace; *1623* becomes seriously ill; *1624* becomes vicar of St. Dunstan's; *1626* appointed governor of the Charterhouse; *1630* becomes seriously ill; *1631* dies March 31.

Author's Bibliography (selected)

Ignatius his Conclave, 1611 (religious polemic); *An Anatomy of the World,* 1611 (poetic eulogy); *The Second Anniversarie. Of the Progres of the Soule,* 1612 (poetic eulogy); *Devotions Upon Emergent Occasions,* 1624 (meditations); *Juvenilia: or Certaine Paradoxes, and Problemes,* 1633; *Poems, By J. D. With Elegies on The Authors Death,* 1633; *LXXX Sermons,* 1640; *Biathanatos,* 1647? (on suicide); *Fifty Sermons,* 1649; *Letters to Severall Persons of Honour,* 1651; *Essayes in Divinity,* 1651.

Overview of Biographical Sources

Donne's life poses numerous problems to the biographer, who must decide how to deal with such difficult issues as the later impact of the poet's Catholic background; how the poems can be used as biographical evidence; the supposed conflict between Donne's youth and maturity; how his interest in self-presentation affects various sources; the frequent difficulties of deciding dates of composition; and the fact that many of the most interesting questions about Donne's life—including controversies about his character, motives, and thought—often cannot be answered readily from the evidence available. The first biography of Donne—Izaak Walton's *The Life and Death of Dr Donne* (1640; subsequently revised and enlarged)—remains one of the most interesting. Walton's influence on many later biographers was very great, but although his book is still an important source for some information, it is no longer considered wholly dependable. In *The Making of Walton's Lives* (Ithaca: Cornell University Press, 1958), David Novarr shows how Walton produced distortions by shaping and selecting some materials while neglecting others. Throughout his book, Novarr offers important comments of his own about Donne's life. Novarr's more recent study, *The Disinterred Muse: Donne's Texts and Contexts* (Ithaca: Cornell University Press, 1980), is especially significant for attempting to situate biographically the poems Donne composed after his ordination.

The standard scholarly biography is R. C. Bald's *John Donne: A Life* (1970), which supersedes previous treatments. Bald's earlier study, *Donne and the Drurys* (Cambridge: Cambridge University Press, 1959), examines the poet's relationships with important patrons. Arthur Marotti discusses Donne and patronage more broadly in "John Donne and the Rewards of Patronage" in *Patronage in the Renaissance,* ed. Guy Fitch Lytle and Stephen Orgel (Princeton: Princeton University Press, 1981), pp. 207–234. More general issues of power and social aspiration are raised in *John Donne: Life, Mind, and Art* (New York: Oxford Univ. Press, 1981), by John Carey. One of the most controversial of recent studies, Carey's book is not a biography *per se,* but its critical orientation is strongly biographical. Edmund Gosse's *The Life and Letters of John Donne, Dean of St. Paul's* (2 vols.; London: Heinemann, 1899), for years the standard work, is unreliable factually and textually, but contains a very full collection of letters. Richard E. Hughes, in *The Progress of the Soul: The Interior Career of John Donne* (New York: William Morrow, 1968), intersperses brief chapters on the "exterior" life with longer discussions of the poetry and prose to chart developments in Donne's psychology and attitudes. Evelyn M. Simpson's *A Study of the Prose Works of John Donne,* 2nd. ed. (Oxford: Clarendon Press, 1948) sketches the life, discusses Donne as a man of letters and theologian, then gives biographical contexts for the prose. William R. Mueller, in *John Donne: Preacher* (Princeton: Princeton University Press, 1962) opens with a brief biography, then discusses Donne's theology and views of the priesthood.

Written for the general reader, Edward LeComte's *Grace to a Witty Sinner: A Life of Donne* (New York: Walker and Co., 1965) contains a bibliography but no notes; some of its assumptions have been questioned. Derek Parker's *John Donne and His World* (London: Thames and Hudson, 1975) is short, with interesting pictures, but has been faulted for "biographizing" from the poems and for offering questionable interpretations of documents. Contemporary biographical comments are printed in Appendix V of Geoffrey Keynes' indispensable *Bibliography of Dr. John Donne,* 4th ed. (Oxford: Clarendon Press, 1973). More recent studies are listed and indexed in John R. Roberts' *John Donne: An*

Annotated Bibliography of Modern Criticism 1912–1967 (Columbia: University of Missouri Press, 1973) and *John Donne: An Annotated Bibliography of Modern Criticism 1968–1978* (Columbia: University of Missouri Press, 1982). The *John Donne Journal* (first volume: 1982) publishes biographical articles, among others.

Evaluation of Selected Biographies

Bald, R. C. *John Donne: A Life.* New York and Oxford: Oxford University Press, 1970. This careful work emphasizes "hard" evidence and uses the poems only within limits. Although criticized by some scholars for not capturing Donne's vitality, it remains the most reliable account yet written, assembling many facts about the poet and his acquaintances. It has been censured for failing to recreate the spirit of the age; for failing to clarify how it uses Walton; and for over-emphasizing insignificant facts while under-emphasizing certain important but less-well-documented characters and events. Some readers find it colorless, but its prose is clear and its manner sensible. It assesses earlier biographies, includes a chronology and notes on Donne's children, and appends biographical documents.

Carey, John, *John Donne: Life, Mind, and Art.* New York: Oxford University Press, 1981. Carey's informal style appeals to some readers but annoys others. Some have admired the book's scholarship and clarity, while others have attacked it for faulty methodology and unconvincing arguments. Criticized for interpreting poems in naively biographical terms, its early chapters emphasize Donne's "apostasy" and "ambition"; the second half discusses the works in terms of such concerns as the body, change, death, and skepticism.

Walton, Izaak, *The Life and Death of Dr Donne.* London: 1640; subsequently revised and enlarged; included in many modern editions of Walton's *Lives.* London: 1670. Walton's biography, itself an important literary work, can be faulted for imbalance and inaccuracy. But as the fullest treatment by one who personally knew Donne and his times, it remains uniquely significant. Changes between 1640 and 1675 emphasized Donne's exemplary holiness.

Autobiographical Sources

How the poems bear on the man will remain a vexing problem for Donne's biographers. Bald considered the love poems generally less reliable sources than the religious poems, because the speaker was more likely to be a persona. The verse letters are clearly important sources; how to deal with them is less clear. Addressed to acquaintances and patrons, they offer interesting glimpses of the poet as friend, suitor, and commentator. The prose works—in whole or in part—often seem autobiographically significant, but frequently pose interpretive problems. Even Donne's *Letters to Severall Persons of Honour* (1651), ed. M. Thomas Hester (Delmar, NY: Scholar's Facsimiles and Reprints, 1977) must often be viewed as self-conscious products of a highly imaginative mind. No comprehensive, authoritative edition of Donne's letters has yet been published although one is in preparation. However, Keynes' *Bibliography* contains a helpful inventory of the scattered surviving texts. In nearly every genre Donne exploited there are autobiographical facts and reflections, but distilling and explicating them is difficult.

Overview of Critical Sources

Partly because Donne has often been central to critical controversy about Renaissance literature, the numerous books and essays on his work frequently go beyond a narrow concern with Donne himself. Once disputed, his major status now seems assured. Some earlier critics saw him as a kind of proto-modern; more recent writers have attempted to view him in historical context, often without agreement. Like all major authors, Donne will continue to attract as many different kinds of critical attention as there are different kinds of critics.

Evaluation of Selected Criticism

Leishman, J. B. *The Monarch of Wit: An Analytical and Comparative Study of the Poetry of John Donne.* London: Hutchinson University Library, 1951. Revised several times since 1951, this remains one of the better introductions. The first chapter compares Donne with Jonson, while the second discusses "Donne the Man." Leishman deals with the elegies, satires, verse letters, and divine poems, but spends most time on the *Songs and Sonnets,* emphasizing their variety of tone and their stylistic features, and generally stressing Donne's dramatic qualities.

Lewalski, Barbara Kiefer, *Protestant Poetics and the Seventeenth-Century Religious Lyric.* Princeton: Princeton University Press, 1979. Partly a response to Martz's *Poetry of Meditation,* this massive work charts Protestant influences on the divine poetry of Donne and others. Scrutinizing religious and rhetorical texts, it suggests that Protestants saw no necessary conflict between art and truth, and indeed regarded the Bible itself as a poetic model. Critics have accused Lewalski of claiming too much, of soft-pedaling Protestant hostility to art, and of over-emphasizing Calvinist influences. But the book remains a mine of valuable information.

Martz, Louis L. *The Poetry of Meditation: A Study in English Religious Literature of the Seventeenth Century.* New Haven: Yale University Press, 1954. Not limited to Donne, this book discusses him repeatedly, arguing that methods of religious meditation influenced the style and structure of many 17th-century poems. Martz contends that intense meditation, like many of Donne's works, creatively unites the senses, intellect, and emotions. Martz devotes special attention to the *Anniversaries* and the divine poems, but touches briefly on some of the *Songs and Sonnets.* The book has been criticized for over-emphasizing Catholic traditions at the expense of Protestant influences.

Tuve, Rosemond, *Elizabethan and Metaphysical Imagery.* Chicago: University of Chicago Press, 1947. Tuve warns against reading Donne and others without awareness of how Renaissance poetic conventions and stylistic criteria influenced them. She emphasizes particularly the impact of rhetorical and logical theories, but has been criticized for underemphasizing Donne's uniqueness and for exaggerating the influence of Ramist logic on metaphysical style.

Other Sources

Alvarez, A. *The School of Donne.* London: Chatto and Windus, 1961. Links the realism and logic of Donne's wit to his original coterie audience.

Andreasen, N. J. C. *John Donne: Conservative Revolutionary.* Princeton: Princeton University Press, 1967. Argues that the love poetry (Ovidian, Petrarchan, and Christian Platonic) teaches morality by positive and negative example.

Eliot, T. S. "The Metaphysical Poets," in *Selected Essays of T. S. Eliot.* 2nd ed. New York: Harcourt, Brace, & World, 1951. Argues that Donne's sensibility united mind and feeling. Although Eliot himself later modified this view, for decades it was both very influential and the target of subsequent criticism.

Fiore, Peter A. ed. *Just So Much Honor: Essays Commemorating the Four-Hundredth Anniversary of the Birth of John Donne.* University Park: Pennsylvania State University Press, 1972. Eleven original essays.

Guss, Donald L. *John Donne: Petrarchist: Italianate Conceits and Love Theory in The Songs and Sonets.* Detroit: Wayne State University Press, 1966. Attempts to define Donne's place and originality in the tradition of Petrarchan poetry.

Hester, M. Thomas, *Kinde Pitty and Brave Scorn: John Donne's Satyres.* Durham, NC: Duke University Press, 1982. Richly detailed analytical and contextual study; sees the satires as illustrating the speaker's progressive regeneration.

Lewalski, Barbara Kiefer, *Donne's Anniversaries and the Poetry of Praise: The Creation of a Symbolic Mode.* Princeton: Princeton University Press, 1973. Studies literary and theological contexts to argue that Donne created a new, meditative mode of praise focused on "potentialities of the human soul as image of God."

Miner, Earl, *The Metaphysical Mode from Donne to Cowley.* Princeton: Princeton University Press, 1969. Uses Donne to define some typical features of metaphysical poetry: private mode; definitional and dialectical wit; satiric denial and lyric affirmation. Two later books deal with "social" and "public" modes.

Pinka, Patricia Garland, *This Dialogue of One: The Songs and Sonnets of John Donne.* University, AL: University of Alabama Press, 1982. Approaches the poems through their different types of personae.

Roberts, John R. ed. *Essential Articles for the Study of John Donne's Poetry.* Hamden, CT: Archon Books, 1975. Extremely useful anthology of recent criticism, with sections on Donne's reputation, impact on English poetry, uses of tradition, prosodic and rhetorical practices, love poetry, religious poetry, *Anniversaries,* and miscellaneous poems.

Roston, Murray, *The Soul of Wit: A Study of John Donne.* Oxford: Clarendon Press, 1974. Examines similarities between the secular and religious verse; discusses Donne's views of empirical and spiritual reality, and compares his poems to mannerist paintings. Emphasizes the serious implications of his wit.

Sanders, Wilbur, *John Donne's Poetry.* London: Cambridge University Press, 1971. Praises the poems of fulfilled love, but censures stylistic faults in others.

Schleiner, Winfried, *The Imagery of John Donne's Sermons.* Providence: Brown University Press, 1970. Claims that Donne innovates upon traditional imagery.

Sherwood, Terry, *Fulfilling the Circle: A Study of John Donne's Thought.* Toronto: University of Toronto Press, 1984. Discusses "Donne's notions of reason, body, and suffering in his epistemology and psychology."

Smith, A. J., ed. *John Donne: Essays in Celebration.* London: Methuen, 1972. A wide-ranging collection of original essays.

Stein, Arnold, *John Donne's Lyrics: The Eloquence of Action.* Minneapolis: University of Minnesota Press, 1962. Treats Donne's style, wit, and consciousness.

Webber, Joan, *Contrary Music: The Prose Style of John Donne.* Madison: University of Wisconsin Press, 1963. Focuses on the sermons and *Devotions.*

White, Helen C. *The Metaphysical Poets: A Study in Religious Experience.* New York: Macmillan Co., 1936. One chapter discusses Donne's religious development and thought; another deals with the divine poems' emphasis on the speaker, sin, mutability, and the "otherness" of God, and with their lack of mysticism.

Robert C. Evans
Auburn University at Montgomery

JOHN DOS PASSOS
1896–1970

Author's Chronology

Born in Chicago on January 14, 1896, out of wedlock, to John Roderigo Dos Passos (a corporate attorney) and Lucy Addison Sprigg; *1896–1907* travels with one or both parents in Mexico, Europe; spends time in Washington, D.C. and at his father's estate in Westmoreland County, Virginia; *1907–1912* attends Choate School as John R. Madison; *1912* enters Harvard at 16 as "John Roderigo Dos Passos, Jr." (his parents having married in 1910); *1912–1916* contributes regularly and significantly to *Harvard Monthly; 1916* graduates from Harvard *cum laude;* makes cultural trip to Spain rather than drive an ambulance in the European war; *1917* his father dies; he joins an ambulance unit until discharged in *1919; 1920* having remained in Europe to write following discharge, publishes *One Man's Initiation—1917* (first novel); *1922* returns to America; *1925* publishes *Manhattan Transfer,* a novel characterized by the impressionistic innovations in form and style which were to become a trademark of Dos Passos' most celebrated work; *1926–1929* works in experimental theatre in New York; pickets for Sacco and Vanzetti (*1927*); travels to Russia (*1928*); *1929* marries Katharine Smith; *1930–1937* writes on *U.S.A.* trilogy (most ambitious work); supports various radical causes and movements, but votes for Roosevelt in *1936; 1937* works in Spain with Hemingway and others on a film of the Civil War there, but grows disillusioned and returns home; *1938* publishes *U.S.A.* (novel trilogy); *1940* publishes *The Living Thoughts of Tom Paine,* the first of several books on topics from early American history; *1943* writes numerous war pieces for *Harper's; 1945* reports on War in Pacific for *Life; 1947* Katharine Dos Passos is killed; Dos Passos loses an eye in the same accident; *1948* decides to settle on the Virginia estate left him by his father; *1949* marries Elizabeth Holdridge; *1951* publishes *Chosen Country,* an autobiographical novel and the first of his "contemporary chronicles"; Lucy, his only child, born; *1958* receives gold medal for fiction from The National Institute of Arts and Letters; *1961* publishes *Midcentury,* another "contemporary chronicle" with an autobiographical cast; *1961–1970* is active in conservative political causes (votes for Barry Goldwater in 1964); combines farming and writing as his livelihood; lectures at various colleges and universities; *1966* publishes *The Best Times,* a memoir; *1970* dies in Baltimore on September 28; is buried near his Virginia estate.

Author's Bibliography (selected)

One Man's Initiation—1917, 1920 (novel); *Three Soldiers,* 1921 (novel); *A Pushcart at the Curb,* 1922 (poems); *Rosinante to the Road Again,* 1922 (essays); *Streets of Night,* 1923 (novel); *Manhattan Transfer,* 1925 (novel); *Orient*

Express, 1927 (travel sketches); *Three Plays,* 1934; *U.S.A.* (reprints the trilogy of novels *The 42nd Parallel,* 1930; *1919,* 1932; and *The Big Money,* 1936); *Chosen Country,* 1951 (novel); *District of Columbia,* 1952 (reprints the trilogy of novels *Adventures of a Young Man,* 1939; *Number One,* 1943; *The Grand Design,* 1949; *The Head and Heart of Thomas Jefferson,* 1954 (biography); *The Men Who Made the Nation,* 1957 (biographies); *Midcentury,* 1961 (novel); *The Best Times: An Informal Memoir,* 1966; *The Portugal Story: Three Centuries of Exploration and Discovery,* 1969 (history); *Century's Ebb: The Thirteenth Chronicle,* 1975 (final novel).

Overview of Biographical Sources

Not long after Dos Passos' death in 1970, serious biographers set to work, assisted by his family, friends, and archivists. The major result of these efforts has been the publication of two full-scale biographies which, appearing within four years of each other, offer two comprehensive treatments of their subject. The first to appear was Townsend Ludington's *John Dos Passos: A Twentieth Century Odyssey* (1980). Ludington had already established himself as an authority on Dos Passos by having edited the autobiographical volume *The Fourteenth Chronicle* (q.v., 1973). Ludington's biography has been generally accepted as the kind of complete treatment that had been needed. Four years after Ludington's study appeared, Virginia Spencer Carr published *Dos Passos: A Life* (1984). Carr's study is done on no less a scale than Ludington's. Though different in many respects, either book could be called with justification a "standard" biography.

Evaluation of Selected Biographies

Carr, Virginia Spencer, *Dos Passos: A Life.* New York: Doubleday, 1984. Carr's biography is meticulously researched and presented in a straightforward, chronological manner. It is impressive for the richness of its source materials and for the completeness with which it treats the many facets of its subject. There is, however, little comment made on the author's work, and few conclusions are drawn. It is not focused upon any consistent theme or idea, but rather lets the subject and the sources speak for themselves. It should stand as a factual, comprehensive biographical source.

Ludington, Townsend, *John Dos Passos: A Twentieth Century Odyssey.* New York: E. P. Dutton, 1980. The central theme of Ludington's biography derives from the metaphor of a journey, an odyssey both physical (Dos Passos' extensive travels) and ideological (from left-wing radicalism in his youth to conservatism in old age). This synthesizing of facts, combined with a polished prose style, makes the complex pattern of Dos Passos' life easy to follow. While giving attention to the sentiments of his subject's personal and ideological adversaries, Ludington's portrayal is laudatory, depicting Dos Passos as a major interpreter of his country in the twentieth century. Though he does not pursue certain biographical questions to the lengths as rigorously as Carr, it is anticipated that Ludington's biography will be regarded as the standard treatment.

Autobiographical Sources

Toward the end of his career, John Dos Passos began calling his novels "contemporary chronicles" (the thirteenth and final one, *Century's Ebb,* was not published until after his death). Having considered himself an active participant in the contemporary milieu of which he wrote, there is always an autobiographical character in these "chronicles," or novels. Perhaps most notable among these depictions is that found in the "Camera Eye" passages of *U.S.A.,* where there is little attempt to disguise the author. Carrying forward Dos Passos' idea of the chronicle, Townsend Ludington edited an imposing volume of letters and diaries and called the collection *The Fourteenth Chronicle* (Boston: Gambit, 1973). Beginning with entries written while Dos Passos was a student at Choate and concluding with selections composed just a few weeks before his death, *The Fourteenth Chronicle* is a voluminous source book of autobiography. The editor's introductory and transitional passages make for continuity and easy reading. Among Dos Passos' final works is a memoir, *The Best Times* (New York: New American Library, 1966). Consisting of autobiographical sketches on selected topics such as his father and his early literary career, and ending with some episodes from the early years of his marriage to "Katy" Smith the memoir, though vivid and telling, omits much interesting material. However, it is structured by the author himself, in much the same loose and impressionistic manner found in his novels. *The Best Times,* like *The Fourteenth Chronicle,* contains illustrations by the author, thus revealing a side of his talent known to few of his readers.

Overview of Critical Sources

Not until the 1960's did Dos Passos attract the kind of critical attention that resulted in book-length studies of his work. The preface to John H. Wrenn's *John Dos Passos* (1961) sets forth the critical climate of that time. Dos Passos had achieved a high degree of fame early in his career with novels of protest innovatively structured. But with the passage of time the issues protested had lost currency and the technical originality had come to be taken for granted. Moreover, Dos Passos had undergone an apparent ideological shift from leftist radicalism to conservatism, thus leaving behind many of the converts he had garnered in the 1920's and 1930's. Wrenn's study and numerous subsequent ones have attempted to evaluate the entire sweep of Dos Passos' career in contemporary terms, with the result that his reputation among critics seems to have been established on a positive, stable basis. Critical activity in the 1960's, 1970's, and 1980's has produced a solid body of secondary literature.

Evaluation of Selected Criticism

Belkind, Allen, ed. *Dos Passos, the Critics, and the Writer's Intention.* Carbondale: Southern Illinois University Press, 1971. This is a generous sampling of essays covering key topics relating to Dos Passos' life, work, and times. Among the authors are many contemporaries who have made solid literary reputations for themselves. The entire scope of Dos Passos' career is covered by these pieces, which were written at various points throughout.

Wagner, Linda W. *Dos Passos: Artist as American.* Austin: University of Texas Press, 1979. In the most complete critical study since Dos Passos' death, Linda Wagner treats the entire canon as well as the issues of theme and technique which have consistently attracted the interest of modern critics. The theme of the study—that Dos Passos explored his country by means of expressing it in his writing—is a central one and therefore illuminating for anyone studying Dos Passos' work either piecemeal or in the aggregate. This is, on the whole, a well-rounded, judicious study epitomizing the interests of present-day scholars.

Wrenn, John H. *John Dos Passos.* New York: Twayne, 1961. Wrenn's study was undertaken for the express purpose of dispelling the cliché that the best of Dos Passos' work lay in the past and that he had become something of an anachronism. By tracing the consistent patterns in Dos Passos' work and by explaining his ideological evolution, Wrenn laid the groundwork for other critics of his generation.

Other Sources

Brantley, John D. *The Fiction of John Dos Passos.* The Hague: Mouton, 1968. An overview which considers Dos Passos' achievements in terms of his relative strengths. Concentrates on the novels.

Davis, Robert Gorham, *John Dos Passos.* Minneapolis: University of Minnesota Press, 1962. A competent pamphlet-length study with good summaries of selected titles.

Rohrkemper, John, *John Dos Passos: A Reference Guide.* Boston: G. K. Hall, 1980. Lists all book-length works by Dos Passos as well as books and articles about him. The latter begin with 1921 and go through 1979 on a year-by-year basis.

Welford Dunaway Taylor
The University of Richmond

SIR ARTHUR CONAN DOYLE
1859–1930

Author's Chronology

Born May 22, 1859, Edinburgh, Scotland, son of Charles Altamont Doyle, civil servant and failed painter, and his wife Mary; *1868* attends Hodder Preparatory School; *1870* enters Stonyhurst College, a Jesuit secondary school, where he spends five years; *1876* begins medical studies at Edinburgh University; *1880* sails as ship's doctor aboard the whaler *Hope; 1881* signs on as ship's doctor for African cargo steamer *Mayumba; 1882* sets up medical practice at Southsea, England; abandons Catholicism; lack of patients leaves him time to start writing to supplement income; *1885* marries Louise "Touie" Hawkins; *1887* begins his lifelong fascination with spiritualism; *A Study in Scarlet,* his first Sherlock Holmes adventure, appears; *1891* studies eye diseases in Vienna in hopes of becoming specialist; moves practice to London; *1893* wife develops tuberculosis after birth of second child, is given only months to live; Conan Doyle kills off Sherlock Holmes in "The Final Problem" to have more time for family concerns; *1897* falls in love with Jean Leckie who becomes his acknowledged "fiancée" although his wife is still alive; *1900* organizes field hospital during Boer War; *1900* enters politics, runs unsuccessfully for parliament in this year and *1906; 1902* knighted for medical efforts in Africa; returns to Holmes with *The Hound of the Baskervilles; 1903* resurrects Holmes in *The Return of Sherlock Holmes; 1906* wife dies; *1907* marries Leckie after year of mourning; becomes known as a champion of public causes; *1914–1918* involved in home defense; argues for civilized treatment of prisoners of war; *1918* deaths of family members increase interest in spiritualism; *1918–1930* abandons fiction almost entirely to pursue role as propagandist for spiritualism; *1930* dies July 30 at Crowborough, England.

Author's Bibliography (selected)

A Study in Scarlet, 1887 (novel); *Micah Clarke,* 1889 (novel); *The Sign of the Four,* 1890 (novel); *The White Company,* 1891 (novel); *The Adventures of Sherlock Holmes,* 1892 (stories); *The Memoirs of Sherlock Holmes,* 1894 (stories); *The Stark Munro Letters,* 1895 (novel); *The Great Boer War,* 1900 (nonfiction); *The Hound of the Baskervilles,* 1902 (novel); *The Return of Sherlock Holmes,* 1903 (stories); *Sir Nigel,* 1906 (novel); *The Lost World,* 1912 (novel); *The Valley of Fear,* 1915 (novel); *His Last Bow,* 1917 (stories); *The New Revelation,* 1918 (nonfiction); *My Memories and Adventures,* 1924 (autobiography); *History of Spiritualism,* 1926, 1927 (nonfiction).

Overview of Biographical Sources

Arthur Conan Doyle's life is, for many readers, of secondary importance to that of his most famous fictional creation, Sherlock Holmes. Because of this, as well as a certain embarrassment in academic circles about his uncritical championship of spiritualism, Conan Doyle did not become the subject of a major biography until nearly twenty years after his death. J. Lamond, his fellow spiritualist, had published *Arthur Conan Doyle, a Memoir, with An Epilogue by Lady Conan Doyle* (London: John Murray, 1931) with the family's blessing. The standard, and for many years unchallenged biography appeared in 1949 by mystery writer John Dickson Carr. His *The Life of Sir Arthur Conan Doyle* (1949) remains the definitive study although its largely laudatory style sometimes obscures its real value. The cooperation of Conan Doyle's surviving children who contributed personal recollections as well as allowed Carr access to reams of unpublished diaries, letters, and personal papers makes this very much the "authorized version" of their father's life. Less favored by the family was Hesketh Pearson's *Conan Doyle* (London: Methuen, 1943; reprinted New York: Walker, 1961). Terming this pseudo-biography, Conan Doyle's son Adrian responded with *The True Conan Doyle* (London: John Murray, 1943), a twenty-four page biographical sketch designed to refute specific inaccuracies in Pearson's book. Dissatisfaction with unauthorized biography led the family to cooperate fully with Carr to produce either a more accurate or more acceptable version of their father's life. Two excellent biographies have appeared in the past two decades: Charles Higham's *The Adventures of Conan Doyle: The Life of the Creator of Sherlock Holmes* (1976); Pierre Nordon's *Conan Doyle: A Biography,* trans. Frances Partridge (1966). Both are assiduously researched from surviving unpublished materials; both are valuable for their extensive bibliographies which detail the location of all available primary sources; both are free from the uncritical admiration for their subject that is the hallmark of the Carr biography.

Evaluation of Selected Biographies

Carr, John Dickson, *The Life of Sir Arthur Conan Doyle.* London: John Murray; New York: Harper Brothers, 1949. Carr's biography represents the first general study of Conan Doyle's life and work to be based on unpublished letters and diaries. Written with the cooperation of his family, the book portrays the author as Victorian knight errant to the extent of seemingly serious references to him as "our hero." Its value lies in its reliance on primary sources and its wholly sympathetic portrayal of Conan Doyle. Carr seems embarrassed about his subject's ardent espousal of spiritualism and thus avoids that aspect of his career as much as possible. Given its limitations, the book remains a valuable resource.

Higham, Charles, *The Adventures of Conan Doyle: The Life of the Creator of Sherlock Holmes.* New York: W. W. Norton, 1976. In his well-researched biography, Higham presents an overview of Conan Doyle's life and a critical review of his fiction, including those works which do not feature Sherlock Holmes.

Many family papers accessible to earlier biographers have been withdrawn, and others have been dispersed to various libraries. Higham has nonetheless attempted to use as much original material as is still available and has augmented it by consulting Conan Doyle's many letters to the London *Times* and other newspapers. He also explores the complicated relationship between Conan Doyle, his wife, and Leckie and speculates on its effect on Conan Doyle's fiction to an extent not possible in Carr's biography.

Nordon, Pierre, *Conan Doyle: A Biography.* trans. Frances Partridge. New York: Holt, Rinehart, and Winston, 1966. Nordon, Head of the Department of English at the University of Nantes, focuses this most scholarly of the Conan Doyle biographies on the author's public career and examines the effects of his various interests on his writings. This biography is helpful for its frank discussion of Conan Doyle's preoccupation with spiritualism. Nordon agrees with Carr that devotion to medieval chivalric virtues influenced the author's life and work but is far more objective in his treatment.

Autobiographical Sources

Conan Doyle's *The Stark Munro Letters* (1895) is thinly-disguised autobiography. It recounts the life of a young doctor in an English seaside town in *roman à clef* fashion. The characters and events of the book directly parallel those of Conan Doyle's own establishment in Southsea. In spite of this, little of the private man is revealed. The villain of the book is as much or more the central character than is the figure who represents young Dr. Doyle.

Thirty years later Conan Doyle again attempted autobiography in *My Memories and Adventures* (1924) which is as unrevealing as the fictionalized *The Stark Munro Letters.* Conan Doyle presents a running commentary on the events of his own life but still leaves the reader ignorant of the real Conan Doyle at the end of the book. *My Memories and Adventures* at least shows the public the Conan Doyle its author wishes the world to know even if it reveals little of his actual personality.

Overview of Critical Sources

Most of the criticism of Conan Doyle's work concerns the Sherlock Holmes canon. Except for discussions in the biographies, his other fiction is usually ignored, and, except for *The White Company,* has long been out of print. Recently, there has been a revival of interest in his science fiction about which some critical studies have appeared.

Sherlockian criticism generally takes two forms: serious study as part of the detective novel genre and what has been termed the Grand Game. Beginning as a spoof on academic scholarship but continuing with great seriousness, this form insists that Holmes and Watson were real individuals and Conan Doyle was at best a literary agent or at worst a plagiarist. The Baker Street Irregulars of London and New York promulgate this view which has spawned literally hundreds of books and articles, some tongue-in-cheek but most deadly in their seriousness.

Evaluation of Selected Criticism

Baring-Gould, William S. *Sherlock Holmes of Baker Street: A Life of the World's First Consulting Detective.* New York: Clarkson N. Potter, 1962. One of the greatest Sherlockians, Baring-Gould has written one of the best, though his fellow critics insist it is not the definitive, biography of a fictional detective. Baring-Gould has an obsession with the minutiae of the Holmes canon, but the book is valuable for its attention to detail.

Harrison, Michael, ed. *Beyond Baker Street: A Sherlockian Anthology.* Indianapolis: Bobbs-Merrill, 1976; *In the Footsteps of Sherlock Holmes.* London: Cassell, 1958; *The London of Sherlock Holmes.* Newton-Abbott: David & Charles, 1972; *The World of Sherlock Holmes.* London: Muller, 1973. *Beyond Baker Street* contains an important collection of Grand Game criticism for those readers who do not wish to plow through hundreds of books and articles themselves. The other three books are interesting studies of the Victorian milieu in which Holmes is supposed to have lived and worked. Harrison is like most Sherlockians in that he can take the slightest reference in one of Conan Doyle's stories, relate it to known events in the nineteenth century, and come up with plausible "facts" about Holmes' life.

Shreffler, Philip A. ed. *The Baker Street Reader: Cornerstone Writings about Sherlock Holmes.* Westport, CT: Greenwood Press, 1984. Shreffler presents a serious anthology of critical material on Conan Doyle's detective stories. His introduction is particularly important as it relates the popularity of Holmes and of Grand Game criticism to the phenomena of popular culture. His book contains a balanced selection of critical material from both the serious and Grand Game schools. Undoubtedly fond of the Holmes stories, Shreffler retains a critical objectivity often missing from Sherlockian criticism.

Waugh, Charles G. and Martin H. Greenberg, eds. *The Best Science Fiction of Arthur Conan Doyle.* Carbondale: Southern Illinois University Press, 1981. In the introduction to this revisionist collection, George Slusser relates much of the Conan Doyle canon to the science fiction genre, seeing its traces in most of the diverse writing experiments attempted by the author. Slusser's essay places Conan Doyle firmly in the mainstream of the British science fiction tradition, ranking him along with such other giants as H. G. Wells.

Mary Anne Hutchinson
Utica College of Syracuse University

MICHAEL DRAYTON
1563–1631

Author's Chronology

Born at Hartshill in north Warwickshire in 1563; spends his early years as a page at Polesworth, Sir Henry Goodere's home; witnesses the will of Sir Henry Goodere, who died on January 26, 1595; *1594–1598* warmly dedicates poems to Lucy, Countess of Bedford, claiming that Sir Henry Goodere had bequeathed him to her care; *1597–1602* intermittently writes plays for the Admiral's players; tries unsuccessfully to attract the attention of James after his accession in 1603; bitterly attacks Lucy and a rival poet, possibly John Donne, in *Poemes Lyrick and pastorall* (*1606*); *1602–1620* depends on the patronage of Sir Walter Aston; acquires as patrons during his final years Edward Sackville, fourth Earl of Dorset, and Lady Sackville; *1631* dies in poverty, leaving an estate worth about twenty-four pounds; buried in Westminster Abbey.

Author's Bibliography (selected)

Idea. The Shepheards Garland, 1593 (pastoral poetry); *Ideas Mirrour,* 1594 (first version of sonnet sequence which was revised in 1599, 1600, 1602, 1605, 1619); *Mortimeriados,* 1596 (historical epic); *Englands Heroicall Epistles,* 1597 (epistolary poems exchanged by lovers who are historical figures; reprinted in 1598, 1602, 1605 and in editions of his complete works); *The Barons Warres,* 1603; *The Owle,* 1604 (satirical fable); *The Legend of Great Cromwell,* 1607 (historical poem); *Poly-Olbion,* 1612 (a topographical poem surveying English landscape and history); *The Shepheards Sirena,* 1627 (topical pastoral); *The Muses Elizium,* 1630 (pastoral poetry).

Overview of Biographical Sources

The standard four-volume edition of *The Works of Michael Drayton* (1941; rpt. 1961) was edited by J. William Hebel. He died before he was able to complete the edition; the fifth and final volume, containing the notes and commentary, was prepared by Kathleen Tillotson and Bernard Newdigate. In addition, Newdigate is the author of the principal biographical source for Drayton's life, *Michael Drayton and his Circle* (1941, 1961). These sources supply an accurate factual outline of Drayton's life. Both the standard edition and the principal biographical study, however, assume without any evidence other than dedications that Drayton fell in love with Anne Goodere, the younger daughter of his patron, and that Drayton's sonnet sequence, *Ideas Mirrour,* is addressed to her. Between 1923 and 1927 a number of articles appeared which discussed allegorical interpretations of Drayton's *The Shepheard's Sirena* as alluding to attacks upon the Spenserians by opposing poetic schools. In "Drayton's Relation to the School of Donne as Revealed in 'The Shepherd's Sirena' " (*PMLA,*

XXXVIII (1923), 557–587), and "Drayton's 'Sirena' Again" (*PMLA,* XLII (1927), 129–139), Raymond Jenkins interprets the poem as a defense of the Spenserians against John Donne. J. William Hebel, in "Drayton's 'Sirena' " (*PMLA,* XXXIX (1924), 814–826), insists that Sirena is Anne Goodere, Olcon is Ben Jonson, the attacking swineherds are the Tribe of Ben, and the defending shepherds the Spenserians.

Evaluation of Selected Biographies

Berthelot, Joseph A[lfred], *Michael Drayton.* Twayne English Author Series. Boston: Twayne, 1967. Berthelot's is a slight discussion of Drayton's biography derived entirely from Newdigate.

Elton, Geoffrey, *Michael Drayton. A Critical Study.* 1905; rpt. New York: Russell & Russell, 1966. Elton offers a sympathetic view of Drayton's life, but a highly uncritical introduction to his works.

Helgerson, Richard, *Self-Crowned Laureates: Spenser, Jonson, Milton and the Literary System.* Berkeley: University of California Press, 1983. Helgerson interprets Drayton as a poet who aspired to become a laureate in the tradition of Spenser, but who failed to achieve that stature and became isolated from his audience.

Newdigate, Bernard, *Michael Drayton and his Circle.* 1941; rpt. Oxford: Basil, Blackwell, & Mott, 1961. Newdigate discusses Drayton's ancestors, education, patrons (especially, the Goodere family, Countess of Bedford, and Walter Aston), literary acquaintances (Jonson, Shakespeare, William Drummond of Hawthornden), sources and antiquarian acquaintances (William Camden, John Stow, John Selden).

Although Newdigate has traced painstakingly Drayton's sources and amassed considerable information concerning them and his patrons, the commentary should be used with care. Newdigate describes Drayton's life-long devotion to Anne Goodere, but other than dedications of poems to his patron's daughter, there is no evidence that Drayton was ever her tutor or that he experienced life-long, unrequited love for her. This study should be used as the basis for further investigation of the way in which poets who were principally interested in writing nondramatic poetry supported themselves by means of the patronage system during the sixteenth and seventeenth centuries.

Overview of Critical Sources

Drayton was an extremely prolific writer who repeatedly revised his sonnets and early historical poetry. Although a number of dissertations have been written on Drayton's revisions, there has as yet been no full-scale study which might suggest the influence of changing taste on Drayton's revised texts.

Richard Hardin's book-length study of Drayton as a patriotic poet is valuable in high-lighting one aspect of his poetic activity and importance. Drayton's pastorals and satires might be further investigated. A full-length study of Drayton in relation to seventeenth-century social and political trends affecting poets dependent upon patronage is needed in order to supply a context for Drayton's repeated complaints about his times.

Evaluation of Selected Criticism

Barkan, Leonard F. *Nature's Work of Art: The Human Body as Image of the World.* New Haven: Yale University Press, 1975. Barkan provides a philosophical discussion of the central metaphor in Drayton's *Poly-Olbion.*

Berthelot, Joseph A[lfred], *Michael Drayton.* New York: Twayne, 1967. Berthelot devotes chapters to most of Drayton's works, but the critical commentary is superficial and the bibliographical facts are sometimes inaccurate.

Cooper, [Elizabeth] Helen, *Pastoral: Medieval into Renaissance.* Ipswich: D. S. Brewer; Totowa, NJ: Roman and Littlefield, 1977. Cooper examines Drayton as a pastoral poet, suggesting that the realistic detail in his pastorals indicates medieval influence.

Corbett, Margery and Ronald Lightbrown, *The Comely Frontispiece: The Emblematic Title-Page in England, 1550–1660.* London: Routledge & Kegan Paul, 1979. Chapter 13 presents an interesting discussion of the frontispiece of *Poly-Olbion.*

Davis, Walter R. " 'Fantastickly I sing': Drayton's *Idea* of 1619," *Studies in Philology.* LXVI (1969), 204–216. Most critical studies of Drayton's sonnets take off from this stimulating analysis of *Idea* (1619) as a comic sequence. Davis argues that Drayton is showing that the love poet cannot evade conventionality.

Grundy, Joan, *The Spenserian Poets.* London: Edward Arnold, 1969. Grundy examines Drayton as a Spenserian poet, one of the sixteenth and seventeenth-century poets who continued to write on the same themes as Edmund Spenser. This study correctly identifies the literary tradition to which Drayton belongs and perceptively analyzes his works, especially *Poly-Olbion.*

Hardin, Richard, *Michael Drayton and the Passing of Elizabethan England.* Lawrence: University of Kansas Press, 1973. Hardin identifies Drayton as preeminently a patriotic poet, devoted to English traditions and landscape. This study examines Drayton's pastoral, historical, and satirical poetry, discussing the interrelationship among these three kinds of genres and arguing that Drayton wrote more for the country gentry than the court. Hardin's analysis of Drayton's work is the best book-length critical commentary available.

Hulse, Clark, *Metamorphic Verse: The Elizabethan Minor Epic.* Princeton: Princeton University Press, 1981. After examining sixteenth-century perceptions of verisimilitude and truth in history and poetry, this study offers a fresh and convincing analysis of *Peirs Gaveston* (1593), *Matilda* (1594), and *Robert Duke of Normandy* (1596).

Nagy, N[icholas] Christoph De. *Michael Drayton's "England's Heroical Epistles": A Study in Themes and Compositional Devices.* Cooper Monographs, 14. Bern: Francke, 1968. Nagy analyzes Drayton's *Epistles* in relation to their Ovidian sources.

Nearing, Homer, Jr. *English Historical Poetry, 1599–1641.* Philadelphia: University of Pennsylvania Press, 1945. Homer offers a general and summary discussion of historical verse with a positive assessment of Drayton.

Turner, James G. *The Politics of Landscape: The Rural Scenery and Society in English Poetry, 1630–1660.* Oxford: Basil Blackwell, 1979. Turner frequently uses examples from Drayton's *Poly-Olbion* for comparison with later landscape poets.

Other Sources

Harner, James L. *Samuel Daniel and Michael Drayton: A Reference Guide,* Boston: G. K. Hall, 1980. Harner provides a useful annotated bibliography for biographical and critical studies of Drayton and his works from 1684 to 1979.

Selected Dictionaries and Encyclopedias

Dictionary of National Biography, 1885–1886; rpt. Oxford University Press, 1921–1922, VI, 8–13. Concise, full biography.

Critical Survey of Poetry, Vol. 2, Salem Press, 1982. Short biography, appraisal of Drayton's importance, and analysis of key poems.

Jeanie R. Brink
Arizona State University

THEODORE DREISER
1871–1945

Author's Chronology

Born 27 August 1871, Terre Haute, Indiana, of German immigrant parents; *1892* works for various newspapers in Chicago, St. Louis, and Pittsburgh; *1895* establishes and edits *Ev'ry Month* and other magazines; *1898* marries Sara "Jug" White; *1900* Doubleday, Page, and Co. reluctantly publishes *Sister Carrie; 1903* enters sanitarium, suffering from nervous exhaustion; *1904* becomes a successful magazine editor for Butterick Publications in New York; *1912* publishes *The Financier,* the first part of a trilogy of novels based on the career of industrial tycoon Charles T. Yerkes; *1914* separates from Sara White Dreiser; *1916* autobiographical novel *The "Genius"* is banned; *1919* meets Helen Richardson; *1923* begins research on the Chester Gillette murder case for *An American Tragedy; 1927* tours Russia; *1931* investigates labor problems in Harlan County, Kentucky; *1942* Sara White Dreiser dies; *1944* receives Award of Merit Medal from the American Academy of Arts and Letters; Marries Helen Richardson; *1945* dies December 28 of heart attack in Hollywood, California.

Author's Bibliography (selected)

Sister Carrie, 1900 (novel); *Jennie Gerhardt,* 1911 (novel); *A Traveler At Forty,* 1913 (sketches from European travels); *The Titan,* 1914 (novel); *Free and Other Stories,* 1918; *Twelve Men,* 1919 (non-fiction); *Hey Rub-A-Dub-Dub,* 1920 (philosophical writings); *An American Tragedy,* 1925 (novel); *The Bulwark,* 1946 (posthumously published novel); *The Stoic,* 1947 (posthumously published novel).

Overview of Biographical Sources

The first book-length biography of Dreiser appeared during his lifetime: Dorothy Dudley's *Forgotten Frontiers: Theodore Dreiser and the Land of the Free* (New York: Smith and Haas, 1932) is interesting for its impressions of Dreiser in his time, but is necessarily limited. Robert H. Elias' *Theodore Dreiser: Apostle of Nature,* (1970) is the only authorized biography. With Dreiser's cooperation, Elias worked on this critical biography the last eight years of the author's life. W. A. Swanberg's *Dreiser* (1965), is more comprehensive than Elias' in factual detail, but presents an unfavorable and inaccurate image of Dreiser. The student should also consult *Letters of Theodore Dreiser: A Selection,* ed. Robert H. Elias, 3 vols. (Philadelphia: University of Pennsylvania Press, 1959), an indispensable record of Dreiser's literary activities. Two of Dreiser's many female companions wrote extended memoirs of their relationships with him: Helen Dreiser, his second wife, published *My Life With Dreiser* (Cleveland: World, 1951) and Marguerite Tjader, his secretary during the last eight years of his life, wrote *Theodore Dreiser: A New Dimension* (Norwalk, CT: Silvermine Publishers, 1965). Both books, however, are non-scholarly, sentimental, and provide no significant interpretations of Dreiser's work.

Evaluation of Selected Biographies

Elias, Robert H. *Theodore Dreiser: Apostle of Nature.* Emended ed. Ithaca: Cornell University Press, 1970. First published in 1949, Elias' biography remains the most thorough treatment of the way Dreiser's life shaped his fiction. Elias explores Dreiser's boyhood experiences with his broken, impoverished family and his restless wanderings from the rural midwest to the emerging metropolises of Chicago and New York, his newspaper experience, and his early readings in social Darwinism to demonstrate the importance of Dreiser's impact on American literary history. What emerges is a sensitive chronicle of Dreiser's life balanced with perceptive analyses of his fiction.

Swanberg, W. A. *Dreiser.* New York: Charles Scribner's Sons, 1965. Swanberg's account of Dreiser's life is a plethora of detail. Swanberg incorporates hundreds of letters, diary entries, autobiographical writings, and interviews with Dreiser's contemporaries, but the result is more a log of Dreiser's life rather than an attempt to understand him. In fact, Swanberg makes no attempt to conceal his intense dislike of Dreiser, seeing the writer as something of a literary barbarian. More diligent and reliable scholarship, however, has refuted that impression.

Autobiographical Sources

Dreiser used much of his own life as material for his fiction, and his best work contains obvious biographical echoes. His two volumes of autobiography, *A Book About Myself* and *Dawn,* are not always trustworthy, but they convey depth of feeling that biographies can only summarize. In *The "Genius",* Dreiser fictionalized the experiences he recounted in the autobiographies.

Two recently-published non-fictional works by Dreiser have made available new and valuable biographical information. *American Diaries, 1902–1926,* eds. Thomas P. Riggio, James L. W. West III, and Neda M. Westlake (Philadelphia: University of Pennsylvania Press, 1982), contains a series of intermittent journals in which Dreiser comments on the social and intellectual atmosphere of his day and wrestles with his feelings about his sometimes turbulent relationships with women. But the diaries are also important in that they show a disciplined and mature man of letters, supplying, in the process, clues to Dreiser's compositional habits. *An Amateur Laborer,* eds. Richard W. Dowell, James L. W. West III, and Neda M. Westlake (Philadelphia: University of Pennsylvania Press, 1983), illuminates a dark period in Dreiser's life that has gone largely unexamined by biographers. The narrative is a searingly emotional account by Dreiser of the period after the "suppression" of *Sister Carrie* when, plagued by doubts about his literary career, he underwent a severe nervous breakdown and briefly took a job as a wage laborer on the New York Central Railroad.

Overview of Critical Sources

The publication in 1981 of the unexpurgated edition of *Sister Carrie* has started a revival in Dreiser studies, which had somewhat fallen behind those of other modern American writers in the late 1960's and through the 1970's. Much new scholarship is forthcoming. Many critical articles and pertinent chapters from book-length studies of Dreiser have been reprinted in one or more of the following three collections of criticism: Alfred Kazin and Charles Shapiro, eds., *The Stature of Theodore Dreiser* (Bloomington: Indiana University Press, 1955); John Lydenberg, ed., *Dreiser: A Collection of Critical Essays* (Englewood Cliffs, N.J.: Prentice Hall, 1971); and Donald Pizer, ed., *Critical Essays on Theodore Dreiser* (Boston: G. K. Hall, 1981).

Evaluation of Selected Criticism

Hussman, Lawrence E. *Dreiser and His Fiction: A Twentieth-Century Quest.* Philadelphia: University of Pennsylvania Press, 1983. The most recent study of the novels and several of the short stories, this volume examines for the first time the apparent shift in Dreiser's attitude near the end of his life from a belief in a fatalistic force in the universe to that of a benevolent, creative force. Through close readings of the earlier fiction, Hussman demonstrates that the seeds of this later belief actually lay in his supposedly "deterministic" novels, *Carrie* and *Jennie Gerhardt.* By identifying this pattern throughout Dreiser's major works, Hussman convincingly lays to rest the prevailing notion that Dreiser was an iron-clad determinist.

Matthiessen, F. O. *Theodore Dreiser.* New York: William Sloane Associates, 1951. Matthiessen's volume is a pioneering critical study of Dreiser's novels as well as an attempt to give Dreiser the credit he deserves as a major American writer. Matthiessen devotes the most space to *Carrie* and the *Tragedy,* emphasizing Dreiser's role as a social critic. Matthiessen also consistently defends the accumulation of detail in Dreiser's fiction, asserting that it supplies a sense of historical truth to the situations Dreiser describes.

Moers, Ellen, *Two Dreisers.* New York: Viking, 1969. Unlike Matthiessen, Moers' approach is primarily biographical. Going beyond the simple identification of fact with fiction, Moers traces important events in Dreiser's life during the composition of *Carrie* and the *Tragedy* and shows how such events helped create the two novels. She points out, for example, the artistic influence of contemporary photographers and painters, of Dreiser's newspaper training, and of his interest in scientific experimentation. She relies on Dreiser's correspondence and on other less obvious materials—such as his early magazine articles—to chart the course of Dreiser's ideas during this most productive period of his literary career.

Pizer, Donald, *The Novels of Theodore Dreiser.* Minneapolis: University of Minnesota Press, 1976. Pizer's study is both a work of textual scholarship—an examination of the development of the novels from manuscript to print—and of literary criticism—an analysis of each of the novel's "themes and form." Pizer seems to shortchange the *Trilogy* and *The "Genius",* but as a study of the genetic development of the fiction it is very useful.

Other Sources

Mencken, H. L. "Theodore Dreiser," *A Book of Prefaces.* New York: Alfred A. Knopf, 1917, pp. 67–148. The first published account of Dreiser's life, written by his friend and literary defender, begins with his midwest origins and continues through the controversy surrounding the publication of *The "Genius".*

Campbell, Louise, *Letters to Louise.* Philadelphia: University of Pennsylvania Press, 1959. Campbell served for many years as Dreiser's editorial assistant and confidante. The letters are interwoven with (mostly anecdotal) commentary.

Selected Dictionaries and Encyclopedias

Literary History of the United States, Macmillan, 1974, 4th ed. I: 1197–1207. Robert Spiller devotes one chapter to Dreiser, in which he interprets the novels as social tragedies and asserts that Dreiser is American literature's foremost naturalist. Spiller's critical interpretations are standard ones, but the piece presents a good summary of Dreiser's life and the fundamentals of his art.

James M. Hutchisson
University of Delaware

JOHN DRYDEN
1631-1700

Author's Chronology

Born August 9, 1631, Alwinckle, Northamptonshire, England; *1646* enters Westminster School; *1649* publishes his first poem "Upon the Death of Lord Hastings;" *1650* admitted to Trinity College, Cambridge; *1654* receives B.A.; *1655* possibly enters into employment with the Protectorate; *1658* publishes *Heroic Stanzas* on the death of Cromwell; *1660* celebrates the Restoration in *Astrea Redux; 1662* elected to the Royal Society; *1663* marries Lady Elizabeth Howard; first play, *The Wild Gallant,* is produced; *1664* his first heroic drama, *The Indian Queen,* written in collaboration with Sir Robert Howard, is produced; *1668* appointed Poet Laureate; begins a contractual arrangement with the King's Theatre; *1670* appointed Historiographer Royal; the first part of *The Conquest of Granada* is produced; *1671 Marriage-A-la-Mode* is produced; *1675 Aureng-Zebe* is produced; *1677 All For Love* is produced; *1681* begins a series of controversial writings relating to the Exclusion Crisis and Popish Plot with the publication of *Absalom and Achitophel; The Spanish Fryar* is produced; *1685* publishes *Threnodia Augustalis* on the death of Charles II; converts to Roman Catholicism; *1688* is deprived of his court appointments upon the deposition of James II; *1690* returns to the theatre with the production of *Don Sebastian; 1693* writes his last play, *Love Triumphant;* dies in London, England, May 1, 1700.

Author's Bibliography (selected)

Annus Mirabilis, 1667 (poem); *Of Dramatick Poesie,* 1668 (criticism); "Of Heroic Plays," 1672 (critical preface); "The Author's Apology for Heroic Poetry and Poetic License," 1677 (critical preface); "The Grounds of Criticism in Tragedy," 1679 (critical preface); *Absalom and Achitophel,* 1681 (poem); *The Medall,* 1682 (poem); *MacFlecknoe,* 1682 (poem); *Religio Laici,* 1682 (poem); *To The Memory of Anne Killigrew,* 1685 (poem); *The Hind and The Panther,* 1687 (poem); "Song for St. Cecilia's Day," 1687 (poem); *Eleonora,* 1692 (poem); *Satires of Juvenal and Perseus,* 1692 (translations); *The Works of Virgil,* 1697 (translations); "Alexander's Feast," 1697 (poem); *Fables,* 1700 (translations, poems, and criticism).

Overview of Biographical Sources

Each of the editors of the major collections of Dryden's work which appeared before 1900—Edmund Malone, Walter Scott, and George Saintsbury—supplied a biographical treatment of the author. Of these, only Scott's biography still has worth, not because his did not contain errors of fact and of interpretation, but because Scott offered an interpretation of Dryden's life and literary career which still retains some integrity.

Understandably, the revivified critical interest in Dryden in the 1920's antedated a concentrated approach to the author's biography. Although a considerable amount of discrete biographical evidence preceded them, the publication in 1939 of Hugh Macdonald's bibliography of the early editions of Dryden and of James Osborne's study of the previous biographies and of various biographical problems offered themselves as catalysts for a more unified approach to the author's life. It was not, however, until 1961, with the appearance of Charles Ward's biography that the material of Dryden's life achieved some sort of synthesis.

Since the publication of Ward's biography, it is not so much the weight of new biographical materials as the accumulation of interpretative work done in collateral areas of Dryden and Restoration studies that makes a new biographical approach to Dryden desirable. James Osborne said of Ward's biography that it would remain definitive for at least a generation; that generation is near an end.

Evaluation of Selected Biographies

McFadden, George, *Dryden: The Public Writer, 1660–1685.* Princeton: Princeton University Press, 1978. Intending his book as a supplement to Charles Ward's biography, McFadden does not offer a comprehensive view of the relationship between Dryden's literary work and contemporary public figures and events. Rather, relying heavily upon Dryden's dedications and his dramatic works, McFadden is not afraid to bring informed inference to bear upon various biographical and critical problems which involve the transformation of Dryden's personal attitudes into public discourse.

Ward, Charles E. *The Life of John Dryden.* Chapel Hill: University of North Carolina Press, 1961. Ward's is the standard biography of Dryden: his marshalling of the available materials relating to Dryden's life was scrupulous, and, except in some details, the documentary outlines of Dryden's life remained virtually unchanged. There are, however, two problems with Ward's biography which may be seen as related. One is the book's status as an "academic" biography: the biography does not allow much to a reader who arrives to it without some familiarity with Dryden's work. Another problem is that, while Ward addressed himself to many aspects of Dryden's life whose perennial misinterpretation had distorted earlier studies, his very scrupulousness served to inhibit him from presenting anything close to a comprehensive interpretation of Dryden as a man, a writer, and a public figure.

Wasserman, George R. *John Dryden.* New York: Twayne, 1964. Although this is a rudimentary biographical and critical introduction, one written without the knowledge of many of the major contemporary critical studies of Dryden, Wasserman's first chapter, a discussion of Dryden's "life and times," does have the virtue of brevity.

Autobiographical Sources

Dryden left no autobiographical record nor do the less than eighty letters remaining form what must certainly have been a more voluminous correspondence, most of them concentrated in Dryden's later years, contain much of biographical interest. This paucity of other autobiographical materials has created a situation in which a perhaps undue reliance has been placed upon those passages in Dryden's criticism which appear to represent Dryden's personal attitudes or to reflect his circumstances.

Dryden's criticism, most of which is occasional in nature, has also been used as a kind of prescriptive guide to the literary works which it accompanies. Unfortunately, the relationship between Dryden's criticism and the poem or play it discusses is often oblique, if not problematic. Moreover, Dryden's criticism as a whole, which has been viewed by many as formative of English literary neoclassicism, seems to support many contradictions on its surface.

Overview of Critical Sources

Dryden was a poet, a critic, a dramatist, a translator, a writer of persuasive and narrative prose. It is Dryden's wide range of literary activities as much as the great bulk of his literary production which has limited the number of truly valuable general studies of his work. The historical model of such a work is, of course, Samuel Johnson's treatment of Dryden in *Lives of the English Poets,* criticism as succinct as it is judgmental. But only rarely in contemporary criticism, in such books as those by Mark Van Doren and Earl Miner, has an effort been made to address Dryden's achievement in various genres or to treat intensively the whole of Dryden's poetic career.

In fact, the more than forty years between the publications of these two books saw the production of nothing comparable to them in breadth, nor until the publication of Arthur Hoffman's book on Dryden's imagery in 1961 and Bernard Schilling's book on *Absalom and Achitophel* in 1962 were any major attempts made to draw upon the advancements in Dryden criticism which were evident in academic periodicals. Subsequently, many valuable book-length studies—of various aspects of Dryden's poetry, of various individual poems or group of poems, of his heroic plays and of his criticism—have been published.

Evaluation of Selected Criticism

Hamilton, K. G. *John Dryden and the Poetry of Statement.* St. Lucia, Australia: University of Queensland Press, 1967. Admitting at the outset of his study that Dryden's poetry involves a use of statement which some concepts of poetry would disallow, Hamilton attempts to show how Dryden's combination of directness and artfulness of expression achieves the status of true poetry. Hamilton's analyses of poems published between 1682 and 1687 are concentrated upon various aspects of these poems which would have been understood by their contemporary audience and should be appreciated by their modern readers.

Harth, Philip, *Contexts of Dryden's Thought.* Chicago: University of Chicago Press, 1968. Harth is primarily concerned with Dryden's religious thought. Although he does consider *Religio Laici* and *The Hind and The Panther* at length, it is with the intention of establishing the contexts of their interpretation as religious discourses rather than as poetic structures. In the process of demonstrating the cooperation of revelation and reason in Dryden's religious faith and the logic of his religious conversion, Harth debunks the once commonly-accepted notion of Dryden's anti-rationalist skepticism.

Hoffman, Arthur W. *John Dryden's Imagery.* Gainesville: University of Florida Press, 1962. Hoffman offered one of the first extended analyses of Dryden's poetry which concentrated upon literary structure rather than historical context. Hoffman's close readings of representative poems from every period of Dryden's career remain valuable for their insight into the function of imagery in the achievement of poetic meaning.

Miner, Earl, *Dryden's Poetry.* Bloomington: Indiana University Press, 1967. Miner's book has no need of a subtitle. He not only offers detailed analyses of the major poems which follow their chronological sequence, but also discusses, in a chapter concerned with the varieties of Dryden's lyric poetry, most of the poems which fill out the standard selections from Dryden. Moreover, although Miner is primarily concerned with "the assumptions, ideas and techniques" of Dryden's poetry, he does devote a separate chapter to a valuable treatment of Dryden's most well-known play, *All For Love.* Perhaps the most interesting part of Miner's book is his argument for the inclusion of *The Fables,* the most popular of Dryden's works in the eighteenth century, within the canon of his major writings.

While nearly every page of Miner's thick book has something valuable to say, it is not easy to read. Miner assumes that the reader will already have the texts of the poems under control. Furthermore, Miner does not simply state his points; he makes his reader work, sometimes through lengthy segments, to understand them.

Van Doren, Mark, *John Dryden: A Study of His Poetry.* Bloomington: University of Indiana Press, 1960. Van Doren's book, originally published in 1920, has a definite historical value since it appeared at the beginning of the period of Dryden's modern critical re-estimation; indeed, as the occasion of T. S. Eliot's promotional essays, it should be considered as one of the primary contributing factors in that re-estimation. Although he virtually ignored Dryden's role as a translator and literary critic and much of his work as a dramatist, Van Doren designed a comprehensive treatment of Dryden's poetic career; nonetheless, his is a book to be valued more for its appreciative and descriptive passages than for its analyses.

Other Sources

Budick, Sanford, *Dryden and the Abyss of Light: A Study of "Religio Laici" and "The Hind and The Panther."* New Haven: Yale University Press, 1970.

Hooker, Edward Niles, *et al.* eds. *The Works of John Dryden.* Berkeley: University of California Press, 1956- . The textual and critical commentaries which accompany the already completed volumes of this ongoing project maintain a high standard of scholarly excellence.

Kirsch, Arthur C. *Dryden's Heroic Drama.* Princeton: Princeton University Press, 1965.

Latt, David J. and Samuel Holt Monk. *John Dryden: A Survey and Bibliography of Critical Studies, 1895–1974.* Minneapolis: University of Minnesota Press, 1976.

McKeon, Michael. *Politics and Poetry in Restoration England: The Case of Dryden's "Annus Mirabilis."* Cambridge: Harvard University Press, 1975.

Miner, Earl, ed. *John Dryden.* Athens: Ohio University Press, 1972. A collection of original articles which address the full range of Dryden's literary activity.

Schilling, Bernard, *Dryden and the Conservative Myth: A Reading of "Absalom and Achitophel."* New Haven: Yale University Press, 1961.

———, ed. *Dryden: A Collection of Critical Essays.* Englewood Cliffs, NJ: Prentice-Hall, 1963.

Swedenberg, H. T. Jr. *Essential Articles for the Study of John Dryden.* Hamden, CT: Archon Books, 1966.

James Maloney
Humber College, Ontario

WILLIAM DUNBAR
c. 1455–1517

Author's Chronology

Any attempt to establish a detailed chronology of William Dunbar's life must fail for sheer lack of information. His date and place of birth are unknown, but most authorities believe that he was born between 1455 and 1460, possibly in the district of Lothian in Scotland. A William Dunbar, presumably the poet, is on record as having graduated from the University of Saint Andrews as Bachelor of Arts in 1477, and as Master of Arts in 1479. From 1479 to 1500, Dunbar's life is a blank. From 1500 onwards, some information about Dunbar's career may be gleaned from the records of the Scottish royal court. In 1500, King James IV granted Dunbar a pension of £10 a year, to be paid until the poet obtained a church benefice or died. In 1504, James made an offering at Dunbar's "first mass"—perhaps an indication that the poet had recently been ordained priest. Between 1504 and 1513, Dunbar apparently continued in James's good graces; his pension was twice increased, and he also received gifts of money and clothing. In 1513, after James's death in the Battle of Flodden, the records break off; when they resume, in 1515, Dunbar's name is missing. It is uncertain whether this disappearance means that Dunbar had finally obtained a benefice, or that he had died soon after his King. If one poem attributed to Dunbar, "Quhen the Governour Past in Fraunce," is indeed his work, then he must have survived at least until 1517, when Albany, the Regent or "Governor" of Scotland, made his first visit to France. Dunbar was certainly dead by 1530, in which year Sir David Lindsay's "Testament of the Papyngo" includes him in a list of deceased poets.

Author's Bibliography

The canon of Dunbar's poetry contains 83 poems. The great majority of these poems are preserved only in manuscripts written some time after his death, in the late sixteenth or early seventeenth century. Under these circumstances, most of Dunbar's poems can be dated, if at all, only on the basis of internal references to historical events or figures. Most scholars have dated Dunbar's productive period approximately 1490–1520. Denton Fox, however, reassesses the available evidence in "The Chronology of William Dunbar," *Philological Quarterly* 39 (1960), 413–425, and concludes that nearly all the poems were composed between 1500 and 1513.

The earliest modern edition of Dunbar's poetry is that of John Small, Aeneas J. G. Mackay and Walter Gregor for the Scottish Text Society: *The Poems of William Dunbar,* 3 vols. (Edinburgh: Blackwood, 1884–1893). For many years, the standard available edition was W. Mackay Mackenzie's *The Poems of William Dunbar* (London: Faber and Faber, 1932; reprinted with corrections

1960). This edition has now been superseded by James Kinsley's *The Poems of William Dunbar* (Oxford: Clarendon Press, 1979), which offers not only a more accurate text, but also a more thorough and helpful commentary and glossary. A convenient selection of forty-six poems, with introduction and notes, may also be found in James Kinsley's *William Dunbar: Poems,* Clarendon Medieval and Tudor Series (Oxford: Clarendon Press, 1958).

Overview of Biographical Sources

The lack of information about Dunbar's life makes the biographer's task extremely difficult. Aeneas Mackay's Introduction to the Scottish Text Society's *The Poems of William Dunbar* (Edinburgh: Blackwood, 1884–1893) remains an important biographical resource, even though Mackay sometimes confuses fact with inference and speculation. The earliest attempt at a book-length biography is J. Schipper's *William Dunbar: Sein Leben und Seine Gedichte* (Berlin: Trübner, 1884), which leans heavily on what one critic has termed "fanciful" readings of the poems. Since then, two more reliable accounts of Dunbar's life have appeared in English: J. W. Baxter's *William Dunbar: A Biographical Study* (1952); and Ian Simpson Ross's *William Dunbar,* Medieval and Renaissance Authors series (1981), which combines biography with critical evaluation of the poetry.

Evaluation of Selected Biographies

Baxter, J. W. *William Dunbar: A Biographical Study.* Edinburgh: Oliver and Boyd, 1952. Baxter produces few new facts, but calls extensively on Dunbar's own poetry and the history of the period to fill in the bare outlines of the poet's life. Readers may not always agree with the biographical conclusions which Baxter draws from the poems, but his book is nevertheless valuable as a competent and interesting account of Dunbar's career.

Ross, Ian Simpson, *William Dunbar.* Medieval and Renaissance Authors series. Leiden: Brill, 1981. Part One of Ross's book is an extended biographical essay, "Tyme, Space and Dait". Ross sets out to place Dunbar in his full historical, social and cultural context. The result is a fascinating study as much of Dunbar's milieu of his life.

Overview of Critical Sources

Until 1966, readers and students of Dunbar had to rely on the relevant sections of literary histories and essays in learned journals for any critical appreciation of his poetry. Since that year, four book-length critical evaluations have been published. These studies reflect widely differing approaches; those by Reiss and Ross are balanced and scholarly, while those by Scott and Hope represent the responses of two poets to a fellow-poet, and hence are more personal and provocative.

Evaluation of Selected Criticism

Hope, A. D. *A Midsummer Eve's Dream: Variations on a Theme by William Dunbar.* New York: Viking Press, 1970. Written by a celebrated Australian poet, this book is, as its title implies, not so much an exposition of the "Tretis of the Tua Mariit Wemen and the Wedo" as an imaginative excursus inspired by the poem. During that excursus, Hope gathers evidence from literature, folklore and anthropology to suggest a new and controversial context in which Dunbar's "gay ladeis" might be viewed. A highly interesting *sui generis* study.

Reiss, Edmund, *William Dunbar.* Boston: Twayne, 1979. This recent book presents Dunbar both as an independent and self-aware artist and as heir to medieval poetic traditions in general and to Chaucer in particular. Reiss stresses that Dunbar is a versatile poet who adopts a wide variety of *personae,* and warns against any oversimple interpretation of the poetry as a direct reflection of Dunbar's experiences or beliefs. A chapter on style and technique includes a rewarding examination of the role of voice in Dunbar's verse.

Ross, Ian Simpson, *William Dunbar.* Medieval and Renaissance Authors series. Leiden: Brill, 1981. Part Two of this book, entitled "Slee Poetry", offers careful readings of Dunbar's poems, with an emphasis on meaning rather than on form or style. The most unusual and ambitious feature of Ross's study is perhaps his attempt to relate Dunbar's imagery to the iconographic traditions of late medieval art, sculpture and drama.

Scott, Tom, *Dunbar: A Critical Exposition of the Poems.* New York: Barnes and Noble, 1966. Towards the end of this volume, Scott confesses that, in order to write it, he had to overcome an initial "spiritual antipathy" towards Dunbar. Apparently he has not tried to overcome a similar antipathy towards the period in which Dunbar lived; indeed, he is happiest when he can portray the poet as a satirist who fiercely attacks the vices of court, city, and Church. Scott is undoubtedly guilty of imposing his own social and political views on his material, but his involvement with his subject generates a vitality and excitement often missing in more orthodox criticism.

Other Sources

Lewis, C. S. "The Close of the Middle Ages in Scotland," in *English Literature in the Sixteenth Century, Excluding Drama.* Oxford: Clarendon Press, 1954. Pp. 90–100. An influential study of Dunbar's virtuosity and craftsmanship.

Dorena Allen Wright
University of Oregon

LAWRENCE DURRELL
1912

Author's Chronology

Born February 27, 1912, Jullundur, India of English-Irish parents; *1923* attends St. Edmund's School, Canterbury; *1935* publishes first novel, *Pied Piper of Lovers;* marries Nancy Myers, an artist; begins corresponding with Henry Miller; moves to Corfu with Nancy, his mother, sister, and two brothers; *1937* publishes *Panic Spring* under pseudonym, Charles Norden; meets Henry Miller in Paris; *1939* teaches in Athens; *1940* daughter Peneolope Berengaria born; begins work in the British Foreign Office; *1941* works in Cairo as Foreign Press Service Officer; *1944* works in Alexandria as Press Attache in the British Information Office; *1945* works in Rhodes as Director of Public Relations, Dodecanese Islands; *1947* marries Yvette Cohen; moves to Argentina and works as Director of the British Council Institute, lecturing on modern poetry; *1949* works in Yugoslavia as Press Attache, British Legation; *1951* daughter Sappho-Jane born; *1953* moves to Cyprus and teaches; works as Director of Public Relations for the British Government in Cyprus; *1956* moves to Dorset, England; *1957* moves to small cottage in Provence; publishes *Justine;* begins correspondence with Richard Aldington; receives Duff Cooper Memorial Prize for *Bitter Lemons; 1961* marries Claude Vincendon, a writer; *1967* Claude dies; *1973* marries Ghislaine de Boysson; Andrew Mellon Visiting Professor, California Institute of Technology; *1979* divorces Ghislaine; *1985* continues to live in Provence.

Author's Bibliography (selected)

Pied Piper of Lovers, 1935 (novel); *The Black Book,* 1938 (novel); *Prospero's Cell,* 1945 (travel book); *Sappho: A Play in Verse,* 1950; *Reflections on a Marine Venus,* 1950 (travel book); *Key to Modern Poetry,* 1952 (criticism); *Bitter Lemons,* 1957 (travel book); *Esprit de Corps: Sketches from Diplomatic Life,* 1957 (short stories); *Justine,* 1957 (novel); *Balthazar,* 1958 (novel); *Mountolive,* 1958 (novel); *Clea,* 1960 (novel); *Collected Poems,* 1960; *The Curious History of Pope Joan,* 1961 (translation); *The Poetry of Lawrence Durrell,* 1962; *The Alexandria Quartet: Justine, Balthazar, Mountolive, Clea,* 1962 (novels); *An Irish Faustus,* 1963 (play); *Selected Poems 1935–1963,* 1964; *Tunc,* 1968 (novel); *Nunquam,* 1970 (novel); *Monsieur,* 1974 (novel); *Sicilian Carousel,* 1977 (travel book); *Livia,* 1978 (novel); *Collected Poems 1931–1974,* 1980.

Overview of Biographical Sources

There is as yet no complete Durrell biography. There are, however, a number of short reminiscences by friends, although none of these traces his life completely. Alfred Perles' *My Friend Lawrence Durrell* (Middlesex: Scorpion Press,

1961) is an admiring sketch spanning the years 1937 to 1961. Gerald Durrell's *My Family and Other Animals* (New York: Viking, 1957) is an account of life on Corfu with his brother. John A. Weigel's *Lawrence Durrell* (New York: Twayne, 1965) contains a general overview combining biographical material with criticism, as does G. S. Fraser's *Lawrence Durrell: A Critical Study* (New York: Dutton, 1968).

Autobiographical Sources

Durrell has often written of the places he has lived, but is not considered an autobiographical writer. There are, however, a number of collections of his correspondence with friends. *Lawrence Durrell and Henry Miller: A Private Correspondence,* ed. George Wickes (New York: Dutton, 1963) begins with Durrell's first fan letter to Miller in 1935 and records their growing friendship through 1959. *Literary Lifelines: The Richard Aldington—Lawrence Durrell Correspondence,* eds. Ian S. MacNiven and Harry T. Moore (New York: Viking Press, 1981) documents the growth of that friendship from 1957 through 1962. Other autobiographical information can be found in the interviews Durrell has given: *The Big Supposer: Lawrence Durrell, A Dialogue with Marc Allyn,* translated from the French by Francine Barker (New York: Grove Press, 1973) contains a series of conversations held in Durrell's home in Provence in 1970 and 1971 in which Durrell responds to questions on his life and work; Julian Mitchell and Gene Andrewski, "The Art of Fiction XXIII: Lawrence Durrell," *Paris Review,* 22 (1960), 32–61 is more oriented toward craft.

Overview of Critical Sources

Although Durrell has published a number of poetry collections, criticism most often focuses on his novels. Because he has written of the places he has lived, either directly in travel sketches or indirectly in settings for his novels, critics frequently interweave biographical information into their studies. G. S. Fraser's *Lawrence Durrell: A Critical Study* (New York: Dutton, 1968) is the most prominent example of this approach. Informed by Fraser's friendship with Durrell since 1940, this informal critical work frequently yields to biographical information in its scholarly analyses.

Evaluation of Selected Criticism

Moore, Harry T. ed. *The World of Lawrence Durrell.* Carbondale: Southern Illinois University Press, 1962. This is a collection of articles through 1961 by various critics on all aspects of Durrell's work. Also included are several interviews and a few letters from Durrell to Jean Fanchette.

Weigel, John A. *Lawrence Durrell.* New York: Twayne, 1965. The first major critical work on Durrell, Weigel allots approximately one-third of the book to consideration of *The Alexandria Quartet.* Short treatments of the other novels, travel books, poetry, and plays comprise the remainder of the book.

Other Sources

Deus Loci: The Lawrence Durrell Newsletter. Okanagan College, Kelowna, British Columbia. Comments on all aspects of Durrell's work.

Hutchens, Eleanor N. "The Heraldic Universe in *The Alexandria Quartet,*" *College English,* 24 (1962), 56–61. Demonstrates the relationship between *The Alexandria Quartet* and *The Waste Land.*

"Lawrence Durrell: Special Number," *Modern Fiction Studies,* 13:3 (1967). Five of the eight articles focus on *The Alexandria Quartet.* Includes considerations of Miller's influence, autobiographical elements, heraldry, and the use of place; also a selected checklist.

Thomas, Alan G. and James A. Brigham, *Lawrence Durrell: An Illustrated Checklist.* Carbondale: Southern Illinois University Press, 1983. Descriptive bibliography of primary and secondary sources. Illustrations of selected book jackets.

Unterecker, John, *Lawrence Durrell.* New York: Columbia University Press, 1964. Pamphlet-length study.

Selected Dictionaries and Encyclopedias

Contemporary Authors, Gale Research, 1974. Resumé of Durrell's life, critical overview of his work, and a full bibliography.

Contemporary Novelists, St. Martin's Press, 1982. Short overview of major works and bibliography.

Lisa M. Schwerdt
Purdue University

RICHARD EBERHART
1904

Author's Chronology

Born April 5, 1904, Austin, Minnesota; *1922* mother dies from lung cancer; *1922* father, vice-president of Hormel Meat Packing Company, resigns after an embezzler makes off with 1.25 million dollars; High School captain of football team, president of Debating League; *1922* enters University of Minnesota; *1923* transfers to Dartmouth College; *1927* works on freighters in the Pacific, then enters St. John's College, Cambridge; *1929* receives Bachelor of Arts degree; *1930* tutors the son of the King of Siam; *1933* begins to teach at Saint Mark's School, Massachusetts; *1941* marries Helen Elizabeth Butcher; *1942* serves as gunnery instructor in Naval Reserve; *1952* leaves Butcher Polish Company to teach at various colleges; *1956* takes permanent position at Dartmouth College; *1962* wins Bollingen Prize; *1966* Pulitzer Prize; *1977* National Book Award.

Author's Bibliography (selected)

Poems, New and Selected, 1945; *Selected Poems,* 1951; *Collected Poems 1930–1960; Collected Verse Plays,* 1962; *Selected Poems 1930–1965*, 1965; *Collected Poems 1930–1976,* 1976; *On Poetry and Poets,* 1979 (criticism).

Overview of Biographical Sources

Because Richard Eberhart is still alive, no complete biography exists. The fullest treatment of his early and middle years appears in Joel Roache's *Richard Eberhart, The Progress of an American Poet* (1971). Roache quotes passages from Eberhart's letters and diaries provided by the poet and found in Baker Library, Dartmouth College. He gives an intelligent overview of Eberhart's career from his early 'metaphysical' style, which was essentially lyrical and apolitical, to his later more 'democratic' poetry which addresses the world's social realities in a more candid way. Ralph J. Mills's pamphlet, *Richard Eberhart* (Minneapolis: University of Minnesota Press, 1966), contains some biographical information but is more of a critical work. Biographical facts may be garnered from Eberhart's prose book, *Of Poetry and Poets* (Urbana: University of Illinois Press, 1979), especially from his chapters about meeting other poets and the five interviews at the end. Bernard F. Engel's *Richard Eberhart* (New York: Twayne, 1971) provides a useful chronology of events and also a concise, informative summary of Eberhart's life. Like Roache's study, however, it ends around 1970, when the poet was still writing and very much a part of the American literary scene.

Evaluation of Selected Biographies

Roache, Joel, *Richard Eberhart, The Progress of an American Poet.* New York: Oxford University Press, 1971. This is the most comprehensive biographical and critical study of Eberhart to date. It discusses family background in detail and reveals many of the incidents in Eberhart's life that appear transformed in his poems. Eberhart and his wife opened the poet's files and home to Roache while he was researching and, as a result, the book gives a particularly intimate view of the poet.

Autobiographical Sources

Although there is autobiographical material contained in Eberhart's poetry, most noticeably in *A Bravery of Earth,* and in *Of Poetry and Poets,* the most important materials can be found in his diaries and letters gathered in the Eberhart Collection of Baker Library, Dartmouth College.

Overview of Critical Sources

No comprehensive survey of Eberhart's poetry exists, but the two books by Roache and Engels (mentioned earlier), the pamphlet by Mills, and numerous articles go some way towards establishing one. The tone of Eberhart criticism was set by Harriet Monroe in the September issue of *Poetry* (1930), when she suggested that the poet discipline his rugged muse without capitulating his abundant energy. Most of the following criticism has praised his virtue of passionate intelligence but scolded him for lapsing into awkward locutions and sententious moralizing.

Evaluation of Selected Criticism

Engels, Bernard F. *Richard Eberhart.* New York: Twayne, 1971. As with most Twayne books, Engel's study is a general examination of Eberhart's poetry, from *A Bravery of Earth* to the *Selected Poems 1930–1965,* with a very helpful bibliography at the end. Engels emphasizes the poet's consistent romanticism, which views poetry as inspired utterance and a celebration of the world's mystery. He also focuses on the poet's contemplative style and its obsessive concern for paradoxes, which he suggests was given impetus by the painful experience of his mother's early death.

Mills, Ralph J., Jr. *Richard Eberhart.* Minneapolis: University of Minnesota Press, 1966. This is the fifty-fifth contribution to the University of Minnesota Pamphlets on American Writers series. Unlike the modernists, who filtered experience through personae and complex, mythical narratives, Eberhart, according to Mills's argument, favors an immediate, lyrical treatment of experience. Mills compares him to his contemporaries, Theodore Roethke and Stanley Kunitz, but concludes that Eberhart is an original. Like other critics he both praises and criticizes Eberhart's inspirational theory of poetry.

Other Sources

Blackmur, R. P. "Reading the Spirit," *Partisan Review,* V (February, 1938), 52–56. Discusses the problem of Eberhart's stylistic infelicities but praises his powerful imagination and his philosophical insights into man's quandaries.

Booth, Philip, "The Varieties of Poetic Experience," *Shenandoah,* XV (Summer, 1964), 62–69. A review of *The Quarry* that comments on Eberhart's originality, moral insight, and indebtedness to the romantics.

Selected Dictionaries and Encyclopedias

Concise Encyclopedia of English and American Poets and Poetry, Hawthorn Books, 1963. Brief sketch of Eberhart's career and summary of some of his philosophical and literary concerns.

Reader's Encyclopedia of American Literature, Thomas Y. Crowell, 1962. Includes a short biography with books published and awards won up to the Bollingen in 1962.

Henry Hart
The Citadel

MARIA EDGEWORTH
1768–1849

Author's Chronology

Born January 1, 1768, Black Bourton, Oxfordshire, third child of Anglo-Irish landowner, educator and inventor, Richard Lovell Edgeworth; *1773* first visits Edgeworthstown, County Longford, Ireland, the family estate; *1775* is sent to school in Derby and subsequently in London; *1782* settles in Edgeworthstown with her father, his wife and family, thereafter educating her younger siblings, keeping the estate records, and managing his affairs; *1795* her first publication appears, *Letters to Literary Ladies,* on women's education; *1796* publishes *The Parent's Assistant,* her first stories for children; *1798* collaborates with her father in writing *Practical Education,* sees him married a fourth time and witnesses some of the effects of the rebellion of that year; *1800* publishes *Castle Rackrent,* as her father votes against the Union; *1802* travels with her father and stepmother to England, France and Belgium, turning down her only proposal of marriage; *1809–1812* publishes *Tales of Fashionable Life* which earns her considerable royalties; *1813* visits London where she receives wide recognition; *1817* father dies; *1820* edits her father's *Memoirs,* returns to France, and visits Switzerland; *1823* visits Sir Walter Scott at Abbotsford; *1825* Scott visits Edgeworthstown; *1834 Helen,* her last novel, is published; *1848* funds for Famine relief are provided by the royalties from her last work, *Orlandino;* May 22, 1849, dies at Edgeworthstown.

Author's Bibliography (selected)

The Parent's Assistant, 1796 (children's stories); *Practical Education,* 1798 (essays); *Castle Rackrent,* 1800 (novel); *Moral Tales for Young People,* 1801 (stories); *Belinda,* 1801 (novel); *Essay on Irish Bulls,* 1802; *Popular Tales,* 1804; *The Modern Griselda,* 1805 (novella); *Leonora,* 1806 (novel); *Ennui,* 1809 (novel); *The Absentee,* 1812 (novel); *Ormond,* 1817 (novel); *Little Plays for Children,* 1827; *Helen,* 1834 (novel); *Orlandino,* 1848 (story).

Overview of Biographical Sources

Since Grace A. Oliver's creditable but dated *A Study of Maria Edgeworth* (Boston: A. Williams, 1882), numerous biographies have appeared, each reflecting the tenor of its times and relative access to the voluminous Edgeworth family papers. These biographies variously address several critical questions. Concerning the literary relationship between father and daughter, the earlier biographers considered that he restricted her talent, and is the source of the didacticism in her lesser works. On her position as a Big House novelist, she has been viewed as typical of the dying Anglo-Irish gentry in a time of rising Catholic expectations, a representative of the new middle class, or by Emily

Lawless, in *Maria Edgeworth* (London: Macmillan, 1904), as an advanced sympathizer with the aspirations of the Irish peasantry. Similarly, it has been argued from her works that she is insensitive to the Irish natives, ignorant of their ways, or the first Anglo-Irish novelist of stature to take them seriously. On the other hand, she has been praised for her socially responsible administration of her Irish properties and for her capacities as an educator of her father's large family and her tenants' children. At all events, it is clear from her wide range of publications, her voluminous letters, her large circle of brilliant friends, and her literary reception and travels in Britain and Europe that she was one of the foremost social observers of her day.

Evaluation of Selected Biographies

Butler, Marilyn, *Maria Edgeworth: A Literary Biography*. New York: Oxford University Press, 1972. This is the authoritative biography in terms of its comprehensive and scholarly use of sources and its informed literary judgments. A scrupulous examination of letters, records and MSS establishes that Richard Lovell was not her controller, but collaborator. A critical evaluation of her literary development establishes *Castle Rackrent* as a more distinguished creation than her novels of instruction, sentiment, or realism.

Clarke, Isabel C. *Maria Edgeworth, Her Family and Friends*. London: Hutchinson, 1950. Clarke's work sketches Edgeworth's relations with her father's circle, his wives and his children, as well as with her own friends and literary acquaintances, including Scott and Wordsworth.

Hurst, Michael, *Maria Edgeworth and the Public Scene*. Coral Gables, FL: University of Miami Press, 1969. Hurst focuses on Edgeworth's observations on contemporary Irish social and political developments.

Inglis-Jones, Elizabeth, *The Great Maria*. London: Faber and Faber, 1959. This is directed to a popular audience, and lacks documentation and critical judgments.

Autobiographical Sources

No formal autobiography exists. However, a wealth of memoirs, family accounts, and letters are available (for repositories, see bibliography in Butler's biography, 505–507), and a considerable proportion of them have been published. Augustus J. C. Hare's *The Life and Letters of Maria Edgeworth*, 2 vols. (London: Arnold 1894) is a pastiche of illuminating correspondence. H. J. and H. E. Butler's edition of *The Black Book of Edgeworthstown and other Edgeworth Memories, 1585–1817* (London: Faber and Faber, 1927) contains valuable material on Edgeworth's relationship with her father. Christina Colvin's editions, *Letters from England, 1813–1844* (Oxford: Clarendon Press, 1971) and *Maria Edgeworth in France and Switzerland* (Oxford: Clarendon Press, 1979), are the largest collections of published correspondence, many with Sir Walter Scott; and Edgar E. MacDonald's *The Education of the Heart* (Chapel Hill: University of North Carolina Press 1977) offers still more. All of these materials provide valuable first-hand accounts of Edgeworth's views of political, literary and social subjects, as well as myriad practical details in the running of a large household in times when the tide of history was beginning to turn against her class in Ireland.

Overview of Critical Sources

Usually consigned to a minor note in histories of the novel, Edgeworth is variously seen as progenitor of the Anglo-Irish literary revival, compared with Jane Austen as a novelist of manners, and a critic of her own class's irresponsibility. She is censured for the didacticism of most of her works, but praised for her wit and adroit ambiguity in her best—*Castle Rackrent* and *Ormond.* She is also seen as a figure of the late Enlightenment, and a regional novelist with influence on Scott. More recently, she has been credited as an originator of the Victorian novel of childhood.

Evaluation of Selected Criticism

Baker, Ernest, *History of the English Novel.* London: Witherby, 1929, Vol. VI, 11–33. Baker offers an authoritative comparison of Edgeworth and Jane Austen in their contributions to the domestic novel of manners, and their independence of the Romantic movement.

Colby, Vineta, *Yesterday's Woman: Domestic Realism in the English Novel.* Princeton: Princeton University Press, 1974, 86–144. This work places Edgeworth's fiction between utilitarianism and female-dominated domestic realism in early 19th century English fiction.

Coley, W. B. "An Early 'Irish' Novelist," in *Minor British Novelists,* ed. Charles Alva Hoyt. Carbondale: Southern Illinois University 1967, 13–31. A general discussion of Edgeworth's life and Irish novels, *Castle Rackrent* especially, which is compared technically with William Faulkner's *The Hamlet.*

Davie, Donald, "Maria Edgeworth," *The Heyday of Sir Walter Scott.* London: Routledge & Kegan Paul, 1961, 65–77. The spirit of the Enlightenment runs throughout Edgeworth's letters and novels, with the exception of *Castle Rackrent* which so impressed and influenced Sir Walter Scott.

Flanagan, Thomas, *The Irish Novelists: 1800–1850.* New York: Columbia University Press, 1959, 3–106. A highly articulate discussion of Edgeworth's social and cultural melieus, together with an assessment of her work as anticipating the modern movement.

Harden, O. Elizabeth McWhorter, *Maria Edgeworth's Art of Prose Fiction.* The Hague: Mouton, 1971. In the fullest discussion of her fictional techniques,

Harden criticizes her moralizing and mechanical plots, but praises *Castle Rackrent* for the adroit handling of narrative point of view.

———. *Maria Edgeworth.* Boston: Twayne, 1984. A comprehensive survey of the life and work with a useful annotated bibliography. This study lays stress on the theme of "the education of the heart" through the various phases of her artistic development, in her works dealing with children, women, and public life.

Newcomer, James, *Maria Edgeworth the Novelist.* Fort Worth: Texas Christian University Press, 1967. Newcomer presents a spirited "defense" of Edgeworth against misjudgments and omissions of literary historians. Newcomer's interpretation of Thady Quirk, narrator of *Castle Rackrent,* as a disingenuous schemer has provoked a lively controversy.

Other Sources

Altieri, Joanne, "Style and Purpose in Maria Edgeworth's Fiction," *Nineteenth Century Fiction,* 23 (1968–1969), 265–278. A perceptive study of the relationship between her didacticism and literary style.

Cronin, John, *The Anglo-Irish Novel: Vol. 1. The Nineteenth Century.* Belfast: Appletree, 1980. Contains a brief biography and a discussion of *Castle Rackrent* that focuses on the narrator as a victim of colonial misrule.

Kilroy, James J. "Maria Edgeworth: Bibliographies, Editions, Critical Studies," in *Anglo-Irish Literature: A Review of Research* (1976), 25–31. ed. Richard J. Finneran. New York: Modern Language Association. An annotated bibliography.

———. "Maria Edgeworth," in *Recent Research on Anglo-Irish Writers* (1983), 14–15. ed. Richard J. Finneran. New York: Modern Language Association. Supplementary to item above.

Rafroidi, Patrick, *Irish Literature in the Romantic Period (1789–1850),* 2 vols. Gerrard's Cross: Colin Smythe, 1980. Briefly treats Edgeworth as an anti-Romantic (1: 5–12), and provides a full bibliography (2: 148–156).

Watson, George, Introduction to *Castle Rackrent.* New York: Oxford, 1964. A comprehensive survey of critical perspectives on the novel.

Cóilín D. Owens
George Mason University

GEORGE ELIOT
1819–1880

Author's Chronology

Born Mary Ann Evans, 22 November 1819 at Arbury, Warwickshire, England; *1828* attends boarding school at Nuneaton, where she is influenced by her teacher, the evangelical Maria Lewis; *1841* meets the Bray family; *1842* disavows Christianity; *1850* meets John Chapman, who later purchases *Westminster Review,* of which George Eliot becomes assistant editor; *1854* travels to Germany with George Henry Lewes, the man with whom she lived until his death; *1856* after having published several translations, publishes "Amos Barton," her first work of fiction; *1863* moves with Lewes to The Priory, where they live until Lewes's death; *1878* Lewes dies on November 30; *1880* marries John Walter Cross on May 6; dies in London on December 22.

Author's Bibliography (selected)

Scenes of Clerical Life, 1858 (stories); *Adam Bede,* 1859 (novel); *The Mill on the Floss,* 1860 (novel); *Silas Marner: The Weaver of Raveloe,* 1861 (novel); *Romola,* 1863 (novel); *Felix Holt, The Radical,* 1866 (novel); *The Spanish Gypsy: A Poem,* 1868; *Middlemarch: A Study of Provincial Life,* 1871–1872 (novel); *Daniel Deronda,* 1876 (novel).

Overview of Biographical Sources

Her unconventional lifestyle, her desire for privacy, and her husband's and friends' caution after her death over the biographical materials that would be made public impeded George Eliot's early biographers from producing a substantial, objective account of her life. Though there are now over twenty biographical treatments, this problem persisted well into the twentieth century. Biographies such as Simon Dewes's *Marian: The Life of George Eliot* (London: Rich and Cowan, 1939) and J. L. May's *George Eliot* (Indianapolis: Bobbs-Merrill, 1930) may purport "to recount the salient incidents" (May) of Eliot's life, but they offer only scanty documentation and no bibliographies. Elizabeth S. Haldane's *George Eliot and Her Times: A Victorian Study* (New York: D. Appleton Company, 1927) plainly declares that its purpose is not "to concentrate attention upon the actual events of George Eliot's life" but rather to reevaluate the relationship between her writings and "the general aim and effort of her epoch." An exception to these other early twentieth century Eliot biographies is Blanche Colton William's *George Eliot: A Biography* (New York: Macmillan, 1936). Though its author did not have access to the material which produced the later, more substantial biographies, she nevertheless claims to have consulted all "sources at present available" and "certain unpublished letters from George Eliot." Focusing on Eliot's early life as being formative in her development as a novelist and treating the significance of the relationship between Eliot and George Henry Lewes, the author acknowledges her debt to John Walter Cross's biography (see below). Still, her attempt at thoroughness is evident in her claim to having visited Eliot's living relatives in an effort to gather information.

Even some of the later biographies suffer from a lack of abundant, careful documentation. Rosemary Sprague claims to have written her biography *George Eliot: A Biography* (Philadelphia and New York: Chilton, 1968) to correct the one-sidedness of Cross's work and to have used "primary sources to the fullest extent possible." Yet, she allows herself "the privilege of a few surmises and suggestions" and has "deliberately avoided all published critical opinion" with the exception of that of F. R. Leavis. The book contains only a brief bibliography of main sources, and its author has been criticized for attempting to make the prosaic poetical. Though the publisher states of Margaret Crompton's *George Eliot: The Woman* (New York: Thomas Yoseloff, 1960) that "this is a thoroughly researched volume" whose purpose is to bring "a woman's insight and understanding" to Eliot's life, its bibliography consists of a brief list of books consulted.

More substantial than these are the biographies written by Gerald Bullet, *George Eliot: Her Life and Books* (Westport, CT: Greenwood, 1948) and Lawrence and Elizabeth Hanson, *Mary Ann Evans and George Eliot: A Biography* (London: Oxford University Press, 1952). Though Bullett's book is based largely upon Cross, the author "had access to material not available to previous biographers." Divided into sections on Eliot's life and books, this work offers some good critical insights and contains a separate chapter on *Middlemarch,* Eliot's masterpiece. The Hansons' book is well documented and contains a good bibliography. Based upon newly discovered letters and material concerning the relationship between Eliot and John Chapman first published by Gordon S. Haight, the book contains an analysis of "the struggle between tradition and progress, between a remarkable intellect and a warm and loving heart."

All subsequent Eliot biographers will benefit from the research of Gordon S. Haight, who is also the major biographer to date. His *George Eliot and John Chapman: With Chapman's Diaries,* 2d ed. (Hamden, CT: Archon Books, 1969), "brought the first significant change in the portrait" of Eliot. He is also the editor of the monumental *The George Eliot Letters,* 9 vols. (New Haven and London: Yale University Press, 1954–1955; 1978), the most important source of biographical information about Eliot.

Lastly, for those new to Eliot's life and work, a commendable starting point is Walter Allen's *George Eliot* (New York: Collier, 1967). Always a dependable critic, Allen deals succinctly with the life and works.

Evaluation of Selected Biographies

Cross, John Walter, *George Eliot's Life: As Related in Her Letters and Journals.* 3 vols. New York and London: Harper and Brothers, 1903. Cross, who married Eliot after the death of her long-time companion, George Henry Lewes, claims to have allowed the life "to write itself in extracts from her letters and journals." However, he also states that the letters have been "pruned." This book is important because it is the source of so many subsequent biographies, but later biographers, including Haight, the Hansons, and Sprague, have noted that Cross omitted and suppressed much information that modern scholarship has uncovered.

Haight, Gordon S. *George Eliot: A Biography.* New York and Oxford: Oxford University Press, 1968. This definitive biography includes letters that Cross omitted and incorporates material from the dairies, journals, and papers of Chapman and Lewes. Haight's focus is on Eliot's "need to be loved" as "a dominant element of her personality" and aspects of her relationship with Cross not previously published. The book's only limitation is that it "is better read as a careful reference work than as an interpretation of the woman behind the novels" (Knoepflmacher, p. 239).

Redinger, Ruby, *George Eliot: The Emergent Self.* New York: Alfred A. Knopf, 1975. Unlike Haight's book, Redinger's is interpretive, tracing Eliot's "painful growth-both emotional and creative." Beginning with Eliot's "unhappy family life" and focusing on her early works, the author treats Evangelicalism as an influence, Eliot's "recurrent confrontation with her desire, her *need* to write," and her need to be loved. Redinger's biography can be considered "a companion volume" to Haight's.

Overview of Critical Sources

Eliot's work, like that of other major Victorian novelists, has received a great deal of critical attention, resulting in a bewildering number of sources among which students must choose. As preparation for reading Eliot's works, the novice or general reader will find Ian Adam's *George Eliot* (New York: Humanities Press, 1969) a useful starting point. The book contains a brief essay on the life and works that is followed by numerous extracts from the novels. Another useful introduction is T. S. Pearce's *George Eliot* (Totowa, NJ: Rowman and Littlefield, 1973). Pearce attempts to give a "straight forward account" of the life and works which avoids critical jargon, and he discusses Eliot's novels within the literary context of the genre.

Extremely useful to those who do not have access to large research libraries are the collections of essays from various sources published in book form. Among the best are *Critics on George Eliot: Readings in Literary Criticism,* ed. William Baker (London: George Allen and Unwin, 1973), which contains critical essays on Eliot from the period 1856–1953 and modern criticism; *Discus-*

sions of George Eliot, ed. Richard Stang (Boston: D.C. Heath, 1960), which contains thirteen essays that trace the critical reputation of Eliot's novels; *A Century of George Eliot Criticism,* ed. Gordon S. Haight (Boston: Houghton Mifflin, 1965), which contains critical appraisals of Eliot's work, written between 1858–1962; *Critical Essays on George Eliot,* ed. Barbara Hardy (London: Routledge and Kegan Paul, 1970); *George Eliot; A Collection of Critical Essays,* ed. George R. Creeger (Englewood Cliffs, NJ: Prentice-Hall, 1970), which contains a well balanced survey of criticism and a good selected bibliography; and *George Eliot: Centenary Essays and an Unpublished Fragment,* ed. Ann Smith (New York: Barnes and Noble, 1980), which contains a fragment probably written between 1877–1878, according to William Baker. A number of collections are devoted exclusively to discussions of *Middlemarch.* Among them are *Middlemarch: Critical Approaches to the Novel,* ed. Barbara Hardy (New York: Oxford University Press, 1967); David Daiches's *Middlemarch: George Eliot* (Woodbury: Baron's Educational Series, 1963); and *This Particular Web: Essays on Middlemarch,* ed. Ian Adam (Toronto: University of Toronto Press, 1975).

The critical reputation of Eliot's novels is covered by two volumes: *George Eliot and Her Readers: A Selection of Contemporary Reviews,* eds. John Holmstrom and and Lawrence Lerner (New York: Barnes and Noble, 1966); and *George Eliot: The Critical Heritage,* ed. David Carroll (London: Routledge and Kegan Paul, 1971).

Finally, every reader of Eliot should be familiar with F. R. Leavis's discussion in *The Great Tradition* (New York: Doubleday, 1954) since it has influenced so much subsequent criticism.

Evaluation of Selected Criticism

Hardy, Barbara, *The Novels of George Eliot: A Study in Form.* New York: Oxford University Press, 1959. Reprinted with corrections, 1963. Often cited as a work of major importance, this book analyzes the form of Eliot's novels. The author extends the concept to imagery and theme, noting that the "elaborate patterns" of Eliot's novels support the author's "moral generalizations."

Harvey, W. J. *The Art of George Eliot.* New York: Oxford University Press, 1969. Harvey's primary concern is "with the novelist as an artist." Dismissing the theory that Eliot was a "natural genius', deficient in art," he attempts through his discussion to "restore her rightful place" as a deliberate artist.

Knoepflmacher, U. C. *George Eliot's Early Novels: The Limits of Realism.* Berkeley: University of California Press, 1968. The author states that the "primary purpose of this book is to discover a rationale for George Eliot's growth as a philosophical novelist." He examines those works "which make up the first stage of her development."

Thale, Jerome, *The Novels of George Eliot.* New York: Columbia University Press, 1959. In this widely acknowledged work, Thale delineates "the specific quality of George Eliot's vision and the general type to which her fiction belongs." Using a variety of critical approaches, he employs Eliot's ideas, life, and development, as well as "recurring situations and patterns" in his analysis.

Other Sources

Pinion, F. B. *A George Eliot Companion.* Totowa, NJ: Barnes and Noble, 1981. A useful compilation including chapters on Eliot's life and relevant history, a survey of essays and reviews, and critical discussion of the works. Contains twenty four pages of illustrations.

Selected Dictionaries and Encyclopedias

British Writers, Vol. 5, Charles Scribner's Sons, 1983. Excellent overview of Eliot's life and works. Contains a good bibliography.

Dictionary of Literary Biography, Vol. 21, Gale Research, 1983. A very useful bio-critical introduction. Contains bibliography.

Eugene Zasadinski
St. John's University

T. S. ELIOT
1888–1965

Author's Chronology

Born Thomas Sterns Eliot, September 26, 1888, in St. Louis, Missouri; lives until *1904* in St. Louis, attending Smith Academy as day student and spending summers with his family near Gloucester, Massachusetts; *1905–1906* attends Milton Academy, Massachusetts; *1906–1910* attends Harvard College; *1910–1911* attends the Sorbonne in Paris; *1911–1914* returns to Harvard as a graduate student in philosophy; begins doctoral dissertation on F. H. Bradley; *1914* enrolls in Marburg University in Germany, July-August, then settles in Oxford, where he begins his close association with Ezra Pound; *1915* marries Vivienne Haigh-Wood; moves to London and takes a post as teacher; first poems published in *Blast* and *Poetry; 1917–1925* works for Lloyd's Bank in London; *1917–1919* serves as assistant editor for *The Egoist; 1922* becomes editor of *The Criterion;* publishes *The Waste Land;* wins the $2000 Dial Award; *1925* joins the firm of Faber and Gwyer (later Faber and Faber); *1927* he becomes an Anglo-Catholic and a British citizen; *1927* attempts writing drama with *Sweeney Agonistes; 1935 Murder in the Catehdral* is staged; *1932–1933* delivers Charles Eliot Norton lectures at Harvard; *1933* separates from Vivienne; *1942* stops writing poetry with the completion of *Four Quartets,* but continues writing plays and essays; *1948* receives the Nobel Prize; *1957* marries Valerie Fletcher; *1965* dies on January 4.

Author's Bibliography (selected)

The Love Song of J. Alfred Prufrock and Other Observations, 1917 (poems); *Ara Vos Prec,* 1919 (poems); *The Sacred Wood,* 1920 (criticism); *The Waste Land,* 1922 (poem); *Four Elizabethan Dramatists,* 1924 (essays); *Poems, 1909–1925; For Lancelot Andrewes,* 1928 (essays); *The Use of Poetry and the Use of Criticism,* 1932 (essays); *Collected Poems, 1909–1935; Murder in the Cathedral,* 1935 (play); *Essays Ancient and Modern,* 1936; *The Family Reunion,* 1939 (play); *The Idea of a Christian Society,* 1939 (essay); *Four Quartets,* 1944 (poetry); *Notes toward a Definition of Culture,* 1949 (essay); *Selected Essays,* 1950; *The Cocktail Party,* 1950 (play); *The Confidential Clerk,* 1954 (play); *The Elder Statesman,* 1959 (play); *Collected Poems, 1909–1962,* 1963; *Knowledge and Experience in the Philosophy of F. H. Bradley,* 1964 (doctoral dissertation, completed in 1916); *To Criticize the Critic,* 1965 (essays); *Poems Written in Early Youth,* 1967; *Complete Poems and Plays,* 1969; *The Waste Land. A Facsimile and Transcript of the Original Drafts Including the Annotations of Ezra Pound,* 1971.

Overview of Biographical Sources

Interest in Eliot's life was held in check for many years by his reticence and by his view that poetry was "an escape from personality" rather than an expression of it. Eliot left instructions in his will that there should be no official biography; the poet's estate has consistently refused permission to quote from correspondence. Consequently, much information is being withheld—for example, some 2,000 letters exchanged between Eliot and Emily Hale will not be available until the year 2020. Inevitably, both critics and public have come to feel that much of Eliot's fascination lies in his concealments, and this attitude has grown during the two decades after Eliot's death, culminating in Michael Hastings' play *Tom and Viv* in 1984, and the prolonged commentary on the play in the *Times Literary Supplement* and other periodicals. Perhaps the interest in Eliot's life had to wait for Eliot's own doctrine of impersonality to lose its force. Some of the recent interest in Eliot's life is perverse or gossipy, and a few biographies should be avoided (by T. S. Matthews, Robert Sencourt, and James E. Miller Jr.). The following biographies—or partial biographies—can be read with profit.

Evaluation of Selected Biographies

Ackroyd, Peter, *T. S. Eliot. A Life.* New York: Simon and Schuster, 1984. The treatment of Eliot's life is objective and generally sympathetic, without being overwhelmed by the Eliot legend. The opening chapters on the American background are less perceptive than those on the English years. Ackroyd was refused permission by the Eliot estate to quote from unpublished correspondence.

Gordon, Lyndall, *Eliot's Early Years.* Oxford and New York: Oxford University Press, 1977. The author thoroughly treats Eliot's youth and first marriage in an objective manner, concluding with Eliot's conversion to Anglo-Catholicism at age 39. There are some flaws, such as an oversimplified view of Eliot's youthful religiosity that was opposed to the material world. It is also disputable that Eliot had a "divine goal" as early as 1910, but the account of Eliot's relationships is good.

Howarth, Herbert, *Figures behind T. S. Eliot.* London: Chatto and Windus, 1965. Valuable descriptions are given of various intellectual figures—professors, writers, reviewers, friends—known by Eliot. The book is admirable in following Eliot's voluminous reading. With most writers it would not qualify as a biography, but in Eliot's case it does.

Simpson, Louis, *Three on a Tower.* New York: William Morrow, 1975. The middle section of the book is on Eliot, and contains one of the finest medium-length accounts—100 pages—of Eliot's life. The ideas and poetry are there too, but always subordinate to the life.

Overview of Critical Sources

The criticism of Eliot's poetry, criticism, and drama is voluminous, and its bulk is intimidating. There is also substantial criticism about his religious thought, philosophy, and social criticism. To use F. W. Bateson's phrase, Eliot's "poetry of learning" attracted an enormous number of critics who found his work conducive to learned criticism, frequently academic. His influence as critic was also strong; the poetry and criticism reinforced one another, creating one of the most potent literary influences in the English-speaking world during the period 1920–1960. With the passage of time, many of the exegetical works on Eliot—the "reader's guides" once thought essential to understanding him—seem less essential, even superficial. Eliot's poems do not equal the sum of their literary references. Critics of Eliot's works tend to fall between two poles: those who stress the relationships in the poems to other literature and texts, and those who stress the relationships in the poems to non-literary situations. The distinction is not a neat one, but can be summed up by the two versions of *The Waste Land,* one without notes (as published in *The Dial* and *The Criterion*), and the Boni and Liveright edition, with notes and perpetuated in subsequent versions of the poem. Some critics consider the notes primary to an understanding of the poem, others as secondary. The most important of the following studies, by Stead, Maxwell, Leavis, and Matthiesson, firmly situate Eliot in the context of late 19th-early 20th century poetry. They describe what was new in his work and the reasons for his significance.

Evaluation of Selected Criticism

Bush, Ronald. *T. S. Eliot. A Study in Character and Style.* New York: Oxford University Press, 1984. A synthesis of the many strands of Eliot's thought and work, this interpretation of individual lines of peoms is sometimes shakey, but the attempt to grasp the whole of Eliot, in all his complexity, is admirable.

Kenner, Hugh, *The Invisible Poet: T. S. Eliot.* New York: McDowell and Obolensky, 1959. Kenner's treatment of Eliot is spirited and always interesting. He was not thrall to the legend of Eliot, and establishes a certain distance from it. Kenner's knowledge of the general period is prodigious, and those seeking more information should consult his other book, *The Pound Era* (Berkeley and Los Angeles: University of California Press, 1971).

Leavis, F. R. *New Bearings in English Poetry.* London: Chatto and Windus, 1932. Eliot is the real subject of this book, though there are other chapters about Pound and Hopkins. Leavis presents one of the strongest cases—perhaps *the* strongest—for Eliot's significance as poet and thinker. Leavis was the editor of *Scrutiny,* and exerted great influence among critics in England.

Margolis, John D. *T. S. Eliot's Intellectual Development 1922–1939.* Chicago: University of Chicago Press, 1972. Margolis offers a thorough study of Eliot's evolution after *The Waste Land,* up to "Burnt Norton" and the outbreak of the war.

Matthiesson, F. O. *The Achievement of T. S. Eliot.* New York and London: Oxford University Press, 1935. Matthiesson's purpose in undertaking his study of Eliot was to broaden the scope of Leavis, and to be more sensitive to the poetry than Edmund Wilson in his study *Axle's Castle.* From the present perspective, however, the books by Matthiesson, Leavis, and Maxwell all suffer from the tendency to see Eliot's work as a single block; given the dates when they were written, this was probably inevitable. The books by Kenner, Margolis, and Bush are less narrowly partisan, and describe Eliot's complex evolution as poet and thinker.

Maxwell, D. E. S. *The Poetry of T. S. Eliot.* London: Routledge and Kegan Paul, 1952. This book is good on the context in which Eliot first formulated his major ideas and poetic style. Eliot's revolt, and his concept of the unified sensibility, are especially well described. The second half of the book suffers from excessive, uncritical partisanship, as do many other studies (e.g., Helen Gardner, Elizabeth Drew) written during the period of Eliot's greatest sway, 1945–1955, and underestimates differences in the stages of Eliot's evolution.

Stead, C. K. *The New Poetic: Yeats to Eliot.* London: Hutchinson, 1964; reprinted by Penguin. The second half of the book is about Eliot, and it remains one of the clearest accounts of the formation of Eliot's style and thought. The relations to his predecessors, the Imperialists, Georgians and W. B. Yeats, and to his contemporaries, the war poets and Imagists, are succinctly delineated.

Evaluation of Selected Essays

There are numerous collections of essays about Eliot. The earlier collections often contain reminiscences, and are only occasionally critical (Richard March and Tambimuttu, eds., *T. S. Eliot,* London: Poetry London, 1948; Leonard Unger, ed., *T. S. Eliot,* New York: Rinehart, 1948; Neville Braybrooke, ed., *T. S. Eliot,* New York: Farrar, Straus, 1958). They are valuable, nevertheless, because of their variety. The following collections of essays are noteworthy.

Kenner, Hugh, ed. *T. S. Eliot. A Collection of Critical Essays.* Englewood Cliffs, New Jersey: Prentice-Hall, 1962. The essays by Kenner, D. W. Harding, and Leavis (on the later poetry) are of particular interest.

Litz, A. Walton, ed. *Eliot in His Time.* Princeton: Princeton University Press, 1973. Essays by Litz, Kenner, and Ellmann, among others.

Martin, Graham, ed. *Eliot in Perspective.* London: Macmillan, 1970. Valuable essays by Bateson ("The Poetry of Learning"), Wollheim, and Cunningham.

Martin, Jay, ed. *A Collection of Critical Essays on 'The Waste Land.'* Englewood Cliffs, NJ: Prentice-Hall, 1968. A variety of interpretations of this key poem by Eliot.

Tate, Allen, ed. *T. S. Eliot: The Man and His Work.* New York: Delacorte, 1966. Among the reminiscences there are fine essays by G. Wilson Knight, Kermode, Cleanth Brooks, and Mario Praz.

Other Sources

Chace, William M. *The Political Identities of Ezra Pound and T. S. Eliot.* Stanford: Stanford University Press, 1974. A useful attempt to come to grips with this aspect of Eliot's thought.

Gallup, Donald, *T. S. Eliot: A Bibliography.* New York: Harcourt Brace, revised edition, 1969. An invaluable catalogue of all Eliot's works that appeared in print, including all periodical publications.

Kojecky, Roger, *T. S. Eliot's Social Criticism.* New York: Farrar, Straus, and Giroux, 1971.

Smith, Carol H. *T. S. Eliot's Dramatic Theory and Practise.* Princeton: Princeton University Press, 1963. A useful introduction to Eliot's dramatic writings. Unfortunately it is weak on staging.

Smith, Grover, Jr., *T. S. Eliot's Poetry and Plays. A Study in Sources and Meaning.* Chicago: University of Chicago Press, 1956. One of the most useful books about Eliot, it remains the best single study to consult about the literary allusions. It does not necessarily answer all questions about individual lines, however; the author tends to treat the allusions as literary references, as if they were "about" literature. This approach can be reductive—though lengthy—failing to make the required interpretive synthesis. The book is clear, and chronological.

Williamson, George, *Reader's Guide to T. S. Eliot. A Poem-by-Poem Analysis.* New York: Farrar, Straus & Giroux, 1953, 1966. Exegesis of individual lines.

John Carpenter
University of Michigan

RALPH WALDO EMERSON
1803–1882

Author's Chronology

Born May 25, 1803, in Boston, of old New England stock; *1810–1817* attends Boston Public Latin School; *1817–1821* attends Harvard College on scholarship; *1821–1825* teaches school; *1825* enters Harvard Divinity School but soon withdraws because of eye problems; *1825–1826* teaches school; *1826–1827* sails to Charleston, South Carolina and St. Augustine, Florida to improve his health; *1827* receives degree in Divinity from Harvard; *1829* called as pastor of Second Church, Boston; marries Ellen Tucker; *1831* wife Ellen dies of tuberculosis; *1832* resigns from his pastorate and sails for Europe; *1833* travels to Italy, Switzerland, France, and England; meets Landor, Coleridge, Wordsworth, and Carlyle; *1834* returns to Boston, delivers first lectures; *1835* marries Lydia Jackson; *1836* publishes "Nature"; first meeting of Transcendental Club; son Waldo is born; *1837* delivers "The American Scholar," Harvard Phi Beta Kappa Address; *1838* meets Thoreau, "Divinity School Address" given at Harvard; *1839* birth of daughter Ellen; *1841* daughter Edith born; *1842* death of son Waldo; edits *The Dial; 1844* son Edward born; *1847–1848* sails for England and France; *1851* speaks out against Fugitive Slave Act; *1871* trip to California; *1872* house burns; travels to Europe and Egypt; *1882* death on April 27 and burial in Concord.

Author's Bibliography (selected)

"Nature," 1836 (essay); "The American Scholar," 1837 (essay); "The Divinity School Address," 1838 (essay); *Essays: First Series,* 1841; *Essays: Second Series,* 1844; *Poems,* 1846; *Nature, Addresses, and Lectures,* 1849; *Representative Men,* 1850 (biographical essays); *English Traits,* 1856 (essays); *The Conduct of Life,* 1860 (essays); *May-Day and Other Pieces,* 1867 (poems); *Society and Solitude,* 1870 (essays); *Letters and Social Aims,* 1875 (essays); *Selected Poems,* 1876. Edward Emerson's edition of *The Complete Works of Ralph Waldo Emerson: Centenary Edition,* 12 vols., 1903–1904, is gradually being replaced by the new Harvard edition of *The Collected Works of Ralph Waldo Emerson,* 1971—, of which two volumes have been issued. There is also a new three-volume edition of *The Early Lectures of Ralph Waldo Emerson, 1833–1842* (1964–1971) as well as twenty-five sermons collected in *Young Emerson Speaks: Unpublished Discourses on Many Subjects,* 1938.

Overview of Biographical Sources

Emerson has never lacked for competent biographers, and every generation seems to bring fresh interpretations of his life as new material comes to light.

Oliver Wendell Holmes's *Ralph Waldo Emerson* (1885, 1968) is a clear, judicious appraisal by one who knew Emerson first-hand; James Elliot Cabot's *A Memoir of Ralph Waldo Emerson,* 2 vol. (1887) was the first full-length authorized biography; George E. Woodbury's *Ralph Waldo Emerson* (1907, 1968) is largely based upon Cabot's memoir; Van Wyck Brooks' *The Life of Emerson* (1932) is an important estimate of Emerson's place in "the flowering of New England"; for a generation Ralph L. Rusk's carefully researched *The Life of Ralph Waldo Emerson* (1949, 1957) remained the definitive biography, since Rusk was also the editor of the six-volume *Letters of Ralph Waldo Emerson* (1939); but it has now been superseded by Gay Wilson Allen's *Waldo Emerson* (1981), a meticulous and thorough study that makes use of the wealth of new Emerson materials that have become available, including the 16 volume Harvard edition of the Emerson *Journals and Miscellaneous Notebooks* (1960–1982); other recent critical-biographical studies include Stephen E. Whicher's controversial *Freedom and Fate: An Inner Life of Ralph Waldo Emerson* (1953); Joel Porte's fine *Representative Man: Ralph Waldo Emerson in His Time* (1979); David Robinson's useful *Apostle of Culture: Emerson as Preacher and Lecturer* (1982); Donald Yannella's brief *Ralph Waldo Emerson* (1982); and a forthcoming title by John McAleer, *Ralph Waldo Emerson: Days of Encounter* (1984). Other important indirect biographical sources include Edith W. Gregg's edition of *One First Love: The Letters of Ellen Louisa Tucker to Ralph Waldo Emerson* (1962) and Delores B. Carpenter's *The Life of Lidian Jackson Emerson* (1981). Edith W. Gregg has also edited a recent collection of *The Letters of Ellen Tucker Emerson,* 2 vols. (1982), which sheds some light on the Emerson family life.

Evaluation of Selected Biographies

Allen, Gay Wilson, *Waldo Emerson.* New York: Viking Press, 1981. In this splendid new biography, Allen performs the important task of incorporating more of Emerson's journals and intimate life along with a thorough assessment of his social and intellectual background. In making use of all newly available papers, Allen's biography goes beyond Rusk's standard *Life of Ralph Waldo Emerson* to offer a new appraisal of Emerson's importance as a central figure in American culture. He manages to fuse the literary and personal lives without neglecting any of the contradictions or dark sides of Emerson's personality. In stressing the perennial freshness and originality of Emerson's thought in shaping the course of American letters, Allen offers an enduring portrait. His biography of Emerson should remain definitive for the forseeable future.

Brooks, Van Wyck, *The Life of Emerson.* New York: E. P. Dutton, 1932. Though some of the information here is dated, Brooks' critical biography remains one of the most lucid and readable studies of Emerson's life. Brooks makes extensive use of Emerson's letters and journals in this lively, impressionistic narrative, which is worth reading just to appreciate the graceful style of an earlier generation of American scholarship.

Porte, Joel, *Representative Man: Ralph Waldo Emerson in his Time.* New York: Oxford University Press, 1979. Porte makes extensive use of the new multi-volume *Journals and Miscellaneous Notebooks* to offer the best of the reappraisals of Emerson's importance as an American poet and critic that appeared during the centennial of his death. Porte's title, *Representative Man,* indicates his recognition of Emerson's moderate and balanced intellect as embodying the best of 19th century American culture, alluding to Emerson's collection of biographical sketches of the men he most admired in history and letters. This biography succeeds, as one reviewer has noted, in making Emerson come alive "as a palpable, vibrant person."

Robinson, David, *Apostle of Culture: Emerson as Preacher and Lecturer.* Philadelphia: University of Pennsylvania Press, 1982. Robinson's recent study focuses selectively on one aspect of Emerson's life, the tension he felt between his love of preaching and lecturing and the duties he felt obliged to perform as a pastor, which eventually led him to resign from the ministry. Robinson speculates on the ways in which Emerson's unitarian beliefs shaped his subsequent lecture and essay style.

Rusk, Ralph L. *The Life of Ralph Waldo Emerson.* New York: Columbia University Press, 1949, 1957. For three decades Rusk's meticulously detailed Emerson biography has been definitive, and it remains the best source to consult, along with Allen's more recent life. Rusk made full use of all available Emerson documents in writing his life of Emerson and it remains an objective and thoroughly researched work. Rusk deliberately avoids speculation about Emerson's personal, intimate life and does not offer much literary interpretation. The portrait of Emerson that emerges is accurate but colorless.

Whicher, Stephen E. *Freedom and Fate: An Inner Life of Ralph Emerson.* Philadelphia: University of Pennsylvania Press, 1953. Whicher's book remains an important study of Emerson's intellectual development, particularly in relation to formative influences. Whicher accounts for Emerson's romantic idealism and individualism in terms of his reading and the New England cultural milieu, examining the dual themes of freedom (or originality) and fate (or skepticism) that appear throughout Emerson's writing. Whicher's study traces the gradual decline of Emerson's optimism, particularly after his son Waldo's death, and the emergence of a more guarded skepticism, even pessimism, in his later thought.

Yannella, Donald, *Ralph Waldo Emerson.* Boston: Twayne, 1982. Another of the Emerson centennial biographies, this brief study adds little that is new to the body of Emerson scholarship, but it may be useful as an overview or introduction to Emerson's life. Yannella's book primarily summarizes received information, but it does present a clear and accurate biographical treatment.

Autobiographical Sources

Since Emerson's journals were a spiritual account of his inner life, his thoughts, emotions and sentiments, as well as a detailed record of his daily life, the best place to find autobiographical information is in the new Harvard edition of *The Journals and Miscellaneous Notebooks of Ralph Waldo Emerson,* vols. 1–16 (1960–1982), which replaces the earlier *Journals of Ralph Waldo Emerson,* 10 vols. (1904–1910). From the complete journals Joel Porte has edited a splendid new one-volume edition, *Emerson in His Journals* (1982), which largely supplants Bliss Perry's edition of *The Heart of Emerson's Journals* (1926). Ralph L. Rusk's six-volume edition of the *Letters of Ralph Waldo Emerson* (1939) is still an important autobiographical source, although Professor Eleanor Tilton is now preparing an expanded edition of Rusk's work, which should include some hitherto unpublished family correspondence. The Emerson *Letters* need to be supplemented by Joseph Slater's edition of the *Correspondence of Emerson and Carlyle* (1964), which supersedes the earlier two-volume *Correspondence of Carlyle and Emerson* (1883).

Overview of Critical Sources

The sheer weight of Emerson scholarship may at first seem overwhelming, but with the help of an annotated bibliography the student should be able to make informed choices from among the many Emerson studies. With the advent of the Emerson centennial, critical opinions have been changing about the importance of Emerson's poetry and of his influence on subsequent American poets, not only Dickinson and Whitman, but Frost and Stevens as well. Scholars have generally recognized Emerson's pervasive influence on American culture, and have distinguished his literary accomplishments from the genteel verse of his contemporaries, the other New England Fireside Poets, Longfellow, Whittier, Lowell, and Holmes. There is a growing recognition in recent scholarship about the importance of Emerson's literary theory and practice, his influence on his contemporaries, and his legacy as a poet and thinker.

Evaluation of Selected Criticism

Burkholder, Robert E. and Joel Myerson, *Critical Essays on Ralph Waldo Emerson.* Boston: G. K. Hall, 1983. A comprehensive one-volume collection of Emerson scholarship, ranging from appreciative essays by Emerson's contemporaries, the later changing critical assessments, and including the most recent scholarship. This edition presents a valuable survey of the history of Emerson scholarship.

Carpenter, Frederic Ives, *Emerson Handbook.* New York: Hendricks House, 1953. Though somewhat dated, this book still provides a useful introduction to Emerson's thought and to Emerson scholarship. Carpenter attempts to systematize a highly unsystematic thinker by discussing Emerson's ideas in logical categories. Students will find this a useful book, with sections on biography, primary works (prose and poetry), philosophical ideas, and Emerson's sources and influences.

Hopkins, Vivian C. *Spires of Form: Emerson's Aesthetic Theory.* Cambridge: Harvard University Press, 1981. Hopkins offers a valuable extended discussion of Emerson's creative theory, exploring his interest in organic form in poetry and the other fine arts.

Leary, Lewis, *Ralph Waldo Emerson: An Interpretive Essay.* Boston: Twayne, 1980. Leary breaks no new ground here, but instead offers a broad introduction to and appreciation of Emerson the man and the thinker. Though brief, this book provides a useful introduction to Emerson's thought and accomplishment for the general reader.

Matthiessen, F. O. *American Renaissance: Art and Experience in the Age of Emerson and Whitman.* New York: Oxford University Press, 1941. This is still the best study of Emerson's organic theory of art and its relationship to his poetry. Matthiessen traces the genesis of Emerson's thoughts about a distinctive, democratic American art form and shows how these concepts became embodied in Emerson's verse and how they subsequently influenced Whitman's poetics.

Paul, Sherman, *Emerson's Angle of Vision.* Cambridge: Harvard University Press, 1952, 1965. Paul has written an important critical study of Emerson's philosophical views, particularly his dualism, and of the ways in which Emerson tried to reconcile idealism and experience through his doctrine of correspondence. The emphasis here is on how Emerson's concepts of vision and unity shaped his thought.

Porte, Joel, *Emerson and Thoreau: Transcendentalists in Conflict.* Middletown: Wesleyan University Press, 1965. As his title suggests, Porte examines the reciprocal though sometimes conflicting influence of these two most prominent Transcendentalists. By juxtaposing their letters, journals, and works, Porte demonstrates that the influence is not all one-sided on Emerson's part, but truly mutual and dialectical, with each benefiting from the other, even after their friendship cooled.

Stovall, Floyd, "Ralph Waldo Emerson," *Eight American Authors.* rev. ed. New York: W. W. Norton, 1971. Although this is the single most comprehensive bibliographic essay and survey of Emerson scholarship through 1971,

Stovall's essay needs to be supplemented by the Emerson essay in the *American Literary Scholarship* annual for more recent work.

Wagenknecht, Edward, *Ralph Waldo Emerson: Portrait of a Balanced Soul.* New York: Oxford University Press, 1974. Despite the title, this is more a critical than a biographical study. Wagenknecht discusses the major categories of Emerson's thought, as reflected in the essays, with chapters on self-reliance, nature, art, friendship, love, politics, and the oversoul.

Waggoner, Hyatt A. *Emerson as Poet.* Princeton: Princeton University Press, 1974. In this first major book-length study of Emerson's poetry, Waggoner argues that Emerson is essentially a poet and visionary in all his work, essays and poems alike. He discusses the merits of Emerson's poems in terms of his aesthetic theory, examining vision and voice, and including a chapter on "the poetry of the prose."

Other Sources

Konvitz, Milton R. and Stephen E. Whicher, *Emerson: A Collection of Criticial Essays.* Englewood Cliffs: Prentice-Hall, 1962. A valuable collection of mid-century Emerson scholarship, with a number of important essays not collected elsewhere.

Carpenter, Frederic Ives, *Emerson and Asia.* Cambridge: Harvard University Press, 1930. Still the best study of Emerson's orientalism, particularly his interest in neoplatonism, Persian poetry, and Hindu thought.

Konvitz, Milton R. *The Recognition of Ralph Waldo Emerson: Selected Criticism Since 1837.* Ann Arbor: University of Michigan Press, 1972. A survey of Emerson's growing reputation, based on a selection of prominent writers and critics.

Anderson, John Q. *The Liberating Gods: Emerson on Poets and Poetry.* Coral Gables: University of Miami Press, 1971. A useful study of Emerson's theory of the poet as orphic seer and visionary.

Bishop, Jonathan, *Emerson on the Soul.* Cambridge: Harvard University Press, 1964. A thorough examination of one of Emerson's basic philosophical concepts.

Packer, Barbara L. *Emerson's Fall: A New Interpretation of the Major Essays.* New York: Continuum, 1982. A penetrating new study of Emerson the writer and of the relationship between his journals and essays.

Andrew J. Angyal
Elon College

WILLIAM EMPSON
1906–1984

Author's Chronology

Born September 27, 1906, Yokefleet Hall, Yorkshire, England, to an old family of the landed gentry; *1920* enters Winchester College as a Scholar; *1924* wins Richardson Prize in mathematics and a mathematics scholarship to Magdalene College, Cambridge; *1925* enters Cambridge; *1926* earns a First in Part 1 of the Mathematics Tripos and switches to studies in English under I. A. Richards; *1929* receives a starred First in Part 1 of the English Tripos; edits undergraduate journals *Granta* and *Experiment* during Cambridge years; *1928* publishes fifteen poems; *1930* publishes *Seven Types of Ambiguity; 1930–1934* teaches English literature at the Tokyo University of Literature and Science; *1934* returns to England; *1937* publishes *Poems* and *Some Versions of Pastoral;* makes hazardous trip through war-stricken Manchuria to teach in southwest China; *1940* returns to England and works for B.B.C.; *1941* marries Hester Henrietta Crouse, a South African; *1947* returns to Peking National University; *1948* and *1950* travels to U.S.A. to participate in Kenyon College Summer School; *1951* publishes *The Structure of Complex Words; 1952* returns to England; *1953* becomes Professor of English Literature at Sheffield University; *1961* publishes *Milton's God; 1971* retires from Sheffield; *1978* made Sir William Empson; *1984* dies in London in April.

Author's Bibliography (selected)

Seven Types of Ambiguity, 1930 (criticism); *Poems,* 1935; *Some Versions of Pastoral,* 1935 (criticism); *Collected Poems,* 1949; *The Structure of Complex Words,* 1951 (criticism); *Milton's God,* 1961 (criticism); *Using Biography,* 1984 (criticism).

Overview of Biographical Sources

Very little is in print on Empson's interesting life. The fullest biographical sketch is found in the introduction to Philip and Averill Gardner's *The God Approached. A Commentary on the Poems of William Empson* (Totowa, NJ: Rowan and Littlefield, 1978). Roma Gill's *Festschrift, William Empson: The Man and His Work* (London: Routledge and Kegan Paul, 1974), presents various personal views of Empson. Kathleen Raine's offering, "Extracts from Unpublished Memoirs," recalls her friendship with Empson at Cambridge; Rintaro Fukahara in "Mr. William Empson in Japan" provides his impressions as Empson's department head in Tokyo; and George Fraser tells of "The Man within the Name: William Empson as Poet, Critic, and Friend." I. A. Richards's "William Empson" (*Furioso,* January 12, 1940. Supplement) describes his experiences as Empson's Director of Studies at Cambridge. George Lanning captures something of Empson's personality in "Memories of the School of English" in *John Crowe Ransom; Gentleman, Teacher, Poet, Editor, Founder of 'The Kenyon Review.' A Tribute from the Community of Letters,* ed. D. David Long and Michael R. Burr. Supplement to *The Kenyon Collegian* (1964).

Autobiographical Sources

In "A Chinese University" (*Life and Letters,* June, 1940) Empson offers a tantalizing glimpse of himself in China; and he comments on his religious feelings in "Final Reflections," an essay appended to the 1981 edition of *Milton's God.*

Overview of Critical Sources

No one book in English covers all aspects of Empson's work. Frank Day's *Sir William Empson: An Annotated Bibliography* (New York: Garland, 1984) covers thoroughly both the primary and the secondary materials, and provides an introduction that chronicles the critical reaction to Empson's work.

Evaluation of Selected Criticism

Gardner, Averill and Philip, *The God Approached: A Commentary on the Poems of William Empson.* Totowa, NJ: Rowan and Littlefield, 1978. This is an excellent and indispensable book that analyzes each of Empson's collected poems, giving the date and place of first publication. The thoughtful explications give many leads to sources and analogues. The Gardners provide an informative introduction, as well as useful notes and a bibliography.

Meller, Horst, *Das Gedicht als Einübung: Zum Dichtungsverständnis William Empsons.* Heidelberg: Carl Winter Universitätsverlag, 1974. Meller's study contains four chapters: (1) an account of Empson's literary theory in reference to the thought of I. A. Richards and Coleridge; (2) a discussion of Empson's poetic practice in the light of his critical ideas; (3) an analysis of *Milton's God* in terms of "The Literary Scene as a Moral Tribunal"; and (4) a reading of Empson's poems as exercises in literary styles and genres. It has not been translated into English.

Norris, Christopher, *William Empson and the Philosophy of Literary Criticism.* London: Athlone Press, 1978. This is the only full-length study of Empson in English, but it is difficult and suitable only for readers thoroughly familiar with contemporary literary criticism. It is very valuable for its analysis of Empson's affinities with—and differences from—the New Critics. Norris also elaborates on Empson's quarrels with other critics (e.g., Hugh Kenner) and traces Empson's opposition to Symbolism and the Neo-Christians. Empson's ideas on language and meaning are studied in a context of modern linguistic theory, and his humanism is identified as having its source in Benthamism.

Sale, Roger, "The Achievement of William Empson," in *Modern Heroism.* Berkeley, Los Angeles, and London: University of California Press, 1973. Sale's long essay concentrates on *Seven Types of Ambiguity* and *Some Versions of Pastoral,* finding these works much influenced by T. S. Eliot's idea of history being continually created by the writer. Sale thinks that *Seven Types of Ambiguity* works subtly to subvert nineteenth-century commonplaces.

Willis, J. H., Jr. *William Empson.* No. 39 in "Columbia Essays on Modern Writers." New York and London: Columbia University Press, 1969. Willis provides a brief, well-written overview of Empson's career, praising him for his reason and balance of mind.

Other Sources

Alpers, Paul, "Empson on Pastoral," *New Literary History,* X (1978), 101–123. Alpers judges *Some Versions of Pastoral* a brilliant book but difficult to use, and identifies its two main themes as (1) the pastoral process transforms the complex into the simple, and (2) the pastoral mode has a unifying social force that helps reconcile social classes.

Burgum, Edwin Berry, "The Cult of the Complex in Poetry," *Science and Society,* XV (Winter, 1951), 31–48. Burgum attacks Empson for ignoring the social or historical referent in *Seven Types of Ambiguity.* Burgum further argues that Empson's ambiguity predisposes him to favor casuistical poetry and charges that Empson values a poem by the amount of ambiguity found in it.

Hough, Graham, *Style and Stylistics.* London: Routledge and Kegan Paul, 1969, pp. 90–95. Hough describes the revolutionary impact that *Seven Types of Ambiguity* had on literary criticism and points out that its main ideas have been quietly absorbed into the main stream of critical thought. He judges Empson's work as enormously important but so rich in implication that literary studies will be some time digesting it.

Hyman, Stanley Edgar, "William Empson and Categorical Criticism," *The Armed Vision: A Study in the Methods of Modern Literary Criticism.* New York: Vintage Books, 1955, pp. 237–277. Hyman ranks Empson among the best critics of his day. He also identifies the sources of Empson's thought in *Some Versions of Pastoral* (an implicitly Marxist work in Hyman's opinion) and sketches the influence of Empson on other critics such as R. P. Blackmur, Kenneth Burke, Cleanth Brooks, and John Crowe Ransom.

Jensen, James, "The Construction of Seven Types of Ambiguity," *Modern Language Quarterly,* XXVII (September 1966), 243–259. Jensen hypothesizes in great detail about the influence of I. A. Richards on the composition of *Seven Types of Ambiguity.* His reconstruction is interesting but it was not well received by Empson or Richards.

Kenner, Hugh, "Alice in Empsonland," *Hudson Review* V (1952), 137–144. Kenner has always been one of Empson's fiercest critics, and in this review of *The Structure of Complex Words* he derides Empson's method of analyzing key words as inadequate in opening up long passages and in dealing with concrete images. Although Kenner praises Empson's enthusiasm and mental agility, he faults him for his underlying assumption that word meanings are only subjective.

Olson, Elder, "William Empson, Contemporary Criticism and Poetic Diction," *Modern Philology,* XLVII (May 1950), 222–252. Olson attacks the whole movement of New Criticism, finding Empson one of its chief exponents. Olson charges Empson with a real ignorance of the history of criticism and with a failure to discriminate between meaning and inference.

Ransom, John Crowe, "Mr. Empson's Muddles," *Southern Review,* IV (July 1938-April 1939), 322–339. This excellent analysis treats mostly the essays in *Some Versions of Pastoral.* Ransom stresses Empson's debt to I. A. Richards for his psychological view of poetry. An important point for criticism emerges in Ransom's assertion that poetic acts and religious acts are both metaphysical affirmations.

Thurlow, Geoffrey, " 'Partial Fires': Empson's Poetry," *The Ironic Harvest: English Poetry in the Twentieth Century.* New York: St. Martin's Press, 1974, pp. 38–53. Thurlow provides one of the better discussions of Empson's poetry, pointing to the dominance in Empson of a kind of constitutional ambivalence and a fondness for the ambiguous and the qualified.

The Review: A Magazine of Poetry and Criticism. (June 1963). This is a special issue devoted to Empson. It includes six useful studies of aspects of Empson's poetry, as well as a good interview with Empson by Christopher Ricks.

Selected Dictionaries and Encyclopedias

Contemporary Literary Critics, St. Martin's Press, 1977, pp. 180–187. Elmer Borklund provides concise, well written, balanced summaries and judgments of Empson's four books of criticism. He includes selected primary and secondary bibliographies, plus a paragraph of biographical data.

Contemporary Poets, 3rd edition, St. Martin's Press, 1980, pp. 437–439. G. S. Fraser claims that it is difficult to trace the themes of Empson's terse poems, and his remark elicits a response from Empson (printed here) in which he grumbles about the tendency of critics to ignore the arguments in his poems.

Frank Day
Clemson University

SIR RICHARD FANSHAWE
1608–1666

Author's Chronology

Born June, 1608 at Ware Park in Hertfordshire; *1623* enters Jesus College, Cambridge, and shows a facility for classical languages; *1626* enters Inner Temple to study law; *1627* leaves Inner Temple to study modern languages abroad; *1635* appointed secretary to British ambassador in Spain; *1640* at the outbreak of Civil War joins the royal army of Charles I; *1644* marries Ann Harrison and receives appointment as secretary of war to Prince Charles; *1646* lives privately in London; *1647* on behalf of imprisoned King Charles carries a message to Spanish court; his first translation published anonymously; *1648* recruits troops for King Charles in Ireland; *1650* returns to Spain on a diplomatic mission; *1651* captured at the battle of Worcester and imprisoned; *1652–1653* under house arrest; *1652* publishes translations of three Roman poets; *1655* publishes a translation of Portugal's national epic; *1660* assists in the Restoration of Charles II; *1661–1662* helps negotiate the king's marriage and is appointed ambassador to Portugal; *1664* becomes ambassador to Spain; *1666* relieved as Spanish ambassador; prior to departure from Madrid dies on June 16.

Author's Bibliography

Il Pastor Fido, The Faithful Shepherd, with an Addition of Divers Poems, 1648 (translation of Battista Guarini's pastoral plus original poems in English); *Selected Parts of Horace,* 1652 (translations from Latin); *The Lusiad, or Portugals Historicall Poem,* 1655; *Fida Pastora,* 1658 (translation into Latin of John Fletcher's *The Faithful Shepherdess*); *Querer por solo querer* (*To Love only for Love Sake*) *together with Fiestas de Aranjuez,* 1671 (translation of Antonio de Mendoza's dramatic romance); *Original Letters of His Excellency Sir Richard Fanshawe,* 1702–1724.

Overview of Biographical Sources

Because he served two kings, Fanshawe's life is well documented. He is frequently mentioned in the diaries and memoirs of political figures such as Samuel Pepys, John Evelyn, and the Earl of Clarendon. In addition many of the letters he wrote while ambassador to Spain and Portugal survive. There have been two collections of his correspondence with Charles II, various ministers, and Spanish or Portugese authorities. One collection, *The Original Letters of His Excellency Sir Richard Fanshawe,* has not been reprinted since 1724 and is difficult to locate. The other collection is contained (with some non-Fanshawe pieces) in a volume compiled by the Historical Manuscripts Commission: *The Manuscripts of J. M. Heathcote of Conington Castle,* Norwich: Her

Majesty's Stationery Office, 1899. It is a volume more readily available. Both collections give a fascinating picture of Fanshawe's ambassadorial work between 1661 and 1665, but neither offers material about the early Fanshawe or about the private man. Surprising in view of the materials available and the colorful peripatetic life Fanshawe lived, no book-length biography has been written. The most extended, readily available account is found in *The Dictionary of National Biography.* The closest thing to a full-scale biography of Fanshawe are the memoirs written by his wife Ann.

Autobiographical Sources

The Memoirs of Anne, Lady Halkett, and Ann, Lady Fanshawe. ed. John Loftis. Oxford: Oxford University Press, 1979. Written to her children as a remembrance of their father, Anne's Memoirs make fascinating reading. She obviously adored her husband and proudly records his achievements in poetry and diplomacy. The most fascinating part of the account is her description of their life during the Civil War together. They faced destitution and death as they traveled around England and across the continent on behalf of the Royalist cause.

Overview of Critical Sources

There is not much critical study of Fanshawe primarily because his literary canon is so diverse. He wrote only a few original poems in English; the bulk of his work was translation into English poetry from Portuguese, Latin, and Italian. It would require a critic fluent in each of those languages to comment on the whole of Fanshawe's work. Another factor limiting critical attention is that a rendering of a poem into another language becomes dated very quickly. Criticism focuses instead either on the original work or the most recent translation. The best commentary on Fanshawe is to be found in introductions to the critical editions of his translations. The principal task to date for Fanshawe scholarship has been understanding and evaluating his method of translation.

Evaluation of Selected Criticism

Bawcutt, N. W. "Introduction to Sir Richard Fanshawe," in *Shorter Poems and Translations.* Liverpool: Liverpool University Press, 1964. A brief commentary that finds Fanshawe's poetic models in Horace, Edmund Spenser, and John Donne.

Bullough, Geoffrey, "Fanshawe and Guarini," in *Studies in English Language and Literature Presented to Professor Dr. Karl Brunner.* ed. Siegfried Korninger. Vienna and Stuttgart: Wilhelm Baumiller, 1957, pp. 17–31. Traces English interest in Italian pastorals during the 1600's and finds that Fanshawe contributed dramatic intensity and humor to the genre.

———, "Introduction to Luiz Vaz de Camoies," in *The Lusiads.* trans. Sir Richard Fanshawe. Carbondale: Southern Illinois University Press, 1963. An introduction for the general reader to the poem, its background, and the skill of the translator.

Buxton, John, "Sir Richard Fanshawe," in *A Tradition of Poetry.* New York: St. Martin's, 1967, pp. 102–131. Sketches Fanshawe's development as a poet by relating his works to his political activity. The tradition Fanshawe represents is that of the amateur poet, the courtier or gentleman who adds verification to his social skills.

Ford, Jeremiah D. M. "Introduction" to *The Lusiad of Luis de Camoens.* Cambridge: Harvard University Press, 1940. Discusses Fanshawe's considerable art as a "free" rather than verbatim translator.

Mackail, J. W. "Sir Richard Fanshawe," in *Studies in English Poets.* London: Longman and Co., 1926; rpt. New York: Books for Libraries, 1968, pp. 31–52. Provides a brief sketch of Fanshawe's life and subsequent reputation, and stresses the importance of the translations to the growth of literary consciousness in seventeenth-century England.

Staton, W. F. and W. E. Simeone, "Introduction to Sir Richard Fanshawe," in *Il Pastor Fido, The Faithful Shepherd.* Oxford: Oxford University Press, 1964. Contrasts Fanshawe's free rendering of Guarini with previous close renderings to show Fanshawe's "notable achievement."

Dictionaries and Encyclopedias

Critical Survey of Poetry, Salem Press, 1982. Brief biography and analysis of major poems.

Dictionary of National Biography, Oxford University Press, 1959–1960. Substantial biography and short bibliography.

Robert M. Otten
Indiana University-Purdue University at Fort Wayne

JAMES T. FARRELL
1904–1979

Author's Chronology

Born James Thomas Farrell, 27 February 1904, in Chicago; attends Parochial schools; *1919–1923* attends high school and works part time as American Railway Express Company clerk (full time in *1923–1924,* after graduation); *1925–1929* attends University of Chicago; *1929* publishes first short story and begins *Young Lonigan; April 1931–April 1932* elopes with Dorothy Butler and resides in Paris, where he makes many friends and useful connections, including Samuel Putnam and Ezra Pound; *June 1931 Young Lonigan* accepted by James Henle of Vanguard Press; begins long association with Henle and Vanguard; *1932* returns to US and divides time between New York City and Yaddo writer's colony; becomes involved in anti-Stalinist, Pro-Trotsky left, an involvement that lasts through the end of the decade; active in fight against censorship; *1936* marriage to Dorothy breaks up; *1937* wins censorship case over *Studs Lonigan; 1941* marries Hortense Alden; *1955* divorces Hortense, remarries Dorothy Farrell; *1957* travels in Israel; *1958* separates from Dorothy; *1979* dies 22 August.

Author's Bibliography

Young Lonigan, 1932 (novel); *Gas-House McGinty,* 1933 (novel); *The Young Manhood of Studs Lonigan,* 1934 (novel); *Judgment Day,* 1935 (novel); *A World I Never Made,* 1936 (novel); *A Note on Literary Criticism,* 1936; *The Short Stories of James T. Farrell,* 1937; *No Star Is Lost,* 1938 (novel); *Father and Son,* 1940 (novel); *Ellen Rogers,* 1941 (novel); *My Days of Anger,* 1943 (novel); *The League of Frightened Philistines,* 1945 (criticism); *Bernard Clare,* 1946 (novel); *Literature and Morality,* 1947 (criticism); *The Road Between,* 1949 (novel); *Yet Other Waters,* 1952 (novel); *Boarding House Blues,* 1961 (novel); *Judith and Other Stories,* 1973.

Overview of Biographical Sources

To date, there is no book-length biography of Farrell. His career was a long one, and he distrusted traditional literary classifications, especially traditional literary biography. In addition, while his somewhat substantial reputation is based almost solely on his writings from the 1930's and 1940's, most of his work since 1950 is at best very lightly regarded, so until recently there has been no great demand for a biography. However, Farrell's long and productive friendship with Edgar M. Branch led Farrell to name Branch his literary executor, and Branch is now writing a definitive biography. Until that work is finished, the primary sources for information about Farrell's life are two works by Branch and one by Alan Wald. Branch's *James T. Farrell* (1963) is a monograph-length biocritical essay that deals with the author's childhood and how it affected his writings. Branch also wrote *James T. Farrell* (1971), which is the standard American Authors series biocritical study of an author's life and works. The latter book contains a more complete summary of Farrell's life and a solid critical introduction to his writings. Finally, Alan Wald's *James T. Farrell: The Revolutionary Socialist Years* (1978) deals primarily with the most important period in Farrell's career, the thirties and forties, though Wald does deal convincingly with how Farrell's early involvement in the Trotskyist faction of the Left affects even his *Universe of Time* series, which began in 1963 with the publication of *The Silence of History*. None of these sources can be described as definitive, though all are certainly both accurate and readable. The Branch books are limited by their length, and Wald deals with only one aspect, albeit an important aspect, of Farrell's intellectual development. The forthcoming Branch biography should remedy the present lack of access to information about Farrell's life.

Evaluation of Selected Biographies

Branch, Edgar M. *James T. Farrell.* Minneapolis: University of Minnesota Press, 1963. The earliest biographical treatment of Farrell's life and work, this monograph is also the shortest (forty-eight pages) and most general of all. Branch briefly summarizes Farrell's life up to about 1955, focusing primarily on the childhood years. The rest of the monograph is more of an introduction to Farrell's writing, with occasional references to how he reworked his experience into his fiction. The study concludes with a very useful selected bibliography of Farrell's fiction and criticism, as well as critical works about Farrell. The information is accurate, and the orientation, while sympathetic, is fair. Branch addresses the major critical objections to Farrell's work and establishes an effective defense on the necessity to view Farrell's canon as a single opus, much like Proust's *Remembrance of Things Past,* which had a pronounced influence on Farrell during the late 1920's and early 1930's.

———. *James T. Farrell.* New York: Twayne, 1971. In many ways this book is an extension of the 1963 monograph described above. The Twayne study begins with a detailed look at Farrell's life, again focusing primarily on the years from birth to about 1940, but continuing in less detail through the 1950's and 1960's. The rest of the book is devoted to a biocritical essay of Farrell's work, but since Branch deals extensively with Farrell's author surrogates—Danny O'Neill, Bernard Carr, and, to a slightly lesser extent, Eddie Ryan—this portion of the study is also of biographical interest. Like the Minnesota pamphlet, this book presents an even-handed but more extensive introduction to Farrell's writing, recognizing the critical objections concerning Farrell's style and subject matter, but also establishing compelling reasons for considering Farrell's work more seriously than is generally the case.

Wald, Alan, *James T. Farrell: The Revolutionary Socialist Years.* New York: New York University Press, 1978. Wald examines Farrell's involvement in the Socialist and Trotskyist causes of the 1930's, commenting primarily on how this aspect of Farrell's life affected his critical and fictional writings. Wald effectively sets out Farrell's rather unconventional version of anti-Stalinism and the literary and political struggles those convictions caused Farrell. While the book deals principally with this most crucial time in Farrell's life, Wald also comments on how these views affected Farrell's later writings. The book is vital to an understanding of Farrell's most important works.

Autobiographical Sources

Farrell never finished an autobiography, though during the last fifteen years of his life he started several, each more detailed and longer than the last, in spiral-bound notebooks. These notebooks, together with practically every letter Farrell ever wrote and copies of most documents he was a party to, are housed in the Charles Patterson Van Pelt Library at the University of Pennsylvania. While these materials are neither fully indexed nor readily available to the public, they serve as the primary basis for the Branch biography in progress, so the general outlines of their contents will eventually be known.

Perhaps the most readily available autobiographical source is Farrell's fiction, for his writing, while less photographic in nature than his critics claim, certainly contains many incidents from his own life, more or less as they happened. Author surrogates Danny O'Neill's, Bernard Carr's, and Eddie Ryan's lives closely parallel Farrell's, especially in their younger days. Most of what happens to Danny actually did happen to Farrell, and the same is true, to slightly lesser degrees, for Carr and Ryan. While one must be cautious about reading an author into his fiction, these parallels do exist, and the reader looking for information about Farrell's life should not be as reluctant to make comparisons between life and art as one would be with Hemingway or others.

Other sources

Beach, Joseph Warren, *American Fiction, 1920–1940.* New York: Russell and Russell, 1941, pp. 273-283. Beach deals sympathetically with Farrell's sparse and ugly style, stating that Farrell cannot be judged by the same standards as a lyric novelist, since lyricism does not fit the city environment of Farrell's fiction.

Cox, Don Richard, "A World He Never Made: The Decline of James T. Farrell," *College Language Association Journal,* 23 (1979) 32–48. Cox analyzes reasons for Farrell's decline in public acceptance after the Bernard Carr series.

Gelfant, Blanche, *The American City Novel.* Norman: University of Oklahoma Press, 1954. Gelfant identifies Farrell as a "city novelist" who shows the cumulative effects of environment on the individual.

Pizer, Donald, "James T. Farrell and the 1930's," in *Literature at the Barricades: The American Writer in the 1930's.* Tuscaloosa: University of Alabama Press, 1982. This essay places much of Farrell's most important writing in its social and political contexts.

Twentieth Century Literature, Farrell number, 22 (February 1976). A collection of critical essays about different aspects of Farrell's career.

Selected Dictionaries and Encyclopedias

Contemporary Authors, Gale Research, first revision, Vols. 5–8. Biographical summary and good basic critical assessment of Farrell's major works. Complete with selected bibliography.

Dictionary of Literary Biography, Gale Research, 1984, Vol. 9, Part I. Excellent, fairly extensive biographical note, complete with author's selected bibliography and selected bibliography of critical sources.

William Condon
Arkansas Tech University

WILLIAM FAULKNER
1897–1962

Author's Chronology

Born September 25, 1897 in New Albany, Mississippi, of an established Mississippi family; great-grandfather had been Confederate colonel, railroad founder, local public figure, and author; *1902* family moves to Oxford, Mississippi where Faulkner will spend most of the rest of his life; *1918* enlists in Canadian R.A.F., is still in training when war ends; *1926* publishes his first novel, *Soldier's Pay; 1929* marries Estelle Franklin; chronic financial troubles begin; publishes *Sartoris* and *The Sound and the Fury; 1931* first daughter, Alabama, is born and dies, putting further strain on already troubled marriage; *Sanctuary,* a popular success, is published; *1932* begins first of several stints in Hollywood as a scriptwriter; *1933* second daughter, Jill, is born; *1935* returns to Hollywood, begins lengthy affair with Meta Carpenter; *1948* elected to the American Academy of Arts and Letters; *1950* wins Nobel Prize; *1950–59* travels to New York and Europe more frequently; tours Japan, Iceland, and Greece for the U.S. State Department; *1957* becomes writer-in-residence at University of Virginia, splits time between Oxford and Charlottesville; *1962 The Reivers* is published in June; July 6 dies of coronary thrombosis at private sanitarium in Byhalia, Mississippi, where he was admitted after a fall from a horse.

Author's Bibliography (selected)

The Marble Faun, 1924 (poems); *Soldier's Pay,* 1926 (novel); *Sartoris* and *The Sound and the Fury,* 1929 (novels); *As I Lay Dying,* 1930 (novel); *Sanctuary,* 1931 (novel); *These 13,* 1931 (stories); *Light in August,* 1932 (novel); *Absalom, Absalom!,* 1936 (novel); *The Hamlet,* 1940 (novel); *Go Down, Moses,* 1942 (novel); *Collected Stories of William Faulkner,* 1950; *A Fable,* 1954 (novel); *The Town,* 1957 (novel); *The Mansion,* 1959 (novel); *The Reivers,* 1962 (novel); *Essays, Speeches and Public Letters,* 1966; *New Orleans Sketches,* 1968 (prose); *Selected Letters of William Faulkner,* 1977; *Uncollected Stories of William Faulkner,* 1979.

Overview of Biographical Sources

For the most part, William Faulkner was successful during his lifetime in achieving his stated goal of hiding his personal life from public view and presenting the novels as his public statement. Living for the most part out of the media centers, granting comparatively few interviews, and not being really well-known for his work until he received the Nobel Prize, Faulkner gave would-be biographers little to work with, and as a result, very little biographical material appeared during his lifetime or shortly after his death. Robert Coughlin's *The Private World of William Faulkner* (New York: Harper and

Brothers, 1954) was largely anecdotal, photographic, and reliant on the local color approach to his work. Malcolm Cowley provided some of the most valuable early information, both in *The Viking Portable Faulkner* (New York: Viking, 1946) and *The Faulkner-Cowley File: Letters and Memories, 1944–1962* (New York: Viking, 1966). His information suffers from a lack of distance and a necessary dependence on Faulkner's not always reliable information and deliberately misleading or arch pronouncements on his work and vision. The author's brother, John Faulkner, published a memoir, *My Brother Bill: An Affectionate Reminiscence* (New York: Trident Press, 1961), which provided a more personal view, but it was not until Joseph Blotner's monumental *Faulkner: A Biography* (1974) that Faulkner scholars and students acquired a really useful biography. Blotner provides a comprehensive study of the author's life, aided by the estate, which allowed him access to a great deal of material it has not yet permitted to be published. Since then, Faulkner biographies and memoirs have been a minor growth industry. Meta Carpenter Wilde, Malcolm Franklin, Ben Wasson, among others, have published their memories of the writer; there was a television study of his life, published as *William Faulkner: A Life on Paper,* ed. Ann J. Abadie (Jackson: University Press of Mississippi, 1980); and there have been critical biographies, notably David Minter's *William Faulkner: His Life and Work* (1980) and Judith Bryant Wittenberg's *Faulkner: The Transfiguration of Biography* (1979). These two works take nearly opposite approaches: Minter's discussing the aspects of the life in terms of its impact on the fiction, while Wittenberg's examines the transformations the life undergoes to find its way into the fiction.

The materials covered in the following memoirs are handled, usually with greater objectivity by Blotner, and the books hold comparatively little scholarly value for the student of the novels. For those interested in Faulkner's life, the voices and perspectives are important in and of themselves.

Cullen, John B. with Floyd C. Watkins. *Old Times in the Faulkner Country.* Chapel Hill: University of North Carolina Press, 1961.

Faulkner, John, *My Brother Bill: An Affectionate Reminiscence.* New York: Trident Press, 1963.

Franklin, Malcolm, *Bitterweeds: Life with William Faulkner at Rowan Oak.* Irving, TX: The Society for the Study of Traditional Culture, 1977.

Wasson, Ben, *Count No 'Count: Flashbacks to Faulkner.* Jackson: University Press of Mississippi, 1983.

Wilde, Meta Carpenter, and Orin Borsten, *A Loving Gentleman: The Love Story of William Faulkner and Meta Carpenter.* New York: Simon and Schuster, 1976.

Evaluation of Selected Biographies

Blotner, Joseph, *Faulkner: A Biography.* 2 vols. New York: Random House, 1974. The definitive biography, this study examines Faulkner's life and background in great depth, making use of all available materials. It may be too comprehensive, in fact, for the casual reader. The One-Volume Edition (Random House, 1984) attempts to address that problem, although what it gains in brevity it loses in pace, sometimes feeling rushed. It also updates the earlier work, making use of new or recently discovered material. These works constitute the greatest single resource for the student of Faulkner.

Blotner, Joseph, ed. *Selected Letters of William Faulkner.* New York: Random House, 1977. A valuable addition to the scholar's arsenal, these letters make interesting reading in their own right.

Minter, David, *William Faulkner: His Life and Work.* Baltimore: Johns Hopkins University Press, 1980. A critical biography, this study has the advantage over Blotner of focusing on those elements that impinge on the novels and stories, and it is more concise. Minter shows how Faulkner uses, disguises, and distorts personal elements in his fiction. It is sometimes glib where it should be thorough, sliding over personal crises (such as the author's youngest brother's death) which do not appear in the fiction but which nevertheless bear heavily on Faulkner's work and outlook.

Wittenberg, Judith Bryant, *Faulkner: The Transfiguration of Biography.* Lincoln: University of Nebraska, 1979. Wittenberg argues that the novels are projections and transformations of Faulkner's own life and personality. She supports her claims with detailed discussions of biographical elements and novels, as for instance, the various changes Gavin Stevens undergoes as Faulkner moves through stages of middle age.

Overview of Critical Sources

While Faulkner's work has never attracted a wide reading public outside the academy, he has been the darling of critics for three decades, and that trend is accelerating. Each year finds more and more new studies, most of them lamentably poor. In the early days, the difficulty and breadth of Faulkner's fiction invited pedestrian treatments; more recently, that same complexity and richness has invited wildly inventive analyses based on each new critical movement as it comes along. Perhaps they add to the body of critical theory, but many of them add little to the general understanding of Faulkner's fiction. A few of them, however, have employed the newer critical methods with reason and sensitivity to produce startling and enlightening insights into the workings of the novels. Certainly the increased availability of biographical materials has allowed critics to speak with greater authority in recent years.

Evaluation of Selected Criticism

Brooks, Cleanth, *William Faulkner: The Yoknapatawpha Country.* New Haven: Yale University Press, 1963. *William Faulkner: Toward Yoknapatawpha and Beyond.* New Haven: Yale University Press, 1978. These two books combine to form an interpretation of the entire Faulkner canon. Brooks discusses the novels thematically in the earlier volume, chronologically in the second. The close readings of the novels focus on the distinctly Southern qualities: social castes, history of loss, provinciality, and in the later book, how those regional qualities inform the larger human picture in the non-Yoknapatawpha works.

Davis, Thadious M. *Faulkner's "Negro": Art and the Southern Context.* Baton Rouge: Louisiana State University Press, 1983. Focusing on the novels from 1926-1936 and on *Go Down, Moses,* Davis discusses Faulkner's use of the "Negro" as an aesthetic and thematic construct with which characters—and the novels—must come to terms if they are to resolve their conflicting and fragmented natures. Although it puts too much emphasis on the black presence—the divided self is hardly limited to Southern writers in the modern age—the study provides an enlightening analysis of black characters and white attitudes toward blacks in the novels.

Irwin, John T. *Doubling and Incest/Revenge and Repetition: A Speculative Reading of Faulkner.* Baltimore: Johns Hopkins University Press, 1975. One of the most illuminating discussions of the psychology of Faulkner's fiction, this study attempts to unravel the historical and psychological intricacies of the major novels, especially *The Sound and the Fury* and *Absalom, Absalom!,* through methods derived from Freud, Nietzsche, and structuralism. Irwin identifies phenomena of spatial doubling between characters and temporal doubling of individual characters, repetitions that lead to vengeance that turns inward, resulting in self-destruction.

Kinney, Arthur F. *Faulkner's Narrative Poetics: Style as Vision.* Amherst: University of Massachusetts, 1978. Kinney argues that Faulkner's work places him in the traditions both of novels of consciousness and of modernism, that he carves out his own special niche, that his narrative poetics are an integral part of his vision, and that they require the reader's "constitutive consciousness" to finally assemble, interpret, judge, understand.

Malin, Irving, *William Faulkner: An Interpretation.* Stanford: Stanford University Press, 1957. Malin presents a thematic overview focusing on psychological elements, particularly father-son tensions and "rigidity" or inflexibility. He discusses Freudian, Jungian, and Biblical elements in the fiction and includes an analysis of *Light in August.*

Millgate, Michael, *The Achievement of William Faulkner.* London: Constable, 1966. A comprehensive critical study, including lengthy biography and examination of all the novels, with a chapter on the short stories, this is one of the first important works to rescue Faulkner from provincialism and place his fiction in the wider European tradition where it belongs. With its humanism, its tragicomic vision, its concern with morality rather than intellect, and its sustained volume and quality, his canon places him with the greatest of novelists. Millgate ranks him with Dickens.

Volpe, Edmond L. *A Reader's Guide to William Faulkner.* New York: Farrar, Straus and Giroux, 1964. As the title suggests, this is not so much criticism as a guided tour through the novels. The discussions are generally accurate and intelligent, often unraveling the tangled threads of narrative. Volpe also provides chronologies of several of the more difficult novels and, perhaps most importantly, genealogical tables for some of the most important—and most bewildering—families of Yoknapatawpha, and for the Faulkners themselves.

Other Sources

McHaney, Thomas L. *William Faulkner: A Reference Guide.* Boston: G. K. Hall, 1976. Bibliographic work providing listings and annotations for writings on Faulkner through 1973.

Bassett, John Earl, *Faulkner: An Annotated Checklist of Recent Criticism.* Kent, OH: Kent State University, 1983. Covers writings from 1971-1981.

Selected Dictionaries and Encyclopedias

Critical Survey of Long Fiction, Salem Press, 1983. Brief biography, and short analysis of some of Faulkner's major works, especially *The Sound and the Fury, Absalom, Absalom!, Light in August,* and *Go Down, Moses.*

Dictionary of Literary Biography, Gale Research, 1981. Concise overview of Faulkner's life, and a discussion of the important works.

Thomas C. Foster
Michigan State University

LAWRENCE FERLINGHETTI
1919

Author's Chronology

Born Lawrence Ferling on March 24, 1919 in Yonkers, New York, the son of Charles S. Ferling and Clemence Mendes-Monsanto; father dies several months before his birth and mother is committed to a mental institution shortly after his birth; *1920* taken to France by his great-aunt Emily; *1925* taken by his great-aunt to live with the wealthy Bisland family in Bronxville, New York: *1927* attends a boarding school near Bronxville where he begins to write poetry; *1929–1933* attends both private and public schools; *1937–1941* attends and graduates from the University of North Carolina with an A.B. in journalism: *1941–1945* serves in U.S. Navy where he reaches the rank of lieutenant-commander; *1948* receives M.A. from Columbia University; *1951* marries Selden Kirby-Smith and receives a doctorate from the Sorbonne in Paris; *1951–1953* teaches French in San Francisco's adult education program; *1953* opens City Lights Bookstore with Peter D. Martin in San Francisco—the first all-paperback bookstore in America; *1955* publishes his first book of poetry. *Pictures of the Gone World,* as part of the "Pocket Poet Series"; *1956* arrested for publishing and selling Allen Ginsberg's *Howl,* a work that was seized by authorities until the courts finally ruled that it was not obscene; *1958* publishes his best-known work of poetry, *A Coney Island of the Mind; 1960* travels to Cuba to report on Castro's revolution; *1962* daughter Julie is born; *1963* son Lorenzo is born; *1967* arrested for demonstration against draft at Oakland Army induction center and serves nineteen days in Santa Rita prison; *1976* divorces Kirby-Smith and children come to live with him; *1979* daughter lives with Ferlinghetti in San Francisco and son lives with mother; *1981 Endless Life: Selected Poems* published by New Directions.

Author's Bibliography (selected)

Pictures of the Gone World, 1955 (poems); *A Coney Island of the Mind,* 1958 (poems); *A Tentative Description of a Dinner Given to Promote the Impeachment of President Eisenhower,* 1958 (broadside); *Her,* 1960 (novel); *Starting from San Francisco,* 1962 (poems); *Unfair Arguments with Existence,* 1963 (plays); *Routines,* 1964 (plays); *An Eye on the World; Selected Poems,* 1967; *The Mexican Night,* 1970 (journal); *Open Eye, Open Heart,* 1973 (poems); *Landscape of the Living and Dying,* 1979 (poems); *Endless Life: Selected Poems,* 1981.

Overview of Biographical Sources

Overzealous contemporary critics sometimes refer to Lawrence Ferlinghetti as the "founder" of the Beat Generation. Although such labels almost invariably lead to oversimplification, it is not difficult to find some justification for such a generalization. The City Lights Bookstore has served as a kind of West Coast literary MECCA. Ferlinghetti bought it in 1953 and his celebrated Pocket Poet Series has published such notables of the Beat Movement as Frank O'Hara, Gary Snyder, Robert Duncan, Allen Ginsberg, Philip Lanatia, Gregory Corso and Jack Kerouac. Furthermore, the artistic output of Ferlinghetti himself, encompassing the genres of poetry, drama, film, painting and the novel, serves as a kind of paradigm of the San Francisco Renaissance.

Despite Ferlinghetti's significant influence, only two book-length biographies have been written about him: Neeli Chervovski's *Ferlinghetti: a Biography* (1979) and Larry Smith's *Lawrence Ferlinghetti: Poet-at-Large* (1983). Biographical material also appears in Ann Charter's *Kerouac: A Biography* (San Francisco: Straight Arrow Books, 1973) where she presents interesting information on the San Francisco Beat scene and the relationship between Jack Kerouac and Lawrence Ferlinghetti. Biographical and critical analysis of Ferlinghetti and his work also appears in Richard Ellman and Robert O'Claire's piece in *The Norton Anthology of Modern Poetry* (New York: W.W. Norton, 1973) as well as in David Meltzer's *The San Francisco Poets* (New York: Ballantine Books, 1971), Thomas McClanahan's essay in *Dictionary of Literary Biography* (Detroit: Gale Research, 1980) and the introduction to Bill Morgan's impressively complete *Lawrence Ferlinghetti: A Comprehensive Bibliography* (New York and London: Garland Publishing, 1982).

Evaluation of Selected Biographies

Cherkovski, Neeli, *Ferlinghetti: A Biography.* New York: Doubleday, 1979. This is a very detailed and accurate account of Ferlinghetti's life based heavily on taped interviews with the poet himself. Besides spending many hours with Ferlinghetti at City Lights Bookstore, Cherkovsky was granted access to the poet's unpublished journals, letters and many rare photographs, several of which appear in the biography. Although it does not provide much analysis of the poetry as Smith's work would do, Cherkovski's work does include several of Ferlinghetti's poems as well as ample discussion of the relationship between Ferlinghetti and other significant figures in the literary world such as Jack Kerouac, Gary Synder, Michael McClure, Robert Bly, Gregory Corso, Kenneth Patchen, Kenneth Rexroth and numerous others. Cherkovski provides a good deal of raw material for future biographical and critical studies.

Smith, Larry, *Lawrence Ferlinghetti: Poet-at-Large.* Carbondale and Edwardsville: Southern Illinois University Press, 1983. Smith's critical biography is extremely helpful to anyone seeking a thorough evaluation of Ferlinghetti as a man and a writer. Beginning with a very useful "Chronology" of major events and works of the poet's life, as well as key publications of City Lights Press, Smith does a very impressive job of relating major events in the poet's life to significant passages in the poetry. The title of Smith's second chapter, "Stance Toward Life and Art," points toward Smith's own assumption that "working out the dynamics of Lawrence Ferlinghetti's poetics is essential to developing an appreciation of his achievement as a writer." (p. 53) In attempting to chronicle this achievement in his biography, Smith devotes separate chapters to critical consideration of Ferlinghetti's prose, poetry and plays. Ferlinghetti scholars and enthusiasts will be pleased to find that Smith provides a well-annotated section of secondary sources on Ferlinghetti.

Autobiographical Sources

The only overtly autobiographical writing that Ferlinghetti has produced is the seven-page poem entitled "Autobiography" from his 1958 book, *A Coney Island of the Mind.* Aside from presenting an occasionally accurate comment on his life, such as references to his unhappy childhood, the poem is essentially the poet's effort to place himself within the context of American mythology, much in the way that Walt Whitman does in this "Song of Myself." In fact, Ferlinghetti even alludes directly to Whitman when he writes that "I hear America singing" and when he asserts that "I am the man/I was there/ I suffered." In his "Autobiography," Ferlinghetti emerges less as a real person than an artifact of popular culture who reads *American Boy* magazine, joins the Boy Scouts, owns a baseball mit, delivers newspapers and sees himself as Tom Sawyer. Such details come closer to myth-making than they do to accurate autobiographical commentary.

Overview of Critical Sources

Although Ferlinghetti's writing has brought him a great deal of popular success, the critical reception to his works has usually been lukewarm to negative, often dismissing his poetry as simplistic, sentimental or sensationalist. His one novel, *Her* (1960), a surrealistic and highly experimental work, has been generally well-received as an important prose work. Although no major critical analysis of Ferlinghetti's work yet exists—with the exception of several dissertations and Larry Smith's critical biography—there are several works that critically discuss Ferlinghetti as a significant representative of the Beat Movement.

Evaluation of Selected Criticism

Charters, Samuel, *Some Poems/Poets: Studies in American Underground Poetry since 1945.* Berkeley, CA: Oyez, 1971. Charters, in his introduction to and analysis of Ferlinghetti, evaluates Ferlinghetti's oral methods as important to an understanding of comtemporary poetry. This analysis points toward a major contribution to American poetry in 1959 when Kenneth Rexroth and Lawrence Ferlinghetti presented their jazz and poetry readings at the Cellar café in North Beach, California. The readings and the recordings that came out of them helped make poetry more accessible to the public and introduced Americans to the language and rhythms of the Beat Generation.

Dugan, Alan, "Three Books, A Pamphlet, and a Broadside," in *Poetry 100* (August 1962). Dugan, like Charters, gives insight into the oral form of Ferlinghetti's poetry. In reviewing *Starting from San Francisco,* Dugan demonstrates a great deal of insight into the poetry as well as to Ferlinghetti's reading method.

Everson, William. *Archetype West: The Pacific Coast as a Literary Region.* Berkeley, CA: Oyez, 1976. Particularly in the fifteenth chapter of this provocative book, Everson combines a literary history of the West with an astute appraisal of Ferlinghetti's role in the cultural developments of the region.

Parkinson, Thomas F. ed. *A Casebook on the Beat.* New York: Thomas Y. Crowell, 1961. In Parkinson's essay, "Phenomenon or Generation," Ferlinghetti's poems and essays are analyzed, from an early perspective, within the context of the Beat movement.

Rexroth, Kenneth, *American Poetry in the Twentieth Century.* New York: Herder and Herder, 1971. In his effort to cover the entire scope of American Contemporary poetry, Rexroth discusses Ferlinghetti in the context of the San Francisco Renaissance as both a poet and a publisher.

Other Sources

Dana, Robert, "An Interview with Lawrence Ferlinghetti," *Midwest Quarterly* #4 (1983), pp. 412–440. Provides a vivid picture of the man as poet and publisher.

Kherdian, David, *Six Poets of the San Francisco Renaissance.* Fresno, CA: Giligia Press, 1967, pp. 2–44. An often impressionistic depiction of the personal and artisitic life of Ferlinghetti.

Wakeman, John, ed. *World Authors: 1950–1970.* New York: H. W. Wilson, 1975, pp. 465–466. Offers a brief biographical overview with some critical comments on his novel, *Her,* and some mention of the literary activities around the City Lights Bookstore.

Selected Dictionaries and Encyclopedias

Dictionary of Literary Biography, Gale Research, 1983, pp. 199–214. This critical and biographical sketch by Ferlinghetti biographer, Larry Smith, is rather slim on biographical details but provides a useful list of Ferlinghetti's works and a brief analysis of his place in comtemporary poetry.

Donald E. Winters
Minneapolis Community College

HENRY FIELDING
1707-1754

Author's Chronology

Born April 22, 1707, at Sharpham Park, Somersetshire England; as boy lives on father's farm in East Stour, later with grandmother in Salisbury; *1719-1724* attends Eton, embroiled in custody battle between father and grandmother; *1724* leaves Eton for life of young man about town; *1725* visits Lyme Regis; proposes unsuccessfully to fifteen-year-old heiress; *1727* established in London by end of year; *1728* his first play produced in London; embarks for Holland to study letters at University of Leyden; *1729* returns to London; *1730-1737* works in London as dramatist producing numerous farces and plays, including an adaptation of Moliere's *The Miser* (1732-33) and *Pasquin* (1736); *1734* marries Charlotte Cradock; *1737* popularity of his political satire provokes passage of Licensing Act in June, effectively ending his dramatic career; in November enters Middle Temple to study law; *1739* contributes to political newspaper, *The Champion; 1740* admitted to the bar; *1741* parodies Richardson's *Pamela* with *Shamela; 1742* publishes first novel, *Joseph Andrews; 1744* first wife dies; *1745-47* edits political newspapers, remarries; *1748* named Justice of the Peace for Westminster; *1749* named Justice for Middlesex; *1751* edits *Covent Garden Journal; 1754* sails to Lisbon, Portugal for health, dies and is buried there.

Author's Bibliography (selected)

Love in Several Masques, 1728 (play); *The Author's Farce, and the Pleasures of the Town,* 1730 (play); *The Mock Doctor; or, the Dumb Lady cur'd,* 1732 (play); *Don Quixote in England. A Comedy,* 1734 (play); *Shamela,* 1741 (prose parody); *Joseph Andrews,* 1742 (novel); *Miscellanies,* 1743 (politics, journalism, some autobiography, includes *Jonathon Wild*); *Tom Jones,* 1749 (novel); *Amelia,* 1751 (novel); *A Journal of the Voyage to Lisbon,* 1755 (autobiography).

Overview of Biographical Sources

Fielding's first biographer, Arthur Murphy, wrote his "Essay on the Life and Genius of Henry Fielding, Esq." for a 1762 edition of the works. His essay emphasizes the life of dissipation Fielding purportedly led in youth, and subsequent biographers repeated Murphy's assessment. Recent scholars, however, have discounted as exaggerated Fielding's early immorality and dissolution. During the two centuries since his death, there have been numerous biographies of varying length—some appended to the several nineteenth-century editions of his work. A succession of nineteenth-century and early twentieth-century literary figures—including Sir Walter Scott, William Makepeace Thackeray, Austin Dobson, Sir Leslie Stephen, Edmund Gosse, and W. E. Henley—have commented on Fielding's life and work. Two twentieth century biographies stand as definitive works. Wilbur Lucas Cross's three volume *The*

History of Henry Fielding (1918, rpt. 1963) is yet regarded as the standard biography. F. H. Dudden's two volume *Henry Fielding: His Life, Works, and Times* (1952), though more recent, does not employ all the research and scholarship available since Cross's study was first published. Both Cross and Dudden offer comprehensive bibliographies of the many works—essays, dramas, novels, articles and journals—which Fielding wrote, and Dudden includes a selected bibliography of criticism to 1952. A recent short biography is Pat Roger's *Henry Fielding: A Biography.* (1979).

Evaluation of Selected Biographies

Banerji, H. K. *Henry Fielding, Playwright, Journalist and Master of the Art of Fiction: His Life and Works.* Oxford: Blackwell, 1929; rpt. New York: Russell and Russell, 1962. In his widely circulated biography, Banerji assesses Fielding's major works in terms of influences of other writers, which he sees as few in number, and reconfirms some of the standard generalizations about Fielding. Its length makes it accessible, but does not compensate for its lack of depth.

Cross, Wilbur L. *The History of Henry Fielding.* 3 vols. New Haven: Yale University Press, 1918; rpt. New York: Russell and Russell, 1963. In this comprehensive consideration of Fielding's life, times and work, Cross discusses not only the major novels but also the dramas and journalistic writings. He comments on the audience, the management, the actors and the productions of Fielding's dramatic works. He includes at least two chapters on each of the major prose works. Since much of Fielding's satire is topical, he relates the themes of the plays and the novels to the social and political events of the time. He is especially helpful in following Fielding's political attitudes as expressed in the papers he wrote for or edited.

Dudden, F. H. *Henry Fielding: His Life, Works, and Times.* 2 vols. Oxford: Clarendon Press, 1952. Dudden parallels Cross in most instances, but fails to take advantage of biographical research which transpired after Cross was published. It does have two advantages over Cross: Dudden offers an especially cogent commentary on Fielding's religious views and he subdivides his chapter sections into numbered and lettered headings which are helpful to a reader scanning the work for specific topics.

Rogers, Pat, *Henry Fielding: A Biography.* New York: Charles Scribner's Sons, 1979. This work is regarded as an important supplement to Cross because it incorporates the relevant biographical information recovered in this century, it presents objectively the environment in which Fielding lived, and it provides sufficient detail to cover the life without becoming pedantic or unreadable.

Autobiographical Sources

Though he did not write an autobiography as such, the breadth and scope of Fielding's writing serve as an informal, running autobiographical commentary.

One piece of some autobiographical interest is his "Preface" to the *Miscellanies.* Unfortunately, most of his letters were destroyed either by family members, by fire, or in the political disturbances of 1780. The precise nature of their destruction remains a mystery, but a valuable source for autobiographical information about most authors is not available for Fielding. The *Journal of the Voyage to Lisbon* gives a detailed commentary on Fielding's final trip and reveals his interest in the personalities of the crew, his fellow passengers, and the ports of call the ship visited.

Overview of Critical Sources

Given his significance in the history of the English novel and the quantity of dramatic and non-fictional works he produced, Fielding has been subjected to critical scrutiny throughout the twentieth century. Most of the numerous book-length critical studies focus on the longer prose pieces with *Joseph Andrews* and *Tom Jones* receiving the bulk of the attention. Opinion is still divided on Fielding's dramatic works, and these along with the essays, journals, and articles are usually studied as means of elucidating the philosophy or cultural milieu of the novels. Important recurrent themes in these works include Fielding's narrative methods, his philosophical and religious thought, his use of satire and irony, and his mastery of language.

Evaluation of Selected Criticism

Battestin, Martin C. *The Moral Basis of Fielding's Art: A Study of Joseph Andrews.* Middleton, CT: Wesleyan University Press, 1959. This work examines Fielding's ethical and religious beliefs as expressed in the novel. Neither another parody of *Pamela* nor a stoic or deistic study of man, *Joseph Andrews* structurally and thematically explores the good man's confrontation with vanity and hypocrisy.

Ehrenpreis, Irwin, *Fielding: Tom Jones. Studies in English Literature.* No. 23. London: Edward Arnold, 1964. This rhetorical study examines Fielding as intrusive author, compares him with contemporaries such as Sterne, and summarizes recent criticism.

Hatfield, Glenn W. *Henry Fielding and the Language of Irony.* Chicago: University of Chicago Press, 1968. Using the novels, dramas and non-ironic essays, Hatfield demonstrates Fielding's sensitivity to language and his concern with the prostitution of language. Hatfield devotes one chapter to Fielding's attack on those who corrupt language: critics, hacks, politicians, professionals. In others, he discusses Fielding's exploration of abstractions such as love, honor and faithfulness.

Hunter, J. Paul, *Occasional Form: Henry Fielding and the Chains of Circumstance.* Baltimore: Johns Hopkins University Press, 1975. Hunter examines the extent to which Fielding is caught between the past and the present, the medieval and the modern world. Through looking at the form of the dramas, he comments on Fielding's view of the relationship between perception and interpretation, and he studies the novels in terms of the kinds of journeys they employ as indications of the growth of the characters.

McCrea, Brian, *Henry Fielding and the Politics of Mid-Eighteenth-Century England.* Athens: University of Georgia Press, 1981. McCrea's study focuses on an important and complicated aspect of Fielding's work. McCrea discusses the political background of the times, the political connections of Fielding's family, and follows the twists of Fielding's own political associations. A specialized and scholarly study, it contains a bibliography limited to Fielding's place in eighteenth-century political life.

Paulson, Ronald and Thomas Lockwood, eds. *Henry Fielding: The Critical Heritage.* New York: Barnes and Noble, 1969. An anthology of criticism of Fielding offered by his eighteenth-century friends, enemies and colleagues. Included in the one hundred eighty selections—subdivided by theme and genre—are letters, journal articles, and excerpts from books. Contains several interesting passages from the Murphy biographical essay.

Paulson, Ronald, ed. *Fielding: A Collection of Critical Essays.* Englewood Cliffs, NJ: Prentice-Hall, 1962. This collection of contemporary academic criticism offers a compendium of comments by leading Fielding scholars. An introductory essay gives an overview of the approaches of the critics represented, and at the end of the selections is found a useful chronology and selected bibliography.

Paulson, Ronald, *Popular and Polite Art in the Age of Hogarth and Fielding.* Notre Dame, IN: University of Notre Dame Press, 1979. Focussing on Fielding and his friend the graphic artist William Hogarth, Paulson shows Fielding's use of and reaction to both popular and polite art of the eighteenth century. In the first section, "Subculture Types," he examines such staples of Fielding's time as the criminal, the crowd and the English dog; in the second section, "Polite Metaphors, Models, and Paradigms," he surveys entertainment, the family and politics.

Rawson, C. J. *Henry Fielding.* The Profiles in Literature Series. London: Routledge and Kegan Paul, 1968. This anthology offers selected passages from various prose works, especially the major novels, with a running explication by the editor—a good introduction to Fielding.

Other Sources

Hahn, H. George, *Henry Fielding: An Annotated Bibliography.* Metuchen, NJ: Scarecrow Press, 1979. Hahn provides a roadmap to the constantly expanding world of Fielding criticism. This work, which covers books, articles and essays published between 1900 and 1979, is divided into sections which include Fielding's biography, general criticism, his plays, his major prose works, and his journalism and miscellaneous pieces. It offers clear judgments of the value of the more significant items.

Morrissey, L. J. *Henry Fielding: A Reference Guide.* Boston: G. K. Hall, 1980. Morrissey's guide overlaps with Hahn to an extent, but they differ in three important ways. First, Morrissey covers from 1755 to 1979; he lists the works chronologically rather than by genre, dividing each year into book-length and shorter pieces. Lastly, though he devotes as much as a page or more to major works, his commentaries are descriptive rather than judgmental.

Stoler, John A. and Richard S. Fulton, *Fielding Criticism: An Annotated Bibliography of Twentieth Century Criticism, 1900–1977.* New York: Garland, 1980.

Selected Dictionaries and Encyclopedias

British Writers, Charles Scribner's Sons, 1983, Vol. III, 94–106. Survey of the life with a brief commentary on the major works.

Chambers Biographical Dictionary, St. Martin's Press, 1962, pp. 469–470. Brief biography with short bibliography.

The Dictionary of National Biography, Oxford University Press, 1917, Vol. VI, 1280–1288. A sympathetic survey of Fielding's life which concludes with a list of the plays and a brief bibliography of biographical sources through Dobson in 1907.

Moulton's Library of Literary Criticism, Moulton, 1902; rpt. Peter Smith, 1959. Includes a chronology and critical excerpts on each genre of Fielding's work and on each of his major works.

Richard H. Beckham
University of Wisconsin-River Falls

F. SCOTT FITZGERALD
1896–1940

Author's Chronology

Born September 24, 1896, St. Paul, Minnesota of Irish Catholic parents; *1898–1903* moves to Buffalo and Syracuse; back to St. Paul after father loses job; *1911–1913* attends Newman School, New Jersey; *1915–1917* in and out of Princeton; *1917* enlists in Army, commissioned 2nd Lieutenant; *1918* meets Zelda Sayre; *1919* discharged from Army; writes advertising copy; *This Side of Paradise* accepted by Scribner's; *1920* marries Zelda; *1921–1925* writes stories, publishes second novel, daughter born, lives abroad; *1925 Great Gatsby* published; meets Hemingway; *1925–1930* lives abroad, works in Hollywood; *1930* Zelda has first breakdown; *1931–1934* works again in Hollywood, father dies, Zelda "cracks up" again; *1934–1937* works in Hollywood; *Tender Is the Night* (1934) published; Zelda placed more or less permanently in sanitarium; *1937–1940* works on screenplays, meets Sheilah Graham, writes *Last Tycoon;* 1940 dies in Hollywood December 21.

Author's Bibliography (selected)

Fie! Fie! Fi-Fi!, 1914 (song lyrics); *The Evil Eye,* 1915 (song lyrics); *Safety First,* 1916 (song lyrics); *This Side of Paradise,* 1920 (novel); *Flappers and Philosophers,* 1920 (stories); *The Beautiful and Damned,* 1922 (novel); *Tales of the Jazz Age,* 1922 (stories); *The Vegetable,* 1923 (play); *The Great Gatsby,* 1925 (novel); *All the Sad Young Men,* 1926 (stories); *Tender Is the Night,* 1934 (novel); *Taps at Reveille,* 1935 (stories); *The Last Tycoon,* 1941 (unfinished novel); *The Crack-Up,* 1945 (non-fiction); *The Stories of F. Scott Fitzgerald,* 1951; *Afternoon of an Author,* 1957 (non-fiction); *The Pat Hobby Stories,* 1962; *The Apprentice Fiction of F. Scott Fitzgerald,* 1965; *The Basil and Josephine Stories,* 1973; *F. Scott Fitzgerald's St. Paul Plays,* 1978; *The Price Was High,* 1979 (stories); *Poems 1911–1940,* 1981.

Overview of Biographical Sources

Beginning with Arthur Mizener's distinguished biography, *The Far Side of Paradise,* which first appeared in 1951, there has been a steady stream of biographies, reminiscences, and autobiographies which have contributed to the view of Fitzgerald and his times. Scott Berg's *Max Perkins: Editor of Genius* (New York: Congdon/Dutton, 1978) traced Fitzgerald's relationship with his editor at Charles Scribner's Sons, and Aaron Latham's *Crazy Sundays: F. Scott Fitzgerald in Hollywood* (New York: Viking Press, 1971) examined Fitzgerald's life in the film world including a look at his screen work. Among the reminiscences are those by Sheilah Graham with whom Fitzgerald spent his last years in Hollywood while Zelda was in the hospital and in whose apartment he died.

Beloved Infidel: The Education of a Woman (New York: Holt, Rinehart & Winston, 1958) was the most infamous and aroused the greatest controversy especially since Miss Graham seemed to be exploiting the growing interest in her one-time mentor/lover. *College of One* (New York: Viking, 1967) explained the education Fitzgerald set out for Miss Graham in a series of reading lists which she apparently worked through and *The Real F. Scott Fitzgerald Thirty-Five Years Later* (New York: Grosset & Dunlap, 1976) rehashed old ground in an attempt to once again lay claim to Sheilah Graham's place in the life of a great writer. Of the other remembrances among the best are Morley Callaghan's *That Summer in Paris: Memories of Tangled Friendships with Hemingway, Fitzgerald and Some Others* (New York: Coward-McCann, 1963) which provides a fascinating portrait of life in Paris following the war and makes good use of Callahan's observant presence; John Dos Passos offers another glimpse of the same period in his *The Fourteenth Chronicle: Letters and Diaries of John Dos Passos* (Boston: Gambit, 1973); finally Ernest Hemingway's *A Movable Feast* (New York: Charles Scribner's Sons, 1964) and *Ernest Hemingway: Selected Letters, 1917–1961,* edited by Carlos Baker (New York: Charles Scribner's Sons, 1981) reveal still another portrait of Fitzgerald, this time through the eyes of a successful yet envious colleague. Fitzgerald's relationship with Hemingway has been set down by Matthew J. Bruccoli in *Scott and Ernest: The Authority of Failure and the Authority of Success* (New York: Random House, 1978) and Fitzgerald's friendship with Sara and Gerald Murphy is chronicled in Calvin Tompkin's study *Living Well Is the Best Revenge* (New York: Viking, 1971). Also, there has been written a number of fascinating studies of the Scott/Zelda relationship. The first of these and the one which opened up the controversies that have fermented ever since is Nancy Milford's *Zelda* (New York: Harper and Row, 1971) in which she exploded the myth that Zelda was responsible for dragging Scott into drinking and for destroying his career. Milford revealed Fitzgerald's use of Zelda's writing and his exploitation of her creativity. James R. Mellow in *Invented Lives: F. Scott and Zelda Fitzgerald* (Boston: Houghton Mifflin, 1984) and Sara Mayfield in *Exiles from Paradise: Zelda and Scott Fitzgerald* (New York: Delacorte Press, 1971) both examined the relationship of the two Fitzgeralds as interdependent, destructive and exhilerating at the same time. One other addition to the collective information on the couple was edited by their daughter in collaboration with Matthew Bruccoli and Jean P. Kerr, *The Romantic Egotists: A Pictorial Biography from the Scrapbooks and Albums of F. Scott and Zelda Fitzgerald* (New York: Charles Scribner's Sons, 1974) which contains a grab-bag of materials collected by the Fitzgeralds during their careers. Two other pictorial works of a biographical nature round out the sources and include Arthur Mizener's *Scott Fitzgerald and His World* (London: Thames and Hudson, 1972) which contains a condensation of his earlier biography with pictures, and John J. Koblas, *F. Scott Fitzgerald in Minnesota: His Homes and Haunts* (St. Paul: Minnesota Historical Society, 1978), which is a fascinating little book and details the locations of Fitzgerald's places of residence in St. Paul and other locations in that city which figure in his life and work.

Evaluation of Selected Biographies

Bruccoli, Matthew Joseph, *Some Sort of Grandeur: The Life of F. Scott Fitzgerald.* With a Genealogical Afterword by Scottie Fitzgerald Smith. New York: Harcourt Brace Jovanovich, 1981. While believing that Fitzgerald's life was a quest for heroism and that the writer himself was heroic, Bruccoli does much in his biography to revise the popular mythology surrounding Fitzgerald's life and to correct the factual errors of Fitzgerald's previous biographers. This study is the most carefully researched of the many books on Fitzgerald's life.

Donaldson, Scott, *Fool for Love: F. Scott Fitzgerald.* New York: Congdon/St. Martin, 1983. Interesting examination of Fitzgerald's life and work through the women who influenced him. This new approach provides insight into Fitzgerald's life missed before.

Le Vot, André, *F. Scott Fitzgerald: A Biography.* Translated from the French by William Byron. Garden City, NY: Doubleday, 1983. Written in response to Fitzgerald's growing reputation in Europe, almost non-existent twenty years ago, Professor Le Vot has fashioned a biographical study which places Fitzgerald in the classic American mold of "paleface" writer, prey to sexual uneasiness and although centrally American in theme and style, perceived here as one writer taken over and used by the forces of American capitalism. A highly psychoanalytical study, it is nevertheless fascinating because of its European perspective.

Mizener, Arthur, *The Far Side of Paradise: A Biography of F. Scott Fitzgerald.* Boston: Houghton Mifflin, 1951. The first full-length study of Fitzgerald and the one in part responsible for the resurgence of interest in the writer. Much remains good about this biography, but it has been superseded by more recent efforts.

Turnbull, Andrew, *Scott Fitzgerald.* New York: Charles Scribner's Sons, 1962. This is a well-written study from an insider's point of view. Turnbull's family knew Fitzgerald and Turnbull himself remembers his subject well. This biography is neither as comprehensive as Bruccoli's nor as groundbreaking as Mizener's.

Autobiographical Sources

Fitzgerald left very little by way of manuscript materials for scholars to mine. Two collections of his non-fiction were published shortly after his death. Edmund Wilson edited *The Crack-Up* (New York: New Directions, 1945) in which he brought together previously uncollected pieces by Fitzgerald along with letters and excerpts from his notebooks. Arthur Mizener also edited a collection of materials *Afternoon of an Author* (Princeton: Princeton University Library, 1957; New York: Charles Scribner's Sons, 1958). Matthew Bruccoli and Jackson R. Bryer collected materials for *F. Scott Fitzgerald in His Own Time: A Miscellany* (Kent, OH: Kent State University Press, 1971) which assembles ephemera by Fitzgerald now hard to find. These three books publish, some for the first time, a fair amount of autobiographical information. Additionally Matthew J. Bruccoli has edited *The Notebooks of F. Scott Fitzgerald* (New York: Harcourt Brace Jovanovich/Bruccoli Clark, 1978) some of which was originally published in *The Crack-Up* but most of which appears here for the first time. Fitzgerald was a confessional writer and his notebooks contain a good deal of a highly personal nature and shed much light on his life as well as his working methods as a writer. See also *F. Scott Fitzgerald's Ledger: A Facsimile,* introduction by Matthew J. Bruccoli (Washington: NCR/Microcard Editions, 1972). Finally the richest source of autobiographical information is contained in Fitzgerald's letters of which there are now five collections. The first two appeared at the same time as Andrew Turnbull's biography. *The Letters of Scott Fitzgerald,* edited by Andrew Turnbull (New York: Charles Scribner's Sons, 1963) contains a selection of letters arranged by addressee and publishes correspondence to Maxwell Perkins, Zelda, Hemingway, Edmund Wilson, John Peal Bishop, Christian Gauss, Harold Ober and Sara and Gerald Murphy among others. The second selection, also edited by Turnbull, *Letters to His Daughter,* with an Introduction by Frances Fitzgerald Lanahan (New York: Charles Scribner's Sons, 1963) contain the author's letters to his daughter, most of them written in the late thirties when Scottie was attending school in the east while Fitzgerald was working in Hollywood. Two more specialized literary collections appeared some eight years later. *Dear Scott/Dear Max: The Fitzgerald-Perkins Correspondence,* edited by John Kuehl and Jackson R. Bryer (New York: Charles Scribner's Sons, 1971) collected the letters between Fitzgerald and his editor at Scribner's, Max Perkins. This correspondence traces the literary relationship between author and publisher from 1920 until Fitzgerald's death in 1940. *As Ever, Scott Fitz—: Letters Between F. Scott Fitzgerald and His Literary Agent Harold Ober, 1919–1940,* edited by Matthew J. Bruccoli (New York and Philadelphia: J. B. Lippincott, 1972) contains Fitzgerald's letters concerning the business side of his career, but as the letters attest, Harold Ober and his family were more than merely business associates of Fitzgerald's. Finally Matthew J. Bruccoli edited another volume of Fitzgerald's letters *Correspondence of F. Scott Fitzgerald,* edited by Matthew J. Bruccoli and Margaret M. Duggan (New York: Random House, 1980). This volume does not reprint letters contained in any of the earlier books and includes some letters to Fitzgerald which provide a semblance of the context of his correspondence as well as supplying biographical facts otherwise not available.

Overview of Critical Sources

Ever since Alfred Kazin first brought together a collection of contemporary assessments of Fitzgerald's work in 1951, there has been a constant flow of critical books on the author. Matthew J. Bruccoli's *F. Scott Fitzgerald: A Descriptive Bibliography* (Pittsburgh: University of Pittsburgh Press, 1972) and his *Supplement to F. Scott Fitzgerald: A Descriptive Bibliography* (Pittsburgh: University of Pittsburgh Press, 1980) contain the definitive bibliography of Fitzgerald's works. The most comprehensive listing of materials about Fitzgerald is to be found in Jackson R. Bryer's *The Critical Reputation of F. Scott Fitzgerald: A Bibliographical Study* (Hamden, CT: Archon Books, 1984). Alfred Kazin edited the first general collection of criticism about Fitzgerald in *F. Scott Fitzgerald: The Man and His Work* (Cleveland: World Publishing Company, 1951) and this was supplemented by Arthur Mizener's *F. Scott Fitzgerald: A Collection of Critical Essays* (Englewood Cliffs, NJ: Prentice-Hall, 1963).

There are available a number of short introductions to Fitzgerald's life and work, many of them part of various series on American writers: Charles E. Shain, *F. Scott Fitzgerald* (Minneapolis: University of Minnesota Press, 1961); K. G. W. Cross, *Scott Fitzgerald* (Edinburgh: Oliver and Boyd, 1970); Milton Hindus, *F. Scott Fitzgerald: An Introduction and Interpretation* (New York: Barnes and Noble, 1968); and Rose Adrienne Gallo, *F. Scott Fitzgerald* (New York: Frederick Ungar, 1978).

There are also a number of studies of Fitzgerald's individual novels with those devoted to *The Great Gatsby* the most numerous: Frederick J. Hoffman, ed. *The Great Gatsby: A Study* (New York: Charles Scribner's Sons, 1962); Ernest Lockridge, ed. *Twentieth Century Interpretations of The Great Gatsby: A Collection of Critical Essay* (Englewood Cliffs, NJ: Prentice-Hall, 1968); Matthew J. Bruccoli, *Apparatus for F. Scott Fitzgerald's The Great Gatsby* (Columbia: University of South Carolina Press, 1974); Andrew Crosland, *Concordance to The Great Gatsby* (Detroit: Gale Research, 1975); John S. Whitley, *F. Scott Fitzgerald: The Great Gatsby* (London: Edward Arnold, 1976); and Robert Emmet Long, *The Achieving of The Great Gatsby: F. Scott Fitzgerald, 1920–1925* (Lewisburg, PA: Bucknell University Press, 1979). In addition there are a number of other studies devoted to Fitzgerald's other novels: James L. W. West, *The Making of This Side of Paradise* (Philadelphia: University of Pennsylvania Press, 1983); Matthew J. Bruccoli, *The Composition of Tender Is the Night: A Study of the Manuscripts* (Pittsburgh: University of Pittsburgh Press, 1963); Marvin J. LaHood, ed., *Tender Is the Night: Essays in Criticism* (Bloomington: Indiana University Press, 1969); and Matthew J. Bruccoli, *"The Last of the Novelists": F. Scott Fitzgerald and The Last Tycoon* (Carbondale: Southern Illinois University Press, 1977).

Finally there are a number of studies of Fitzgerald's work in general: Joan M. Allen, *Candles and Carnival Lights: The Catholic Sensibility of F. Scott*

Fitzgerald (New York: New York University Press, 1978); John F. Callahan, *The Illusions of a Nation: Myth and History in the Novels of F. Scott Fitzgerald* (Urbana: University of Illinois Press, 1972); Richard Daniel Lehan, *F. Scott Fitzgerald and the Craft of Fiction* (Carbondale: Southern Illinois University Press, 1966); Sergio Perosa, *The Art of F. Scott Fitzgerald,* translated by Charles Matz and the author (Ann Arbor: University of Michigan Press, 1965); Linda Stanley, *The Foreign Critical Reputation of F. Scott Fitzgerald: An Analysis and Annotated Bibliography* (Westport, CT: Greewood Press, 1980); Thomas J. Stavola, *Scott Fitzgerald: Crisis in an American Identity* (London: Vision, 1979); and Milton R. Stern, *The Golden Moment: The Novels of F. Scott Fitzgerald* (Urbana: University of Illinois Press, 1970).

Other Sources

Eble, Kenneth, *F. Scott Fitzgerald.* Boston: G. K. Hall, 1963. The best of the short life-and-works books on Fitzgerald. Contains a nice overview of his work with a balanced assessment.

Miller, James E. *F. Scott Fitzgerald: His Art and His Technique.* New York: New York University Press, 1967. Still probably the best single work on Fitzgerald's art of fiction.

Piper, Henry Dan, *F. Scott Fitzgerald: A Critical Portrait.* New York: Holt, Rinehart and Winston, 1965. Contains the best balance between biographical and critical evaluation of Fitzgerald's life and work.

Sklar, Robert, *F. Scott Fitzgerald: The Last Laocoon.* New York: Oxford University Press, 1967. The most controversial of the Fitzgerald books, these provocative ideas still generate an interesting analysis of Fitzgerald's work.

Collected Dictionaires and Encyclopedias

Critical Survey of Long Fiction, Salem Press, 1983. Contains a brief biographical sketch of Fitzgerald's life and a summary of his work.

Dictionary of Literary Biography, Gale Research, 1981. Concise study and a good introduction to Fitzgerald's life and career.

Charles L. P. Silet
Iowa State University

JOHN GOULD FLETCHER
1886–1950

Author's Chronology

Born January 3, 1886 in Little Rock, Arkansas; *1896* enters a private academy; subsequently attends Phillips Academy, Andover; *1903* enters Harvard; *1907* resigns from Harvard prior to graduation after being left an annuity upon his father's death; *1908* sails for Italy; *1909* relocates to London; *1913* publishes five books of verse at his own expense; meets Ezra Pound in Paris and offers financial support to Pound's literary review, *The Egoist;* becomes a fringe member of the expatriates in Europe; meets Ford Madox Ford, W. B. Yeats, T. E. Hulme, H. D., and Amy Lowell; *1914* contributes to *Some Imagist Poets; 1915* contributes to *Poetry,* the *Dial,* and the *Little Review;* becomes close friends of Conrad Aiken; *1916* marries Daisy Arbuthnot; *1919* meets Robert Graves and Van Wyck Brooks; contributes regularly to *The Freeman; 1921* invited to contribute to *I'll Take My Stand,* the symposium published by the Fugitives; *1933* after 24 years residence in Europe returns to the United States to live; *1935* marries children's writer Charlie May Simon; *1937* writes autobiographical *Life Is My Song; 1938* wins Pulitzer Prize for *Selected Poems; 1950* dies by suicide, Little Rock, Arkansas, April 10.

Author's Bibliography (selected)

Irradiations: Sand and Spray, 1915 (poems); *Goblins and Pagodas,* 1916 (poems); *Japanese Prints,* 1918 (poems); *The Tree of Life,* 1918 (poems); *Breakers and Granite,* 1921 (poems); *Paul Gauguin; His Life and Art,* 1921 (biography); *Preludes and Symphonies,* 1922 (poems); *Parables,* 1925 (short prose poems); *Branches of Adam,* 1926 (poem); *The Black Rock,* 1928 (poems); *John Smith—also Pocahontas,* 1928 (historical biography); *The Crisis of the Film,* 1929 (essay); *The Two Frontiers; A Study in Historical Psychology,* 1930; *Elegies,* 1935 (poems); *Life Is My Song,* 1937 (autobiography); *Selected Poems,* 1938 (poems); *South Star,* 1941 (poems); *The Burning Mountain,* 1946 (poems); *Arkansas,* 1947 (history).

Overview of Biographical Sources

Fletcher played a prominent role in two modern literary movements—the Imagists (1909–1925) and the Southern Agrarian Movement of the 1920's and 1930's. There is little published material dealing exclusively with Fletcher and his life. Fletcher's wife's *Johnswood* (1953) is the most comprehensive treatment but is far from objective. A good deal of information about Fletcher the man could be gleaned from reviewing the voluminous correspondence and papers held by the University of Arkansas, Fayetteville, Special Collections Library, and from the papers of Charlie May Simon at the University of Arkansas,

Little Rock, Special Collections Library. Fletcher does not emerge as an appealing personality nor as a public individual and has not attracted much attention, even though he has been categorized as occupying a unique place in American literature. His wide knowledge and eclectic interests distinguish him from other poets.

Evaluation of Selected Biographies

de Chasca, Edmund S. *John Gould Fletcher and Imagism.* Columbia: University of Missouri Press, 1978. Part I of this biocritical study documents Fletcher's role in the Imagist movement, particularly the years 1913–1917; and his relationship with Amy Lowell, Ezra Pound, and other prominent literary contemporaries. In Part II, de Chasca provides additional biographical data, but the emphasis is on ideas, on an assessment of Fletcher's poetry, and not the individual.

Simon, Charlie May, *Johnswood.* New York: E. P. Dutton, 1953. Fletcher's second wife, three years after his death, published a biographical, fragmentary reminiscence of the last years of their married life and the difficulties in their relationship. She did have high praise for her husband's poetic accomplishments and always seemed awed by and dedicated to his genius, but as one might expect from a devoted wife, Simon's biography of her husband is laced with sentimentality. Earlier, in 1943, Simon had published a brief biographical sketch of her husband, "John Gould Fletcher," in *Lays of the New Land: Stories of Some American Poets* (New York: E. P. Dutton, 1943). This article is similarly saccharine.

Stephens, Edna B. *John Gould Fletcher.* New York: Twayne, 1967. Stephens provides a two-page chronology of Fletcher's life, but limits biographical information in the study to occasional remarks woven into her discussion about various influences on his work. Stephens focuses more on Fletcher's oriental religious interests and how they are reflected in his work than on details of his life. Her study seems primarily a re-working of her dissertation, a study of religious influences on Fletcher's life. The chronology printed at the beginning of the Stephens' book is a quick and useful reference.

Autobiographical Sources

In 1937 Fletcher published his autobiographical work, *Life Is My Song* (New York: Farrar & Rinehart, 1937), in which he related many anecdotes of literary celebrities of his acquaintance. The narrative style is unexciting and undramatic. Fletcher probably took himself and his work too seriously. This weakness is very apparent and Fletcher cannot show any humor in his work. That is to say, the man is not necessarily without humor, but the body of his work fails to reveal the light touch. Only in his history of his home state, *Arkansas* (Chapel Hill: University of North Carolina Press, 1947), are there even patches of humor. In his lifetime, Fletcher corresponded with hundreds of literary figures. A large assembly of these letters are stored at the Special Collections Library at the University of Arkansas, Fayetteville. Two dissertations catalogue this extensive correspondence.

Overview of Critical Sources

There is no definitive work available on Fletcher, except for a half-dozen doctoral dissertations and the biographical works mentioned above. Discussion of Fletcher's work can be found only in book-length studies of other subjects or in short articles. Fletcher's interest in music and color and how they related to his poetry; his philosophical stance; and his interest in his native state's folklore are some of the subjects.

Evaluation of Selected Criticism

Fairchild, Hoxie Neale, *Religious Trends in English Poetry.* New York: Columbia University Press, 1962. Fairchild claims that Fletcher never grew up, that he was terrified as a child by the Old Testament and unmoved as an adult by the New Testament.

Hughes, Glenn, *Imagism and Modern Poetry.* New York: Humanities Press, 1931. Hughes provides an analysis of the Imagist movement and in the context of this gives an insight into Fletcher's life and his work.

Osborne, William R. "The Poetry of John Gould Fletcher: A Critical Analysis." Dissertation: Peabody College, 1955. Osborne hypothesizes that Fletcher's thought and his writings were in opposition.

Other Sources

Kreymborg, Alfred, *A History of American Poetry: Our Singing Strength.* New York: Tudor, 1934. Contains a short article which evaluates Fletcher as an individual and as a poet.

Rock, Virginia, "The Twelve Southerners: Biographical Essays," in *I'll Take My Stand, By Twelve Southerners: The South and the Agrarian Tradition.* New York: Harper and Row, 1962. Provides a brief biographical sketch and observes that Fletcher could experiment with various literary forms but generally chose the traditional for his works.

Lyman B. Hagen
Arkansas State University

FORD MADOX FORD
1873–1939

Author's Chronology

Born Ford Hermann Hueffer on December 17, 1873, into a Pre-Raphaelite family; *1881–1889* attends Praetoria House boarding school in Folkestone; *1891* publishes his first work, a fairy tale; *1894* elopes with Elsie Martindale and leaves London to live in the Kentish countryside; *1897* daughter Christina born; *1898* meets Henry James, Stephen Crane, W. H. Hudson, and others, and begins collaboration with Joseph Conrad; *1900* daughter Katherine born; *1906* first American lectures; *1907* returns to London; *1908–1910* founds and edits *The English Review; 1911* "divorces" Elsie in Germany; lawsuits and scandal over his relationship with Violet Hunt; *1915* enlists, commissioned 2nd lieutenant in the Welsh Regiment; *1916* gassed; *1917* wounded; *1919* discharged from service with rank of Acting Brevet Major; breaks with Violet Hunt; changes his name by deed poll to Ford Madox Ford; lives with Stella Bowen in West Sussex countryside; *1920* daughter Esther Julia born; *1922* leaves England for Paris; attends Proust's funeral; *1924* edits *the transatlantic review; 1927* visits New York; *1928* separates from Stella Bowen; *1929* begins living with Janice Biala in Provence and New York; *1937–1938* teaches at Olivet College, Michigan, which awards him an honorary doctorate; *1939* dies of heart failure in Deauville, France, on June 26.

Author's Bibliography (selected)

Romance, 1903 (novel, with Joseph Conrad); *The Fifth Queen,* 1906–1908 (novel trilogy); *Ancient Lights,* 1911 (reminiscences); *Henry James,* 1914 (critical essay); *The Good Soldier,* 1915 (novel); *Joseph Conrad: A Personal Remembrance,* 1924 (critical memoir); 1924–1928 the four "Tietjens" novels republished in 1950 as *Parade's End; No Enemy,* 1929 (disguised autobiography); *Return to Yesterday,* 1931 (reminiscences); *It Was the Nightingale,* 1933 (reminiscences); *Provence,* 1935 (impressions); *Collected Poems,* 1936 (poetry); *Great Trade Route,* 1937 (impressions); *Portraits from Life,* 1937 (critical memoir); *The March of Literature,* 1938 (impressionistic history of literature "from Confucius's Day to Our Own").

Overview of Biographical Sources

In addition to three full biographies by Douglas Goldring, Frank MacShane, and Arthur Mizener, there exist a great many references to Ford in the memoirs of the many literary figures he knew in England, France, and America. Many of these remarks are cited in David Dow Harvey's bibliography, *Ford Madox Ford, 1873–1939: A Bibliography of Works and Criticism* (Princeton: Princeton University Press, 1962). All biographers of Joseph Conrad have something to say about the collaboration, usually unsympathetic to Ford. Ford's pre-war years in London are described by Douglas Goldring in *South Lodge: Reminiscences of Violet Hunt, Ford Madox Ford, and the English Review Circle* (London: Collins, 1941). Violet Hunt's own views are expressed in *The Flurried Years* (London: Hurst & Blackett, 1926). Ford's Paris editorship is chronicled in Bernard J. Poli, *Ford Madox Ford and the Transatlantic Review* (Syracuse: Syracuse University Press, 1967). Stella Bowen has written a beautiful memoir of her life with Ford in *Drawn From Life: Reminiscences* (London: Collins, 1941). Ford is also mentioned in poems by Ezra Pound, William Carlos Williams, James Joyce, and e. e. cummings. Ernest Hemingway paints a rather unflattering portrait of Ford in one chapter of *A Moveable Feast* (New York: Charles Scribner's Sons, 1964), although this curious encounter may also be read as if Ford were teasing Hemingway deliberately. Ford's friendship with Pound is discussed in *Pound/Ford & Faber,* ed. Brita Lindberg-Feyersted (London: Faber, 1982).

Evaluation of Selected Biographies

Goldring, Douglas, *The Last Pre-Raphaelite.* London: Macdonald, 1948; American title, *Trained for Genius.* New York: E. P. Dutton, 1949. This first biography of Ford, written by his former sub-editor on *The English Review,* makes less interesting reading than Goldring's own earlier *South Lodge,* and is now regarded as superseded by MacShane and Mizener.

MacShane, Frank, *The Life and Work of Ford Madox Ford.* London: Routledge & Kegan Paul, 1965. The first critical biography of Ford is readable and carefully documented. MacShane treats Ford's poetry seriously, but the critical sections generally seem rather simplistic and peremptory. Although less thorough than Mizener, this remains an accurate and useful introductory biography.

Mizener, Arthur, *The Saddest Story: A Biography of Ford Madox Ford.* New York and Cleveland: World Publishing, 1971. The most authoritative and thorough biography of Ford to date, Mizener devotes great and careful attention to the intricacies of Ford's various tangled "affairs," and the work is nicely illustrated with original documentary material. Mizener also includes a useful descriptive survey of Ford's many neglected fictions.

Autobiographical Sources

Ford's own memoirs and reminiscences may be read in sequence as a nearly complete impressionistic autobiography. In *Ancient Lights* (1911, published in America as *Memories and Impressions*), Ford described the impressions left by his childhood in the Pre-Raphaelite circles of Ford Madox Brown and the Rossettis. *Return to Yesterday* offers a charming series of anecdotes and reflections concerning Ford's life among writers in London and Kent from 1894 to the outbreak of war in 1914, and includes a number of delightful and revealing portraits of Henry James, Joseph Conrad, H. G. Wells, and others. *No Enemy* is a thinly-disguised record of Ford's experiences in the trenches of Flanders during the war. Written in 1920, it introduces the themes of husbandry and gardening that will be elaborated in the Tietjens novels and in *It Was the Nightingale,* which describes Ford's life in Sussex and Paris after the war. His later works of "sociological impressionism," *Provence* and *Great Trade Route,* also contain a great many personal anecdotes, as do Ford's works of literary criticism, all written in his characteristically fluent and conversational style.

Ford's tribute in *Joseph Conrad: A Personal Remembrance,* which was the occasion of a scandal when first published, is now recognized not only as an inside account of Ford's collaboration with Conrad, but also as the best exposition of the "impressionistic" techniques practiced by both literary craftsmen. Ford elaborated this doctrine of a literary impressionism based on the work of Flaubert and Maupassant in his other critical works as well. A selection of these has been published by Frank MacShane as *The Critical Writings of Ford Madox Ford* (Lincoln, NB: University of Nebraska Press, 1964).

Overview of Critical Sources

Of the more than seventy volumes Ford produced in his lifetime, including over twenty novels, only three of Ford's fictions have received critical notice: *The Fifth Queen,* a trilogy of historical novels about the life of Katherine Howard; *The Good Soldier,* which is Ford's novel usually taught in classrooms; and *Parade's End,* the "Tietjens" tetralogy. Critics have tended to focus their attention on various psychological aspects of the protagonists of Ford's works, or to seek out thematic or archetypal patterns in the major novels. In general, Ford's ideas as a social theorist have never been taken very seriously, and critics often have cause to complain of the unreliable exaggerations to which Ford was prone. *Magill's Bibliography of Literary Criticism,* ed. Frank N. Magill (Englewood Cliffs: Salem Press, 1979) lists recent articles on *The Fifth Queen, The Good Soldier,* and *Parade's End.*

Evaluation of Selected Criticism

Cassell, Richard A. ed. *Ford Madox Ford: Modern Judgements.* London: Macmillan, 1972. Cassell has compiled a representative cross-section of Ford criticism, including contributions by Ezra Pound, Morton Dauwen Zabel, and William Carlos Williams.

MacShane, Frank, *Ford Madox Ford: The Critical Heritage.* London & Boston: Routledge & Kegan Paul, 1972. This is a chronological survey of reviews of Ford's work, with an introduction describing the ups and downs of Ford's literary reception.

Moser, Thomas C. *The Life in the Fiction of Ford Madox Ford.* Princeton: Princeton University Press, 1981. Moser explores the relationship between Ford and his friend Arthur Marwood, who served as the model for Christopher Tietjens.

Wiley, Paul L. *Novelist of Three Worlds: Ford Madox Ford.* Syracuse: Syracuse University Press, 1962. Wiley traces Ford's career through the "three worlds" of pre-war London, post-war Paris, and America in the thirties. This is a fine study of the social and literary contexts in which Ford's novels took shape.

Other Sources

Harvey, David Dow, *Ford Madox Ford, 1873–1939: A Bibliography of Works and Criticism.* Princeton: Princeton University Press, 1962. Extremely thorough, precise, and beautifully annotated, this, together with Mizener's biography, remains the most useful single work on Ford. Harvey quotes extensively from other sources in his section entitled "Books Significantly Mentioning Ford."

Homage to Ford Madox Ford. New Directions, Number Seven, 1942. An early memorial tribute to Ford by many of the writers he had helped.

Ludwig, Richard M. ed., *Letters of Ford Madox Ford.* Princeton: Princeton University Press, 1965. A selection of Ford's letters.

Moore, Gene M. "The Tory in a Time of Change: Social Aspects of Ford Madox Ford's *Parade's End,*" in *Twentieth Century Literature,* 28:1 (Spring 1982), 49–68. Moore explores *Parade's End* as a work of social history.

Stang, Sondra J. ed. *The Presence of Ford Madox Ford.* Philadelphia: University of Pennsylvania Press, 1981. A handsome collection, including letters Ford wrote to Conrad from the trenches.

Gene M. Moore
Virginia Commonwealth University

E. M. FORSTER
1879–1970

Author's Chronology

Born Edward Morgan Forster, January 1, 1879, London, England, of English and remotely French descent; *1890* enters Kent House School, Eastbourne, and in *1893* Tonbridge School; *1897* enters King's College, Cambridge; *1901–1902* travels in Italy to prepare for career as journalist and art lecturer; *1904* begins writing fiction and settles in Weybridge; *1905* serves as tutor to children of Count and Countess von Arnim, and publishes first novel, *Where Angels Fear to Tread; 1906* meets Syed Ross Masood, a major influence on Forster; *1912* first visit to India; *1915* goes to Egypt as Red Cross worker and meets Mohammed el Adl; *1919* returns to England; *1921* visits India again as private secretary to Maharaja of Dewas Senior; *1924* publishes *A Passage to India* and inherits Surrey home, West Hackhurst; *1929* visits South Africa; *1930* meets Robert Buckingham; *1934* becomes first President of National Council for Civil Liberties; *1935* addresses International Congress of Writers in Paris; *1945* attends All-India P.E.N. conference, third and last visit to India; *1946* loses West Hackhurst and moves to Cambridge; *1947* lectures in the United States; *1949–1951* collaborates with Eric Crozier on libretto for Benjamin Britten opera *Billy Budd; 1969* awarded Order of Merit; *1970* dies on June 6; *1971* novel *Maurice* published posthumously.

Author's Bibliography (selected)

Where Angels Fear to Tread, 1905 (novel); *The Longest Journey,* 1907 (novel); *A Room with a View,* 1908 (novel); *Howards End,* 1910 (novel); *The Celestial Omnibus,* 1911 (short fiction); *Alexandria,* 1922 (history and guide book); *A Passage to India,* 1924 (novel); *Aspects of the Novel,* 1927 (criticism); *Goldsworthy Lowes Dickinson,* 1934 (biography); 'What I Believe', 1939 (essay); *Two Cheers for Democracy,* 1951 (essays); *The Hill of Devi,* 1953 (memoir); *Marianne Thornton,* 1956 (biography).

Overview of Biographical Sources

At Forster's wish, P. N. Furbank began the authorized biography in the late 1960's, *E. M. Forster: A Life.* This will stand for some time as the definitive biography, since Furbank both knew Forster during the last decade of his life, and had access to all available Forster materials. Francis King's *E. M. Forster and His World* (1978) is a brief illustrated biography. Two other works may be classed as complementary biographical material, for both provide essential materials that elaborate Forster's visits to India. These are *E. M. Forster's India,* by G. K. Das (1977), and *E. M. Forster's Passages to India,* by Robin Jared Lewis (1979). At present, other biographical material consists principally of recollections and comments in biographies and memoirs of Forster's contemporaries.

Evaluation of Selected Biographies

Das, G. K. *E. M. Forster's India.* London: Macmillan, 1977. This study may be classed among biographical materials because it recreates Forster's view of political and spiritual India at the times of his visits there. The book began as a doctoral thesis at Cambridge University but is unmarked by pedantry.

Furbank, P. N. *E. M. Forster: A Life.* London: Sidgwick and Jackson; New York: Harcourt Brace Jovanovich, 1977–1978. Furbank's biography is authoritative not only because of his personal knowledge of Forster but also because of acquaintance with many of Forster's friends and associates. Furbank also commands a prose style of great elegance and charm; he has an understated wit and a gift for the unexpected turn of phrase, not unlike Forster's own. The biography is most detailed on the years up to World War II; thereafter, with the move to Cambridge in 1946, his life maintained a generally even tenor. However, Furbank stresses particularly the importance of Forster's later nonfiction, his work for the British Broadcasting Corporation, and his association with Benjamin Britten. The biography closes with Furbank's eloquent and moving memoir of his friendship with Forster.

King, Francis, *E. M. Forster and His World.* London: Thames and Hudson; New York: Charles Scribner's Sons, 1978. This concise basic biography, also by a friend of Forster, provides a good introduction to Forster and his work, enhanced by 122 illustrations not previously available in one publication.

Lewis, Robin Jared, *E.M. Forster's Passages to India.* New York: Columbia University Press, 1979. This study, also originating as a dissertation, recreates Forster's 1912–1913 and 1921 visits to India, viewing the country geographically and socially through Forster's eyes. Lewis followed Forster's routes, collecting details such as the authentic sound of the echo in the Barabar [Forster's Marabar] Caves. The Das and Lewis books complement not only Furbank's biography, but each other.

Autobiographical Sources

Whatever autobiographical material of substance Forster provided, up to 1953 and publication of *The Hill of Devi,* may be found principally in his letters. He was a conversational letter-writer and much preferred the pen to the telephone. *Selected Letters of E. M. Forster* (2 volumes, eds. Mary Lago and P.N. Furbank. London: William Collins; Cambridge, MA: Harvard University Press, 1983, 1985) includes 446 letters out of an estimated 15,000 extant. Portions of additional letters are included in annotations. The edition is supplemented by *Calendar of the Letters of E. M. Forster,* compiled by Mary Lago

(London: Mansell Publishing, 1985), which lists all the letters available as of 1984, with information on their owners. *The Hill of Devi* draws upon letters written during his sojourn at Dewas Senior and has the Forster hallmarks of thoughtful wit and an affectionate sense of the absurd.

Overview of Critical Sources

The enormous literature of criticism of Forster's work concentrates principally on his fiction. Forster himself tended to dismiss analyses that leaned heavily on symbolism (intentional or unintentional). The dominant themes that inform his fiction, his non-fiction, and many of his personal writings are the importance of personal relations and the saving power of the arts as a guide for civilization. Critics tend increasingly to study the importance of Forster's humanist principles in relation to their present-day applications.

Evaluation of Selected Criticism

Bradbury, Malcolm, *Forster: A Collection of Critical Essays.* Englewood Cliffs, NJ: Prentice-Hall, 1966. This collection of essays by leading literary critics investigates the ways in which Forster is modern in both technique and ideas.

Crews, Frederick, *E.M. Forster: The Perils of Humanism.* Princeton: Princeton University Press; London: Oxford University Press, 1962. Crews discusses Forster as an Edwardian in point of time and in spirit; he examines Forster's understated style as an element that has somewhat obscured the historical weight of his ideas.

Gardner, Philip, ed. *E.M. Forster: The Critical Heritage.* The Critical Heritage Series. London and Boston: Routledge and Kegan Paul, 1973. Reprints representative contemporary reactions to Forster's works and includes reviews that assess Forster's place in literary history.

Macaulay, Rose, *The Writings of E. M. Forster.* London: Hogarth Press; New York: Harcourt, Brace, 1938. Macaulay studies Forster in relation to his background and its effect on his libertarianism and humanism.

Stone, Wilfred, *The Cave and the Mountain: A Study of E. M. Forster.* Stanford: Stanford University Press; London: Oxford University Press, 1966. Stone views Forster as a Coleridgean, dedicated to the search for ways of bridging the gap between poetry and fact. In discussing Forster's works, Stone investigates Forster's devices for establishing connection between the best of the old, and whatever in the new promises best for the future. Stone analyzes and admires Forster's high literary standards.

Trilling, Lionel, *E. M. Forster.* New York: New Directions, 1943. This examination of Forster's work as the product of an imaginative liberal mind greatly accelerated post-World War II interest in his writings, both fiction and non-fiction. Trilling stresses the importance to Forster of the continuity of tradition.

Other Sources

Borrello, Alfred. *An E. M. Forster Dictionary.* Metuchen, NJ: The Scarecrow Press, 1971. Under alphabetical headings, lists and annotates summaries of Forster's works, chapter headings, and characters.

———. *An E. M. Forster Glossary.* Metuchen, NJ: The Scarecrow Press, 1972. Annotates allusions in Forster's works.

Kirkpatrick, B. J. *A Bibliography of E. M. Forster.* The Soho Bibliographies, No. 19. London: Rupert Hart-Davis, 1968. Kirkpatrick has compiled detailed analytical descriptions of Forster's works, including newspaper and periodical articles, dramatizations, broadcasts, and some unpublished materials. This is the standard Forster bibliography. A revised and expanded edition is in progress.

McDowell, Frederick, *E. M. Forster: An Annotated Bibliography of Writings about Him.* Annotated Secondary Bibliography Series on English Literature in Transition, 1880–1920. De Kalb: Northern Illinois University Press, 1976. This collection of 1,119 annotated items is the most extensive such listing of secondary sources on Forster. Entries are fully annotated and documented; deal with both literary and biographical commentary and criticism; and are indexed by author, title of secondary work, periodicals and newspapers, foreign languages, and primary titles.

Mary Lago
University of Missouri-Columbia

BENJAMIN FRANKLIN
1706–1790

Author's Chronology

Born 6 January, 1706 in Boston, Massachusetts the tenth of fifteen children; father a Protestant English tallow chandler and soap boiler; *1718* apprenticed to brother as printer; *1722* first essay published under name of "Silence Dogood;" edits paper while brother is politically imprisoned; *1723* in Philadelphia; *1724–26* in England; *1726* Clerk of Pennsylvania Assembly; *1730* owner, editor and publisher of the *Pennsylvania Gazette* in Philadelphia; *1737–1753* Deputy Postmaster for Philadelphia, marries Deborah Read, becomes a father, invents a fire chimney, establishes a fire company, helps organize an academy which becomes the University of Pennsylvania and serves as secretary to the American Philosophical Society; *1746* retires after accumulating wealth; *1751* publishes observations on electricity in England; *1757–1785* serves at diplomatic table in London, Paris and Philadelphia; *1759* awarded L.L.D. by St. Andrews and D.L.C. by Oxford; *1775* chosen representative to second Continental Congress; serves on committee to draft Declaration of Independence; *1776* appointed Minister to France and successfully negotiates treaty of allegiance; *1781* member of the American delegation to the Paris peace conference; *1783* assists in signing the Treaty of Paris which ends Revolutionary War; *1785* returns to Philadelphia and serves as delegate to Constitutional Convention; dies April 17, 1790, one of the most beloved Americans.

Author's Bibliography (selected)

Pennsylvania Gazette, 1729–1749 (essays); *Poor Richard's Almanac,* 1732–1757 (almanacs); *Way to Make Money Plenty,* 1736 (economic treatise); *Account of Pennsylvania Fire Place,* 1744 (invention pamphlet); *Reflections on Courtship and Marriage,* 1746 (marriage essay); *Association for Defense,* 1747 (warfare/political pamphlet); *Plain Truth,* 1747 (political pamphlet); *Advice to Young Tradesmen,* 1748 (business essay); *Education of Youth,* 1749 (education proposal); *Electrical Experiments,* 1751, rpt. with additions 1753, 1760–1762 (scientific pamphlet); *Plan of School,* 1751 (educational proposal for the Philadelphia Academy); *Increase of Mankind,* 1751 (diplomatic political pamphlet regarding the encroachment of French upon British Colonies in America); 1751 *Introduction to Preface to Hopkins' Memoirs,* 1757 (historical introduction); *Way to Wealth, Boston: 1757,* 1757 (economic treatise); *State of Pennsylvania,* 1759 (political tract); *Interest of Great Britain Considered With Regard to Her Colonies,* 1760 (political pamphlet); *Cool Thoughts* 1764 (political pamphlet); *Preface to Galloways' Speech,* 1764 (political preface); *Examination in Parliament,* 1766 (relative to the Repeal of the American Stamp Act); *Preface to Dickinson's Letters,* London, 1768 (political essay); *Curious Note,* 1769 (political note); *Autobiography,* 1771–1789; *Plan for New Countries,* 1771 (economic treatise); *Rules by Which a Great Empire May be Reduced to a Small One,* 1773 (political essay); *Notes on Trade,* 1774 (trade treatise); *Articles of Confederation,* 1775 (government articles); *Direction to Postmasters,* 1775 (political essay); *American Credit,* 1777 (political paper); *The Ephemera,* 1778 (bagatelle); *The Morals of Chess,* 1779 (moral essay).

Overview of Biographical Sources

From Franklin's own lifetime until this decade, many significant biographical treatments have been rendered. Outstanding biographers include John Bigelow, Bernard Fay, J. B. McMaster, Theodore Parker and James Parton. These biographers represent both nineteenth and twentieth century scholars who possess a desire to know and to render the life of Franklin in context to both his environment and motivation. They approached the task of conquering his biography by including all forms of literary materials which he wrote. Because of the voluminous amount of materials, biographers resorted to putting their work in several volumes or concentrating on certain events and major highlights of Franklin's life and career. Although they use basically the same materials, Franklin is explored from different points of view. All scholarly biographers are grateful to Franklin for supplying this overwhelming amount of literary material which includes his own *Autobiography* and serves as the core of their information.

Evaluation of Selected Biographies

Bigelow, John, *Life of Benjamin Franklin.* Volumes I, II and III. Philadelphia: J. B. Lippincott, 1893. This three volume biography is one of the most comprehensive and informative. Bigelow condenses the more important of Franklin's own memorials into a single compact work while giving convenient order and attractiveness of a continuous narrator. In Volume I, Bigelow covers the *Autobiography* with later autobiographical writings arranged as a continuation of it. Volume II covers the period from 1768 to 1780. Bigelow includes in this volume Franklin's early marriage, his sensitivity to old age, his scientific endeavors, advice to the colonists, problems with taxation, as Agent for Massachusetts Bay and as a contributing force to solving the country's political problems. Volume III is concerned with Franklin's life in Paris and includes Franklin's letters from September 6, 1778 to April 8, 1790, just nine days before his death. While these three volumes are basically an accounting of Franklin's life based on his own writings, Bigelow gives attention to blank spaces left by Franklin. The reader leaves this work with a greater understanding of both Franklin and Colonial America.

Bruce, William Cabell, *Benjamin Franklin Self-Revealed.* New York: G. P. Putnam's Sons, 1917. This biography and critical study is based mainly on

Franklin's own writings. A study of Franklin's varied aspects rather than a narrative biography, Bruce explores Franklin's moral standing and system, religious beliefs, success as Philanthropist and citizen, his family relations, his American, British, and French friends, his personal characteristics, his life as a man of business, a statesman, a man of science and as a writer. Using excerpts from various Franklin letters, Bruce unveils Franklin as the Colonial man.

Van Doren, Carl, *Benjamin Franklin.* New York: Viking Press, 1938. Van Doren, aware of the problem of capturing Franklin's biography in one book, is successful in his attempt to cover certain parts of Franklin's life. He analyzes Franklin's relationship with his father, his early life and talents, his relationship with his brother, his first publishing success, his life in Philadelphia as a journeyman, as a leader of his society, as a scientist, as an organizer of the militia, the Academy, the hospital and the first American fire insurance company. The reader follows Franklin in London as an American Agent; in Paris, as a commissioner, Minister and peacemaker and, back in the United States, as the President of Pennsylvania. This book is easy to read and includes incidents that are often left out of more historical biographies.

Autobiographical Sources

The *Autobiography,* Franklin's own recollection of his life, was begun in 1771 but never finished. It recounts his life until 1759 and is perhaps the most lasting monument to his wisdom and to his persistence in the belief that all men may better themselves. His plain style, his practical approach and his humor, touched with a hint of sentimentality, make him a truly representative man of his age. In this autobiography, Franklin recounts in journal form events from his childhood, his work experiences, his escape to Philadelphia and his mature years in Boston and England as a printer and writer, as a family man, politician and statesman.

In addition to this extensive memoir, Franklin produced many letters and tracts, both religious and political, which reflect a firm conviction of his belief and a changing portrait of his theories as he matured and became more tolerant. Franklin possessed a clear, precise view of his beliefs and fought for his convictions in every way he could, especially with his pen. The last part of *Autobiography* was written by an aging Franklin after his health was on the wane. Thus the reader sees a more reflective Franklin than the earlier author.

Overview of Critical Sources

Although the reading public knows Franklin primarily for his political life and as author of the *Autobiography,* critics in science, education, foreign affairs, religion, literature and government have been interested in Franklin because of his originality and successful treatments of inventions, foreign relations, religious tracts and especially his moral tracts, which were taught in schools until the nineteenth century. There has always been an abundance of criticism that attempted to access Franklin's work fairly.

Evaluation of Selected Criticism

Amacher, Richard E. *Benjamin Franklin.* New York: Twayne, 1962. In this book of essays, Amacher limits his approach to the life and activity of Franklin as a writer. This is particularly interesting if the reader wishes to comprehend Franklin's literary career as a whole. The essays present representative samples of significant aspects of Franklin as a craftsman in different literary genres.

Barbour, Brian M. ed. *Benjamin Franklin, A Collection of Essays.* Englewood Cliffs, NJ: Prentice-Hall, 1979. This collection includes essays by several authors, among D. H. Lawrence and Bruce Granger who approach Franklin from the twentieth century point of view and are both complimentary and critical of Franklin as a writer and moralist. For a modern perspective, this book is valuable in assessing Franklin's value and contribution to the literary world. The reader should keep in mind, however, that these contemporary writers are looking at Franklin in retrospect and in regard to the "new American experience."

Granger, Bruce Ingham, *Benjamin Franklin, An American Man of Letters.* Ithaca, NY: Cornell University Press, 1964. Ingham looks at Franklin's achievements in the world of letters with a focus on various of his writings studied in their historical and biographical context.

Other Sources

Franklin, William Temple, *Memoirs of the Life and Writings of Benjamin Franklin . . . Written by Himself . . . and Continued . . . by His Grandson, William Temple Franklin . . .* 3rd edition, London, 1818. Temple Franklin continues his grandfather's life in more thorough and objective terms than other early biographers. He contends that the statesman should not be held responsible for certain schemes undertaken by men who used his name. Temple shows Franklin to be a moderate philosophic man whose plans and efforts were always considered and directed toward the public good.

Selected Dictionaries and Encyclopedias

American Writers, a Collection of Literary Biographies, Charles Scribner's Sons, 1974. A twenty-four page biography with overview of Franklin's achievements and literary works.

The Reader's Encyclopedia of American Literature, Thomas Y. Crowell, 1962. Concise overview of Franklin's entire life and a discussion of his more outstanding achievements.

Wanda LaFaye Seay
Oklahoma State University

MARY E. WILKINS FREEMAN
1852–1930

Author's Chronology

Born October 31, 1852 as Mary Ella Wilkins in Randolph, Massachusetts; changes her middle name to Eleanor after her mother; *1867* family moves to Brattleboro, Vermont; *1873* family's business fails; *1880* mother dies; *1883* father dies; *1902* marries Dr. Charles Freeman, an alcoholic; couple moves to Metuchen, New Jersey; begins publishing as Mary E. Wilkins Freeman; *1920* Dr. Freeman committed to a New Jersey state hospital; *1923* Dr. Freeman dies; successfully contests her husband's will in which Dr. Freeman had disinherited her; *1926* receives the William Dean Howells Medal for Fiction from the American Academy of Letters and is elected to the National Institute of Arts and Letters; March 13, 1930 dies in Metuchen; buried in Plainfield, New Jersey; had written approximately two hundred stories.

Author's Bibliography (selected)

A Humble Romance and Other Stories, 1887; *A New England Nun and Other Stories,* 1891; *Jane Field,* 1893 (novel); *Giley Corey, Yeoman,* 1893 (play); *Pembroke,* 1894 (novel); *The Love of Parson Lord and Other Stories,* 1900; *Understudies,* 1901 (stories); *The Portion of Labor,* 1901 (novel); *Six Trees,* 1903 (stories); *The Wind in the Rose-Bush and Other Stories,* 1903; *The Givers,* 1904 (stories); *The Fair Lavinia and Others,* 1907 (stories); *Doctor Gordon,* 1907 (novel); *The Shoulders of Atlas,* 1908 (novel); *The Winning Lady and Others,* 1909 (stories); *The Butterfly House,* 1912 (novel); *Edgewater People,* 1918 (stories); *The Best Stories of Mary E. Wilkins,* 1927.

Overview of Biographical Sources

While Mary E. Wilkins Freeman's works are not strictly autobiographical, she relied heavily on her own background and observations of New England life to create her fiction. Therefore, almost any author who discusses Freeman's work in detail also describes her life. Two book-length biographies exist: Edward Foster's *Mary E. Wilkins Freeman* (1956) and Perry D. Westbrook's *Mary Wilkins Freeman* (1967). Both are important to the Freeman scholar.

Evaluation of Selected Biographies

Foster, Edward, *Mary E. Wilkins Freeman.* New York: Hendricks House, 1956. Foster's sympathetic portrayal of Freeman is valuable because of the sources he uses. He bases his study on his interviews with thirty of Freeman's friends and relatives, Freeman's correspondence kept by her friends and relatives, and accounts of her life in local newspapers and town records. He defines local color (the form Freeman most often used), defends its value, points out the sources that influenced her, and describes her own special contribution to the form. Aware that the local color apparent in her fiction derives from her own observations, Foster gives meticulous details about her family's heritage and the New England community's social and religious mores. He largely ignores her poetry and work for children but pays special attention to her best work, *A Humble Romance and Other Stories* and *A New England Nun and Other Stories.* The end of his book includes a bibliography of her published works and a bibliography of secondary sources. Foster is highly sympathetic to Freeman but is not totally uncritical, observing, for example, that she was not a good critic and she had little concern for style.

Westbrook, Perry D. *Mary Wilkins Freeman.* New York: Twayne, 1967. Westbrook also carefully describes Freeman's heritage and the traditions of New England villages that colored her stories. Of particular value is his chapter on the religious and philosophical beliefs of New England in the late nineteenth century. He also explains her use of local color although he prefers to describe her work as regionalism since it does not have the pejorative connotations of the other term. Westbrook spends more time analyzing Freeman's work than Foster does, so his book is also useful as a critical study. Westbrook's last chapter concludes with a valuable description of the rise and decline of her reputation as a writer. His bibliography of Freeman's work is less detailed than Foster's, but his bibliography of secondary sources is annotated and more recent.

Overview of Critical Sources

Critical analyses of Freeman's work usually exist in books that discuss the history of the short story or local color. Critics generally believe that Freeman, as one of the best local colorists of the nineteenth century, deserves serious consideration; however, they believe she lacked the discipline or talent necessary to produce consistently first-rate works.

Evaluation of Selected Criticism

Brooks, Van Wyck, *New England: Indian Summer 1865–1915.* New York: E. P. Dutton, 1940. Critics today reinforce Brooks' opinions of Freeman's works. He observes that her best work is her earliest; her later work is too sentimental. He notes that she is a better short story writer than a novelist and that she writes best when she writes about New England villagers and their decaying way of life.

Donovan, Josephine, *New England Local Color: A Women's Tradition.* New York: Frederick Ungar, 1983. A chapter in this feminist approach shows that Freeman's stories depict the decay of the matriarchy in rural New England. Donovan analyzes stories that emphasize mother-daughter relationships, depict strong women, and show Freeman's anti-Calvinist position.

Hamblen, Abigail Ann, *The New England Art of Mary E. Wilkins Freeman.* Amherst: The Green Knight Press, 1966. Hamblen discusses the importance of pride and the Puritan heritage in Freeman's early stories.

Pattee, Fred Lewis, *The Development of the American Short Story: An Historical Survey.* New York: Harper, 1923. His book provides one of the earliest and still one of the best treatments of Freeman as a local colorist. He points out that both Nathaniel Hawthorne and Freeman depended on their Puritan heritage to write their fiction, but Freeman did not have the dedication necessary to become a first-rate artist. Pattee also discusses the difference between Sarah Orne Jewett's conscious and Freeman's unconscious artistry. He observes that Freeman's stories center on women and depict a decaying way of life. Many Freeman critics have simply provided support for Pattee's early observations.

Westbrook, Perry D. *Acres of Flint.* Washington, D.C.: The Scarecrow Press, 1951. This book on New England local color compares Freeman's concern with Puritan values to Hawthorne's. Westbrook points out the theme of hopelessness in some of Freeman's stories. He astutely observes that most of Sarah Orne Jewett's works are better than Freeman's, but that Freeman's best work is unexcelled by Jewett.

———. *The New England Town: Fact and Fiction.* East Brunswick, NJ: Associated University Presses, 1982. Westbrook describes the pessimism in Freeman's stories, calls her a realist, and points out that obsessive pride and conscience dominate the lives of her characters.

Other Sources

Spiller, Robert, *et al. Literary History of the United States,* third edition, revised. New York: Macmillan, 1963. Describes the characteristics of Freeman's fiction by comparing it to Jewett's work; states that Freeman's early work is her best.

Warren, Austin, *The New England Conscience.* Ann Arbor: University of Michigan Press, 1967. Includes a chapter showing the importance of pride and conscience in the characters of Freeman's stories.

Selected Dictionaries and Encyclopedias

Notable American Women, 1607–1950, Belknap Press of Harvard University Press, 1971. A concise, valuable biography of Freeman's life and analysis of her fiction; written by Edward Foster, who wrote her first full-length biography.

Margaret Ann Baker
Iowa State University

PHILIP MORIN FRENEAU
1752–1832

Author's Chronology

Born on January 2, 1752 to Philip and Agnes Fresneau (Philip Morin was the first to change the spelling of the family name) in New York City; *1753* family moves to a thousand-acre estate called Mount Pleasant in Monmouth County, New Jersey; *1754–1766* probably attends a boarding school in New York City; *1767* enters Latin school at Penolopen, New Jersey to prepare for entry into the College of New Jersey—later Princeton; October, *1767* father dies; *1768* enters College of New Jersey, where Hugh Henry Brackenridge, James Madison, and Aaron Burr are fellow students; *1771* writes with Brackenridge "Father Bombo's Pilgrimage" and "The Rising Glory of America;" graduates with a B.A.; *1775* has published several of his first poems, including *The American Village* and other poems relating to the Revolutionary War; *1779* contributes to the *United States Magazine* under Brackenridge's editorship; *1780* imprisoned on a British prison ship in New York harbor; *1781* publishes his famous "The British Prison Ship," along with other occasional poems dealing with the war; *1784–1790* serves as master of a merchant ship; *1786* publishes first collection of poems, *The Poems of Philip Freneau; 1790* journalist for the New York *Daily Advertiser;* marries Eleanor Forman after a lengthy courtship; *1791* founds the *National Gazette* in Philadelphia; *1792* after several supportive articles in the *National Gazette,* is accused of being Thomas Jefferson's tool; *1794* sets up own press in Mount Pleasant and publishes *The Monmouth Almanac; 1797* edits the New York *Time Piece and Literary Companion; 1802–1803* earns living as ship's captain; *1809* publishes *Poems Written and Published during the American Revolutionary War; 1815* gathers *A Collection of Poems Chiefly on American Affairs; 1832* dies on December 18 at eighty, from exposure during a snow storm.

Author's Bibliography (selected)

The American Village, a Poem, 1772; *The British Prison-Ship: A Poem,* 1781; *The Poems of Philip Freneau,* 1786; *Poems Written and Published During the American Revolutionary War,* 2 vols., 1809; *Poems of Philip Freneau,* 1902; *Poems of Philip Freneau,* ed. Philip M. Marsh, 1955; *The Last Poems of Philip Freneau,* ed. Lewis Leary, 1945.

Overview of Biographical Sources

Despite the fact that some eighty years have passed since its appearance, Fred Lewis Pattee's long sketch prefacing his edition of *The Poems of Philip Freneau* (3 vols. Princeton: Princeton University Press, 1902–1907) continues to be valuable. Though this edition is not widely available today, in its introduction appears for the first time the assessment of Freneau as precursor of such English Romantics as Coleridge and Wordsworth, with his portraying gothicism in "The House of Night," his treating the common and ordinary in *The American Village,* and his centering on nature in "The Wild Honey-Suckle." In an interpretation which unfortunately persists to this day, Pattee sees Freneau as a poet endowed with wondrous potential but whose circumstances thwarted full realization of his talents.

Evaluation of Selected Biographies

Axelrad, Jacob, *Philip Freneau: Champion of Democracy.* Austin: University of Texas Press, 1967. This author emphasizes Freneau's inflammatory personality, which caused him frequent trouble—once even with President Washington. Axelrad attempts to make of Freneau a popular poet of the American Revolution and a herald of American democracy. The author relies heavily on the technique of invention, such as making up Freneau's daily feelings and thoughts.

Bowden, Mary W. *Philip Freneau.* Boston: G. K. Hall, 1976. Bowden argues that "Freneau's greatest claim to attention is the variety shown in his works." Unlike earlier views of the poet's work, Bowden does not find Freneau to be a romantic; instead she emphasizes Freneau's rationalism. This corrective view of the poet is valuable, though its author's reading of some of the poems should be viewed in conjunction with other commentary.

Leary, Lewis, *That Rascal Freneau: A Study in Literary Failure.* New Brunswick: Rutgers University Press, 1941. Now generally judged to be the standard biography, the book opens with this arresting declaration: "Philip Freneau failed in almost everything he attempted." Leary, as have others, centers his explanation for Freneau's "failures" on his impulsiveness and emotions. His assessment of Freneau dominates even today literary anthologies and survey courses. It must be cautioned, however, that a new and growing critical interpretation sees Freneau as much less a literary failure than Leary's book suggests. Leary has himself mitigated his view in recent years.

Marsh, Philip M. *Philip Freneau: Poet and Journalist.* Minneapolis: Dillon Press, 1967. Perhaps the most popular biography, this work does both Freneau and the history of journalism a great service by establishing the substantial contribution Freneau has made to the foundation of journalism in the United States. He seems to accept in large part, however, the traditional view that Freneau's volatile personality leaves his readers a poetry in which the poet is at the mercy of his feelings.

Overview of Critical Sources

Even though Philip Freneau has been called, erroneously, the Father of American Poetry and even though Freneau promoted himself as Poet of the

American Revolution, until very recent times the trend in criticism has been to treat him and his work as failures. As shown above, his biographers, though they have acknowledged his great potential, universally agree that he never quite attained the reaches of that potential, either financially or artistically. Recently, however, critics have begun to be more generous toward this poet. One critic, Richard Vitzthum, claims to have discovered the "key" to interpreting the body of Freneau's poetry.

Evaluation of Selected Criticism

Adkins, Nelson F. *Philip Freneau and the Cosmic Enigma: The Religious and Philosophical Speculations of an American Poet.* New York: New York University Press, 1949. Adkins presents an admirable attempt to trace Freneau's reading and the evolution of his thought through his poetry. He closes this monograph with the observation that Freneau's philosophy is riddled with "religious uncertainties" and "metaphysical gropings," but then, after all "no age ever so seethed with contending and conflicting modes of thought as the eighteenth century."

Leary, Lewis, "Philip Freneau: A Reassessment," *Major Writers of Early American Literature.* ed. Everett Emerson. Madison: University of Wisconsin Press, 1972, pp. 245–271. In this brief portrait written thirty years after his long biographical study, Leary somewhat mollifies his view of Freneau's "failure" as a poet. Claiming that there are no poets who could be considered Freneau's "descendents," he maintains Freneau should be read as a transitional figure between neoclassicism and romanticism.

Marsh, Philip M. *The Works of Philip Freneau: A Critical Study.* Metuchen, NJ: Scarecrow Press, 1968. Largely a descriptive treatment of Freneau's poems and prose, this book-length essay concludes that Freneau wrote his best poems before the 1790's.

Vitzthum, Richard C. *Land and Sea: The Lyric Poetry of Philip Freneau.* Minneapolis: University of Minnesota Press, 1978. Vitzthum's volume points a new and revolutionary direction in Freneau criticism. In this fascinating and most competent book, Vitzthum holds that at the core of Freneau's poetic opus are about one hundred poems which, when taken together, map a discernable evolution in Freneau's philosophical, theological, and aesthetic thought. This critic further maintains that within this group of poems—among them are such works as *The American Village,* "The Beauties of Santa Cruz," "The Hurricane," "The Departure," and "On Arriving in South Carolina"—Freneau develops an equation wherein the land represents fecund, benevolent security, or the female principle, while the sea stands for the aggression, even destructiveness associated with the male principle. Finally and most significantly, Vitzthum declares that Freneau's most substantial contribution to romanticism was not his usually voiced celebration of nature, freedom and the common man, but "his internalization of poetic symbol," manifested by his land-sea polarity.

Selected Dictionaries and Encyclopedias

American Writers Before 1800: A Biographical and Critical Dictionary, Greenwood Press, 1983. Brief overview of Freneau's variegated life and concise discussion of his principal works.

Critical Survey of Poetry, Salem Press, 1982. Brief biography and succinct analysis of some of Freneau's most important and most frequently anthologized poems.

The Reader's Encyclopedia of American Literature, Crowell, 1962. Still one of the most popular treatments of American letters, it contains a useful and pithy survey of Freneau's life, major themes, and most significant works.

John C. Shields
Illinois State University

ROBERT FROST
1874–1963

Author's Chronology

Born March 26, 1874, in San Francisco, California, to a Scottish mother and New England father; *1885* settles with family in Salem, New Hampshire upon father's death; *1892* graduates as co-valedictorian (with Elinor White) and class poet from Lawrence High School, studies at Dartmouth for less than a semester; *1895* marries Elinor and teaches for two years in Lawrence; *1897–1899* enters Harvard as a special student; *1900* moves family to a farm in Derry, New Hampshire; *1912* sells Derry property and takes family to England; *1913* publishes *A Boy's Will* in England, with *North of Boston* immediately after (*1914*), both to critical acclaim; *1915* returns to a farm in Franconia, New Hampshire, both volumes of poetry now published in America; *1916* publishes *Mountain Interval* and is elected to the National Institute of Arts and Letters; *1917–1920* undertakes first of several appointments as Professor of English, Amherst College; *1919* relocates family to farm in South Shaftsbury, Vermont; *1920* co-founds Bread Loaf School of English, Middlebury College; *1921–1923* becomes poet-in-residence at the University of Michigan; *1924* receives the Pulitzer Prize for *New Hampshire; 1930* is elected to the American Academy; *1931* wins Pulitzer Prize for *Collected Poems; 1936* selected Charles Eliot Norton Professor of Poetry at Harvard; *1937* awarded Pulitzer Prize for *A Witness Tree; 1943–1949* selected as Ticknor Fellow in the Humanities, Dartmouth College; *1949* and *1959* is accorded formal greetings on his 75th and 85th birthdays by the United States Senate; *1957* awarded honorary degrees from Oxford and Cambridge; *1961* reads "The Gift Outright" at the Presidential Inaugural of John F. Kennedy; *1962* publishes *In the Clearing* and takes an official State Department trip to the U.S.S.R., meeting with Premier Krushchev; January 29, 1963 dies after cancer operation and heart attack.

Author's Bibliography (selected poetry)

A Boy's Will, 1913, 1915; *North of Boston,* 1914; *Mountain Interval,* 1916; *New Hampshire,* 1923; *Selected Poems,* 1923; rev. 1928, 1934; *West-running Brook,* 1928; *Collected Poems,* 1930; *A Further Range,* 1936; *A Witness Tree* 1942; *A Masque of Reason,* 1945 (poetic drama); *Steeple Bush,* 1947; *A Masque of Mercy,* 1947 (poetic drama); *Complete Poems,* 1949; *In the Clearing,* 1962; *Selected Poems of Robert Frost,* 1963; *The Poetry of Robert Frost,* 1969 (ed. Edwin Connery Lathem; at present the standard edition).

Overview of Biographical Sources

During Frost's life of nearly ninety years, he experienced years of frustration and neglect, the excitement of "discovery" at age 39, and subsequent decades of admiring attention, even veneration. His peripatetic existence as poet-in-residence on college campuses brought him into contact with many who later sought to record their impressions of him. Over the years Frost himself carefully crafted his public image as the homely backwoods artist-philosopher, a mask which so endeared him to his public that reading at the Kennedy Inaugural merely sanctioned his unofficial role as the nation's poet laureate. His life received its first book-length scrutiny in 1927 with Gorham Munson's *Robert Frost: A Study in Sensibility and Good Sense* (New York: George H. Duran). The biography neglects the darker contours of those years. Elizabeth Shepley Sargeant's *Robert Frost: The Trial by Existence* (New York: Holt, Rinehart and Winston, 1960), contains factual errors and interprets Frost's life from an overtly sentimental bias. Other writers have more successfully penetrated Frost's public facade. One of Frost's long-time friends discusses him in *From Another World: The Autobiography of Louis Untermeyer* (New York: Harcourt, 1939) and shares his experience of the fuller person Frost allowed him to see. Untermeyer speculates that the complexities of Frost's personality would defy any potential biographer since "his life, like his poetry, is a maze of disguised simplicities and delicate double meanings." In 1964 Untermeyer gave a lecture published as *Robert Frost: A Backward Look* (Washington: Library of Congress). C. P. Snow included a remembrance of Frost in *Variety of Men* (London: Macmillan, 1967); he records his conversations and meetings with Frost after 1957. Donald Hall's *Remembering Poets* (New York: Harper & Row, 1978), describes Frost as tough, solitary, and quite human. With the publication of Lawrance Thompson's three-volume revisionist biography, *Robert Frost: The Early Years, The Years of Triumph,* and *The Later Years,* completed in 1976, the image of Frost as benign sage was exploded, creating a controversy which has since dominated the biographical study of the poet. A third volume of essays celebrating Frost's centennial was published specifically to present "the real Frost" whom Thompson "misrepresented." (*Frost: Centennial Essays III,* ed. Jac Tharpe, University Press of Mississippi, 1978). Most recently, William Pritchard has published a major biographical reevaluation, *Robert Frost: A Literary Life Reconsidered* (1984).

Evaluation of Selected Biographies

Cox, Sidney, *A Swinger of Birches: A Portrait of Robert Frost.* New York: New York University Press, 1957. Cox's study delineates his forty-year association with Frost, and in its absolute identification of Frost the man and Frost the public figure offers an unqualified tribute to its subject. Cox discusses the poet's complex sense of humor, his theories of poetic expression, and his dedication to the concrete experiences of ordinary life as the source of his creativity.

Frost, Lesley, *New Hampshire's Child: The Derry Journals of Lesley Frost.* Albany: State University of New York Press, 1969. This work covers four years of Lesley's childhood on the Derry farm where her parents struggled to earn a livelihood for the family. The author illuminates the strains inflicted on the Frosts' marriage by their very different temperaments; she also reveals how literature stood at the center of the Frost children's education.

Mertins, Louis, *Robert Frost: Life and Talks-Walking.* Norman: University of Oklahoma Press, 1965. This volume provides an uncritical account of the author's lengthy relationship with Frost. While it includes many of Frost's anecdotes about his life and art, it suffers from the inaccuracies that abounded in the poet's multiple versions of events. Nonetheless, the vitality of Frost's personality emerges in his conversations with Mertins.

Pritchard, William H. *Frost: A Literary Life Reconsidered.* New York: Oxford University Press, 1984. Pritchard's study is the fullest effort yet undertaken to redress the imbalance many believe Thompson's biography has introduced into the discussion of Frost the poet. He criticizes Thompson for his harsh interpretation of Frost's character and his heavy-handed analysis of the poet's style. His own method approaches the man through his art; he investigates each volume of Frost's poetry as an aesthetic whole and elucidates the events of his life during the period in which each was written. His critical focus remains on the evolution of Frost's poetic voice, and he employs the writer's notebooks, letters and talks to support his analysis. This biography elaborates Pritchard's earlier study of Frost in *Lives of the Modern Poets* (New York: Oxford University Press, 1980).

Reeve, F. D. *Robert Frost in Russia.* Boston: Atlantic-Little, Brown, 1964. Reeve documents Frost's 1962 visit to the Soviet Union as an emissary of the State Department. Stewart Udall published "Robert Frost's Last Adventure" in *The New York Times Magazine,* 11 June 1972, to provide his eye-witness account of those events.

Sutton, William A. ed. *Newdick's Season of Frost: An Interrupted Biography of Robert Frost.* Albany: State University of New York Press, 1976. This volume draws upon the files of Professor Robert Spangler Newdick of Ohio State University, whose friendship with Frost extended from 1934 to 1939. Newdick composed the first thirteen chapters of a tentative biography before his death in 1939; the bulk of the text contains research information.

Thompson, Lawrance, *Robert Frost: The Early Years, 1874–1915* (1966); *Robert Frost: The Years of Triumph, 1915–1938* (1970); *Robert Frost: The Later Years, 1938–1963* (completed by R. H. Winnick in 1976). New York: Holt, Rinehart and Winston. Having met Frost while still a college student, Thompson was chosen in 1939 as the poet's official biographer. His decades-long association with Frost, combined with his exhaustive scholarly investigation and documentation, make this biography the centerpiece for any discussion of

Frost's life. Thompson approaches his subject without the sentimentality of so many of the memoirists, and his dissection of Frost's public image has produced a firestorm of debate. Thompson sets straight the facts of Frost's life and deliberately demythologizes Frost's self-created mask by exposing the darker facets of his personality—his petty jealousies, his tendency toward self-pity, his harshness within the family circle. Frost's agnosticism and his hunger for public acclaim receive attention in this narrative, as do the numerous personal tragedies of Frost's life. Biographical information is carefully integrated with poetic output to allow Thompson new interpretations of many poems. In 1981, Edward Connery Lathem edited a one-volume abridgement of this work entitled *Robert Frost: A Biography* (New York: Holt, Rinehart and Winston).

Autobiographical Sources

Other essential sources for information about Frost's life and art include several collections of correspondence. *Selected Letters of Robert Frost,* edited by Lawrance Thompson (New York: Holt, Rinehart and Winston, 1964), contains some 566 letters written to 123 persons. The book captures his conversational and idiomatic prose style and provides a corrective to any simple reading of Frost as either sainted bard or maniacal egotist. *The Letters of Robert Frost to Louis Untermeyer* (New York: Holt, Rinehart and Winston, 1963) collects some 270 letters and telegrams spanning nearly fifty years. In them Frost reveals himself honestly, demonstrating the complexity of his personality without subterfuge. Many of the letters contain drafts of poems later published in very different form; others offer memorable remarks on poetic technique. *Family Letters of Robert and Elinor Frost,* edited by Arnold Grade (Albany: State University of New York Press, 1972), contains 182 letters not published in Thompson's volume, 133 of which were written by Frost, 50 by his wife. This collection represents most of the remaining family correspondence.

Several important books provide a look at Frost's own critical commentaries on his art. *Interviews with Robert Frost,* edited by Edward Connery Lathem, collects the major interviews conducted with Frost from 1915 until just before his death in 1963. *Selected Prose of Robert Frost,* edited by Hyde Cox and Edward Connery Lathem (New York: Collier Books, 1968), contains Frost's major prose statements about poetry and other American poets. Reginald L. Cook has compiled two valuable collections of Frost's remarks in "Robert Frost's Asides on His Poetry" (*American Literature,* January 1948) and "Frost on Frost: The Making of Poems" (*American Literature,* March 1956).

Overview of Critical Sources

The effort of critics to elucidate Frost's *oeuvre* has grown steadily since the publication of his first book of verse. Among the controversies energizing discussions of Frost is the question of his status within the pantheon of modern poets. The revisionist criticism prominent since the poet's death has helped to separate the myth of Frost from the dynamics of the poetry itself, and as such has generated exciting new interpretive works. Concern with Frost's religious belief, as well as with his debt to literary forebears, both English and American, continues to prompt scholarly examination.

Evaluation of Selected Book-Length Critical Studies

Brower, Reuben, *The Poetry of Robert Frost: Constellations of Intention.* New York: Oxford University Press, 1963. Brower offers an incisive commentary on Frost's imaginative debt to and divergence from William Wordsworth and Ralph Waldo Emerson. He examines Frost's nature poetry in the light of those poets' response to the natural world, and distinguishes Frost the sceptical naturalist from the more transcendental Wordsworth and Emerson.

Kemp, John C. *Robert Frost and New England: The Poet as Regionalist.* Princeton: Princeton University Press, 1979. Kemp continues the reevaluation of Frost's public image by examining the Yankee regionalism so regularly associated with him. Kemp demonstrates that Frost evolved his Yankee persona to build upon the critical response given his work in England. Frost was in fact an outsider to New England culture and derived his sense of pastoral from a knowledge of the classics and the poetry of the English Romantics.

Lynen, John F. *The Pastoral Art of Robert Frost.* New Haven: Yale University Press, revised ed. 1964. A thorough analysis of Frost as a nature poet, this study sees the pastoral form as central to Frost's shaping of his poetic materials. The rural world is the framework for his artistic investigations into the nature of reality. Frost transforms his regional subject, New England, into a mythic and universal imaginative Arcadia, but he does so with decidedly modernist systems of belief and perception.

Nitchie, George W. *Human Values in the Poetry of Robert Frost: A Study of a Poet's Convictions.* Durham, NC: Duke University Press, 1960. Nitchie synthesizes all the attacks leveled at Frost by critics who fault his provincialism, spiritual drifting and reactionary politics. His own reading of Frost presents the poet as incoherent, evasive and anti-intellectual. Nitchie's study articulates the argument against Frost as a major modern poet.

Poirier, Richard, *Robert Frost: The Work of Knowing.* New York: Oxford University Press, 1977. Poirier's study is considered one of the most illuminating analyses of Frost yet to appear. He uncovers the philosophical profundity too often overlooked in Frost's work because of its deceptive simplicity, and delineates the influence of William James and Pragmatism upon Frost's poetic vision. Poirier also investigates Frost's formalist preoccupations.

Thompson, Lawrance, *Fire and Ice.* New York: Russell & Russell, 1942. Thompson's work was crucial in redefining the terms of Frost criticism by focusing attention upon the aesthetic theories and accomplishments of Frost the poet. His close scrutiny of Frost's canny use of metaphor leads him to characterize the poet as "a self-styled synecdochist."

Other Sources

Cox, James M. ed. *Robert Frost: A Collection of Critical Essays.* Englewood Cliffs, NJ: Prentice-Hall, 1962. Cox's selection provides many essayists who have played a major part in the critical controversy surrounding Frost's reputation, among them Yvor Winters, Malcolm Cowley, Randall Jarrell and Lionel Trilling.

Gerber, Philip L. ed. *Critical Essays on Robert Frost.* Boston: G. K. Hall, 1982. This volume includes an introductory overview of the history of Frost criticism. It also contains a selection of reviews and a number of essays written by important figures in the debate over Frost's status as a modern poet.

Greiner, Donald, *Robert Frost: The Poet and His Critics.* Chicago: The American Library Association, 1974. This book-length study describes and evaluates the major scholarly material available on Frost the man and Frost the poet.

Lentricchia, Frank and Melissa Christensen Lentricchia. *Robert Frost: A Bibliography, 1913–1974.* Metuchen, NJ: The Scarecrow Press, 1976.

Tharpe, Jac, ed. *Frost: Centennial Essays I, II, III.* Jackson: University Press of Mississippi, 1974, 1976, 1978. These essays were collected in honor of the centennial of Frost's birth. Compiled for the general reader, they represent a goodly number of the major Frost critics.

Van Egmond, Peter, ed. *The Critical Reception of Robert Frost.* Boston: G. K. Hall, 1974. This compilation lists reviews of each of Frost's works in the order of publication and itemizes Frost scholarship.

Barbara Seidman
Linfield College

JOHN GALSWORTHY
1867–1933

Author's Chronology

Born August 14, 1867, at Kingston Hill, Surrey, the second of four children and elder son of John Galsworthy III, a prosperous solicitor, and Blanche Bartleet Galsworthy, daughter of a manufacturer; *1876* sent to Saugeen preparatory school; *1881–1886* attends Harrow, distinguishing himself more as an athlete than an intellectual; *1886–1889* attends New College, Oxford, taking a degree in jurisprudence; *1890* admitted to the Bar; *1891–1893* travels widely (as he was to do throughout his life), inspecting his family's foreign investments and preparing for a career in marine law; *1893* returning to England from Adelaide, meets Joseph Conrad, his lifetime friend, then a first-mate on the *Torrens; 1897* bored with law, writes and publishes, at own expense, his first stories; *1904* death of his revered father; *1905* marries the recently-divorced wife of his first cousin, Ada Cooper Galsworthy, who had been his lover for ten years; *1906* simultaneous success of his first play, *The Silver Box,* and most famous novel, *The Man of Property; 1911* reputedly platonic affair with a dancer, Margaret Morris; *1914–1918* active support of war charities and relief efforts; *1918* returns to the subject matter of *The Man of Property,* beginning his lengthy "Forsyte" novel sequences; rejects knighthood; *1929* awarded the Order of Merit; *1932* awarded the Nobel Prize; *1933* dies of a brain tumor, January 31.

Author's Bibliography (selected)

Jocelyn, 1898 (novel); *The Island Pharisees,* 1904 (novel); *The Man of Property,* 1906 (novel); *The Country House,* 1907 (novel); *Fraternity,* 1909 (novel); *The Silver Box,* 1909 (play); *Strife,* 1909 (play); *Justice,* 1910 (play); *The Dark Flower,* 1913 (novel); *The Skin Game,* 1920 (play); *Loyalties,* 1922 (play); *The Forsyte Saga,* 1922 (collects the novels: *The Man of Property,* 1906; *In Chancery,* 1920; *To Let,* 1921); *Caravan: The Assembled Tales,* 1925; *Escape,* 1926 (play); *The Plays of John Galsworthy,* 1929; *A Modern Comedy,* 1929 (collects the novels: *The White Monkey,* 1924; *The Silver Spoon,* 1926; *Swan Song,* 1928); *End of the Chapter,* 1934 (collects the novels: *Maid in Waiting,* 1931; *Flowering Wilderness,* 1932; *One More River,* 1933); *Letters from John Galsworthy, 1900–1932,* ed. Edward Garnett, 1934; "The Letters," in *The Life and Letters of John Galsworthy,* ed. H. V. Marrot, 1935.

Overview of Biographical Sources

The biographical literature on Galsworthy is both more varied and of better quality than the criticism of his works. Two memoirs by his wife Ada, *Our Dear Dogs* (London: Heinemann, 1935) and *Over the Hills and Far Away* (London:

Hale, 1937), are less informative than the "authorized" biography by H. V. Marrot (below), with whom she collaborated closely. The most valuable memoirs are by his long-time friend and fellow novelist Ralph H. Mottram, *For Some We Loved: An Intimate Portrait of Ada and John Galsworthy* (London: Hutchinson, 1956), Hermon Ould's *John Galsworthy* (London: Chapman and Hall, 1934), and two books by family members, his sister M. E. Reynolds's *Memories of John Galsworthy* (London: Hale, 1936) and his nephew Rudolf Sauter's *Galsworthy the Man: An Intimate Portrait* (London: Owen, 1967). Margaret Morris's *My Galsworthy Story* (London: Owen, 1967), contains an intriguing account of Galsworthy's apparently platonic liaison with Morris, in 1911. James Gindin's recent *The English Climate: An Excursion into a Biography of John Galsworthy* (Ann Arbor: University of Michigan Press, 1979), which mixes travelogue and interviews with persons remembering Galsworthy, contains some additional biographical materials. Popular biographies have also been published by Dudley Barker (*The Man of Principle: A View of John Galsworthy* [London: Heinemann, 1963]), and, more recently, by Catherine Dupré (*John Galsworthy* [London: Collins, 1976]). Both are readable, Barker presenting a balanced critical view of the major works and Dupré, avoiding critical commentary, incorporating the affair with Morris into her narrative. Neither is as uncritically eulogistic as Marrot.

Evaluation of Selected Biographies

Marrot, H. V. *The Life and Letters of John Galsworthy.* London: Heinemann, 1935. Despite its early date, admiring perspective, and ignorance or concealment of some materials (e.g., the Morris "affair"), Marrot's is still the standard biography. Marrot has the advantage of access to numerous personal documents, provided by Galsworthy's wife Ada, which have since been lost or destroyed. Adding to his volume's documentary value is his edition of Galsworthy's letters, which is appended, and his citation of numerous additional letters and diary entries throughout. Marrot does not, however, offer any critical observations on Galsworthy's writings.

Autobiographical Sources

Galsworthy wrote no autobiography, and remarkably few personal reminiscences are found in his numerous collections of nonfiction. His diaries for the years 1910–1918 have been preserved, but have not yet been published (except in extracts, in Marrot, above). The greatest sources of autobiographical information are Galsworthy's novels, particularly those published through *The Man of Property* and the entire Forsyte sequence.

Overview of Critical Sources

Despite considerable popular success during his lifetime, as both novelist and playwright, Galsworthy has never enjoyed the critical attention and favor given to the writers with whom he is frequently associated, such as Arnold Bennett or H. G. Wells, or even to many lesser writers of this century. The most representative, damaging, and influential critiques of Galsworthy's work, published by D. H. Lawrence and Virginia Woolf, and evaluated below, pinpoint the chief reasons for his low critical reputation. However, in France, Japan, and Russia, beyond the immediate influence of Lawrence's and Woolf's criticisms, Galsworthy's artistic reputation has grown. To date, the best critical studies of his drama and fiction have been published in France (see Dupont and Fréchet, below).

Evaluation of Selected Criticism

Bellamy, William, *The Novels of Wells, Bennett, and Galsworthy: 1890–1910.* New York: Barnes and Noble, 1971. pp. 88–102, 165-204. Bellamy's study concentrates on the "post-Darwinian cultural crisis" reflected in the transition from nineteenth-century to twentieth-century fiction. Selecting *Jocelyn, The Man of Property, The Country House,* and *Fraternity* for discussion, Bellamy considers Galsworthy, like Wells and Bennett, a prototype of the modern existentialist who has learned to "live with human animality."

Dupont, V. *John Galsworthy: The Dramatic Artist.* Paris: M. Didier, 1942. Dupont's is the most extensive and detailed study of Galsworthy's symbolic, naturalistic, and experimental plays, pursuing throughout his thesis that the drama demonstrates Galsworthy's "philosophical sincerity," "artistic conscientiousness," and "profound humanity."

Fisher, John C. *The World of the Forsytes.* New York: Universe Books, 1976. This lavishly illustrated, entertaining, but lightweight social history of the English upper-middle class, 1886–1926, was stimulated by the successful B.B.C. dramatizations of the Forsyte novels (1967), but discusses much more than Galsworthy's fiction.

Fréchet, Alec, *John Galsworthy: A Reassessment.* 1979. trans. Denis Mahaffey. Totowa, NJ: Barnes and Noble, 1982. Fréchet's excellent biographical sketch and systematic discussion of Galsworthy's fiction, while perhaps excessively admiring, is the most recent and best commentary on the novels. His summary of the chief themes and technical characteristics of the "Galsworthian" novel is clear and concise, and his persuasive analyses of Galsworthy's philosophic individualism, artistic pragmatism, and social criticism present a strong case for reevaluating Galsworthy's achievement.

Other Sources

Lawrence, D. H. "John Galsworthy," in *Scrutinies.* ed. Edgell Rickword. London: Wishart, 1928, pp. 51–72. Lawrence's savagely insightful attack on Galsworthy for joining the philistines whom he had earlier, so brilliantly exposed, centers on the novelist's evident, growing sympathy for the "villain" Soames Forsyte, who literally becomes the "hero" of the later Forsyte novels. Lawrence's dismissal of Galsworthy's satire as ineffectual and sentimental has only recently begun to provoke counter-argument (see Fréchet, above). This essay has been frequently reprinted and is most readily available in *Phoenix: The Posthumous Papers of D. H. Lawrence,* ed. Edward D. McDonald (New York: Viking, 1936), or in *The Selected Literary Criticism of D. H. Lawrence,* ed. Anthony Beal (New York: Viking, 1956).

Marrot, H. V. ed. *A Bibliography of the Works of John Galsworthy.* New York: Charles Scribner's Sons, 1928. Though published several years before the end of Galsworthy's career, this is still the only reasonably complete bibliography of his writings.

Mottram, Ralph H. *John Galsworthy.* 1953. 2nd ed. London: Longmans, 1963. Mottram's introduction to the "writer and his works" comments briefly on the major plays and novels. (Pamphlet.)

Stevens, Earl E. and H. Ray Stevens, eds. *John Galsworthy: An Annotated Bibliography of Writings About Him.* DeKalb: Northern Illinois University Press, 1980. The editors list, with extensive abstracts, an impressive number of reviews and studies of Galsworthy's works, published through the 1970's.

Woolf, Virginia, *Mr. Bennett and Mrs. Brown.* London: Hogarth, 1924. Although Arnold Bennett is the primary target of Woolf's influential attack on the Edwardian realists, both H. G. Wells and Galsworthy are prominently victimized by her criticism of conventional narrative techniques and unimaginative, documentary realism. This essay has been frequently reprinted, and is most readily available in Woolf's *The Captain's Death Bed* (London: Hogarth, 1950), or her *Collected Essays* (4 vols., London: Hogarth, 1966–1967).

Selected Dictionaries and Encyclopedias

Dictionary of Literary Biography, Vol. 10, Detroit: Gale Research, 1982, pp. 194–206. Fine critical overview of Galsworthy's plays.

Dictionary of Literary Biography, Vol. 34, Detroit: Gale Research, 1985, pp. 151–174. Concise biographical summary and insightful survey of Galsworthy's major fiction.

Thomas J. Rice
University of South Carolina

HAMLIN GARLAND
1860–1940

Author's Chronology

Born September 16, 1860, West Salem, Wisconsin, of Richard Hayes and Isabelle McClintock Garland, Scotch-Irish descendents; spends childhood and youth on an Iowa farm and in Ordway, South Dakota; educated in rural schools and Cedar Valley Seminary, graduating 1881; *1881* tours New England on foot with brother Franklin; after securing and holding a land claim in North Dakota for a year, returns East to attend Boston University, but is unable to enroll; begins writing and lecturing; publishes first "significant" piece, "The Western Corn-Husking" in *American Magazine; 1887* on a visit home writes "Mrs. Ripley's Trip," later included in first book *Main-Travelled Roads* (*1891*); back in Boston joins Anti-Poverty Society, coming under the influence of *Arena* editor Benjamin O. Flowers, publisher of Garland's story "A Prairie Heroine"; returns to West Salem upon his mother's illness and younger sister's death; travels West several times seeking new locales and character types for his writing; *1899* marries Zulime Taft, fathers two daughters; moves to Chicago; *1915* moves his family to New York; receives four honorary doctorates, a Pulitzer Prize for the autobiographical *A Daughter of the Middle Border* (*1921*), and *1918* elected to board of directors of American Academy of Arts and Letters; *1930* moves to Los Angeles; *1940* dies there of a cerebral hemorrhage March 4.

Author's Bibliography (selected)

Main-Travelled Roads, 1891 (stories); *Crumbling Idols,* 1894 (essays); *A Little Norsk,* 1892 (novel); *Rose of Dutcher's Coolly,* 1895 (novel); *The Captain of the Gray-Horse Troop,* 1902 (novel); *A Son of the Middle Border,* 1914 (autobiography); *A Daughter of the Middle Border,* 1921 (autobiography).

Overview of Biographical Sources

Book-length biographies of Garland are scarce. Standard sources, such as Stanley J. Kunitz and Howard Haycraft, eds., *Twentieth Century Authors* (New York: H. W. Wilson, 1942), provide useful chronologies. Unpublished dissertations examining his life or aspects of it are also available, but the two most recent and most-often cited book-length biographies are by Jean Holloway and Donald Pizer.

Evaluation of Selected Biographies

Holloway, Jean, *Hamlin Garland: A Biography.* Austin: University of Texas, 1960. Holloway enjoyed the cooperation of Garland's two daughters and the use of the UCLA Garland collection in preparing this biography, which includes family photographs of Garland from childhood to old age. It begins with

Garland in Boston in 1884 and traces his self-study, lecturing career, literary associations, and family relationships, concluding with his death in 1940.

Pizer, Donald, *Hamlin Garland's Early Work and Career.* Berkeley: University of California Press, 1960. This book traces Garland's early career from 1884 to 1895. It examines influences on his writing, and his personal drives and motivations, showing how and why his early career took the direction it did.

Autobiographical Sources

Garland's autobiographical quartet chronicles his family's life from his father's 1850 move from Maine to Wisconsin (in *Trailmakers of the Middle Border,* 1926) to Garland's transplantation back East in 1915 (in *Backtrailers from the Middle Border,* 1928). *Trailmakers,* being a fictionalized, romanticized version of Garland's father's early life, has less reliably factual information than the other books of the quartet. *Backtrailers* describes the commercial success of Garland's career, his two-year sojourn in England with his family, and the eventual break-up of his family unit when his two daughters marry. *A Son of the Middle Border* (1914) picks up where *Trailmakers* leaves off, describing both Garland's mother's family and the Garlands as they settle first in Iowa, then Dakota. It covers Garland's childhood, his early schooling and enrollment in and graduation from Cedar Valley Seminary, his first trip east, his involvement with the Anti-Poverty Society, and his early writing career. *A Daughter of the Middle Border* (1921) details his marriage to Zulime Taft, his daughters' births and childhood, their life in Chicago and West Salem. As it describes his association with such literary figures as Henry James and William Dean Howells, it also reveals his gradual disenchantment with the Midwest as a home and as a setting for his fiction.

Four other autobiographical books, based on notebooks and records Garland had kept since 1885, detail his literary career and associations and serve to place Garland among his literary contemporaries. They are very useful in revealing his sometimes grand, sometimes petty eccentricities, delineating an often intriguing personality. *Roadside Meetings* (1930) and *Companions on the Trail* (1931) deal with the years from 1884 to 1914. *My Friendly Contemporaries* (1931) and *Afternoon Neighbors* (1934) are laden with anecdotes about his friendships and associations with other celebrated figures of his time. These volumes might be more valuable for the views they give of Garland's contemporaries than of the view they give of him.

Overview of Critical Sources

Critics have been most concerned with Garland's contributions to developing "naturalism" through his early short and long fiction, and with his penchant for reform propaganda. His commercially successful Western novels have received little attention, although *The Captain of the Gray-Horse Troop* is occasionally considered. The best critical material on Garland, outside of scholarly articles in such journals as *American Literature,* is to be found in three enduring sources.

Evaluation of Selected Criticism

Parrington, Vernon Louis, *Main Currents in American Thought.* New York: Harcourt, Brace, and Company, 1930. Vol. III. Chapter 3. "Hamlin Garland and the Middle Border" devotes 12 pages to Garland's literary and intellectual antecedents and analyzes his best-known novels and short stories. His theory of veritism is compared to realism and naturalism.

Pattee, Fred L. *The Development of the American Short Story.* New York: Harpers, 1923. A very early but still highly recommended source, Pattee's book contains critical commentary on the early short stories, particularly as they represent the trend toward realism.

Spiller, Robert, *et al. Literary History of the United States.* 3rd ed. rev. New York: Macmillan Company, 1963. Chapter 62, "Toward Naturalism in Fiction," discusses Garland's role in shaping modern American fiction, addressing particularly *Main-Travelled Roads, Rose of Dutcher's Coolly,* and the Middle Border autobiographical books.

Selected Dictionaries and Encyclopedias

Critical Survey of Long Fiction, Salem Press, 1983. Brief biography. Analysis of novels *A Spoil of Office, A Little Norsk, Rose of Dutcher's Coolly,* and *The Captain of the Gray-Horse Troop.*

Critical Survey of Short Fiction, Salem Press, 1981. Brief biography. Analysis of several short stories, including "A Branch Road," "Under the Lion's Paw," and "The Return of the Private."

Jane L. Ball
Wilberforce University

GEORGE GASCOIGNE
1539–1577

Author's Chronology

Born 1539 in Cardington, Bedfordshire, England, of a well-to-do landowner; as an adolescent begins his education at Cambridge but does not complete a degree; *1555* begins legal studies at Gray's Inn; *1558* leaves Gray's Inn to seek illusive advancement at court; *1561* marries widow Elizabeth Breton; *1566* *Jocasta* and *Supposes* are performed at Gray's Inn, where the poet is again studying law; by this time his fortunes are in ruin; *1572* volunteers as a gentleman-soldier in the Holland wars; while in England to supervise publication of *A Hundreth Sundry Flowers,* is appointed to Parliament but returns to Holland when his creditors oppose his being seated; *1574–1575* returns to England to republish his first book in a revised version, *The Posies; 1575–1577* publishes various moral works; his prospects improve as he receives some court employment; *1577* after an illness of some months, dies on October 7 in Stamford, Lincolnshire, England.

Author's Bibliography (selected)

Supposes: A Comedy Written in the Italian Tongue by Ariosto, 1566 (play); *Jocasta, A Tragedy Written in Greek By Euripides,* 1566 (play, coauthored by Francis Kinwelmarsh); *A Hundreth Sundry Flowers,* 1573 (original poetry); *A Discourse of the Adventures Passed by Master F. J.,* 1573 (prose narrative with interspersed poems); *The Posies of George Gascoigne,* 1575 (revised version of *Hundreth Sundry Flowers*); "Certain Notes of Instruction Concerning the Making of Verse or Rhyme in English," 1575 (criticism); *The Glass of Government,* 1575 (original drama); *The Spoil of Antwerp,* 1576 (nonfiction); *The Steel Glass, A Satire,* 1576 (long poem); *The Drum of Doomsday* and *A Delicate Diet for Dainty-Mouthed Drunkards,* 1577 (prose tracts); *The Grief of Joy,* 1577 (long poem).

Overview of Biographical Sources

The life histories of most Elizabethan figures must be pieced together from a scattered, fragmentary record. The biographers of Gascoigne have been assisted not only by the poet's frequent autobiographical writings but also by the fact that, as a litigious and controversial man, he left relatively many references in legal documents and other records. Nevertheless, such information is fragmentary, calling for much scholarly detective work. Furthermore, imaginative interpretations must be applied as the biographer seeks to recreate the man from such records.

Evaluation of Selected Biographies

Buxton, John, *A Tradition of Poetry.* New York: St. Martin's, 1967. The third chapter of this book presents an accurate, readable, and critically acute bio-critical introduction. Sensitively interpreting the facts for a sense of the actual man and writer, this account is especially valuable for readers new to Gascoigne.

Prouty, Charles T. *George Gascoigne: Elizabethan Courtier, Soldier, and Poet.* New York: Columbia University Press, 1942. All modern accounts of Gascoigne's life are based on this book's exhaustive literary-historical scholarship. Although Prouty overstates the autobiographical significance of such works as *The Adventures of Master F. J.,* he has resolved many questions surrounding Gascoigne's marriage, legal troubles, and activities; and his derivation of a birthdate of 1539 is now generally accepted. The book's survey of Gascoigne's works contains usually accurate and always detailed expositions and valuable material on contexts and analogues, but reflects little grasp of important critical issues.

Autobiographical Sources

Threads of autobiography run throughout Gascoigne's *oeuvre.* The poet recognized significant patterns in his own experiences as he reflected on his youthful follies and the vanity of many of his life's pursuits. His autobiographical writings are honest, introspective, and critical of his times; nevertheless, one suspects that the entire, complex person remains obscured as the poet seeks near the end of his life to show himself as newly reformed, worthy of employment and patronage. In the final analysis the man remains half revealed, half hidden behind the various *personae* which he created for himself.

In his long poem "Dulce Bellum Inexpertis" Gascoigne shows himself a victim of circumstance and illusion in his Netherlands soldiering (stanzas 92–end). Another evocation of this period of his life is found in "The Green Knight's Farewell to Fancy." Many other pieces or passages seem autobiographical as they evoke a realistic world of Elizabethan society; such realism has led some critics to overstate the autobiographical elements in two amatory narratives, *The Adventures of Master F. J.* and "The Dolorous Discourses of Dan Batholomew of Bath." Perhaps his best shorter poem of autobiography, which achieves a significant self-analysis, is "Gascoigne's Woodmanship."

Gascoigne reveals many details of his personal "reformation" in the three prefatory letters to *The Posies of George Gascoigne.* These letters, together with the "Certain Notes of Instruction in the Making of Verse or Rhyme in English" which concludes that volume, give revealing insights into Gascoigne's aims and methods as a writer. He shows himself a patriot in his search for an English idiom and diction. His comments on the need for "invention" in a poem's content, metrical consistency, and perspicuity of language make an important statement of principles of Elizabethan—indeed of most pre-Romantic—poetry.

Overview of Critical Sources

Most recent commentators have sought to revise the too-simple notion of a dull or dead period in literary history between Thomas Wyatt and Edmund

Spenser. Gascoigne is now acknowledged to have been an innovator who made significant contributions and achieved his own poetic voice. One work of criticism underlies this reevaluation not only of Gascoigne but of the entire canon of Elizabethan poets: Yvor Winters, "The 16th Century Lyric in England," reprinted in *Elizabethan Poetry: Modern Essays in Criticism,* edited by Paul J. Alpers (London: Oxford University Press, 1967). Winters finds Gascoigne's achievement to be among the most important of the century for realizing a candid, morally-perceptive, immediate verse. Winters identifies Gascoigne as working within the sixteenth-century tradition of "the native plain style." The existence of such a "style," however, remains a matter of debate, while a number of commentators have stressed Gascoigne's indebtedness to eloquent—as well as "plain"—traditions and to Petrarchism.

As showing innovations in Elizabethan prose fiction, Gascoigne's *The Adventures of Master F. J.* has stimulated a considerable interest in scholarly articles, although no book-length study has given a significant treatment.

Evaluation of Selected Criticism

Guss, Donald L. *John Donne, Petrarchist.* Detroit: Wayne State University Press, 1966. A chapter on Gascoigne and the earlier English poet Thomas Wyatt finds richly contrasting styles in their uses of Italianate models. This study explores the great variety of effects and emphases made available to the century's poets by imitation of foreign models, and it resists simple oppositions between ornate and plain styles or foreign and native influences. Guss describes Gascoigne's social poetry as witty, worldy-wise, often cavalier, and showing an enjoyment of verbal and social play for their own sakes.

Johnson, Ronald C. *George Gascoigne.* New York: Twayne, 1972. This general bio-critical introduction to Gascoigne's works concentrates on his poetry, neglecting the dramatic and moralistic pieces. It is the only book-length study in addition to Prouty's. Unlike Prouty, however, Johnson seeks to demonstrate a thesis, which is that Gascoigne is best understood as a rebel against the Petrarchism and poetic artificiality popular in his day. This approach simplifies the poet's aims and especially the achievements of his social and amatory poems. The matter of Elizabethan literary imitation is more complex than can be encompassed by the partitioning of poets into Petrarchist and anti-Petrarchist "camps."

Other Sources

Helgerson, Richard, *The Elizabethan Prodigals.* Berkeley: University of California Press, 1976. Reveals Gascoigne as exemplifying a pattern of improvidence and reform in his life and writing.

Pooley, Roger, ed. *George Gascoigne: " 'The Green Knight', Selected Poetry and Prose."* Manchester: Carcanet, 1982. Presents a perceptive, brief introduction and useful notes, but edits *The Adventures of Master F. J.* too severely.

Rowe, George E., Jr. "Interpretation, Sixteenth-Century Readers, and George Gascoigne's 'The Adventures of Master F. J.' " in *ELH* 48 (1981), 271–289. A new, comprehensive article, latest in a series of studies of this fictional narrative.

Schmidt, Michael, *A Reader's Guide to Fifty British Poets.* Totowa, NJ: Barnes & Noble, 1980. Brief but critically perceptive account of the life and works.

Thompson, John, *The Founding of English Metre.* New York: Columbia University Press, 1961. Recounts the key role of Gascoigne in the evolution of poetic meter in the sixteenth century.

Selected Dictionaries and Encyclopedias

Critical Survey of Poetry, Salem Press, 1982. Concise overview of Gascoigne's life and writings, with short interpretations of key poems.

Great Writers of the English Languages: Poets, St. Martin's, 1979. Bibliography, and analyses of selected works.

Richard J. Panofsky
New Mexico Highlands University

ELIZABETH GASKELL
1810–1865

Author's Chronology

Born Chelsea, England, 1810 youngest daughter of William Stevenson, former Unitarian minister, and Elizabeth Holland Stevenson; *1811* sent to live with maternal aunt at Knutsford after mother's death; *1822–1827* attends Avonbrook School, Stratford-upon-Avon; *1832* marries William Gaskell, Unitarian minister; *1833–1846* gives birth to six children, one daughter dying at birth; *1845* only son dies of scarlet fever at age nine months; *1850* meets Charlotte Brontë; *1853* Brontë invites her to Haworth; *1854* husband becomes senior minister at Cross Street Chapel, Manchester; *1855* asked to write biography of Brontë; *1864* arranges purchase of retirement home, The Lawn, Holybourne; *1865* shortly after moving there, dies suddenly on November 10 while talking with her daughters.

Author's Bibliography (selected)

1848, *Mary Barton* (fiction); 1853 *Ruth* (fiction), *Cranford* (fiction); 1855, *North and South* (fiction); 1857 *The Life of Charlotte Brontë* (biography); 1863 *Sylvia's Lovers* (fiction); 1866 *Wives and Daughters* (fiction).

Overview of Biographical Sources

No serious full-length biographical study of Elizabeth Gaskell could be attempted until nearly a half century after her death. Her youngest daughters, having overheard Gaskell remark that she wished no life of herself to be written, refused to co-operate with would-be biographers or to release their mother's personal papers and correspondence for study. Even the information they provided for the first entry in the *Dictionary of National Biography* is incomplete and incorrect. When biographical details were included in Mrs. Ellis Chadwick's *Mrs. Gaskell: Haunts, Homes, and Stories* (1910), Meta Gaskell disputed them in a published article and insisted that the material given to Chadwick had never been intended for publication. Marianne Holland, Gaskell's oldest daughter, attempted unsuccessfully to convince her sisters to collaborate with her in writing what she saw as a much-needed biography of their mother. So adamant were the younger daughters about refusing to authorize a biography that their wills were drawn up to prevent the release of Gaskell's correspondence even after their deaths. Consequently, when Gerald Sanders began his major study *Elizabeth Gaskell* (New Haven: Yale University Press, 1929), he was legally prevented from using much of Gaskell's correspondence although her descendants wished him to do so. The expiration of these legal restrictions at mid-century led to Annette Hopkins' definitive biography *Elizabeth Gaskell: Her Life and Work* (1952). Gaskell's correspondence was finally published in 1966 and subsequent biographers, such as Arthur Pollard in *Mrs.*

Gaskell: Novelist and Biographer (1965, 1967) and Coral Lansbury in *Elizabeth Gaskell: The Novel of Social Crisis* (1975), have made extensive use of it.

Evaluation of Selected Biographies

Hopkins, Annette B. *Elizabeth Gaskell: Her Life and Work.* London: John Lehmann, 1952. Long regarded as the definitive biography of Gaskell, this book was one of the first to make use of personal papers and correspondence previously prohibited to scholars. As such, it was long thought to have exhausted available biographical materials. Hopkins' treatment is as sympathetic as it is thorough, and she is largely responsible for rescuing Gaskell from the unenviable distinction of being a minor Victorian female novelist.

Lansbury, Coral, *Elizabeth Gaskell: The Novel of Social Crisis.* London: Paul Elck, 1975; rpt. New York: Harper and Row, 1975. Although primarily interested in a re-evaluation of Gaskell the novelist, Lansbury assesses Gaskell's writings in light of the major events of her life. She adds little to Hopkins' biographical information but makes an important examination of Gaskell's Unitarianism and its influence on her writing.

Pollard, Arthur, *Mrs. Gaskell: Novelist and Biographer.* Cambridge: Harvard University Press, 1965, 1967. As co-editor of Gaskell's correspondence, Pollard uses his familiarity with this material to examine her life, her relationships with family members, especially her daughters, and her literary friendships. Although appreciative of Gaskell as individual and as author, he is more critical of her skill as a writer than is Hopkins. Pollard begins by examining her reputation among her contemporaries and concludes with an assessment of her current standing. Pollard is particularly valuable for the review of Gaskell criticism in his introduction.

Autobiographical Sources

The primary autobiographical source for the study of Gaskell's life is *Letters of Mrs. Gaskell* edited by J. A. V. Chapple and Arthur Pollard (Manchester: University of Manchester Press, 1966). This edition allows scholars access to writings of Gaskell previously unavailable due to her daughters' desire to carry out what they believed were their mother's wishes concerning this material. The *Letters of Mrs. Gaskell* supplements earlier correspondence published in *Letters of Mrs. Gaskell and Charles Eliot Norton,* edited by Jane Whitehill (Oxford: Oxford University Press, 1932) and parts of her diary published as *My Diary: The Early Years of My Daughter Marianne,* edited by Clement Shorter King (privately printed 1923).

Overview of Critical Sources

Much of the critical material written since mid-century has concerned itself with the establishment of Gaskell's "place" in Victorian literature. Highly acclaimed by her contemporaries, Gaskell's reputation suffered in comparison with other mid-Victorian novelists, so much so that she came to be regarded as a minor "female novelist." The availability of major autobiographical sources led to a renewed interest in Gaskell and an attempt to revise the general scholarly opinion of her work. In the last twenty years feminist critics have looked at Gaskell's novels to determine their role in the development of women's literature. Most critics ignore her *Life of Charlotte Brontë* although it remains an extremely important example of literary biography.

Evaluation of Selected Criticism

Beer, Patricia, *Reader, I Married Him: A Study of the Women Characters of Jane Austen, Charlotte Brontë, Elizabeth Gaskell and George Eliot.* London: Macmillan, 1974. Beer ranks Gaskell as one of the four major women writers of the nineteenth century. In this study, which involves both a biographical and a social history approach, she finds a progression in the attitudes of these four writers towards the "Woman Question" and sees Gaskell as the most typically feminine and yet also the most perceptive in her examination of the male-female relationship in her novels.

Craik, W. A. *Elizabeth Gaskell and the English Provincial Novel.* London: Methuen, 1975. Craik examines Gaskell's affinity with a group of novelists (the Brontës, Trollope, Eliot, and Hardy) who examine the Victorian world from a perspective that sees London as atypical of English life. His intention is to rescue Gaskell from her undeservedly modest reputation by assessing her development as a novelist from *Mary Barton* to *Wives and Daughters.* He finds her more of an innovator than do many earlier critics, seeing her as a writer who extends the form of the novel for later authors.

Mews, Hazel, *Frail Vessels: Woman's Role in Women's Novels from Fanny Burney to George Eliot.* London: Athlone, 1969. One of the earliest feminist critics of Gaskell's novels, Mews finds her totally representative of the average Victorian woman, dismissing Gaskell's style as typically feminine. Mews does, however, admire Gaskell for being one of the first authors to address the plight and concerns of working women in a sympathetic manner.

Showalter, Elaine, *A Literature of Their Own: British Women Novelists from Brontë to Lessing.* Princeton: Princeton University Press, 1977. In a major critical study, Showalter attempts to examine the achievements of English women novelists who do not necessarily rank with Austen or the Brontës. She places Gaskell in the first phase of the female literary tradition as a typical writer who absorbed the standards of a male-dominated culture and also slavishly imitated its artistic models.

Wright, Edgar, *Mrs. Gaskell: The Basis for Reassessment.* Oxford: Oxford University Press, 1969. Feeling that Gaskell's achievement has been oversimplified, Wright has undertaken a major re-evaluation of her work in an attempt to show that she is a much more important novelist than generally believed. He examines her artistic development and technical expertise in a discussion of all her major writings, seeing her biography of Charlotte Brontë as central to her own development as a writer.

Other Sources

Lucas, John, *The Literature of Change: Studies in the Nineteenth-Century Provincial Novel.* Sussex: Harvester Press, 1977. Sees Gaskell as a novelist who attempts to examine the effects of the Industrial Revolution on English provincial life.

Sanders, Andrew, *The Victorian Historical Novel, 1840–1880.* New York: St. Martin's, 1979. Studies Gaskell's novels from the perspective of the influence of Sir Walter Scott.

Tomlinson, T. B. *The English Middle-Class Novel.* London: Macmillan, 1979. Feels Gaskell's novels are flawed by her conventionality and sentimentality.

Victorian Fiction: A Guide to Research. Cambridge: Harvard University Press, 1964. Reviews Gaskell's biography and critical reputation with intention of suggesting possible areas of research.

Selected Dictionaries and Encyclopedias

British Writers of the Nineteenth Century, H. W. Wilson, 1936. Brief, highly laudatory biography presents a typically feminine Gaskell followed by analysis of her as a "moral" writer.

Dictionary of National Biography, Oxford University Press, 1917. First major attempt to relate Gaskell's life and work. Biographical details are incomplete and often inaccurate due to her daughters' reluctance to cooperate in any attempt to write about her life.

Great Writers of the English Language: Novelists and Prose Writers, St. Martin's, 1979. Short commentary on each of the major novels stressing difficulty in establishing Gaskell's reputation.

Mary Anne Hutchinson
Utica College of Syracuse University

JOHN GAY
1685–1732

Author's Chronology

Born in Barnstaple, Devon, and baptized at Barnstaple Old Church on September 16, 1685; *1702* apprenticed to a mercer in London; *1707* becomes secretary to Aaron Hill; *1708* publishes first poem, *Wine; 1712* appointed secretary or domestic steward to the Duchess of Monmouth; *1713* becomes a member of the Scriblerus Club; *1714* publishes *The Shepherd's Week,* which he had been encouraged by Alexander Pope to write "after the true and ancient guise of Theocritus;" upon resignation from the household of the Duchess of Monmouth, becomes secretary to Lord Clarendon and accompanies him on a diplomatic mission to the Court at Hanover; *1715 The What D'Ye Call It* performed at Drury Lane; *1716* publication of *Trivia; Or, the Art of Walking the Streets of London* brings Gay large financial return; *1717 Three Hours After Marriage,* advertised as written "by John Gay and others," performed at Drury Lane; accompanies William Pulteney, later Earl of Bath, to Aix; *1719 Acis and Galatea,* music by Handel, performed privately at Cannons, home of the Duke of Chandos; *1720* publishes *Poems on Several Occasions* through large subscription sale; loses his profits after investing them in South Sea stock; accepts patronage of Duke and Duchess of Queensberry, who become his lifelong friends; *1723* appointed Commissioner of State Lotteries; *1727* publishes *Fables,* First Series, dedicated "To His Highness, William, Duke of Cumberland;" declines appointment as gentleman-usher to Princess Louisa; *1728 The Beggar's Opera* performed at Lincoln's Inn Fields and becomes immediate theatrical and financial success; production of *Polly,* sequel to *The Beggar's Opera,* forbidden by the Duke of Grafton, then Lord Chamberlain; *1729 Polly* published through large subscription sales; Gay takes up residence with Duke and Duchess of Queensberry; *1732 Acis and Galatea* performed at Haymarket; Gay dies on December 4 and is interred in Westminster Abbey.

Author's Bibliography (selected)

Wine, 1708 (poetry); *The Mohocks,* 1712 (drama); *The Shepherd's Week,* 1714 (poetry); *The What D'Ye Call It,* 1715 (drama); *Trivia: Or, the Art of Walking the Streets of London,* 1716 (poetry); *Three Hours After Marriage,* 1717 (drama); *Poems on Several Occasions,* 2 vols. 1720; *Fables,* First Series, 1727 (poetry); *The Beggar's Opera,* 1728 (musical drama); *Polly,* 1729 (musical drama).

Overview of Biographical Sources

Perhaps because so much attention has been lavished on his most celebrated work, *The Beggar's Opera,* John Gay, the man, has received relatively little attention. Interestingly, one of the earliest biographies, that by Samuel Johnson in *Prefaces, Biographical and Critical, to the Works of the English Poets,* 10 vols. (1779), remains one of the best in its blending of biographical data and historical context. Lewis Melville's (pseudonym for Lewis S. Benjamin) *Life and Letters of John Gay* (London: D. O'Connor, 1921) presented new biographical material through Gay's then unknown letters, but the book is weakened by its rather superficial treatment of biographical detail. William Henry Irving's biography, *John Gay, Favorite of the Wits* (1940), is both sound and interesting. The work is written with style and verve and treats its subject with respect: "He was a serious artist, . . . and a serious artist is inevitably a man of character."

Evaluation of Selected Biographies

Irving, William Henry, *John Gay, Favorite of the Wits.* Durham, NC: Duke University Press, 1940. Irving examines the biographical data carefully, placing judgment upon the literary works in relation to the facts of the biography. He depicts Gay as personally honest, loyal, fastidious, affectionate and somewhat indolent. Noting that he was secretary to the Scriblerians, Irving studies Gay's satisfying relationships with Swift, Pope and Arbuthnot; he also describes Gay's association with the Queensberrys in considerable detail. Irving considers Gay a first-rate songster and believes that he "epitomizes the art of poetry as men practiced it in his time." The biography concludes with a useful account of Gay's popularity from the eighteenth to the twentieth centuries.

Johnson, Samuel, "John Gay," in *Prefaces, Biographical and Critical, to the Works of the English Poets.* 10 vols. London: J. Nichols, 1779. Johnson's brief account of Gay's life is valuable in examining all facets of his experience: his personal entanglements, his literary successes and failures, and his reactions to both. Discussions of Gay's literature derive naturally from the circumstances of his life, and the biography is accordingly laced with Johnson's critical judgments. Johnson sees the essential humanity of the man: he describes Gay as one who alternated between hope and the depression which followed if his hopes were disappointed. While Johnson admits that this is not the makeup of a hero, he perceives that "it may naturally imply something more generally welcome, a soft and civil companion. Whoever is apt to hope good from others is diligent to please them. . . ."

Autobiographical Source

Burgess, C. F. ed. *The Letters of John Gay.* Oxford: Clarendon Press, 1966. This slender volume of eighty-one letters seeks to provide a convenient single source for all of Gay's extant letters. Letters to Gay are not included. The letters, many of them to Swift, others to Pope, to Mrs. Howard, to Thomas Parnell and to other friends, confirm the impression of the man that has evolved from eighteenth century writings and that has been documented by recent scholarship: that of a talented, personable, but somewhat indolent man. In a letter to Thomas Parnell, Gay states the chief reason for the paucity of letters in the collection: "I don't care for the trouble of writing." Nevertheless, *The Letters of John Gay* provides valuable insights into the life and personality of an important literary figure.

Overview of Critical Sources

During the last sixty years, considerable critical energy has been directed to the works of Gay. William Schultz's study, *Gay's Beggar's Opera: Its Content, History & Influence* (New Haven: Yale University Press, 1923), has been followed by assessments of his overall accomplishments in poetry in James Sutherland's essay, "John Gay" in *Pope and His Contemporaries: Essays Presented to George Sherburn* (Oxford: Clarendon Press, 1949), and in Adina Forsgren's *John Gay: Poet "of a Lower Order"* (1971). Only two critics have surveyed the whole of Gay's work, Oliver Warner in a brief sketch, *John Gay: Writers and Their Work,* #171 (London: British Council Pamphlet, 1964), and Patricia Meyer Spacks in a book-length study, *John Gay* (1965).

Evaluation of Selected Criticism

Brown, Wallace Cable, "Gay: Pope's Alter Ego," in *The Triumph of Form.* Chapel Hill: The University of North Carolina Press, 1948. In a larger study of the variations in the use of the heroic couplet made by eighteenth-century poets after Pope, Brown makes a careful analysis of Gay's handling of the form. He considers the balance of syntax and the propriety of sound and sense of primary importance. Under these two large umbrellas, elements such as end-stop, the placement of the caesura, alliteration, the handling of consonant and vowel music, parallelism, and antithesis are scrutinized. Brown notes that, in Gay's poetry, the full effects of the couplet appear in larger units, the couplets grouping themselves into a kind of verse paragraph, which is unified by the interplay of thought, syntax, cadence and music. In his judgment, Gay's handling of the heroic couplet, along with Pope's, most closely approximates the neoclassic norm. Brown concludes: "Gay's management of the heroic couplet is always skillful and, at its best, excellent."

Forsgren, Adina, *John Gay: Poet "Of a Lower Order."* Stockholm: Natur och Kultur, 1971. This careful study of Gay's poetry places it within its historic and cultural context. Forsgren maintains that Gay wrote neither panegyric poetry nor literary caricature. Rather, he chose a middle path between those extremes, writing pleasant comic verse which employed realistic characters and situations. Forsgren believes that Gay was committed in his poetry to teach morality "of some sort," to correct manners, and to profess his political allegiance. Approximately two-thirds of the book is devoted to a survey of the historical and cultural background and a treatment of individual poems; the last third is a discussion of "some general features" of his poetry; namely, characters, modes, machines, and descriptions.

Noble, Yvonne, ed. *Twentieth Century Interpretations of The Beggar's Opera.* Englewood Cliffs, NJ: Prentice-Hall, 1975. In this slender volume, Noble has collected nine of the most stimulating and provocative essays on *The Beggar's Opera* written by modern critics, and has written an introductory essay. Included are Ian Donaldson's consideration of the methods of comic levelling and inversion; Roger Fiske's discussion of the practices of Italian opera which were mocked in *The Beggar's Opera;* and a selection from Bertrand Bronson's classic essay, "*The Beggar's Opera,*" and a study of the quality of irony in the play.

Spacks, Patricia Meyer, *John Gay.* New York: Twayne, 1965. Spacks discusses Gay's work in terms of his attempt to master the use of the persona. The persona was a necessary element in his work, she believes, because his instincts were essentially those of the entertainer and lyric singer. Mastery of the persona, she argues, enabled Gay to assume the authority of a commentator, which authority was demanded of the writer at that time. His most successful use of the persona occurred in *The Beggar's Opera* and in *The Fables,* in which the use of the simple man as persona allowed Gay to reveal and order his own complexity.

Other Sources

Armens, Sven M. *John Gay, Social Critic.* New York: King's Crown Press, 1954. Armens argues for the seriousness of Gay's purpose as a writer and sees *The Beggar's Opera* as the fullest expression of Gay's criticism of his time.

Gagey, Edmond McAdoo, *Ballad Opera.* New York: Columbia University Press, 1937. Gagey studies the genre which developed from *The Beggar's Opera.* He appends a useful bibliography of ballad operas, both published and unpublished, and includes an extended discussion of possible sources of *The Beggar's Opera.*

Schultz, William Eben, *Gay's Beggar's Opera: Its Content, History and Influence.* New Haven: Yale University Press, 1923. This is a carefully researched study that provides much valuable information on identifying sources of the play, sketching its history through the twentieth century, and suggesting the extent of its influence.

Warner, Oliver, *John Gay: Writers and Their Work,* #171. London: British Council Pamphlet, 1964. This briskly written, brief study gives a sympathetic view of Gay and his literature.

Phyllis T. Dircks
Long Island University

ALLEN GINSBERG
1926

Author's Chronology

Born June 3, 1926, Newark, N.J. of Louis Ginsberg, the lyric poet and teacher and his Russian émigrée wife Naomi; *1943* leaves Paterson High School at age 17 to attend Columbia University; is dismissed from Columbia in *1943* for allegedly scrawling anti-Semitic slogans on a classroom window and for alleged sexual improprieties; holds a variety of odd jobs including welder, dishwasher, literary agent, night porter, and newspaper reporter; *1948* readmitted to Columbia, graduating with a B.A. and A– scholastic average; remains at Columbia for graduate study; experiences mystic visions of William Blake in sublet apartment in Harlem; *1949* undergoes psychiatric counseling followed by an eight-month stay at Rockland (New York) State Hospital; *1950* is a book reviewer for *Newsweek; 1951* serves as market research consultant in New York and San Francisco; relocates to San Francisco *1954; 1956* "obscenity trial" over *Howl* begins (ruled not obscene by courts in *1957*); *1957–1959* travels to the Arctic, Tangier, Venice, Amsterdam, Paris, London, and Oxford; begins series of poetry readings at Harvard, Columbia and Princeton; *1960* experiments with Yage drug in the Peruvian jungles and experiences terrifying visions of a Death/God; *1961* journeys to the Far East and meets with Martin Buber and various Oriental holy men; appears in motion picture *Pull My Diasy; 1962* appears in motion picture *Guns of the Trees;* undergoes basic change toward existence as recorded in the poem "The Change"; tours Europe again and is crowned *Kral Majales* (King of May) by Czech students before being expelled from the country; *1965* wins Guggenheim Fellowship; *1966* wins National Endowment for the Arts Grant; *1967* appears in motion picture *Chappaqua; 1969* National Institute of Arts and Letters Award; *1974* National Book Award for *The Fall of America; 1979* National Arts Club Gold Medal; signs lucrative contract with Harper & Row for five volumes of future works.

Author's Bibliography (selected)

Howl and Other Poems, 1956; *Empty Mirror: Early Poems,* 1961; *Kaddish and Other Poems: 1958–1960,* 1961; *Reality Sandwiches: 1953–1960,* 1963 (poems); *The Yage Letters* (correspondence between Ginsberg and William S. Burroughs), 1963; *Wichita Vortex Sutra,* 1967 (poems); *T.V. Baby Poems: 1961–1967,* 1968; *Planet News: 1961–1967,* 1968 (poems); *Ankor Wat,* 1968 (poems); *Airplane Dreams: Compositions from Journals,* 1968 (poems); *Notes After an Evening with William Carlos Williams,* 1970 (poems); *Indian Journals: March 1962–May 1963,* 1970 (prose); *The Fall of America: Poems of These States: 1965–1971,* 1972; *The Gates of Wrath: Rhymed Poems: 1948–1952,* 1972; *Iron Horse* (poetry), 1974; *Allen Verbatim: Lectures on Poetry, Politics,*

Consciousness, 1974; *The Visions of the Great Rememberer,* 1974 (prose); *Chicago Trial Testimony,* 1974 (prose); *First Blues: Rags, Ballads & Harmonium Songs: 1971–74,* 1975; *Journals: Early Fifties–Early Sixties,* 1977; *Poems All Over the Place: Mostly Seventies,* 1978; *Mind Breaths: Poems 1972–1977,* 1978; *Plutonium Ode,* 1982 (poem); *Collected Poems 1947–1980,* 1984.

Overview of Biographical Sources

Because he is a cultural phenomenon as well as a poet, Ginsberg's life continues to be unusually well-documented in the popular press, although care must be taken to separate sensationalist distortions from authentic fact. The first formal biographical treatment is Jane Kramer's *Allen Ginsberg in America* (1969), a popular, journalistic profile of the poet and the sixties Beat milieu. Eric Mottram's *Allen Ginsberg in the Sixties* (Brighton, Sussex: Unicorn Bookshop, 1972) provides some updating to that along with good criticism of the poetry. John Tytell's *Naked Angels, The Lives and Literature of the Beat Generation* (1976) contains two substantial sections specifically addressed to Ginsberg. Among the standard biographical sources are Thomas Wiloch's account in *Contemporary Authors* (New Revised Series), Thomas Merrill's *Allen Ginsberg* (New York: Twayne, 1969), and Christine Tysh's *Allen Ginsberg* [in French] (Paris: Seghers, 1974), but perhaps the frankest and most interestingly authentic biography comes from Ginsberg's own "lectures," letters, and interviews [see *Autobiographical Sources*].

Evaluation of Selected Biographies

Kramer, Jane, *Allen Ginsberg in America.* New York: Random House, 1968. This is an informal expansion of Kramer's earlier *New Yorker* profile on the poet which provides biography but features a contemporary narrative description of his present and recent past in the later sixties. It is entertainingly written and generally maintains an objectivity not always common in commentaries on Beat figures.

Tytell, John, *Naked Angels, The Lives and Literature of the Beat Generation.* New York: McGraw-Hill, 1976. Tytell provides close biographical treatments of William Burroughs, Jack Kerouac and Ginsberg, including a number of photographs of Ginsberg and friends. Two long sections are specifically addressed to Ginsberg. This is an important, well-written, well-researched book.

Autobiographical Sources

Ginsberg is probably one of the most interviewed literary figures in the twentieth century and one of the reasons may be that he is so consistently frank and open about the details of his private life. Thomas Clark's *Paris Review* interview (Spring, 1966) is a good case in point and an excellent place to begin for a sense of the poet's life and thought. *Allen Verbatim* (New York: McGraw-

Hill, 1974) is precisely what its title suggests: a wide-ranging compilation of taped interviews, lectures, and conversations on all subjects. James McKenzie's "Interview" in *The Beat Journey* (*unspeakable visions of the individual*), (1978) is autobiographically revealing, and Paul Portugs' *The Visionary Poetics of Allen Ginsberg* (Santa Barbara, CA: Ross-Erikson, 1979) contains three "conversations" with Ginsberg. Allen Young's *Gay Sunshine Interview: Allen Ginsberg* (Bolinas, CA, 1974) provides candid expressions of the poet's views on controversial personal subjects such as homosexuality. Two published collections of letters, *To Eberhart From Ginsberg: A Letter About Howl* (Lincoln, MA, 1976) and *As Ever: The Collected Correspondence of Allen Ginsberg & Neal Cassady,* ed. Barry Gifford (Berkeley, 1977), are also helpful in filling out the complexity of Ginsberg's life and times. Ginsberg wrote an interesting "Autobiographical Precis" for Michelle P. Kraus' *Allen Ginsberg: An Annotated Bibliography 1969–1977* (1980) which contains some biographical "addenda" to the official record.

Overview of Critical Sources

Thomas Merrill's *Allen Ginsberg* (1969) is the first major critical study of the poet. Eric Mottram's shorter forty-page monograph *Allen Ginsberg in the Sixties* (1971) discusses the value and development of his work in the sixties. Christine Tysh provides a Gallic view of Ginsberg's achievement [in French] in *Allen Ginsberg* (Paris: Seqhers, 1974). *The Visionary Poetics of Allen Ginsberg* (Santa Barbara, CA: Ross-Erikson, 1979) by Paul Portugs is as much interested in religion, politics and drugs as in the poetry. An interesting socio-literary discussion of Ginsberg's work emerges in *Howl and the Censor,* ed. J. W. Ehrlich (San Carlos, CA: Nourse Publishing, 1961). Excellent shorter discussions of Ginsberg's work appear in M. L. Rosenthal's *The New Poets* (New York: Macmillan, 1967) and Stephen Stepanchev's *American Poetry Since 1945* (New York: Harper Colophon Books, 1967).

Evaluation of Selected Criticism

Merrill, Thomas F. *Allen Ginsberg.* New York: Twayne, 1969. Merrill provides a good introduction to the philosophical and literary concerns of the Beat Generation and places Ginsberg in that context. The study is consciously and deliberately objective in its determination to "avoid the carnival aspects of Ginsberg's career . . . and to focus upon the question of his worth as a poet." *Empty Mirror, Howl, Kaddish, Reality Sandwiches,* "Wichita Vortex Sutra," and "The Change" are analyzed in detail.

Mottram, Eric, *Allen Ginsberg in the Sixties.* Brighton, England: Unicorn Bookshop, 1972. A shorter 40-page monograph which sympathetically urges that the "theme of power and paranoia is the center of Ginsberg's concern. . . . The Beat had a violent freshness which barely concealed a suicidal retreat into self-exploration and cosmic consciousness." Ginsberg cites this as "one of the few serious textual exams of what I've written."

Other Sources

Bartlett, Lee, ed. *The Beats: Essays in Criticism.* Jefferson, NC: McFarland, 1981. Contains general commentary on Ginsberg and other Beat figures along with specific essays and extensive bibliographies. Contains essay on Ginsberg's *Reality Sandwiches.*

Charters, Ann, *Scenes Along the Road.* New York: Gotham Book Mart, 1970. A photographic study of Ginsberg and other Beat writers containing three poems and a commentary by Ginsberg.

Dowden, George, *A Bibliography of Works by Allen Ginsberg, October, 1943 to July 1, 1967.* San Francisco: City Lights Books, 1971. A detailed catalog of all Ginsberg's works including films, paintings, drawings, translations, etc. Useful, but now out of date.

Kraus, Michelle P. *Allen Ginsberg: An Annotated Bibliography, 1969–1977.* Metuchen, NJ: Scarecrow Press, 1980. Supersedes Dowden's work and provides a totally comprehensive catalog of Ginsberg's works, including the poet's own introductory "Contemplation on Bibliography." An invaluable scholarly tool.

Selected Dictionaries and Encyclopedias

Contemporary Authors, Gale Research, 1980. Brief biography and critical commentary. Selected bibliography.

Dictionary of Literary Biography, Vol. 16, Gale Research, 1983. Comprehensive overview of Ginsberg's life and works with selected bibliography. See also the Ginsberg entry in *DLB 5, American Poets Since World War II.*

Thomas F. Merrill
University of Delaware

GEORGE GISSING
1857–1903

Author's Chronology

Born November 22, 1857, Wakefield, England of Margaret Bedford-Gissing and Thomas Gissing, pharmacist, agnostic, amateur botanist, and local liberal politician; December *1870* father Thomas dies; January *1873* enters Owens College on scholarship; early *1876* meets Marianne Helen ("Nell") Harrison; June *1876* is expelled from Owens College for theft and serves a one-month prison sentence; September *1876* travels to United States; March *1877* publishes first short story, "The Sins of the Fathers," in the *Chicago Tribune;* October *1877* returns to England, moves to London to begin his literary career; October *1879* marries Nell; *1880* publishes first novel, *Workers in the Dawn;* April *1886* travels in France; March *1888* wife Nell, destitute and separated from her husband, dies as a result of alcoholism; September *1888* to March *1889* travels in Europe; *1890* meets Edith Underwood; February *1891* marries Edith, September *1898* leaves Edith after years of discord, travels in Italy and throughout Europe; July *1898* meets Gabrielle Fleury in France; May *1899* marries Gabrielle though not divorced from Edith, lives in France; May *1901,* his health deteriorating, revisits England, convalesces in Suffolk sanitorium; September *1901* returns to France; January *1903* publishes *The Private Papers of Henry Ryecroft;* December 28, 1903 dies of myocarditis in southern France.

Author's Bibliography (selected novels)

The Unclassed, 1884; *Demos,* 1886; *The Nether World,* 1889; *New Grub Street,* 1891; *Born in Exile,* 1892; *The Odd Women,* 1893; *In the Year of Jubilee,* 1894; *Sleeping Fires,* 1895; *The Paying Guest,* 1896; *The Whirlpool,* 1897; *The Private Papers of Henry Ryecroft,* 1903; *Will Warburton,* 1905.

Overview of Biographical Sources

From the time of the publication of his first short story in March 1877, George Gissing referred to his own experience as material for his writing of fiction. Thus a thorough understanding of the major events of Gissing's life is essential for a study of his works. Gissing's close friend Morley Roberts published the first book-length biography of the author, *The Private Papers of Henry Maitland* (1912); H. G. Wells reminisced about him in *Experiment in Autobiography* (London: Gollancz, 1934); and Mabel Collins Donnelly provided an early critical biography, *George Gissing: Grave Comedian* (Cambridge, MA: Harvard University Press, 1954). Since 1960, with the renewal of scholarly interest in the author, two fine biographies have appeared, Jacob Korg's *George Gissing: A Critical Biography* (1963) and John Halperin's *Gissing: A Life in*

Books (1982). Both of the latter give thorough and useful accounts of the novelist's life and its importance for his *oeuvre.*

Evaluation of Selected Biographies

Halperin, John, *Gissing: A Life in Books.* New York: Oxford University Press, 1982. Halperin suggests that Gissing's novels consider primarily sex, money, and class, the three areas that produced the most concern for the author in his own life. He contends that Gissing believed that his problems in marriage were due to these three factors, a belief that translated itself into the author's extensive and very personal treatment of marriage in most of his novels. According to Halperin, Gissing's choice of subject matter is characteristically Victorian, with frequent excursions into his own experience; he was a man of his time who drew on autobiographical materials regularly.

Korg, Jacob, *George Gissing: A Critical Biography.* Seattle: University of Washington Press, 1963. Korg provides a thorough, scholarly, in-depth critical biography which considers the great majority of Gissing's works. This study places the author in his intellectual, philosophical, political, and socio-historical context and includes a considerable amount of literary criticism, as well as accurate and pertinent accounts of the events of Gissing's life. Korg also delves into the possible motivations of many of the author's actions; his theories are interesting and credible.

Roberts, Morley, *The Private Papers of Henry Maitland.* New York: George H. Doran, 1912. Roberts models his biography after Gissing's autobiography, *The Private Papers of Henry Ryecroft,* creating a fictional Henry Maitland who, with small deviations here and there, closely resembles George Gissing. For example, Maitland is expelled from school for theft, travels to the United States and writes for the *Chicago Tribune,* publishes critically under appreciated novels, and is generally a victim of pessimism. Although this book remains of some interest because Roberts was a personal friend of Gissing and because it includes candid discussion of Gissing's often disastrous relationships with women, it presents on the whole an overly negative, unsympathetic, and even hostile view of Gissing. These last qualities bring its reliability into question.

Autobiographical Sources

The Private Papers of Henry Ryecroft, one of Gissing's last and perhaps most brilliant novels, is a thinly veiled autobiographical account. In his preface to the novel, the author claims that he came upon three manuscript books, evidently diaries, while rummaging through the papers of his recently deceased (fictional) friend, Henry Ryecroft. According to Gissing, the novel consists of a compilation of Ryecroft's diaries: "a thought, a reminiscence, a bit of reverie, a description of his state of mind, and so on." He then presents a short history of

Ryecroft's life, a description whose details correspond so exactly to the events of Gissing's own life that it leaves little doubt that Ryecroft and Gissing are one. One finds, for example, accounts of Gissing's boyhood, his early literary career and poverty, his lifetime of financial insecurity and homelessness, and his opinions on social democracy, education, class, and religion—in short, a personal portrait of the author's life and psyche. Singularly lacking is any attention to Ryecroft's (or Gissing's) lifelong troubles with women. Because *The Ryecroft Papers* constitute a fictional self-portrait, they often make impossible close critical scrutiny of the real author.

Overview of Critical Sources

In his lifetime, Gissing never appealed to the English popular reading audience, yet he could boast a small, ardent band of well-educated followers, many of whom were the novelist's fellow writers. Although a handful of reviewers praised Gissing's early works, the novels were generally received negatively by literary critics. With the publication of *New Grub Street,* he finally won critical praise; the novel was widely read and discussed, and Gissing became a literary force in his time.

Gissing's reputation suffered greatly after his death, with the publication of Roberts' subjective biography *The Private Papers of Henry Maitland* and Frank Swinnerton's deprecative *George Gissing: A Critical Study* (1923) doing much to destroy the earlier approbation he had earned. Although there existed a limited amount of critical interest after 1912, intensive study of Gissing and his works began only in the late 1950's. Since 1960 scholars have been concerned primarily with biographical and bibliographical research on the author, as well as collection of his letters and private papers. Fresh, positive appraisals of the novels have appeared alongside socio-historical considerations of Gissing's canon.

Evaluation of Selected Criticism

Coustillas, Pierre, ed. *Collected Articles on George Gissing.* London: Frank Cass, 1968. This is an impressive and helpful group of sixteen (mostly critical) essays, and a sound critical introduction to Gissing.

Coustillas, Pierre and Colin Partridge, eds. *Gissing: The Critical Heritage.* London: Routledge and Kegan Paul, 1972. This is the first exhaustive collection of contemporary reaction to Gissing's works.

Gapp, Samuel Vogt, *George Gissing: Classicist.* Philadelphia: University of Pennsylvania Press, 1936. An expert evaluation of the effect of Gissing's lifelong study of the classics on his writings.

Michaux, Jean-Pierre, ed. *George Gissing: Critical Essays.* London and Totowa, NJ: Vision and Barnes & Noble, 1981. In a wide-ranging collection of twenty-one important reprinted essays, the first part consists of general studies of Gissing the man, while the second focuses on Gissing's writings, specifically their theme, style, and structure.

Poole, Adrian, *Gissing in Context.* Totowa, NJ: Rowman and Littlefield, 1975. Poole relates Gissing's work to that of his predecessors and contemporaries, suggesting that the author's vision was neither completely personal nor a product of "a general atmosphere of late-Victorian malaise."

Swinnerton, Frank, *George Gissing: A Critical Study.* New York: George H. Doran, 1923. In this first book-length critical study of Gissing, Swinnerton openly attempts to demolish the language, style, and characterization of Gissing's works.

Tindall, Gillian, *The Born Exile.* London: Temple Smith, 1974. Tindall suggests in this psychoanalytical study that it is insufficient merely to uncover biographical facts and to explicate the author's works accordingly. She maintains that since Gissing was born a compulsive writer, many subtle but fundamental truths concerning his mentality manifest themselves in his novels.

Other Sources

Coustillas, Pierre, ed. *London and the Life of Literature in Late Victorian England: The Diary of George Gissing, Novelist.* Hassocks, Sussex: Harvester Press, 1978.

Gettmann, Royal A. ed. *George Gissing and H. G. Wells: Their Friendship and Correspondence.* Urbana: University of Illinois Press, 1961.

Korg, Jacob, ed. "George Gissing's Commonplace Book," in *Bulletin of the New York Public Library,* LIV (1961), 417-434, 534-546, 588-614. A diary.

Wolff, Joseph J. *George Gissing: An Annotated Bibliography of Writings About Him.* DeKalb: Northern Illinois University Press, 1974.

Young, Arthur C. ed. *The Letters of George Gissing to Eduard Bertz 1887-1903.* New Brunswick, NJ: Rutgers University Press, 1961. Correspondence with his lifelong intellectual associate.

Selected Dictionaries and Encyclopedias

Critical Survey of Long Fiction, Vol. 3, Salem Press, 1983. Divides Gissing's career into stages, and analyzes a novel from each period.

Dictionary of National Biography (second supplement), Oxford University Press, 1912, pp. 114–116.

Anne-Marie Foley
University of Missouri/Columbia

ELLEN GLASGOW
1873–1945

Author's Chronology

Born April 22, 1873, Richmond, Virginia of Scotch-Irish parents; *1888* Glasgow family moves to One West Main Street, Richmond, where she lives for remainder of her life; *1889* hearing problems begin; *1893* death of mother causes severe depression; *1895* publishes first story "A Woman of To-morrow;" *1897* anonymously publishes first novel *The Descendant; 1899–1904* love affair with unidentified man called Gerald B— in her autobiography; *1905* Gerald B— dies; *1911–1915* lives in New York and travels to Europe; *1917* engaged to Henry W. Anderson; *1919* engagement broken; *1924* becomes president of the Richmond Society for the Prevention of Cruelty to Animals; *1932* elected to National Institute of Arts and Letters; *1938* suffers heart attack; *1942* Pulitzer Prize for *In This Our Life; 1945* dies on November 21 of heart complications.

Author's Bibliography (selected)

The Descendant, 1897 (novel); *Phases of an Inferior Planet,* 1898 (novel); *The Voice of the People,* 1900 (novel); *The Freeman and Other Poems,* 1902; *The Battle-Ground,* 1902 (novel); *The Deliverance,* 1904 (novel); *The Wheel of Life,* 1906 (novel); *The Ancient Law,* 1908 (novel); *The Romance of a Plain Man,* 1909 (novel); *The Miller of Old Church,* 1911 (novel); *Virginia,* 1913 (novel); *Life and Gabriella,* 1916 (novel); *The Builders,* 1919 (novel); *One Man in His Time,* 1922 (novel); *The Shadowy Third and Other Stories,* 1923; *Barren Ground,* 1925 (novel); *The Romantic Comedians,* 1926 (novel); *They Stooped to Folly,* 1929 (novel); *The Sheltered Life,* 1932 (novel); *Vein of Iron,* 1935 (novel); *In This Our Life,* 1941 (novel); *A Certain Measure,* 1943 (criticism); *The Woman Within,* 1954 (autobiography); *The Collected Stories,* 1963; *Beyond Defeat,* 1966 (novel).

Overview of Biographical Sources

Despite a long life during which she published nineteen novels, a book of poetry, a collection of critical prefaces, and numerous letters, essays, and reviews, until 1971 only one full-length biographical study was available: Blair Rouse's *Ellen Glasgow* (1962). The same year, Monique Parent published *Ellen Glasgow: Romancière* (Paris: A. G. Nizet, 1962), a 574-page study that remains the most exhaustive and definitive biographical source, though still not translated into English. J. R. Raper's *Without Shelter: The Early Career of Ellen Glasgow* (1971), though limited to Glasgow's life through 1906, is an excellent source for her formative years. E. Stanly Godbold, Jr.'s *Ellen Glasgow and The Woman Within* (1972) comes the closest to satisfying its advertised claim as the first definitive account of Glasgow's life. See also the special issue of *Mississippi Quarterly*—31 (1977-1978)—devoted to the early career of the author.

Evaluation of Selected Biographies

Godbold, E. Stanly Jr. *Ellen Glasgow and The Woman Within.* Baton Rouge: Louisiana State University Press, 1972. Godbold's is the only full-length biography of Glasgow in English. Based in part on the notes of novelist Marjorie Kinnan Rawlings, who died before writing a proposed biography of Glasgow, *Ellen Glasgow and the Woman Within* focuses on the author's personal, psychological and literary life. Because Godbold only touches on those parts of Glasgow's novels which bear directly on her life, several critics have faulted his overly autobiographical readings of the fiction as being somewhat misguided. While the book is thorough and accurate, especially when dealing with the latter years, a number of Glasgow scholars have noted its non-critical acceptance of Rawling's notes and its lack of reference to Parent's earlier work. Godbold is careful to balance the various aspects of Glasgow's life so that his book is neither overly romantic nor unnecessarily harsh.

Raper, J. R. *Without Shelter: The Early Career of Ellen Glasgow.* Baton Rouge: Louisiana State University Press, 1971. Raper's study is specifically designed both to analyze Glasgow's early novels and to present an intellectual and psychological biography of her years through 1906. Though not as much concerned with her personal life as Godbold's book, Raper's is also excellent for its many details about the daily life of the writer. Raper focuses on Glasgow's rebellion against the evasive idealism often associated with Southern writers of the time, which she wished to replace with an application of Darwinian realism more complex than sometimes thought.

Rouse, Blair, *Ellen Glasgow.* New York: Twayne, 1962. Following the standard format of the Twayne series, Rouse combines biography and criticism in a clear, informative, thorough, and straightforward style. Having previously edited a selection of Glasgow's letters—*Letters of Ellen Glasgow* (New York: Harcourt, Brace, 1958)—Rouse was thoroughly knowledgeable about his subject. The book is an excellent introductory overview of Glasgow's life and work, and its annotated bibliography is helpful, though the author tends to underemphasize negative criticism.

Autobiographical Sources

Published posthumously, at Glasgow's request, *The Woman Within* (New York: Harcourt, Brace, 1954) is an autobiography reflective of its author: outspoken, honest, at times neurotic and boastful, often melodramatic, inexact and sometimes unnecessarily vindictive. Begun in 1934, her autobiography was initially called "The Autobiography of An Exile," an indication of the themes of suffering, loneliness, alienation, sensitivity, and maladjustment that pervade the book. Although she is sometimes inaccurate—changing dates, obscuring names and events—Glasgow is often brutally frank about such subjects as her deafness, her relations with family, her love affairs, her quarrel with fellow Richmond writer James Branch Cabell, her views on feminism, and her idea of her place in American literary history. Additional autobiographical material is available in her essay in *I Believe: The Personal Philosophies of Certain Eminent Men and Women of Our Time,* ed. by Clifton Fadiman (New York: Simon and Schuster, 1938), and throughout Glasgow's *A Certain Measure.* See also Cabell's *As I Remember It* (New York: McBride, 1955) for the other side of a literary feud.

Overview of Critical Sources

For an author whose literary reputation is still less than major, Glasgow has been well served by a steady body of literary criticism. While early critics concentrated on her place in the Southern literary tradition and the overall plan of her novels, recent scholars have found in her life and work a strong source for feminist thought. She has been the subject of dissertations, bibliographies, textual studies, and a centennial symposium. Her life and literary work is covered in the *Ellen Glasgow Newsletter,* edited by Edgar E. MacDonald, which features a frequently updated annotated bibliography.

Evaluation of Selected Criticism

McDowell, Frederick P. W. *Ellen Glasgow and the Ironic Art of Fiction.* Madison: University of Wisconsin Press, 1960. In this first full-length study of Glasgow, McDowell sorts out the bulk of Glasgow's novels in an attempt to give her a more accurate place in literary history. Once considered a popular writer, then an equal with Willa Cather and Edith Wharton, Glasgow was almost totally neglected by 1960. McDowell's separate analysis of each novel is clear, fairminded, and thorough, though necessarily more basic than the books that followed.

Raper, Julius Rowan, *From the Sunken Garden: The Fiction of Ellen Glasgow, 1916–1945.* Baton Rouge: Louisiana State University Press, 1980. Far from being a sequel to his earlier book, cited above, Raper's second study contains little biography, and little attempt at continuing his study of Glasgow's biological and cultural themes. Instead, this book is concerned with such non-Freudian psychological literary techniques as the double, the foil, and psychological projection. Covering the fiction from the author's later years, Raper's book is excellent, full of psychological insights and free of psychological jargon.

Other Sources

Holman, C. Hugh, "Ellen Glasgow: The Novelist of Manners as Social Critic," *Three Modes of Southern Fiction* (Athens: University of Georgia Press,

1966). One of the best Southern literary critics compares Glasgow to Faulkner and Wolfe, and distinguishes between her form of comedy of manners and others.

Inge, M. Thomas, ed. *Ellen Glasgow: Centennial Essays.* Charlottesville: University Press of Virginia, 1976. Nine essays by the best known of Glasgow scholars, plus an excellent bibliographical essay.

Rubin, Louis D., Jr., *No Place on Earth: Ellen Glasgow, James Branch Cabell, and Richmond-in-Virginia.* Austin: University of Texas Press, 1959. Another of the best of Southern literary critics argues in an early essay that Richmond's influence on Glasgow and Cabell was particularly important.

Thiébaux, Marcelle, *Ellen Glasgow.* New York: Frederick Ungar, 1982. Biographical/critical study arranged thematically. Part of Ungar's Modern Literature Series.

Wagner, Linda W. *Ellen Glasgow: Beyond Convention.* Austin: University of Texas Press, 1982. Brief but valuable study of Glasgow's developing interest in women characters who attempted to defy convention.

Selected Dictionaries and Encyclopedias

American Women Writers: A Critical Reference Guide from Colonial Times to the Present, 2, Frederick Ungar, 1980. Brief biographical and critical sketch.

American Writers: A Collection of Literary Biographies, 1981. Among the best short biographical and critical assessments of Glasgow, this reprint of Louis Auchincloss's pamphlet in the University of Minnesota Pamphlets on American Writers Series, was originally published in 1964. Auchincloss used the same material in his *Pioneers and Caretakers* (Minneapolis: University of Minnesota Press, 1965).

Critical Survey of Long Fiction, Salem Press, 1983. Except for inaccurate birthdate, this is a good analysis of Glasgow's important novels and a brief study of her life.

Dictionary of Literary Biography, Gale Research, 1983. A major entry on Glasgow provides thorough coverage of her life and career, plus a bibliography.

Timothy Dow Adams
West Virginia University

WILLIAM GODWIN
1756–1836

Author's Chronology

Born March 3, 1756, Wisbech, England, the son of a nonconformist minister; *1773* follows his father's calling and enters Hoxton Dissenting Academy; *1778* becomes a dissenting minister and for five years serves at various parishes; comes under the influence of skeptical and radical thinkers, notably philosophers of the French Revolution; *1783* resigns his ministry and goes to London to regenerate society by his writing; *1787* becomes a "complete unbeliever"; *1793* publishes the *Enquiry concerning Political Justice,* which establishes his reputation as the leading radical thinker of his time; *1794* adds to his fame with *Caleb Williams,* a novel written to illustrate the ideas advanced in *Political Justice; 1797* marries Mary Wollstonecraft, author of a *Vindication of the Rights of Woman,* who dies shortly after childbirth the same year; their daughter Mary Godwin later marries the poet Shelley; *1801* marries Mrs. Mary Jane Clairmont, whose daughter Clara Mary Jane becomes Byron's mistress; *1805* establishes a small publishing business and continues to write novels and miscellaneous works; *1822* becomes bankrupt after years of pecuniary struggles; *1833* receives the small sinecure post of Usher of the Exchequer; dies April 7, 1836.

Author's Bibliography (selected)

Enquiry Concerning Political Justice, 1793 (political theory); *Adventures of Caleb Williams, or Things as They Are,* 1794 (novel); *St. Leon: a Tale of the Sixteenth Century,* 1799 (novel); *Fleetwood: or, The New Man of Feeling,* 1805 (novel); *Mandeville, a Tale of the Seventeenth Century in England,* 1817 (novel); *Cloudesley; a Tale,* 1830 (novel); *Deloraine,* 1833 (novel); miscellaneous sermons, essays, histories, biographies, plays, and children's stories.

Overview of Biographical Sources

Godwin defies the biographer who would interpret his genius and character. He emerges from the impressions of his contemporaries as cold, stiff, and passionless. Later biographers have sustained this view of him. At present there are two major biographies of Godwin: C. Kegan Paul's *William Godwin: His Friends and Contemporaries.* 2 vols. (1876) and Ford K. Brown's *The Life of William Godwin* (1926).

C. Kegan Paul's two-volume study was for many years the standard life and for some readers is still the best. His biography is a classic work of scholarship with its accuracy, thoroughness, and scrupulous impartiality. Paul builds up a composite picture of his subject with a wealth of interesting material. Yet Godwin's inner life is essentially missing, and in the end he remains an enigma.

Ford K. Brown's biography of Godwin is probably definitive. Although he adds little new material to Paul, his critical insights, fresh perceptions of the author's life, and fine treatment of Godwin's relationship to his time make it the best study. Unlike his predecessor, Brown was fascinated with the psychology of his subject. However, the inner Godwin apparently inspired in him a contempt that he could not altogether conceal. The sardonic irony with which he treats the events of Godwin's tragic life strikes the reader as a flaw in this admirable work.

Evaluation of Selected Biographies

Brown, Ford K. *The Life of William Godwin.* London: J. M. Dent and Sons, 1926. Although distinctly ironic in tone, and not as exact in its scholarship as Paul's work, Brown's study is a thorough and reliable biography. The book is an engaging account of Godwin and his circle of friends. Godwin emerges as egotistical, childish, and morally obnoxious in his relationship with Shelley, from whom he sponged outrageously. Ford is at his best in treating Godwin's relations with his contemporaries and the potent influence he exerted on many of them, especially on Wordsworth, Coleridge, and Shelley.

Grylls, Rosalie Glynn, *William Godwin and His World.* London: Odhams Press, 1953. While Grylls' study is useful, it is not intended to be exhaustive biography. To avoid plagiarism, she omitted reading contemporary standard biographies. Her style is vivid and lively, the life of Godwin reading like fiction, perhaps with an eye to the general rather than to the scholarly reader. She knows the age well, and her portrayal of Godwin is balanced and objective, although she never quite brings him to life.

Paul, C. Kegan. *William Godwin: His Friends and Contemporaries.* 2 vols. London: Henry S. King, 1876. This study is an indispensable source for details on Godwin's life, friends, family affairs, and literary relationships. It presents excerpts from his unpublished Diary, as well as from letters and documents now scattered or lost. In Paul's portrait, he emerges as a man both feared and admired by his contemporaries. With little native feeling, Godwin advocated that all men be guided by reason.

Autobiographical Sources

While few references to himself appear in Godwin's published works, an autobiographical sketch and extracts from his Diary, letters, and reminiscences are included in the standard source, C. Kegan Paul's *William Godwin: His Friends and Contemporaries* (see above). A good edition of selected correspondence is *Godwin and Mary: Letters of William Godwin and Mary Wollstonecraft,* edited by Ralph M. Wardle (Lawrence: University of Kansas Press, 1967).

Overview of Critical Sources

For many years William Godwin was known chiefly as the father-in-law of Shelley and the husband of Mary Wollstonecraft. He was rescued from almost complete oblivion by C. Kegan Paul's *William Godwin: His Friends and Contemporaries.* With the appearance of later critical studies, Godwin's reputation has risen steadily. Criticism in recent years has divided almost exactly between the author as political thinker and as novelist. If F. E. L. Priestley's facsimile third edition of *Enquiry concerning Political Justice* (1946) gave a powerful impetus to the re-study of Godwin's political thought, B. J. Tysdahl's *William Godwin as Novelist* (1981) directed a beam of fresh light on the other side of Godwin's genius with the first full-length study of his novels.

Evaluation of Selected Criticism

Monro, D. H. *Godwin's Moral Philosophy, an Interpretation of William Godwin.* London: Oxford University Press, 1953. In his study of Godwin's ideas, D. H. Monro views Godwin not in the traditional way as a political reformer but as a moral philosopher. With his dissenting background, Godwin was essentially a moralist who wished to regenerate society with his writing. Monro's study is especially valuable for its examination of the link between *Political Justice* and the six novels. He suggests that the novels, especially *Caleb Williams* and *St. Leon,* are vehicles for conveying Godwin's moral vision and dramatizing his social theories.

Priestley, F. E. L. ed. Critical Introduction to *Enquiry concerning Political Justice.* 3 vols. Toronto: University of Toronto Press, 1946. To a long-needed critical edition of *Political Justice,* F. E. L. Priestley has supplied in the form of Volume III a careful and scholarly essay. This critical introduction to a superb edition compares the first, second, and third editions and provides an account of the development of Godwin's thought, its sources and its influence. Priestley reveals that Godwin traced all social ills to institutions—government, church, marriage, court system, and schools. Yet Godwin would eradicate these not by violent overthrow but gradually through enlightened education.

Tysdahl, B. J. *William Godwin as Novelist.* London: The Athlone Press, 1981. While Godwin's stature as the author of *Political Justice* is secure, his place as a novelist is far less certain. In literary histories his first two novels, *Caleb Williams* and *St. Leon,* are praised for their absorbing plots, while the later novels are often dismissed as dull and tedious. Tysdahl's illuminating study is the most convincing of the critics who find all the novels worthwhile and successful as fiction. He points out that all of the novels are experimental in form with significant themes reflecting tenets of *Political Justice.*

Other Sources

Fleisher, David, *William Godwin: a Study in Liberalism.* London: G. Allen and Unwin, 1951. Excellent analysis of Godwin's thought in the context of *Political Justice.*

Pollin, Burton R. *Godwin Criticism: a Synoptic Bibliography.* Toronto: University of Toronto Press, 1967. An indispensable aid to Godwin studies.

Sherburn, George, ed. Introduction to *Caleb Williams.* New York: Rhinehart and Co., 1960. Sherburn treats *Caleb Williams* as the best of the revolutionary novels of the eighteenth century.

———. "Godwin's Later Novels," *Studies in Romanticism,* I (Winter 1962), 65–82. A critical survey of the novels after *Caleb Williams* (*St. Leon, Fleetwood, Mandeville, Cloudesley,* and *Deloraine*).

Smith, Elton Edward and Esther Greenwell Smith. *William Godwin.* New York: Twayne, 1965. Best for its summary of the ideas of *Political Justice* and its gloss of the novels.

Woodcock, George, *William Godwin.* London: The Porcupine Press, 1946. A good critical life, which argues that Godwin's ideas and influence have been underestimated.

Selected Dictionaries and Encyclopedias

Dictionary of National Biography, Oxford University Press, 1885–1900. A lucid brief sketch of Godwin and his principal works.

Great Writers of the English Language: Novelists and Prose Writers, St. Martin's Press, 1979. A survey of Godwin's work, especially of the significance of his novels.

George E. McCelvey
Western Kentucky University

WILLIAM GOLDING
1911

Author's Chronology

Born September 19, 1911, St. Columb Minor, near Newquay in Cornwall; attends grammar school in Marlborough, where father is schoolmaster; *1930* enters Brasenose College, Oxford University, majoring in natural sciences; *1934* publishes *Poems,* an unsuccessful work that leads him to abandon the notion of becoming a poet; *1935* graduates from Brasenose with major in English literature; *1935–1938* takes miscellaneous jobs as lecturer and as part-time actor, writer, and producer for small theater company; *1939* marries Ann Brookfield and becomes schoolmaster at Bishop Wordsworth's School, Salisbury; *1940–1945* serves in Royal Navy as lieutenant commanding rocket-launcher; *1945* returns to Bishop Wordsworth's School; *1954* publishes first novel, *Lord of the Flies; 1955* made a Fellow of the Royal Society of Literature; *1961* is writer-in-residence at Hollins College, Virginia; *1962* leaves teaching to devote time solely to writing; *1983* awarded the Nobel Prize for Literature.

Author's Bibliography (selected)

Poems, 1934; *Lord of the Flies,* 1954 (novel); *The Inheritors,* 1955 (novel); *Pincher Martin,* 1956 (novel); *The Brass Butterfly,* 1958 (play); *Free Fall,* 1959 (novel); *The Spire,* 1964 (novel); *The Hot Gates and Other Occasional Pieces,* 1965 (essays); *The Pyramid,* 1967 (novel); *The Scorpion God,* 1971 (three novellas); *Darkness Visible,* 1979 (novel); *Rites of Passage,* 1980 (novel); *A Moving Target,* 1982 (essays); *The Paper Men,* 1984 (novel).

Autobiographical Sources

Critics have pointed to autobiographical elements in Golding's novels—his experience as a schoolmaster and his experience in World War II in *Lord of the Flies;* his navy and theater experience in *Pincher Martin;* his struggle between the rational and the irrational in *Free Fall;* and the setting and the protagonists's career dilemma in *The Pyramid.* Certainly *The Paper Men* reflects Golding's feeling of being plagued by persistent academicians.

Golding's essays in *The Hot Gates and Other Occasional Pieces* and in *A Moving Target* reflect his ideas and relate personal experiences. Three essays from *The Hot Gates and Other Occasional Pieces* provide a picture of his early years: "Egypt from My Inside" discusses his childhood interest in Egypt and its relation to the intrigue of mystery for him; "Billy the Kid" depicts the author learning early social skills; and "The Ladder and the Tree" describes his home life and delineates the conflict between the irrational and the rational. Four essays from *A Moving Target* deal with Golding the writer: "Rough Magic" describes his writing process; "My First Book" discusses his interest in the sound and rhythm of language; "A Moving Target" focuses on the way Golding finds a theme and transmutes it into fiction; and "Belief and Creativity" describes his struggle to find and communicate truth.

Overview of Critical Sources

Of the several book-length studies and one collection of essays, most were written after *The Pyramid* and do not include discussion of the later works. In fact, no study includes the last two novels. Critics focus primarily on sources, biographical elements, and Golding's concentration on the themes of evil and human guilt. In addition to the book-length studies, numerous articles and two special issues of literary journals have appeared.

Evaluation of Selected Criticism

Babb, Howard S. *The Novels of William Golding.* Columbus: Ohio State University Press, 1970. Close formal critical analyses of the first six novels concentrate on the significance of Golding's structural trademark, a narrative building steadily to a dramatic climax.

Baker, James R. *William Golding: A Critical Study.* New York: St. Martin's Press, 1965. Baker focuses on Golding's adaptation of techniques of Greek tragedy in the first five novels.

Biles, Jack I. and Robert O. Evans, eds. *William Golding: Some Critical Considerations.* Lexington: University Press of Kentucky, 1978. This book offers commentary from several critical perspectives, both on Golding's work as a whole and on individual works. Of great value is the extensive bibliography of primary and secondary sources.

Dick, Bernard F. *William Golding.* New York: Twayne, 1967. Dick traces the writer's development from his early poems through *The Hot Gates and Other Occasional Pieces.* He dismisses any influence by contemporary writers and concentrates instead on the strong Greek influence in Golding's work.

Hodson, Leighton, *William Golding.* Edinburgh: Oliver and Boyd, 1969. Following a biographical introduction that traces the background of Golding's major themes, Hodson analyzes the first six novels. He examines the literary strategies that lead the reader to awareness of the dichotomous nature of the human condition.

Johnston, Arnold, *Of Earth and Darkness, The Novels of William Golding.* Columbia: University of Missouri Press, 1980. The only critic to include *Darkness Visible,* Johnston explores Golding's development as a literary artist. Furthermore, he points out that protagonists who are often artists in their own right convey the difficulty of identifying and communicating truth, an important theme for Golding.

Kinkead-Weekes, Mark, and Ian Gregor, *William Golding: A Critical Study.* London: Faber & Faber, 1967. These authors explicate the first five novels, emphasizing Golding's imagination and his ability to transport the reader into the world he creates.

Tiger, Virginia, *William Golding: The Dark Fields of Discovery.* London: Calder and Boyars, 1974. Tiger posits an "ideographic structure," which forces the reader to link two seemingly contradictory perspectives and discover the complementary coexistence of opposites. She uses extensively Golding's commentary from interviews and correspondence to discuss the first seven works.

Other Sources

Baker, James R. ed. "William Golding Issue," *Twentieth Century Literature,* XXVIII, #2 (Summer 1982). This special number of the journal is valuable because it concentrates on the later Golding. It includes articles on *Darkness Visible* and *Rites of Passage* as well as an interview with Golding.

Biles, Jack I. ed. "A William Golding Miscellany," *Studies in the Literary Imagination,* II, #2 (October 1969). The essays in this special number of the journal treat Golding's imagery in specific works.

———.*Talk: Conversations with William Golding.* New York: Harcourt, Brace, Jovanovich, 1970. Falling into two categories, autobiography and criticism, this collection of conversations with Golding offers valuable author commentary on Golding's life, his writing, his themes, and some specific works.

Rebecca Kelly
Southern Technical Institute

OLIVER GOLDSMITH
1730?-1774

Author's Chronology

Born on November 10, 1730? the exact year uncertain, at Pallas, County Westmeath, Ireland, the son of Charles Goldsmith, a curate, and Ann Jones, the daughter of Rev. Oliver Jones, a school-master; educated at schools in Elphin, Athlone, and Edgeworthstown before being admitted to Trinity College Dublin as a sizar on June 11, 1745; *1747* father dies early in the year; *1750* takes his B.A. degree despite being publicly admonished for participating in a riot in 1747 and having quarreled with his tutor; *1750–1752* fails in effort to be ordained; becomes tutor to the family of a Mr. Flinn; plans unsuccessfully to emigrate to America; leaves for London to study law but loses his money gambling in Dublin; *1752* begins study of medicine at the University of Edinburgh; *1754* leaves Edinburgh to continue studies at Leyden where he remains until 1755 when he begins to travel through France, Germany, Switzerland and Italy; *1756* returns to London; works as an apothecary's assistant and as a physician; becomes an usher in the school of the Rev. John Milner at Peckham in Surrey where he meets Ralph Griffiths, editor of the *Monthly Review,* to which he begins to contribute articles; *1758* fails to pass examination for certificate as a hospital mate; *1759–1760* publishes *An Enquiry into the Present State of Polite Learning in Europe,* and begins contributing to a number of periodicals, including *The Critical Review, The Bee, The Busy Body, The Weekly Magazine, The Royal Magazine, The British Magazine,* and *The Lady's Magazine; 1760* contributes papers called "Chinese Letters" to *The Public Ledger,* which establishes his reputation as an author when published as *The Citizen of the World* two years later; *1761* meets Samuel Johnson and Sir Joshua Reynolds; *1764* founding member of The Club with Johnson and others; begins career as poet with *The Traveller; 1766* publishes his novel, *The Vicar of Wakefield; 1768* embarks on career as dramatist with production of *The Good Natured Man; 1773* publishes essays on the theatre in *The Westminster Magazine;* assures his permanent fame as dramatist with the production of *She Stoops to Conquer* at Drury Lane; *1774* becomes seriously ill and dies on April 4, his last poem, *Retaliation,* unfinished.

Author's Bibliography (selected)

Enquiry into the Present State of Polite Learning in Europe, 8 vols. 1759 (social history); *The Bee,* 1759 (essays); *The Citizen of the World,* 2 vols. 1762 (essays); *A History of England,* 2 vols. 1764 (history); *The Traveller,* 1764 (poetry); *Essays,* 1765 (collected essays); *The Vicar of Wakefield,* 2 vols. 1766 (novel); *The Good Natured Man,* 1768 (drama); *The Roman History,* 2 vols. 1769 (history); *The Deserted Village,* 1770 (poetry); *The History of England,* 4 vols. 1771 (history); *She Stoops to Conquer,* 1773 (drama); *Retaliation,* 1774 (poetry); *The Grecian History,* 2 vols. 1774 (history); *History of the Earth and Animated Nature,* 8 vols. 1774 (natural history); *The Haunch of Venison,* 1776 (poetry).

Overview of Biographical Sources

Goldsmith, as a prominent member of the intellectual circle that surrounded Samuel Johnson, is included in a number of significant contemporary letters, memoirs, and incidental accounts. The earliest major effort to compose a life of Goldsmith was that of the Reverend Thomas Percy who offered to prepare one for an edition of Goldsmith's works shortly after his death. He had a personal acquaintance with Goldsmith and possessed biographical material supplied by the author. The project was completed by others, including Thomas Cambell, Henry Boyd, and Samuel Rose, but it is generally known as the "Percy Memoir," and was published with the *Miscellaneous Works* (London: Johnson, Robinson and others, 1801). In this connection, see Katherine C. Balserston's *The History and Sources of Percy's "Memoir of Oliver Goldsmith"* (Cambridge: University Press, 1926). The first important nineteenth-century biography, that of James Prior *The Life of Oliver Goldsmith* (London: J. Murray, 1837), contains material drawn from relatives of the poet, from Percy, and from other contemporary sources including anecdotes drawn from Boswell's *Life of Johnson.* Other good accounts are: Joseph Cradock's *Literary and Miscellaneous Memoirs* (London: J. B. Nichols, 1828), Richard Cumberland's *Memoirs* (London: Lackington, Allen & Co., 1807), Thomas Davies' *Memoirs of the Life of David Garrick* (London: Davies, 1780), Sir John Hawkins' *Life of Johnson,* (London: J. Buckland, 1787); James Northcote's *Memoirs of Sir Joshua Reynolds,* (London: H. Colburn, 1813); and Sir Joshua Reynolds' *Portraits,* ed. Frederick Hilles (London: Heinemann, 1952). John Forster's (1848) became the standard biography. Modern lives of Goldsmith begin with the excellent short biography of Austin Dobson (London: W. Scott, 1888), which contains a bibliography by J. P. Anderson. Important to the study of Goldsmith is *The Collected Letters of Oliver Goldsmith,* edited by Katharine C. Balderston (Cambridge: University Press, 1928) and her *A Census of the Manuscripts of Oliver Goldsmith* (New York: Brick Row Book Shop, 1926). Significant also is Temple Scott's *Oliver Goldsmith Bibliographically and Biographically Considered* (New York: Bowling Green Press, 1928). William Freeman's *Oliver Goldsmith* (London: Herbert Jenkins, 1951) is a reliable short biography. Of much greater significance is Ralph Martin Wardle's *Oliver Goldsmith* (1957), combining the accuracy and documentation required by contemporary scholarship with the use of twentieth-century discoveries about Goldsmith. Elizabeth E. Kent's *Goldsmith and his Booksellers* (Ithaca: Cornell University Press, 1933) studies an important phase of Goldsmith's career. Oscar Shawn's *Goldy, The Life and Times of Oliver Gold-*

smith (1961) is a popularly written, anecdotal account, and A. Lytton Sells' *Oliver Goldsmith* (1974) is a carefully researched study.

Evaluation of Selected Biographies

Forster, John, *The Life and Adventures of Oliver Goldsmith,* London, 1848; 2nd ed. 2 vols. London, 1854; New York: Frederick A. Stokes, 1903; rpt. Westport, CT: Greenwood Press, 1971, Roger Ingpen, ed. Forster's biography incorporates the contemporary material included in that of Prior who preceded him and adds to it. Forster's study was amplified into two volumes and went through six editions by 1877. It is carefully written, with close attention to the evaluation of evidence.

Sells, Arthur Lytton, *Oliver Goldsmith, His Life and Works.* New York: Barnes and Noble, 1974. Sells re-examines existing evidence with considerable energy and provides a large amount of background material that sets Goldsmith's career in its eighteenth-century milieu and makes more intelligible much of Goldsmith's work.

Shawn, Oscar, *Goldy, The Life and Times of Oliver Goldsmith.* New York: Twayne, 1961. Shawn's biography is popularly written and anecdotal in form. Basically sound in its facts about and knowledge of its subject, it does not add much of scholarly significance to modern understanding of Goldsmith or his works. Its primary value is in making interesting and readable the life of an important eighteenth-century man of letters.

Wardle, Ralph M. *Oliver Goldsmith.* Lawrence, KS: University of Kansas Press, 1957. Wardle's study is the first attempt to write a biography of Goldsmith employing modern scholarly approaches. Wardle has re-examined existing biographical material providing admirable documentation. It amplifies many aspects of Goldsmith's career by using manuscripts and original sources not previously available to or used by Goldsmith's biographers, including manuscripts and texts at major research libraries.

Overview of Critical Sources

A good deal of significant criticism is to be found in Goldsmith's biographies, especially in the modern lives by Wardle and Sells mentioned above. Recent critical studies by Norman Jaffares, *Oliver Goldsmith,* (London and New York: Longmans, Green, 1959) and Ricardo Quintana (1967) reflect modern critical approaches. George S. Rousseau's *Goldsmith: The Critical Heritage* (London: Routledge and Kegan Paul, 1973) gathers in one volume critical material from many sources. Important critical comment is also included in the modern editions of Goldsmith's works by Arthur Friedman in *Collected Works* (Oxford: Clarendon Press, 1966), and *The Vicar of Wakefield* (London and

New York: Oxford University Press, 1974). Samuel Woods's *Oliver Goldsmith, a Reference Guide* (Boston: G. K. Hall, 1982) is a recent bibliography.

Evaluation of Selected Criticism

Kirk, Clara M. *Oliver Goldsmith.* New York: Twayne Publishers, 1967. Kirk's study provides an accessible and valuable critical study of Goldsmith's major works. The evaluation of his career as a master in four important literary areas, poet, novelist, dramatist, and biographer reveals the versatility and depth of Goldsmith's contribution to literature.

Quintana, Ricardo, *Oliver Goldsmith: A Georgian Study.* New York: Macmillan; London: Collier-Macmillan Limited, 1967. Quintana's chronological study of Goldsmith's career provides the most authoritative critical discussion of the major literary works of the author that is available in a single volume, and adds, in an appendix, definitive information on his biographical and historical writing.

Smith, Hamilton Jewell, *Oliver Goldsmith's The Citizen of the World: A Study,* Yale Studies in English, LXXI, New Haven, CT: Yale University Press, 1926. In undertaking the series of anonymous periodical essays for *The Public Ledger* that were eventually published as *The Citizen of the World,* Goldsmith was writing in one of the most popular and influential literary genres. He was also capitalizing on the popularity of eastern culture as a literary motif. Smith's study sets Goldsmith's work effectively in these traditions and indicates the specific sources from which he drew his knowledge of the orient.

Selected Dictionaries and Encyclopedias

Dictionary of National Biography, Oxford University Press, 1939. This authoritative biographical account of Goldsmith provides most of the factual data available concerning his life and works, and lists most of the biographical sources available.

The Oxford Companion to English Literature, Oxford University Press, Fourth Edition, 1967. A concise, useful summary of Goldsmith's life and works, indicating biographical and critical source material.

Richard J. Dircks
St. John's University

JOHN GOWER
c. 1330–1408

Author's Chronology

Born c. 1330, probably in Kent or Yorkshire, England, into prominent family; c. *1365–1375* may have held some civil or legal office in Kent; *1376* begins *Mirour de l'Omme,* first major work; c. *1377* takes up residence at Priory of St. Mary Overey in Southwark where he spends most of the rest of his life; *1386* Geoffrey Chaucer dedicates *Troilus and Criseyde* to "moral Gower" and "philosophical Strode;" *1390* dedicates first recension of *Confessio Amantis* to Richard II and Chaucer; *1392–1393* revises *Confessio Amantis,* adding dedication to Henry of Lancaster (later Henry IV) and deleting praise of Richard from conclusion; *1398* marries Agnes Groundolf; *1399* granted annual gift of wine by new king Henry IV shortly after Richard's deposition; c. *1400* writes last poem in English, "In Praise of Peace;" c. *1402* becomes blind; *1408* dies and is buried in Priory Church of St. Mary Overey, now Southwark Cathedral.

Author's Bibliography (selected)

Cinkante Balades, before 1380? (lyric poems); *Mirour de l'Omme* (alternate Latin titles: *Speculum Hominis* and *Speculum Meditantis*), 1376–1379 (long moral allegory in Anglo-Norman verse); *Vox Clamantis,* c. 1377–1381/1382 (allegorical, apocalyptic vision of society in Latin verse); *Confessio Amantis,* 1386–1390 (collection of tales in English verse); *Cronica Tripertita,* c. 1399–1400 (political poem).

Overview of Biographical Sources

The intriguing gaps in Gower's career and the uncertainty surrounding the sparse extant life-records have tantalized and exasperated scholars interested in the poet's biography. G. C. Macauley in Vol. IV of the authoritative edition, *The Collected Works of John Gower* (Oxford: Clarendon Press, 1899-1902) gathered and reviewed much of this documentary evidence. The material has since been corrected and supplemented by John H. Fisher in the now standard study *John Gower: Moral Philosopher and Friend of Chaucer* (1964). Fisher presents a general critical biography that stresses the historical context and structure of Gower's social and political ideas throughout the three major works. Fisher's longest and most stimulating section re-examines the literary relationship between Gower and Chaucer. Brief, earlier articles of a biographical nature, still valuable for the light they shed on Gower's views toward contemporary political figures and issues, include Gardiner Stillwell, "John Gower and the Last Years of Edward III," *Studies in Philology,* XLV (1948), 454–471 and George R. Coffman, "John Gower, Mentor for Royalty: Richard II," *Publications of the Modern Language Association,* LXIX (1954), 953–964.

Evaluation of Selected Biographies

Fisher, John H. *John Gower: Moral Philosopher and Friend of Chaucer.* New York: New York University Press, 1964. Fisher's is the only full-length study of Gower's life and entire corpus of nearly 80,000 lines in three languages. It is likely to remain the standard work for a long time. Brief chapters trace the changes in Gower's critical reputation, re-evaluate the life-records, and present an overview of the literary career. Here Fisher is valuable in clarifying the vexing questions concerning the poet's ethical integrity and shifting political allegiance. More than half the book is devoted to Fisher's compelling argument that Gower's significance is not as a great literary artist but as a moral idealist and social critic. These qualities unify his major poems, which may be regarded as "one continuous work" in their coherent structure and vision. Moreover, Fisher believes Gower's moral concerns exerted a shaping influence upon Chaucer's poetic practice, greatly affecting the superior poet's artistic development.

Although some of Fisher's conclusions are debatable, his study is an impressive, scholarly contribution which no student of Gower—or Chaucer—should neglect.

Overview of Critical Sources

Predictably most Gower criticism focuses on the *Confessio Amantis.* Discussion of this poem centers around two general approaches: one emphasizes Gower's rhetorical artistry, storytelling skills, and creative use of source materials. The other sees the moral and political instruction as central, the courtly love element somewhat peripheral, the poetry dull. Despite this growing body of critical commentary, there is no single full-length treatment which deals satisfactorily with both Gower's thought and esthetics. The long Latin and French poems have received less attention, though ever since Fisher's biography gave impetus to the belief that Gowerian studies should be directed to the social and political aspects of his writings, both works have been more widely discussed. The *Vox Clamantis* is now accessible in a prose translation by Eric W. Stockton. There is unfortunately no similar translation of the *Mirour de l'Omme.*

Evaluation of Selected Criticism

Burrow, J. A. *Ricardian Poetry.* London: Routledge and Kegan Paul, 1971. Although he does not focus exclusively on Gower, Burrow contributes to an understanding of his significance by situating Gower in the context of late fourteenth-century English literature. Moving easily among the writings of the four 'Ricardian' poets he studies—Chaucer, Gower, William Langland, and the *Gawain*-poet—Burrow defines and illuminates common features of style, narrative design, and theme which link these writers and constitute in Burrow's estimation a literary *period.*

Gallacher, Patrick J. *Love, the Word, and Mercury: A Reading of John Gower's "Confessio Amantis."* Albuquerque: University of New Mexico Press, 1975. Intended for specialists, this scholarly examination of twenty-two tales from the *Confessio Amantis* discusses a thematic pattern, based on the act of speech, which links courtly love conventions, Christian notions of God as Word (Logos), and the pagan god Mercury, emblematic of perfect speech. Gallacher relentlessly pursues the theme of speech throughout Gower's work but also creates a distorted image of the poem by his narrow focus. A dense, sometimes brilliant, finally unconvincing reading of the poem, this study will be of value to those interested in medieval traditions of rhetoric for whom it provides a rich quarry of information.

Peck, Russell A. *Kingship and Common Profit in Gower's "Confessio Amantis."* Carbondale: Southern Illinois University Press, 1978. Written in a clear and lively style, this is the best extensive study of Gower's moral purpose and structural design in his masterpiece. The keys to Gower's scheme are found, according to Peck, in the concepts of "kingship"—good governance, a form of rational maturity both social and individual—and "common profit"—the mutual enhancement of all parts of a community for the general welfare. Though Peck is more concerned with elucidating Gower's argument than the literary qualities of the tales, his observations on plot, style, irony, and other devices are sensitive and illuminating.

Stockton, Eric W. *The Major Latin Works of John Gower: The Voice of One Crying and The Tripartite Chronicle.* Seattle: University of Washington Press, 1962. The first complete translation into modern English prose, this is an invaluable aid for readers interested in Gower's political and social thought but unfamiliar with Latin. The translations are literal but fluent and idiomatic. A substantial introduction includes a clear, detailed discussion of Gower's ideas in the two poems and the connections between them.

Other Sources

Bennett, J. A. W. "Gower's 'Honeste Love,' " in *Patterns of Love and Courtesy.* ed. John Lawlor. Evanston, IL: Northwestern University Press, 1966, pp. 107–121. A careful, graceful examination of Gower's ideal of chaste love in the *Confessio Amantis* which Bennett links to the poet's concern for the good of the commonweal.

Legge, M. Dominica, *Anglo-Norman Literature and Its Background.* Oxford: Clarendon Press, 1963. Contains brief, intelligent discussion of the Balades, viewed against the tradition of French lyric poetry.

Lewis, C. S. *The Allegory of Love.* Oxford: Oxford University Press, 1936, pp. 198–222. A sympathetic, engagingly written appreciation of Gower's poetic skills in the *Confessio Amantis:* his easy, plain style; moral sentiments; and handling of love-allegory.

Pearsall, Derek, "Gower's Narrative Art," *Publications of the Modern Language Association,* LXXXI (1966), 475–484. In contrast to recent appraisals of Gower as moral philosopher and political critic, this is a judicious analysis of the *literary* success of the *Confessio Amantis.*

———, "John Gower," in *British Writers,* Vol. I, ed. Ian Scott-Kilvert. New York: Charles Scribner's Sons, 1979; originally 1969 in #211 British Council series *Writers and Their Work.* Brief, perceptive survey of the major poems and the best short introduction to Gower's poetic achievement.

Selected Editions and Translations

Confessio Amantis. ed. Russell A. Peck. Toronto: University Press of Toronto, 1980. Medieval Academy Reprint for Teaching of 1968 Rinehart edition. Generous selection of tales in Middle English, full critical apparatus, and valuable introduction on the poem's philosophical and social ideas.

Selections from John Gower. ed. J. A. W. Bennett. Oxford: Clarendon Press, 1968. Brief biographical sketch but full, scholarly notes on best tales from *Confessio Amantis* and several non-English poems (selections).

Selected Dictionaries and Encyclopedias

Critical Survey of Poetry, Salem Press, 1982. Biographical overview and a succinct analysis of Gower's major works.

The Critical Temper: A Survey of Modern Criticism, Frederick Ungar, 1969. Collection of twentieth-century critical excerpts on Gower's work, especially the *Confessio Amantis.*

Joseph Marotta
St. John's University

ROBERT GRAVES
1895

Author's Chronology

Born July 26, 1895, Wimbledon, England of Irish-German parents; *1910* enters Charterhouse School on a scholarship; wins varsity letter for boxing; *1914* commissioned second lieutenant in Royal Welch Fusiliers; *1916* publishes first poetry collection, *Over the Brazier;* wounded by shellfire in France; *1918* marries Nancy Nicholson, a militant feminist; *1919* enters St. John's College, Oxford, on a war veteran's grant; *1926* invites Laura Riding to England as a household guest; accepts a faculty position at the University of Cairo, Egypt; *1927–1928* returns to England to found Seizen Press with Riding; *1929* divorces Nicholson and settles in Majorca, Spain, with Riding; *1934* wins Hawthornden Prize for *I, Claudius; 1936* departs Majorca because of the Spanish Civil War; *1939* tours America, then separates from Riding; *1939–1945* marries Beryl Pritchard Hodge; resides in Devon, England during World War II; *1946* returns to Majorca which becomes his permanent home; *1954* delivers Clark Lectures at Cambridge University; *1961* elected Professor of Poetry at Oxford University; *1976* gives his last interview; ceases to write or talk about literature; *1985* continues to live on Majorca.

Author's Bibliography (selected)

Over the Brazier, 1916 (poems); *Poetic Unreason,* 1925 (criticism); *Good-bye to All That,* 1929 (autobiography); *I, Claudius,* 1934 (novel); *Collected Poems,* 1938; *King Jesus,* 1946 (novel); *The White Goddess,* 1948 (novel); *The Greek Myths,* 1955 (prose); *Collected Short Stories,* 1964; *New Collected Poems,* 1976.

Overview of Biographical Sources

Because of his long life, eccentric and polemical critical theories, and bellicose personality, Robert Graves' life presents a complex, and often conflicting, problem for biographers. Until 1977, there were only three, comparatively brief biographical treatments: J. M. Cohen's *Robert Graves* (Edinburgh: Oliver and Boyd, 1949), Martin Seymour-Smith's monograph, *Robert Graves: Writers and Their Work,* #58 (London: British Council Pamphlet, 1956), and George Slades's *Robert Graves: Columbia Essays in Modern Writers,* #25 (New York, 1967). The last two are pamphlet length studies which combine selected biographical material with criticism. The only "definitive" biography is Seymour-Smith's *Robert Graves: His Life and Works* (1982). It cannot, however, be regarded as truly definitive because many biographical materials will not become available until after Graves' death. Graves did, however, cooperate with Seymour-Smith, which gives the book the status of an authorized biography since it reflects access to diaries, correspondence, and other confidential documents provided by Graves. In 1983 another biographical source was published, *In Broken Images: Selected Letters of Robert Graves, 1914–1946,* edited by Paul O'Prey (London: Hutchinson, 1983). This collection of correspondence focuses mostly on literary matters, but many details about Graves' life emerge. Both Seymour-Smith and O'Prey are former members of Graves' inner circle on Majorca, and both books give the appearance of a somewhat partisan view of Graves' story.

Evaluation of Selected Biographies

Canary, Robert H. *Robert Graves.* Boston: Twayne, 1980. Canary presents a general bio-critical introduction to Graves' life and works. It does not discuss any material in great detail, and focuses more on Graves as poet than as novelist or literary critic. Canary discounts Graves' mythographic theories, but does believe that Graves used his creativity to resolve his internal conflicts, and free himself to write his best poetry, the love lyrics. While he does not focus on the Graves-Riding partnership, he acknowledges her influence.

Matthews, T. S. *Jacks or Better.* New York: Harper and Row, 1977. (British title, *Under the Influence.* London: Cassell, 1978.) Matthews, an editor for *Time* magazine and frequent guest in Graves' home on Majorca, introduced Graves and Riding to the poet, Schuyler Jackson, when they toured America in 1939. Riding fell in love with Schuyler and married him. Matthews' account of the Graves-Riding partnership, combined with his revelations about Graves' life during this period, is distorted by his envy of Graves and his dislike of Riding. Readers should be aware of Matthews' biases. In spite of its errors, *Jacks or Better* is the most vivid published account of Graves' breakup with Riding and his subsequent marriage to Beryl Hodge. Matthews writes in readable, journalistic style.

Seymour-Smith, Martin, *Robert Graves.* New York: Holt, Rinehart and Winston, 1982. Seymour-Smith has known Graves personally for many years, spending considerable time since 1975 working with him on this book. Although he writes with objectivity and integrity, Seymour-Smith devotes two-fifths of the book to the thirteen years which Graves spent with Riding. The result is that Riding is negatively portrayed as the cause of Graves' substantial unhappiness. After the book was published, Riding felt so wronged by the account that she published a rebuttal in the *New York Review of Books* (December 22, 1983). In contrast to Riding, Seymour-Smith depicts Graves' second wife, Beryl, as a heroine who provided Graves with an idyllic existence during the last half of his life. Both accounts seem to be overstated, as is Seymour-Smith's continued insistence that Graves is the "foremost love poet of this century."

Because this book was written with Graves' cooperation, it is to be expected that Seymour-Smith reflects Graves' interpretations. Written in an informal and readable style, the biography includes both correspondence and conversations between Graves and Seymour-Smith. Graves also gave Seymour-Smith access to much unpublished material that could provide primary sources for future biographies.

Autobiographical Sources

Graves attempted to fictionalize his experiences in World War I in order to "rid himself of war memories," but the final result of his story became a memoir rather than any published fiction. Written in three months, *Good-bye to All That* is factual, sparse, and non-literary. Graves recounts events from his childhood and school experiences, his war service, and his first marriage. Interestingly, he omits all reference to Riding, even though she lived with him during the late 1920's, when the book was published.

The focus of *Good-bye to All That* is Graves' life as an infantry officer on the western front. Of the book's thirty-one chapters, sixteen deal with the war and the years between 1914–1918. Although an important book for understanding Graves' domestic and artistic development, *Good-bye to All That* is also an excellent artistic account of the horrors and disillusionment of World War I. A sequel to this first memoir is Graves' play entitled *But It Still Goes On* (1930). Despite rearranging many specific autobiographical events, Graves admits in an appendix that this is an autobiography. In 1930, Graves' father published his own autobiography which "corrects" much of Robert Graves' information.

In addition to these memoirs, Graves produced many books of criticism and mythic theory. His inconsistent use of Freudian, anthropological, and textual criticism to explain artistic connections diminishes his credibility as a critic, so that his evaluations of his peers, such as W. B. Yeats, D. H. Lawrence, W. H. Auden, Dylan Thomas, Ezra Pound, and T. S. Eliot, appear to be cranky attacks rather than valid criticism.

Overview of Critical Sources

Although the reading public knows Graves primarily for his historical novels, critics in literature, history, religion, and the classics have been interested in Graves because of his original and unorthodox treatments and translations of Homer, biblical texts, *Rubáiyát of Omar Khayyám,* the life of Christ, and the matriarchal goddesses of the ancient world. While there is a growing body of criticism that attempts to assess Graves' work fairly and accurately, there is still no single book-length critical study that gives a detailed and systematic treatment of the entire *oeuvre.* The focus of the existing criticism is on facets of Graves' poetry and prose, and on the interrelationship between his work, and between his critical theory and personal life.

Evaluation of Selected Criticism

Day, Douglas, *Swifter Than Reason: The Poetry and Criticism of Robert Graves.* Chapel Hill: University of North Carolina Press, 1983. In this first full-length study of the poetry and criticism, Day focuses on Graves' early critical essays. He explores textual alterations among the numerous collections of Graves' poems, showing how the poet has pruned and excised his work. Day also contributes to understanding Graves as a poet and critic by discussing the literary, historical, and personal forces that have shaped Graves' career.

Hoffman, Daniel, *Barbarous Knowledge: Myth in the Poetry of Yeats, Graves, and Muir.* New York: Oxford University Press, 1967. Although not exclusively devoted to Graves, this is regarded by many scholars to be the most illuminating single piece of criticism on Graves. Hoffman explicates Graves' difficult story, "The Shout," and includes a chapter, "The Unquiet Graves," which is an imaginary conversation between a poet and a professor explaining Graves' theories on ballad origins.

Kirkham, Michael, *The Poetry of Robert Graves.* New York: Oxford University Press, 1969. Kirkham explores Graves' intellectual and stylistic debts to Laura Riding. Conversant with the works of both poets, Kirkham illustrates the mutual borrowing between them during their years of association.

Vickery, John E. *Robert Graves and the White Goddess.* Lincoln: University of Nebraska Press, 1972. This is the best extensive study of the mytho-poetic element in Graves' work. Vickery theorizes that the greatest influence on Graves is the genesis of the divine female figure in ancient literature who is the source of inspiration for all art and religion. Vickery underestimates the influence of other anthropological influences on Graves, leaving the reader with the impression that the only way to understand Graves is through critical interpretations of how Graves deploys myth throughout his work.

Other Sources

Graves, Alfred Perceval, *To Return to All That.* London: Jonathan Cape, 1930. Graves' father's autobiography, which devotes the last chapters to correcting his son's inaccurate facts in *Good-bye to All That.*

Green, Peter, "All That Again," in *Grand Street,* II, #2 (Winter 1983), 84–120. A witty and useful summary of Graves' entire life.

Jackson, Laura (Riding), "Some Autobiographical Corrections of Literary History," in *Denver Quarterly,* VIII (Winter 1974), 1–13. Riding's corrections to Graves' account of their association.

Jarrell, Randall, "Graves and the White Goddess," in *The Third Book of Criticism.* New York: Farrar, Straus, and Giroux, 1969. The Jungian aspects of Graves' poetic myth.

McKinley, James, "Subject: Robert Graves: Random Notes of a Biographer," in *New Letters,* XL, #4 (1974), 75–100. Full biographical introduction to Graves' *New Collected Poems,* which McKinley edited.

Wexler, Joyce, *Laura Riding's Pursuit of Truth.* Athens: Ohio University Press, 1979. The only book-length study of the Riding—Graves relationship.

Selected Dictionaries and Encyclopedias

Critical Survey of Long Fiction, Salem Press, 1983. Brief biography, and short analysis of some of Graves' important novels.

Dictionary of Literary Biography, Gale Research, 1983. Concise overview of Graves' entire life, and a discussion of the principal works.

Hallman B. Bryant
Clemson University

THOMAS GRAY
1716–1771

Author's Chronology

Born December 26, 1716 in London to parents of the merchant middle class; *1725* enters Eton where two of his maternal uncles are masters and where he meets Thomas Ashton, Richard West, and Horace Walpole; *1734* enters Peterhouse College, Cambridge University; *1738* leaves Cambridge without a degree, intending to study law; *1739* begins tour of Europe with Walpole; *1741* quarrels with Walpole in Italy and returns to England; father dies; *1742* West dies in June, and Gray returns to Peterhouse as a Fellow-commoner and composes some of his early poems; *1743* receives an LL.B. degree; *1745* reconciles with Walpole; *1753* mother dies; *1756* moves from Peterhouse to Pembroke College; *1757* declines Poet Laureateship; *1759* moves to London to read at the British Library; *1761* returns to Cambridge, his primary residence for the remainder of his life; *1768* named Regius Professor of Modern History; *1771* dies on July 30.

Author's Bibliography

"An Ode on a Distant Prospect of Eton College," 1747; "Ode on the Death of a Favourite Cat" and "Ode on the Spring," 1748; *Elegy Written in a Country Churchyard,* 1751; *Designs by Mr. R. Bentley for Six Poems by Mr. T. Gray* (adds "Ode to Adversity" and "A Long Story"), 1753; *Odes by Mr. Gray* (includes "The Progress of Poesy" and "The Bard"), 1757; *Poems by Mr. Gray* (adds "The Fatal Sisters," "The Descent of Odin," and "The Triumphs of Owen"), 1768; *The Poems of Mr. Gray. To Which are Prefixed Memoirs of His Life and Writings,* ed. 1775 William Mason (includes many of Gray's other poems including "Sonnet on the Death of Mr. Richard West").

Overview of Biographical Sources

Because Gray's life was seemingly uneventful, biographers have focused on his melancholic personality, his limited production of poetry, his scholarship, his friendships, and his reticence before the public. Of specific interest have been the difficult family setting during his childhood, the pleasant days at Eton, his paradoxical distaste for Cambridge, the Grand Tour and his falling out with Walpole, his refusal of the Poet Laureateship, and his association in his later years with Charles-Victor de Bonstetten. Biographical information is relatively complete in part through his letters and in part as a result of his friendship with William Mason, his first biographer.

Evaluation of Selected Biographies

Ketton-Cremer, R. W. *Thomas Gray.* Cambridge: Cambridge University Press, 1955. Ketton-Cremer, in writing what is the standard biography, depends heavily on Leonard Whibley's footnotes and addenda to the *Correspondence of Thomas Gray,* as well as on Whibley's own notes for a projected biography. While this scholarly study does speculate on important aspects of Gray's life, his friendships with Walpole, Mason, and Bonstetten, for example, Ketton-Cremer is always circumspect in his use of facts. He is particularly convincing in his discussion of Gray's aesthetic development in the 1740's with the concomitant of Gray's "white melancholy." He places Gray's relatively few poems in the perspective of other interests, particularly in antiquarian studies, and explains Gray's real isolation as a man and a poet. His discussion of Gray's self-view as a private man of letters who agonized over the publication of the poetry is convincing.

Lytton Sells, A. L. *Thomas Gray: His Life and Works.* London: George Allen & Unwin, 1980. In this most recent critical biography, Lytton Sells finds virtue in his having approached this work with very limited prior knowledge of either Gray the man or the poet, thus presumably establishing his own objectivity. He speculates about Gray's possible attachments to or infatuations with Walpole, West, and Bonstettin, but concludes that Gray suffered from a "deficiency of heart." His treatment of the poetry is as hostile as his treatment of the man, and he decides that "Gray must be denied a significant place among the pre-romantics." Readers unfamiliar with Gray or his period should be advised against undue reliance on this source.

Autobiographical Sources

Much attention has been given to how much of Gray is in his best known poems. Why, for example, does the "Sonnet on the Death of Richard West" reveal so little apparent emotion? Similarly, in "Elegy Written in a Country Churchyard," is Gray revealing his private sympathy for the anonymous dead, or is he expressing his barely concealed condescension toward them? A possible answer to the first question may lie in a Latin poem written shortly after West's death that does indeed express personal grief. The answer to the second can only be speculative. The single most important autobiographical source is the *Correspondence of Thomas Gray,* edited by Paget Toynbee and Leonard Whibley (Oxford: Clarendon Press, 1935, reprinted 1971). This standard edition contains 557 letters indexed and carefully annotated. Gray reveals little about his poems in these letters, although he does discuss his idea of poetry in general and makes critical comments about other writers. Moreover, an image of Gray as a witty intellect as well as a retired observer comes through clearly.

Overview of Critical Sources

As many have noted, despite Gray's slender production of poetry, his verse has always drawn considerable commentary, particularly since the publication of "Elegy Written in a Country Churchyard," and especially by other poets, among them the famous critical judgments of Samuel Johnson, William Wordsworth, and Matthew Arnold. Ironically, Johnson's essentially negative view of the poems probably did much to keep them in the eyes of the public as well as to elicit defenses from Gray's admirers. Wordsworth's criticism of the the diction was amplified by Samuel Taylor Coleridge, Lord Byron, and William Hazlitt, who also questioned Gray's apparent lack of emotion. Early in this century are the usual unsuccessful attempts in defining the era to "place" Gray as either a neoclassic or a "pre-romantic." While "Elegy Written in a Country Churchyard" has always drawn the most attention, considerable concern of late has been devoted to the other poems, particularly the Pindaric odes, "Sonnet on the Death of Mr. Richard West," and "Ode on a Distant Prospect of Eton College."

Evaluation of Selected Criticism

Downey, James and Ben Jones, eds. *Fearful Joy: Papers from the Thomas Gray Bicentenary Conference at Carleton University.* Montreal: McGill-Queens University Press, 1974. Eminent scholars provide provocative and conflicting statements on the merits of Gray's poetry in terms of diction and genre, and assess him in contrast to Johnson and William Blake within the eighteenth century context.

Golden, Morris, *Thomas Gray.* New York: Twayne, 1964. In an accessible introduction, Golden outlines Gray's career paying particular attention to the man as he sees reflected in the poems. He devotes separate chapters to the poems of the 1740's, "Elegy Written in a Country Churchyard," and the Pindaric odes respectively, and concludes with a discussion of Gray's place among the eighteenth century poets. He disputes Matthew Arnold's view that Gray was out of place in an "age of prose," arguing that emotional outpourings were not expected of Gray or of his contemporaries. In the usual classic versus romantic cleavage, Golden sensibly shows that Gray shares both tendencies.

Starr, Herbert, ed. *Twentieth Century Interpretations of Gray's "Elegy."* Englewood Cliffs, NJ: Prentice Hall, 1968. This readily available collection contains scholarly approaches from the thirty years prior to its publication. Generally discussed are Gray's sources of inspiration, the nature of the concluding epitaph, the identity of the narrator, the autobiographical issue, and the question over whether or not the theme of the poem is death as the great leveller. Most useful to students will be Cleanth Brook's "Gray's Storied Urn," Lyle Glazier's "Gray's *Elegy:* 'The Skull Beneath the Skin,' " and Morse Peckham's "Gray's 'Epitaph' Revisited" for their respective readings of the poem.

Other Sources

McKenzie, Alan T. *Thomas Gray: A Reference Guide.* Boston: G. K. Hall, 1982. An annotated bibliography that is indispensable to students and scholars.

Spack, Patricia M. "Thomas Gray: Action and Image," in *The Poetry of Vision: Five Eighteenth Century Poets.* Cambridge: Harvard University Press, 1967. A close analysis of the major poems with particular attention to the deliberate artifice of Gray's diction and the distinctions between artifice and reality.

James M. O'Neil
The Citadel

GRAHAM GREENE
1904

Author's Chronology

Born October 2, 1904, Berkhamsted, Hertfordshire, England; *1912–1922* attends Berkhamsted School, of which his father is headmaster; *1920* undergoes six months of psychoanalysis in London; *1922* enters Balliol College, Oxford; *1923* experiments with Russian roulette; *1926* is received into Roman Catholic Church; becomes sub-editor for *The Times,* London; *1927* marries Vivien Dayrell-Browning; *1929* publishes his first novel, *The Man Within; 1932* begins reviewing books and, later, films for *The Spectator; 1934* travels to Liberia; *1938* commissioned to visit Tabasco, Mexico, to report on religious persecution; *1941* works with British Foreign Office; *1942–1943* posted to Sierra Leone by the Secret Service, and works under Kim Philby; *1948–1950* works on film adaptations of *The Third Man* and *The Fallen Idol; 1951* covers Mau Mau rebellion in Kenya and the Malayan Emergency; *1953* writes *The Living Room,* his first produced play; *1954–1955* travels three times to Vietnam during French Indochina War; *1959* visits a leproserie in the Congo; *1963* visits Haiti and Cuba; *1966* settles permanently in Antibes, France; *1969–1970* travels to Paraguay, Argentina, and Chile; *1976* makes the first of several trips to Panama, at the personal invitation of General Omar Torrijos; *1985* continues to live and work in Antibes.

Author's Bibliography (selected)

Novels: *Stamboul Train,* 1932; *England Made Me,* 1935; *A Gun for Sale,* 1936; *Brighton Rock,* 1938; *The Confidential Agent,* 1939; *The Power and the Glory,* 1940; *The Ministry of Fear,* 1943; *The Heart of the Matter,* 1948; *The End of the Affair,* 1951; *The Quiet American,* 1955; *Our Man in Havana,* 1958; *A Burnt-Out Case,* 1961; *The Comedians,* 1966; *Travels with My Aunt,* 1969; *The Honorary Consul,* 1973; *The Human Factor,* 1978; *Monsignor Quixote,* 1982; *A Sort of Life,* 1971 (autobiography); *Ways of Escape,* 1980 (autobiography).

Overview of Biographical Sources

It is curious that a writer of Graham Greene's stature should have attracted so little serious biographical scrutiny. Of course Greene, now in his eighty-first year, is still very much alive and actively working. It seems, for the moment, that he may have stolen the biographers' thunder by producing two autobiographical volumes, *A Sort of Life* and *Ways of Escape.* Still, these works are impressionistic and evocative, concealing as much as they reveal; thus it is welcome news that Norman Sherry is preparing a fully documented life, apparently with Greene's cooperation. Until Sherry's biography appears, one must rely on Greene's memoirs and those of his family and friends. Among the latter, anecdotes about Greene may be found in Peter Quenell, *The Sign of the Fish* (London, 1960); Barbara Greene, *Land Benighted* (London: Geoffrey Bless, 1938); *The Diaries of Evelyn Waugh,* edited by Michael Davie (Boston: Little, Brown, 1976); and *Like It Was: The Diaries of Malcolm Muggeridge,* selected and edited by John Bright-Holmes (1982).

Evaluation of Selected Biographical Sources

Strafford, Philip, *Faith and Fiction: Creative Process in Greene and Mauriac.* Notre Dame, IN: Notre Dame University Press, 1964. Drawing on Greene's autobiographical essays, Stratford writes perceptively of Greene's adolescent crisis at Berkhamsted School where, as the headmaster's son, he felt his loyalties divided between "enemy camps" neither of which accepted him fully. Stratford provides no new information about this experience but persuasively demonstrates that it shaped Greene's persona as a man forever living on a border as much psychological as physical and, later, political.

Autobiographical Sources

Although Greene's travel books—*Journey Without Maps* (1936), *The Lawless Roads* (1939), *In Search of a Character: Two African Journals* (1961), and *Getting to Know the General: The Story of an Involvement* (1984)—have considerable autobiographical interest both as accounts of his journeys and as occasions for other personal reminiscences, all but the last are superseded by *A Sort of Life* and *Ways of Escape.* The main focus of *Getting to Know the General* is Greene's close personal friendship with General Omar Torrijos during the period of the new Panama Canal Treaty. The narrative is accompanied by Greene's exposition of his evolving political commitments, which have moved decisively to the left since his denunciation of Mexican socialism in 1939. *A Sort of Life* covers only the first twenty-seven years of Greene's life, concluding with the years of struggle and failure after the publication of *The Man Within.* Yet it is certainly one of his finest and most important books, not only because of the information it provides but also because of the suggestive shape given to the formative experiences of his life. With its pointed emphasis on "the lost childhood," the pivotal experience at Berkhamsted School, his psychoanalysis which purged his fear but left him afflicted by chronic boredom, his first attraction to the world of espionage, his obsession with psychological borders, and his conversion to Catholicism, *A Sort of Life* provides a remarkably complete map of the imaginative territory he would inhabit for more than fifty years as novelist. *Ways of Escape* is not a true sequel, although its materials are arranged so as to extend the account from 1931 to 1980. Consisting of the introductions Greene wrote for the Collected Edition of his works, interspersed with fugitive pieces of journalism, extracts from his diaries and correspondence, and tributes to friends such as Herbert Read and Evelyn Waugh, this "memoir" is diffuse, repetitive, and uneven in quality, lacking the shapeliness and economy of *A Sort of Life.*

Overview of Critical Sources

There is not yet a full-length critical treatment that adequately addresses the richness and diversity of Greene's achievement in several genres over more than five decades. Of the fifteen or so books and monographs on his work, the majority appeared more than twenty years ago, when his so-called Catholic novels—*Brighton Rock, The Power and the Glory, The Heart of the Matter, The End of the Affair,* and perhaps *A Burnt-Out Case*—still appeared to be his greatest achievement. Hence most interpreters over-emphasized the centrality of these works, conveniently downplaying significant, but "non-Catholic," works such as *The Ministry of Fear* and *The Quiet American.* This selective emphasis resulted in tiresomely repetitive and reductive discussions of theological matters, at the expense of analyzing the more significant artistic elements of Greene's canon. His later works, beginning with *The Comedians,* have been unduly neglected, in part because they do not readily lend themselves to a predominently "theological" approach. In short, Greene's *oeuvre* is seriously in need of detailed analysis and reassessment.

Evaluation of Selected Criticism

Allott, Kenneth and Mariam Farris, *The Art of Graham Greene.* London: Hamish Hamilton, 1951. This first book in English on Greene remains one of the best, despite its essentially thematic approach. The chapter titles are chosen to illustrate Greene's "obsessive" subjects: the terror of life, the divided mind, the fallen world, and the universe of pity. Nevertheless, Allott and Farris include discussion of the early "pre-Catholic" novels and the "entertainments" as well as the Catholic novels written through 1948. Given their rather narrow focus, the readings are remarkably penetrating and cogent.

Consolo, Dominick P. "Graham Greene: Style and Stylistics in Five Novels," in *Graham Greene: Some Critical Considerations.* edited by Robert O. Evans. Lexington: University of Kentucky Press, 1963. By far the most significant article in this early collection of essays, Consolo's pioneering study of four "Catholic" novels and *The Quiet American* provides a detailed, rigorous analysis of Greene's recurring techniques of characterization, narrative viewpoint, structure, and syntax.

DeVitis, A. A. *Graham Greene.* New York: Twayne, 1964. DeVitis mounts a vigorous attack on critics who treat Greene's work as a species of theological argument; yet his book devotes so much attention to this dispute that it seldom succeeds in looking at Greene's writing in artistic terms. Though the Catholic works are highlighted, DeVitis also discusses the early novels, the entertainments, and the three plays written in the 1950's; the annotated bibliography is useful.

Hoggart, Richard, *Speaking to Each Other.* London: Oxford University Press, 1970. Hoggart's essay on "The Force of Caricature: Aspects of the Art of Graham Greene," which has been widely reprinted, is the most penetrating and persuasive attack on Greene's fiction yet to appear. Focusing on *The Power and the Glory* as representative of Greene's novels, Hoggart analyzes the "seedy" setting, the "allegorical" symbols, the "nervous, vivid, astringent" style, the puppet-like characters, and the melodramatic plot, finding them all to be powerful but unrealistic contrivances—manipulations imposed from outside the material as the vehicles of Greene's peculiarly obsessive view of life.

Stratford, Philip, *Faith and Fiction: Creative Process in Greene and Mauriac.* In this comparative study of two Catholic novelists, Stratford succeeds in demonstrating the distinctness of each yet also finds interesting parallels. Despite his initial focus on religious issues, Stratford deftly modulates his discussion to include questions of genre and fictional technique and provides suggestive readings of several works. In his hands, the "Catholic writer" label is given maximum elucidation, and one is enabled to see how it might be extended to include the later Greene, usually regarded as typical of the "lapsed" Catholic.

Wolfe, Peter, *Graham Greene the Entertainer.* Carbondale: Southern Illinois University Press, 1972. Wolfe addresses a key issue, the relationship of Greene's popular "entertainments" to his more "serious" novels—a question on which Greene's own views have undergone significant change, until he no longer subscribes to the distinction. Unfortunately, Wolfe's book lacks methodological rigor and, although offering salutary attention to comparatively neglected works, it provides little clarification of the issue of genre.

Other Sources

Lodge, David, *Graham Greene,* Columbia Essays on Modern Writers, #17. New York: Columbia University Press, 1966. A sympathetic and often perceptive survey of the novels, by an important critic.

Spurling, John, *Graham Greene,* Contemporary Writers, #14. London: Methuen, 1983. Concise overview of Greene's life and career, with due attention to the later works.

Ronald G. Walker
University of Houston-Victoria

FULKE GREVILLE
1554–1628

Author's Chronology

Born, 1554, at Warwickshire, England, of titled parentage; *1564* enters grammar school with Philip Sidney, with whom he forms the principal friendship of his life; *1568* matriculates at Cambridge; *1576* begins his long service at Elizabeth's court under the patronage of Sidney; *1577–1579* undertakes diplomatic missions to the continent; *1583* named Secretary to Wales, a position he maintains until his death; *1591* serves in Normandy under Henry of Navarre; *1592–1593* begins his first of several terms as Member of Parliament for Warwickshire; *1596* pallbearer at Sidney's funeral; *1597* named Knight of the Bath; *1598* designated Treasurer of the Wars and Treasurer of the Navy; *1603* Elizabeth dies; *1605* granted Warwick Castle by James I; *1612* adopts only son, Robert Greville; *1614–1621* serves as Chancellor of the Exchequer; *1621* created Baron (First Lord) Brooke; *1624* named to Council of War; *1625* appointed to the Council of Foreign Affairs; *1628* murdered by disaffected servant and buried in St. Mary's Church, Warwick.

Author's Bibliography

Life of Sir Philip Sidney, edited by Nowell Smith, 1907; *Poems and Dramas of Fulke Greville,* edited by Geoffrey Bullough, two volumes, 1938; *The Remains Being Poems of Monarchy and Religion,* edited by G. A. Wilkes, 1965; *Selected Poems of Fulke Greville,* edited by Thom Gunn, 1968; *Selected Writings of Fulke Greville,* edited by Joan Rees, 1973; *The Works in Verse and Prose Complete of the Right Honourable Fulke Greville, Lord Brooke,* edited by Alexander B. Grosart, 4 Vols. 1870.

Overview of Biographical Sources

Because of his long and public life at the courts of Elizabeth, James, and Charles, more primary biographical sources exist for Greville than for virtually any other Renaissance figure. Nevertheless, no full-length biography of Greville existed until 1971, when two such works appeared: Joan Rees's *Fulke Greville, Lord Brooke, 1554–1628: A Critical Biography* (Berkeley: University of California Press, 1971) and Ronald Rebholz's *The Life of Fulke Greville, First Lord Brooke* (Oxford: Clarendon Press, 1971). Rees confines her biographical comments to four opening chapters; she does not pretend to be comprehensive, but rather seeks to provide an adequate background for her investigation of Greville's works. Accordingly, Rebholz's book stands as the fullest treatment of Greville's life; it falls short of being "definitive" only in the sense that the wealth of materials on Greville requires judicious selection. Prior to these studies, students of Greville could rely only on the brief biography provided in

Morris W. Croll's *The Works of Fulke Greville* (Philadelphia: Lippincott, 1903) and the biographical sketch prefacing Geoffrey Bullough's *Poems and Dramas of Fulke Greville, First Lord Brooke* (London: Oliver and Boyd, 1938). More recently, a helpful bio-critical review of Greville's life and works has become available in Charles Larson's *Fulke Greville* (Boston: Twayne, 1980). An edition of Greville's letters has been long promised.

Evaluation of Selected Biographies

Rebholz, Ronald, *The Life of Fulke Greville, First Lord Brooke.* Oxford: Clarendon Press, 1971. Contrary to Rees and others, Rebholz believes that Greville's works can be dated with a fair degree of accuracy and that his writings describe a personal movement away from an initially optimistic humanism and toward a darkly fatalistic Calvinism. Rebholz's aim, therefore, is to document this development by correlating his reading of Greville's works with the chief divisions of the poet's life. Rebholz's success in this endeavor is debatable, but it is certain that he has provided the closest account available of Greville's life. The book is minutely researched and dense with detail.

Rees, Joan, *Fulke Greville, Lord Brooke, 1554–1628.* Berkeley: University of California Press, 1971. As mentioned above, Rees subordinates biography to the role of supporting her views about Greville's poetry, and her approach to his life is often anecdotal. Nonetheless, Rees chooses her anecdotes with precision in an effort to depict Greville as an artist whose thought and work is remarkably consistent from first to last. The more common idea is that Greville was essentially torn between the competing calls of his religion and the world, but Rees, in this eminently readable biography, sees his life's work as a seamless whole and argues compellingly that no fundamental rift can be inferred from Greville's sustained effort to serve both God and his earthly sovereign.

Autobiographical Sources

Greville wrote no autobiography, but his *Life of Sidney,* a memorial to his closest friend, offers considerable information about Greville himself, including the early years at court, travels to the continent, and the aesthetic, religious, and political convictions behind his and Sidney's writings.

Overview of Critical Sources

Greville's critical star is clearly rising. His identification in this century as the last of the major Renaissance writers to be "discovered" has prompted many recent articles and dissertations. However, it is plain from the scholarly work being done that Greville's reputation will rest with his sonnet sequence *Caelica;* comparatively little interest has been paid to his long verse treatises or to his Senecan closet dramas *Mustapha* and *Alaham.* Further, full-length published criticisms of Greville's canon remain very few in number; for this reason alone,

Rees's and Rebholz's bio-critical works, cited above, are of major importance. A discernible trend in recent Greville criticism is an attempt to place him more firmly in the context of the wide-ranging group of Protestant thinkers with which he shared his religious beliefs and to which he tied his hopes for political advancement.

Evaluation of Selected Criticism

Croll, Morris W. *The Works of Fulke Greville.* Philadelphia: Lippincott, 1903. This early assessment of Greville's works remains useful, especially to students new to the poet and his themes. Croll sparked the current interest in Greville by insisting on his status as a major poet who imposed "a new character upon the forms and conventions" of the genres within which he worked.

Waswo, Richard, *The Fatal Mirror: Themes and Techniques in the Poetry of Fulke Greville.* Charlottesville: University Press of Virginia, 1972. Waswo's study stands as perhaps the single most luminous commentary on Greville. Waswo touches upon the entire Greville corpus, but his point of focus is a close and informed reading of the *Caelica* sequence, a work which he sees as unified in terms of its literary and religious traditions. He argues for the given sequential order in *Caelica* and explicates Greville's relation to such figures as Petrarch, Sidney, Donne, and Herbert.

Winters, Yvor, *Forms of Discovery: Critical and Historical Essays on the Forms of the Short Poem in English.* Chicago: Alan Swallow, 1967. Winters' high praise of Greville—he calls him, with Jonson, "one of the two great masters of the short poem in the Renaissance"—has done much to elevate the poet's reputation. His discussion of the native English "plain" style provides a historical framework whereby the aims of Greville and his contemporaries may be better understood. And Winters, in his role as teacher, has influenced subsequent editors and critics of Greville, including Richard Waswo, Thom Gunn, and Douglas Peterson.

Other Sources

Maclean, Hugh N. "Fulke Greville: Kingship and Sovereignty," *Huntington Library Quarterly,* 16 (1953), 237–271. The best short introduction to Greville's theory of statecraft in the *Monarchy* treatise.

Peterson, Douglas, "Fulke Greville's *Caelica,*" *The English Lyric from Wyatt to Donne: A History of the Plain and Eloquent Styles* (Princeton: Princeton University Press, 1967). More on Winters' views of Greville as a "plain" stylist.

Bennett, Paula, "Recent Studies in Greville," *English Literary Renaissance,* 2 (1972), 376–382. A good annotated bibliography of research on Greville through 1971.

Levy, F. J., "Fulke Greville: The Courtier as Philosophic Poet," *Modern Language Quarterly,* 33 (1972), 433–448. A review of the Rebholz and Rees biographies and a plea for contextual studies of Greville.

Waller, G. F. "Fulke Greville's Struggle with Calvinism," *Studia Neophilologica,* 44 (1972), 295–314. A fine summary of Greville's Calvinism and its relationship to his works.

Williams, John, "Fulke Greville: The World and God," *Denver Quarterly,* 10 (Summer 1975), 106–120. A brief introduction to Greville's life and works.

Selected Dictionaries and Encyclopedias

Biographia Britannica, Volume 3, London, 1750. A venerable but still useful précis of Greville's life.

Dictionary of National Biography, Volume 8, Oxford University Press, 1890. Occasionally erroneous overview of Greville's life; contains an early assertion of his debt to Sidney.

William R. Drennan
University of Wisconsin
Center-Baraboo/Sauk County

H. D.
1886–1961

Author's Chronology

Born Hilda Doolittle September 10, 1886, Bethlehem, Pennsylvania; *1904* enters Bryn Mawr College; *1905* becomes engaged to Ezra Pound; *1906* withdraws from Bryn Mawr; *1906–1911* lives at home and begins serious writing; *1911* leaves America for London; *1913* first Imagist poems published; marries Richard Aldington; *1915* loses first child; *1918* meets Bryher (Winifred Ellerman) who becomes her benefactor and lifelong companion; *1919* daughter, Perdita, is born; separates from Aldington; *1920* travels to Greece with Bryher; *1922* takes up residence in Switzerland; *1925* publishes *Collected Poems; 1930* makes film *Borderline; 1933–1934* analysis with Freud; *1938* receives Helen Haire Levinson Prize of *Poetry* magazine; is divorced from Aldington; *1939* returns to London to live throughout the war; *1942–1944* writes *Trilogy's* three sections; *1946* returns to Switzerland; *1948* writes *Tribute to Freud; 1951–1954* writes *Helen in Egypt; 1959* receives Brandeis University Creative Arts Award for Poetry; *1960* becomes first woman to receive Award of Merit Medal for Poetry of the American Academy of Arts and Letters; *1961* dies September 28, near Zurich, Switzerland.

Author's Bibliography (selected)

Collected Poems of H. D., 1925; *Euripides' Ion,* 1937 (translation and commentary); *Tribute to Freud,* 1956 (memoir); *Selected Poems of H. D.,* 1957; *Bid Me to Live,* 1960 (novel); *Helen in Egypt,* 1961 (poem); *Hermetic Definition,* 1972 (poem sequence); *Trilogy,* 1973 (poem); *End to Torment: A Memoir of Ezra Pound,* 1979; *Hermione,* 1981 (novel); *The Gift,* 1982 (memoir); *H. D.: Collected Poems 1912–1944,* 1983 (includes *Trilogy*).

Overview of Biographical Sources

H. D.'s circle of friend's and intimate associates included such literary figures as Ezra Pound, William Carlos Williams, Amy Lowell, D. H. Lawrence, Marianne Moore, T. S. Eliot, and Richard Aldington, and much biographical information about H. D. is present in books by and about these other writers. At the present time, however, H. D.'s own life is the subject of only three book-length studies: Vincent Quinn's *Hilda Doolittle: (H. D.)* (1967), Janice S. Robinson's *H. D.: The Life and Work of an American Poet* (1982), and Barbara Guest's *Herself Defined: The Poet H. D. and Her World* (1984). Quinn's and Robinson's books are as much criticism as biography, but Guest's book tells the story of H. D.'s life quite objectively and in vivid detail.

Evaluation of Biographies

Guest, Barbara, *Herself Defined: The Poet H. D. and Her World.* Garden City, NY: Doubleday, 1984. H. D. authorized no biography, but she left behind her a biographer's treasure-trove: letters, notebooks, memoirs, unpublished manuscripts of poetry, prose, and fiction. Barbara Guest has drawn on these sources, on works written by and about H. D.'s friends and intimates, and on interviews with numerous people including H. D.'s daughter, Perdita Schaffner, in writing this comprehensive biography. A poet herself, Guest holds H. D.'s poetry in the highest regard. Nevertheless, she neither canonizes her subject nor focuses on the product rather than the poet. Guest's account is compassionate but objective. She gives the facts of H. D.'s life and the lives of those who inhabited the colorful, indeed bizarre circle in which she moved, while refusing to indulge in mere speculation.

Quinn, Vincent, *Hilda Doolittle: (H. D.)*. New York: Twayne, 1967. Quinn presents a basic introduction to H. D.'s life and works. The biographical section is limited to the years 1886-1925, years encompassing H. D.'s childhood, engagement to Pound, acclaim as an Imagist poet, marriage and separation, mental and physical breakdown, and convalescence with Bryher. The section contains enough detail to be interesting while remaining brief enough for quick reference.

Robinson, Janice S. *H. D.: The Life and Work of an American Poet.* Boston: Houghton Mifflin, 1982. Robinson amasses an impressive array of sources as she attempts a synthesis of H. D.'s life and work, saying in her introduction that she constructs a "literary biographical narrative" by using H. D.'s life to "illuminate" her work, and vice versa. The book begins with H. D.'s birth, proceeds chronologically, and ends with her death, events are described and interpreted by means of poems, novels, and other writings in which H. D.'s experiences are fictionalized. This can be most confusing if one has had no previous introduction to H. D. In addition, some scholars question Robinson's interpretations, speculations, and conclusions.

Autobiographical Sources

H. D. wrote no autobiography as such, and no work which shows concern for names and dates or for exact, factual recollection. Nevertheless, much of her work is highly autobiographical, with *Bid Me to Live, Hermione, The Gift, Tribute to Freud,* and *End to Torment* offering insights into H. D.'s life.

Bid Me to Live is, H. D. admitted, a *roman à clef.* It takes place during World War I in England and tells the story of the troubled marriage of Hilda and Richard Aldington ("Julia" and "Rafe") during the years 1916-1918. Featuring D. H. and Freida Lawrence ("Rico" and "Elsa") among its cast of characters, *Bid Me to Live* offers insight into the complex personalities and relationships of gifted artists during a time when their lives and the world they knew were crumbling to bits. *Hermione,* a novel, and *The Gift,* a novelistic memoir, tell of earlier times. In *The Gift,* H. D. recalls her early childhood days first in Bethlehem and then in Philadelphia. Although H. D. wrote it in 1941, *The Gift's* voice is that of a small child who observes and tries to understand her circumscribed world of home and family. *Hermione,* written in 1927, tells a more troubled tale of H. D.'s years living at home after the trauma of her failure at Bryn Mawr, years which encompassed her engagement to Ezra Pound, her infatuation with a cousin, Frances Josepha Gregg, and the first of a series of mental breakdowns. *Tribute to Freud* and *End to Torment,* both affectionate memoirs, offer additional insights. In the first, H. D. describes her analysis with Sigmund Freud in 1933 and 1934; in the second, which was prompted by H. D.'s hope in 1958 that Pound would soon be released from federal custody, she reminisces about their early relationship as lovers and later as friends.

No one volume, then, gives a complete picture, and in all of them H. D. fictionalizes her experience to a greater or lesser extent. All are written in H. D.'s distinctively poetic and difficult prose style.

Overview of Critical Sources

Acclaimed for her early Imagist poems but for nothing else, H. D. was long neglected or panned by critics. However, the past fifteen years or so bear witness to a fast-increasing body of appreciative critical commentary. Because many of H. D.'s published volumes were long out of print, and because other manuscripts remain unpublished, no detailed and systematic book-length study of the entire *oeuvre* has been possible.

Evaluation of Selected Criticism

Dembo, L. S. *Conceptions of Reality in Modern American Poetry.* Berkeley: University of California Press, 1966. One of the first critics to rank H. D. among great poets of the twentieth century, Dembo has high praise for the neo-epics *Trilogy* and *Helen in Egypt.*

Friedman, Susan Stanford, *Psyche Reborn: The Emergence of H. D..* Bloomington: Indiana University Press, 1981. In this groundbreaking work of feminist criticism, Friedman focuses in depth on H. D.'s psychoanalysis, her interest in hermetic tradition, and the effect of these on her writing.

Holland, Norman N. *Poems in Persons: An Introduction to the Psychoanalysis of Literature.* New York: W. W. Norton, 1973, pp. 5–59. Although Holland's focus is on the methods of psychoanalytic criticism, he chooses H. D. as his primary subject and devotes one of the book's three chapters to a discussion of her works.

Ostriker, Alicia, *Writing Like a Woman.* Ann Arbor: University of Michigan Press, 1983, pp. 7–41. In the section entitled "The Poet as Heroine: Learning to Read H. D.," Ostriker defines and discusses the early, middle, and late "phases" of H. D.'s poetry, and she praises H. D. as a visionary poet and revisionist mythmaker.

Quinn, Vincent, *Hilda Doolittle: (H. D.)*. New York: Twayne, 1967. Quinn's overview is a useful introduction to the wide range of H. D.'s work. After discussing her early poetry, her translations and adaptations, and her prose fiction, he devotes a chapter each to *Trilogy* and to *Helen in Egypt*. After making his review, however, Quinn concludes that H. D.'s early lyric poetry is her best work.

Other Sources

Contemporary Literature, Vol. 10, Autumn 1969. This special issue on H. D. is entitled "H. D.: A Reconsideration" and includes essays by Joseph Riddel, Norman Holland, Bernard Engel, Linda Wagner, A. Kingsley Weatherhead, Cyrena Pondrom, and L. S. Dembo.

Gubar, Susan, "The Echoing Spells of H. D.'s *Trilogy*." *Contemporary Literature,* 19 (1978), 196–218. rpt. in *Shakespeare's Sisters: Feminist Essays on Women Poets.* eds. Sandra M. Gilbert and Susan Gubar. Bloomington: Indiana University Press, 1979, pp. 200–218. In this much-quoted essay, Gubar discusses H. D.'s creation of a female mythology in *Trilogy.*

Selected Dictionaries and Encyclopedias

American Women Writers, Vol. 1, Frederick Ungar, 1979. Brief biography and a good, sympathetic critical overview.

Contemporary Authors, Vol. 97–100, Gale Research, 1981. Good biographical essay and an excellent bibliography.

Dictionary of Literary Biography, Vol. 4, Gale Research, 1980. Excellent overview of H. D.'s life and works.

Margaret M. Dunn
Indiana University

ARTHUR HENRY HALLAM
1811–1833

Author's Chronology

Born 1 February 1811 in Bedford Place, London; son of noted historian Henry Hallam; *1819* begins formal education at Putney; studies at Eton, *1822–1827; 1825* elected to Eton Debating Society; becomes friends with Gladstone and with James Gaskell; Winter *1827–1828* tours Italy; October *1828* wishes to attend Oxford but enters Trinity College, Cambridge, at father's insistence; early spring, *1829* begins close friendship with Tennyson; May *1829* elected to Cambridge Apostles Society; early *1830* visits Tennyson's home in Lincolnshire and falls in love with Emily Tennyson; December *1830* proposes to Emily; Henry Hallam discourages match, exacts promise that Arthur will not see Emily until his twenty-first birthday; *1831* wins Declamation Prize at Cambridge; summer *1831* brings together Tennyson and Edward Moxon, Tennyson's lifelong publisher; 21 January *1832* receives BA; Spring *1832* announces engagement to Emily; marriage delayed by financial arrangements; August *1833* Hallam and father take European tour; 15 September 1833 Hallam dies in Vienna of a cerebral hemorrhage, probably brought on by an aneurism.

Author's Bibliography

Timbuctoo, 1829 (private printing of poem); *Poems by A. H. Hallam, Esq,* 1830 (private printing); "On Some of the Characteristics of Modern Poetry, and on the Lyrical Poems of Alfred Tennyson," *Englishman's Magazine,* August 1831; *Essay on the Philosophical Writings of Cicero,* 1832; *Oration, on the Influence of Italian Works of the Imagination on the Same Class of Compositions in England,* 1832; *Remarks on Professor Rossetti's "Disquisizioni Sullo Spirito Antipapale,"* 1832; *Remains, in Verse and Prose, of Arthur Henry Hallam,* ed. Henry Hallam, 1834; *The Writings of Arthur Henry Hallam,* ed. T. H. Vail Motter, 1943; "Some Unpublished Poems by Arthur Henry Hallam," ed. Sir Charles Tennyson and F. T. Baker, *Victorian Poetry* 3, supplement, 1965.

Autobiographical Sources

Arthur Henry Hallam is best remembered as the A.H.H. of Tennyson's *In Memoriam A.H.H.,* rather than for any lasting contribution of his own, so there is no book-length biography of him, and since he died at the age of twenty-two, he wrote no autobiography. The best source of information about Hallam's life is Jack Kolb's *The Letters of Arthur Henry Hallam* (Columbus: Ohio State University Press) 1981. Because Hallam's letters and manuscripts are in libraries scattered across England and the United States, making access a problem, and since previous publications of Hallam's letters have been fragmentary and often erroneous, Kolb's edition is welcomed. This collection of all known letters and fragments shows Hallam's combination of brilliance and emotional immaturity. The letters give a fair picture of this man, who, upon his death at the age of twenty-two, had already heavily influenced Tennyson and Gladstone and was almost universally admired by his peers. Hallam's critical views had already begun to swing opinion away from Byron and toward the Shelleyan and Keatsian verse practiced by the young Tennyson. Had he lived, critics believe that Hallam might have offset the influx of German criticism introduced and championed by such strong minds as Carlyle and George Eliot.

Other Sources

Allen, Peter, *The Cambridge Apostles: The Early Years.* Cambridge: Cambridge University Press, 1978. A history of the Apostles' beginnings, the book deals with Hallam's role as guiding spirit of that august group during his time at Cambridge.

Brook, John and Mary Sorensen, eds. *The Prime Minister's Papers: W. E. Gladstone. I: Autobiographica.* London: Her Majesty's Stationery Office, 1971. Scattered details of Hallam's life, together with testimony to the high regard his friends and acquaintances had for him.

Gladstone, William Ewart, *Diaries.* Vols. 1 and 2. ed. M. R. D. Foot. New York: Oxford University Press, 1968. An important contemporary source, and by far the more reliable. Though Tennyson and Hallam were ultimately much closer than were Hallam and Gladstone, Gladstone's diary entries provide a somewhat more objective view of Hallam, and they focus more on Hallam's potential in public life, whereas the Tennyson memoir deals with the personal relationship between the poet and Hallam.

———. "Personal Recollections of Hallam," London *Daily Telegraph* 5 January 1898. A late-in-life reminiscence of a friend of Gladstone's youth, the article is almost necessarily romanticized.

Kolb, Jack, "Arthur Hallam and Emily Tennyson," *Review of English Studies* 28 (1977), 32–48. Based on the long weekly letters Hallam wrote to his fiancee, the essay gives a detailed account of Hallam's courtship and engagement.

Pearce, Helen, "Homage to Arthur Henry Hallam," in *The Image of the Work: Essays in Criticism.* ed. B. H. Lehman. Berkeley: University of California Press, 1955. Provides an assessment of Hallam's reputation among his contemporaries and deals with their views of his potential accomplishments.

Tennyson, Hallam, *Alfred, Lord Tennyson: A Memoir of My Father.* London, 1897. Primary source for information about Hallam's relationship with the poet. The book's understandable bias dictates that it must be used with caution, since it primarily contains second-hand reminiscences written by the son of the subject, who also happens to be Arthur Hallam's namesake.

Selected Dictionaries and Encyclopedias

Dictionary of Literary Biography, Vol. 32, Gale Research, 1984. The excellent entry on Hallam, written by Jack Kolb, is in the form of an extended biographical essay, complete with author's bibliography and selected critical bibliography.

William Condon
Arkansas Tech University

THOMAS HARDY
1840–1928

Author's Chronology

Born June 2, 1849, eldest of four children to Thomas and Jemina Hardy in Dorset, at Higher Bockhampton; *1856* articled to John Hick, a Dorchester architect; *1862* travels to London and begins work for Arthur Blomfield, an architect; *1870* goes to Cornwall to inspect St. Juliot Church and meets Emma Gifford for the first time; *1871* publishes *Desperate Remedies,* first successful novel, to mixed reviews; *1872* publishes *Under the Greenwood Tree;* begins the serialization of *A Pair of Blue Eyes* in the September issue of *Tinsleys' Magazine; 1873* suicide of friend, Horace Moule; December, begins first installment of *Far From the Madding Crowd* in *Cornhill Magazine; 1874* marries Emma Gifford in Paddington, honeymoons in France and collects material for next novels; *1880* onset of serious illness; *1885* moves to a house which he designs, Max Gate, just on the outskirts of Dorchester; *1887* publishes the first number of *The Woodlanders* in *Macmillan's Magazine* which sold out its first printing of 10,000 copies immediately; later that year visits Italy; *1891* publishes *Tess of the D'Urbervilles* which ignites a storm of controversy over its explicit mention of sexual matters; *1893* publishes *Jude the Obscure* which results in such negative criticism that Hardy resolves to return to poetry writing exclusively; *1898* publishes *Wessex Poems; 1910* receives the Order of Merit; *1912* death of his wife Emma; *1914* marries Florence Dugdate at St. Andrew's Church, Enfield; *1927* last public appearance is an address at a stone-laying at Dorchester Grammar School; January 11, 1928 dies at Max Gate.

Author's Bibliography (selected)

Desperate Remedies, 1871 (novel); *Under the Greenwood Tree,* 1872 (novel); *Far from the Madding Crowd,* 1874 (novel); *The Return of the Native,* 1878 (novel); *The Mayor of Casterbridge,* 1886 (novel); *Wessex Tales,* 1888 (stories); *Tess of the D'Urbervilles,* 1891 (novel); *Jude the Obscure,* 1896 (novel); *Wessex Poems,* 1898; *Poems of the Past and Present,* 1901; *A Changed Man and Other Tales,* 1913; *Moments of Vision,* 1917 (poems); *Later Lyrics and Earlier,* 1922 (poems); *Winter Words,* 1928 (poems).

The history of the printing of Hardy's works, especially his novels, has the complexity typical of the nineteenth century British novelist. Many of his novels appeared first in serial fashion in periodicals and then were published in multi-volume sets afterward. In Hardy's case, his novels were serialized in such magazines as *Tinsleys' Magazine, Cornhill Magazine* and *Macmillan's Magazine.* These versions often show the evidence of heavy-handed editing as a result of the fears of the journals' publishers that Hardy's explicitness in regard to matters of sexuality and religious belief would harm the circulation. Hence, it is only in the full-length versions that the more explicit scenes appear.

The Wessex Editions of the novels and verse are the best editions available. The earlier version, 1912–1931, was compiled under Hardy's supervision. The more recent, the New Wessex Edition, begun in 1974, not only provides accurate texts but introductions in the individual volumes by such Hardy authorities as J. Hillis Miller, Harold Orel and Robert Gittings.

Overview of Biographical Sources

Hardy's biographers have been many. No 'definitive' biography exists, but numerous studies shed a good deal of light on Hardy's inspirations, early influences and interaction with publishers. Among such include: Florence Emily Hardy's two volumes, *The Early Life of Thomas Hardy: 1840–1891* (London: Macmillan Company, 1928) and *The Later Years of Thomas Hardy: 1892–1928* (New York: Macmillan Company, 1930); Clive Holland's *Thomas Hardy, O.M.: The Man, His Works and the Land of Wessex* (London: Herbert Jenkins Limited, 1933). These three works represent early attempts at biography. The former two contain primary material that Hardy dictated to his wife and so represent the closest thing to an autobiography by Hardy which exists.

Evaluation of Selected Biographies

Blunden, Edmund, *Thomas Hardy*. London: Macmillan, 1942. This short work, among one of the more influential earlier biographies, concentrates on Hardy's background and earlier days. It precedes the vast research done in the past two decades but has merit as an early view of Hardy's life.

Gittings, Robert, *Young Thomas Hardy*. Boston: Little, Brown, 1975. This first volume in a two-volume set includes material on Hardy's early life, especially his work as an architect's apprentice, his friendship with Horace Moule, his marriage to Emma Gifford and general attitudes toward subjects such as religion. A number of photographs of the young Hardy and his surroundings are included.

Guerard, Albert J. *Thomas Hardy*. Cambridge, MA: Harvard University Press, 1949. This work, only somewhat a biography, places Hardy in the tradition of the modern novelist such as Andre Gidé and Conrad. This is a fine reading of a number of important works and their relation to Hardy's development as a 'modern' novelist.

———, *Thomas Hardy's Later Years*. Boston: Little, Brown, 1978. This work follows the earlier by Gittings. It covers the final fifty years of Hardy's life and seeks to uncover the hidden currents of Hardy's life as they are revealed in the later novels and the poetry. The work is well-documented and contains some interesting photographs of both of Hardy's wives.

Millgate, Michael, *Thomas Hardy: A Biography*. New York: Random House, 1982. As a co-editor of the Clarendon Press edition of the letters of Hardy,

Millgate brings to this full-length study an extraordinary knowledge of Hardy's life, background and attitudes. A richly documented work, this may be the most complete biography available at the present time. Among the illustrations and photographs is one interesting plate entitled "The Hardy Pedigree" which is a family tree written out by Hardy around 1917.

Orel, Harold, *The Final Years of Thomas Hardy: 1912–1928.* Lawrence: The University Press of Kansas, 1976. This volume deals primarily with the poetry, beginning with *The Dynasts, Part Third* in 1908 through *Winter Woods* in 1928. Two chapters in particular shed light on the relationship of biography to art: "Emma" which examines Hardy's first marriage and "Hardy's Views on Christianity" which explores Hardy's later theological position as reflected in his work.

Autobiographical Sources

In addition to the two volumes by Florence Hardy which were dictated by Hardy, two useful sources for autobiographical information are Harold Orel's edition of *Thomas Hardy's Personal Writings: Prefaces, Literary Opinions, Reminiscences* (Lawrence: The University Press of Kansas, 1966) and *The Collected Letters of Thomas Hardy* edited by Richard Little Purdy and Michael Millgate (Oxford: The Clarendon Press, 1980). The former is an excellent source of primary material on Hardy's views in relation to literature. Included are all the prefaces he wrote for the Wessex Edition of his writings and other commentaries on the literature of others such as H. J. Moule's *Dorchester Antiquities.* The annotated appendix of minor writings is useful for anyone wishing to examine Hardy's views on such disparate subjects as English country dances and the hunting of animals. The latter series, the collected letters, is still in process. The several volumes already available, represent the most complete collection of the letters available and will probably be as close to a definitive edition of the letters as possible. They reveal, among other things, the Hardy who was a careful manager of his finances and his legal affairs.

Overview of Critical Sources

Hardy and his works have been the subject of hundreds of articles, dissertations and full-length studies. As an influence on twentieth-century poetry and fiction, he has been examined in numerous additional essays. The *MLA Annual Bibliography* lists an ever-expanding bibliography. Although no single work covers this complex and prolific writer a number of works listed below will indicate the range and diversity of the criticism he has inspired.

Evaluation of Selected Criticism

Bailey, J. O. *The Poetry of Thomas Hardy: A Handbook and Commentary.* Chapel Hill: University of North Carolina Press, 1970. This is a very helpful work which provides background to the people and places prominent in Hardy's poetry. The second section of the work provides background for over a thousand poems. Useful especially for the beginning reader of Hardy's poetry.

Drabble, Margaret, ed. *The Genius of Thomas Hardy.* New York: Alfred A. Knopf, 1976. This is an excellent beginning text for readers of Hardy. The sections are three: "The Life," "The Work," and "The Genius of Thomas Hardy," with essays written by such authorities as Harold Orel, Lord David Cecil and Drabble herself. Easily readable, the text provides excellent photographs of Hardy, his family and his milieu.

Hawkins, Desmond, *Hardy: Novelist and Poet.* New York: Barnes and Noble, 1976. This work attempts to survey the whole of Hardy's work, both in poetry and in prose. It provides biographical background and several appendices which are useful, including one with brief synopses of the novels.

Miller, J. Hillis, *Thomas Hardy: Distance and Desire.* Boston: Belknap Press of Harvard University Press, 1970. This work centers on the novels and provides some fine commentary on the principal ones. Miller then turns to a study of Hardy's shift to poetry in the later part of his life and explores such notions as the pessimism in the poetry and the novels.

Murphin, Ross C. *Swinburne, Hardy and Lawrence.* Chicago: University of Chicago Press, 1978. This is a good example of criticism which attempts to 'place' Hardy in the tradition of British literature. Murphin demonstrates the influence which Swinburne had on Hardy and the effect that both Hardy and Swinburne had on D. H. Lawrence.

Pipkin, Charles, ed. *The Southern Review,* 6 (1940). The entire number of this journal is given over, in the Centennial year, to Hardy and contains such articles as W. H. Auden, "A Literary Transference" and F. R. Leavis, "Hardy the Poet." Other distinguished contributers include Delmore Schwartz and R. P. Blackmur.

Zitelow, Paul, *Moments of Vision: The Poetry of Thomas Hardy.* Cambridge: Harvard University Press, 1974. This is an excellent full-length study of the *Collected Poems.* It attempts to describe, poem by poem, Hardy's method and intent in the poetry. It is a readable study and an excellent introduction to Hardy's poetic method.

Other Sources

Cox, R. G. ed. *Thomas Hardy: The Critical Heritage.* New York: Barnes & Noble, 1970. The Hardy volume of this series provides the same coverage of contemporary reaction and evaluation as other works in this series. It begins with early reviews of *Desperate Remedies* in 1871 and is a good source of understanding of the range of critical reaction to Hardy's more controversial novels, *Tess of the D'Urbervilles* and *Jude the Obscure.* Of the seventy-eight entries, the first sixty concern the novels and the final eighteen the poetry.

Davis, W. Eugene and Helmut E. Gerber, *Thomas Hardy: An Annotated Bibliography of Writings About Him. Volume II 1970–1978 and Supplement for 1871–1969.* DeKalb: Northern Illinois University Press, 1983. This is an excellent source of annual bibliography on secondary sources for the works of Hardy. It is exhaustive in its coverage and it provides useful annotations.

Taylor, Richard H. ed. *The Personal Notebooks of Thomas Hardy.* New York: Columbia University Press, 1979. This volume present the texts of four of Hardy's notebooks: Memoranda, I; Memoranda II; Schools of Painting Notebook; Trumpet-Major Notebook. Despite Hardy's explicit directions that the notebooks be destroyed, these survived and provide a good deal of insight into the creation of the novels and poems.

Selected Dictionaries and Encyclopedias

Encyclopedia of World Literature in the Twentieth Century, revised edition, Frederick Ungar, 1982. This work provides a lengthy entry on Hardy which includes biography, a list of principal works with synopses, bibliography and excerpts from critics on Hardy ranging from Virginia Woolf to Donald Davie.

Critical Survey of Long Fiction, Salem Press, 1983. This series, concentrating on long fiction, provides seventeen pages on Hardy, including biography, achievements, analysis of works and bibliography.

Twentieth Century Literary Criticism: Excerpts from Criticism of the Works of Novelists, Poets, Playwrights, Short Story Writers, and other Creative Writers Who Lived between 1900 and 1960, from the First Published Critical Appraisals to Current Evaluations, Gale Research, 1983. These volumes extract from assorted reviewing sources from the time of the author's writing to the present. Included also is a brief biography and list or principal works. Volumes Four and Ten contain entries on Hardy.

Joan Lescinski, CSJ
College of St. Rose
Albany, New York

JOEL CHANDLER HARRIS
1848–1908

Author's Chronology

Born December 9, 1848, illegitimately near Eatonton, Georgia; *1856* begins school; *1862–1866* printer's devil for *The Countryman* and informal apprentice to Joseph Addison Turner; unconsciously learns folklore and dialect from slaves on Turner's plantation, Turnwold; publishes first work in *The Countryman; 1864* witnesses Sherman's demoralizing but not destructive visit to Turnwold; *1866–1867* typesetter for *Macon Telegraph* and secretary to publisher of New Orleans *Crescent Monthly;* returns, homesick, to Eatonton; *1870–1876* associate editor of *Savannah Morning News; 1873* marries Esther LaRose who bore him nine children of whom five survived childhood; *1876* flees to Atlanta from yellow fever epidemic; becomes associate editor for *Atlanta Constitution;* publishes first Uncle Remus sketch; *1881* moves to permanent home, Wren's Nest; *1882* meets Mark Twain, George Washington Cable and James Osgood in New Orleans; declines to join them in a lecture tour; *1886* visited by A. B. Frost who would become his favorite illustrator; *1896* evinces interest in Catholicism; *1900* retires from *Constitution;* visited for two weeks by James Whitcomb Riley; *1902* awarded honorary degree by Emory College; *1905* elected to American Academy of Arts and Letters; honored by Theodore Roosevelt in Atlanta; *1907* visits Roosevelt at the White House; *1907–1908* edits *Uncle Remus Magazine; 1908* baptized a Catholic in June; dies July 3 from cirrhosis of the liver.

Author's Bibliography (selected)

Uncle Remus: His Songs and Sayings, 1880 (folklore); *Nights With Uncle Remus,* 1883 (folklore); *Mingo and Other Stories,* 1884; *Free Joe and Other Georgia Sketches,* 1887; *On the Plantation,* 1892 (autobiographical fiction); *Uncle Remus and His Friends,* 1892 (folklore); *Stories of Georgia,* 1896; *Sister Jane: Her Friends and Acquaintances,* 1896 (novel); *Plantation Pageants,* 1899 (children's narrative); *The Chronicles of Aunt Minervy Ann,* 1899 (extended narrative); *Gabriel Tolliver: A Story of Reconstruction,* 1902 (novel); *Told by Uncle Remus,* 1905 (folklore); *Uncle Remus and Brer Rabbit,* 1907 (folklore).

Overview of Biographical Sources

Point-of-view is the one distinguishing feature between the various biographical accounts of Joel Chandler Harris. Whether it be an affectionate tribute by his daughter-in-law, a chronicle of his boyhood and youth for younger readers or a scholarly literary biography, all biographers agree that Harris was an insecure, near-recluse, fearful of public appearances but graciously at home to well-screened friends and admirers. They also agree that his apparently paradoxical predilection for practical jokes resulted from his ambivalence about the

South, the black race, and his own impoverished and illegitimate background. Each considers his four years as printer's devil and germinating journalist at Turnwold plantation to be the most influential experience in his development. There he was exposed to black folklore that became the backbone of his most important work; there he was tutored by Joseph Addision Turner in the art of writing; and there his exposure to the Civil War and General Sherman was painful but not devastating. The rest of his life is important because his self-imposed seclusion and his reluctance to appear publicly made possible a volume of literary and journalistic work that would have taxed more active writers of comparable talent.

Evaluation of Selected Biographies

Cousins, Paul M. *Joel Chandler Harris: A Biography.* Baton Rouge: Louisiana State University Press, 1968. Cousins began his scholarly biography when he could still interview friends and acquaintances of Harris, abandoned it for forty years, and resumed it when he had the advantage of perspective and intervening scholarship. The book stresses the themes of reconciliation between North and South and affection toward blacks that permeate Harris' life and work.

Harris, Julia Collier, *The Life and Letters of Joel Chandler Harris.* Boston: Houghton Mifflin, 1918. Although she was his daughter-in-law, Julia Harris refers to her subject as father throughout her book. This extensive collection of Harris' letters has been selected, edited and excerpted to illuminate the author's affectionate view of her subject. Though the book includes scholarly paraphernalia and a complete bibliography to date, it is as readable as it is reliable.

———, *Joel Chandler Harris: Editor and Essayist, Miscellaneous Literary, Political, and Social Writings.* Chapel Hill: University of North Carolina Press, 1931. Not precisely biography, both the selections and the author's commentary in this collection cast light on the subject's life.

Wiggins, Robert Lemuel, *The Life of Joel Chandler Harris From Obscurity in Boyhood to Fame in Early Manhood with Short Stories and Other Early Literary Work Not Heretofore Published in Book Form.* Nashville, TN: Publishing House Methodist Episcopal Church, South, 1918. About one third of this volume is a detailed account of Harris' development until *Uncle Remus: His Songs and Sayings* brought him fame. This book has one noteworthy feature for the scholar and the curious. Its last two-thirds is a collection of Harris' otherwise uncollected works: poetry and essays more notable for their sentimentality and naiveté than for any literary merit.

Autobiographical Sources

Shy and lacking confidence in his own artistry, Harris wrote no autobiography. The only published autobiographical materials are Julia Harris' two collections of his personal writings and his fictional narrative, *On the Plantation,* which is said to be autobiographical. A Texas A & M University dissertation (Joseph Matthew Grisa, Jr. "Selected Letters of Joel Chandler Harris, 1863–1885") reproduces seventy-seven letters with headnotes and commentary. The Harris papers reside in the Harris Memorial Collection at Emory University.

Overview of Critical Sources

Critical opinion has remained uniform over the years in its respect for Harris as recorder of authentic black dialect and collector of black folk tales. And it uniformly considers his fiction to be less successful than his "folklore." Beyond that the criticism has evolved as public opinion of blacks and the South has evolved. Early Harris was lauded for his theme of reconciliation between American regions, his sympathetic treatment of plantation life and freed blacks and his efforts to develop a literature that was Southern in tone and content while it was American in spirit. Later he was dismissed as "merely" a local colorist whose only value was as collector of black folklore. More recently, he has been roundly criticized for the character of Uncle Remus—an Uncle Tom if ever there was one—and the omission of black oral lore that demonstrate the existence of a southern black culture separate from and existing alongside the white one. Today, he is respected for his efforts to collect black lore while his omissions are understood as a function of the historical period in which he wrote. His fiction is treated as an indication that the South did produce a local colorist, and his journalism is studied historically. While journal articles on Harris and essays in studies of American literature are legion, only one critic, Bruce R. Bickley, Jr. has devoted much of his career to the study of Harris.

Evaluation of Selected Critical Sources

Bickley, R. Bruce, Jr. *Critical Essays on Joel Chandler Harris.* Boston: G. K. Hall, 1981. The first, brief, section of this book anthologizes contemporary reviews of Harris' work. In the second are gathered critical articles representing the most important views on Harris from his day to the present.

———, *Joel Chandler Harris: A Reference Guide.* Boston: G. K. Hall, 1978. An annotated list of every identifiable publication about Harris from 1862 to 1976. The annotations make no value judgments on the material but rather attempt to describe the viewpoints of the authors.

———, *Joel Chandler Harris.* Boston: Twayne, 1978. Here Bickley provides an overview of the subject's life and career with particular attention to content in the published works. It includes sections on biography, and on Harris' various careers: cornfield journalist, folklorist, fiction writer, and children's writer. Bickley sees Harris as having negligible "Literary" value, but he honors his contributions to folklore, black dialect transcription, the development of a

Southern literature and the preservation of material about the frequently neglected ante-bellum middle class South.

Brookes, Stella Brewer, *Joel Chandler Harris—Folklorist.* Athens: University of Georgia Press, 1950. A traditional folklore classification of the tales in the Uncle Remus canon as Trickster Tales, Myths, Supernatural Tales, Proverbs, Dialect and Songs.

Other Sources

Bone, Robert, *Down Home: A History of Afro-American Short Fiction from Its Beginnings to the End of the Harlem Renaissance.* New York: G. P. Putnam's Sons, 1975. Shows that Harris' Brer Rabbit represents a black survival code wherein blacks may play a role but do not actually succumb to white domination.

Davidson, Marshall B. *et al.* eds. *The American Heritage History of the Writers' America.* New York: American Heritage Publishing. Demonstrates how American Regionalism of the 1920's and 1930's harks back to Chandler's writing.

"Uncle Remus": Joel Chandler Harris as Seen and Remembered by a Few of His Friends including a Memorial Sermon by the Rev. James W. Lee, D. D. and a poem by Frank L. Stanton. Privately printed in a limited edition of 300 copies, Christmas 1908. Illustrations and some photographs. Affectionate reminiscence. Worthy of mention because its existence has not been noted elsewhere.

Selected Dictionaries and Encyclopedias

Dictionary of American Biography, Charles Scribner's Sons, 1932. Includes tidbits about Harris' life; takes the usual standpoint that folklore is major contribution, literary value negligible, and fiction worth only passing note. Brief critical bibliography.

Dictionary of Literary Biography, Gale Research, 1982. Considers Harris as humorist but includes critical material, especially on the relationship between the black lore in the Harris canon and race relations. Shows Harris to be more aware of black survival strategies than is usually imagined. Includes critical bibliography and illustrations.

Sue Bridwell Beckham
University of Wisconsin-Stout

BRET HARTE
1836–1902

Author's Chronology

Born Francis Brett Harte, August 25, 1836, in Albany, New York; reads widely as a child; *1854–1860* works at various odd jobs; *1860* typesetter for the *Golden Era,* which publishes his short sketches; *1862* marries Anna Griswold; *1867* publishes first collection of poems, *The Lost Galleon and Other Tales; 1868* edits the *Overland Monthly;* publishes his first mature story, "The Luck of Roaring Camp," followed (January *1869*) by "The Outcasts of Poker Flat"; these two stories secure his literary reputation; *1871* leaves for the East, receiving a $10,000 contract from *Atlantic Monthly;* the contract is not renewed; financial difficulties follow; *1877* establishes the *Capitol Magazine,* which fails; *1878* accepts a U.S. Consulate in Prussia; *1880* receives the consulate in Glasgow; *1885* dismissed from his post by Grover Cleveland; "grinds out" stories until his death of throat cancer, May 5, 1902, in England.

Author's Bibliography (selected)

Condensed Novels, and Other Papers, 1867 (satire); *The Luck of Roaring Camp, and Other Sketches,* 1870; *Poems,* 1871; *Mrs. Skaggs's Husbands, and Other Sketches,* 1872; *Tales of the Argonauts,* 1875 (stories); *Echoes of the Foothills,* 1875 (poems); *Gabriel Conroy,* 1876 (novel); *Two Men of Sandy Bar,* 1876 (drama); *Ah Sin,* 1877 (drama, with Mark Twain); *On the Frontier,* 1884 (stories); *A Protegee of Jack Hamlin's, and Other Stories,* 1894; *Tales of Trail and Town,* 1898; *The Writings of Bret Harte,* 20 volumes (1896–1914).

Overview of Biographical Sources

The life of Bret Harte has proven to be of greater interest than his prodigious literary output. Fascination with his early, meteoric success and subsequent decline has produced a range of biographical studies. Two biographies appeared within a year of his death: Henry W. Boynton's *Bret Harte* (New York: McClure, Phillips, 1903), and Thomas Edgar Pemberton's *The Life of Bret Harte* (London: C. Arthur Pearson, 1903). Pemberton had the advantage of a personal friendship with Harte, but the work suffers from lack of distance, objectivity and adequate information. Henry Childs Merwin's *The Life of Bret Harte* (Boston and New York: Houghton Mifflin, 1911) presents a more solid, comprehensive view of Harte's life, but has since been surpassed. The biography by George R. Stewart, Jr., *Bret Harte: Argonaut and Exile* (1931), remains the "definitive" biography, and the most readable. Richard O'Connor's *Bret Harte: A Biography* (1966), the most recent full-length study, seeks to present an informative, objective description of Harte's life. Margaret Duckett's *Mark Twain and Bret Harte* (1964) is the most scholarly, focusing upon the literary relationship between Twain and Harte.

Evaluation of Selected Biographies

Duckett, Margaret, *Mark Twain and Bret Harte.* Norman: University of Oklahoma Press, 1964. In an effort to account for the bitter divergence between these two writers, Duckett rigorously explores the personal and literary relationships between Twain and Harte. Meticulously documented, including numerous letters, this in-depth study examines their early friendship, their literary collaboration, and probes into the causes for the eventual rift and bitter animosity between them. Duckett illuminates one's understanding of both writers, each in terms of the other.

Howells, William Dean, "A Belated Guest," *Literary Friends and Acquaintance.* New York: Harper, 1900. As a faithful supporter of Bret Harte, Howells devotes a chapter of this reminiscence to him, presenting a measured, but gracious, view of Bret Harte among the literary and social circles of Cambridge and Boston.

O'Connor, Richard, *Bret Harte: A Biography.* Boston: Little, Brown, 1966. Written by an experienced biographer, O'Connor's book is a particularly descriptive account, emphasizing the picturesque moments of Harte's experience. This book has been criticized for drawing freely upon the work of earlier biographers, and, consequently, adding nothing new; nevertheless, O'Connor's work is lucidly written, and presents an evenly distributed view of three stages in Harte's life: argonaut, celebrity, and expatriate.

Stewart, George. R., Jr. *Bret Harte: Argonaut and Exile.* Boston and New York: Houghton Mifflin, 1931. Beautifully written, this book is still recognized by many scholars to be the "definitive" biography of Bret Harte. The book strives, not to offer any theory about Harte's successes and failures, but to present the character and personality of Bret Harte as richly as possible. The book assumes a leisurely pace, uncluttered by any critical material, even when discussing Harte's writings, and remains eminently readable.

Walker, Franklin, *San Francisco's Literary Frontier.* New York: Alfred A. Knopf, 1939. A "group biography" which has the advantage of viewing Harte's literary beginnings in context with other literary figures—Mark Twain, Ambrose Bierce, Joaquin Miller and more than forty others. Much more than biography, this book offers a rich, cultural and social history of San Francisco's literary and journalistic milieu between 1848 and 1875.

Autobiographical Sources

Very little of Bret Harte's life is revealed through his fiction. *The Letters of Bret Harte,* edited by Geoffrey Bret Harte (Boston and New York: Houghton Mifflin, 1926), serve as the only major autobiographical document. Though ranging from 1866–1902, most of these letters were written during his later years abroad, and many are addressed to his wife. Often undramatic and trivial, they nevertheless record much of his unhappiness and anguish during those difficult years.

Unpublished letters occasionally appear in various literary journals. Of particular interest are those edited by Bradford A. Booth, "Bret Harte Goes East: Some Unpublished Letters," in *American Literature,* 19 (1948), 318–335. These letters, written between 1866–1875 to Howells, Longfellow, Bierce, Lowell and others, provide a keen insight into Harte's hopes, ambitions and frustrations during those early years in the East. Another 28 letters to Harte's friend and fellow writer, John Hay, were recently published by Brenda Murphy and George Monteiro, "The Unpublished Letters of Bret Harte to John Hay," in *American Literary Realism, 1860–1920,* 12 (1979), 77–110.

Overview of Critical Sources

Because Harte's literary reputation rests primarily upon two stories, there is no full-length study of his fiction. Indispensible to an understanding of Harte's place in American literary criticism is Patrick D. Morrow's *Bret Harte Literary Critic* (1979), which rigorously examines Harte's own critical views. Morrow also edited a special issue of *Western American Literature* (1973) devoted to critical studies of Harte's work. The five essays included in that issue discuss: (1) the power of sex in Harte's work, (2) the character of Jack Hamlin, (3) Harte's place in "local color" fiction, (4) Harte's Civil War poems, (5) Harte's later work. Other criticism of Harte's work appears only in various literary journals and as parts of larger studies.

Evaluation of Selected Criticism

Morrow, Patrick D. *Bret Harte Literary Critic.* Bowling Green: Bowling Green State University Popular Press, 1979. Recognizing Harte's greater role as a literary critic, Morrow masterfully traces Harte's critical development—from his letters, through his influence upon other American writers, his practical ideas and concepts of literature, and through his own craft of fiction. This book, meticulous in scholarship, yet written with clarity and grace, provides a coherent view of Harte's widely scattered criticism, and secures a prominent position for Harte in nineteenth-century literary criticism.

Pattee, Fred Lewis, "Bret Harte," in *The Development of the American Short Story.* New York: Harper, 1923, 220–244. Pattee justifies Harte's place in American literature by identifying six distinctive contributions Harte's work made to the short story form.

Quinn, Arthur H. "Bret Harte and the Fiction of Moral Contrast," in *American Fiction.* New York: Appleton-Century, 1963, 232–242. A good beginning point for discussing Harte's artistry, Quinn argues that Harte's method, rather than his material, and his use of dramatic contrasts, make him an artist who reveals human nature.

Other Sources

Barnett, Linda D. *Bret Harte: A Reference Guide.* Boston: G. K. Hall, 1980. A comprehensive guide for Harte scholars.

Broggan, J. R. "The Regeneration of 'Roaring Camp,' " in *Nineteenth Century Fiction,* 22 (1967), 271–280. Raises questions challenging a conventional, Christian reading of "The Luck of Roaring Camp."

Spingarn, Lawrence P. "Journey of Bret Harte," in *Yale Review,* 41 (Summer 1952), 591–593. A narrative poem imagining Harte's social failure in the East.

Thomas, Jeffrey F. "Bret Harte and the Power of Sex," in *Western American Literature,* 8 (1973), 91–109. Shows that the same power of sex, celebrated by Whitman and insisted upon by Henry Adams, energizes Harte's characters. Illuminates a dynamic quality to Harte's fiction which is often ignored.

Walterhouse, Roger R. *Bret Harte, Joaquin Miller and the Western Local Color Story.* Chicago: University of Chicago, 1939. Describes Harte's place in the development of "local color" fiction.

Selected Dictionaries and Encyclopedias

Critical Survey of Short Fiction, Salem Press, 1981. Examines "The Outcasts of Poker Flat" to illustrate both strengths and limitations of Harte's work.

Dictionary of American Biography, Charles Scribner's Sons, 1943. A succinct summary of Harte's successes and failures.

Dictionary of Literary Biography, Gale Research, 1982. A solid summary of Harte's life and literary reputation. Also presents a helpful description and evaluation of his most important stories, "M'Liss," "The Luck of Roaring Camp," and "The Outcasts of Poker Flat," justifying Harte's place in American literature.

Thomas Becknell
Bethel College (Minnesota)

NATHANIEL HAWTHORNE
1804–1864

Author's Chronology

Born July 4, 1804 in Salem, Massachusetts; *1813* suffers injury to his foot, which limits his physical activity for almost two years, thereby fostering a love of reading; *1821–1825* attends Bowdoin College in Brunswick, Maine; *1828* publishes anonymously his first novel, *Fanshawe: A Tale; 1830–1837* publishes tales and sketches in periodicals; *1839–1840* works as a measurer of salt and coal at the Boston Custom House; *1841* participates in the utopian community of Brook Farm in West Roxbury, Massachusetts; *1842* marries Sophia Peabody; *1842–1845* resides at the Old Manse, the ancestral home of the Emerson family; *1846–1849* serves as Surveyor in the Salem Custom House; *1850–1851* lives in Lenox, Massachusetts, where he becomes friends with Herman Melville; *1851–1852* resides in West Newton, Massachusetts; *1852-1853* lives at the Wayside in Concord, Massachusetts; *1853–1857* serves as United States Consul at Liverpool, England under the administration of Franklin Pierce; *1858–1859* lives in Rome and Florence; *1860* returns home to the Wayside; *1864* dies on May 19 at Plymouth, New Hampshire and is buried four days later at Sleepy Hollow Cemetery in Concord; Leaves four unfinished romances: *Dr. Grimshawe's Secret, The Ancestral Footstep, Septimius Felton,* and *The Dolliver Romance.*

Author's Bibliography (selected)

Fanshawe: A Tale, 1828 (historical romance); *Twice-Told Tales,* 1837; *Grandfather's Chair,* 1841 (historical story collection for children); *Mosses from an Old Manse,* 1846 (collection of tales and sketches); *The Scarlet Letter,* 1850 (romance); *The House of the Seven Gables,* 1851 (romance); *The Snow-Image and Other Twice-Told Tales,* 1851; *A Wonder Book for Girls and Boys,* 1852 (children's stories); *The Blithedale Romance,* 1852 (romance); *Life of Franklin Pierce,* 1852 (biography); *Tanglewood Tales for Girls and Boys,* 1853; *The Marble Faun,* 1860 (romance); *Our Old Home,* 1863 (collection of sketches).

Overview of Biographical Sources

Because of Nathaniel Hawthorne's preeminent position in American literary history as one of the first writers not to have, as Emerson complained, "listened too long to the courtly muses of Europe, but instead to have forged art out of the materials of his native land and because of his enigmatic character—part coldly observant recluse, part loving family man and cheerful public servant," Hawthorne has intrigued biographers. Indeed, there is probably no other American literary figure who has inspired more biographies from the time of his death to the present day. A wealth of biographical information is located in the personal collections published by Hawthorne's relatives, friends, and acquaintances. The most significant of these is Julian Hawthorne's *Nathaniel Hawthorne and His Wife* (Boston: J. R. Osgood, 1884), which, its author announces, presents no literary criticism or theory but rather "a simple record of lives." This two-volume work offers Julian Hawthorne's memories of his parents, friends' reminiscences, and valuable excerpts from Hawthorne's letters. Hawthorne's youngest daughter, Rose Hawthorne Lathrop, also published a book. In her *Memories of Hawthorne* (Boston: Houghton Mifflin, 1897), she presents a collection of Sophia Peabody Hawthorne's letters from 1820–1871, with brief commentary. This work is most important for providing a glimpse into the early years of Hawthorne's marriage. Among other useful early sources are George Parsons Lathrop's *A Study of Hawthorne* (Boston: James R. Osgood, 1876), a highly laudatory account by Hawthorne's son-in-law; the *Life of Nathaniel Hawthorne* (New York: Scribner and Welford, 1890) by Moncure D. Conway, a follower of Emerson and acquaintance of Hawthorne; and *Personal Recollections of Nathaniel Hawthorne* (New York: Harper, 1893) by Horatio Bridges, Hawthorne's close friend from college. Certainly one of the most interesting assessments of Hawthorne's career comes from Henry James in his contribution to the English Men of Letters Series entitled *Hawthorne* (1879). James's book adds no new information about Hawthorne's life, as it relies heavily upon Lathrop's study; however, it is fascinating for James's evaluations of Hawthorne's fiction. In 1902, George Woodberry published the first scholarly biography of Hawthorne for the American Men of Letter Series. His *Nathaniel Hawthorne* (Boston: Houghton Mifflin, 1902) stresses Hawthorne's tendency to withdraw from society, as does Newton Arvin's *Hawthorne* (1929). In reaction against what he believed were grossly distorted portraits of Hawthorne as the brooding, guilt-laden, misanthropic hermit, Robert Cantwell in *Nathaniel Hawthorne: The American Years* (New York: Rinehart, 1948) emphasizes Hawthorne's roles as politician, journalist, and customs official and describes his social milieu. One of the most balanced and intelligent treatments of Hawthorne is contained in Randall Stewart's *Nathaniel Hawthorne: A Biography* (1948). Also helpful as introductions to Hawthorne's life and fiction are two well-written, critically sound works: Mark Van Doren's *Nathaniel Hawthorne* (New York: William Sloane Associates, 1949) and Terence Martin's *Nathaniel Hawthorne* (New York: Twayne Publishers, 1965), which includes an excellent annotated bibliography of secondary sources. More recent biographies have been psychological in orientation, as evidenced by Edward Wagenknecht's *Nathaniel Hawthorne: Man and Writer* (1961), a study of Hawthorne's personality and interests, and Hubert H. Hoeltje's *Inward Sky: The Mind and Heart of Nathaniel Hawthorne* (Durham: Duke University Press, 1962). One of the latest additions to the corpus of Hawthorne biographies is Arlin Turner's *Nathaniel Hawthorne: A Biography* (1980).

Evaluation of Selected Biographies

Arvin, Newton, *Hawthorne.* Boston: Little, Brown, 1929. Because Newton Arvin relied solely on published source material, his book reflects the limitations of the early biographies in exaggerating Hawthorne's unsociability. Rather melodramatically, Arvin describes Hawthorne as "growing more and more apart from ordinary humanity, losing gradually his capacity for warm and open relations with men and women, allowing a cold, inquiring, analytic interest in them to take more and more entire possession of his mind." Arvin provides thematic analyses of Hawthorne's major tales and four romances, concluding that Hawthorne was not a writer of the first rank because he lacked imaginative vigor. Arvin's thesis is that Hawthorne's fictional preoccupation with the sin of intellectual pride mirrors "the essential tragedy of pride" found in his life.

James, Henry, *Hawthorne.* London: Macmillan, 1879. James's work tells almost as much about himself as it does about Hawthorne, for the cosmopolitan James, who had first confronted European culture at the age of six months, reacts strongly against Hawthorne's New England provincialism. In fact, James observes with disdain that Hawthorne's life "had few perceptible points of contact with what is called the world, with public events, with the manner of his time, even with the life of his neighbours." An ardent Realist, James, as one might expect, is unappreciative of Hawthorne's use of allegory, viewing it as "one of the lighter exercises of the imagination." He therefore praises *The Blithedale Romance* above *The Scarlet Letter.* Despite his reservations about Hawthorne's technique, however, James recognizes Hawthorne as the greatest example of literary genius that America has yet produced.

Stewart, Randall, *Nathaniel Hawthorne: A Biography.* New Haven: Yale University Press, 1948. This thoroughly researched biography provides one of the most reliable sources of information about Hawthorne's life. In editing *The American Notebooks* and *The English Notebooks,* Stewart discovered that Mrs. Hawthorne had revised and suppressed passages from her husband's work. The Hawthorne that emerged from the original text was less morbid and isolated than early biographers had thought. Thus Stewart's book attempts to correct previous misconceptions about Hawthorne and to present a man actively engaged with the world about him. Stewart emphasizes Hawthorne's attraction to the Puritan view of life, although not to its intolerance. For Stewart, Hawthorne is essentially a moral writer whose message is "the importance of understanding mankind in whole, and the need of man's sympathy with man based upon the honest recognition of the good and evil in our common nature." This book is factual in its orientation; it does not address fully the complexities of Hawthorne's character.

Turner, Arlin, *Nathaniel Hawthorne: A Biography.* New York: Oxford University Press, 1980. Turner began publishing articles on Hawthorne in the

1930's. Then in 1961 he produced *Nathaniel Hawthorne: An Introduction and Interpretation* (New York: Barnes and Noble, 1961), in his words, "a brief history" of Hawthorne's mind. His purpose in this recent biography is "to present the rich variety of Hawthorne's personality, and the individuality and complexity of his thought." In this goal he succeeds, defining Hawthorne's paradoxical nature, yet not exaggerating his tendency toward isolation. The product of extensive research, Turner's biography provides numerous quotations from Hawthorne's letters, notebooks, prefaces, sketches, and fiction. Turner does not offer critical evaluations but instead describes where Hawthorne got ideas and names for his characters, what happened in his life at the time he was composing his various works, and how the critics and readers responded to them. Among the most interesting material is Turner's examination of Hawthorne's relationships with Emerson, Thoreau, and Melville. With its short, clearly titled chapters and its variety of illustrations, this book is one of the most highly readable of the biographies.

Wagenknecht, Edward, *Nathaniel Hawthorne: Man and Writer.* New York: Oxford University Press, 1961. Wagenknecht labels his book a "psychograph," that is, a work that attempts to describe what sort of man Hawthorne was and to define his experience of life. Rejecting a chronological presentation of the chief events in Hawthorne's life, Wagenknecht instead arranges his chapters according to topics. Among the subjects he considers are Hawthorne's attitudes toward science, literature, art, nature, politics, religion, love and passion. Showing extensive knowledge of Hawthorne's fiction, letters, journals, and the works written about him, Wagenknecht provides a provocative study of Hawthorne's character.

Woodberry, George, *Nathaniel Hawthorne.* Boston: Houghton Mifflin, 1902. Woodberry provides a comprehensive account of Hawthorne's life, beginning with his first ancestor to come to America, William Hathorne, and ending with details of his death and burial. Throughout his book, Woodberry quotes liberally from Hawthorne's diary and letters. As is typical of the early biographers, he emphasizes Hawthorne's solitude, particularly concerning the period from 1825 to 1837 in which in his "haunted chamber" Hawthorne read voraciously and devoted himself to the craft of writing. According to Woodberry, Hawthorne inherited from Puritanism an obsession with spirituality; he explains, "The moral world, the supremacy of the soul's interests, how life fared in the soul, was his region; he thought about nothing else." The darkness of Hawthorne's fiction disturbs Woodberry; indeed, he labels *The Scarlet Letter* as "a false book" because love and light are absent from it. He is, however, able to find love and light in Hawthorne's personal life and to recognize Hawthorne's ability to evoke deep affection from his family and friends.

Autobiographical Sources

The major autobiographical material on Hawthorne is contained in his notebooks. Randall Stewart has masterfully edited *The American Notebooks by Nathaniel Hawthorne* (New Haven: Yale University Press, 1932) and *The English Notebooks by Nathaniel Hawthorne* (New York: Modern Language Association of America, 1941), providing reliable texts and illuminating introductions that explain the extent to which Sophia Hawthorne altered her husband's work in terms of both style and content. Through these editions, Stewart proved that Hawthorne was not as aloof as experts had previously considered him to be. Thomas Woodson has edited *The French and Italian Notebooks* for *The Centenary Edition of The Works of Nathaniel Hawthorne* (Columbus: Ohio State University Press, 1980). Published volumes of Hawthorne's letters include *Love Letters of Nathaniel Hawthorne, 1839–1863* (Chicago: Society of the Dofobs, 1907) and *Letters of Nathaniel Hawthorne to William D. Ticknor, 1851–1864* (Newark, NJ: Carteret Book Club, 1910).

Overview of Critical Sources

Hawthorne scholars and students can find a wealth of critical sources examining Hawthorne's work. Some focus upon the tragic darkness of his themes, whereas others study his techniques, including symbolism, allegory, ambiguity, imagery patterns, and the use of fine-art devices. Still other sources focus upon Hawthorne's reading, his composing process, and the difficulties he had completing romances at the end of his career. Several book-length works present enlightening comparisons of Hawthorne with his fellow American Romantics. Since the 1960's psychoanalytical and mythic approaches to Hawthorne have become popular.

Evaluation of Selected Criticism

Bell, Millicent, *Hawthorne's View of the Artist.* New York: State University of New York, 1962. Millicent Bell examines Hawthorne's treatment of the artist figure in his fiction, observing that his artist characters are never fully integrated into society. This alienation reflects Hawthorne's awareness that a life devoted to idealism and beauty is often misunderstood. She finds his view of the artist ambivalent, for as a man who frequently had to abandon writing for public service, he knew the danger of "self-absorbed artistic activity."

Crews, Frederic, *The Sins of the Fathers: Hawthorne's Psychological Themes.* New York: Oxford University Press, 1966. Crews bemoans two recent trends in Hawthorne criticism: the emphasis upon his social affability and the interest in his symbolism and didacticism. He believes those approaches deny Hawthorne's fundamental ambivalence. Crews studies Hawthorne's fiction from a psychological perspective and finds it dominated by a "tyrannical superego."

Crews believes the death of his father when Hawthorne was quite young caused an Oedipal conflict that is revealed in the concern with incest, sin, and guilt found in his fiction.

Fogle, Richard Harter, *Hawthorne's Fiction: the Light and the Dark.* Norman: University of Oklahoma Press, 1952. Fogle applies the methods of New Criticism to Hawthorne's major tales and his four romances. Fogle contends that Hawthorne's work shows a blend of light and dark; the light is his clarity of design and the dark is his tragic complexity. According to Fogle, one cannot approach Hawthorne's works successfully with a prejudice against allegory, since allegory is his legacy from the Puritans and an essential ingredient of his art. Fogle's interpretations are intelligent and well-supported.

Male, Roy R. *Hawthorne's Tragic Vision.* New York: Austin: University of Texas Press, 1957. Male states that readers value Hawthorne for penetrating to the deep truths of the human heart. Hawthorne's central concern is with moral growth, which he believes cannot be accomplished without sin and suffering. Male examines the quest for home theme in "The Gentle Boy" and "My Kinsman, Major Molineux," treats "Rappaccini's Daughter" as a precursor to *The Scarlet Letter,* and considers each of the four romances as a love story centered upon Original Sin. He suggests we can recognize Hawthorne's greatness only when we view him as a "romancer" who blends poetry and fiction.

Pearce, Roy Harvey, ed. *Hawthorne Centenary Essays.* Columbus: Ohio State University Press, 1964. This work is a collection of essays commemorating the centenary of Hawthorne's death. It includes analyses of Hawthorne's fiction by Terence Martin, Charles Feidelson, Harry Levin, R. W. B. Lewis, Hyatt Waggoner, and Daniel Hoffman. It also includes essays examining Hawthorne scholarship, studying his influence abroad, and noting the difficulties he presents to textual critics. This volume concludes with an afterword by Lionel Trilling, who considers Hawthorne's relevance to modern readers.

Waggoner, Hyatt, *Hawthorne, a Critical Study.* Cambridge: Harvard University Press, 1955. Waggoner's work provides one of the most indispensable sources of Hawthorne criticism. He gives detailed readings of the major tales and the four romances, emphasizing imagery patterns. Hawthorne's major talent, he concludes, lies in portraying the truths of the human heart through combining traditional allegory with modern symbolism.

Other Sources

Fiedler, Leslie, *Love and Death in the American Novel.* New York: Criterion Books, 1960. Contains an essay entitled "*The Scarlet Letter*: Woman as Faust."

Hoffman, Daniel, *Form and Fable in American Fiction.* New York: Oxford University Press, 1961. Discusses Hawthorne's use of folklore in "My Kinsman, Major Molineux," "The Maypole of Merry Mount," "Young Goodman Brown," *The Scarlet Letter,* and *The Blithedale Romance.*

Lawrence, D. H. *Studies in Classic American Literature.* New York: T. Seltzer, 1923. Examines *The Scarlet Letter* to promote the thesis that American literature is "goody-goody" on the surface but diabolic on a deeper level.

Levin, Harry, *The Power of Blackness.* New York: Alfred A. Knopf, 1958. Studies the tragic visions of Hawthorne, Poe, and Melville.

Lewis, R. W. B. *The American Adam: Innocence, Tragedy, and Tradition in the Nineteenth Century.* Chicago: University of Chicago Press, 1955. In a chapter entitled "The Return into Time: Hawthorne" discusses Hawthorne's recreation of the story of Adam in his fiction, particularly *The Scarlet Letter* and *The Marble Faun.*

Matthiessen, F. O. *American Renaissance: Art and Expression in the Age of Emerson and Whitman.* New York: Oxford University Press, 1941. Offers an illuminating discussion of Hawthorne's techniques and themes by placing him in his historical context and relating him to four other nineteenth-century writers—Emerson, Thoreau, Melville, and Whitman.

Lynne Shackelford
Furman University

ROBERT HAYDEN
1913–1980

Author's Chronology

Born Asa Bundy Sheffey, August 4, 1913, Detroit; raised by neighbors who renamed him Robert Earl Hayden; *1918* public school education augmented by violin classes at Detroit Institute of Musical Art and by special classes for severe vision problems; *1932–1936* attends Detroit City College (now Wayne State University); *1936* works for WPA Federal Writers' Project; *1940* publishes first poetry collection, *Heart-Shape in the Dust; 1940* marries Erma Inez Morris; *1942* joins Baha'i World Faith; *1944* receives M.A. from University of Michigan; *1946* accepts teaching position at Fisk University; *1954* receives Ford Foundation grant for travel in Mexico; *1966* awarded Grand Prize for Poetry at First World Festival of Negro Arts, Dakar, Senegal; *1969* appointed full professor at University of Michigan; *1970 Words in the Mourning Time* nominated for National Book Award; *1975* appointed Consultant in Poetry to the Library of Congress; 1980 dies on February 24 in Ann Arbor, Michigan of respiratory embolism.

Author's Bibliography

Heart-Shape in the Dust, 1940 (poems); with Myron O'Higgins, *The Lion and the Archer,* 1948 (poems); *Figure of Time,* 1955 (poems); *A Ballad of Remembrance,* 1962 (poems); *Selected Poems,* 1966; *Kaleidoscope: Poems by American Negro Poets,* 1967 (poetry anthology); *Words in the Mourning Time,* 1970 (poems); with David Burrows and Frederick Lapides, eds., *Afro-American Literature: An Introduction,* 1971 (anthology); *The Night-Blooming Cereus,* 1972 (poems); *Angle of Ascent,* 1975 (poems); *American Journal,* 1982 (poems).

Overview of Biographical Sources

Only one book devoted solely to Hayden's life and work exists: Fred M. Fetrow's *Robert Hayden* (1984). The next best source for biographical information is the memorial number of *Obsidian: Black Literature in Review,* 8 (Spring 1982), which was not actually in print until 1984. This special issue contains more than thirty sketches, remembrances, and poems about Hayden, plus a bibliography. See also Rosey E. Pool's early "Robert Hayden: Poet Laureate," *Negro Digest,* 15 (1966), 39–43; and Michael S. Harper's two articles—"Remembering Robert E. Hayden," *Carleton Miscellany,* 18 (1980), 231–234 and "Remembering Robert Hayden," *Michigan Quarterly Review,* 21 (1982), 182–188.

Evaluation of Selected Biographies

Fetrow, Fred M. *Robert Hayden.* Boston: Twayne, 1984. Fetrow provides the most complete account of Hayden's life in his opening chapter "Living is the

Thing." Based on previously published interviews, as well as his own talks with the poet, Fetrow carefully and accurately presents a complete biographical portrait, focusing both on personal and on professional details. Fetro is particularly good at providing specific information about Hayden's early work at the University of Michigan with W. H. Auden, about his frustrating years at Fisk University, and about the changes in the poet's life once his national reputation finally emerged. Fetrow is specific and knowledgable about such matters as Hayden's revisions, editors, and publishers, and particularly adept at maintaining a fairminded tone about such controversial subjects as the poet's years of critical neglect, or his being attacked for failing to subscribe to the ethnocentric argument that a black writer should avoid any poetic or political connection to the white world. On the other hand, Fetrow's otherwise excellent annotated bibliography is marred by an occasional harsh or unnecessarily dismissive tone.

Autobiographical Sources

Although Hayden wrote no full-length autobiography, he spoke candidly and at length about his writing in both philosophical and practical terms with Paul McCluskey, who published the results as *How I Write/1* (New York: Harcourt, Brace, Jovanovich, 1972), pp. 133–213. Another full interview is "Richard Hayden" in *Interviews with Black Writers,* ed. by John O'Brien (New York: Liveright, 1973), pp. 108–123. Since Hayden's national reputation only began after 1966, those interested in later interviews should consult Richard Layman's "Robert Hayden," *Conversations with Writers* (Detroit: Gale Research, 1977), 156–179. For an interview oriented to the poet's Bahai faith see "Conversations with Americans," *World Order,* 10 (1975–1976), 46–53. Hayden can be heard reading from his own poetry on *Spectrum in Black: Poems by 20th Century Black Poets* (Scott-Foresman) and on the *Inauguration Series of Poetry Readings, Folger Shakespeare Library.* He appears, with Derek Walcott, on the PBS documentary "Middle Passage and Beyond," made at WETA, Washington, D.C. in 1968.

Overview of Critical Sources

The only published book on Hayden's poetry is the previously cited *Robert Hayden* by Fred Fetrow. Since 1977 a growing body of critical articles has appeared in scholarly books and journals, including the following major pieces: Michael G. Cooke, "Robert Hayden: At Large at Home in the World," in his *Afro-American Literature in the Twentieth Century* (New Haven: Yale University Press, 1984), 137–157; Charles T. Davis, "Robert Hayden's Use of History," in *Modern Black Poets,* ed. by Donald B. Gibson (Englewood Cliffs, NJ: Prentice-Hall, 1973), pp. 96–111; and Wilburn Williams, Jr., "Covenant of Timelessness and Time: Symbolism and History in Robert Hayden's *Angle of Ascent,*" *The Massachusetts Review,* 18 (1977), 731–749.

Evaluation of Selected Criticism

Fetrow, Fred M. *Robert Hayden.* Boston: Twayne, 1984. Following the standard format prescribed by the Twayne's United States Authors Series, Fetrow covers virtually all of Hayden's poetry, moving chronologically from 1940 to 1982, subdividing each of the book's five critical chapters into sub-sections labelled "Personals," "People," "Places," and "Heritage." Fetrow's analysis is clear, readable, thorough, and unstrained.

Other Sources

Faulkner, Howard, " 'Transformed by Steeps of Flight'; The Poetry of Robert Hayden," *CLA Journal,* 21 (1977), 282–291.

Post, Constance J, "Image and Idea in the Poetry of Robert Hayden," *CLA Journal,* 20 (1976), 164–175.

Potter, Vilma Raskin, "Reconsiderations and Reviews: A Remembrance for Robert Hayden, 1913-1980," *MELUS,* 8 (1981), 51-55.

Turco, Lewis, "Angle of Ascent: The Poetry of Robert Hayden," *Michigan Quarterly Review,* 16 (1977), 199–219.

Selected Dictionaries and Encyclopedias

American Writers: A Collection of Literary Biographies. Charles Scribner's Sons, Supplement II, part 1 1981. An excellent introduction to the life and work of Hayden. This biographical series replaces the University of Minnesota Pamphlets on American writers.

Critical Survey of Poetry, Vol. 3, Salem Press, 1982. Brief biography, which incorrectly claims that Hayden was married twice, and a clear discussion of his poetry.

Dictionary of Literary Biography, 5, *American Poets Since World War II,* Gale, 1980. Concise portrait of Hayden and important study of his work.

Timothy Dow Adams
West Virginia University

WILLIAM HAZLITT
1778–1830

Author's Chronology

Born April 10, 1778 in Maidstone, Kent, son of a dissenting minister; *1783–1787* lives with his family in America; *1787–1793* grows up in village of Ulem, Shropshire, educated by father; *1793–1794* subsidized student for the ministry at Unitarian New College at Hackney, near London; *1795* withdraws from college, abandons ministry, returns to Ulem, tries to write philosophical essays; *1798* "first acquaintance" with Coleridge and Wordsworth; *1799–1806* studies painting under his brother; *1802–1803* lives in Paris; *1808* marries Sarah Stoddart; *1812* lectures on English philosophy in London and hired as Parliamentary reporter for the leading Wig newspaper, London *Morning Chronicle; 1813–1814* first journalistic successes are reviews of art and theater; *1815–1816* mounting celebrity as critic and political satirist; *1818* lectures on English Poets and English theatre at Surrey Institution, attended by Keats; *1819* lives apart from his wife; *1820* contributes "table talks" to *London Magazine;* becomes infatuated with Sarah Walker, daughter of his lodging-house keeper in London; *1822* journeys twice to Scotland to obtain a divorce; despairs to find Sarah Walker involved with other lodgers; *1824–1825* tours Europe with second wife, Isabella Bridgewater; *1827* separates from Isabella; *1826–1829* declining health and increasing isolation; *1830* dies in lodgings in Soho, London, September 18.

Author's Bibliography (selected)

An Essay on the Principles of Human Action, 1805 (philosophical essays); *A Reply to the Essay on Population,* by Rev. T. R. Malthus, 1807 (political pamphlet); *Characters of Shakespeare's Plays,* 1817 (essays); *A View of the English Stage,* 1818 (essays); *Lectures on the English Poets,* 1818 (essays); *Lectures on the English Comic Writers,* 1819 (essays); *Table Talk,* 1821 (essays); *Liber Amoris,* 1823 (anonymous narrative of the Sarah Walker affair); *The Spirit of the Age,* 1825 (essays); *The Life of Napoleon Bonaparte,* 1828–1830 (biography).

Overview of Biographical Sources

There are three major biographical treatments of Hazlitt. While all three tend to concentrate on the events of Hazlitt's life, this is especially true of P. P. Howe's *The Life of William Hazlitt* (London: Martin Secker, 1922, rev. 1947) which is little more than a straight chronological account. Herschel Baker's *William Hazlitt* (1962) and Ralph M. Wardle's *Hazlitt* (1971) both give a complete and accurate picture of the writer's career and the development of his ideas. In 1978 Hazlitt's letters were collected and published by Hershel Moreland Sikes, William Hallam Bonner, and Gerald Lakey, *The Letters of William*

Hazlitt (New York: New York University Press, 1978). These letters, most of which were already in print, are not especially useful nor are they well edited.

Evaluation of Selected Biographies

Baker, Hershel, *William Hazlitt.* Cambridge: Harvard University Press, 1962. Concerned with every facet of Hazlitt's life and work, including the political writing, Baker places Hazlitt in his literary, philosophical, and political milieu; however, Baker has little sympathy with his subject. Although Baker sometimes slights Hazlitt's intellectual and literary development and complexity in the interests of narrative chronology, the information is accurate and useful.

Wardle, Ralph, *Hazlitt.* Lincoln: University of Nebraska Press, 1971. Wardle offers a complete and accurate account of Hazlitt's development as a writer and critic. The political writing is not discussed in enough detail, but the intricacies of Hazlitt's relationship with women are. This book represents an important attempt to bring Hazlitt's public persona and private life together.

Autobiographical Sources

Hazlitt is generally a reliable autobiographer in his essays; however, he never published a formal autobiography. The fictionalized narrative of the Sarah Walker affair, *Liber Amoris,* is often treated autobiographically.

Overview of Critical Sources

An appreciation of Hazlitt as a literary and aesthetic critic is relatively recent. Within the last twenty years there has been a growing body of criticism that attempts to assess Hazlitt's work fairly, accurately, and sympathetically. There have been a number of book length studies on the entire *oeuvre,* and some very good books and articles on his aesthetic and literary theory. The focus of most of this criticism is on Hazlitt's centrality in English Romanticism, and upon the relationship between his theory, his journalism, and his conception of politics. He has recently come to be seen as a complex exponent of an expressive poetics, and a major influence on the later generation of Romantic poets.

Evaluation of Selected Criticism

Albrecht, W. P. *Hazlitt and the Creative Imagination.* Lawrence: University of Kansas Press, 1965. This is a very useful and concise book on Hazlitt's aesthetic theories, and has detailed information and an assessment of Hazlitt's relationship with eighteenth-century philosophy and literary theory.

Bromwich, David, *Hazlitt: The Mind of a Critic.* London: Oxford, 1983. This is a very well written examination of Hazlitt as a critic of literature, philosophy, and society. It is especially useful on examining individual essays and in showing Hazlitt's debts to Montague and Samuel Johnson. Hazlitt's connections, both personal and aesthetic, with other Romantic writers are emphasized as are parallels, sources, and influences.

Kinnaird, John, *William Hazlitt: Critic of Power.* New York: Columbia University Press, 1978. Kinnaird offers a convincing overview of Hazlitt's mental development, his relationship to eighteenth-century philosophy, and the structure of his argument in certain works, especially in his lectures on literature and the *Spirit of the Age.*

Other Sources

Albrecht, W. P. "Structure in Two of Hazlitt's Essays," *Studies in Romanticism,* 21(2), Summer, 1982, 181–190. Useful discussion of essay structure and role of metronymy.

Mahoney, John L. *The Logic of Passion: The Literary Criticism of William Hazlitt.* New York: Fordham, 1981. A short, concise introduction to Hazlitt's literary criticism. The author looks closely at the principles of the criticism, without detailing the structure of the essays.

Noxon, James, "Hazlitt as Moral Philosopher," *Ethics,* 72 (1963), 279–283. A good essay on Hazlitt's speculations about personal identity.

Park, Roy, *Hazlitt and the Spirit of the Age: Abstraction and Critical Theory.* Oxford: Clarendon Press, 1971. Concise account of Hazlitt's critical theories; however, Park often takes Hazlitt literally rather than investigating the metaphoric complexity of his prose.

Schneider, Elizabeth, *Aesthetics of William Hazlitt.* Philadelphia: University of Pennsylvania Press, 1933. One of the first expository accounts of Hazlitt's literary and art criticism. Useful documentation on what Hazlitt read in eighteenth-century philosophy and criticism.

Stephen F. Wolfe
Linfield College

SEAMUS HEANEY
1939

Author's Chronology

Born April 13, 1939 to Catholic parents on a farm near Castledawson, County Derry, Northern Ireland; *1951–1957* attends St. Columb's College, Londonderry on a scholarship; *1957–1961* studies at Queen's University, Belfast; receives a B.A. degree with first-class honors in English; does postgraduate work at St. Joseph College of Education, Belfast; *1962–1966* teaches one year at a secondary school; returns to St. Joseph as English lecturer; marries Marie Devlin in *1965;* first of three children born in 1966; *1966* publishes first major collection of poems, *Death of a Naturalist;* receives four literary awards; *1966–1972* lecturer in Modern Literature at Queen's University, with one-year leave in *1970* for guest lectureship at University of California, Berkeley; participates in civil rights action in Belfast; *1972–1975* resigns teaching position and moves to Ashford, County Wicklow, Republic of Ireland; continues to write poetry, free-lances, and edits two poetry anthologies; *1976* moves to Dublin to join faculty at Carysfort College of Education, as lecturer and, later, as administrator; *1976–1984* lecturer at Queen's University, Dublin, with frequent guest lectures and poetry readings at American and European universities, and interviews on radio and television; contributes criticism to journals, edits others; receives Bennett Award in *1982;* poet-in-residence at Harvard University; *1985* continues to teach and engage in a range of literary endeavors in both Ireland and America; primary residence in Dublin.

Author's Bibliography (selected)

Eleven Poems, 1965; *Death of a Naturalist,* 1966 (poems); *Door into the Dark,* 1969 (poems); *Wintering Out,* 1972 (poems); *Stations* (prose-poem sequence), 1975; *North,* 1975 (poems); *Field Work,* 1979 (poems); *Poems: Nineteen Sixty-five to Nineteen Seventy-five,* 1980; *Preoccupations: Selected Prose 1968–1978,* 1980; *Sweeney Astray: A Version from the Irish,* 1984 (prose and poetry); *Station Island,* 1985 (poems).

Overview of Biographical Sources

With Heaney, these are still early days in terms of a poet's life; thus, no extensive biographical studies exist. In *Seamus Heaney* (London and New York: Methuen, 1982), Blake Morrison offers a brief biographical account as he relates Heaney's works to matters of ancestry, nationality, religion, history, and politics. Monie Begley's reminiscences with Heaney in *Rambles in Ireland* (Old Greenwich, CT: The Devin-Adair Company, 1977) are mostly biographical. Because much of Heaney's poetry is of the self, most of the longer critical studies include biographical details. The best short introduction to Heaney's life is in *Current Biography Yearbook 1982* (New York: The H. W. Wilson Company, 1982), pp. 148–151.

Autobiographical Sources

In the first part of *Preoccupations: Selected Prose 1968–1978* (London and Boston: Faber and Faber, 1980), Heaney recalls his formative years in County Derry and his literary apprenticeship at Queen's University, Belfast. In the section entitled "Mossbawn," Heaney reminisces about the widening of his childhood world, recounts his childhood reading, and traces his absorption of Irish and English rhythms from roadside rhymes, recitations for relatives, and school poetry. In the "Belfast" section, Heaney notes the effects Philip Hobsbaum, poet-professor, and the Group at Queen's University had on his poetic beginnings; recounts a particular Christmas in Belfast among Army forces and vigilantes; and probes his early poetic principles. The literary essays and lectures and the short reviews and radio talks, in the second and third parts of *Preoccupations: Selected Prose 1968–1978,* provide a context for the reading of Heaney's poems.

Heaney's frequent interviews with literary critics and reviewers contain autobiographical insights and personal statements about his art. These include interviews with John Haffenden in *Viewpoints: Poets in Conversation* (London and Boston: Faber and Faber, 1981), pages 57–75; two with Seamus Deane: "Unhappy and at Home," *The Crane Bag,* I (Spring 1977), 61–67, and "Talk with Seamus Heaney," *New York Times Review,* 84, No. 48 (1979), pp. 79–101; with James Randall, "An Interview with Seamus Heaney," *Ploughshares,* 5, No. 3 (1979), pp. 7–22; and two published in *Irish Times,* with Harriet Cooke, December 28, 1973, p. 8, and with Caroline Walsh, December 6, 1975, p. 5.

Overview of Critical Sources

The wide sale of Heaney's poetry attests to his public acclaim, and an ever-increasing body of critical commentary affirms his importance and growing reputation as a post-Yeatsian Anglo-Irish poet. Other poets now write about Heaney's works, and critics are measuring the poems of other contemporary poets against Heaney's. Most of the critical assessments appear in popular periodicals or academic journals. To date, there are two relatively short book-length studies of Heaney's work—one is now outdated. In addition, a collection of essays overviewing Heaney's major works has been published in Wales. No critical study thoroughly and systematically analyzes and evaluates Heaney's poems and essays. Many of the available studies trace Heaney's development from a regional poet of Northern Ireland, one who depicts rural farm and domestic life, to a significant, perhaps major, poet with a widening poetic vision. In scanning Heaney's evolution, the critics mark Heaney's shaping of Ulster history, landscape, and violence into a broader northern European and more universal perspective, as he mixes the familiar with legend and myth.

Early acclaim of Heaney, on the one hand, as the greatest poet since Yeats, and his dismissal, on the other, as a bard of the Ulster bogs are being tempered by critics assessing the range and depth of Heaney's poetic achievement. In general, his reputation has increased with each collection.

Evaluation of Selected Criticism

Brown, Terence, *Northern Voices: Poets from Ulster.* Totowa, NJ: Rowman and Littlefield, 1975. Brown sees a sublimial violence in the poet's vision of Ireland as territory, from which Heaney constructs a natural-historical-religio-sexual complex. Brown's appraisal is less enthusiastic than that of most Heaney critics.

Buttel, Robert, *Seamus Heaney.* Lewisburg, PA: Bucknell University Press, 1975. Part of the Irish Writers Series, this slim volume, now somewhat dated, traces the maturing of Heaney's vision through his first three volumes. Buttel's explications of individual poems are useful for first-time readers.

Curtis, Tony, *The Art of Seamus Heaney.* Bridgend, Mid Glamorgan, Wales: Poetry Wales Press, 1982. With diverse, even opposing, views of Heaney's achievement, this essay collection traces thematically and chronologically the development of Heaney's poetic voice. It also has essays on the draft manuscripts of the poem "North"; on Heaney sequence of twenty-one prose poems called *Stations* (1975); and on his essay collection *Preoccupations: Selected Prose 1968-1978.*

Kiely, Benedict, "A Raid Into Dark Corners: The Poetry of Seamus Heaney," *The Hollins Critic,* VI (October 4 1970), 1-12. The first protracted study of Heaney's work, this essay argues that Heaney's images, arising from his native country, become symbols of life's continuity. Much of the discussion focuses on "A Lough Neagh Sequence" in *Door into the Dark,* and places the origin of Heaney's poetry in dark corners of wells, bogs, and love beds.

King, P. R. *Nine Contemporary Poets: A Critical Introduction.* London and New York: Methuen, 1979. King's chapter on Heaney, in this simple, systematic introduction to important post-war English poets, overviews the subject matter, themes, sources, imagery, diction, and rhythms of the poems in Heaney's first four volumes.

Morrison, Blake, *Seamus Heaney.* London and New York: Methuen, 1982. In this first major study of Heaney—a relatively short yet incisive one, Morrison corrects the early labeling of Heaney's poetry as simple and direct by probing its tensions, allusions, and its personal-political-cultural complexity. Morrison also unearths the sources of the poems and locates them in the matrices of Irish, British, and American poetic traditions.

Other Sources

Dunn, Douglas, ed. *Two Decades of Irish Writing.* Manchester: Carcanet Press, 1975. Survey of recent Irish literature, probing Heaney's poetic growth, themes, influences, and relationship to his Ulster contemporaries.

Finneran, Richard, ed. *Recent Research on Anglo-Irish Writers,* MLA, 1983. First-rate, chronological survey of significant critical analyses of Heaney's poetry.

Foster, John Wilson, "The Poetry of Seamus Heaney," *The Critical Quarterly,* XVI (Spring 1974), pp. 35–48. Early study of Heaney's poetry in the context of English and Irish traditions and cultures.

McGuinness, Arthur E. " 'Hoarder of the Common Ground': Tradition and Ritual in Seamus Heaney's Poetry," *Eire-Ireland,* XIV (Summer 1978), 71-92. Examination of Heaney's linkage of early Irish traditions and rituals with current Ulster violence.

Parini, Jay, "Seamus Heaney: The Ground Possessed," *Southern Review,* XVI (Winter 1980), 100–123. Excellent introduction to Heaney's poetry, tracing his use of the metaphor of possession.

Selected Dictionaries and Encyclopedias

Critical Survey of Poetry, Salem Press, 1983. Brief biography, and short analysis of Heaney's first five collections, with bibliography.

The Macmillan Dictionary of Irish Literature, Macmillan, 1980. Brief biography; overview of Heaney's first four volumes, with commentary on representative poems; useful bibliography.

Glenn A. Grever
Illinois State University

ERNEST HEMINGWAY
1899–1961

Author's Chronology

Born July 21, 1899, in Oak Park, Illinois, the son of a doctor; *1917* graduates from Oak Park High School and works as a reporter in Kansas City; *1918* volunteers as Red Cross ambulance driver, is wounded in Italy; *1921* marries Hadley Richardson; *1922* settles in Paris and begins literary life, travelling frequently in Europe; *1923* first fiesta in Pamplona, Spain; son John Hadley Nicanor (Bumby) born; *1927* divorces Hadley and marries Pauline Pfeiffer; *1928* first visits to Key West and Wyoming; son Patrick born; *1929 A Farewell to Arms* a best-seller; *1931* son Gregory born; *1932* buys house in Key West; *1933* fishing the Gulf Stream, first African safaris; *1937–1938* three trips to Spain during the Civil War; *1940* divorces Pauline and marries Martha Gellhorn; settles in the Finca Vigía, near Havana, Cuba; *1941* travels to China, meets Chiang Kai-Shek; *1942–1943* patrols for German submarines off the Cuban coast; *1944* suffers a concussion in an automobile accident; witnesses D-day landings and takes part in liberation of Paris; *1945* divorces Martha; *1946* marries Mary Welsh; *1953* Pulitzer Prize for *The Old Man and the Sea; 1954* injured in two plane crashes in Uganda; awarded Nobel Prize for Literature; *1959* buys house in Ketchum, Idaho; *1960–1961* hospitalized and given shock treatments for depression; *1961* commits suicide by shotgun on July 2.

Author's Bibliography (selected)

The Sun Also Rises, 1926 (novel); *A Farewell to Arms,* 1929 (novel); *Death in the Afternoon,* 1932 (bullfighting); *Green Hills of Africa,* 1935 (novel-memoir); *To Have and Have Not,* 1937 (novel); *The Fifth Column and the First Forty-Nine Stories,* 1938 (play, stories); *For Whom the Bell Tolls,* 1940 (novel); *Across the River and Into the Trees,* 1950 (novel); *The Old Man and the Sea,* 1952 (novel); *A Moveable Feast,* 1964 (memoir); *Islands in the Stream,* 1970 (novel); *Selected Letters, 1917–1961,* 1981 (letters).

Overview of Biographical Sources

Hemingway is probably the best-known novelist of this century, and the great and growing mass of bibliographical material attests to his continuing popularity. He tried to prevent the publication of biographical studies during his lifetime, and as a result, all the important full biographies have appeared since 1961. There was a great "boom" of books on Hemingway in the early 1960's, including book-length reminiscences by his older sister Marcelline Hemingway Sanford, *At the Hemingways: A Family Portrait* (Boston: Atlantic-Little, Brown, 1962) and by his brother Leicester Hemingway, *My Brother, Ernest Hemingway* (Cleveland: World Publishing, 1962). His son Gregory added *Papa: A Personal Memoir* (New York: Houghton, 1976). The most authoritative of all the biographies remains Carlos Baker's splendid *Ernest Hemingway: A Life Story* (1969), and the best of the family tributes is the work of Hemingway's widow Mary, *How It Was* (1976).

The first book-length biographical study of Hemingway was Charles A. Fenton's *The Apprenticeship of Ernest Hemingway: The Early Years* (New York: Farrar, Straus, & Young, 1954), which examines Hemingway's earliest work up to the first collection of stories, *In Our Time.* Hemingway figures in most classic accounts of literary life in Paris in the twenties, including Sylvia Beach, *Shakespeare and Company* (New York: Harcourt Brace, 1959); Malcolm Cowley, *Exile's Return* (1934; rpt. New York: Viking Press, 1951); John Dos Passos, *The Best Times: An Informal Memoir* (New York: New American Library, 1966); and *The Autobiography of Alice B. Toklas,* by Gertrude Stein (New York: Harcourt Brace, 1933). For anecdotes about Hemingway in Key West, see James McLendon, *Papa: Hemingway in Key West* (Miami: E. A. Seemann, 1972). Audre Hanneman's excellent bibliography and supplement together list over 900 items in the category of "Books On or Significantly Mentioning Hemingway" through 1975, and the number continues to grow.

Evaluation of Selected Biographies

Baker, Carlos, *Ernest Hemingway: A Life Story.* New York: Charles Scribner's Sons, 1969. This splendid work, written with the cooperation of Hemingway's widow Mary and with access to his unpublished manuscripts and letters, remains by far the most authoritative of the biographies. It is based chiefly on documented sources, and is extensively annotated. However, this is not a critical biography, and Hemingway's works are mentioned only in direct connection with the author's life. There is also no bibliography except for references incorporated in the notes.

Bruccoli, Matthew J. *Scott and Ernest.* New York: Random House, 1978. A "documentary reconstruction" of the troubled friendship between Hemingway and F. Scott Fitzgerald, which reveals some discrepancies in Hemingway's account in *A Moveable Feast.*

Fenton, Charles A. *The Apprenticeship of Ernest Hemingway: The Early Years.* New York: Farrar, Straus, & Young, 1954. This early biography remains an important source of information about Hemingway's development from reporter to novelist during the years 1916 to 1924, although both Hemingway and Baker have noted minor inaccuracies or misleading impressions.

Hemingway, Mary Welsh, *How It Was.* New York: Alfred A. Knopf, 1976. Complementing Baker's work for the years after 1945, this is an honest and personal account of the final fifteen years of Hemingway's life, spent mostly in

Cuba and Idaho. The final months leading up to Hemingway's suicide are recalled with candor and compassion.

Hotchner, A. E. *Papa Hemingway: A Personal Memoir.* New York: Random House, 1966. This work celebrates the larger-than-life image of Hemingway as sportsman and battler, written by a journalist who first met him in 1948 and became a friend. Although Mary Hemingway lost a court suit in an attempt to prevent the publication of this work on the grounds that it violated her right to privacy, Hotchner's account remains one of the most vivid and popular portraits of the legendary Hemingway.

Autobiographical Sources

Hemingway believed that a writer should write about what he knew first hand, and all of Hemingway's fiction is thus in principle autobiographical. Shortly before he died, he wrote a series of sketches of his life in Paris in the twenties which were published posthumously as *A Moveable Feast* (New York: Charles Scribner's Sons, 1964). This bittersweet tribute to the Paris of his youth contains a number of memorable critical portraits of F. Scott Fitzgerald, Gertrude Stein, Ford Madox Ford, and other famous figures. Written in Hemingway's classic lean clean style, this remains an essential work for anyone interested in his early years as a writer.

He also wrote an incredible number of letters, and the selection assembled by Carlos Baker, *Selected Letters, 1917-1961* (New York: Charles Scribner's Sons, 1981) is well annotated and can easily be read as a fascinating epistolary autobiography of Hemingway's moods.

Many of Hemingway's manuscripts still remain unpublished. In 1968 Hemingway's widow Mary transferred her collection of Hemingway materials to the John F. Kennedy Memorial Library in Boston, which has published a 2-volume *Catalogue of the Ernest Hemingway Collection at the John F. Kennedy Library* (Boston: G. K. Hall, 1982).

Overview of Critical Sources

Hemingway rose to world fame by the 1930's, but except for reviews and magazine articles, his work received little critical notice before about 1950. According to Carlos Baker, the *Viking Portable Hemingway* edition of his works, edited by Malcolm Cowley (New York: Viking, 1944), was responsible for initiating the first serious critical study of Hemingway's works. The first book-length critical study was Philip Young's *Ernest Hemingway* (1951), which sought to explain Hemingway's work in terms of the neuroses and obsessions of the author. This psychological approach has established itself as a major trend in Hemingway studies, and has recently received added impetus from the wave of feminist criticism that has attacked Hemingway as an irresistible symbol of *macho* style.

Hemingway's works have been subjected to a great many critical approaches, but the two most dominant currents appear to involve either stylistic studies or attempts to understand the character of his protagonists. The best shorter essays have been collected and republished; the major collections of critical essays are listed in Linda Welshimer Wagner, *Ernest Hemingway: A Reference Guide* (Boston: G. K. Hall, 1977).

Evaluation of Selected Criticism

Baker, Carlos, ed. *Hemingway and His Critics: An International Anthology.* New York: Hill & Wang, 1961. This early collection includes essays by Lionel Trilling, Edmund Wilson, and Harry Levin, together with a checklist of Hemingway criticism up to 1960.

Benson, Jackson J. ed. *The Short Stories of Ernest Hemingway: Critical Essays.* Durham: Duke University Press, 1975. A comprehensive collection of essays on the stories, dealing particularly with Hemingway's characters and language. Contains a bibliography.

Burgess, Anthony. *Ernest Hemingway and His World.* New York: Charles Scribner's Sons, 1978. A lavishly illustrated photo-introduction to Hemingway, with an accompanying text by a major novelist.

McCaffery, John K. M. ed. *Ernest Hemingway: The Man and His Work.* Cleveland: World Publishing, 1950. This was the earliest collection of essays about Hemingway, including contributions by Malcolm Cowley, Gertrude Stein, and Delmore Schwartz, among others.

Meyers, Jeffrey, ed. *Hemingway: The Critical Heritage.* London, Boston & Henley: Routledge & Kegan Paul, 1982. A chronological survey of reviews and critical commentary from 1924 to 1972, with several essays on each of the major works.

Weeks, Robert P. ed. *Hemingway: A Collection of Critical Essays.* Englewood Cliffs: Prentice-Hall, 1962. A representative cross-section of Hemingway criticism, which is especially strong on Hemingway's style, including essays by Leon Edel, Cleanth Brooks and Robert Penn Warren, and Philip Young.

Young, Philip. *Ernest Hemingway.* New York: Rinehart Critical Studies, 1951; rev. and enlarged ed. by Harcourt Brace & World, 1966. This early psychological approach to Nick Adams set the tone for much of later Hemingway criticism. Hemingway appealed to Young not to publish this work. Young is now regarded as one of the leading authorities on Hemingway.

Other Sources

Bruccoli, Matthew J. and C. E. Frazer Clark, Jr. eds. *Hemingway at Auction, 1930–1973.* Detroit: Gale Research, 1973. This volume reproduces pages from over 100 auction sale and dealer catalogues, including many illustrations from Hemingway letters and manuscripts.

Hanneman, Audre, *Ernest Hemingway: A Comprehensive Bibliography.* Princeton: Princeton University Press, 1967. This work, together with its 1975 *Supplement,* provides the most comprehensive survey to date of books and articles by and about Hemingway. It is carefully annotated and, as bibliographies go, a pleasure to read.

Nagel, James, ed. *Ernest Hemingway: The Writer in Context.* Madison: University of Wisconsin Press, 1984. A fine recent collection of essays, with contributions from Hemingway's son Patrick, playwright Tom Stoppard, and publisher Charles Scribner, Jr.

Wagner, Linda Welshimer, *Ernest Hemingway: A Reference Guide.* Boston: G. K. Hall, 1977. This work includes a useful introduction outlining the history of Hemingway criticism, and surveys works by and about Hemingway chronologically from 1923 to 1975. It also lists the major collections of critical essays.

White, William, ed. *By-Line: Ernest Hemingway: Selected Articles and Dispatches of Four Decades.* New York: Charles Scribner's Sons, 1967. This is the most complete collection to date of Hemingway's journalism from 1920 to 1956.

Gene M. Moore
Virginia Commonwealth University

ROBERT HENRYSON
c.1425–1505

Author's Chronology

The life of Robert Henryson is poorly documented even by fifteenth-century standards, and the task of reconstructing it is complicated by the fact that his name appears to have been quite common in late medieval Scotland. The year of his birth is unknown; estimates range from c. 1420–1435. He may perhaps be identified with the "Magister Robertus Henrisone" who was incorporated into the University of Glasgow in 1462, and with the Robert Henryson who was acting as a public notary in Dunfermline in 1477–1478. Sixteenth-century Scottish sources repeatedly describe Henryson as "Maister" (usually the vernacular equivalent of *Magister* or Master of Arts) or "scolmaister", and link his name with that of Dunfermline. The introductory note to Sir Francis Kinaston's Latin version of "The Testament of Cresseid" (1639) quotes a tradition that Henryson was "sometimes cheife schoole maister in Dumfermling," presumably at a grammar school attached to the Benedictine abbey. Kinaston also reports that Henryson died "very old" of a "fluxe." Apart from this possibly apochryphal tale, all that is known of Henryson's death is that it must have taken place before c. 1505, when William Dunbar's "Timor Mortis Conturbat Me" included "Maister Robert Henrisoun" of "Dumfermelyne" in its catalog of dead poets.

Author's Bibliography

The chronology of Henryson's works is as obscure as that of his life. The Henryson corpus consists of fifteen poems: "The Morall Fabillis", "The Testament of Cresseid," "Orpheus and Eurydice," and twelve shorter pieces. Most of these poems survive only in manuscripts and early printed editions produced after the likely date of Henryson's death; worse still, they contain too few unambiguous allusions to historical events or figures to be datable on internal evidence. Henryson's *floruit* is often placed in the late fifteenth century because of his supposed indebtedness to Caxton's translations, but Denton Fox, the most recent editor of Henryson, rejects this argument and proposes a somewhat earlier date. Readers interested in the problem are recommended to consult Fox's Introduction to *The Poems of Robert Henryson* (Oxford: Clarendon Press, 1981), pp. xix–xxi, for a survey of the evidence.

The earliest modern edition of Henryson's work is that of G. Gregory Smith for the Scottish Text Society: *The Poems of Robert Henryson,* 3 vols. (Edinburgh: Blackwood, 1906–1914). H. Harvey Wood's *Poems and Fables of Robert Henryson* (Edinburgh: Oliver and Boyd, 1933; revised 1958) is compact and convenient, but the scholarship on which it is based is now partly outdated. The standard edition is Denton Fox's *Poems of Robert Henryson* (Oxford: Clarendon Press, 1981). Fox's introduction, text and commentary incorporate the most important recent developments in Henryson research and criticism, and are indispensable for a serious study of the poetry. A broad selection of Henryson's work is offered by Charles Elliott's *Robert Henryson: Poems,* Clarendon Medieval and Tudor Series (Oxford: Clarendon Press, 1963; revised 1975).

Overview of Biographical Sources

A life as poorly documented as Henryson's does not lend itself to biography, and no book-length biographical treatment has in fact appeared. Denton Fox presents and evaluates the most important biographical evidence in *The Poems of Robert Henryson* (Oxford, Clarendon Press, 1981), pp. xiii–xxv. Douglas Gray provides a more extensive account in his biographical and critical study, *Robert Henryson,* Medieval and Renaissance Authors (1979).

Evaluation of Selected Biographies

Gray, Douglas, *Robert Henryson.* Medieval and Renaissance Authors. Leiden: Brill, 1979. The first chapter of Gray's book, "Dunfermline and Beyond", rehearses the few known facts of Henryson's life, and then carefully reconstructs his social and cultural milieu, from the architectural achievements of fifteenth-century Scotland to its popular amusements and customs. On the issue of Henryson's relation to Humanism, Gray adopts a moderate position, seeing the poet as a product of late scholasticism rather than as a Humanist in the strict sense.

Overview of Critical Sources

For the first half of this century, Henryson was overshadowed by the other Scottish Chaucerians, especially his younger contemporary William Dunbar. The earliest book-length study of his poetry in English is Marshall Stearns's *Robert Henryson* (1949), which focuses primarily on the poet's role as a social and political commentator. Since the mid-1960's, three more comprehensive treatments of Henryson's art have been published.

Evaluation of Selected Criticism

Gray, Douglas, *Robert Henryson.* Medieval and Renaissance Authors. Leiden: Brill, 1979. Gray depicts Henryson as Chaucerian in the fullest sense, in that he draws on both learned and popular literary traditions. About half Gray's study is devoted to "The Morall Fabillis", which he praises as achieving an imaginative harmony "reminiscent in miniature of *The Canterbury Tales.*" He also argues that the minor poems show a distinctively Henrysonian assurance in the handling of traditional subjects and forms, and deserve more critical respect than they are usually accorded.

Kindrick, Robert L. *Robert Henryson.* Boston: Twayne, 1979. Kindrick sees Henryson's poetry as a blending of three literary traditions: the Chaucerian, the native Scots, and the European (French and Italian). He particularly admires "The Morall Fabillis", in which he finds an intellectual and artistic richness equal to that of the more famous "Testament of Cresseid". Kindrick's final chapter claims that Henryson was the true founder of the Scots literary tradition, and provided the model for later poets, among them Robert Burns.

MacQueen, John, *Robert Henryson: A Study of the Major Narrative Poems.* Oxford: Clarendon Press, 1967. MacQueen is one of the first critics fully to recognize Henryson's intellectual and artistic stature. He describes Henryson not only as a learned poet by medieval standards, but also as a precursor of Humanism, "the first of the University Wits". Whether or not this particular claim is seen as over-enthusiastic, MacQueen's study represents a milestone in Henryson scholarship.

Stearns, Marshall, *Robert Henryson.* New York: Columbia University Press, 1949. This pioneering study portrays Henryson chiefly as a champion of the poor and oppressed in a turbulent age. Stearns's examination of the sources of "The Testament of Cresseid", however, anticipates later views of Henryson as an erudite poet.

Dorena Allen Wright
University of Oregon

GEORGE HERBERT
1593–1633

Author's Chronology

Born April 3, 1593 at Montgomery, England; *1596* father dies leaving ten children; *1601* moves with family to London where Magdalene Herbert, his mother, maintains a well-known household, reflecting her dedication to literary, musical, and religious values; c.*1604* attends Westminster School; *1609* matriculates at Trinity College, Cambridge; *1613* awarded Bachelor of Arts and in the following year becomes a fellow of Trinity College; *1616* awarded Master of Arts after which he remains at the university in various academic posts; *1620* named University Orator; *1623* takes leave of absence from position in the university to serve in Parliament for Montgomery borough; c.*1625* ordained as deacon and returns to Cambridge as University Orator, a position which he maintains until 1628; *1627* Magdalene Herbert dies and John Donne preaches the funeral sermon; *1628* apparently leaves Cambridge to live with his step-father in Wiltshire; *1629* marries Jane Danvers, a cousin of his step-father Sir John Danvers; *1630* instituted as rector of Bemerton and ordained as priest; writes *The Country Parson* and probably many of the English poems during his years at Bemerton; *1631–1632* corresponds with Nicholas Farrar; *1633* (March) dies in Bemerton Rectory; *1633 The Temple, Sacred Poems and Private Ejaculations* printed by Thomas Buck at Cambridge.

Author's Bibliography

The Temple, Sacred Poems and Private Ejaculations, 1633 (poems); *A Priest to the Temple or, the Country Parson his Character and Rule of Holy Life,* 1652 (prose). There are a limited number of reliable modern editions: *The Latin Poetry of George Herbert: A Bilingual Edition,* translated by Mark McCloskey and Paul R. Murphy, (Athens, OH: Ohio University Press, 1965); *The Works of George Herbert,* ed. with a commentary by F. E. Hutchinson, (Oxford: Clarendon Press, 1941); *The English Poems of George Herbert,* ed. by C. A. Patrides, (London: J. M. Dent & Sons, 1974).

Overview of Biographical Sources

The most significant biography of George Herbert is, without doubt, that written by Izaak Walton and published in 1670. Walton had access to the Herbert family and some of its papers. His biography includes poems and letters which would not have otherwise been preserved. Walton, however, was guided by didactic interest in writing the story of the poet's life. Though he respected documentary evidence of his subject's achievements, he did not feel bound to confine himself to commentary based on his documents. In George Herbert's case, he imagined his subject to be an example of perfect piety, a piety to be emulated by the reader. The gushing compliment to Herbert originating in Walton's biography spilled over into virtually every biography published until Hutchinson's "Introduction" in *The Works of George Herbert* which included the first brief notice of Herbert's parliamentary service and cooled Walton's enthusiasm for the thesis that Herbert was torn between the lures of secular preferment and the call of spiritual duty. Herbert had clearly not seen the demands as conflicting. Joseph H. Summers supported Hutchinson's view in *George Herbert: His Religion and Art* (1954). The definitive biography based upon an exhaustive search of the relevant documents and sources is Amy M. Charles' *A Life of George Herbert* (1977). Because it is still not known exactly when Herbert composed his poems, scholars have not been able to trace strict relationships between the poet's life and his works.

Evaluation of Selected Biographies

Charles, Amy M. *A Life of George Herbert.* Ithaca and London: Cornell University Press, 1977. Amy M. Charles' authoritative biography of George Herbert is based upon an exhaustive search of documents related to the poet, his family, the places he lived, and the institutions he served. Her approach is thorough and academic, based upon a knowledge of political, academic, and religious institutions of the seventeenth-century. In a straight forward style she unfolds the puzzling aspects of a life for which few documents exist. Charles occasionally includes speculations about the place of the poetry in Herbert's life, but her attention is drawn primarily to charting his career and describing his relationships with members of his family and his many famous acquaintances.

Chute, Marchette, *Two Gentle Men: The Lives of George Herbert and Robert Herrick.* New York: E. P. Dutton, 1959. Chute presents an imaginative account of the life of George Herbert, based on her knowledge of life in England in the seventeenth-century and the outlines of Herbert's life. Though certainly not as reliable as scholarly attempts to reconstruct Herbert's life, Chute's lively narrative gives the beginning reader of seventeenth-century poetry a sense of the spirit of the age.

Hutchinson, F. E. "Introduction," *The Works of George Herbert.* Oxford: Clarendon Press, 1941. Hutchinson summarizes the documented facts of Herbert's life, correcting errors in Walton's account. Unlike Walton, he restricts his narrative to events pertinent to the chronology of Herbert's life.

Summers, Joseph H. *George Herbert: His Religion and Art.* Cambridge, MA: Harvard University Press, 1968. Summers' chapter on George Herbert's life tells the story of the poet in a somewhat more readable style than Hutchinson. He argues that for Herbert there would have not been a conflict between a career in civil affairs and a career in the church. Summers examines Herbert's political aspirations and his acquaintanceship with Nicholas Farrar.

Walton, Izaak, "The Life of Mr. George Herbert," in *The Lives of John Donne, Sir Henry Wotton, Richard Hooker, George Herbert, and Robert Sanderson,* with an introduction by George Saintsbury. London: Oxford University Press, 1927. In addition to some poems and letters, Walton preserved many details of fact concerning Herbert's life. He is especially inspired by Herbert's great learning and his pious character. He shows him to be an humble servant of God dedicated to the service of his Bemerton congregation, "a saint, unspotted of the world, full of alms-deeds, full of humility, and all the examples of a virtuous life." Walton had never met Herbert and lacked knowledge of several aspects of his career, particularly his parliamentary service, which have since come to light.

Autobiographical Sources

A Priest to the Temple or, The Country Parson His Character, and Rule of Holy Life, probably written during Herbert's years at Bemerton, sets out his view of the proper behavior for a country parson. Though it is not autobiographical in any strict sense, it does reflect Herbert's thoughts on his chosen vocation, based, no doubt, on his pastoral experience. He describes the problems faced by such a clergyman and the ideals which he sought to attain in his personal life and to instill in his congregation. The treatise is characterized by an emphasis on Protestant values and religious practices and by a regard for the place of humility in the disposition of a country parson.

Overview of Critical Sources

The primary stimulous for the study of George Herbert's poetry in the twentieth century was the rediscovery by Herbert Grierson, George Saintsbury, T. S. Eliot and other men of letters of a group of seventeenth-century lyric poets now known as "Metaphysical Poets." Interest in John Donne dominated the discussion until the mid-1950's when George Herbert came to be recognized as a poet of merit in his own right. The focus of the recent critical study of Herbert has been on the close reading of individual poems, the evaluation of the poems in the context of Herbert's theology, and the understanding of the poems in the context of seventeenth-century meditative practices. More recent studies consider the relationship between the reader and the poem.

Evaluation of Selected Criticism

Benet, Diana, *Secretary of Praise: The Poetic Vocation of George Herbert.* Columbia: University of Missouri Press, 1984. Benet attempts to read the poems in the light of Herbert's personal uncertainties regarding the proper Christian vocation for himself. Careful to explain that the poems are not strictly autobiographical, Benet shows that the persona instructs the reader on the important question of vocation and that Herbert's personal conflict between serving the church or living the life of a Christian statesman informs his writing.

Fish, Stanley, *The Living Temple: George Herbert and Catechizing.* Berkeley: University of California Press, 1978. Fish considers Herbert's poems to be a series of shifting structures and ploys designed to bring the reader into the rhetorical process of the poem. Both Herbert the poet through his lyrics and Herbert the parson through his Catechism both teach the reader about personal insufficiency. Fish shows the process of reading Herbert to be that of interplay between the reader and the text, with the text proding and guiding the reader to a refined understanding of the human-divine relationship.

Lewalski, Barbara Kiefer, *Protestant Poetics and the Seventeenth-Century Religious Lyric.* Princeton: Princeton University Press, 1979. Though not devoted exclusively to the poetry of Herbert, Lewalski's treatment of the Biblical backgrounds of seventeenth-century lyric poetry is of considerable use to the reader concerned with understanding the religious aspects of his poetry. She is especially interested in the relationship between the religious and poetic vocations. A chapter, "George Herbert: Artful Psalms from the Temple in the Heart," focuses on genres, themes, and images which have Biblical roots.

Summers, Joseph H. *George Herbert: His Religion and Art.* Cambridge, MA: Harvard University Press, 1954. Summers was one of the pioneers in the critical reassessment of Herbert which began in the mid-1950's. His study of Herbert's poetry recognizes the formal complexity of Herbert's language and structures, especially the great variety of poetic forms which Herbert incorporated into *The Temple.*

Tuve, Rosamund, *A Reading of George Herbert.* Chicago: University of Chicago Press, 1952. Tuve relates Herbert's poetry to the traditions of Christian symbolism, especially those reflected in the visual arts and less well known to twentieth-century readers. Her study is particularly useful for an understanding of "The Sacrifice."

Vendler, Helen, *The Poetry of George Herbert.* Cambridge, MA: Harvard University Press, 1975. Vendler provides close readings of many of the shorter poems. Her readings are detailed and attentive to the subtle complexity of the lyric mode which contrasts with the apparent simplicity of expression. She groups the poems according to rhetorical strategies and patterns.

Other Sources

DiCesare, Mario A. ed. *A Concordance to the Complete Writings of George Herbert.* Ithaca, NY: Cornell University Press, 1977. Useful for tracing images and themes in Herbert's writing.

Gottlieb, Sidney, ed. *George Herbert Journal.* Published by Sacred Heart University, Bridgeport, Connecticut, 1978–present. This journal publishes essays concerning the life and works of George Herbert and related writers.

Patrides, C. A. ed. *George Herbert: The Critical Heritage.* London: Routledge & Kegan Paul, 1983. A collection of critical commentaries from the seventeenth century to 1936 through which the reader can assess the development of Herbert's literary reputation.

Roberts, John R., ed. *Essential Articles for the Study of George Herbert's Poetry.* Hamden, CT: Archon Books, 1979. A carefully selected group of essays representing the best critical articles written between 1957 and 1977. The emphasis is on the images, style, and structure of Herbert's poems. Several essays are close readings of individual poems.

Roberts, John R. *George Herbert: An Annotated Bibliography of Modern Criticism, 1905–1974.* Columbia and London: University of Missouri Press, 1978. A chronological list of the critical writings about Herbert with useful, descriptive comments reflecting the content and scope of each title.

Summers, Claude J. and Ted-Larry Pebworth, ed. *"Too Rich to Clothe the Sunne": Essays on George Herbert.* Pittsburgh: University of Pittsburgh Press, 1980. A collection of fifteen informative essays written in 1978 representing a wide range of contemporary critical approaches to the study of Herbert's poetry. Several of the essays emphasize the study of Herbert's poems in their intellectual and religious contexts.

Selected Dictionaries and Encyclopedias

Dictionary of National Biography, Macmillan, 1891. A biographical summary which (as the date suggests) shows the influence of Walton's biography. Includes the publishing history of *The Temple.*

Faye Pauli Whitaker
Iowa State University

ROBERT HERRICK
1591–1674

Author's Chronology

Born 1591, London, England, the son of a goldsmith who died (possibly by suicide) the following year; *1592–1607* residence and place of schooling unknown; *1607* apprenticed to his uncle, Sir William Herrick, a successful London goldsmith; *1613* enters St. John's College, Cambridge, as a wealthy student; *1617* transfers to Trinity Hall, Cambridge, to save money; receives B.A. degree; *1620* receives Cambridge M.A.; *1623* ordained an Anglican deacon and priest; *1623–1627* probably visits London often, acquainting himself with literary and artistic figures (including Ben Jonson) and making a name for himself as a poet; *1627* serves as chaplain to the Duke of Buckingham during the calamitous expedition to the Isle of Rhé; *1630* installed as Vicar of Dean Prior; *1640* returns to London to arrange publication of a volume of his verse, apparently not issued; *1647* expelled from his vicarage because of his royalist sympathies; probably returns to London, perhaps supported by charity from relatives; *1648 Hesperides* published, after which Herrick probably wrote few other poems; *1660* successfully petitions Parliament for the return of his vicarage and resumes his duties there; *1674* dies; buried at Dean Prior.

Author's Bibliography

Hesperides: or, The Works both Humane and Divine, 1648 (poems; includes, with separate title and pagination, *His Noble Numbers: or, His Pious Pieces*).

Overview of Biographical Sources

No truly satisfying biography of Herrick exists, partly because "hard" sources are so scanty. The poems can be used in reconstructing aspects of the life, but must be used cautiously since their relevance and reliability vary. L. C. Martin outlines the life in his standard edition, *The Poetical Works of Robert Herrick* (Oxford: Clarendon Press, 1956). F. W. Moorman's *Robert Herrick: A Biographical and Critical Study* (London: John Lane, 1910) has been criticized for depending too heavily on the poems. Although called outdated and sometimes unreliable, it can still be of some value if used with care. The most recent biography, George Walton Scott's *Robert Herrick, 1591–1674* (London: Sidgwick and Jackson, 1974) has been dismissed as derivative and inconsequential, but it prints some interesting photographs. Many works on Herrick's life seem either thin or padded; truly interested readers should probably consult and collate all, without fully trusting any.

Evaluation of Selected Biographies

Chute, Marchette, *Two Gentle Men: The Lives of George Herbert and Robert Herrick.* New York: E. P. Dutton, 1959; London: Secker and Warburg, 1960.

In her readable popular study, Chute sets the meagre biographical data against the background of the times and milieu. Although she provides a good bibliography, lack of notes makes checking her facts difficult. The tone is occasionally either too speculative or too definite; but for the time being, this remains one of the sounder treatments in English.

Delattre, Floris, *Robert Herrick: Contribution à l'Etude de la Poésie Lyrique en Angleterre au Dix-septième Siècle.* Paris: F. Alcan, 1911. Although dated, this is still considered a more reliable treatment than some published later. An opening section surveys the life. Delattre then discusses the thematic, stylistic, and metrical characteristics of the poems. She comments on the order and chronology of works in *Hesperides,* and appends biographical records. The book has been faulted for excessive impressionism and for too often reading the poems in naively biographical terms.

Autobiographical Sources

Fifteen letters from Herrick are printed in Martin's edition of *The Poetical Works.* Written during Herrick's stay at Cambridge, they frequently solicit money from his uncle William. Autobiographical comments of varying credibility are scattered throughout the poems.

Overview of Critical Sources

Herrick has only recently been seen as a major 17th century poet, and much modern criticism has been concerned with assessing his precise importance. His frequent deftness, brevity, humor, and charm encouraged some earlier readers to regard him as a minor poet chiefly interested in light or minor subjects; recent criticism has therefore often highlighted his underlying seriousness. Critics have dealt, for instance, with his treatments of death and change; with the poetic impact of contemporary political and religious controversies; with the balance between classicism (or even "paganism") and Christianity in his writings; with specific classical influences; with the influence of his immediate poetic predecessors, especially Jonson; with his pastoralism and his tendencies towards poetic ceremony and ritual; with his fairy poems; and with the connections between his poetry and contemporary music. They have also explored unities of theme, tone, technique, and personae in his many writings.

Evaluation of Selected Criticism

Deneef, A. Leigh, *"This Poetick Liturgie": Robert Herrick's Ceremonial Mode.* Durham, NC: Duke University Press, 1974. This important book argues that Herrick typically uses poetic ceremony to "isolate specific and limited instants of human experience and to transform them into significant and static celebratory rites in which both poet and reader participate." Deneef identifies four major personae (pastoral, courtly, realistic, and artistic) in Herrick's verse and discusses their various voices. "By using different personae, Herrick is able to pit one ceremonial approach to existence against another, to show that each is significant on its own terms and within its own limits, and to demonstrate that the *poetic* ceremonial, the rite of artistic or imaginative creation, is one means of actualizing all these approaches simultaneously." Deneef stresses Herrick's poetic confrontation with death and mutability.

Deming, Robert H. *Ceremony and Art: Robert Herrick's Poetry.* The Hague: Mouton, 1974. Deming's book attempts to "place Herrick's poetry in its own milieu, literary and historical, social and artistic." At the same time, it seeks to highlight such aspects of his work as "the self-conscious and the ironic, the playful and the miniature, the paradoxical and the Baroque, and, most importantly, the ritualistic and ceremonial elements." Deming stresses Herrick's negative reaction to contemporary Puritanism, and emphasizes the connections between classical and Christian ceremonies and between ceremony and art. Praised for its emphasis on the Christian elements in Herrick's work, Deming's book has also been criticized for offering few technical insights and for being written in a style that is sometimes unclear.

Rollin, Roger, *Robert Herrick.* New York: Twayne, 1966. Rollin proposes to read Herrick's poems *as poems* rather than as mere imitations or as versified autobiography. He emphasizes Herrick's artistic variety but also stresses the intellectual unity that results from his "conception of himself as a pastoral poet . . . who uses his artistry to portray an idyllic, ideal world that can serve as an overt or covert criticism of 'the real world.' " Individual chapters show how Herrick responds to transience and death through such themes as the good life, love, faith, and artistic immortality. The closing chapter makes a case for Herrick's importance by comparing him with other 17th century authors.

Rollin, Roger B. and J. Max Patrick, eds. *"Trust to Good Verses": Herrick Tercentenary Essays.* Pittsburgh: University of Pittsburgh Press, 1978. This handsome volume brings together a wide variety of approaches to Herrick's achievement, with essays on his debts to and use of the classics; on his epigrams of praise; on his political poetry; on the Christian aspects of his verse; on his contemporary reputation; on the visual elements in his work; on the developmental structure of his book; on his "poetry of song;" on his passion for poetry; on his meditative poems; on the names of his poetic mistresses; and even on "Herrick and Japanese Classical Poetry." The volume closes with a helpful selected and annotated bibliography that identifies the most important previous Herrick criticism.

Other Sources

Braden, Gordon, "Robert Herrick and Classical Lyric Poetry," in *The Classics and English Renaissance Poetry: Three Case Studies.* New Haven: Yale

University Press, 1978, pp. 154–258, 269–275. Emphasizes Herrick's use of Martial, Anacreon, and Horace; an appendix discusses "Herrick's Edition of 'Anacreon.' "

Brooks, Cleanth, "What Does Poetry Communicate?" in *The Well Wrought Urn: Studies in the Structure of Poetry*. New York: Harcourt, Brace, 1947, pp. 62–73. Influential discussion of the poem "Corinna's going a Maying."

Hageman, Elizabeth H. *Robert Herrick: A Reference Guide*. Boston: G. K. Hall, 1983. A fully annotated bibliography stretching from 1648 to 1981.

Musgrove, Sydney, *The Universe of Robert Herrick*. Auckland University College Bulletin, no. 38; English series, no. 4. Auckland: Pelorus Press, 1951; rpt. Folcroft, PA: Folcroft Library Editions, 1967, 1971. Emphasizes Herrick's seriousness, importance, his Christianity, and his sacramental view of nature.

Selected Dictionaries and Encyclopedias

British Writers, Charles Scribner's Sons, 1979. A short biography precedes this reassessment of Herrick's importance and discussion of his typical stances, styles, and subjects.

Critical Survey of Poetry, Salem Press, 1982. Brief biography, followed by a discussion of characteristic themes and analysis of some important poems.

Robert C. Evans
Auburn University at Montgomery

GERARD MANLEY HOPKINS
1844–1889

Author's Chronology

Born July 28, 1844, Stratford, Essex England; *1854* attends Highgate Grammar School mostly as a boarder; *1857* tours Belgium and the Rhineland with his father and brother; *1860* wins school poetry prize with "The Escorial"; tours south Germany with his father; *1863* attends Balliol College, Oxford, on a Classical Exhibition scholarship; *1864* meets Christina Rossetti; *1865* has religious crisis; *1866* decides to leave the Church of England, visits John Henry Cardinal Newman, and is received by Newman into the Roman Catholic Church; *1867* graduates from Oxford with a Double-First in "Greats"; teaches at the Oratory School, Birmingham; *1868* resolves to become a Jesuit priest, burns his early poems, and writes only two occasional poems in the next seven years; *1870* studies philosophy at St. Mary's Hall, Stonyhurst; *1872* discovers Duns Scotus; *1873* teaches Rhetoric at Roehampton; *1875* writes *The Wreck of the Deutschland* ending a seven year silence; *1877* ordained to the priesthood; *1878–1881* preaches in London, Oxford, and Liverpool; *1882–1884* teaches classics at Stonyhurst College; *1884–1889* Professor of Greek at University College, Dublin and Fellow of the Royal Academy; *1889* dies in Dublin of typhoid fever; *1918* first edition of his *Poems,* edited by Robert Bridges.

Author's Bibliography

The Poems of Gerard Manley Hopkins, 4th edition. eds. W. H. Gardner and N. H. MacKenzie. London: Oxford University Press, 1970; *The Letters of Gerard Manley Hopkins to Robert Bridges, The Correspondence of Gerard Manley Hopkins and Richard Watson Dixon,* and *Further Letters of Gerard Manley Hopkins,* 2nd edition. all edited by C. C. Abbott. London: Oxford University Press, 1970; *The Journals and Papers of Gerard Manley Hopkins.* eds. Humphry House and Graham Storey. Oxford, 1966; *The Sermons and Devotional Writings of Gerard Manley Hopkins.* ed. Christopher Devlin, S.J., London: Oxford University Press, 1967; *A Selection of Poems and Prose.* ed. W. H. Gardner. Hammondsworth: Penguin, 1953, rev. 1969; *A Hopkins Reader.* ed. John Pick. London: Oxford University Press, 1953, rev. and enlarged 1966.

Overview of Biographical Sources

Hopkins's biographers have had little difficulty chronicling and elucidating the main outlines of his life. The facts are indisputably clear. What is of interest, however, resulting in differences of biographical focus and emphasis, is the relationship between Hopkins the priest and Hopkins the poet. The dialectic between his religious sensibility and his poetic inclination provides the focal point of his biographers' interest. Of particular importance in this regard is his conversion from Anglicanism to Roman Catholicism and his subsequent ordination as a Jesuit priest, with consequent tensions and repercussions among his family and friends.

Hopkins's first biographer, Father G. F. Lahey, S.J., provides a useful starting point for the study of his religious sensibility: *Gerard Manley Hopkins* (London: Oxford University Press, 1930). This early work, however, suppresses Hopkins's struggle to integrate his priestly and poetic vocations. Like other biographies by Jesuit writers such as Alfred Thomas's *Hopkins the Jesuit* (London: Oxford University Press, 1969), Father Lahey's pioneering effort tends toward hagiography. Other useful biographies varying in their degree of accuracy and their focus include John Pick's *Gerard Manley Hopkins* (New York: Oxford University Press, 1966), a critical biography that relates Hopkin's religion and his art; *Gerard Manley Hopkins* (New York: W. W. Norton, 1944), by Eleanor Ruggles, a colorful and sometimes fanciful, novelistic account; and more recently, Paddy Kitchen's detailed, psychologically speculative work, *Gerard Manley Hopkins* (New York: Atheneum, 1979).

Evaluation of Selected Biographies

Bergonzi, Bernard, *Gerard Manley Hopkins.* New York: Macmillan, 1977. An introductory critical biography. The advantage of this book as biography is its limitation as criticism: Bergonzi interprets Hopkins's poems as reflections of his experience of life. More descriptive than analytical, Bergonzi's discussion draws heavily on Hopkins's journals and correspondence. Focusing on Hopkins's intellectual development, Bergonzi places him accurately in the contexts of Victorian England, Oxford, the Catholic Church, and the Jesuit order. In the final chapter Bergonzi presents an assessment of Hopkins's small body of poetry, concluding that "his was a narrow, even constricted triumph; but he was able . . . to enclose infinite riches in a little room."

Storey, Graham, *A Preface to Hopkins.* London: Longmans, 1981. The bulk of this informative book focuses on familial, religious, and literary background. Storey's facts are accurate and his writing is lucid. He includes photographs of prominent people and places in Hopkins's life, as well as reproductions of a few of Hopkins's sketches and manuscript copies of selected poems. The brief critical comments accompanying the poems, which are conveniently reprinted in the book, provide a useful starting point for textual analysis.

Autobiographical Sources

Hopkins's autobiography is contained in his extensive correspondence, journals, and devotional writings. All of his biographers have drawn on this rich fund of materials. What is revealed strikingly throughout these personal documents is Hopkins's artistic sensibility, especially his interest in historical linguistics and prosody, his intense spirituality, his physical debility, and his deep love of nature. In addition, these autobiographical documents contain information about his poetic theory and practice, especially about instress, inscape, and sprung rhythm.

Overview of Critical Sources

Hopkins's poems have invited considerable scrutiny. Nearly all the critical works offer analyses and explications of many individual poems. A few, in fact, offer commentaries on Hopkins's complete *oeuvre.* In addition, nearly all explain the technical aspects of Hopkins's verse. Finally, each of the critical books contains some biographical background, for Hopkins's most complex and successful poems derive directly from his religious experience and his experience of nature.

Evaluation of Selected Criticism

Bump, Jerome, *Gerard Manley Hopkins.* Boston: Twayne, 1982. While surveying Hopkins's life and works, Bump explores issues overlooked by many other critics: Hopkins's concept of providence, his affinities with Romanticism, literary influences in both directions, and the dialectic of modernity and medievalism in his work. This is a solid, provocative study that goes beyond introductory matters.

Gardner, W. H. *Gerard Manley Hopkins: A Study of Poetic Idiosyncrasy in Relation to Poetic Tradition.* 2 vols. London: Secker and Warburg, 1949. This pioneering critical study emphasizes technical matters, especially the subtleties of Hopkins's versification. Gardner's immensely detailed and informative work, though occasionally daunting, is the most comprehensive account of the poems available.

Johnson, Wendell Stacy, *Gerard Manley Hopkins: The Poet as Victorian.* Ithaca: Cornell University Press, 1968. This concise and illuminating book focuses on the Victorian concern with self and nature in four poems: *The Wreck of the Deutschland,* "The Windhover," "Spring and Fall," and "That Nature is a Heraclitean Fire." Johnson provides brief glosses on other poems as they relate to the concerns of these four.

Mariani, Paul, *A Commentary on the Complete Poems of Gerard Manley Hopkins.* Ithaca: Cornell University Press, 1970. The most comprehensive and readable of the commentaries, Mariani's book offers persuasive and reasonable interpretations of the poems. His discussion of Hopkins's prosody is brief but clear, and he includes an excellent appendix on "Hopkins and the Sonnet." This is the best single critical account of Hopkins's work.

MacKenzie, Norman H. *A Reader's Guide to Gerard Manley Hopkins.* Ithaca: Cornell University Press, 1981. Not a beginner's book, MacKenzie's *Guide* is a rich source of information on matters technical, historical, biographical, and speculative. The prose is dense and the interpretations of the poems often are strained, but the book is scrupulously well informed and researched.

Robinson, Ian, *In Extremity: A Study of Gerard Manley Hopkins.* Cambridge: Cambridge University Press, 1978. Robinson's central concern is how successfully Hopkins's religious beliefs are transmuted into poetry. His book is a subtle and rigorous work of refined critical analysis.

Other Sources

Davie, Donald, "Hopkins as a Decadent Critic," *Purity of Diction in English Verse,* London, 1952. A perceptive discussion of Hopkins's criticism.

Dunne, Tom, *Gerard Manley Hopkins: A Comprehensive Bibliography.* Oxford: Clarendon Press, 1976. Can be supplemented by the annual bibliographies in *The Hopkins Quarterly* and *The Hopkins Research Bulletin.*

Hartman, Geoffrey, *Hopkins: A Collection of Critical Essays.* Twentieth-century Views Series. Englewood Cliffs: Prentice Hall, 1966. Includes a number of fine, important essays by distinguished critics. Provides the best critical overview by diverse hands representing varied points of view.

Miller, J. Hillis, "Gerard Manley Hopkins," *The Disappearance of God.* Cambridge: Harvard University Press, 1963. A brilliant, influential discussion of Hopkins's mind and art. Indispensable.

Milward, Peter, S.J. and Raymond V. Schoder, S.J. *Landscape and Inscape: Vision and Inspiration in Hopkins's Poetry.* Grand Rapids: William B. Eerdman's, 1975. Texts and analyses of selected poems coupled with stunning photographs.

Schneider, Elizabeth W. *The Dragon in the Gate: Studies in the Poetry of Gerard Manley Hopkins.* Berkeley and Los Angeles: University of California Press, 1968. Essays on aspects of Hopkins's poetry, containing some outstanding criticism, especially on prosody.

Selected Dictionaries and Encyclopedias

Critical Survey of Poetry, Salem Press, 1984. Brief biography and critical overview of the major poems.

Dictionary of Literary Biography, Gale Research, 1983. Concise overview of Hopkins's life, and a brief description of selected poems.

The New Catholic Encyclopedia, 15 vols. McGraw Hill, 1967. General discussion of Hopkins's life and work.

Robert DiYanni
Pace University

A. E. HOUSMAN
1859–1936

Author's Chronology

Born Alfred Edward Housman, March 26, 1859, Bournheath, England; *1870* attends Bromsgrove School; *1871* mother dies on his twelfth birthday; *1877–1880* attends St. John's College, Oxford; rooms with A. W. Pollard and Moses J. Jackson; *1881* fails final examination in Classics and leaves with no degree; *1882–1892* works in Government Patent Office; publishes classical papers; *1889* Jackson marries and later goes to Canada; *1892–1911* Housman becomes Professor of Latin, University College, London; *1896 A Shropshire Lad* published; *1903–1930* edits Manilius' *Astronomica* (Latin work on astronomy); *1911–1936* Kennedy Professor of Latin, Cambridge University; *1922 Last Poems; 1923* Jackson dies; *1933* Housman gives the Leslie Stephen Lecture, published as *The Name and Nature of Poetry; 1936* dies April 30 at Cambridge, England.

Author's Bibliography (selected)

"The Death of Socrates," 1874 (poem); "Horatiana," 1882 (classical paper); *A Shropshire Lad,* 1896 (poems); *Introductory Lecture,* 1892, 1933, 1937 (criticism); "The Application of Thought to Textual Criticism," 1921 (criticism); *Last Poems,* 1922; *The Name and Nature of Poetry,* 1933 (criticism); *More Poems,* 1936; *Additional Poems,* 1937.

Overview of Biographical Sources

A. E. Housman's long, deliberately private, curiously divided life has produced much reminiscence and speculation. His habitual reserve is countered by flashes of genial humor and kindness; the austere university professor is opposed by the poignant poet. His homosexual, ungratified, attraction for a college roommate, Moses J. Jackson, has been variously cited as the basis, first and foremost, for his poems, although no solid evidence concerning that relationship is available. Just after his death a spate of personal recollections appeared. In the 1950's two speculative biographies, one highly romanticized, the other so unsympathetic toward its subject as to undermine it, appeared. Henry Maas's *The Letters of A. E. Housman* (Cambridge: Harvard University Press, 1971) made available much information. Richard Perceval Graves's *A. E. Housman: The Scholar-Poet* (1980) synthesized the best of previous materials. It was followed by Norman Page's *A. E. Housman: A Critical Biography* (1983), which challenged some of Graves's speculations, but admitted how essential speculation is in chronicling Housman's life. The biography is eminently readable and sound. These two recent books, along with the biographical information, in more compact form by Tom Burns Haber in *A. E. Housman* (1967), furnish the best accounts of Housman's life.

Evaluation of Selected Biographies

Gow, A. S. F. *A. E. Housman.* Cambridge: At the University Press, 1936. A terse, sympathetic portrait of a very human personality by a colleague who knew him well.

Graves, Richard Perceval, *A. E. Housman: The Scholar-Poet.* London: Routledge and Kegan Paul, 1979; rpt. New York: Charles Scribner's Sons, 1980. Using Maas's and other correspondence, as well as a wealth of scholarship since the 1930's, Graves deftly draws upon earlier biographies and reminiscences to balance the long classical scholar-professor career with the brief outbursts of poetic publication. One criticism is that Graves insufficiently analyzes the poetry, but two lengthy sections entitled "A Literary Life" do ample justice to Housman's verse. Graves thinks the autobiographical nature of the poems is evident and the craftsmanship superb. A stated purpose of this book is to promote a revival of enjoyment of Housman's poetry.

Haber, Tom Burns, *A. E. Housman.* New York: Twayne, 1967. The condensed biographical portions of this book afford a reasonable view of Housman's life by one of the most productive Housman scholars of the mid-twentieth century.

Page, Norman, *A. E. Housman: A Critical Biography.* London: Macmillan Press; New York: Schocken Books, 1983. Page's book opens with an excellent overview of earlier biographies, charting their strengths and weaknesses. One need only consult this section to become readily informed about other biographical sources. His one weakness is an uncharitable attitude toward Graves, whom he chastises as overspeculative. Page thus contradicts his own views, which, he admits, are speculative, as must be the case in any approach to Housman's biography. Nonetheless, he offers sound syntheses of previous biocritical work, forming his own opinions into a readable portraiture. The relationship with Moses and Adalbert Jackson is treated dispassionately and sensibly. Page believes that Laurence Housman's thoughts about his brother's homosexuality are not trustworthy. Page defers examination of the verse until the close of his book.

Overview of Critical Sources

Although Housman's poetic reputation enjoyed great currency for much of the early twentieth century, and although it has recently revived, just two book length critical studies exist. Many terse explications appear in journals like *The Explicator* and *Notes & Queries,* and articles of critical substance continue to appear. A Housman Society was founded in England in 1973; its interests embrace the lives and writings of the family. Too often, A. E. Housman's poetry is analyzed in contexts other than that of literary art. His present reputation is that of a significant second-rank poet of the late Victorian and Edwardian eras. His theories of poetry have gained recent acclaim.

Evaluation of Selected Criticism

Gosse, Edmund, *The Making of a Shropshire Lad.* Seattle: University of Washington Press, 1966. This study of Housman's manuscripts offers many insights into his poetic aims and art.

Haber, Tom Burns, *A. E. Housman.* New York: Twayne, 1967. Haber brings together many of his ideas about Housman's sources and methods. This is the best introduction to his writings.

Housman, A. E. *The Name and Nature of Poetry.* Cambridge: At The University Press, 1933. Housman's summing up his essentially Romantic conception of poetry provides personal comments about some of his verse.

Leggett, B. J. *Housman's Land of Lost Content: A Critical Study of "A Shropshire Lad."* Knoxville: University of Tennessee Press, 1970. To date the best book length study of Housman's greatest poetic work. Leggett suggests a loose unity among the sixty-three poems in *A Shropshire Lad,* thematically and otherwise. The motif of a lost Eden, with consequent conflicts between ideas of permanence versus impermanence in life, is central. This view is also consistent with observations in *The Name and Nature of Poetry.* Leggett's command of scholarship is impressive.

———. *The Poetic Art of A. E. Housman: Theory and Practice.* Lincoln: University of Nebraska Press, 1978. Leggett's consideration here encompasses all of Housman's poetry, which, he thinks, is in accord with views expressed in *The Name and Nature of Poetry.* That document aligns Housman with the theories and practices of T. S. Eliot and thus makes Housman not so far removed from the poetics of the 1930's as his detractors have suggested. The later poems receive thorough analysis. Housman's views of poetry resemble those of Samuel Taylor Coleridge and Matthew Arnold: taste becomes the final arbiter in judging it. Irony, wit, and ambiguity inform much of Housman's own verse; consequently it resembles Eliot's, whose critical theories and poetic methods are often held up in opposition to Housman's.

Ricks, Christopher, ed. *A. E. Housman: A Collection of Critical Essays.* Englewood Cliffs, NJ: Prentice-Hall, 1968. Ricks's introduction, a fine display of opinion about Housman, is followed by fifteen essays on varied aspects of the poet-scholar by such writers as Ezra Pound, Richard Wilbur, Randall Jarrell, Cleanth Brooks, and John Sparrow. A brief chronology and a succinct bibliography of additional study material appear.

Other Sources

White, William, "Alfred Edward Housman," *The New Cambridge Bibliography of English Literature,* ed. George Watson. Cambridge: At the University Press, 1969. Vol. III. Cols. 601–606. Compiled by the foremost Housman scholar of our time, this list is a standard reference from which to begin research.

Benjamin Franklin Fisher IV
University of Mississippi

WILLIAM DEAN HOWELLS
1837–1920

Author's Chronology

Born March 1, 1837, Martin's Ferry, Ohio, to a Welsh newspaper editor and his Irish-German wife; *1851* works as compositor on *Ohio State Journal;* writes poems for *Atlantic Monthly; 1860* travels to New England to meet James Russell Lowell, Nathaniel Hawthorne, Henry David Thoreau, Ralph Waldo Emerson, and Oliver Wendell Holmes; *1861* serves as consul to Venice; *1862* marries Elinor Gertrude Mead; *1866* serves as assistant editor of *Atlantic Monthly* and begins friendship with Henry James; *1869* begins friendship with Mark Twain; *1871* becomes editor of *Atlantic Monthly; 1881* resigns editorship; *1886* writes "Editor's Study" for *Harper's; 1892* resigns from "Editor's Study;" *1900* writes "Editor's Easy Chair" for *Harper's; 1908* serves as first president of the American Academy of Arts and Letters; *1910* wife dies; *1915* receives gold medal for fiction from the Academy of Arts and Letters; dies May 11, 1920 in New York City; ashes buried in Cambridge, Massachusetts.

Author's Bibliography (selected)

Venetian Life, 1866 (travel sketches); *A Foregone Conclusion,* 1875 (novel); *A Modern Instance,* 1882 (novel); *The Rise of Silas Lapham,* 1885 (novel); *A Hazard of New Fortunes,* 1889 (novel); *Annie Kilburn,* 1889 (novel); *A Boy's Town,* 1890 (nonfiction); *Criticism and Fiction,* 1891 (essays); *My Year in a Log Cabin,* 1893 (nonfiction); *My Literary Passions,* 1895 (nonfiction); *The Landlord at Lion's Head,* 1897 (novel); *Literary Friends and Acquaintance,* 1900 (nonfiction); *Literature and Life,* 1902 (nonfiction); *The Son of Royal Langbrith,* 1904 (novel); *My Mark Twain,* 1910 (nonfiction); *The Leatherwood God,* 1916 (novel); *Years of My Youth,* 1916 (nonfiction); *The Vacation of the Kelwyns,* 1920 (novel); *Selected Letters,* 6 vols. 1979; *Editor's Study,* 1983 (essays).

Overview of Biographical Sources

William Dean Howell's long and productive life has been explored by many authors. James L. Woodress, Jr. has written *Howells and Italy* (Durham: Duke University Press, 1952) which describes Howells' life in Italy and the influence his travels had on his work, particularly *Venetian Life.* Edward Wagenknecht's *William Dean Howells: The Friendly Eye* (New York: Oxford University Press, 1969) is a psychography of Howells' life. Kenneth S. Lynn's *William Dean Howells: An America Life* (New York: Harcourt Brace Jovanovich, 1971) is valuable both as a biography of Howells and a critical analysis of his work. Kenneth E. Eble has written, for the beginning scholar of Howells, the biocritical book, *William Dean Howells,* second edition (Boston: Twayne: 1982). The most complete biography of Howells' life is Edwin Cady's two volume work, *The Road to Realism* and *The Realist at War* (1956, 1958).

Biographies of Howells stress that he was a self-educated man who willingly defended and unselfishly supported the efforts of serious artists, even those who did not practice his brand of realism. Biographers of Howells are highly sympathetic to the man they have studied and believe he should not be treated by critics and the public as a lesser figure than Mark Twain and Henry James.

Evaluation of Selected Biographies

Brooks, Van Wyck, *Howells: His Life and World.* New York: E. P. Dutton, 1959. A highly readable book, this is an excellent introduction to Howells' life. Brooks provides detailed descriptions of Howells' friendship with and support of Mark Twain and Henry James. Interesting anecdotes concerning Robert Louis Stevenson and other important literary figures of the time increase one's understanding of Howells. Brooks judges the novels written between 1880 and 1890 as Howells' best fiction.

Cady, Edwin H. *The Road to Realism: The Early Years 1837–1885 of William Dean Howells.* Syracuse, NY: Syracuse University Press, 1956. This book provides the most complete picture of Howells' early life and self-education. Cady emphasizes the important influence Howells' parents and wife had on his life. He describes Howells' well-known pilgrimage to New England in 1860 when he met important literary figures as well as the less well-known details of Howells' neurotic illnesses that lasted until he married. Cady identifies Howells as an agnostic and explains how such skepticism led him to realism. He divides Howells' literary career into three periods—the Poetic Period which ended in Venice, the Experimental Period which began with travel literature, and the Realistic Period which began with *A Modern Instance.* Critical analysis includes a discussion of *A Foregone Conclusion* as an early international novel and *The Rise of Silas Lapham* as the first American novel on the businessman.

———. *The Realist at War: The Mature Years 1885–1920 of William Dean Howells.* Syracuse, NY: Syracuse University Press, 1958. Cady identifies Howells as the first to recognize the emergence of the American realistic novel, and he classifies *A Modern Instance* as Howells' first fully realistic novel. Because *Criticism and Fiction,* excerpts from Howells' essays for "Editor's Study," was hastily compiled, Cady wisely concludes it is unreliable. He defends Howells against the charge that he was naively optimistic and prudish, and describes the support Howells gave writers such as Frank Norris, Stephen Crane, Paul Laurence Dunbar, and Hamlin Garland. Cady blames Alexander Harvey's work, *William Dean Howells: A Study of the Achievement of a Literary Artist* (New York: Huebsch, 1917) for the decline of Howells' reputation.

Kirk, Clara M. and Rudolf Kirk, *William Dean Howells.* New York: Twayne, 1962. This book, which examines Howells as a product of nineteenth-century America, is appropriate for someone just beginning to study Howells' life and literary influence. The book rushes through Howells' life prior to his becoming editor of the *Atlantic Monthly;* however, important observations that the Kirks make include the fact that in "Editor's Study" Howells defended such controversial artists as Leo Tolstoy, Gustave Flaubert, Thomas Hardy, Henrik Ibsen and Stephen Crane.

Autobiographical Sources

Howells wrote several books about his life, both as a young man from Ohio and as a literary figure in New England and New York. Works concerning his early years include *A Boy's Town,* describing his life from three to eleven in Hamilton, Ohio, and *My Year in a Log Cabin,* describing his family's life in 1850 when his father's business failed. Both of these periods in his youth are included in the larger work, *Years of My Life.* This book begins with his birth and a description of his family's background, and ends when he received his appointment as consul in Venice.

An important book describing his life as a literary figure is *Literary Friends and Acquaintance.* This recounts his first trip to New England when he met Emerson, Thoreau, and Hawthorne; his first trip to New York when he met Walt Whitman; his stay in Venice; and his work as assistant editor of the *Atlantic Monthly.* It also includes chapters on Oliver Wendell Holmes, Henry Wadsworth Longfellow, and James Russell Lowell.

Another important book, both a biography and an autobiography, is *My Mark Twain.* It describes Howells and Samuel Clemens' first meeting in 1869 at the office of James Fields, their business relationship when Howells was editor of the *Atlantic Monthly* and Mark Twain was a contributor, and Mark Twain's death. Howells provides revealing details about his friend's personality, literary preferences, and religious beliefs.

Overview of Critical Sources

Howells wrote short stories, novels, drama, poetry, literary criticism, and travel literature. Critics find that his short stories, drama, and poetry are less important than his novels and essays. Critics admire *A Modern Instance* but often disagree about which other novels are among Howells' best works. They also disagree about which terms best describe his fiction and how God is represented in his fiction. Authors of book-length works on Howells agree, however, that he was not unreasonably optimistic and prudish. They also defend him against the charge that his work has little to do with later twentieth century fiction.

Evaluation of Selected Criticism

Bennett, George N. *The Realism of William Dean Howells, 1889–1920.* Nashville: Vanderbilt University Press, 1976. In this valuable book, Bennett discusses the influence of Ivan Turgenev and the characteristics of Howells' realism. He analyzes the economic novels and psychological novels, observing that Howells wrote serious comedy throughout his career. According to him, Howells' fiction shows a belief in a benevolent God who has given people free will.

Carrington, George C., Jr. *The Immense Complex Drama: The World and Art of the Howells Novel.* Columbus: Ohio State University Press, 1966. This good but rather pretentious book analyzes sixteen of Howells' novels. Carrington identifies Howells' best works as, among others, *A Modern Instance, A Hazard of New Fortunes,* and *The Landlord at Lion's Head.* Carrington discusses the theme of alienation in Howells' novels and states that there is no god in Howells' world of fiction. He calls Howells' novels satires that grew grimmer as the novelist aged. In his analysis of Howells' characters, Carrington identifies the self-destructive artist, the demon, the moving observer, and those (usually women) who try to comprehend their world. The last of his book points out Howells' flaws as a novelist, including his abstract and mechanical style and his inability to reveal preconscious thoughts well.

Carter, Everett, *Howells and the Age of Realism.* Hamden, CT: Archon Books, 1966. This is one of the best book-length critical studies of Howells' fiction. It expertly places Howells within his literary period by describing the romanticism he respected but could not understand, the sentimentalism he abhorred, the early realism he admired, and the naturalism he rejected. Carter provides an excellent explanation of Howells' realism and discusses all its important aspects including the emphasis on characterization and the commonplace; the rejection of conventional plot; the use of the dramatic method; the influence of impressionism, pragmatism, and positivism; and the importance of writing ethically without moralizing. He also analyzes Howells' use of critical realism in *Annie Kilburn* and *A Hazard of New Fortunes.* Carter calls Howells a social satirist and adherent of Christian socialism.

Fryckstedt, Olov W. *In Quest of America: A Study of Howells' Early Development as a Novelist.* Cambridge: Harvard University Press, 1958. This author discusses Howells' novels up to 1882 when he wrote one of his best works, *A Modern Instance.* The book provides an excellent description of how Howells gradually developed his definition of realism. Fryckstedt discusses the influence of Turgenev's psychological fiction on Howells' novels and defends his contribution to twentieth-century literature by showing his influence on Stephen Crane, Frank Norris, and Theodore Dreiser.

Kirk, Clara Marburg, *W. D. Howells and Art in His Time.* New Brunswick, NJ: Rutgers University Press, 1965. In this first study of Howells as an art critic, Kirk emphasizes Howells' belief that art should be an integral part of society and appreciated by all types of people. Artists discussed include Joseph Pennell, Augustus Saint-Gaudens, William Powell Frith, and James Whistler.

Other Sources

Brenni, Vito J. *William Dean Howells: A Bibliography.* Metuchen, NJ: The Scarecrow Press, 1973. Works by and about Howells are divided by genres.

Dean, James L. *Howells' Travels toward Art.* Albuquerque: University of New Mexico Press, 1970. On the genre of travel literature.

Eble, Kenneth E. ed. *Howells: A Century of Criticism.* Dallas: Southern Methodist University Press, 1962. Includes comments by James Russell Lowell, Hamlin Garland, George Bernard Shaw, Mark Twain, Henry James, Edwin Cady, and Everett S. Carter.

McMurray, William, *The Literary Realism of William Dean Howells.* Carbondale: Southern Illinois Press, 1967. A study of twelve of Howells' novels including *A Foregone Conclusion, A Modern Instance, The Rise of Silas Lapham* and *The Vacation of the Kelwyns.*

Vanderbilt, Kermit, *The Achievement of William Dean Howells.* Princeton: Princeton University Press, 1968. Discusses the religious and philosophical emphasis of *The Undiscovered Country* and *A Modern Instance,* the theme of social status in *The Rise of Silas Lapham,* and the relationship of art to the world in *A Hazard of New Fortunes.*

Selected Dictionaries and Encyclopedias

The Oxford Companion to American Literature, Oxford University Press, 1983. Brief biography of Howells' life and analysis of his most important works; overvalues *Criticism and Fiction.*

Margaret Ann Baker
Iowa State University

LANGSTON HUGHES
1902–1967

Author's Chronology

Born James Langston Hughes, February 1, 1902, Joplin, Missouri; *1919–1920* spends summers in Mexico with his father who lived there since 1904; *1920* graduates from Central High School, Cleveland, Ohio; writes "The Negro Speaks of Rivers;" *1921–1922* attends Columbia University; *1923–1924* works on ships bound for Africa and Europe; lives in Paris; stranded in Genoa; *1926–1929,* attends Lincoln University, A.B. 1929; *1930* works with Zora Hurston on *Mule Bone; 1931* receives Harmon Gold Award for Literature; receives Rosenwald Fund Fellowship; journeys to Haiti and Russia; *1935* receives Guggenheim Fellowship; *1937* correspondent reporting Civil War in Spain; *1940* receives second Rosenwald Fund Fellowship; *1942* moves to Harlem; *1943* receives honorary Litt. D. from Lincoln University; *1946* receives grant from American Academy of Arts and Letters; *1949* teaches in Laboratory School, University of Chicago; *1953* receives Anisfield-Wolfe Award; *1960* receives NAACP's Spingarn Medal; *1961* elected to National Institute of Arts and Letters; *1963* receives honorary Litt. D. from Howard University and Case Western Reserve University; *1967* dies in New York City on May 22.

Author's Bibliography (selected)

The Weary Blues, 1926 (poetry); *Fine Clothes to the Jew,* 1927 (poetry); *Not Without Laughter,* 1930 (novel); *The Dreamkeeper and Other Poems,* 1932; *Scottsboro Limited: Four Poems and a Play in Verse,* 1932; *The Ways of White Folks,* 1934 (stories); *Mulatto,* 1935 (play); *The Big Sea,* 1940 (autobiography); *Shakespeare in Harlem,* 1942 (poems); *Freedom's Plow,* 1943 (play); *Fields of Wonder,* 1947 (poems); *Street Scene,* 1947 (lyrics only); *One Way Ticket,* 1949 (poems); *Simple Speaks His Mind,* 1950 (stories); *Montage of a Dream Deferred,* 1951 (poems); *Laughing to Keep from Crying,* 1952 (stories); *Simple Takes a Wife,* 1953 (stories); *Simple Stakes a Claim,* 1957 (stories); *Tambourines of Glory,* 1958 (stories); *Selected Poems,* 1959; *Something in Common and Other Stories,* 1963; *The Prodigal Son,* 1965 (play).

Overview of Biographical Sources

No thoroughgoing, authoritative biography of Hughes has yet appeared. Faith Berry's *Langston Hughes: Before and Beyond Harlem* (1983) presents the most thoroughgoing biography of Hughes, although she concentrates on the years up to 1940, when Hughes began his long residence in Harlem. Berry's twenty-two page epilogue covers sketchily the years from 1940 to Hughes' death in 1967. James A. Emanuel's *Langston Hughes* (1967) covers Hughes' whole life and is critical as well as biographical. Therman B. O'Daniel's *Lang-*

ston Hughes: Black Genius (1971) is a collection of essays. O'Daniel's bibliography, though not so comprehensive as Donald C. Dickinson's *A Bio-Bibliography of Langston Hughes. 1920–1967* (1967), is serviceable.

Evaluation of Selected Biographies

Berry, Faith, *Langston Hughes: Before and Beyond Harlem.* Westport, CT: Lawrence Hill, 1983. Berry's book, both biographical and critical, is most interesting for its biographical presentation, which makes some needed corrections and additions to what is known about Hughes as an artist and as an ardent spokesman for his race. Berry provides considerable information about Hughes' ancestry. This book cannot be regarded as the authoritative biography because it deals with the last twenty-seven years of Hughes' life briefly and superficially.

Dickinson, Donald C. *A Bio-Bibliography of Langston Hughes. 1902–1967.* Hamden, CT: The Shoestring Press, 1967. The biography in this book is limited but accurate. Dickinson lists forty-eight volumes, fifteen of them poetry, of which Hughes was author, coauthor, or editor and explodes Calverton and Cruse's contentions that Hughes showed little artistic development during the 1930's, demonstrating that this decade was one of exceptional artistic development and literary experimentation for him.

Emanuel, James A. *Langston Hughes.* New York: Twayne, 1967. This is the first full-length study of Hughes. The format and space limitations of the Twayne series prevented Emanuel from presenting the exhaustive critical biography that this book shows him clearly capable of writing. This slim volume is a standard reference for those embarking on Hughes research. Despite its limitations, Emanuel's book is effective in pinpointing Hughes' most salient themes and in demonstrating through reference to a substantial number of poems Hughes' artistic techniques and artistic development. Valuable for its chronology and bibliography, the book is readable and dependable.

O'Daniel, Therman B. ed. *Langston Hughes: Black Genius.* New York: Morrow, 1971. This collection is at times biased and occasionally substitutes enthusiasm for sharp critical insight. Nevertheless, the essays in it are valuable because they cover a broad spectrum and because they show quite clearly and consistently Hughes' development as a conscious artist whose literary mission was connected to his racial identity.

Autobiographical Sources

Hughes' first autobiography, *The Big Sea* (1940), covers the years from his birth to the late 1920's. Divided into three sections, *The Big Sea* deals with the young Hughes and tells of his tortured relationship with his father. Hughes' great break from his father came in June 1923 when, having withdrawn after a year in the mining engineering curriculum at Columbia University, he set sail as a mess boy on the *S. S. Malone* bound for Africa. The second portion of *The Big Sea* traces Hughes' adventures in Africa and in Europe, and sees him returning to the United States to work as a busboy in the Wardman Park Hotel in Washington and to be discovered as a poet. The final section focuses on the Harlem Renaissance of which Hughes was a major part. This section provides information about his days as a student at Lincoln University. Told with verve and wit, *The Big Sea* is a valuable if somewhat selective resource.

I Wonder as I Wander (1956), Hughes' second autobiography, focuses on the author's life in the 1930's, a time when he enjoyed considerable celebrity as a writer. The book is valuable for its assessment of the status of black artists in the United States in the 1930's.

Overview of Critical Sources

Most of the criticism deals with Hughes' poetry, even though only about one-third of his published work was verse. There exists no critical volume that considers the whole of Hughes' poetry. Extant critical works give scant attention to his tales, his one novel, his dramas, his political writing, and his books for children.

Evaluation of Selected Criticism

Barksdale, Richard K. *Langston Hughes: The Poet and His Critics.* Chicago: American Library Association, 1977. This short book gives a comprehensive overview of Hughes criticism to 1977. Particularly strong is its chapter on Hughes' use of blues and jazz rhythms in his poetry. Barksdale views Hughes as a prose writer and dramatist as well as a poet.

Dodat, François, *Langston Hughes.* Paris: Éditions Pierre Seghers, 1964. This book, written in French, offers criticism of a number of Hughes' poems and provides French translations of sixty-one of them. Dodat gives an historical perspective for his French audience.

Jemie, Onwuchekwa, *Langston Hughes: An Introduction to the Poetry.* New York: Columbia University Press, 1976. Jemie deals with Hughes' collected poems, examining his themes and techniques, particularly as they relate to Afro-American oral tradition. He explains the reasons that Hughes has been somewhat neglected critically despite his prolific literary output. The book shows Hughes as a masterful technician and as an exciting innovator. Jemie explains Hughes' use of blues and jazz rhythms in his poetry.

Other Sources

Barksdale, Richard K. "Langston Hughes: His Times and His Humanistic Techniques," in R. B. Miller, ed. *Black American Literature and Humanism.*

Lexington: University of Kentucky Press, 1981, 11–26. Comments on Hughes' use of persona and of dramatic dialogue. Traces his sources in folklore.

Davis, Arthur P. "The Harlem of Langston Hughes' Poetry," *Phylon,* 13 (Winter 1952), 276–283. Considers Hughes' poetry from 1926, showing how his later poems reflect a disenchanted Harlem.

Jackson, Richard, "The Shared Vision of Langston Hughes and Black Hispanic Writers," *Black American Literature Forum,* 15 (Fall 1981), 89–92. Documents Hughes' influence on Afro-Hispanic writers.

Kinnamon, Keneth, "The Man Who Created Simple," *Nation,* 147 (December 1967), 599–601. Succinct, incisive commentary on Hughes as a prose writer.

Martin, Dellita L. "Langston Hughes's Use of the Blues," *College Language Association Journal,* 22 (1978), 151–159. A close analysis of Hughes' use of blues rhythms in his poetry.

Redding, J. Saunders, *To Make a Poet Black.* Chapel Hill: University of North Carolina Press, 1939. One of the earliest serious appraisals by a black scholar of Hughes as a literary artist. Relates Hughes' work to his times.

Schatt, Stanley, "Langston Hughes: The Minstrel as Artificer," *Journal of Modern Literature,* 1 (September 1974), 115–120. Traces Hughes' poetic revisions and relates them to changes in his philosophy.

Selected Dictionaries and Encyclopedias

Contemporary Authors, Vols. 1–4, Gale Research, 1967. Biographical overview and selected bibliography.

Contemporary Literary Criticism, Vols. 1 (1973), 5 (1976), 10 (1979), and 15 (1980), Gale Research. Lengthy excerpts from selected critical works on Hughes.

Encyclopedia of World Literature in the 20th Century, 2nd ed. Vol 2, Frederick Ungar, 1983. Brief biographical essay and limited bibliography.

Great Writers of the English Language: Poets, New York: St. Martin's, 1979. Extensive bibliography and concise biographical-critical essay.

R. Baird Shuman
University of Illinois at
Urbana-Champaign

LEIGH HUNT
1784–1859

Author's Chronology

Born James Henry Leigh Hunt at Southgate, Middlesex, on October 19, *1784,* son of Isaac Hunt, an American lawyer and minister; *1791* enrolls at Christ's Hospital; *1801* his first work, *Juvenilia,* published by his father; *1805* begins writing theatrical reviews for his brother John's paper, the *News; 1808* begins editing the *Examiner; 1809* marries Marianne Kent; *1813* sentenced to two years' imprisonment at Horsemonger Lane Gaol for libelling the Prince Regent; *1816* publishes *The Story of Rimini; 1817 Blackwood's Magazine* attacks Hunt in its series "The Cockney School of Poetry"; *1822* sets sail for Italy, where he planned to join with Byron and Shelley to edit the *Liberal;* Shelley's death ended this project after only four numbers; *1828* publishes *Lord Byron and Some of His Contemporaries; 1840* his play *A Legend of Florence* staged at Covent Garden; *1844* publishes *Imagination and Fancy;* granted a 200-pound pension by government; *1850* publishes *Autobiography; 1853* caricatured by Dickens in *Bleak House* as Skimpole; *1859* dies on August 28 and buried at Kensal Green Cemetery.

Author's Bibliography (selected)

Juvenilia, 1801 (poems); *Examiner,* 1808–1821 (periodical); *The Story of Rimini,* 1816 (poem); *Poetical Works,* 3 vols., 1819, revised 1832 and 1844; *Amyntas: A Tale of the Woods, from the Italian of Tasso,* 1820 (translation); *Indicator,* 1822 (periodical); *Lord Byron and Some of His Contemporaries,* 1828 (non-fiction); *Christianism; or Belief and Unbelief Reconciled,* ed. John Forster, 1832, rev. as *The Religion of the Heart,* 1853 (non-fiction); *Hunt's London Journal,* 1834–1835 (periodical); *Captain Sword and Captain Pen,* 1835 (satire); *A Legend of Florence,* 1840 (drama); *Imagination and Fancy,* 1844 (anthology and criticism); *Autobiography,* 1850, rev. 1860; *Correspondence,* 2 vols., ed. Thornton Hunt, 1862; *Poetical Works,* ed. H. S. Milford, 1923; *Leigh Hunt's Dramatic Criticism,* ed. L. H. and C. W. Houtchens, 1949; *Leigh Hunt's Literary Criticism,* ed. L. H. and C. W. Houtchens, 1956; *Leigh Hunt's Political and Occasional Essays,* ed. L. H. and C. W. Houtchens, 1962.

Overview of Biographical Sources

In light of the exceptionally prominent position Leigh Hunt held among his nineteenth-century contemporaries as a poet, critic, essayist, drama reviewer, and diarist, an extensive, well-researched, and recent biography would help to organize some important aspects of the Romantic Period and after. No such book exists in English, however. Of the four English biographies of Hunt, two are nineteenth-century studies flawed both by their proximity to the subject and by an unquestioning acceptance of his autobiography: R. Brimley Johnson's *Leigh Hunt* (London: Swan-Sonnenschein, 1896) and Cosmo Monkhouse's *Life of Leigh Hunt* (London: Walter Scott, 1893). Edmund Blunden's *Leigh Hunt and His Circle* (1930), which was titled *Leigh Hunt: A Biography* in its London edition (Cobden-Sanderson, 1930), remains the standard full-length study of Hunt's life. James R. Thompson's *Leigh Hunt* (1977) is too short at 176 pages to serve as a comprehensive study. Easily the most thorough and authoritative biography of Hunt is Louis Landré's two-volume *Leigh Hunt (1784–1859): Contribution á l'histoire du Romantisme* (Paris: Societé d'édition, 1935); unfortunately, it has not been translated into English.

Evaluation of Selected Biographies

Blunden, Edmund, *Leigh Hunt and His Circle.* New York: Harper and Brothers, 1930. Although thin of documentation and slightly old-fashioned now in its tone of admiration, this book remains the best single source in English for information about Hunt's life, works, and famous friends. It suffers under the liability of having been written without recourse to the Hunt papers in the Luther A. Brewer Collection at the University of Iowa. However, Blunden was the first biographer to pay much attention to Hunt's life after 1825, and the vitality of his writing has helped to secure for Hunt studies a lively beginning in the twentieth century.

Thompson, James R. *Leigh Hunt.* Boston: Twayne, 1977. This critical biography does a much better job than might be expected in handling masses of information and material accurately and intelligently in a relatively short space; yet the want of room to explore complexities is ultimately felt. In uncluttered prose, Thompson presents a balanced view of Hunt's achievements. He is at his best explaining the significance of Hunt's contributions to dramatic criticism.

Autobiographical Sources

Abandoned by Byron in Italy at Shelley's death, Hunt secured an advance from publisher Henry Coburn to finance his return to England. Back home in 1825, he began work for Coburn on what was to become *Lord Byron and Some of His Contemporaries* (1828), which contained a lively, though embittered, picture of his association with Byron, as well as with Shelley, Keats, Lamb, Coleridge, and others. Containing an autobiographical section, this work was eventually reformed into his *Autobiography* (1850), which was updated by an additional chapter in 1859.

The reader should expect to learn in this little book more about Hunt and his views than might be expected from a chronicle of his friendships. Irrepressibly optimistic, affectionate, and outgoing, Hunt was unable even within the limits of autobiography to resist putting most of his energies into praising excellence where he saw it. Although Hunt provided interesting detail about the lives and works of many talented friends—most notably Percy Shelley—, the reader is left wondering about such matters as his problematical domestic life, his tangled financial difficulties, and the caricature of him as Harold Skimpole in *Bleak House.* Written in a graceful nineteenth-century style and with a loose, almost rambling structure, Hunt's *Autobiography* provides us with a lively view of an important circle of friends.

The only edition of Hunt's letters was done by his son, Thornton, in two volumes in 1862.

Overview of Critical Sources

Hunt's unusually long, diverse, and productive life poses problems which are compounded by the uneven quality of his writings. He was a poet, a literary critic, an editor of literary works, an anthologist, a journalist, an essayist, a drama and music critic, a political writer, a memoirist, and a dramatist. Modern critics in English have responded to his voluminous writings only selectively, and book-length investigations of any aspect of his work are rare. There are, however, four studies of his journalistic career, plus one of his contribution to opera criticism.

Evaluation of Selected Criticism

Blunden, Edmund, *Leigh Hunt's "Examiner" Examined.* London: Harper, 1928. This provides information on the literary, dramatic, and artistic contents of the *Examiner,* offering selections both by and about many Romantic writers.

Fenner, Theodore, *Leigh Hunt and Opera Criticism: the Examiner Years, 1808–1821.* Lawrence: University of Kansas Press, 1972. In giving his account of London opera in the first quarter of the nineteenth century, Fenner traces its backgrounds in England and Italy. He offers information about Hunt's musical talents and experience, analyzes Hunt's opera criticism, and compares Hunt's observations with those of other Romantic opera critics, though perhaps exaggerating Hunt's understanding of music theory.

Kendall, Kenneth E. *Leigh Hunt's "Reflector."* The Hague: Mouton, 1971. Kendall names the authors of most of the major pieces in the *Reflector* and provides valuable biographical information about those authors. Though marred by some factual errors, this remains the only book-length study of the *Reflector.*

Marshall, William H. *Byron, Shelley, Hunt, and the "Liberal."* Philadelphia: University of Pennsylvania Press, 1960. This scholarly, though somewhat narrow, work provides a careful description of the contents of the *Liberal,* gives the reception of each of the four numbers received, and traces the deteriorating relationship between Byron and Hunt after Shelley's death.

Stout, George Dumas, *The Political History of Leigh Hunt's "Examiner."* St. Louis: Washington University Studies, 1949. Whereas Blunden had dealt with the literary concerns of Hunt's most important journal, Stout concentrates on the considerable political aspects. It was in the *Examiner* that Hunt began his attacks on the Prince Regent which led to his incarceration for libel.

Other Sources

Thorpe, Clarence DeWitt, "Leigh Hunt As Man of Letters," in *Leigh Hunt's Literary Criticism.* ed. Lawrence Huston Houtchens and Carolyn Washburn Houtchens. New York: Columbia University Press, 1956, pp. 3–73. Thorpe seeks to raise the general estimate of Hunt's worth as a writer. Beginning with a history of the issue of his Cockneyism and admitting the weakness of Hunt's poetry, he emphasizes Hunt's contributions as a journalist, anthologist, translator, and critic. Thorpe formulates Hunt's critical principles, especially those concerning economy, unity, the imagination, and metrics, contrasting and comparing them favorably with those of Wordsworth and Coleridge.

Woodring, Carl R. "Leigh Hunt as Political Essayist," in *Leigh Hunt's Political and Occasional Essays.* ed. Lawrence Huston Houtchens and Carolyn Washburn Houtchens. New York: Columbia University Press, 1962, pp. 3–71. Woodring gives a brief political history of early nineteenth-century Britain as background for a study of Hunt's imprisonment for libel and its influence on Hunt's later political writing. He analyzes the *Examiner* for both tone and contents, noting the opinions expressed regarding important issues of the day, including Utilitarianism, Castlereagh, and the French Revolution.

Jack Wright Rhodes
The Citadel

ZORA NEALE HURSTON
1901?-1960

Author's Chronology

Born January 7 around the turn of the century in all black Eatonville, Florida; *1904* mother dies; *1915* travels as maid with a Gilbert and Sullivan troupe; *1923* attends Howard University; *1924* begins working friendship with Langston Hughes; *1925* moves to New York in search of publishing opportunities; lives with Fannie Hurst; wins scholarship to study anthropology at Barnard College; *1927* accepts sponsorship of "Godmother," Mrs. Rufus Osgood Mason; graduates from Barnard; comes to attention of Franz Boaz; *1928–1931* collects black tales in Florida and voodoo lore in New Orleans; *1933–1934* teaches drama at Bethune Cookman College; *1937–1938* receives two Guggenheim fellowships to collect folklore in Jamaica, Haiti, and Bermuda; *1938* collects folklore for WPA in Florida; *1939* marries Albert Price III; *1941* writes for Paramount Studios; *1943* divorces Price; *1945* contracts chronic gallbladder and colon infection from which she never recovers; *1947* writes in Honduras; *1948* faces groundless but widely publicized charge of child sexual abuse; *1950* works as maid in Florida; *1951–1956* lives idyllic life gardening and writing unsuccessfully in Florida; *1956–1958* holds part time jobs in Florida as librarian, teacher and reporter; *1959* suffers stroke and enters County Welfare Home; *1960* dies on January 28.

Author's Bibliography (selected)

Jonah's Gourd Vine, 1934 (novel); *Mules and Men,* 1935 (folklore); *Their Eyes Were Watching God,* 1937 (novel); *Tell My Horse,* 1938 (folklore); *Moses, Man of the Mountain,* 1939 (novel); *Dust Tracks on a Road,* 1942 (autobiography); *Seraph on the Suwanee,* 1948 (novel); *I Love Myself When I Am Laughing . . . and Then Again When I Am Looking Mean and Impressive,* 1979 (collection). A complete bibliography of Hurston's shorter work, published and unpublished, appears in an Appendix to Robert Hemenway's *Zora Neale Hurston: A Literary Biography.*

Overview of Biographical Sources

Since Hurston was only recently rescued from literary oblivion, serious study of her life and work has just begun. Although biographical sketches have appeared regularly in magazines and reference works on Black American authors, only recently have such questions as the date of Hurston's birth, her relationship with her parents and her mysterious final years been seriously studied. Still today, only one complete biography exists, but from its positive reception by students of her work as well as by her family, it must be considered as definitive.

Hemenway's *Zora Neqle Hurston: A Literary Biography* covers almost all that is known about her enigmatic life and evaluates her work in terms of it. Notes, acknowledgements and bibliography reveal the whereabouts of sources for further biographical study. Although Hemenway is a white male, black feminists such as Alice Walker and Mary Helen Washington not only endorse but praise the book. Those searching for further interpretation of Hurston's biography might consult the Introduction, Afterword and commentary in *I Love Myself When I Am Laughing . . . and Then Again When I Am Looking Mean and Impressive,* edited by Walker and introduced by Washington (The Feminist Press, 1979) for a more reverent but compatible viewpoint on Hurston's attitudes toward herself as a black and as a woman. In *The Big Sea* (New York: Hill and Wang, 1940), Langston Hughes reports his firsthand observations of Hurston, and in "Zora Neale Hurston: A Personality Sketch," (*Yale University Library Gazette* 35, 1960, pp. 17–22), Fannie Hurst reminisces about her own life with Hurston as unsatisfactory amanuensis but highly attractive companion.

Evaluation of Selected Biographies

Hemenway, Robert, *Zora Neale Hurston: A Literary Biography.* Urbana: University of Illinois Press, 1977. In this highly readable story of a troubled woman, the author's life is seen in terms of her writing, and her literary output is evaluated in terms of events in her life. Hemenway's book based almost exclusively on primary sources—frequently unpublished archival materials—reveals Hurston to be ambivalent about her role as a black American but never as woman or writer. The biographer analyzes and occasionally criticizes fiction, autobiography, and folklore alike but seldom actually summarizes content. A folio of rare photographs of Hurston and her family is included.

Autobiographical Sources

Hurston's autobiography, *Dust Tracks on a Road* (1942; rpt. 1985), is praiseworthy as revelation of black folk culture and exegesis on Eatonville, Florida, but as the author's life story, it reveals more about Hurston's difficulty sharing her innermost self than it does about Hurston. Of her birth date, she concludes that "it is pretty well established that [she] did get born." Her published story is further complicated by changes made for the publishers. An unedited draft in the James Weldon Johnson Collection at Yale University reveals changes mandated by the market and the times—during war a black dared not question American values. Hurston's novel, *Jonah's Gourd Vine,* though fiction, is assumed to be based on her own experiences growing up in an all black town as the daughter of a minister.

Overview of Critical Sources

Early critics hail Hurston as collector of black folklore and celebrant of her people while they often find the dearth of race politics in her work and her use of the black vernacular objectionable. More recently, she is praised as an exponent of black culture, a precursor of modern feminism, and a masterful but unorthodox prose stylist. She is chiefly praised for her ability to blend black folklore into insightful fiction. Considered her fictional masterpiece, *Their Eyes Were Watching God,* is the story of one woman's struggle for a sense of self within an all black community rich in folklore and strategies for survival. *Jonah's Gourd Vine,* a story of family in Eatonville, and *Moses Man of the Mountain,* a black rendering of the Old Testament story are also widely acclaimed. *Seraph on the Suwanee,* with a white protagonist and an all white culture, seems to be Hurston's effort to prove a black can write about the dominant culture. Unfortunately, it is considered by most to have failed. *Mules and Men,* a very early effort to apply anthropological method to American blacks, is acknowledged as masterful folklore. Even though the fascinating *Tell My Horse,* supposedly a collection of Haitian folklore, is too cluttered with Haitian politics to be good folklore, it still deserves reading, not only for background on Haiti, but for voodoo and zombie lore as well.

Only one booklength critical study of Hurston has been done. Lillie P. Howard's *Zora Neale Hurston* (1980) is much more a traditional literary study than Hemenway's. Whereas both authors acknowledge that the definitive work on Hurston remains to be done, each aims through literary study to establish her as an important American literary figure. Closely related in philosophy and content, the two books differ in two primary ways. In Hemenway, literary work is closely associated with biography while in Howard, the stress is on literary analysis. And whereas Hemenway evaluates Hurston's writings, Howard summarizes and analyzes. In these two books, all past Hurston criticism has been examined and summarized, and since their publication, published criticism has acknowledged their authority as general references and concentrated on particular works or particular elements in Hurston's work.

The single other recent general consideration of Hurston is the bibliographic sketch by Daryl C. Dance in *American Women Writers: Bibliographic Essays* (Westport, CT: Greenwood Press, 1983, pp. 321–351). For an unsympathetic reading, scholars should consult Darwin Turner's *In A Minor Chord* (Carbondale: University of Illinois Press, 1971). Contemporary views of Hurston's work can be found in Hugh Gloster's essay in *Negro Voices in American Fiction* (Chapel Hill: University of North Carolina Press, 1948) and the essay by Sterling Brown in *The Negro in American Fiction* (Washington, DC: Associates in Negro Folk Education, 1937).

Evaluation of Selected Criticism

Howard, Lillie P. *Zora Neale Hurston.* Boston: Twayne, 1980. In her research guide to Hurston, Howard sees Hurston as chiefly a literary figure giving fiction works much more attention than she gives the folklore and other non-fiction writings. Although she uses some unpublished letters, much of this work is dependent on the writing of other scholars. Howard organizes her biographical sections in terms of Hurston's professional development, and the parts on the fiction are "new-critical" analyses of the works themselves. Thus, each section on a novel includes a detailed plot summary. This is, so far, the only place where a serious consideration of *Seraph on the Suwanee* can be found.

Selected Dictionaries and Encyclopedias

American Women Writers: A Critical Reference Guide from Colonial Times to the Present, Frederick Ungar, 1980, pp. 363-366. Treats Hurston's as feminist writer, but only as a writer of fiction. Brief critical bibliography included.

Contemporary Literary Criticism, Gale Research, Vol. 7, pp. 170–172; Vol. 30, pp. 207–229. An invaluable compendium of excerpts from published criticism.

Southern Writers: A Biographical Dictionary, Louisiana State University Press, 1979, pp. 239–240. Cooly dispassionate recital of biographical facts by a less than sympathetic critic of Hurston's work. Includes brief bibliography.

Twentieth Century Authors: A Biographical Dictionary of Modern Literature, H. W. Wilson, 1942, pp. 694–695. Brief but warm account of the facts of Hurston's biography and publication. Sees her as exponent of black culture. Includes brief critical bibliography.

Sue Bridwell Beckham
University of Wisconsin-Stout

WASHINGTON IRVING
1783–1859

Author's Chronology

Born April 3, 1783, in New York City, the eleventh child of middle-class Scotch-English parents; *1799* begins work in law offices; *1802* contributes *Letters of Jonathan Oldstyle, Gent.* to *Morning Chronicle; 1804–1806* makes his first tour of Europe; *1806* passes bar examinations; *1807* publishes *Salmagundi* with William Irving and James Kirke Paulding; *1809* publishes *A History of New York; 1812–1814* edits *Analectic Magazine; 1815–1818* lives in England; *1819–1820* publishes *The Sketch Book* in America and England in installments; *1820–1832* travels in Europe; publishes *Bracebridge Hall, Tales of a Traveller, The Alhambra; 1835* lives in New York; publishes *The Crayon Miscellany; 1836* publishes *Astoria; 1842–1845* ambassador to Spain; *1855–1859* publishes *Life of Washington; 1859* dies on November 28, at his home at Sunnyside in New York state.

Author's Bibliography (selected)

Letters of Jonathan Oldstyle, Gent., 1802 (essays); *Salmagundi,* 1807 (sketches); *Diedrich Knickerbocker's A History of New York,* 1809 (satire); *The Sketch Book,* 1819–1820 (tales and sketches); *Bracebridge Hall,* 1822 (sketches); *Tales of a Traveller,* 1824 (tales and sketches); *The Life and Voyages of Christopher Columbus,* 1828 (biography); *The Alhambra,* 1832 (tales and sketches); *Astoria,* 1836 (history); *The Life of Goldsmith,* 1849 (biography); *Wolfert's Roost,* 1855 (tales and sketches); *Life of George Washington,* 1855–1859 (biography).

Overview of Biographical Sources

Because Washington Irving was the first American author of world-wide renown, his death stimulated much speculation about who would write his biography. The task fell to Pierre M. Irving, his nephew, who served as researcher on some of his historical works. Pierre Irving's four-volume *The Life and Letters of Washington Irving* (1862–1863) contains a wealth of materials which Irving made available to his nephew, but is primarily a sentimental account of Irving's life. George S. Hellman's *Washington Irving, Esquire* (1925) makes use of previously unpublished journals, notebooks, and letters. Informally-written and largely undocumented, Hellman presents Irving as a somewhat lazy, pleasure-loving gentleman. More authoritative and more soundly documented is the two-volume *The Life of Washington Irving* by Stanley T. Williams (1935). This is perhaps the most detailed and best-researched biography yet to be written, one that all subsequent biographers of Irving refer to. The most recent biography is the somewhat unusual study by Philip McFarland, *Sojourners* (1979). Although the book focuses on Irving, it also presents biographical accounts of figures who impinged on his life.

Evaluation of Selected Biographies

Hellman, George S. *Washington Irving, Esquire: Ambassador at Large from the New World to the Old.* New York: Alfred A. Knopf, 1925. This is an informal and anecdotal biography which makes use of previously unpublished journals, letters, and notebooks. As the title suggests, it focuses on Irving's travels, his association with influential people of the time, and his role as an ambassador of American good will to the world. Hellman portrays Irving as the most beloved American of his time.

McFarland, Philip, *Sojourners.* New York: Atheneum, 1979. This most recent account of Irving's life focuses as much on contemporaries of Irving as it does on Irving himself. In its account of Aaron Burr, Sir Walter Scott, Mary Shelley, and John Jacob Astor, it paints a picture of a literary and social world that Irving helped create.

Irving, Pierre M. *The Life and Letters of Washington Irving.* 4 vols. New York: G. P. Putnam's, 1863; rpt. Gale Research, 1967. This is the first biographical account of Irving, written by his nephew at his own wish. The book is highly respectful and made up to a great extent of quoted material from Irving's notebooks, letters, and journals. The chapter on Matilda Hoffman is based on Pierre Irving's discovery of a journal entry after his uncle's death, which makes him believe that Irving remained a bachelor all of his life because of his love for Matilda.

Williams, Stanley T. *The Life of Washington Irving.* 2 vols. New York: Oxford University Press, 1935. This is still the authoritative biography, the result of extensive research in original manuscripts of Irving's journals, notebooks, travel notes, and letters. It is often disparaging of the uneven quality of Irving's writing, even *The SketchBook,* of which Williams says, probably rightly, only a few sketches are worthy of serious attention.

Autobiographical Sources

Although Irving did not write an autobiography, a large number of his letters, journals, and notebooks have been published. Stanley T. Williams edited several collections in the 1920's. More recently Twayne Publishers has taken over the job, started by the University of Wisconsin Press, of publishing the complete works of Irving. Already completed are three volumes of letters and three volumes of journals and notebooks, edited by Ralph Aderman, Wayne Kime, and Walter Reichart.

Overview of Critical Sources

Although several books have been written about Washington Irving, most are purely biographical and lack any real critical approach to his work. The general consensus seems to be that although Irving is important historically for making American writing respectable world-wide, there is little intrinsic merit in his work. The only exceptions are, of course, his two most famous works, "Rip Van Winkle" and "The Legend of Sleepy Hollow," both of which depend heavily on German legends and folktales which Irving was familiar with. Because these stories are so widely anthologized and familiar, and because both Rip and Ichabod Crane are icons of American culture, many essays have been published on them. However, there are few book-length critical studies of Irving's work, and these are uneven in quality.

Evaluation of Selected Criticism

Bowden, Mary Weatherspoon, *Washington Irving.* Boston: Twayne, 1981. This is a routine critical study of Irving, which attempts to chart his literary development. It contains only sketchy biographical discussions, and its critical commentary is heavily biased by the author's own interest in the influence of politics on literature. By insisting on this political focus, she ignores the essential mythic nature of his sketches and tales.

Hedges, William L. *Washington Irving: An American Study, 1802–1832.* Baltimore: The Johns Hopkins Press, 1965. This first full-length critical study of Irving is valuable, for it places him solidly within his cultural and literary milieu, explores the various literary genres Irving made use of, and makes helpful and sound critical remarks about his best-known works. Hedges quite rightly sees Irving as a writer focusing on dreams, fantasies, and symbolic projections.

Myers, Andrew B. ed. *A Century of Commentary on the Works of Washington Irving.* Tarrytown, NY: Sleepy Hollow Restorations, 1976. A collection of essays on Irving from William Cullen Bryant's 1860 "Discourse" to Philip Young's influential 1973 essay, "Fallen From Time: The Mythic Rip Van Winkle." Other important pieces are Terrence Martin's 1959 essay, "Rip, Ichabod, and the American Imagination," and Daniel Hoffman's chapter on "Sleepy Hollow" from his *Form and Fable in American Fiction* (1961).

Roth, Martin, *Comedy and America: The Lost World of Washington Irving.* Port Washington, NY: Kennikat Press, 1976. This is an interesting and helpful study of the literary genres of burlesque and satire that Irving used, especially in *The History of New York.* Roth argues that Irving owes his "burlesque comedy" primarily to Sterne and Rabelais.

Other Sources

Cracroft, Richard H. *Washington Irving: The Western Works.* Boise, ID: Boise State University Press, 1974. A pamphlet focusing on such works as *The Adventures of Captain Bonneville; Astoria;* and *A Tour of the Praries.*

Wayne R. Kime, *Pierre M. Irving and Washington Irving: A Collaboration in Life and Letters.* Waterloo, Ontario: Wilfrid Laurier University Press, 1977. A detailed account of the professional relationship between Irving and his nephew.

Leary, Lewis, *Washington Irving.* Minneapolis: University of Minnesota Press, 1963. A good pamphlet introduction to Irving's works, although it does not always show much regard for what Leary calls Irving's primarily undistinguished writing.

Reichart, Walter A. *Washington Irving and Germany.* Ann Arbor: University of Michigan Press, 1957. An account of Irving's tour of Germany and Austria in 1822-1823.

Wagenknecht, Edward, *Washington Irving: Moderation Displayed.* New York: Oxford University Press, 1962. A routine study focused more on familiar biographical information than on original criticism.

Warner, Charles Dudley, *Washington Irving.* Boston: Houghton Mifflin, 1881; rpt. Chelsea House Publishers, 1980. A brief and general biography written with affection, conciseness, and accuracy—still a good introduction to Irving and his work.

Charles E. May
California State University,
Long Beach

CHRISTOPHER ISHERWOOD
1904

Author's Chronology

Born August 26, 1904, Cheshire, England; *1914* attends St. Edmund's School and meets W. H. Auden; *1919* attends Repton; *1923* enters Corpus Christi College, Cambridge on a history scholarship; *1925* deliberately fails examinations and leaves Cambridge; works as a secretary; *1926* tutors in London; *1928* enrolls as a medical student, King's College, London; *1928* publishes *All the Conspirators; 1929* visits Auden in Germany; *1930* teaches English in Berlin; *1933* leaves Berlin; lives in various European countries for the next five years; *1938* visits China with Auden; *1939* emigrates to U.S.; settles in California and meets Swami Prabhavananda; becomes a Vedantist; *1940* writes for films in Hollywood; *1946* becomes U.S. citizen; *1947* visits South America; *1949* elected member of the U.S. National Institute of Arts and Letters; *1953* meets and begins living with Don Bachardy; *1959* guest professor at California colleges; *1962* delivers lectures at the University of California at Berkeley entitled "The Autobiography of My Books"; *1964* visits India; *1973* delivers talk at the Modern Language Association convention on "Homosexuality and Literature"; *1983* is awarded the PEN-Los Angeles Center Award and the Common Wealth Award for Distinguished Service in Literature from the Modern Language Association; *1984* receives the Robert Kirsh Award; *1985* continues to live in California.

Author's Bibliography (selected)

All the Conspirators, 1928 (novel); *The Memorial: Portrait of a Family,* 1932 (novel); *The Last of Mr. Norris,* 1935 (novel); *Lions and Shadows: An Education in the Twenties,* 1938 (autobiographical novel); *Goodbye to Berlin,* 1939 (novel); with W.H. Auden, *Journey to a War,* 1939 (travel book); *Prater Violet,* 1945 (novel); *The Condor and the Cows: A South American Travel-Diary,* 1949 (travel book); *Down There on a Visit,* 1962 (novel); *An Approach to Vedanta,* 1963 (prose); *A Single Man,* 1964 (novel); *Ramakrishna and His Disciples,* 1965 (biography); *A Meeting by the River,* 1967 (novel); *Kathleen and Frank: The Autobiography of a Family,* 1971 (autobiography); *Christopher and His Kind: 1929–1939,* 1976 (autobiography); *My Guru and His Disciple,* 1980 (autobiography); *October,* 1981 (diary).

Overview of Biographical Sources

Because Isherwood's work is so autobiographical in nature, his critics have been forced to include biographical material in their analyses even as his biographers have needed to comment upon his work. All of the major critical studies include biographical information and there are two Isherwood biographies, both written with the cooperation of Isherwood.

Evaluation of Selected Biographies

Finney, Brian, *Christopher Isherwood: A Critical Biography.* New York: Oxford University Press, 1979. This is an excellent and thoroughly researched presentation resulting from Finney's unrestricted access to Isherwood's private archives, letters, and manuscripts and interviews with scores of his friends, many of whom lent him letters received from Isherwood. Although concentrating on the biographical, Finney also includes full chapter analyses of the novels as well. The book is heavily documented, yet the prose is lively and clear. He also includes a lengthy list of interviews Isherwood has given.

Fryer, Jonathan, *Isherwood: A Biography.* Garden City, NY: Doubleday, 1978. Fryer's book is informal in tone and much less scholarly than Finney's. Primarily supported by quotes from Isherwood or his friends, there is little or no bibliographical information supplied, making the text somewhat difficult to work with. Fryer treats Isherwood's work primarily through synopses. The first of the Isherwood biographies, it was superseded by Finney's the following year.

Autobiographical Sources

All of Isherwood's work contains autobiographical elements. Of chief interest, however, are *Lions and Shadows: An Education in the Twenties* (1938; rpt. New York: New Directions, 1947) which Isherwood calls an "autobiographical novel" tracing his life from just prior to entering Cambridge to his departure for Berlin. Friends are disguised by pseudonyms and Isherwood freely admits he has used a novelist's license in recounting incidents. *Christopher and His Kind: 1929–1939* (New York: Farrar, Strauss, and Giroux, 1976) picks up Isherwood's life where *Lions and Shadows* left off, but is much more factual, eschewing the pseudonyms of the earlier book. Isherwood considered this an autobiography; he substituted facts for fiction wherever possible just as the earlier book did the opposite. *Kathleen and Frank: The Autobiography of a Family* (New York: Simon and Schuster, 1971), ostensibly Isherwood's biography of his parents, is largely autobiographical in nature with Isherwood frequently injecting himself into the text, presenting his perceptions of his parents and exploring the impact they had on his own life. *My Guru and His Disciple* (New York: Farrar, Straus, and Giroux, 1980) is Isherwood's account of his relationship with Swami Prabhavananda, his Vedanta teacher, and contains both diary entries made during the 1940's as well as contemporary commentary. In *October* (Los Angeles: Twelvetrees Press, 1980), diary entries from the month of October, 1979, Isherwood comments upon everyday events and recalls the past as anniversaries occur.

Overview of Critical Sources

Isherwood criticism flourished in the 1970's with five published studies, as well as numerous articles. The first, Carolyn G. Heilburn's *Christopher Isher-*

wood (New York: Columbia University Press, 1970) is pamphlet-length, as is Francis King's *Christopher Isherwood* (Essex, England: Longman Group, 1976), both of which include brief biography along with cursory analyses of the books. The criticism, in general, has found it impossible to fully separate Isherwood's life from his novels and comments upon this connection to a greater or lesser degree.

Evaluation of Selected Criticism

Piazza, Paul, *Christopher Isherwood: Myth and Anti-Myth.* New York: Columbia University Press, 1978. Piazza believes Isherwood's work is the result of his rebellion against the establishment and its various representatives. The only critic to find a unifying theme in Isherwood's work, Piazza makes strong connections between Isherwood's life and his novels. Although Piazza's approach is psycho-biographical in its grounding, psychological references and/or support are curiously unmentioned. He includes a selected bibliography.

Summers, Claude J. *Christopher Isherwood.* New York: Frederick Ungar, 1980. Summers finds a solid link between Isherwood's life and works, although he makes no attempt to explain it. There are analyses of all of Isherwood's work, interspersed with biographical information, and concentrating more on matters of form and content rather than style. There is a selected bibliography of primary and secondary sources.

Wilde, Alan, *Christopher Isherwood.* New York: Twayne, 1971. The first full-length critical study of Isherwood, Wilde focuses on his handling of language, use of irony, and moral thinking. The usual biographical information is included, although Wilde is less apt than other critics to view Isherwood's work autobiographically. A selected bibliography of primary and secondary sources is also included. Because of Wilde's dense prose style, his analyses are often difficult to unravel.

Other Sources

Finney, Brian, "Christopher Isherwood: A Profile," *New Review,* 2 (1975), 17–24. Compact and useful overview of Isherwood's life and work.

Funk, Robert W. *Christopher Isherwood: A Reference Guide.* Boston: G. K. Hall, 1979. Annotated bibliography through 1977.

Geherin, David J. "An Interview with Christopher Isherwood," *Journal of Narrative Technique,* 12 (1972), 143–158. Primarily discusses technique, point of view, and autobiographical connections.

Hynes, Samuel, *The Auden Generation: Literature and Politics in England in the 1930s.* New York: Viking Press, 1977. Places Isherwood in the context of his times.

Kamel, Rose, "Unravelling One's Personal Myth: Christopher Isherwood's Autobiographical Strategies," *Biography,* 5:2 (1982), 161–175. Examines style in Isherwood's autobiographies.

Scobie, W. I. "The Art of Fiction: Christopher Isherwood," *Paris Review,* 14 (1974), 138–182. Isherwood comments on most of his novels, friends, writing habits, and vendetta.

Thomas, David P. "*Goodbye to Berlin:* Refocusing Isherwood's Camera," *Contemporary Literature,* 13 (1972), 44–52. Intelligently rebuts the common notion that Isherwood's narrator is passive and uninvolved.

Selected Dictionaries and Encyclopedias

Contemporary Authors, Vol. 13–66 R, Gale Research, 1975. Resumé of Isherwood's life, critical overview of his work, and a full bibliography.

Contemporary Literary Criticism, I, Gale Research, 1973. Short excerpts from selected critical studies and a brief biographical outline.

Lisa M. Schwerdt
Purdue University

HENRY JAMES
1843–1916

Author's Chronology

Born April 15, 1843 in New York City of Irish-American parents; at the age of six months is taken by his parents to England and France; *1845–1847* resides with his family in Albany, New York, where many of his relatives lived; *1847–1855* lives in New York and visits the museums and theaters; *1855–1858* lives abroad in Geneva, London, Paris, and Boulogne-sur-mer; *1858–1859* resides in Newport, Rhode Island; *1859–1860* returns to Europe with his family and is educated at a technical preparatory school in Geneva and then in a German *gymnasium* at Bonn; *1860* returns to Newport and studies art with William Morris Hunt; *1861* receives an "obscure hurt" while helping to fight a fire in Newport; *1862–1863* attends Harvard Law School; *1864* lives in Boston; publishes anonymously the tale "A Tragedy of Error;" *1865* publishes his first signed work, "The Story of a Year," in the *Atlantic Monthly* and begins writing reviews; *1869* takes a grand tour of Europe and meets some of the leading intellectuals of the day, including Ruskin, Morris, Rossetti, Burne-Jones, and George Eliot; *1870–1872* resides in Cambridge, Massachusetts; *1872–1874* travels in Europe; *1875* decides to reside permanently abroad; the next several decades lives in England, travels frequently on the Continent, and becomes a leading literary figure; *1897* purchases Lamb House in Rye, England; *1915* becomes a British citizen in protest against America's delay in entering World War I; February 28, *1916* dies after an illness following a stroke; is buried in Cambridge, Massachusetts.

Author's Bibliography (selected)

A Passionate Pilgrim and Other Tales, 1875; *Transatlantic Sketches,* 1875 (travel essays); *Roderick Hudson,* 1875 (novel); *The American,* 1877 (novel); *French Poets and Novelists,* 1878 (critical essays); *The Europeans,* 1878 (novel); *Daisy Miller,* 1878 (nouvelle); *Hawthorne,* 1879 (critical biography); *Washington Square,* 1880 (nouvelle); *The Portrait of a Lady,* 1881 (novel); *Portraits of Places,* 1883 (travel essays); *A Little Tour in France,* 1883 (travel essays); *The Bostonians,* 1886 (novel); *The Princess Casamassima,* 1886 (novel); *Partial Portraits,* 1888 (critical essays); *The Tragic Muse,* 1890 (novel); *The Spoils of Poynton,* 1897 (novel); *What Maisie Knew,* 1897 (novel); *The Awkward Age,* 1899 (novel); *The Sacred Fount,* 1901 (novel); *The Wings of the Dove,* 1902 (novel); *The Ambassadors,* 1903 (novel); *The Golden Bowl,* 1904 (novel); *The American Scene,* 1907 (travel essays); *The Novels and Tales of Henry James,* "New York Edition," 1907–1909; *A Small Boy and Others,* 1913 (autobiography); *Notes of a Son and Brother,* 1914 (autobiography); *The Middle Years,* 1917 (autobiography).

Overview of Biographical Sources

Henry James has proved a difficult subject for biographers. A scrupulous protector of his privacy, he burned many of his papers to keep them from prying eyes. As his story "The Aspern Papers" indicates, he feared exploitation by those anxious to possess literary documents; thus he tried to thwart their efforts. Another problem for biographers has been that James's life lacked adventure and romance; his biography had to be a history of his mind—a challenge few proved capable of confronting. Yet a third difficulty has been the magnitude of the task. Not only was James's life long, but his literary production was prodigious. One of the earliest biographies is Rebecca West's *Henry James* (New York: Holt, 1916), a provocative study that, after briefly summarizing the major events in James's life, analyzes his most important works. Rebecca West acknowledges James's genius, particularly as manifested in the middle period of his career, but she berates him for a lack of passion. Van Wyck Brooks in *The Pilgrimage of Henry James* (New York: Dutton, 1925) emphasizes rather heavy-handedly James's dilemma of being alienated from both American and European society. In response to Brooks, Pelham Edgar in *Henry James: Man and Author* (Boston: Houghton Mifflin, 1927) suggests that rather than being alienated from America, James simply exhausted his American material and therefore needed the stimulation of a more complex culture. Pelham presents clearly James's themes and techniques. Furthermore, he holds the distinction of being the first critic to recognize the later novels as the author's finest work. Two works that are invaluable for examining James's intellectual development within the context of his family are: Clinton Hartley Grattan's *The Three Jameses, A Family of Minds: Henry James, Sr., William James, Henry James* (1932) and F. O. Matthiessen's *The James Family: Including Selections from the Writings of Henry James, Senior, William, Henry & Alice James* (1947). Several biographers have focused upon a particular period of James's life. Extremely helpful for portraying the mature James as the literary lion of England is Simon Nowell-Smith's *The Legend of the Master: Henry James* (London: Constable, 1947; New York: Charles Scribner's Sons, 1948). Smith collected material from over one hundred of James's relatives, friends, and acquaintances, including Alice James, Edith Wharton, Edmund Gosse, and F. M. Hueffer. Robert Le Clair in *Young Henry James, 1843–1870* (New York: Bookman Associates, 1955) directs his attention to the childhood and youth of the author. One of the first of the modern biographies to benefit from access to the James family papers is F. W. Dupee's *Henry James* (1951), a concise, informative contribution to the American Men of Letters Series. The definitive biography of Henry James is Leon Edel's five-volume study. The result of over a quarter of a century of research, Edel's work has been widely acclaimed as one of the major biographical achievements of the twentieth century. For the reader seeking a concise, pleasurable introduction to James and his major works, Harry T. Moore's *Henry James* (New York: Viking Press, 1974) is a good choice. His book contains over one hundred illustrations, a chronology, and a selective bibliography.

Evaluation of Selected Biographies

Dupee, F. W. *Henry James.* New York: William Sloane Associates, 1951. For the student just becoming acquainted with Henry James, Dupee provides a readable, straightforward account of the biographical facts of James's life. He begins with James's grandfather, William James, and ends with James's burial. Although offering little original critical insight, Dupee does achieve his goal of revealing to his readers that James led an eventful life. In doing this, he emphasizes James's extensive travel experiences, wide social circle, and intelligent response to the literary currents of America, England, and France. Dupee bases his discussion of James's works upon the antitheses of past and present, experience and innocence, Europe and America.

Edel, Leon, *Henry James: The Untried Years, 1843–1870; Henry James: The Conquest of London, 1870–1881; Henry James: The Middle Years, 1882–1895; Henry James: The Treacherous Years, 1895–1901;* and *Henry James: The Master, 1901–1916.* New York: J. B. Lippincott, 1953–1972. Leon Edel has produced a mammoth achievement in literary biography, as evidenced by the awarding of the Pulitzer Prize for Biography and the National Book Award for Nonfiction for Volumes II and III of his study of Henry James. The extent of Edel's research is staggering, involving perusal of thousands of letters, journals, and newspapers—many included in the collection of the James family papers given to the Houghton Library at Harvard University by the novelist's nephew and literary executor, also named Henry James. Edel writes in rebellion against the stereotyped conception of James as "a kind of disembodied Mind, a writing machine riveted to a desk creating characters without flesh and stories without passion." Instead he gives his readers memorable intimate glimpses of James as son, brother, friend, and uncle. Henry James believed the best way to know an artist was through his art, and Leon Edel remains true to that belief. He analyzes James's fiction to reveal the author's experiences and personality. Critics have found two major limitations in Edel's biography. Some think it is overly psychological, cautioning against the danger of interpreting James's characters as reflections of himself. Another limitation is that Edel is so enamored of his subject that he sometimes loses necessary critical objectivity. Edel asserts, "With Henry James the novel in English achieves its greatest perfection" and also says that James became "the first great theorist and scholar in the art which he himself practiced with such distinction." Nevertheless, despite its Freudian orientation and eulogistic tone, Edel's biography is the most comprehensive and fascinating source concerning the life, personality, and works of Henry James.

Grattan, Clinton Hartley, *The Three Jameses, A Family of Minds: Henry James, Sr., William James, Henry James.* New York: Longmans, Green, 1932.

In his interesting account that is both a factual biography and an intellectual history, Grattan covers three generations of the James family. He begins with William James, the Irish immigrant who came to America and amassed a huge fortune. He then discusses as representative of the second generation Henry James, Sr., a man of great intellect, who, however, failed to gain fame. With the third generation came the flowering of genius and international recognition through William James, the psychologist, and Henry James, the author. Grattan comments upon the childhood, personality, education, and principal works of Henry James, Sr. and his two sons. Stressing their similarities, he concludes in his epilogue, "All of the Jameses were psychologists; all of them were biased toward social values; and all of them were individualists."

Le Clair, Robert, *Young Henry James, 1843–1870.* New York: Bookman Associates, 1955. Robert Le Clair's book covers the early years of Henry James's life, describing his childhood experiences with art and theater, his travels in Europe as a baby and as an adolescent, his education in Switzerland and Germany and then at Harvard Law School, and his close relationship with his cousin Minny Temple. Le Clair is especially interested in the influence of Henry James, Sr. upon his second son and Henry's relationship with his elder brother William. Depending heavily upon James's three volumes of autobiography, Le Clair avoids psychoanalyzing his subject and instead strives for objectivity. His work is most valuable for revealing how the shy, sensitive, introspective child who loved nothing more than to gape at the life around him grew into the keenly observant writer.

Matthiessen, F. O. *The James Family: Including Selections from the Writings of Henry James, Senior, William, Henry & Alice James.* New York: Alfred A. Knopf, 1947. Labeling his work as an internal biography of "a family of minds," F. O. Matthiessen examines the ideas of Henry James, Sr. and his children about religion, philosophy, literature, politics, and society. Matthiessen confesses in his introduction that his work is also an anthology; for, believing that the most revealing material about the James family is contained in their letters, journals, and essays, he subordinates authorial commentary to a direct presentation of the family members' formal and informal writings. Among the most interesting material are William's and Henry's critiques of each other's works and the father's and his two sons' observations about some of the important figures of the times, including Emerson, Whitman, Carlyle, Hawthorne, and Howells. The book, enhanced by an excellent set of illustrations, makes the James family come alive for the reader.

Autobiographical Sources

Autobiographical sources are plentiful. Among the greatest treasures are Henry James's three volumes of reminiscences: *A Small Boy and Others, Notes of a Son and Brother,* and *The Middle Years*—the last just a fragment at the time of the author's death. In 1911—a year after his brother William died, James began a work intended to present a selection of William's early letters followed by a memoir of him. However, as James began dictating to his secretary, Theodora Bosanquet, inspired by only a handful of family letters, his phenomenal memory asserted itself. The result was an autobiographical record of his own intellectual development, particularly his discovery of his vocation as a writer. These three volumes of memories are charming, often humorous, and always revealing of James's penetrating mind.

Other glimpses into Henry James's mind are offered in his letters. In 1920 Percy Lubbock published two volumes of *The Letters of Henry James* (London: Macmillan, 1920; New York: Charles Scribner's Sons, 1920) with the assistance of James's relatives. Lubbock groups the letters according to chronological periods and provides informative introductions to each period. Supplementing the Lubbock collection are Leon Edel's four volumes entitled *Henry James Letters* (Cambridge, MA: Belknap Press of the Harvard University Press, 1974, 1975, 1980, 1984). Edel notes, "The present edition is the first to draw upon the full *epistolarium,* now available after half a century." Most of the letters Edel publishes are from the collection of the James family papers at Harvard.

The best insight into James as a writer of fiction comes from his prefaces to the New York Edition. These reveal his thematic interests and major techniques, as well as highlighting the similarities he perceives between literature and the visual arts. Also useful are *The Notebooks of Henry James,* edited by F. O. Matthiessen and Kenneth B. Murdock (New York: Oxford University Press, 1947), which illuminate James's creative process and record the seminal ideas for many of his works. James's many art and literary reviews and his travel essays shed light upon his aesthetic values.

Overview of Critical Sources

From the time James published his early tales and novels to the present, he has received much critical attention. And, indeed, beginning with William Dean Howells' review of *A Passionate Pilgrim and Other Tales* in the *Atlantic Monthly* in 1875, James has been fortunate in attracting intelligent critical minds that have recognized his craftsmanship. Many of the critical books on James provide readings of his major works or of periods of his works, such as the early tales or the last three major novels. Other volumes concentrate upon his technique, especially his use of point of view, ambiguity, irony, imagery, and the character types of the reflector and the confidante. A number of works compare James with other writers, including Twain, T. S. Eliot, Conrad, Turgenev, Chekhov, and Proust. Still others place him in a cultural and historical context, and emphasize the philosophical influence that his father and brother William exerted upon him. Two recent critical concerns have been James's interest in the visual and dramatic arts and his treatment of female characters.

Evaluation of Selected Criticism

Beach, Joseph Warren, *The Method of Henry James.* New Haven: Yale University Press, 1918. This book is a pioneer study in James's use of storytelling techniques, including idea, picture, point of view, and dialogue. After defining the building blocks of James's fiction, Beach discusses individual works, grouping them into six periods.

Dupee, Frederick W. ed. *The Question of Henry James: A Collection of Critical Essays.* New York: Henry Holt, 1945. This important collection of criticism contains essays on James by such eminent writers as William Dean Howells, Ford Madox Ford, Joseph Conrad, W. H. Auden, Stephen Spender, and André Gide and such noted Jamesian critics as Edmund Wilson, Percy Lubbock, F. O. Matthiessen, and R. P. Blackmur.

Matthiessen, F. O. *Henry James: The Major Phase.* New York: Oxford University Press, 1944. Disagreeing with Van Wyck Brooks' theory that James's expatriation caused his talent to decline, Matthiessen asserts that James's later work has greater depth and richness than his previous writings. He provides intelligent analyses of *The Wings of the Dove, The Ambassadors, The Golden Bowl, The American Scene,* and *The Ivory Tower* and relates these works to the culture of the times in which James wrote them.

Putt, S. Gorley, *Henry James: A Reader's Guide.* London: Thames and Hudson, 1966; Ithaca, NY: Cornell University Press, 1966. Putt addresses his book "to the ordinary lover of good fiction who has yet to discover the rich merits of Henry James as a poet and scholar of the human heart." To introduce the reader to James, he provides systematic commentary on the author's twenty-two novels and one hundred and twelve short stories, which he arranges according to themes. Putt's clear, commonsensical, and appreciative approach to James provides one of the most helpful critical guides for students.

Other Sources

Andreas, Osborn, *Henry James and the Expanding Horizon: A Study of the Meaning and Basic Themes of James's Fiction.* Seattle: University of Washington Press, 1948. Asserts that James's central method in his fiction is that sensitivity to others expands one's consciousness.

Bewley, Marius, *The Complex Fate: Hawthorne, Henry James and Some Other American Writers.* London: Chatto and Windus, 1952. Discusses Cooper, Melville, Hawthorne and James as American writers who confronted the problem of being both separated from and connected with European culture. Relates the romances of Hawthorne to the novels of James, noting especially the similarities between the *Blithedale Romance* and *The Bostonians,* and between *The Marble Faun* and *The Wings of the Dove.*

Canby, Henry Seidel, *Turn West, Turn East: Mark Twain and Henry James.* Boston: Houghton Mifflin, 1951. Compares Twain's and James's fictional interest in American innocence and independence, and contrasts their family backgrounds and cultural orientations.

Kelley, Cornelia Pulsifer, *The Early Development of Henry James.* Urbana: University of Illinois Press, 1930; rev. 1965. Studies James's reviews, travel sketches, and fiction from 1864 to 1881.

Krook, Dorothea, *The Ordeal of Consciousness in Henry James.* Cambridge: Cambridge University Press, 1962. Considers the theme of "being and seeing" in James's principal works.

Leavis, F. R. *The Great Tradition: George Eliot, Henry James, Joseph Conrad.* London: Chatto and Windus, 1948. Defines Eliot, James and Conrad as great novelists for their awareness of life's possibilities and their preoccupation with form.

Poirier, Richard, *The Comic Sense of Henry James: A Study of the Early Novels.* New York: Oxford University Press, 1960. Studies the comic clash between James's "free" and his "fixed" characters in six novels written between 1875–1881.

Wagenknecht, Edward, *The Novels of Henry James.* New York: Frederick Ungar, 1983. Provides source studies, plot summaries, and brief interpretations of James's major works presented in chronological order.

Selected Dictionaries and Encyclopedias

Critical Survey of Long Fiction, Salem Press, 1983. Brief biography and analysis of the major works.

Dictionary of Literary Biography. Gale Research, 1982. Discussion of James's life and works, and a bibliography of primary and secondary sources.

Lynne P. Shackelford
Furman University

RANDALL JARRELL
1914–1965

Author's Chronology

Born May 6, 1914 in Nashville, Tennessee, first child of Anna Campbell Jarrell and Owen Jarrell; *1915* poses for statue of Ganymede in full-scale model of the Parthenon in Nashville's Centennial Park; *1926* lives in Hollywood with his grandparents after the separation of his parents; returns to Nashville to live with his mother; *1931* enters Vanderbilt University; studies with John Crowe Ransom; edits the humor magazine; *1934* first published poem, "Above the waters in their toil," in *American Review; 1935* graduates from Vanderbilt with B.A. in psychology; enters graduate school for degree in English; forms close friendship with Peter Taylor, a life-long friend and colleague; *1937* secures position at Kenyon College; forms close friendship with Robert Lowell, then a student at Kenyon; *1940* marries Mackie Langham; *1942* enlists in Army Air Corps; "washes out" as a pilot trainee; serves as instructor for crewman and as a celestial navigation tower operator; *1946* receives Guggenheim Fellowship; joins Peter Taylor on faculty of the Woman's College of the University of North Carolina at Greensboro; poetry editor of the magazine *The Nation; 1949* poetry critic for *Partisan Review; 1951* visiting professor at Princeton; *1952* divorces Mackie; marries Mary Eloise von Schrader; teaches at Indiana School of Letters, then University of Illinois; *1956* Consultant in Poetry at the Library of Congress; *1960* wins the National Book Award for *The Woman at the Washington Zoo;* summers in Italy; *1963* receives second Guggenheim fellowship; spends five months in Europe; *1965* hospitalized; fatally hit by car on October 14; buried in Guilford Cemetery in Greensboro, North Carolina.

Author's Bibliography (selected)

The Rage for the Lost Penny, in *Five Young American Poets,* 1940 (poems); *Little Friend, Little Friend,* 1945 (poems); *Losses,* 1948 (poems); *Poetry and the Age,* 1953 (criticism); *Pictures from an Institution,* 1954 (fiction); *The Seven-League Crutches,* 1957 (poetry); *The Woman at the Washington Zoo,* 1960 (poetry); *A Sad Heart at the Supermarket,* 1962 (criticism); *The Bat-Poet,* 1964 (children's book); *Selected Poems,* 1964; *The Animal Family,* 1965 (children's book); *The Lost World,* 1965 (poetry); *The Three Sisters,* 1969 (translation and production of play); *The Complete Poems,* 1969; *The Third Book of Criticism,* 1969; *Kipling, Auden & Co./Essays and Reviews, 1935–1964,* 1980 (criticism); *Randall Jarrell's Letters.* ed. by Mary Jarrell, 1985.

Overview of Biographical Sources

Surprisingly, given the importance of Jarrell as a poet and critic, there is still no biography. His letters, edited by Mrs. Jarrell, *Randall Jarrell's Letters* (Boston: Houghton Mifflin, 1985) provide the best testimony to his importance as a man of letters as well as to his wit and critical acumen. The most complete account is Sister Bernetta Quinn's biographical sketch in *Randall Jarrell* (Boston: Twayne, 1981). Suzanne Ferguson's critical study, *The Poetry of Randall Jarrell* (Baton Rouge, Louisiana State University Press, 1971) includes a remarkable collection of Jarrell photographs, many of which she obtained from the poet's mother. There are also many photographs in *Randall Jarrell 1914-1965,* edited by his friends Robert Lowell, Peter Taylor, and Robert Penn Warren (New York: Farrar, Straus & Giroux), as well as remembrances by Peter Taylor, Elinor Ross Taylor, Robert Lowell, and Robert Watson. Of special value in this book is Mary Jarrell's essay on Jarrell and his literary friend, "A Group of Two."

Evaluation of Selected Biographies

Quinn, Sister Bernetta, *Randall Jarrell.* Boston: Twayne, 1981. Sister Bernetta's biographical chapter in a very general bio-critical account of Jarrell's work details the bare facts of his life without going into much detail. She corresponded with many of Jarrell's friends, many of his colleagues and former students, his first wife Mackie Jarrell, and consulted on numerous occasions with Mary Jarrell. This is very much a pro-Jarrell account, presenting him as an important literary figure, perhaps the man of letters for the 1950's, who was a critic and friend of many important writers. There are, unfortunately, factual errors and biographical gaps. Sister Bernetta does not, for instance, discuss the circumstances of Jarrell's death or his health problems prior to it. She does not treat sufficiently the decline in Jarrell's reputation in the 1960's. Until a biography is written this will, however, be the most useful source for facts about his life.

Autobiographical Sources

The major autobiographical source, covering only a brief episode in Jarrell's life is his last volume of poetry, *The Lost World,* published posthumously, which recounts vividly his days in Hollywood at the home of his grandparents. It was written during the vogue of confessional poetry. Jarrell is personal, but, intentionally, not confessional. If he gives only the minimal information about his personal life at a crucial moment in his childhood, he does reveal much of his inner life. Some readers have regarded his comic exposé of life at a woman's college in his novel, *Pictures from an Institution,* as comic autobiography, based on faculty life at Sarah Lawrence and the Woman's College at Greensboro.

Overview of Critical Sources

Randall Jarrell was known first for his brilliant but often acerbic reviews in literary magazines. He was probably the best southern reviewer of poetry since Edgar Allan Poe, and just as effective, winning respect for his critical judgments, but making a few enemies. The reputation of *Poetry and the Age* remains undiminished as an important forerunner of post-modernism in literary taste and as an alternative in the 1950's to the formalism of the New Criticism.

Jarrell's critics praise him for his war poems, for his blend of realism and compassion, and for his use of childhood innocence to depict the pathos of the human situation. He received less praise then, but more later, for his sensitivity to the plight of women. The greatest critical compliment paid Jarrell was a comparison with Rilke, whom he sensitively translated.

In the 1950's Jarrell's poetry came under attack for his colloquial, flat, unvaried, and, generally undistinguished style. At a time when southern writers were critically in vogue, Jarrell seemed to be trying to become a European writer, having more in common with Grimm or Rilke than with Robert Penn Warren or Allen Tate. His last book of poems, *The Lost World,* was, with a few dissenting opinions, judged as an attempt at confessional poetry that failed because of sentimentality.

Because of structuralist and deconstructionist critics, the 1980's promise an upturn in Jarrell's critical reputation. As a result of reexaminations by Sister Bernetta Quinn, Suzanne Ferguson, and William Pritchard, there has even been a new appreciation of his last volume, *The Lost World,* not as an attempt at confessional poetry, but as evocation of a place, the Hollywood of the 1920's from the memories of an adult through the eyes of a sensitive child whose parents have separated.

Evaluation of Selected Criticism

Dickey, James, *Babel to Byzantium Poets & Poetry Now.* New York: Farrar, Straus and Giroux, 1968. In a collection of mostly unfavorable reviews of poets who mostly write dull, academic poetry of the "garden variety" type, Dickey includes a self-argument over his enthusiasm as a poet for the poetry of Jarrell, and his disdain as a critic for the failure of his poems to show the vitality that Dickey demands in modern poetry. The poetry lacks the power of style to evoke a world that is "realer than the real," but the compassion, the caring, for the people in his poems almost makes up for the deficiencies. This essay is not only a remarkable testimony by a poet who admires Jarrell in spite of himself but a good introduction to the poetry.

Ferguson, Suzanne, *The Poetry of Randall Jarrell.* Baton Rouge: Louisiana State University Press, 1971. Ferguson's first book-length study of Jarrell's poetry began the revaluation of Jarrell's poetry that has taken place. Book by book, she takes up Jarrell's poetry and examines, if not explicates, all the major poetry. She shows the variety of his themes, and argues persuasively for the importance of his treatment of woman. Especially influential was her case for *The Lost World,* contending that it is not a major departure or mistake. There is a brief biographical sketch, accurately presented, and a bibliography.

———, *Critical Essays on Randall Jarrell.* Boston: G. K. Hall, 1983. Ferguson offers the only thorough collection of essays on Jarrell, from early reviews of his books to a few essays written for this book.

Lowell, Robert, Peter Taylor, and Robert Penn Warren, eds. *Randall Jarrell 1914–1965.* New York: Farrar, Straus & Giroux, 1967. In the absence of a biography this collection is important as a source for Jarrell's importance as a man of letters and his character as poet by those who knew him best.

Quinn, Sister Bernetta, *Randall Jarrell.* Boston: Twayne, 1981. In addition to presenting the most detailed biographical sketch, Sister Bernetta Quinn, Jarrell's strongest advocate over the years, presents in a general introduction a strong case for Jarrell as poet, critic, and translator, and as the key literary figure in his age.

Other Sources

Beck, Charlotte, *Worlds and Lives: The Poetry of Randall Jarrell.* Port Washington, NY: Associated Faculty Press, 1983. Beck provides a good brief account, at its best stressing Jarrell's special affinities for Rilke.

Hagenbüchle, Helen, *The Black Goddess: A Study of the Archetypal Feminine in the Poetry of Randall Jarrell.* Bern: Francke Verlag, 1975. The archetypal female is an important subject for an understanding of Jarrell's poetry, but the treatment here is narrowly Jungian.

Jarrell, Mary, ed. *Randall Jarrell's Letters: An Autobiographical and Literary Selection.* Boston: Houghton Mifflin, 1985. Four hundred of nearly 2,500 of Jarrell's letters from 1935 to 1965. Subjects range from his friendships with other writers to his literary positions as a "new critic." Witty and engaging correspondence.

Selected Dictionaries and Encyclopedias

Critical Survey of Poetry, Vol. 4, Salem Press, 1982. Brief biography, and short analysis of Jarrell's poetry.

Great Writers of the English Language: Poets, St. Martin's Press, 1979. Biographical sketch, and brief critical essay.

Richard J. Calhoun
Clemson University

ROBINSON JEFFERS
1887–1962

Author's Chronology

Born January 10, 1887, Pittsburgh, Pennsylvania, to educated and talented parents; *1899–1902* travels; educated in Europe; *1903* family moves to California; enters Occidental College; *1906* begins graduate studies University of Southern California; *1907* studies medicine U.S.C.; *1910* studies forestry University of Washington; *1911* returns to Los Angeles then to University of Washington; *1913* marries Una Call Kuster; *1914* moves to Carmel, California; *1916* twin sons born; *1919* begins "Tor House"; *1937* honorary degree Occidental College; elected National Institute of Arts and Letters; *1939* receives degree from U.S.C.; *1940* Levinson Prize; *1941* reads poetry in eastern cities; *1947 Medea* produced on New York stage; elected American Academy of Arts and Letters; *Dear Judas* produced; *1951* Tietjens Memorial Prize; *1952* Union League Arts Foundation Prize; *1954* Pulitzer Prize; *1958* Academy of American Poets fellowship; *1961* Shelley Memorial Award; dies January 20, 1962.

Author's Bibliography (selected)

Californians, 1916 (poems); *Tamar and Other Poems,* 1924; *Roan Stallion, Tamar and Other Poems,* 1925; *The Women at Point Sur,* 1927 (poems); *Cawdor and Other Poems,* 1928; *Dear Judas and Other Poems,* 1929; *Thurso's Landing and Other Poems,* 1932; *Give Your Heart to the Hawks and Other Poems,* 1933; *Solstice and Other Poems,* 1935; *Such Counsels You Gave to Me and Other Poems,* 1937; *The Selected Poems of Robinson Jeffers,* 1938; *Be Angry at the Sun,* 1941 (poems); *Medea,* 1946 (poems); *The Double Axe and Other Poems,* 1948; *Tower Beyond Tragedy,* 1950 (poems); and *Hungerfield and Other Poems,* 1954.

Overview of Biographical Sources

Of three early biographies of Robinson Jeffers, two containing interesting material are *Robinson Jeffers, A Portrait* by Louis Adamic (Seattle: University of Washington, 1929) and *Robinson Jeffers, The Man and His Work* by Lawrence Clark Powell (Pasadena: San Pasquel Press, 1940). Both were published almost a quarter century before Jeffers died, are not complete studies, and are not always available in most libraries. Frederic I. Carpenter's *Robinson Jeffers* (1962) manages to cover a good deal of Jeffers' life and writing succinctly, and without losing the flavor of the man or the poet. Melba Berry Bennett's *The Stone Mason of Tor House, The Life and Work of Robinson Jeffers* (1966), while a sympathetic study, proves to be an extensive biography with a wealth of autobiographical material. *The Selected Letters of Robinson Jeffers, 1897–1962,* edited by Ann N. Ridgeway (Baltimore: The Johns Hopkins Press,

1968), adds immeasurably to a better understanding of the man, and the foreward, by Mark Van Doren, makes some significant points regarding Jeffers as a poet. The volumes listed in the overview of critical sources all contain some references to the life of Jeffers but not to an extent that would make them prime biographical sources.

Evaluation of Selected Biographies

Bennett, Melba Berry, *The Stone Mason of Tor House, The Life and Work of Robinson Jeffers.* Los Angeles: The Ward Ritchie Press, 1966. In a foreward to this book one of Jeffers' earlier biographers, Lawrence Clark Powell, said, "The prospect for Jeffers studies is furthered and brightened by" her work. Una Jeffers had intended to write *the* biography of her husband, kept notes with that purpose in mind, but died before she could start. During this time Mrs. Bennett had enjoyed the privilege of spending months at Tor House, going over manuscripts, letters, notes and clippings; catching both Una and Jeffers in their moods, discussing his works and the critics with both, and storing up many impressions. When Una died Mrs. Bennett was eminently qualified to write what Powell described as the "first biography" of Robinson Jeffers. While not the definitive biography it contains considerable detail, and a wealth of autobiographical material.

Carpenter, Frederic I. *Robinson Jeffers.* New York: Twayne, 1962. As with practically all of the Twayne series on American authors, this book compresses in relatively few pages not only an essential biography and bibliography, but a readable assessment of a number of Jeffers' long narrative poems and some of his short ones. The book is a good introduction to the writings of one of the most controversial poets America has produced.

Autobiographical Sources

Robinson Jeffers never wrote his autobiography probably because he never attached importance to self adulation and disliked personal recognition of any sort. There is, however, some autobiographical material in Mrs. Bennett's book worth reading. In her long sessions with Una and Jeffers, Mrs. Bennett managed to record many personal and family matters. She was also permitted to use Una's notes. Ridgeway's *Selected Letters of Robinson Jeffers* is another source of some autobiographical material. In many of the 400 letters in this well-designed book Jeffers explains himself as a man and as a poet.

Overview of Critical Sources

Despite the paucity of biographies about Robinson Jeffers there is a respectful body of critical studies attesting to the growing interest in the poet and his work. Some critics suggest that Jeffers was influenced by his exposure to old legends, myths, and fables, while others see an intense religious quality in his poems. Others claim his writings reflect everything from mysticism to modern science. After reviewing this list of critical views Carpenter concludes that "Few authors in the history of literature have excited greater differences of opinion." He also echoes the view of most critics when he says Jeffers' "poetry awaits the gradual verdict of posterity."

Evaluation of Selected Criticism

Brophy, Robert J. *Robinson Jeffers, Myth, Ritual and Symbol in His Narrative Poems.* Cleveland: The Press of Case Western Reserve University, 1973. The fact that he studied Latin and Greek at a very early age, and was a voracious reader gives Brophy cause to consider Jeffers' "amazing background." As a boy, traveling, living, and studying in Europe, Jeffers became steeped in Old World legends, myths and fables. "The preparation which he brought to his poetry," Brophy believes, "is one of the most varied and rich among American poets." The end result of this background is a "myth-ritual approach" which Brophy explores in his penetrating explication of five of Jeffers' major narrative poems.

Coffin, Arthur B. *Robinson Jeffers, Poet of Inhumanism.* Madison: University of Wisconsin Press, 1971. Coffin believes the poet was influenced by Nietzsche's ideas and that Jeffers called the ideological position which developed, "Inhumanism." Just what "inhumanism" represented has been difficult to explain, not only by the poet himself but by his friends as well. Jeffers preferred to call it a "philosophical attitude." Coffin attempts to explain its meaning in a book of careful scholarship. How well he succeeds to illuminate some of Jeffers' more complex themes must be left to his reader's judgement.

Gilbert, Rudolph, *Shine, Perishing Republic, Robinson Jeffers and the Tragic Sense in Modern Poetry.* New York: Haskell House, 1965. Gilbert attributes qualities to Jeffers which other critics do not see in quite the same hue. Jeffers admitted to the inconsistencies of his complex philosophy, and accepted what people read into his poetry. He thought it was natural that they did. In that light he might not have questioned Gilbert who sees Jeffers as a "poet of transition," one who is prophetic, a mystic influenced by Buddha's teachings, and one who had found the "tragic note" in modern American life. While somewhat excessive in adulation, and not always accurate with facts, few would question Gilbert's belief that Jeffers brought 'something fiery' into American poetry.

Nolte, William H. *Rock and Hawk, Robinson Jeffers and the Romantic Agony.* Athens: University of Georgia Press, 1978. While a partisan and defender of Jeffers and his work, Nolte must assuredly win the respect of scholars in the field with this dispassionate study. He reminds readers that the interest in Jeffers is on the rise, and that anyone who likes poetry knows his work. The author of this excellent book has cleared the underbrush of obtuseness, so much a part of Jeffers study, to show that the poet reveals "a larger world than any other poet of his time has given us."

Squires, Radcliffe, *The Loyalties of Robinson Jeffers.* Ann Arbor: University of Michigan Press, 1956. Squires, who regards Jeffers as one of the three great poets (with Eliot and Frost) America has produced "in the century which has seen her rise to greatness," believes his world needs discovery. He is disenchanted with the "new critics" for treating Jeffers with silence. Squires is also puzzled that in selecting the American minor and major poets of the last fifty years John Crowe Ransom did not even "obliquely" mention Jeffers. This author believes Jeffers was first and foremost a thinking man, and one who does not merit silence but the attention of thinking critics to evaluate and reevaluate his philosophy.

Selected Dictionaries and Encyclopedias

American Writers, A Collection of Literary Biographies, Supplement II, Part 2. Charles Scribner's Sons, 1981, pp. 413-440. A well rounded survey in twenty-seven pages.

Literary History of the United States, Bibliography, 4th edition, Macmillan, pp. 593-595, 1238-1239. Brief but useful.

Robert A. Gates
St. John's University

SARAH ORNE JEWETT
1849–1909

Author's Chronology

Born September 3, 1849, South Berwick, Maine, U.S.A., daughter of a country doctor, descendant of seagoing people of the Maine coast; *1855–1866* has delicate health in childhood, is educated at Miss Raynes's school and Berwick academy; perhaps most importantly rides in her father's buggy visiting upcountry patients and at the local store where she hears old seamen tell stories; *1863* reads Harriet Beecher Stowe's *The Pearl of Orr's Island* (*1862*), an important influence on her decision to write and on her choice of subject; *1868* publishes first short story, "Jenny Garrow's Lovers," a "magazine" story; *1877* publishes first long work, *Deephaven,* with the encouragement of William Dean Howells, then an editor at *Atlantic Monthly; 1880* begins friendship with Annie Fields, wife of publisher James T. Fields, which develops on his death, into a "Boston Marriage," the two women living and travelling together until Jewett's death; *1882* first travels to Europe with Fields; in their American and European travels they continue friendships with or become acquainted with such important literary figures as Henry James, Robert Lowell, John Greenleaf Whittier, Oliver Wendell Holmes, H. B. Stowe, R. W. Emerson, Henry Wadsworth Longfellow, Mark Twain, Alfred, Lord Tennyson, Rudyard Kipling, and many contemporary American women writers; *1886* publishes *A White Heron and Other Stories,* her first highly regarded collection of short stories and enters into her most productive period; *1896* publishes *The Country of the Pointed Firs,* considered her masterpiece; *1902* injured in a fall from a carriage, she feels unable to write fiction though she continues to correspond with her friends; *1907* meets Willa Cather in Boston, beginning an influential literary friendship; *1909* dies of cerebral hemorrhage at South Berwick on June 24.

Author's Bibliography (selected)

Deephaven, 1877 (novel); *A White Heron and Other Stories,* 1886; *The King of Folly Island and Other People,* 1888; *Strangers and Wayfarers,* 1890 (stories); *A Native of Winby and Other Tales,* 1893; *The Life of Nancy,* 1895 (stories); *The Country of the Pointed Firs,* 1896 (novel); *The Queen's Twin and Other Stories,* 1899; *The Uncollected Short Stories of Sarah Orne Jewett,* edited by Richard Cary, 1971.

Overview of Biographical Sources

Because Jewett's circle of friends was large and because she corresponded so faithfully with many of them, there is a good quantity of material available. Her biographers have, therefore, made available solid and useful accounts of her life. However, a definitive critical biography remains to be written. Much of the material for such a biography will be found in the collections of the Houghton Library of Harvard University and at Colby College in Waterville, Maine. Short biographical treatments include Margaret Farrand Thorp, *Sarah Orne Jewett* (Minneapolis: University of Minnesota Pamphlets on American Writers, No. 61, 1966) and various encyclopedia sketches. Longer treatments are few and various: F. O. Mathiessen, *Sarah Orne Jewett* (Boston: Houghton Mifflin, 1929), John Eldridge Frost, *Sarah Orne Jewett,* (1960), and Richard Cary, *Sarah Orne Jewett* (1962).

Evaluation of Selected Biographies

Cary, Richard, *Sarah Orne Jewett.* New York: Twayne, 1962. Cary writes an introduction to Jewett's work which contains a good deal of biography; he creates a literary portrait. Drawing on a wide variety of Jewett's materials, he produces the most authoritative longer study to date. He also provides a useful annotated, selective bibliography.

Frost, John Eldridge, *Sarah Orne Jewett.* Kittery Point, ME: Gundalow Club, 1960. This is a detailed and documented account of Jewett's personal and public life.

Autobiographical Sources

By far the most important known autobiographical sources are Jewett's letters. A number appear as parts of journal articles. Two collections have been published.

Cary, Richard, ed. *Sarah Orne Jewett Letters.* Waterville, ME: Colby College Press, 1956. Revised and expanded, 1967. Especially useful for information about her personal and daily life.

Fields, Annie, ed. *Letters of Sarah Orne Jewett.* New York: Houghton Mifflin, 1912. Especially useful for her literary opinions, this collection includes letters to literary acquaintances such as Cather.

Overview of Critical Sources

Outside of the scholarly journals, Jewett has received relatively little close critical attention. There is general agreement that she produced, in *The Country of the Pointed Firs,* the best novel to come out of the Local Color and Regional Movements. Most critical treatments of her work have focused on her regional subjects and themes. She is praised for her development of techniques which are particularly adapted to her chosen material, techniques which help her to avoid sentimentality while portraying the dignified and often pathetic members of a withering culture, techniques which help her to produce interesting fiction out of the pointedly uneventful, mundane lives of her New England characters.

Recent criticism has begun to apply various feminist perspectives to her writing.

Evaluation of Selected Criticism

Cary, Richard, *Sarah Orne Jewett.* New York: Twayne, 1962. Cary provides an excellent introduction to Jewett's work, combining biography with summary and analysis of most of her significant writing. He shows how her New England childhood, her family backgound, and her literary education contributed to her interest in regional New England subjects. He attempts to estimate the value of her contribution to American literature, concluding that *The Country of the Pointed Firs* and perhaps twenty of her stories rank with the best of American fiction.

Cary, Richard, ed. *Appreciation of Sarah Orne Jewett.* Waterville, ME: Colby College Press, 1973. This is a collection of twenty-nine critical and appreciative essays published between 1885 and 1972. The essays range from general evaluations to discussions of her themes and techniques. The foreword offers a summary of Jewett's critical reception.

Donovan, Josephine, *Sarah Orne Jewett.* New York: Frederick Ungar, 1980. Donovan makes interesting use of Jewett's diaries and letters to discuss her literary theory and her ideas about "women's literature." She gives special attention to Jewett's influence on other American woman writers, to her treatment of the roles of women and to the development of characteristic themes during her career.

Other Sources

Auchincloss, Louis, *Pioneers and Caretakers.* Minneapolis: University of Minnesota Press, 1965. Places Jewett in a tradition of American women writers interested in conserving what they see as best in the American Heritage.

Cather, Willa, *The Country of the Pointed Firs and Other Stories.* New York: Doubleday, 1956; originally published as *The Best Stories of Sarah Orne Jewett,* Boston: Houghton Mifflin, 1925. In her preface, Cather notices Jewett's love of her country and its language. She calls attention to Jewett's humor and rates *The Country of the Pointed Firs* with *The Scarlet Letter* and *Adventures of Huckleberry Finn.* Cather revises and expands her reflections on Jewett in *Not Under Forty* (1936).

Mathiessen, F. O. *Sarah Orne Jewett.* Boston: Houghton Mifflin, 1929. Mathiessen's treatment is primarily appreciative and attends to relationships between her life and works.

Nagel, Gwen L. and James Nagel, *Sarah Orne Jewett: A Reference Guide.* Boston: G. K. Hall, 1978. A fully annotated list of secondary writing on Jewett through 1976. The introduction is an important survey of Jewett criticism and scholarship.

Thorp, Margaret Farrand, *Sarah Orne Jewett.* Minneapolis: University of Minnesota Pamphlets on American Writers, No. 61, 1966. Thorp discusses connections between Jewett's fiction and her New England background.

Weber, Clara C. and Carl J. *A Bibliography of the Published Writings of Sarah Orne Jewett.* Waterville, ME: Colby College Press, 1949.

Westbrook, Perry, *Acres of Flint.* Washington: Scarecrow Press, 1951. Places Jewett at the center of New England regional writers, 1870–1890. Studies her work in relation to Cather, Helen Hunt Jackson and others.

Selected Dictionaries and Encyclopedias

American Women Writers, Vol. 2, Frederick Ungar, 1980. Brief biography and analysis of her career.

Critical Survey of Short Fiction, Salem Press, 1981. Biographical sketch and brief analysis of several short stories.

Dictionary of Literary Biography, Vol. 12, Gale Research, 1982. Concise overview of Jewett's life and work.

Terry Heller
Coe College

SAMUEL JOHNSON
1709–1784

Author's Chronology

Born September 18, 1709, Lichfield, Staffordshire, England, son of a bookseller; *1727* attends Pembroke College, Oxford for thirteen months; *1735* marries Mrs. Elizabeth Porter, twenty years his senior, and sets up as a schoolmaster; *1737* goes to London accompanied by David Garrick; *1738* publishes *London. A Poem* anonymously; *1741–1744* reconstructs parliamentary debates from notes for *Gentleman's Magazine; 1746* begins *Dictionary of the English Language; 1749* finishes *Irene,* which ran for nine nights; *1752* wife Tetty dies; *1755* finally completes his *Dictionary; 1759* mother dies; *1762* receives lifetime annual pension of three hundred pounds from George III; *1763* meets James Boswell; *1764* founds the Literary Club with Joshua Reynolds; *1765* brings out eight-volume edition of Shakespeare; and made Doctor of Laws by Trinity College, Dublin; *1765* meets Mr. and Mrs. Henry Thrale; *1773* tours Scotland and Hebrides with Boswell; *1774* tours North Wales; *1775* made Doctor of Laws by Oxford; *1779–1781* produces *Lives of the Poets; 1781* Henry Thrale dies; dies December 13, 1784 and buried in Westminster Abbey.

Author's Bibliography (selected)

London. A Poem, 1738; *An Account of the Life of Mr. Richard Savage,* 1744 (biography); *The Vanity of Human Wishes,* 1749 (poem); *Irene,* 1749 (tragedy); *Rambler,* 1750–1752 (essays); *Adventurer,* 1753–1754 (essays); *Dictionary of the English Language,* 1755 (dictionary); *Idler,* 1758–1760 (essays); *The History of Rasselas, Prince of Abyssinia,* 1759 (philosophical tale); *Edition of The Plays of William Shakespeare with preface and notes,* 1765 (criticism); *A Journey to the Western Islands,* 1775 (travel book); *Prefaces, Biographical and Critical, to the Works of the English Poets* (*Lives of the Poets*), 1779–1781 (critical biography).

Overview of Biographical Sources

Johnson is the subject of what many have called the greatest biography ever written—James Boswell's *Life of Johnson* (1964). Any reader wishing to know about Johnson should begin here. Other biographies written by friends of Johnson and illuminating different aspects of his character include Sir John Hawkins' *The Life of Johnson, LL.D.* (London, 1787) and Hester Lynch Piozzi's *Anecdotes of the Late Samuel Johnson, LL.D.* (ed. Arthur Sherbo, London: Oxford University Press, 1974). Johnson left a few personal papers, collected in *Diaries, Prayers, and Annals,* ed. E. L. McAdam Jr. with Donald and Mary Hyde, Volume 1 of the *Yale Edition of the Works of Samuel Johnson* (1958). His letters have been edited by R. W. Chapman in three volumes, *The Letters of Samuel Johnson* (1952). Good modern biographies produced by leading Johnsonian scholars include J. L. Clifford's *Young Sam Johnson* (1955) and *Dictionary Johnson: The Middle Years of Samuel Johnson* (1979) and W. Jackson Bate's *Samuel Johnson* (1977).

Evaluation of Selected Biographies

Bate, W. Jackson, *Samuel Johnson.* New York: Harcourt Brace Jovanovich, 1977. Called a "model literary biography," Bate's work provides fresh literary assessments of Johnson's work and a psychological study of his character. Bate is especially perceptive about Johnson's moral writings and gives a clear picture of Johnson's humanity. Bate analyzes Johnson's motives, his fears of insanity, his marriage, the fluctuations between his repression and his imagination, and his combative wit. As Johnson himself did in *Lives of the Poets,* Bate tries to find continuity between the life and work of his subject.

Boswell, James, *Life of Johnson.* ed. G. B. Hill; rev. and enlarged by L. F. Powell, 6 vols. Oxford: Clarendon Press, 1934, 1950; 2nd ed. V and VI, 1964. Boswell met Johnson in 1763 at the height of Johnson's literary fame. The greatness of this biography lies in Boswell's recreation of Johnson's conversations, recreations based on notes Boswell jotted down, journal entries, and memory. Johnson was Boswell's hero, and in many ways this is a book about what Johnson meant to Boswell. It obviously emphasizes Johnson in his later years in mostly masculine situations (at the club, at dinners, etc.) with skimpier treatment of Johnson's early years, rise to fame, and life in a family (with his parents, his own wife Tetty, and the Thrales).

Clifford, J. L. *Dictionary Johnson: Samuel Johnson's Middle Years.* New York: McGraw-Hill, 1979. The sequel to *Young Sam Johnson,* this biography covers Johnson's life from 1749 to his meeting with Boswell in 1763, one-fifth of Johnson's life which makes up only one-tenth of Boswell's biography. During this period Johnson produced much of his great work: the essays, the *Dictionary,* and *Rasselas.* This biography details Johnson's daily life: his literary labors, marriage, friendships, eccentricities, financial struggles, and charity.

———. *Young Sam Johnson.* New York: McGraw-Hill, 1955. (British title, *Young Samuel Johnson.* London: Heinemann, 1955). Clifford begins with Johnson's early years in Lichfield and closes with his work on the *Dictionary* in 1749. This detailed biography acquaints the reader with both Johnson and his age. For his information Clifford draws on Boswell's *Life of Johnson* but more on Aleyn Lyell Reade's *Johnsonian Gleanings* (privately printed 1909–1946; facsimile, New York: Octagon Books, 1955).

Wain, John, *Samuel Johnson.* London: Macmillan, 1974. Written by a poet-novelist, this very readable biography is aimed at the general reader. Its material is derived mainly from Boswell and the *Letters of Samuel Johnson* and is presented in a less scholarly format than Bate's or Clifford's: there are no footnotes and only a limited bibliography.

Autobiographical Sources

Before his death, Johnson burned almost all his own papers, including two large quarto diaries and his letters to his wife. What remains is found in *Diaries, Prayers, and Annals,* Volume 1 of the *Yale Edition of the Works of Samuel Johnson,* ed. E. L. McAdam, Jr. with Donald and Mary Hyde (New Haven: Yale University Press, 1958). Arranged chronologically, these give information on the events of Johnson's life, his health, and his reading. Altogether, they reveal the inner Johnson—his guilt feelings, his resolutions, the conflicting pressures he felt, his fears for the future, his feelings of incapacity to reform, and his longing for forgiveness and peace. They contain examples of his earliest writing, earlier than any known letters. Though many of the entries are short jottings or abbreviated observations, they record the state of Johnson's mind. The prayers on the death of his wife, for example, are Johnson's working through of his grief and supplicating for his own welfare. Some prayers center on his work: his need for help with the *Dictionary* and his dedication of the *Rambler* essays to God for the promotion of His glory.

Johnson's correspondence, collected in *The Letters of Samuel Johnson,* ed. R. W. Chapman, 3 vols. (Oxford: Clarendon Press, 1952), reveal the more public Johnson. Over 1500 of Johnson's letters are known to have survived, and they complement his published writing and oral wisdom. The surviving letters are fairly representative of Johnson's correspondence of his middle and later years, though there are few letters remaining from his early years. Chapman's edition also contains Mrs. Thrales' replies to Johnson's letters.

Corrections to Chapman by T. M. Knox can be found in *Notes and Queries,* July 1962; additions in Mary Hyde, "Not in Chapman," in *Johnson, Boswell and Their Circle,* ed. Mary Lascelles et al (Oxford: Clarendon Press, 1965) and Duncan Isles, "The Lennox Collection," *Harvard Library Bulletin,* 1970–1971.

Overview of Critical Sources

As well as having several excellent biographies about Johnson, readers can choose from numerous book-length studies of Johnson's work as a whole, as well as various aspects of his thought and works: his style, his poetry, his biographical writings, his criticism, his moral thought, his scientific thought, his tragic sense, his allegory, and his thoughts about reason and imagination. The many articles written about him cover even more limited topics.

Evaluation of Selected Criticism

Bate, W. Jackson, *The Achievement of Samuel Johnson.* Chicago: University of Chicago Press, 1955. Earlier than Bate's comprehensive biography of Johnson, this work emphasizes the overall themes of Johnson's writing and character of his thinking. The first chapter summarizes Johnson's life while the final chapter focuses on Johnson as a critic. The middle three chapters—"The Hunger of the Imagination," "The Treachery of the Human Heart and the Stratagems of Defense," and "The Stability of Truth"—are most insightful.

Bronson, Bertrand H. *Johnson Agonistes and Other Essays.* Berkeley: University of California Press, 1965 (first three essays originally printed in *University of California Publications in English,* vol. 3, no. 9, 1944). The four essays combined in this volume cover Johnson's mind and character, the duality of Boswell's temperament, Johnson's only play *Irene,* and Johnson's reputation. The third essay, on *Irene,* is mostly for scholars with its examination of the play's literary sources, first draft, and biographical material. The last essay, in particular, is helpful in distinguishing the Johnson of the "learned" tradition and the "popular" tradition, Johnson the author and Johnson the personality.

Greene, Donald J. *The Politics of Samuel Johnson.* New Haven: Yale Univeristy Press, 1960. Exploding Boswell's and subsequent critics' myth of Johnson as the great Tory and monarchist, Greene carefully examines Johnson's political ideas, activities and milieu. Johnson's political views, of course, also take in his critical principles, religion and morality. Greene bases much of his discussion on Johnson's own writings and relies on the redefinition of Toryism made by historians in the middle part of this century. Greene considered this study to be an introductory sketch, but it has been enormously influential. More recent comments by Greene can be found in his introduction to *Political Writings,* volume 10 of the *Yale Edition of the Works of Samuel Johnson* (New Haven: Yale University Press, 1977).

Hagstrum, Jean H. *Samuel Johnson's Literary Criticism.* Minneapolis: University of Minnesota Press, 1952; rpt. with new preface, Chicago: University of Chicago Press, 1967. The value of Hagstrum's work lies in his attempts to find the theoretical bases for Johnson's criticism rather than in reliance upon Johnson's single judgments on individual works. Proceeding deductively rather than inductively, Hagstrum uses a topical approach to set forth Johnson's theories of literature. According to Hagstrum, Johnson used empirical grounds for his judgment and, unlike other eighteenth-century critics, based his opinions on perception rather than principle.

Other Sources

Brack, O. M., Jr. and Robert E. Kelley, *The Early Biographies of Samuel Johnson* (Iowa City: University of Iowa Press, 1974). Fourteen biographical accounts of Johnson that appeared 1762–1786.

Chapin, Chester F. *The Religious Thought of Samuel Johnson.* Ann Arbor: University of Michigan Press, 1968. Discussion of Johnson's religious convictions which emphasizes the rationality of Johnson's beliefs, and the lack of inward peace they gave him.

Folkenflik, Robert, *Samuel Johnson, Biographer.* Ithaca and London: Cornell University Press, 1978. Johnson's biographical writings and techniques.

Greene, Donald J. *Samuel Johnson* (New York: Twayne, 1970). A general introduction to Johnson's thought and writings.

———. *Samuel Johnson: A Collection of Critical Essays* (*Twentieth Century Views*). Englewood Cliffs, NJ: Prentice-Hall, 1965. Excerpts from critical books on Johnson and original modern essays.

Selected Dictionaries and Encyclopedias

British Writers, Vol. 3, Charles Scribner's Sons, 1980. Short biography with survey of Johnson's principal writings and assessment of his work.

Critical Survey of Poetry, Salem Press, 1982. Brief biography and analysis of major poems and *Irene.*

Critical Survey of Short Fiction, Salem Press, 1981. Brief biography and analysis of *Rasselas.*

Moulton's Library of Literary Criticism of English and American Authors, Vol. 2, Frederick Ungar, 1966. Concise overview of Johnson's life and short quotations from contemporaries and nineteenth-century writers on his works, letters and personality.

Ann W. Engar
University of Utah

BEN JONSON
1572(?)-1637

Author's Chronology

Born in either 1572 or 1573, probably in or near London, one month after the death of his father, a minister; within several years his mother remarries a master-bricklayer; as a boy Jonson studies under William Camden at Westminster School; *1588?* withdrawn from school and apprenticed as a bricklayer; early *1590's* perhaps works as a bricklayer; serves briefly as a military volunteer in Flanders; *1594* marries Anne Lewis; *1597* acts in a company of transient players; employed as a playwright; imprisoned for part authorship of allegedly seditious play; *1598* kills a fellow actor in a duel; is imprisoned; converts to Catholicism; freed after pleading benefit of clergy; *1599–1601* feuds with John Marston and Thomas Dekker in the "War of the Theatres"; *1603* begins writing aristocratic entertainments; *1604–1625* becomes chief masque-writer for the Jacobean court; *1605* imprisoned, with Marston and George Chapman, for anti-Scottish satire detected in their play *Eastward Ho!; 1612–1613* travels in France as tutor; *1616* publishes folio *Works;* pensioned by King James; *1618–1619* tours Scotland on foot; *1619* receives honorary Oxford M.A.; *1623* manuscripts destroyed in fire; *1628* suffers paralytic stroke; appointed Chronologer of London; *1630* receives increased pension from Charles I; *1631* resumes long-standing feud with Inigo Jones; *1637* dies August 6.

Author's Bibliography (selected)

Every Man in His Humour, 1598 (comedy); *Sejanus his Fall,* 1603 (tragedy); *Masque of Blackness,* 1605; *Volpone,* 1606 (comedy); *Epicoene,* 1609 (comedy); *The Alchemist,* 1610 (comedy); *Bartholomew Fair,* 1614 (comedy); folio *Works,* 1616, including *Epigrammes* and *The Forrest* (poems); *Chloridia,* 1631 (final masque); *A Tale of a Tub,* 1633 (final complete play); *Love's Welcome at Bolsover,* 1634 (final entertainment); second folio *Works,* 1640–1641, including *The Under-wood* (poems), *The English Grammar,* and *Timber, or Discoveries* (prose notes).

Overview of Biographical Sources

Writing Jonson's life is no easy task. His early years are obscure, and his suppression of some early writings makes them obscurer. The later loss of important manuscripts further distorts the record, and much of the surviving evidence is fragmentary, vague, or questionable. His complex relations with superiors, rivals, colleagues, and the law are not always easy to interpret, while his frequent concern with self-presentation complicates matters even more. Still, numerous data about Jonson *do* exist, although no completely satisfying biography has yet been built from them. Many materials are collected in the

11-volume standard edition of his works, *Ben Jonson,* ed. C. H. Herford and Percy and Evelyn Simpson (1925–1952). Volume I includes a short biography; although usually reliable, its effectiveness is limited by its brevity. However, other biographical discussions are dispersed throughout the edition in introductions, commentaries, and appendices. Marchette Chute's *Ben Jonson of Westminster* (1953) is lively, comprehensive, and well-researched, but unfortunately lacks documentation.

Documentation abounds in Barbara De Luna's *Jonson's Romish Plot: A Study of "Catiline" and Its Historical Context* (Oxford: Clarendon Press, 1967). De Luna argues that Jonson's play parallels aspects of the 1605 Gunpowder Plot. The book surveys much of Jonson's career, but its evidence and arguments are not always convincing. Although valuable, it illustrates the pitfalls and difficulties involved in writing about Jonson's life. Eric Linklater's *Ben Jonson and King James: Biography and Portrait* (London: Jonathan Cape, 1931) is a popular, undocumented account that has been criticized for stylistic flaws and factual errors. John Palmer's *Ben Jonson* (London: George Routledge, 1934) is similarly vulnerable. While not strictly biographical, Richard Helgerson's *Self-Crowned Laureates: Spenser, Jonson, Milton and the Literary System* (Berkeley: University of California Press, 1983) does contain an intriguing discussion of Jonson's career.

Evaluation of Selected Biographies

Chute, Marchette, *Ben Jonson of Westminster* (New York: E. P. Dutton, 1953). Written for a popular audience, Chute's book is generally a reliable, sensible account of Jonson's life and times. It effectively blends background discussion with personal information, and sets Jonson's works—especially the plays—in a clear context. Some of its critical judgements have been questioned; although the absence of notes is a defect, the index is helpfully full.

Herford, C. H. and Percy and Evelyn Simpson, eds. *Ben Jonson,* 11 vols. (Oxford: Clarendon Press, 1925–1952). A brief biography in volume I surveys the entire life; appendices include contemporary notes and records, Jonson's letters, legal and official documents, and books in Jonson's library. Volume II introduces his works and their biographical contexts. Introductions in subsequent volumes concentrate on textual matters, but often supply added biographical facts. The commentary in volumes IX–XI is often biographically pertinent. Volume X includes an appendix on Jonson's relations with George Chapman and Inigo Jones. Volume XI prints contemporary and later reactions to Jonson; additional notes on his life, masques, and library; and a very full index.

Autobiographical Sources

William Drummond of Hawthornden's fragmentary notes of his 1618/19 conversations with Jonson constitute a crucial but controversial source of information about Jonson's life and mind. Jonson apparently did not know that Drummond was keeping a record of their talks: this fact either enhances the notes' revelatory interest or makes them suspect, depending upon one's point of view. Drummond's portrait of Jonson is sometimes unflattering; some later writers have accused him of various deficiencies that supposedly made him an unreliable witness to his guest's character. But the notes remain a uniquely valuable catalogue of biographical data by one of Jonson's contemporaries. Valuable for different reasons are the twenty-two surviving letters to various patrons and acquaintances that Jonson wrote over a number of years; they provide important glimpses of his character, his opinions, and the milieu in which he operated. Drummond's notes, as well as the letters, are printed in Volume I of the Herford and Simpson *Ben Jonson.*

Autobiographical elements figure prominently in many of Jonson's creative works, especially in the non-dramatic poems, in the dedications, prologues, inductions, and epilogues of the plays, and in the introductions and marginalia to the masques. Jonson was very concerned with effective self-presentation, and he shaped public images of himself repeatedly during his career. His critical views are reflected in many of these pronouncements, but a good collection of the ideas and ideals—not all literary—that he found congenial is his commonplace book, *Timber, or Discoveries* (printed in Volume VIII of the Herford and Simpson *Ben Jonson*). James D. Redwine, Jr. has helpfully culled and edited *Ben Jonson's Literary Criticism* (Lincoln: University of Nebraska Press, 1970).

Overview of Critical Sources

Until the past few decades, most critical attention focused on Jonson's plays, but his non-dramatic poetry has now become the subject of intense, interesting criticism in its own right. Jonson's is recognized as one of the most distinctive and most influential voices in 17th century literature. He and John Donne have often been seen as the central figures of two poetic "schools," although it is easy to exaggerate the differences between them. Because Jonson often appeals less immediately to modern readers than Donne does, earlier writers frequently sought to champion or defend the poems and to define their special qualities. Discussion of Jonson's "plain" style, of his forthright moral stance and conservative social attitudes, and of his typical themes has proven very fruitful, but more recent criticism has begun to explore the tonal and thematic ambiguities and complexities of his writing. Issues of power and self-presentation are important in his poems and will undoubtedly receive further attention from his critics. His relations with poetic predecessors and heirs has been and is likely to remain a central topic, while exploration of the thematic unity of his works in various genres will probably continue.

Evaluation of Selected Criticism

Miner, Earl, *The Cavalier Mode from Jonson to Cotton.* Princeton: Princeton University Press, 1971. Jonson looms large in this discussion of "the social voice." Chapters on the good life, on the ruins and remedies of time, on order and disorder, on love, and on friendship treat characteristic Jonsonian themes. Part of a trilogy whose two other volumes discuss the period's private and public modes, this book stresses Jonson's influence on later writers.

Peterson, Richard S. *Imitation and Praise in the Poems of Ben Jonson.* New Haven: Yale University Press, 1980. Arguing that *imitatio* is Jonson's central stylistic principle, Peterson sees the poems as carrying on a subtly allusive and creative dialogue with earlier classical texts. He focuses on the celebratory poems to show how Jonson fuses aesthetic and moral concerns and discusses the poet's uses of "a coherent and characteristic pattern of metaphors" to communicate his artistic and social ideals. The book includes very full analyses of some important poems.

Summers, Claude J. and Ted-Larry Pebworth, *Ben Jonson.* Boston: Twayne, 1979. This superb introduction sums up the best insights of modern Jonson studies while charting new approaches of its own. An opening chapter focuses on "The Man and His Age" is followed by sections on the comedies, tragedies, and masques. There is a long and substantial discussion of the non-dramatic poems, then a survey of "Jonson's Reputation." The poems are said to mingle the public and private, Christian and classical, idealism and realism, celebration and satire. The authors stress the diversity of Jonson's art while also emphasizing the typical features of his "social vision."

———. *Classic and Cavalier: Essays on Jonson and the Sons of Ben.* Pittsburgh: University of Pittsburgh Press, 1982. Focused on Jonson's non-dramatic poems and, to a lesser extent, on the writings of other poets influenced by him, this collection brings together important essays that discuss Jonson's debt to classical poetry; the impact of printing on his concept of the literary text; his prosody, formalism, and linguistic ideas; his epitaphs; the "Celebration of Charis" sequence; and his rivalries with other poets. The book concludes with essays on Jonson and Herbert; on a poem by Carew; on a "Jonsonian sequence" by Vaughan; on Suckling and "low seriousness;" on Marvell's Cavalier poetry; and on Jonson, Milton, and the Sons of Ben. There is a helpful index of works cited.

Trimpi, Wesley, *Ben Jonson's Poems: A Study of the Plain Style.* Palo Alto: Stanford University Press, 1963. Still considered one of the best studies of Jonson's poetry, Trimpi's book examines the impact of classical and native plain style traditions on Jonson's writing. The first four chapters treat Jonson's *Discoveries* as a stylistic handbook and as "a consistent exposition of a stylistic position." Part II applies these stylistic ideas to discussions of particular poems.

Wayne, Don E. *Penshurst: The Semiotics of Place in the Poetics of History.* Madison: University of Wisconsin Press, 1984. This is an extended examination of Jonson's important country-house poem, "To Penshurst." Wayne also confronts issues of more general significance to Jonson's poetry and to the interpretation of Renaissance text. Studying the "social, moral, intellectual, and psychological context" of both the house and the poem, it explores the tensions and ambiguities, and the ideological contradictions implicit in each.

Other Sources

Brock, D. Heyward, *A Ben Jonson Companion.* Bloomington: Indiana University Press, 1983. An encyclopedic reference work on Jonson's writings, life, and times.

Gardiner, Judith Kegan, *Craftsmanship in Context: The Development of Ben Jonson's Poetry.* The Hague: Mouton, 1975. Attempts to show how different principles affected the poems produced in four phases of Jonson's career.

Judkins, David C. *The Non-Dramatic Works of Ben Jonson: A Reference Guide.* Boston: G. K. Hall, 1982. A useful bibliography.

Leggatt, Alexander, *Ben Jonson: His Vision and His Art.* London: Methuen, 1981. Offers a synthetic view of Jonson's work in various genres, stressing unifying motifs and emphasizing the tension between idealism and realism.

Maclean, Hugh, ed. *Ben Jonson and the Cavalier Poets.* New York: W. W. Norton, 1974. Gathers poems by Jonson and his "sons," with accompanying critical essays.

Nichols, J. G. *The Poetry of Ben Jonson.* New York: Barnes and Noble, 1969. Claims the poems deserve more readers; treats their typical styles and themes.

Parfitt, George, *Ben Jonson: Public Poet and Private Man.* London: Dent, 1976. Includes chapters on Jonson's personality and early life; on the tension between his "natural" personality and his ideal self; on his self-projections and teacher figures; on different periods in his art; on his language and classicism; on his reputation and theatricality; and on his social views.

Robert C. Evans
Auburn University at Montgomery

JAMES JOYCE
1882–1941

Author's Chronology

Born February 2, 1882, Dublin, Ireland; *1888* enters Clongowes Wood College; *1893* enrolls at Belvedere College; *1898* enters University College, Dublin; *1900* first important publication, an essay, 'Ibsen's New Drama'; *1902–1903* samples bohemianism and penury in Paris; *1903–1904* adrift in Dublin; *1904* leaves Ireland with wife-to-be, Nora Barnacle, for teaching position with Berlitz School at Trieste; *1904–1905* teaches at Pola, now Pulj, Yugoslavia; *1905–1906* teaches at Trieste; *1906–1907* bank official in Rome; *1907–1915* teaches at Trieste; *1913* befriended by Ezra Pound; *1915–1919* resides at Zurich composing *Ulysses; 1917* lifelong financial support from Harriet Shaw Weaver commences; *1919–1920* resides in Trieste; *1920–1939* resides in Paris; *1930* undergoes eleventh eye operation since 1917; *1931* marriage to Nora Barnacle legalised; *1940* war forces a second retreat to Zurich; *1941* dies January 13, Zurich.

Author's Bibliography (selected)

Chamber Music, 1907 (poems); *Dubliners,* 1914 (stories); *A Portrait of the Artist as a Young Man,* 1916 (novel); *Exiles,* 1918 (play); *Ulysses,* 1922 (novel); *Pomes Penyeach,* 1927 (poems); *Collected Poems,* 1936; *Finnegans Wake,* 1939 (novel); *Stephen Hero,* 1944 (novel); *Epiphanies,* 1956 (prose sketches); *Critical Writings,* 1956 (essays and reviews); *Giacomo Joyce,* 1968 (prose poem).

Overview of Biographical Sources

The integrity of Joyce's egotism, the intimate biographical detail contained in all his works, his frequently-voiced fear of betrayal by friends present the biographer with two approaches. One is the authorized variety, which was attempted during Joyce's lifetime under his rigorous supervision: Herbert Gorman, *James Joyce* (1939; rev. ed. 1948), and an enlargement of his *James Joyce: His First Forty Years* (1924). The other approach combines sympathy and objectivity, working with scholarship as mentor, such as Richard Ellmann's *James Joyce* (1959; rev. ed. 1982).

Joyce's letters have been published in three volumes. The first of these was edited, a little casually, by Joyce's friend, Stuart Gilbert (1957). Richard Ellmann has brought his immense expertise to the editing of the two subsequent volumes (1966). Ellmann has also edited a Selected Letters (1976), which contains previously unpublished material.

Evaluation of Selected Biographies

Ellmann, Richard, *James Joyce.* New York: Oxford University Press, 1959. In terms of exhaustiveness, patience, resources and scope, Ellmann's work stands as a monument both to its subject and to contemporary biographical method. Its great advantages over Gorman's work are its scholarship and its willingness to see Joyce as a man as well as an artist. As a work of scholarship it treats with deft assurance such matters as the diversity of forces which contributed to the genesis of 'The Dead,' the autobiographical provenance of much of *Finnegans Wake,* Joyce's attitude to Ireland and Irish culture, and a host of similar matters which hitherto had hardly received their share of the scrupulous evaluation which scholarly research entails. The portrait of Joyce the man also benefits from Ellmann's researches among Joyce's friends, as well as his access to letters and other important documents. In addition, Ellmann tactfully and sympathetically reveals his subject's weaknesses and misfortunes. The result is an imposing work of synthesis which keeps its focus largely on the man, while at the same time not losing sight of his consummate artistry. Encyclopedic in scale and modestly suave in tone, minutely detailed yet always aware of larger perspectives, designed as a chronology but executed as a mosaic, Ellmann's biography has, with due respect, learned from Joyce. Critical acclaim has, with reason, placed it, in order of importance, immediately next to Joyce's own works.

Gorman, Herbert, *James Joyce.* New York: Farrar and Rinehart, 1939. It is easy to dismiss this biography, because it does not begin to compare with Ellman's standard work. Nevertheless, readers should bear in mind that it was composed with the active, if intermittent, collaboration of its subject. Thus, its depiction of Joyce serves a different purpose than does Ellmann's biography. In fact, Gorman's purpose is largely that which Joyce dictated to him. The biography heavily favors a heroic representation of Joyce the artist. The result is a book which is stronger on journalistic rhetoric than on a patient review of fact. But the overall image it projects is important and influential, and given the author's perspective and circumstances, this image is certainly not inaccurate.

Autobiographical Sources

Joyce is one of the most autobiographical of writers. Under the pseudonym Stephen Dedalus he appears authoritatively in *Stephen Hero, A Portrait of the Artist as a Young Man,* and *Ulysses.* In addition, some of the stories in *Dubliners* are strongly autobiographical, and there is an overriding personal element in the dramatic situation in *Exiles.* As for *Finnegans Wake,* its inclusion of a character named Shem the Penman and innumerable allusions to the author's own history, also give it a prominent autobiographical aspect.

The most accessible autobiographical material occurs in *A Portrait of the Artist as a Young Man,* which is a brilliantly streamlined remodelling of *Stephen Hero,* and in *Ulysses.* Taking these novels together, there is a history of the author from infancy to the age of twenty-two. The history is conveyed less chronologically than in a series of dramatic encounters. These encounters are with cultural and circumstantial forces capable of depriving Joyce/Dedalus of his individuality. The forces are family, nationality, education and religion. The hero's struggles at home, at school, in language and in morals are graphically depicted throughout *A Portrait of the Artist as a Young Man.* As a result of his struggles, Stephen is able to redefine himself as an artist. In *Ulysses,* however, he realizes that the redefinition causes problems of its own, problems of ego, will, spirit and vision. "*A Portrait of the Artist as a Young Man* is not an autobiography; it is an artistic creation." This declaration by Joyce's brother, Stanislaus, must be borne in mind at all times with regard to all of Joyce's work. Nevertheless, Joyce draws more explicitly and in more detail on his own life in his work than any other major author, while at the same time ensuring that his work is not merely or totally autobiographical. The accuracy in fact of Joyce's autobiographical materials is less important than the realization that his art has its roots in the recollection of lived experience.

Overview of Critical Sources

The phrase 'the Joyce industry' is a cliché which attempts to describe the scale and volume of critical commentary devoted to Joyce. Particularly since World War II, Joyce has attracted critical attention of every conceivable kind. In part, the artistic ambition and intellectual sophistication of Joyce's work requires and tolerates such exhaustive critical scrutiny. Moreover, for cultural reasons Joyce's life and work have struck chords of awe, empathy and fascination in the imagination of the contemporary literary world. As Richard Ellmann says in the opening sentence of his biography: "We are still learning to be James Joyce's contemporaries, to understand our interpreter." With this in mind, it has seemed most sensible to devote the following section to works dealing with the whole of Joyce's artistic career.

Evaluation of Selected Criticism

Kenner, Hugh, *Dublin's Joyce.* Bloomington: Indiana University Press, 1956. Kenner presents a complex, even tortuous, argument dealing with the question of verbal tone in such a way as to extend the inquiry to evaluations of aesthetic form and moral vision. Localized reading in the main Joyce texts produce brilliant insights. The overall approach, however, has not won universal assent. Despite its controversial reception by professional Joyceans, this study has remained influential.

Levin, Harry, *James Joyce.* New York: New Directions, 1941; rev. ed. 1960. A pioneering study when it first appeared, it still has much to offer the newcomer to Joyce. Its main attraction is the author's obviously sympathetic understanding of Joyce's artistic methods and preoccupations.

Litz, A. Walton, *James Joyce.* New York: Twayne, 1966; rev. ed. 1972. Complete with a thorough familiarity with all phases of Joyce scholarship. Litz's is a succinct account of the subject's life and work by a leading Joyce scholar. The manner in which life may become work is one of Joyce's key artistic preoccupations, which the author patiently and incisively assesses.

Peake, C. H. *James Joyce: The Citizen and the Artist.* London: Edward Arnold. 1977. Extremely well received by the critical community, this study is patient, clear and devoid of scholarly flashiness. As in the case of all the best work on Joyce, it operates from within Joyce's own texts, rather than attempting to align those texts with a predetermined idiom of interpretation. Particularly valuable for its sense of *Ulysses'* intricate integrity.

Tindall, William York, *A Reader's Guide to James Joyce.* New York: Farrar, Straus and Giroux, 1959. This critic's method has been widely influential in teaching Joyce. The method's advantages and limitations may be seen to good effect here. Essentially, the approach consists of the identification and interpretation of Joyce's symbols. Some abuses of Joyce's texts result, since the relative importance of each symbol in its context is not sufficiently appreciated. However, the method sharpens awareness of Joyce's use of language.

Other Sources

Budgen, Frank, *James Joyce and the Making of Ulysses.* London: Oxford University Press 1934; 1972. A fascinating, informative and judicious view of Joyce in Zurich in the throes of writing his most celebrated work.

Byrne, J. F. *Silent Years.* New York: Farrar, Straus & Young, 1953. The idiosyncratic autobiography of 'Cranly' in *A Portrait of the Artist as a Young Man.* As well as some interesting sidelights on Joyce as a friend companion, the book also illuminates the lower middle-class Dublin to which Joyce and the author belonged.

Curran, C. P., *James Joyce Remembered.* London: Oxford University Press, 1968. A balanced account of Joyce's student days and of the social and cultural *milieux* in which they were spent.

Joyce, Stanislaus, *My Brother's Keeper.* London: Faber and Faber, 1958; New York: Viking, 1958. A critical contribution to studying Joyce, this memoir by his younger brother conveys in splendid detail and with admirable candor the whole story of James Joyce's Dublin years. Family atmosphere, spiritual and educational development, personal outlook and disposition are all dealt with in tones of unimpeachable honesty.

Potts, Willard, ed. *Portraits of the Artist in Exile.* Seattle: University of Washington Press, 1979. A wide-ranging compilation of memoirs and recollections by some of Joyce's wide circle of European friends and acquaintances.

George O'Brien
Georgetown University

JOHN KEATS
1795–1821

Author's Chronology

Born October 31, 1795, Swan and Hoop Livery Stables, 24 Moorfields Pavement Row, London, to Thomas and Frances Keats; *1787* brother George born; *1799* brother Thomas born; *1803–1811* attends Clarke's school at Enfield; *1804* father dies; mother marries William Rawlings; *1811* apprenticed to Hammond, a surgeon of Edmonton; *1814* writes first poems including "Imitation of Spenser," "To Lord Byron," and "On Death;" *1815* enters Guy's Hospital as a student; July *1816* passes examination and becomes eligible to practice as a surgeon and an apothecary; October *1816* writes sonnet on Chapman's Homer; March *1817* sees Elgin Marbles and, later, starts *Endymion;* early *1818* receives negative reaction to his verse in both the *British Critic* and *Blackwood's;* August *1818* meets Fanny Brawne to whom he later becomes engaged; December *1818* brother Thomas dies; February *1819* writes "Eve of St. Mark" and begins extremely prolific period; April to May *1819* writes odes "Grecian Urn," "Nightingale," "Melancholy," and "Indolence;" *1829* health begins seriously to fail; February *1820* offers to break engagement to Fanny Brawne; July *1820* ordered to Italy for the sake of his health; September to November *1820* travels by ship to Italy, reaching Rome in November; November 30, *1820* writes last known letter; February 23, 1821 dies in Rome and is buried three days later in the Protestant Cemetery.

Author's Bibliography

The definitive edition of the poetic works is edited by Jack Stillinger, *The Poems of John Keats* (Cambridge: The Belknap Press, 1978). It supersedes the prior editions which include H. W. Garrod, *Poetical Works* (Oxford: Oxford University Press, 1958). It contains one hundred and forty-eight poems, the collaborative play, *Otho the Great,* and the dramatic fragment, *King Stephen.* Its scholarly apparatus is complete and represents, in a one-volume edition, the most complete collection of the poems presently available.

Overview of Biographical Sources

Keats has been the subject of numerous biographical studies and, while there is no 'definitive' biography, several are quite useful. Beginning chronologically, there are: Sir Sidney Colvin's *John Keats: His Life and Poetry, His Friends, Critics, and After-Fame* (New York: Charles Scribner's Sons, 1920), Amy Lowell's *John Keats,* 2 vols. (Boston: Houghton, 1925), Dorothy Hewlett's *A Life of John Keats* (2nd ed., rev. New York: Barnes & Noble, 1950), Aileen Ward's *John Keats: The Making of a Poet* (1963), Walter Jackson Bate's *John Keats* (1963) and Robert Gitting's *John Keats* (1968). The latter two incorporate more successfully than the earlier works some of the more recent criticism on Keats and his circle and profit from the editing of Keats' letters which were published in 1958. Another work of biographical assistance is Hyder E. Rollins' edition of *The Keats Circle: Letters and Papers 1816–1878,* 2 vols. (Cambridge: Harvard University Press, 1965, 2nd ed.).

Evaluation of Selected Biographies

Bate, W. Jackson, *John Keats.* Cambridge: The Belknap Press of Harvard University Press, 1963. This work, winner of the Pulitzer Prize for Biography, is probably the best American edition of the life of Keats presently available. Besides incorporating the kind of biographical detail interesting to the general reader, the biography relates Keats' life to his works in a way that illuminates both. The illustrations, thirty-two in number, complement the text and include portraits, manuscript pages and scenes important in the life of Keats. Bate's own sure critical eye allows him to give the reader important insight into the entire corpus, especially the odes of April-May 1819 and *Lamia.* Though not as easily readable as Ward, this work is the most useful.

Gittings, Robert, *John Keats.* Boston: Little, Brown, 1968. This biography presents Keats in the same exhaustive detail as does Bate's work. Written from a British, not an American, perspective, the work complements Bate's *John Keats* and includes numerous insightful sections which shed light on the poems. Especially useful in this regard is Part III, "The Living Year" which comprises a fifth of the text and creates the odes of 1819 in great detail. Richly illustrated (fifty-one in all), the text is readable though the smaller print size makes it less so than Bate's work.

Ward, Aileen, *John Keats: The Making of a Poet.* New York: Viking, 1963. This biography centers on the personality of Keats and presents his life in a readable, pleasing style easily accessible to anyone interested in the poet. It superseded the Hewlett work in this regard.

Autobiographical Sources

Keats did not leave a formal autobiography, but the nineteenth-century tendency to correspond, particularly among the artists and intellectuals, has resulted in the letters of the poet which are equally revealing of the man and the artist. The definitive edition is the two-volume set edited by Hyder E. Rollins, *The Letters of John Keats 1814–1821* (Cambridge: Harvard University Press, 1958). Not only does this set include three hundred and twenty letters to family members, friends, personal and business acquaintances and his fiancée, Fanny Brawne, but it provides a detailed biography in the form of a 'calendar' of events in the life of the poet and brief, but useful sketches of Keats's correspondents. As previously mentioned, this work supersedes Rollins' earlier edition of *The Keats Circle.* The letters reveal an intense Keats for whom poetry appeared to come as naturally as breathing. They do not settle the multiple questions around works so complex as the odes or *Endymion,* but they attest in a more personal way to the incredibly imaginative intensity which his works possess.

Overview of Critical Sources

The critical outpouring on Keats's work is almost overwhelming. In addition to the hundreds of short articles and scores of full-length studies devoted specifically to Keats, there are hundreds more in which he figures significantly, especially in works which deal with Victorian and twentieth-century poetry on which he had enormous impact. Each year, as a glance at the *MLA Annual Bibliography* will prove, scholars find an unending source of critical debate in this poetry and his life. Hence, no single work of criticism can hope to encompass this richness. Several of the works listed below, however, are quite useful.

Evaluation of Selected Criticism

Bate, Walter Jackson, ed. *Keats: A Collection of Critical Essays.* Englewood Cliffs: Prentice-Hall, 1964. In the tradition of the Twentieth Century Series this collection represents some of the major critics on Keats and the Romantic period in eleven essays ranging from general and biographical pieces by such critics as T. S. Eliot, Douglas Bush and Richard Fogle to discussions of individual poems such as "The Eve of St. Agnes," "Ode to Autumn" and "Ode on a Grecian Urn," A useful collection, though now twenty years old, the work brings together a good sampling of various approaches to Keats's poetry.

Harris, William Meg, *Inspiration in Milton and Keats.* Totowa, NJ: Barnes & Noble Books, 1982. This recent work is a good example of the numerous studies which offer comparative criticism of Keats with some other major author, in this case Milton. Williams explores Milton's influence on Keats in some detail.

Matthews, G. M. ed. *Keats: The Critical Heritage.* London: Routledge & Kegan Paul, 1971. This work, part of a distinguished series of major writers, brings together the evaluation of Keats by his contemporaries and near-contemporaries. The pieces include comments on Keats's early work by Hunt and Wordsworth, among others, reviews, not always complimentary, of the individual poems and the collection published in 1818, three obituaries from 1821 and posthumous reputation as late as 1863. As always in this series, there is a useful introduction to Keats, as well as careful identification of sources.

O'Neill, Judith, ed. *Critics on Keats: Readings in Literary Criticism.* Coral Gables: University of Miami Press, 1968. This work gathers for the reader some of the best criticism available on Keats by selecting short, now famous, sections from the works of such Keats's experts as Kenneth Alcott, Cleanth Books, Kenneth Muir, Lionel Trilling and Aileen Ward. It is probably the best book with which to begin a reading of Keats's criticism. A useful select bibliography with annotations is attached.

Walsh, William, *Introduction to Keats.* New York: Methuen, 1981. This slim volume is a fine introductory study of Keats meant for the general reader and the beginning student of Keats. It offers a good exploration in its beginning chapter, "The Opening Sensibility," of Keats early development as a poet. The most significant treatment of the poems is given to *Endymion* and the Odes with relatively little attention given to the other works. It is quite readable and well-documented.

Other Sources

Green, David Bonnell and Edwin Graves Wilson, eds. *Keats, Shelley, Byron, Hunt and Their Circles: A Bibliography: July 1, 1950–June 30, 1962.* Lincoln: University of Nebraska Press, 1964. This is a collection of bibliographies annually provided in the *Keats-Shelley Journal.* It is thorough and provides very brief descriptive annotations.

Hearn, Ronald B. *et al. eds. Keats Criticism Since 1954: A Bibliography.* Salzburg: Institut fur Anglistik and Amerikanistik, 1981. This small work provides a more complete supplement to the MacGillivray work listed below. It is, however, without annotations, but it does provide not only articles and full-length studies, but dissertations as well.

MacGillivray, J. R. *Keats: A Bibliography and Reference Guide with an Essay on Keats' Reputation.* Toronto: University of Toronto Press, 1949. Up to its publication date it represents the best bibliography available on Keats.

Selected Dictionaries and Encyclopedias

British Writers, Charles Scribner's Sons, 1981. This series provides extended entries on major British writers. The entry on Keats by Miriam Allott gives an excellent introduction to the poet and his work. It gives comments and evaluation of his works by notable critics with brief citations from the poems, and lists an excellent selected bibliography.

The Cambridge History of English Literature, G. P. Putnam's Sons, 1916. A classic in reference tools, this work provides extended essays on major writers and brief entries on minor ones. Keats's entry, fifteen pages long, includes information on biography, artistic development and major works.

A Chronological Outline of British Literature, Greenwood Press, 1980. This work provides a year-by-year list of literary activity in England, including births, deaths, events and works in British literature from 516 A.D. to 1979. Useful for locating the key literary events in a writer's life.

Critical Survey of Poetry, English Language Series, Salem Press, 1982. This series provides lengthy entries on authors including biography, achievements, analysis of works and bibliography. The sixteen pages on Keats are useful for an overview of the author.

The Critical Temper: A Survey of Modern Criticism on English and American Literature from Beginnings to the Twentieth Century in Three Volumes, Frederick Ungar, 1969. This series provides entries, in Keats's case twenty-six pages long, which include information on biography, and comments by biographers and critics.

Cyclopedia of World Authors, rev. ed. Salem Press, 1974. This series provides 2–3 page entries on authors with brief introductions on biography, works and bibliography.

English Literature: An Illustrated Record in Four Volumes, Grosset & Dunlap, 1904. A standard reference work, this set contains general information on writers in English up to the 'Age of Tennyson.' The entry on Keats, in Volume Four, provides lengthy biographical information, including photos in his home and grave, reproductions of manuscripts in Keats's hand of several important works including "Ode on a Grecian Urn."

The Oxford Companion to English Literature, 4th ed., rev., Clarendon Press, 1967. This work contains short articles on authors, characters and works. The brief entry on Keats includes information on biography, works and some comments on bibliography.

Joan Lescinski, CSJ
College of St. Rose
Albany, New York

JACK KEROUAC
1922–1969

Author's Chronology

Born March 12, 1922, Lowell, Massachusetts of French-Canadian parents, baptized Jean Louis Lebris de Kerouac; *1939* graduates from Lowell High School; *1939–1940* attends Horace Mann Prep School, New York City; *1940–1941* attends Columbia College, on a football scholarship; *1942–1943* serves in the Merchant Marine and U.S. Navy, receives medical discharge; *1944* meets Lucien Carr, William Burroughs and Allen Ginsberg, core members of the Beat Generation; *1946–1948* meets Neal Cassady, writes first novel, *The Town and the City,* published in *1950; 1947–1951* early cross-country trips with Cassady, first attempts to write *On the Road, 1951; 1952–1953* continues writing in San Francisco, New York, North Carolina and Mexico City; works as a brakeman on the Southern Pacific Railroad; *1953–1957* travels around the U.S. and Mexico, serves as a fire lookout for U.S. Agricultural Service in northwestern Washington; *1957–1969* period of celebrity and decline, publishes many works written earlier; *1966* marries Stella Sampas; dies October 21, 1969, St. Petersburg, Florida.

Author's Bibliography (selected)

The Town and the City, 1950 (novel); *On the Road,* 1957 (novel); *The Subterraneans,* 1958 (novel); *The Dharma Bums,* 1958 (novel); *Doctor Sax,* 1959 (novel); *Maggie Cassidy,* 1959 (novel); *Mexico City Blues,* 1959 (poetry); *Visions of Cody,* 1960 (novel); *Tristessa,* 1960 (novel); *Lonesome Traveler,* 1960 (autobiography); *Big Sur,* 1962 (novel); *Desolation Angels,* 1965 (novel); *Satori in Paris,* 1966 (novel).

Overview of Biographical Sources

Few writers have written so autobiographically as Jack Kerouac, yet as has become increasingly apparent, he was a highly conscious artist and not a mere recorder of scenes from his life. With Walt Whitman, he could say that he celebrated himself and contained multitudes. One of the earliest studies is that of Ann Charters, now a pre-eminent Kerouac scholar. Her *Kerouac: A Biography* (1973) provides a year-by-year chronicle and reflects the author's friendship with Kerouac, dating from 1956. Charles E. Jarvis grew up in Lowell, a close friend and contemporary of Kerouac; his study, *Visions of Kerouac: The Life of Jack Kerouac* (Lowell, MA: Ithaca Press, 1974) incorporates a number of extended conversations. In *Naked Angels: The Lives and Literature of the Beat Generation* (1976) John Tytell combines biographical essays with practical criticism. Barry Gifford and Lawrence Lee undertook a biographical experiment in *Jack's Book: An Oral Biography of Jack Kerouac* (New York: St. Martin's Press,

1978); the co-authors gathered and provided connecting matter between excerpts from interviews with friends and acquaintances of Kerouac. Dennis McNally, in *Desolate Angel: Jack Kerouac, the Beat Generation, and America* (1979), chronicles Kerouac's life and places the author and his work in sociohistorical context. A notable expansion of interest in Kerouac's life and work has become apparent in the 1980's. Thus 1983 witnessed the publication of two complementary biographies. Joyce Johnson's *Minor Characters* (Boston: Houghton Mifflin, 1983) offers a well-drawn impressionist portrait of the King of the Beats. Much the longest, most detailed, and most nearly definitive biography yet to appear is Gerald Nicosia's *Memory Babe: A Critical Biography of Jack Kerouac* (1983).

Evaluation of Selected Biographies

Charters, Ann, *Kerouac: A Biography.* San Francisco: Straight Arrow Books, 1973. Charters' is an eminently readable and well researched study. Included in the appendices are an identity key, which associates fictional characters with their real life counterparts, and a bibliographical chronology, which establishes the period in Kerouac's life with which each of the novels is concerned. If the reader is to consult only one secondary source, this should be it.

McNally, Dennis, *Desolate Angels: Jack Kerouac, the Beat Generation, and America.* New York: Random House, 1979. McNally seeks to show that the art and the lives of the Beats are dramatic reflections of apocalyptic change in post-World War II America.

Nicosia, Gerald, *Memory Babe: A Critical Biography of Jack Kerouac.* New York: Grove Press, 1983. Nicosia's is a total-immersion study which meshes well with Kerouac's own works, paraphrasing at length. It captures well the frenetic creativity, desperation and self-destructiveness of Kerouac's life.

Tytell, John, *Naked Angels: The Lives and Literature of the Beat Generation.* New York: McGraw-Hill, 1976. Tytell is particularly useful as he draws analogies to writers and movements of the past, thus establishing a sense of continuity often absent in studies of the Beats. Tytell also relates Kerouac's theories regarding the composition of "spontaneous prose" to the be-bop movement in Jazz, which is of particular importance to understanding Kerouac's achievement in *On the Road.*

Autobiographical Sources

Kerouac was throughout his career an intensely autobiographical writer. "The Legend of Duluoz," which he conceived of as his life's work, is a fictionalized autobiography, one of the most ambitious projects envisioned by any modern American writer. Kerouac regarded his eighteen published books as one vast autobiographical statement.

Overview of Critical Sources

Kerouac's works were for some years widely regarded more as manifestations of quasi-literate popular culture than as literary products meriting serious critical and scholarly attention. It was Truman Capote who said that what Kerouac did was not writing: "it's typing." During the 1970's and 1980's, however, Kerouac came to be more widely studied, though still disregarded or condescended to by many in the academic community. Most Kerouac criticism is biographically oriented; many critics are disinclined to explore the limitations of Kerouac's work.

Evaluation of Selected Criticism

Cook, Bruce, *The Beat Generation.* New York: Charles Scribner's Sons, 1971. In this popular literary history Cook contends that the Beat literary movement of the 1950's prefigured much of what happened in American culture in the 1960's. Thus the first half of the book focuses on Allen Ginsberg, Kerouac, and Gregory Corso, while the second half focuses on Norman Mailer, William Burroughs, and Ken Kesey.

Hipkiss, Robert A. *Jack Kerouac: Prophet of the New Romanticism.* Lawrence: Regents Press of Kansas, 1976. Professor Hipkiss's thesis, that Kerouac's work was the most uncompromising of the romantic rebirth after World War II, is demonstrated by brief comparative considerations of the work of J. D. Salinger, James Purdy, John Knowles and Ken Kesey. Hipkiss is clear-eyed in his scrutiny of Kerouac's strengths and weaknesses.

Nicosia, Gerald, *Memory Babe: A Critical Biography of Jack Kerouac.* New York: Grove Press, 1983. Nicosia provides a sympathetic and exhaustive account of Kerouac's life and work. Virtually every scrap of known information is included in its 767 pages, which move very slowly.

Other Sources

Charters, Ann, *A Bibliography of the Works of Jack Kerouac, 1939–1975.* New York: Phoenix Bookshop, 1975. The standard bibliography.

———, "Kerouac's Literary Method and Experiments: The Evidence of the Manuscript Notebooks in the Berg Collection," in *Bulletin of Research in the Humanities,* 84 (1981), 431–450. Although celebrated during his career as an undisciplined writer of "spontaneous prose," Kerouac wrote and revised carefully, according to a lifetime grand design for literature.

Duberman, Martin, *Visions of Kerouac.* Boston: Little, Brown, 1977. A play inspired by Kerouac's life and work.

Feied, Frederick, *No Pie in the Sky.* New York: Citadel Press, 1964. In this brief, popularly written study, Feied focuses on the representation in American literature of tramps and the traveling life, as depicted in the works of Jack London, Kerouac, and John Dos Passos.

Holmes, John Clellon, *Nothing More to Declare.* New York: E. P. Dutton, 1967. A gifted friend of Kerouac provides at once a definition, explanation and description of himself and his generation.

Hunt, Tim, *Kerouac's Crooked Road: Development of A Fiction.* Hamden, CT: Archon Books, 1981. An extensive study of the "Beat Bible," *On the Road.*

Selected Dictionaries and Encyclopedias

Critical Survey of Long Fiction, Salem Press, 1983. Biographical sketch and brief account of some of Kerouac's better known works.

Dictionary of Literary Biography: American Novelists Since World War II, Gale Research, 1978. Overview of Kerouac's life and works.

Allen Shepherd
University of Vermont

RUDYARD KIPLING
1865–1936

Author's Chronology

Born Joseph Rudyard Kipling December 30, 1865 in Bombay, India, where his father was a professor in the School of Art; left in England at five, boards unhappily with the Holloways; *1878–1882* attends United Services College; *1882* returns to India, working as journalist for the *Civil and Military Gazette* in Lahore; *1887* promoted to the *Pioneer* in Allahabad; *1886* and *1888* poems and short stories reprinted as *Departmental Ditties* and *Plain Tales from the Hills; 1889* moves to London where his reputation expands rapidly; *1892* marries Caroline Balestier, sister of his American collaborator on the novel *The Naulahka;* moves to Brattleboro, Vermont, near her family; *1892* and *1894* daughters Josephine and Elsie born as Kipling redirects his subject material toward children's literature; *1896* publicity over a quarrel with his brother-in-law drives the Kiplings back to England, where they settle in Sussex; *1897* "Recessional" published for Queen Victoria's second Jubilee; refuses knighthood; *1899* is seriously ill at the time of Josephine's death and winters abroad from 1900–1908 in South Africa on the Rhodes estate; *1907* accepts Nobel Prize and several honorary degrees, but continues to refuse all politically linked honors, including the Poet Laureateship; awareness of German threat and support for compulsory military service cost him popularity; *1915* only son John killed in France; *1917–1922* serves on Imperial War Graves Commission; *1927* Kipling Society founded, publishing *Kipling Journal;* dies London, January 18, 1936.

Author's Bibliography (selected)

Departmental Ditties and Other Verses, 1886; *Plain Tales from the Hills,* 1888; *Life's Handicap,* 1891 (stories); *The Jungle Book,* 1894 (stories); *Stalky & Co.,* 1899 (stories); *Kim,* 1901 (novel); *Just So Stories,* 1902; *Puck of Pook's Hill,* 1906 (stories); *Actions and Reactions,* 1909 (stories); *A Diversity of Creatures,* 1917 (stories); *Letters of Travel,* 1920 (essays); *Debits and Credits,* 1926 (stories); *Something of Myself for My Friends Known and Unknown,* 1937 (autobiography); *Rudyard Kipling's Verse, Definitive Edition,* 1940.

Overview of Biographical Sources

With Kipling's early fame and controversial attitudes, his reputation varied widely in his own lifetime and since. *The Age of Kipling,* edited by John Gross (New York: Simon and Schuster, 1972), contains solid essays on reputation, verse, and imperialism, among others. The autobiographies of L. C. Dunsterville, *Stalky's Reminiscences* (London: Jonathan Cape, 1928) and G. C. Beresford (McTurk), *Schooldays with Kipling* (London: Victor Gollancz, 1936) provide background for the period spent at United Services College and *Stalky &*

Co. Kipling's time in India is detailed by Louis L. Cornell in *Kipling in India* (New York: St. Martin's, 1966), stressing the separation between the English and middleclass Indians; he appends a careful listing of newspaper writing from this period, collected and uncollected. Harold Orel's *Kipling: Interviews and Recollections* (New York: Barnes & Noble, 1983) has little new material and poor notes but includes material published in the *Kipling Journal* which may not be readily available elsewhere.

Four of the shorter biographical/critical accounts offer different values for general reading: James Harrison's *Kipling* (Boston: Twayne, 1982) offers recent coverage and extensive solid criticism. Amis' Rudyard Kipling and His World (London: Thames & Hudson, 1975), heavily illustrated, makes brief iconoclastic attacks on assumptions about Kipling, including his skill in narrative technique. J. I. M. Stewart's *Rudyard Kipling* (New York: Dodd, Mead, 1966) is easily readable with long descriptions of prose works but little on poetry; Hilton Brown's *Rudyard Kipling* (New York: Harper, 1945), stylistically more complex, criticizes Kipling's failure to observe the Indian political revolution, suggesting that his knowledge of India was limited. The definitive biography is C. E. Carrington's *The Life of Rudyard Kipling* (1955); is accurate and unusually readable, if somewhat shallow in interpretation of personality and writings. The Birkenhead biography, *Rudyard Kipling* (1978) is unbalanced and highly colored in tone; it should be used cautiously. Angus Wilson's *The Strange Ride of Rudyard Kipling: His Life and Works* (1977) contains better critical analysis and a more negative evaluation of Kipling's personality.

Evaluation of Selected Biographies

Birkenhead, Lord, (F. W. F. Smith), *Rudyard Kipling.* New York: Random House, 1978. Originally intended as an authorized biography, it draws on contact with family and unpublished correspondence. The first draft, however, led Elsie Kipling Bambridge to ban publication, considering that no rewriting could correct the problems. The biography was revised in the 1960's, but the ban continued until her death in 1976. As a retired army officer, Birkenhead's interests lay in Kipling's political activities, so that the biography is unbalanced. The less tightly controlled analysis of Kipling's neurotic tendencies and contact with lower social classes could be valuable, but the main difficulty is that, though apparently objective, Birkenhead tends to distort the picture stylistically by using highly polarized terms. While this trait contributes to the interest of the narrative, it is often unclear whether a reading is supported by documentation. New primary source material, such as Kipling's account of his delirium during his 1899 illness, is introduced, but any interpretative material should be verified if possible.

Carrington, C. E. *The Life of Rudyard Kipling.* Garden City, NY: Doubleday, 1955. This is the definitive biography, with access to private papers, extensive quotations from letters, interviews with contemporaries, and an appended memoir by Mrs. Bambridge. It is readable, detailed in background, clear, and factually accurate. While it is generally objective, there is a trace of the tendency in an authorized biography to soften material that could be interpreted unfavorably. Carrington is enthusiastic about Kipling's work, but his criticism lacks depth of penetration into theme and strucutre; he is excellent in describing connections between Kipling's experiences and subject matter.

Wilson, Angus, *The Strange Ride of Rudyard Kipling: His Life and Works.* New York: Viking, 1977. Less valuable for unpublished sources, though many new illustrations are added and a responsible effort is made to evaluate sources independently, this is the first of the major biographies to include sophisticated thematic and structural criticism. Biographical material is integrated closely with related writings, so that analyses are not in chronological order and references to one work may be scattered. Psychological analysis of Kipling is less timid than Carrington's; Wilson investigates negatives like love of cruelty and lack of introspective self-knowledge. Wilson also had a close relationship with a native world in childhood and considers Kipling's outstanding gift his ability to retain a child's approach to the world. A coherent picture emerges, but the original and sometimes controversial analyses should be compared with others of the same work.

Autobiographical Sources

The title of Kipling's autobiography, *Something of Myself for Friends Known and Unknown,* suggests an effort in old age—internal references date the latter part to 1935—to break through his privacy and reticence to share something of his experiences. Primarily reminiscences, it includes accounts of indebtedness to friends, impressions of places, some description of sources and the compositon process, especially the role of his father in stimulating ideas and revisions for *Kim* and *Puck of Pook's Hill.* Ideas are not discussed at length, though background for their development can be located. Sharp prejudices are evident, but may reflect his age more than his attitudes at the time recalled. Sections on childhood and school memories reflect the significantly autobiographical "Baa Baa, Black Sheep" and *Stalky & Co.* Painful material from his adult years is omitted or screened by reserve, as is his relationship with his wife; coverage ends with the Nobel Prize in 1907.

Kipling's letters have not been collected and many papers were destroyed by his wife and daughter after his death because of his desire for privacy in personal affairs. His correspondence with H. Rider Haggard has been edited by Morton Cohen in *Rudyard Kipling to Rider Haggard: The Record of a Friendship* (London: Hutchinson, 1965). His first unsuccessful novel *The Light that Failed* (1890 and 1891 for the two opposed endings) is generally considered to contain autobiographical material. The nonfiction collections of articles and essays provide insight into his attitudes and background, from the early Indian accounts in *From Sea to Sea* (1899) to *Letters of Travel* (1920). During and after World War I Kipling wrote extensively on patriotic topics: *France at War* (1915) is an account of visits to the fighting lines in France and *Sea Warfare* (1916) collects material on the navy; and there are some other small and difficult-to-obtain collections of speeches and articles. These provide a vivid picture of the war and English and French attitudes toward it.

Overview of Critical Sources

The two studies regarded as landmarks in the revival of interest in Kipling are Edward Shanks' *Rudyard Kipling: A Study in Literature and Political Ideas* (Garden City, NY: Doubleday, 1940) and J. M. S. Tompkins' *The Art of Rudyard Kipling* (London: Methuen, 1959). For the poetry, T. S. Eliot's introduction to his anthology *A Choice of Kipling's Verse* (London: Faber and Faber, 1941) is also a landmark. The polemic controversy over Kipling's imperialism includes K. Bhaskara Rao's *Rudyard Kipling's India* (Norman: University of Oklahoma Press, 1967), an Indian nationalist's viewpoint; John A. McClure's *Kipling & Conrad: The Colonial Fiction* (Cambridge: Harvard, 1981), a progressive viewpoint that childhood mistreatment led Kipling to accept the suffering inflicted by imperialism as part of the natural order; and Lewis D. Wurgaft's *The Imperial Imagination: Magic and Myth in Kipling's India* (Middletown, CT: Wesleyan University Press, 1983), a psychohistorical analysis that evaluates his contribution to the imperial myth of the British Raj. More balanced analyses are provided by Alan Sandison in *The Wheel of Empire* (London: Macmillan, 1967) and Richard Faber in *The Vision and the Need: Late Victorian Imperialist Aims* (London: Faber and Faber, 1966), a general discussion with a lengthy treatment of Kipling. Three collections of essays provide an overview: Roger Lancelyn Green's *Kipling: The Critical Heritage* (New York: Barnes & Noble, 1971); Elliot L. Gilbert's *Kipling and the Critics* (New York: New York University Press, 1965), with an excellent review of early criticism, key early selections, and a wide range of approaches and time periods; and Andrew Rutherford's *Kipling's Mind and Art: Selected Critical Essays* (Stanford: Stanford University Press, 1964) including the Edmund Wilson essay, several essays evaluating imperialism, and a thematic/technique section drawing together material on vision, soldiers and officers, and the later stories.

Evaluation of Selected Criticism

Dobrée, Bonamy, *Rudyard Kipling: Realist and Fabulist.* London: Oxford University Press, 1967. Dobrée is distinguished for his sensitive reading of texts. Balancing cruelty and compassion as qualities, he suggests that Kipling's imperialism is less racism than a recognition that the contribution England had to make at that time was their art of government. Most of the work explores central ideas such as work, law, empire; a brief section discusses types of poetry.

Mason, Philip, *Kipling: The Glass, the Shadow and the Fire.* New York: Harper & Row, 1975. Primarily concerned with Kipling's prose, Mason correlates biographical detail with lengthy descriptions and analyses of the works. He finds Kipling uneven and contradictory as a writer, intuitive but not thinking issues through, because of an outer social shell induced by cruel treatment. Mason prefers the later stories, the shallowness of his anlaysis casts doubt on his viewpoint.

Shahane, Vasant A. *Rudyard Kipling: Activist and Artist.* Carbondale: Southern Illinois University Press, 1973. Shahane combines Indian background with scrupulous fairness; he includes a brief neutral biography, an extensive bibliography, a section linking Kipling to Victorian activism, and an excellent application of Indian perspective in the discussion of Buddhism in *Kim.*

Other Sources

Bodelsen, C. A. *Aspects of Kipling's Art.* Manchester: University of Manchester Press, 1964. Combines essays on mirth, the artist, and the late style with analyses of five related problem short stories.

Gilbert, Elliot L. *The Good Kipling: Studies in the Short Story.* Athens: Ohio University Press, 1970. Imperialism as metaphor for work; Kipling's viewpoint of a chaotic world with imminent disaster on which man can never impose order.

Selected Dictionaries and Encyclopedias

British Writers, Vol. VI, Charles Scribner's Sons, 1983. Excellent analysis of prose but weak on poetry; bibliographic sections include criticism and index of short stories to source collection.

Dictionary of Literary Biography: British Poets 1880–1914 Vols. 19 and 34; *British Novelists, 1890–1929,* Gale Research, 1983, 1985. Superb treatment of poetry with integrated biography.

Marilyn K. Nellis
Clarkson University

ARTHUR KOESTLER
1905–1983

Author's Chronology

Born September 5, 1905, Budapest, Hungary, of Hungarian-Jewish parents; *1922–1926* studies science at polytechnic in Vienna and becomes devoted Zionist; goes to Palestine in service of Revisionist Party; *1927–1930* hired by Germany's Ullstein newspaper chain as Middle Eastern correspondent; moves to Paris; *1930* becomes science editor of *Vossische Zeitung* and foreign editor of *Berliner Zeitung am Mittag,* both in Berlin; *1931* accompanies *Graf Zeppelin* on Arctic Expedition as its only journalist; joins German Communist Party; *1932* loses Ullstein job because of Party work; visits Russia to study Five Year Plan; *1933–1935* involved with Comintern affairs in Paris; *1935* marries Dorothy Asher; *1936–1937* goes to Spain during Civil War as correspondent for *London News Chronicle;* captured and sentenced to death by Nationalists; jailed in Seville but released with help of British; publishes *Spanish Testament; 1938* resigns from Communist Party; *1939–1940* writes *Darkness at Noon;* released from French prison camp for aliens and joins French Foreign Legion; escapes to England; *1941–1942* publishes *Darkness at Noon* in English translation and a revision of *Spanish Testament* under title *Dialogue with Death; 1946* publishes *Darkness at Noon* in France as *Le Zero et l'Infini; 1948–1949* makes Cold War publicity tour of America; *1950* publishes *The God That Failed;* divorces Dorothy Asher and marries Mamaine Paget; returns to United States and buys farm on the Delaware River; *1953* divorces Mamaine Paget; *1955* publishes *The Trail of the Dinosaur* and stops political writing; *1957* becomes a Fellow of the Royal Society of Literature; *1965* marries his secretary, Cynthia Jefferies; *1971–1974* publishes several works on biology and parapsychology; made a Commander of the Order of the British Empire and a Companion of Literature of the Royal Society of Literature; March 3, *1983* commits suicide with his wife; leaves money to establish a chair in parapsychology at a university in the United Kingdom.

Author's Bibliography (selected)

Spanish Testament, 1937 (autobiography); *The Gladiators,* 1939 (novel); *Darkness at Noon,* 1941 (novel); *Scum of the Earth,* 1941 (autobiography); *Arrival and Departure,* 1943 (novel); *The Yogi and the Commissar and Other Essays,* 1945; *Thieves in the Night,* 1946 (novel); *The God That Failed* (written with others), 1950 (autobiographical essay); *The Age of Longing,* 1951 (novel); *Arrow in the Blue: An Autobiography,* 1952; *The Invisible Writing: An Autobiography,* 1954; *The Sleepwalkers: A History of Man's Changing Vision of the Universe,* 1959; *The Act of Creation,* 1964 (psychology); *The Case of the Midwife Toad,* 1971 (science history); *The Thirteenth Tribe: The Khazar Empire and Its Heritage,* 1976 (social history).

Overview of Biographical Sources

There is only one full-length biography of Koestler: Iain Hamilton's *Koestler: A Biography* (1982). Hamilton stresses the 1940–1970 period in Koestler's life, providing a narrative of events with little analysis. Hamilton's conservative bias shows at times, but his summaries of Koestler's political positions are helpful. He offers a good picture of Koestler's stand against capital punishment. Some fascinating personal glimpses of Koestler are seen in the posthumously published volume co-written with his wife: Arthur and Cynthia Koestler, *Stranger on the Square,* ed. Harold Harris (London: Hutchinson and Company, 1984). Of the twelve essays in this volume, nine are by Cynthia Koestler. She tells of her first meeting with Koestler in 1948 when he hired her as his secretary. The essays cover events in her life with Koestler through 1956. A very personal monograph of a close relationship is given in George Mikes's *Arthur Koestler: The Story of a Friendship* (London: Andre Deutsch, 1983). Mikes met Koestler in 1952 as a result of their common interest in Hungarian literature, and Mikes's short book is the story of shared talk, company, and Hungarian cuisine over three decades.

Evaluation of Selected Biographies

Hamilton, Iain, *Koestler: A Biography.* London: Macmillan, 1982. Hamilton's biography is strong on the period of Koestler's life from 1940 through 1970 but less helpful on the rest. Some reviewers were critical of his failure to analyze Koestler's work in any detail, and some noted a conservative bias in his presentation. His book remains, however, a useful guide to Koestler's political stances as well as the fullest account of the life and work as a whole.

Autobiographical Sources

Koestler has left an especially rich body of autobiographical works, beginning in 1937 with *Spanish Testament,* a chronicle of his experiences as a correspondent in the Spanish Civil War. He produced a shorter version, *Dialogue with Death,* focusing on his capture and imprisonment under sentence of death by Franco's forces. In *Scum of the Earth* Koestler narrates his wartime experiences beginning in 1938 with his confinement with other "undesirable aliens" in a French concentration camp.

Arrow in the Blue is the first of two formal autobiographical volumes, carrying Koestler from childhood through his decision to join the Communist Party on December 31, 1931. His extraordinarily eventful youth is given here in detail: his initiation into a duelling fraternity in Vienna; his struggles as a Zionist immigrant in Palestine; and his early work as a journalist for the Ullstein newspaper chain, culminating in his trip to the North Pole on the *Graf Zeppelin.* The second volume, *The Invisible Writing,* follows his life until 1940 and is essentially the story of his years as a Communist. Koestler himself described his account of his Communist days in Berlin and Russia as trivial and boring, but anyone who is interested in the mentality and the activities of the revolutionaries of that period may well find this an absorbing narrative. It is, at least, an important historical document. Koestler also wrote three of the essays in the posthumous *Stranger on the Square* co-authored with his wife. The most important of them is a recollection of his acquaintance with Jean Paul Sartre and Simone de Beauvoir.

Overview of Critical Sources

The diverse concerns in Koestler's *oeuvre* have not yet been treated comprehensively in a single volume. Students of his work have been drawn mostly to his fiction, his political writing, and the connections between them and his life.

Evaluation of Selected Criticism

Atkins, John, *Arthur Koestler.* London: Neville Spearman, 1956. Atkins is concerned exclusively with Koestler's political ideas. He shuns the scholarly apparatus of footnotes and bibliography and writes a popular exposition of the place of Koestler's thought in modern ideology.

Calder, Jenni, *Chronicles of Conscience. A Study of George Orwell and Arthur Koestler.* London: Martin Secker and Warburg, 1968. This comparative study identifies Orwell and Koestler both as outcasts who put literature to the service of propaganda. Both are judged important spokesmen of their day, but Orwell's superior literary abilities suggest a longer life for his fiction than for Koestler's.

Levene, Mark, *Arthur Koestler.* New York: Frederick Ungar, 1984. Levene's book is an excellent introduction to Koestler's fiction. He provides a detailed chronology of Koestler's life at the beginning, followed by an introductory biographical chapter, and then gives six chapters of deft summary and judicious criticism of the fiction. A helpful bibliography is included.

Merrill, Reed, and Thomas Frazier, *Arthur Koestler: An International Bibliography.* Ann Arbor, MI: Ardis, 1979. This enormously useful work includes all the appearances of Koestler's works in print through July, 1978. It is enhanced by its organization which corresponds to the categories in the definitive Danube edition of the works. An extensive secondary bibliography and several appendices complement the primary bibliography. Almost none of the entries are annotated.

Pearson, Sidney A., Jr. *Arthur Koestler.* Boston: Twayne, 1978. Pearson gives a balanced overview of the whole Koestler, stressing Koestler's rationalism. This short study, with a helpful secondary bibliography, is a good introduction to all of Koestler's main ideas. Pearson finds an essential unity in Koestler's many works, despite their great diversity.

Sperber, Murray A. ed. *Arthur Koestler: A Collection of Critical Essays.* Englewood Cliffs, NJ: Prentice-Hall, 1977. This is an excellent collection of fourteen pieces on Koestler's politics and fiction, and another eight on his interests in science and mysticism. The contributors are distinguished scholars like Edmund Wilson, Stephen Spender, George Orwell, and William Empson.

Other Sources

Harris, Harold, ed. *Astride the Two Cultures: Arthur Koestler at 70.* New York: Random House, 1976. Harris collects here thirteen essays on the various interests reflected in Koestler's works: science, politics, fiction writing, and the paranormal. Roy Webberley's introductory essay, "An Attempt at an Overview," offers a useful introduction to the whole Koestler. Another excellent inclusion is Goronwy Rees's "*Darkness at Noon* and the 'Grammatical Fiction.' "

Mays, Wolfe, *Arthur Koestler.* Guildford and London: Lutterworth, 1973. Mays's monograph is very short (57 pages) but it is a useful introduction to Koestler's main ideas. It is divided into two sections, one on political and social thinking and another on creativity and science.

Selected Dictionaries and Encyclopedias

Critical Survey of Long Fiction, Salem Press, 1983. Provides a biographical sketch and short analyses of the novels.

Frank Day
Clemson University

CHARLES LAMB
1775–1834

Author's Chronology

Born February 10, 1775, London, to John and Elizabeth Field Lamb; *1782–1789* student at Christ Hospital where friendship with Coleridge begins; *1792* joins the East India House as clerk; *1794* writes poetry with Coleridge; *1795* committed to an insane asylum for six weeks; *1796* contributes to *Poems On Various Subjects;* his sister Mary, temporarily insane, fatally stabs their mother; Lamb takes responsibility for Mary; *1797* summer holidays with Coleridge at Nether Stowey; begins friendship with the Wordsworths; *1798* publishes *Blank Verse* with Charles Lloyd, publishes *A Tale Of Rosamund Gray; 1802–1820* active career writing and publishing; *1820* contributes essays by "Elia" to London magazine; *1823* adopts Emma Isola; *1825* retires with pension from East India House; *1825–1827* contributes to Hone's *Every-Day Book, New Monthly Magazine,* and Hone's *Table Book; 1827* moves from London to Enfield; *1830* publishes *Album Verses,* moves to London, then returns to Enfield in November; *1833* publishes *The Last Essays of Elia. Being a Sequel to Essays Published under that Name.,* Emma marries Lamb's publisher, Edward Moxon; *1834* Lamb dies on December 27 of an infection.

Author's Bibliography (selected)

A Tale of Rosamund Gray and Old Blind Margaret, 1798 (fiction); *Tales From Shakespeare Designed for the Use of Young Persons,* 1807, 2 vols. (Lamb wrote six, Mary Lamb wrote fourteen); *Specimens of English Dramatic Poets, Who Lived About the Time of Shakespeare,* 1808 (extracts plus notes which are important Lamb criticism); *The Works of Charles Lamb,* 2 vols. 1818 (poetry and prose); *Elia, Essays which have appeared under that signature in the London Magazine,* 1823 (essays); *The Last Essays of Elia. Being a Sequel to Essays Published under that Name,* 1833 (essays); *The Works of Charles Lamb,* ed. Thomas Hutchinson, 1908; *The Letters of Charles Lamb: To Which Are Added Those of His Sister Mary Lamb,* 1935; *The Letters of Charles Lamb and Mary Anne Lamb,* Vol. I (1796–1801), 1975; Vol. II (1801–1809), 1976; Vol. III (1809–1817), 1978.

Overview of Biographical Sources

Because Lamb's life provides much of the subject matter of his work, there has been consistent and abundant interest in Lamb's biography. A good collection of comments by Lamb's contemporaries is found in Edmund Blunden's *Charles Lamb: His Life Recorded by His Contemporaries* (London: Hogarth Press, 1934). An early biography, Alfred Ainger's *Charles Lamb* (London: Macmillan, 1888) offers some critical insights and is comfortable reading; it includes generous samplings from Lamb's writings. As is true of all of the biographers to follow, Ainger writes with great positive feeling for Lamb. Later biographies add newly uncovered facts, but the prevailing emphasis on Lamb's charm and kind-heartedness limits the possibilities for a sound well-rounded critical appraisal of his life.

The definitive biography is E. V. Lucas' *The Life of Charles Lamb* (1905). Two volumes of copious extracts from Lamb's work and amazing detail make this a complete and engaging life of the author although there is little criticism. Much shorter, but a good introduction to the world and friends of Charles Lamb is Edmund Blunden's *Charles Lamb and his Contemporaries.* (Cambridge: University Press, London and New York: Macmillan, 1933; rpt. Shoestring Press, 1967). Several biographies focus on particular periods or aspects of Lamb's life. Ernest Carson Ross' *The Ordeal of Bridget Elia* (Norman: University of Oklahoma Press, 1940) gives dependable information on Mary Lamb, whose life and illness were closely interwoven with the life of the author, while Reginald L. Hine in *Charles Lamb and His Hertfordshire* (New York: Macmillan, 1949) offers, in minute detail, Lamb's life as it was connected with Hertfordshire, England. Ernest Carson Ross in *Charles Lamb and Emma Isola* (London: The Charles Lamb Society, 1950) examines the details of Charles Lamb's relationship with his adopted daughter. A concise but substantial and traditional biography of Lamb may be found in George L. Barnett's *Charles Lamb* (1976), which reviews both the life and the work. Most recent works are Winifred F. Courtney's *Young Charles Lamb, 1775–1802* (New York: New York University Press, 1982) which investigates Lamb's early years, describing his connections with the radical thinkers of his day and the articles he contributed to *Albion,* a radical newspaper, a dimension of Lamb not covered earlier, and, the most recent biography, Lord David Cecil's *A Portrait of Charles Lamb* (New York: Charles Scribner's Sons, 1983), not a scholarly presentation since it lacks references and bibliography, and has some minor errors, but widely available and gracefully written.

Evaluation of Selected Biographies

Barnett, George L. *Charles Lamb.* Boston: Twayne, 1976. This is an excellent place to begin the study of Lamb although it offers little in the way of new interpretations or new critical outlook. Barnett points out the main features of Lamb's personality and stresses the significance of that personality, for all of Lamb's work. This is the traditional approach. The first chapter contains essential biographical information told with admirable concision. Within the context of the biographical background, the rest of the volume discusses Lamb's experimentation with literary form, his letters, the "Elia" essays, his criticism and his place in English literature.

Lucas, E. V. *The Life of Charles Lamb.* New York and London: G. P. Putnam's Sons, 1905. Not now in print, this is the standard, complete biography of

Lamb. The 1905 edition has marvelous illustrations and four appendices reviewing Lamb's portraits, commonplace books, and library. The 1921 edition omits all of these, but has corrections and some additions. The two volumes run over five hundred pages with such extensive quotation that they are, to a large extent, written in the words of Lamb himself. Although new facts have emerged since this was written, Lucas gives a full life. There is, however, little critical insight offered.

Autobiographical Sources

Lamb's letters record his life, and in their style and substance they suggest the direction of his essays. As with many other Romantic period writers, Lamb was an astute and prolific correspondent, and although there are four voluminous volumes of his letters in print, there is still no definitive edition which has been annotated and corrected. Lamb's critical theories as well as his personal life and feelings are meticulously recorded in his letters. Anyone interested in Lamb's many famous friends, or in the Romantic period, will find much informed material and opinion here. The letters have been collected in the following editions. *The Letters of Charles Lamb: To Which Are Added Those of His Sister Mary Lamb.* ed. Edward V. Lucas. London: Dent and Methuen, 1935. *The Letters of Charles Lamb and Mary Lamb.* ed. Edwin W. Marrs. Ithaca: Cornell University Press, Vol. I. (1796–1801), 1975; Vol. II. (1801–1809), 1976; Vol. III. (1809–1817), 1978.

Overview of Critical Sources

Praise of Lamb's morality or interest in his biography has overshadowed sound criticism of his writing. Although there are useful insights in the comments of contemporaries, it is only recently that there has been some truly critical scholarly reassessment. There is no one satisfactory book-length study that examines all aspects of his work.

Evaluation of Selected Criticism

Barnett, George L. *The Evolution of Elia.* Bloomington: Indiana University Press, 1964. Exploring the influence of Lamb's schooling, friendships, reading, and occupation on the development of his essays, Barnett studies the essays analyzing twenty manuscripts for insights into Lamb's methods of composition. This provides a useful introduction to Lamb's style.

Frank, Robert, *Don't Call Me Gentle Charles! An Essay on Lamb's Essays of Elia.* Studies in Literature 2; Oregon State Monographs. Corvallis: Oregon State University Press, 1976. Frank attacks the view that Lamb's essays are inextricably bound up with his biography, analyzing seven essays from the standpoint of their relationship to Romantic poetry and demonstrating that they will support close critical reading, without connection to Lamb's life.

McKenna, Wayne, *Charles Lamb and the Theatre.* New York: Harper & Row, 1978. McKenna reviews the state of the English theatre from 1737 to

1843 and compares Lamb's views to those of his contemporaries, arguing that Lamb's theater criticism was not, as many have claimed, whimsical or gentle hearted but rather was serious, honest, sophisticated and based on fundamental principles.

Park, Roy, ed. *Lamb as Critic.* Lincoln: University of Nebraska Press, 1980. In the introductory essay, Parker summarizes the reception of Lamb's criticism and argues that Lamb has been denied his place as a great critic in the central English tradition. Refuting charges that Lamb's criticism lacks sufficient theoretical underpinnings, and is limited in scope, Park underscores the parallels between Lamb's critical concerns and those of his contemporaries, providing a solid defense.

Randal, Fred. V. *The World of Elia: Charles Lamb's Essayistic Romanticism.* Port Washington, NY and London: Kennikat Press, 1975. Randal reads Lamb's essays closely, enriched by a psychoanalytical perspective, and examines the place of individual essays in the larger Romantic context and within the tradition of the familiar essay. He refutes the claim that Lamb's essays are an escape from his psychological and social suffering, arguing instead that they represent a universality and transmutation of those distresses into art.

Other Sources

De Quincey, Thomas, "Recollections of Charles Lamb," *Works,* III. ed. David Masson (Edinburgh, 1889–1897). An early admirer recalls Lamb.

Talfourd, Thomas Noon, "Sketch of Lamb's Life," in *The Letters of Charles Lamb.* London: Moxon, 1837. A reliable early biographical glimpse written by a close friend.

Selected Dictionaries and Encyclopedias

Collier's Encyclopedia, Vol. 14, P. F. Collier, 1981. Brief biography and discussion of the work.

The Dictionary of National Biography, Vol. XI, Oxford University Press, 1917; rpt. 1964. Essential biographical information.

Phyllis Fahrie Edelson
Pace University

WALTER SAVAGE LANDOR
1775–1864

Author's Chronology

Born January 30, 1775, Warwick, England; *1783* sent to study at Rugby; *1791* sent home from Rugby because he antagonized people with his satirical wit; *1792* tutored by Reverend William Langley; *1793* enters Trinity College, Oxford; *1794* leaves Oxford; *1795* publishes first book, *The Poems of Walter Savage Landor; 1805* father dies, leaving him a large fortune; *1808* purchases Llanthony Abbey in Wales; outfits and leads his own regiment to fight the French in Spain; *1811* marries Julia Thuillier (they have four children and a miserably unhappy marriage); *1814* begins tour of Continent; *1816–1818* resides in Como, Italy; *1821–1828* travels through Italy; *1829–1835* lives in Fiesole, Italy; *1835* returns to England, leaving wife and children in Fiesole; *1842–1843* daughter and two eldest sons variously visit him; *1848–1855* writes on foreign affairs for the *Examiner; 1857* sued for libel; *1858* convicted of libel; *1859* returns to Fiesole but is turned away by his family; Robert Browning provides him with a home in Florence; dies September 17, 1864, Florence, Italy.

Author's Bibliography (selected)

Gebir: A Poem, in Seven Books, 1798; *Imaginary Conversations of Literary Men and Statesmen,* 1824–1829, five volumes (prose); *The Siege of Ancona,* 1846 (verse drama); *Dry Sticks Fagoted,* 1858 (short fiction); *Heroic Idyls, with additional poems,* 1863; *The Complete Works of Walter Savage Landor,* ed. T. Earle Welby, sixteen volumes, 1927–1936; *The Poetical Works of Walter Savage Landor,* ed. Stephen Wheeler, three volumes, 1937.

Overview of Biographical Sources

Most biographies of Landor have followed, or at least borrowed from John Forster's *Walter Savage Landor: A Biography* (two volumes. London: Chapman and Hall, 1869), which includes letters since lost. Forster's biography is almost unbearable to read because of its plot summaries and recitation of the statistics of Landor's life. Sidney Colvin's *Landor* (New York: Harper, 1881) does a much better job of capturing the drama of Landor's life and is the most readable biography. The two major modern biographies both lack the elegance of writing found in Colvin's book.

Evaluation of Selected Biographies

Elwin, Malcolm, *Landor: A Replevin.* London: Macdonald, 1958 (revision of *Savage Landor.* New York: Macmillan, 1941). Elwin believes that most modern accounts of Landor have been unduly unsympathetic, and he hopes to correct

impressions of the author with this book. In addition to providing a readable account of the events of Landor's life, Elwin places Lander in the context of the Romantic era.

Super, R. H. *Walter Savage Landor: A Biography*. New York: New York University Press, 1954. This well documented biography lacks the vigor of Colvin's book and the sympathy of Elwin's work but is much more accessible to both student and scholar than is Forster's difficult book. Although Super makes Landor seem less pleasant than he probably really was, his accumulation of facts and resources for research has made his biography the standard one for reference.

Autobiographical Resources

The best places to look for autobiographical references are the biographies by Forster and Super. Other sources are the *Letters of Walter Savage Landor, Private and Public,* edited by Stephen Wheeler (London: Duckworth, 1899), H. C. Minchin's *Walter Savage Landor: Last Days, Letters and Conversations* (London: Methuen, 1934), and William Howitt's *Homes and Haunts of the Most Eminent British Poets* (London: Bentley, 1847; reprinted 1857 with Landor's corrections). The first two books contain letters by Landor and the last contains information that was provided by Landor. Students should beware of errors as to date and place in Minchin's notes.

Overview of Critical Sources

Although widely admired as a superb prose stylist, Landor has received attention primarily as a poet. Colvin's *Landor* contains the most intelligent of early criticism, providing a balanced evaluation of both the poetry and the prose. Another early study that is valuable for its insights is Algernon Charles Swinburne's "Landor" (*Encyclopedia Britannica,* ninth edition, volume 14, 1882. Reprinted in *Swinburne as Critic,* ed. Clyde K. Hyder. London: Routledge and Kegan Paul, 1972). Swinburne declares that Landor "won for himself such a double crown of glory in verse and in prose as has been won by no other Englishman but Milton." Swinburne valued Landor as an influence, which prompted W. B. Drayton Henderson to write *Swinburne and Landor* (London: Macmillan, 1918). Even though the book focuses on Swinburne, it contains some fine critical evaluations of Landor's poetry. Most twentieth-century criticism has focused on narrow aspects of Landor's work. Andrea Kelly's "The Latin Poetry of Walter Savage Landor" (*The Latin Poetry of English Poets,* ed. J. W. Binns. London: Routledge and Kegan Paul, 1974) provides an introduction to the poet's work in Latin. Also of interest is Thomas B. Brumbaugh's "Walter Savage Landor as Romantic Classicist" (*Topic,* 23 [1972], 14–21), which examines Landor's aesthetics. The most detailed study of Landor's achievement is in French: Pierre Vitoux's *L'Oeuvre de Walter Savage Landor* (Paris: Presses Universitaires de France, 1964).

Evaluation of Selected Criticism

Dilworth, Ernest, *Walter Savage Landor.* New York: Twayne, 1971. This book provides a broad introduction to Landor's verse and prose writings. Dilworth's emphasis on Landor's style yields some informative insights into Landor's literary achievement. Students in particular may find the discussion of Landor's efforts to write economically to be helpful. Landor's neoclassicism is pointed out but perhaps not discussed in as much detail as it ought to be.

Pinsky, Robert, *Landor's Poetry.* Chicago: University of Chicago Press, 1968. Pinsky tries to place Landor's poetry in a modern perspective. He examines the responses of Ezra Pound and Donald Davie to the poetry and then traces some of the major poetic themes. His classifications of the poems into such categories as "Poems Treating 'Universal Sentiments' " and "Poems about Recalling the Past" provide a clear introduction to Landor's themes. Although this book too often reads like a dissertation, it is as good an overview of Landor's poetic achievement as is currently available.

Other Sources

Aldington, Richard, "Landor's 'Hellenics,' " in *Literary Studies and Reviews.* New York: Dial, 1924. An appreciation of Landor's neoclassical poetry.

Selected Dictionaries and Encyclopedias

Critical Survey of Poetry, Salem Press, 1982. Brief biography and bibliography with a short analysis of Landor's principal poetic works.

Kirk H. Beetz
National University, Sacramento